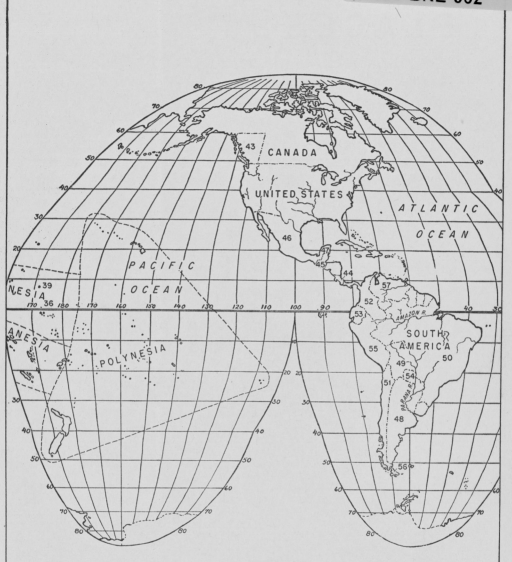

AMERICAS

NORTH
43 BRITISH COLUMBIA

CENTRAL
44 COSTA RICA
45 GUATEMALA
46 MEXICO
47 YUCATAN

SOUTH
48 ARGENTINA
49 BOLIVIA
50 BRAZIL
51 CHILE
52 COLOMBIA
53 ECUADOR
54 PARAGUAY
55 PERU
56 TIERRA DEL FUEGO
57 VENEZUELA

AN INTRODUCTION
TO ANTHROPOLOGY

THE MACMILLAN COMPANY
NEW YORK · CHICAGO
DALLAS · ATLANTA · SAN FRANCISCO

THE MACMILLAN COMPANY
OF CANADA, LIMITED
TORONTO

AN INTRODUCTION
TO ANTHROPOLOGY

BY

RALPH L. BEALS AND HARRY HOIJER

University of California, Los Angeles

With the Collaboration of
VIRGINIA MORE ROEDIGER

THE MACMILLAN COMPANY   *New York*

PREFACE

An Introduction to Anthropology is an elementary textbook for first and second-year college students who are beginning work in anthropology. It attempts to present, in as simple a fashion as possible, the basic materials and ideas of modern anthropology. Its purpose is twofold: to give a well-rounded view of the discipline to students who take only an introductory course, and to provide, for those who plan to concentrate in anthropology, the necessary groundwork for further study.

Two major themes dominate the text. The first is the origin, development, and differentiation of man as a biological organism, the second the concept of culture. These themes, in our belief, may not be separated. Culture, in all its diversity, may best be understood against the background of man's biological inheritance and make-up. Though human cultures are remarkably diverse and offer almost unlimited solutions to common human problems, all of them are in the end limited by the fact that they must serve basic biological imperatives, or the societies that live under them will cease to exist.

In treating the field of physical anthropology we have emphasized as far as possible the newer genetic approach, as it is now being developed by S. L. Washburn, Joseph Birdsell, William Boyd, and others. Important as this approach may be, however, it is evident that it does not as yet provide a comprehensive picture of man's development as a biological organism nor an adequate classification, in biological terms, of modern men. Consequently we have found it necessary to include much of the older data on racial history, the criteria of race, and modern racial classification, though with the caution that these data, based as they are on phenotypic characters, must be regarded as tentative, and that the whole concept of race may be profoundly modified in the light of current researches.

Our discussion of cultural anthropology frankly emphasizes the more recent structural and functional approach, and gives less emphasis to the older historical studies. Archeological and historical materials are therefore greatly simplified, even to the extent of treating the Old World Paleolithic, for example, in terms of the traditional time periods rather than attempting to include the more elaborate, but as yet confused and unstabilized, modern terminology. An effort has been made, nevertheless, to give the student a sense of the historical depth of culture, and to make him aware that neither culture as such nor any particular culture may be wholly understood apart from its historical background.

Much of our space has been devoted to the nature of culture and to a careful exposition of its major aspects, illustrated as concretely as possible by data from particular cultures chosen for their diversity. We have therefore done less than justice to certain studies marginal to cultural anthropology, such as, for example, the field of culture and personality. This is not of course to deny the importance of these studies, which today form perhaps some of the most significant areas of research in the social sciences. But it is clear, to us at any rate, that these marginal and recently developed fields are as yet too rapidly changing to warrant an important place in an elementary text. The beginning student needs a clear understanding of culture itself, backed by a wide acquaintance with a variety of cultures, before he can make much progress in areas like culture and personality.

We have followed customary usage in anthropological writings of using the present tense in describing the cultures of the world, even where it is clear that these cultures, by reason of modern contacts, no longer exist in their aboriginal form. The reader will understand that this usage is simply for consistency and convenience; we do not imply, for example, that American Indians still engage in inter-tribal warfare, or that their clothing, shelters, tools, and weapons have not changed since the time of the discovery of America. Unless another time is specified, all cultures are described as they existed before the spread of modern civilizations had materially affected them in form or content.

Though the text is intended for a year course covering both physical and cultural anthropology, we believe that it may also be used in courses devoted primarily to cultural anthropology. Numerous collateral references have been supplied for each chapter and we have attempted to select for this purpose only those books that are easily available in most college and university libraries. In addition we have provided an Ethnographic Bibliography to supplement and expand the descriptions of particular cultures given in the chapters on cultural anthropology.

An Introduction to Anthropology has been a joint work in the fullest sense of that term. Originally we planned to divide the chapters, each of the authors to prepare roughly one-half of the total. As it worked out, however, both of us worked on nearly every chapter, each of which has been rewritten and revised by both authors to the point where it is in most cases quite impossible to assign responsibility for the final version.

The book has its origin in the experience of the authors in teaching introductory anthropology for many years. We owe, therefore, a considerable debt of gratitude to the many hundreds of students who have unconsciously directed much of our teaching and whose reactions to textbooks and other assigned readings have helped in the preparation of this one. An earlier version of Chapters 1–7 was used in planographed form by some of our colleagues and students for some years; their comments and criticisms assisted us materially in the preparation of the version here presented.

We have of course depended in large part on the writings and researches of our fellow anthropologists, probably far more than can be indicated by footnotes and bibliography. To all these, and to the publishers who have given us permission to quote from extant works, we offer our sincere thanks.

RALPH L. BEALS

HARRY HOIJER

University of California, Los Angeles

CONCERNING THE ILLUSTRATIONS

The illustrations in *An Introduction to Anthropology* are prepared by Dr. Virginia More Roediger and set a new standard for the illustration of anthropological textbooks. Every effort has been made to integrate the illustrations fully with the text and in many cases to substitute an illustration for text material. Each illustration makes a particular point, and Dr. Roediger's skill has brought out the salient point clearly through suppression of unnecessary detail without distorting the facts. The illustrations are the product of considerable research and make a substantial contribution to the value of the text.

Dr. Roediger brought unique qualities to this task of collaboration. Besides her great skill in draftsmanship, a doctorate in Theater Research and Dramatic Criticism from Yale University imparted a sense of the dramatic as well as an understanding of art as communication. Later Dr. Roediger became interested in anthropology and was both a graduate student and for some years a Research Associate in Anthropology at the University of California, Los Angeles. She is the author and illustrator of *Ceremonial Costumes of the Pueblo Indians.*

CONTENTS

LIST OF ILLUSTRATIONS,
MAPS, AND CHARTS

Chapter 1

THE NATURE AND SCOPE
OF ANTHROPOLOGY

1. WHAT ANTHROPOLOGISTS DO

Early in January, 1944, the Bushmasters of the United States Army extended the Arawe bridgehead in the South Pacific one thousand yards. The Bushmasters were the only United States Army unit prepared before World War II for jungle-fighting. They were trained and equipped largely through the efforts of an anthropologist, whose experience in his scientific field had fitted him for this task. Another anthropologist, a specialist in the South Pacific, helped to increase the efficiency of native fishing industries in that area. And in South America, a rich source of raw rubber, anthropologists who knew both the people and the country attacked the complex problem of replenishing our limited supply of this essential war material.

These are only a few dramatic instances of the participation of anthropologists in the war effort. There were few war agencies which did not in some way make use of professional anthropologists or of data which anthropologists had made available. As early as 1942 anthropologists were used to help train army and navy personnel for military government and administration in occupied regions. Later, in colleges and universities throughout the country, anthropologists who had special knowledge of the languages and customs of the peoples of Asia, Africa, and the South Pacific assisted materially in the Army Specialized Training Program, which prepared men for liaison and other services on the many fighting fronts of World War II. Similarly, anthropologists who had lived and worked in little known regions of the earth contributed heavily to the work of the Office of War Information, the Office of Strategic Services, the Board of Economic Warfare, the Supply and Intelligence services of both the army and navy, and to other governmental agencies.

Equally diverse tasks engage the attention of anthropologists in times of peace. Ruins of ancient civilizations all over the world are excavated and reconstructed. Earlier forms of man uncovered in the course of these and other excavations are measured and minutely described. Detailed physical descriptions of present-day populations are compared and classified to lay the groundwork for studies of man's development in bodily form. In scores of remote places in Australia, Central and South Africa, the Far East, Oceania, and North and South America, anthropologists record for the first time the ways of life of little known peoples and put their languages into writing. In many frontier regions anthropologists working under government auspices aid administrators in finding solutions to problems of social control, education, and public welfare. At home anthropologists not only apply their special techniques to the study of American cities, towns, and rural areas, but also to the study of interracial and intercultural problems, problems of education, the administration of the American Indian, child-training, personality growth, and industrial relations.

These and many other activities of anthropologists at first seem to be a hodgepodge of unrelated undertakings. Underlying all anthropological research, however, is a common theme to which each individual project, whether in the field of research alone or in the application of anthropological data and method to practical affairs, is in some measure related. It will be our first task to define this theme as clearly as possible, and so to learn what is common to the many activities in which anthropologists engage.

2. THE CENTRAL PROBLEM OF ANTHROPOLOGY

Etymologically, the word "anthropology" is derived from the Greek stem *anthropo-* ("man") and the noun ending *-logy* ("science"). Its literal meaning is therefore "the science of man." The manifold activities we have listed suggest that anthropologists have taken the literal definition of their science seriously and so intend to study man and all his works.

This is true, however, only in the sense that anthropology is probably the most comprehensive of the sciences dealing with man and his works. It is certainly not the only one. Biological sciences also study man. Anatomy, for example, is concerned with the physical structure of man, both in itself and in contrast to that of the other animals. Physiology, embryology, and many others have also to do with special aspects of man's bodily apparatus. Man's behavior is a subject treated by several disciplines, among which psychology, sociology, and history loom prominently.

The anthropologist, in contrast, combines in one discipline the approaches of both the biological and the social sciences. His problems center, on the one hand, on man as a member of the animal kingdom, and on the other, on man's behavior as a member of society. Furthermore, he does not limit himself to any particular group of men or to any one period of history. On the contrary, he is as much interested in the earlier forms of man and his behavior as in those of the present day. Both the structural evolution of mankind and the growth of civilizations are studied from the earliest times for which any record survives to the present. Similarly, in his concern with contemporary human groups and civilizations, the anthropologist places particular emphasis on comparative studies. He seeks, in one branch of his science, to discover and describe the physical criteria differentiating mankind from all other living creatures, as well as those which are useful in distinguishing the many varieties within the human family itself. The comparative study of civilizations (or "cultures," as the anthropologist calls them) centers its attention on the differences and similarities in culture to be noted among the many human groups that inhabit the earth, and attempts to isolate and define the laws or principles which govern the formation and development of human societies and cultures.

It is apparent almost at once, from studies such as these, that man is unique in the animal kingdom. For despite many similarities in bodily structure which make him indisputably akin to the animals, man possesses certain bodily attributes wholly lacking among even his closest relatives in the animal kingdom. Man has a more complex brain than any other animal. He walks and stands in a completely erect position and has, as a result, a distinctive foot structure. His pelvis is broader and shallower than that of the other animals, his legs longer in proportion to body and arm length, and his backbone is S-shaped rather than straight or bowshaped. Since man uses his hands exclusively for handling rather than as an aid in walking, they, too, are distinctive in structure as compared to other animals.

But it is in the field of behavior that we may best appreciate man's uniqueness. Wherever man is found and however simple his culture, we find that he possesses tools and other material artifacts, more or less complex techniques for obtaining food, some degree of arbitrary division of labor, a social and political organization, a system of religious beliefs and rituals, and the ability to communicate with his fellows by means of a spoken language. All of these cultural characteristics have only the crudest analogs among even the most manlike animals. In other words, even the simplest of human societies possesses cultural characteristics far more complex than any found among animals, however advanced the animal group may be.

All animal species, excepting only those which man has domesticated, are restricted to specific environments. By reason of their inherited physical structures they have become so adapted to the particular area of the earth's surface in which they live as to be unable to survive any drastic change in environment. Man, because of his cultures, has freed himself from most environmental restrictions. Where the climate is unsuited to his physical nature (like his close relative, the ape, man is by nature a tropical animal), he has learned to make clothing and build shelters to protect himself from the elements. Where food in its raw state is unfit for him to eat, he has devised ways of making it edible. In hundreds of other details man has discovered how to extend and supplement his physical powers and to reshape his environment to meet his needs. More important, perhaps, is the fact that man has learned, albeit imperfectly as yet, to cooperate with others of his species. He always lives in groups and has often discovered that tasks beyond the powers of a single individual are well within those of a group working together.

Both the development of culture and the habit of living and working together would have been impossible without language, probably the most valuable of man's possessions. Language not only enables man to communicate directly with his fellows and so more easily to achieve cooperative and coordinated labor, but it also permits him to store up his experiences and knowledge, and to pass these on to successive generations. Men, unlike animals, are not obliged to learn all they know by direct experience or by observing and imitating the actions of others. They gain most of their knowledge through the medium of the spoken and written word. This permits them not only to share the experiences of their contemporaries, but also to share those of the many generations who lived before them. Even in societies which lack a system of writing, the useful inventions and discoveries of long past generations of men are handed down, often with successive improvements, to those who succeed them.

The fact that man has so freed himself that he may live almost anywhere on the surface of the earth has had a profound influence on his physique, his behavior, and his culture. Thus, the men of today, though all belong to a single species, are far more divergent in physical form than most other species of animal. In the same way, though man's cultures and languages are everywhere similar in broad outline, differences in the physical environment, in the nature and amount of contact with other groups, as well as in the specific historical events peculiar to individual human groups have together brought about a bewildering cultural and linguistic diversity.

It is very probable that the first men came into being more than a million years ago. The place of origin was probably in some tropical area of southern Asia or northeastern Africa. The earliest men, once they had acquired a rudimentary language and culture, spread rapidly over the Old World, gradually adapting, through the medium of their cultures, to a variety of environments. So, shortly after the opening of the present geological epoch, we find small groups of primitive humans, characterized by diverse but very simple cultures, in numerous areas extending from the British Isles to northern China and the island of Java. At this time and for many thousands of years afterward there were many species—and perhaps even differing genera—of humans. Gradually these were reduced until, by the middle of the present geological epoch or shortly thereafter, a single genus with only one species *(Homo sapiens)* survived. Today this is the species to which all varieties of man belong, though there is some evidence that earlier species have left their traces in modern forms.

Our record of cultural and linguistic change is much less complete. It is probably impossible to reconstruct the earlier stages of man's cultural and linguistic development except in very broad and general terms. Nevertheless, it can be shown that cultural diversity has on the whole increased with the passage of time. Intensive comparisons of present-day languages and cultures reveal differences so wide and numerous that they must have had their origins far in the past. This cultural and linguistic diversity, it must be emphasized, cannot be attributed to inherited psychological differences. All races of men appear to be equally variable insofar as their behavior unaffected by the cultural environment can be described at all. The many thousands of years of contact and interbreeding between diverse forms of man plus the fact that cultural or learned behavior profoundly modifies even the "drives" or "needs" (such as eating, sleeping, or breathing) necessary to the sustenance of life itself make it difficult, if not impossible, to establish any significant variations among men in terms of inherited nonphysical characteristics.

We are now better able to state the central theme which underlies all anthropological research. Primarily, this is the search for a set of principles which governs man's physical and cultural development. Why has man changed physically? Why are there so many distinctive human types despite their common origin? And if it is true that man's cultural and linguistic diversity is not the result of biologically inherited differences in behavior, what accounts for the many wide differences in languages and cultures? What is the nature of culture and how do cultures change? How do individuals respond to the ideals and goals set by their cultures? What relations exist between culture and personality? Solutions to such problems demand the intensive study and comparison of all kinds of humans, as well as similarly intensive comparative studies of as many human cultures as are available to research. In place of the experimental approach, obviously impossible when dealing with man and his civilizations, the anthropologist must substitute the comparative method. The world of today, together with the rare and fragmentary remains of its past history, is the only laboratory for anthropological research.

There are a great many different problems related to the central theme we have just defined. Each set of problems requires the development of specific and highly technical methods. Anthropology therefore, like many other disciplines, is divided into numerous branches, each having to do with some specialized aspect of the general field. These may best be defined under two principal headings: physical anthropology and cultural anthropology.

3. PHYSICAL ANTHROPOLOGY

Physical anthropology studies man, the animal. Its principal interest is, then, the history, evolution, and present nature of man's bodily structure. What varieties of man existed formerly and what forms do we find in the world today? How do these differ from one another? What explanations may be found for these differences? These are some of the more important questions to which the physical anthropologist seeks an answer.

It follows, then, that much of physical anthropology has to do with the history of man's physical characteristics. The physical anthropologist searches the earth for traces of early man. Such early forms are carefully compared with one another and with modern man. In this way a given structural feature, or a whole set of them, may be traced from the earliest populations in which it appears to populations of the present day. We may discover when a given trait first appeared among men, how it became more widespread, and in some cases we may also note its gradual disappearance. Where sets or clusters of physical traits are studied historically, we may note their first occurrence among a population and what happened to the trait or cluster when the population in which it occurred came into contact with structurally diverse groups. Though there are still many gaps in the historical sequences reconstructed by physical anthropologists, questions like the following may be answered, at least in part: Where and when did the earliest human beings first appear? What did these people look like and how did they resemble or differ from one another? How have the physical characteristics of man changed during their time on earth?

The men of today are all quite similar to one another in basic structure despite their differences in outward appearances. All of them belong to a single species, *Homo sapiens,* the history of which is fairly well known. In early prehistoric times, however, there appear to have been other species and perhaps genera. If we go back far enough in time we find a period in which no human forms existed. It is evident, then, that man as we know him today has emerged from earlier nonhuman forms. The study of the processes whereby man developed from his nonhuman ancestors and the continuing processes of change still slowly altering his bodily form is also a part of physical anthropology. From such studies we learn how men gradually became different from the other animals and assumed the bodily characteristics which mark them today. We also learn how men diversified among themselves, and something of the factors responsible for the infinite variety of human forms.

Men do not live in a vacuum; they are constantly interacting with the environment. The environment includes of course not only the land, the sea, the air, and the many other physical features of the world, but also the multitude of living beings who share the world with man. No study of man would be complete which overlooked his relationship, at all times and places, with the environment. We want to know just how the environment has affected and continues to affect man's structure. A third important phase of physical anthropology is, then, the study of the ways in which man interacts with the environment in which he lives and the effects this interaction may have upon his bodily structure. So we may add to our knowledge of the conditions responsible for diversity in human forms.

Finally, it is clear that man never lives by himself. He belongs to a family and to a tribe or state or nation, and even in his most isolated societies, there are interactions of some sort between separate tribes, states, and nations. These facts also may affect man's structure and the changes it is undergoing. Peoples relatively isolated from others apparently change very slowly in physical form, while populations having contacts with many structurally diverse peoples may change radically in bodily structure in a relatively short time. Contacts between diverse peoples may also bring up problems concerning the nature and meaning of the differences between men. So, for example, the physical anthropologist may be called upon to answer such questions as the following: What happens when peoples of different varieties interbreed? Are some varieties of men innately superior to others? Is there any relationship between man's physical type and his temperament, intelligence, special aptitudes, or behavior in general?

We have not of course given anything like a complete inventory of the problems of physical anthropology. There are many other problems and regions of research, some of which will become apparent in later chapters. Our purpose here is only to delimit the field of physical anthropology in broad and general terms and to illustrate by a few examples the nature of the problems proper to the field.

4. *CULTURAL ANTHROPOLOGY*

Cultural anthropology studies the origins and history of man's cultures, their evolution and development, and the structure and functioning of human cultures in every place and time. It is concerned with culture per se, whether it belongs to the primitive men of the Stone Age or to the European city-dwellers of today. All cultures interest the cultural anthropologist, for all contribute some evidence of men's reactions in cultural forms to the ever-present problems posed by the physical environment, the attempts of men to live and work together, and the interactions of human groups with one another.

Since cultural anthropology covers so wide a range of human activities, it is traditionally divided into three main branches: archeology, ethnology, and linguistics. Each of these has its own subject matter, and as a result has developed a distinctive methodology.

More recently a new type of division has been developing which divides the whole field of anthropology into two main branches, one emphasizing a historical approach, the other a nonhistorical, generalizing approach. No really satisfactory terminology has yet been developed for these two approaches, which differ not so much in subject matter as in ways of dealing with the data.

A recent suggestion is that the first approach, emphasizing history, be called "descriptive integration." In this area would be included much of prehistory and ethnology, together with the strictly historical emphases of physical anthropology and linguistics. The purpose of this approach to anthropological data would be so to organize the data, whether on man's physical structure or his cultures, as to bring to light significant historical relationships. The second approach, with emphasis on generalization, would then seek to establish general principles applying to many sorts of data, regardless of the period in history to which they apply or their geographical distribution.

in Europe were not understood until educated missionaries pointed out their resemblance to the tools of the American Indian. Similarly, no adequate time scale or chronology was possible for anthropology until the science of geology was well developed, nor could an understanding of human biology advance greatly until the development of the more general sciences of paleontology and zoology.

The first efforts to develop the study of anthropology were handicapped by inadequate data. Scholars in the field of cultural anthropology long depended upon fragmentary and often biased reports of traders, explorers, and missionaries. Not until the middle of the last century did students visit nonliterate peoples for the express purpose of studying them and their cultures, while professionally trained field workers were almost unknown until 1900.

Ethnology, in large part because it is so dependent on accurate descriptive studies of a wide variety of cultures, was the last of the anthropological disciplines to achieve scientific status. Archeology, physical anthropology, and linguistics reached this status earlier, since considerable data for these disciplines were readily available in Europe itself. However, this early concentration on European prehistoric periods, races, and languages also severely limited archeology, physical anthropology, and linguistics. The major periods of European prehistory, established early in the last century, were regarded until recently as applicable to the entire world. Methods of racial classification, similarly based on European data in large part, are misleading when applied to other peoples, but are so firmly intrenched in usage that change is difficult. In linguistics, recent studies of non-European languages are only now beginning to have an effect on general theory and method; for a long time the study of American Indian, Oceanic, or South African languages (the so-called "primitive" languages) was considered unimportant if not actually unscholarly.

The earliest anthropological studies, like those of today, were comparative; the central aim of anthropology has been from the beginning to include in its studies all men and all cultures, wherever found. Most of the early treatment of man's cultures, however, was evolutionary; scholars like Edward B. Tylor, Herbert Spencer, and Lewis H. Morgan were interested mainly in determining how our own cultures had grown and developed from their earlier "savage" beginnings, while others, in physical anthropology, were equally concerned with the problem of man's biological evolution.

While studies of evolution are still an important part of physical anthropology, cultural evolution, as defined in earlier theory, has long been abandoned. Cultural anthropologists have turned instead more to precise descriptive studies, comparative and historical, as exemplified by the work of Franz Boas, Clarke Wissler, A. L. Kroeber, and Robert H. Lowie. Concepts such as "diffusion" (the spread of cultures and elements of culture through contact; opposed to independent invention) and the "culture area" (an attempt to classify cultures regionally) became increasingly important, especially in the work of American scholars.[3]

Others, notably the British anthropologist Malinowski, emphasized intensive studies of contemporaneous cultures, not to work out their histories, but rather to study them as integrated wholes. By so studying cultures and paying especial attention to the interfunctioning of the several aspects of culture, attempts were made to formulate laws or generalizations in respect to culture which would hold for all times and places.

Although the functionalist group aroused considerable controversy because of its scornful attitude toward historical studies, many other anthropologists paid more and more attention to nonhistorical investigations. Margaret Mead devoted herself to the study of personality formation and child maturation in various cultures. Ruth Benedict wrote on the configurations of culture, while Ralph Linton explored problems of personality along psychiatric lines earlier roughed out by Edward Sapir. Robert Redfield, Melville Herskovits, and Ralph Linton formulated the problems of acculturation, that is, the results of continuing contact between divergent cultures.

As in the case of the earlier controversies over diffusion and independent invention, anthropologists today tend less and less to regard the historical and nonhistorical methods as being in conflict. Research increasingly is conducted in terms of problems to which historical or nonhistorical methods, or both, are applied in accordance with the nature of the problem and the type of data available.

Such a development to some extent parallels the history of other and older sciences. Botany and zoology originally were mainly devoted to the systematic classification of life forms and the discovery of their place in evolutionary and historical sequences. Subsequently interest shifted to such problems as the environmental adjustments and physiological functioning of plants and animals. Historical and evolutionary studies for a time were criticized severely but now are regarded as complementary techniques of study.

Physical anthropology and archeology exhibit, in less pronounced form, something of the same history as ethnology. Early physical anthropology

[3] A more detailed discussion of the history of theory in cultural anthropology will be found in Chapter 20.

was mainly concerned with the classification of man and the process of his evolution. Today physical anthropologists, although perhaps making greater progress than ever before in unraveling the development of the human species, are also greatly concerned with such problems as the effect of environment on physical characteristics, the effects of racial intermixture, problems of growth and development, and a host of others in which historical or evolutionary methods are of little or no importance. Despite these new interests, though, the application of the newer studies of blood types and the young science of genetics are leading to a wholesale revision of the nineteenth-century concepts of race.

Similarly archeology, although by its nature concerned primarily with time sequences, has developed more varied interests. Problems of culture contact and interrelations, the analysis of past cultures in terms of their environments, and analysis of archeological cultures in terms of ethnological problems are among the essentially nonhistorical studies made by archeologists.

We cannot of course give here anything like a detailed history of anthropological thought; our purpose is only to summarize, very briefly, the main currents of anthropological thinking. There are many other directions and tendencies we have not mentioned at all. It should be noted, however, that anthropology, despite its youth and the diversity of its special interests, has contributed markedly to social science theory. This contribution lies primarily (1) in the gradual clarification of the concept of race and the freeing of this concept from its earlier confusion with language, nationality, and culture, and (2) in the concept of culture, that is, that human behavior must be studied with respect to the particular framework of modes, manners, and customs, historically created, in which it takes place and by which it is directed or influenced.

6. THE RELATIONS OF ANTHROPOLOGY TO OTHER SCIENCES

Though anthropology is commonly, and quite correctly, regarded as a social science, with primary relations to disciplines like sociology, psychology, geography, economics, and political science, it by no means stands apart from either the biological sciences or the humanities. Its connection, through physical anthropology, with such fields as anatomy, physiology, embryology, and genetics is perhaps evident, for the physical anthropologist is, in one sense, only a biologist who concentrates his attention on man. But there is an equally important link between anthropology and humanistic disciplines like history, literature, art, and music, for these, like ethnology, archeology, and linguistics, are concerned with both an understanding and appreciation of man's cultures.

To some sciences anthropology is related in the sense that it could not itself have developed until those sciences had achieved a certain degree of maturity. Thus we pointed out in § 5 that no true idea of the age of man and his culture could have been developed until geology had provided a chronology or time sequence with which to measure it. Similarly, paleontology and zoology had to rest on a firm foundation before the nature of man and his relation to the other animals could be understood. These relationships still continue for both physical anthropology and archeology, and there is indeed an increasing cooperation in the solution of problems common to all the sciences concerned.

Archeologists must use the stratigraphic methods of geology (the determination of the relative age of layers of materials by establishing their position in deposits; see Chapter 2, § 5) in establishing the relative time of different cultures, although the archeologist usually works in much shorter time spans and with much greater detail than does the geologist. This relationship becomes even more evident when the archeologist is dealing with very old cultures. Then the archeologist depends almost entirely upon the geologist and the paleontologist to establish the age of his finds. The geologist may be able to determine that given cultural remains lie on terraces, lake deposits, or in strata which belong to a given geological time. On other occasions, the paleontologist, by examining the bones of animals found with cultural remains, may also determine the geological time of the deposits.

In similar fashion the physical anthropologist may depend upon the geologist and paleontologist to establish the age of specimens of prehistoric man. Many of the present problems about the evolution of man would be solved if the geologist and paleontologist could place all fossil remains definitely in time. The physical anthropologist also uses the criteria of classification developed by the zoologists and botanists. Physical anthropology is also closely related to anatomy and other fields of medical investigation.

A second type of interrelationship of anthropology and other sciences involves the use of the techniques or findings of other sciences for the solution of specific problems. For example, the calendar of a primitive people often may be understood only in relation to certain data from astronomy. The methods of chemistry and physics are widely employed in the study of prehistoric ceramics to determine the techniques of manufacture and the origins of the materials. Similarly, the mineralogist may be able to tell that a given stone tool is made of material from a long distance away. The discovery of one of the major types of prehistoric man, Peking Man, resulted from finding a piece of quartz in a location a thousand miles from the nearest known quartz deposit. Ethnologists use the data of botany and zoology to determine the extent to which a primitive people utilize the potentialities of their environment or to reconstruct the environment of a prehistoric one. Even engineering may be involved in anthropological work, for every archeologist must know how to survey an archeological site and how to make maps. Architects may be called on to solve problems connected with building construction, metallurgists to determine the composition of metal tools, and pharmacologists to solve the problems of a primitive arrow poison. The anthropologist hence must be aware of the potentialities of many disciplines and be ready to call on specialists for the solution of his problems.

A third type of relationship between anthropology and other disciplines may be described as one of interdependence in problems, techniques, methods, and theories. In this class of relationship, not only does anthropology make use of data or techniques from other fields but it also contributes to the development of techniques and theories and the solution of common problems. Relationships of this sort exist between anthropology and various disciplines in biology, the humanities, and the social sciences.

From its earliest history, anthropology had close relations with biology. This situation arose in part from the application of evolutionary concepts in early theories of cultural anthropology and in part from the rapid early development of physical anthropology. Although biological concepts of evolution no longer are employed in cultural anthropology, an understanding of man's biology is essential to cultural theory. Culture is more than a biological phenomenon, but every society apparently attempts, through its culture, to provide satisfactions for the basic biological and psychological necessities of man, and, in some cases, at least, it may, through the same means, profoundly modify the operation of biological factors. The study of culture and the study of human biology are constantly interrelated.

Relations of anthropology with psychology have been less close in the past than might be expected. Both subjects are deeply concerned with problems of behavior, but for a considerable period of time most psychologists were interested primarily in problems of individual behavior while the anthropologists tended to make group generalizations phrased in cultural terms. It is true that the comparative studies of the anthropologist helped to break down some of the older "instinct" theories of psychology, but not until anthropologists turned their attention to the relation of culture to the individual did the possibilities of closer relations with psychology develop.

Interest in individual problems in anthropology occurred at a time when psychologists were concentrating on problems of animal behavior. As a result, anthropologists turned to psychoanalytic and psychiatric workers for their psychological concepts, and this trend is still marked. With revived interest in problems of human psychology in recent years, increasing interchange may be expected between the two fields.

The development of the concept of culture and the emphasis upon cultures as an integrated whole have been the major contributions of anthropology to the social sciences. Although not widely used in political science and economics, the idea of culture and its integration has become commonplace in history, geography, and sociology. The field of human geography, indeed, rests upon the cultural concept, and as Forde has said,

> The Geographer who is unversed in the culture of the people of the land he studies, or in the lessons ethnology as a whole has to teach, will, as soon as he begins to consider the mainsprings of human activity, find himself groping uncertainly for geographic factors whose significance he cannot truly assess. Human geography demands as much knowledge of humanity as of geography.[4]

Although perhaps not so clearly recognized by the anthropologist, understanding of geographical factors is equally important in the study of human activity.

The relationships between anthropology and sociology have never been developed to the extent they should be. Many anthropologists and sociologists have long recognized that the two disciplines have much in common. It is true that the subject matter has tended to be different, anthropology concentrating upon the simpler and more isolated peoples, while sociology has been concerned primarily with western European civilization. This difference in subject matter has also brought about differences in methods of study. The anthropologist, studying a small group, has only rarely been aware of or needed to concern himself with problems of sampling, to mention but a single difference. Neither has the schedule, a commonplace tool of the sociologist, found much use among anthropologists.

On the other hand, the fundamental problems of anthropology are such that the general body of theory should ultimately be similar, if not the same. Culture as a concept today is widely used by sociologists and has proved a useful tool. Both sociologists and anthropologists in their theories have increasingly attempted to include each other's data. Essentially the

4 C. Daryll Forde, *Habitat, Economy, and Society,* 2nd edition (New York: E. P. Dutton, 1950), p. 465.

function of the anthropologist is to integrate the various disciplines dealing with man. Most of the sciences dealing with man tend to concentrate on a limited number of aspects. Anthropology has tended to concentrate on the over-all problems, particularly through the concept of culture. Where the economist, for example, has tended to see his problems as part of an isolated system of ideas and behaviors, the anthropologist is concerned with structure of the total culture and perceives the interrelationships between economic institutions and other aspects of culture.

Anthropology also has brought to the various sciences dealing with man a greater objectivity and relativity of viewpoint. Through examination of a wide range of cultures differing greatly from our own, it becomes possible to see the nonrational character of much of Euro-American culture. Types of behavior differing from our own are also seen as not necessarily inferior or less logical but as alternative solutions to general human problems. Behaviors and institutions that, viewed by themselves, do not make sense to us, are discovered to be parts of integrated wholes and hence necessary or inevitable parts of a specified culture. Others are found to be the inescapable responses to particular types of cultural conditioning of the individual.

7. THE APPLICATIONS OF ANTHROPOLOGY

Not until after World War I was anthropology generally recognized as having practical application. Suggestions for the use of anthropology had, it is true, been made earlier, but few attempts were made. One argument for the founding of the Bureau of American Ethnology by the United States government in 1879 was that it would provide a research agency for the Bureau of Indian Affairs, but not until the 1930's did the Bureau of Indian Affairs address its first request for information and assistance to the Bureau of American Ethnology.

The first, and still the most widely recognized, application of anthropology has been in connection with the administration of so-called dependent peoples. Anthropology has been used extensively by the French, British, and Dutch colonial administrations, and more recently by the United States in the Indian Service and in the administration of Trust Territories in the Pacific. It appears that the administration has been more effective and more satisfactory from both the native and the administrative viewpoint where anthropological techniques and knowledge have been most widely used. In recent years anthropologists and anthropological techniques have been useful in a wide variety of applied situations such as discovering and removing causes of labor-management friction in industry, in dealing with minority groups and securing fair employment practices, and in better organizing resettlement projects. Anthropology is also being used increasingly in connection with programs designed to raise living standards and to improve health and education in underdeveloped areas. All these applications will be discussed in the final chapter.

To summarize the last three sections, the modern period in anthropology has been marked by the rise of new approaches utilizing historical methods and by the development of nonhistorical methods. Both approaches have been increasingly interested in the processes of culture and in seeking generalizations or laws about culture. In general the followers of the historical approach have tended toward searching for a science of culture, that is, culture as it appears at all times and places. Followers of the nonhistorical methods have in general concentrated on developing what might be called a science of cultures, emphasizing the individual societies and their characteristics. In both cases, research has tended increasingly to center upon seeking the answers to specific questions or problems. In modern times also there has been an increasing tendency to utilize the results of anthropology to solve practical problems.

COLLATERAL READING

Boas, Franz. *Anthropology and Modern Life*. New York: W. W. Norton and Co., 1928.

————. "Anthropology," *Encyclopedia of the Social Sciences*. New York: The Macmillan Co., 1930. II, 73–110.

————. "The Aims of Anthropological Research," *Race, Language and Culture*. New York: The Macmillan Co., 1940. Pp. 243–259.

Kluckhohn, Clyde. *Mirror for Man*. New York: McGraw-Hill Book Co., 1944.

Linton, Ralph. "The Scope and Aims of Anthropology," *The Science of Man in the World Crisis,* ed. Ralph Linton. New York: Columbia University Press, 1945. Pp. 3–18.

Chapter 2

MAN AND THE ANIMALS

1. THE CLASSIFICATION OF MEN AND ANIMALS

As a first step toward the understanding of man's physical structure, we shall study the problem of man's relationships to the other animals that inhabit the earth. Is man a separate creation who has always been distinct from the animals? Or are there similarities between men and animals which point to their common origin? Has man always possessed his present-day physical form? If not, how did he look in prehistoric times? Was prehistoric man more, or less, similar to the animals than the men of modern times?

To answer these and other related questions we must consider the animal kingdom as a whole. Zoologists and anatomists have described and classified the animals, whereas physical anthropologists have done the same for man. The problem that now arises is as follows: Are there two systems of classification, one restricted to animals, the other to man? Or may the various human types be included in that of the animal kingdom taken as a whole?

As we shall presently see, man is in fact to be included in the animal kingdom. All comparative research in zoology, anatomy, and physical anthropology demonstrates unmistakably that man is, bone for bone and organ for organ, fundamentally like the animals. To some animals, such as the chimpanzee and the gorilla, man has numerous and obvious resemblances; to others, like the frog and the fish, his resemblances are fewer and not so easy to see. But all the animals in the great classes of

21

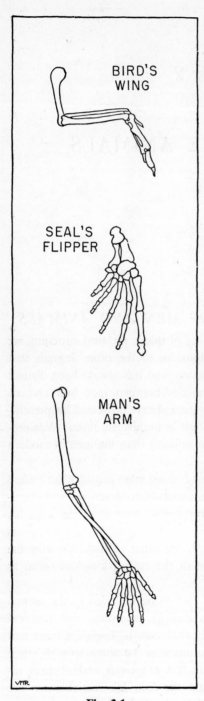

BIRD'S
WING

SEAL'S
FLIPPER

MAN'S
ARM

Fig. 2:1.

fishes, amphibians, reptiles, birds, and mammals, up to and including man himself, are definitely interrelated. Further, it is almost equally clear that this relationship extends also to all living forms.

Relationships among members of the animal kingdom are based upon *homologies,* structural similarities in the organs of animals concerned. These must not be confused with *analogies,* which are resemblances between organs brought about by a common function or use to which the organs are put. Careful comparison reveals that the arms of men, the wings of birds, and the flippers of the seal are basically alike in structure, though widely different in function. These organs are thus homologous; the fact that arms, wings, and flippers are put to different uses may obscure their fundamental similarities in structure but does not deny it. Similarly, it may be observed that the chimpanzee's foot is used much as a man's hand may be; the chimpanzee can, for example, grasp a limb or other object with his foot in much the same way, if not as efficiently, as man grasps objects with his hand. Man's foot, on the other hand, is normally employed as a supporting and locomotory organ; man rests his weight on and walks by means of his feet. He can only rarely use them to grasp or pick up objects. But a careful comparison of the structure of the feet of men and chimpanzees shows them to be basically alike, despite their differing functions, and quite different structurally, in both men and chimpanzees, from the hands.

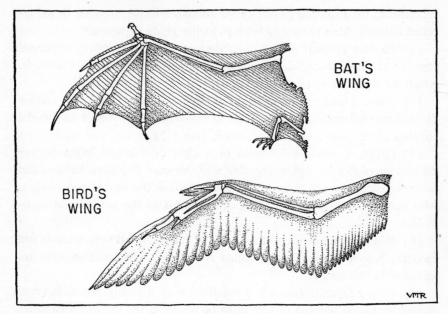

Fig. 2:2.

Analogous organs may be exemplified by the wings of bats and birds. Superficially these appear to be alike, an impression gained largely from the fact that in both animals the wings serve the function of flying. When, however, we come to examine these organs carefully, we find that the wings of birds consist of feathers supported by tissues attached to the forelimbs alone, while those of bats are composed of thin membranes stretched between the fore and hind limbs. In structure, then, the two organs are wholly different and cannot be taken as homologous points of resemblance between the two animals.

It is evident of course that there is not the same degree of resemblance between all animals. Men resemble one another far more than they resemble any other animal. Men, apes, and monkeys have a great many more homologies in common than any of them has with birds, reptiles, or fish. Therefore, though all members of the animal kingdom have a few homologies in common, it is clearly evident that the kingdom as a whole can be broken down into many divisions and subdivisions. This breakdown is usually given in the following terms:

(1) *Kingdom,* the classification which includes all animals and men, as opposed to plants and other nonanimal organisms. There are relatively few homologous traits shared by all the animals; their number increases as the subdivisions (listed below) become smaller.

(2) *Grade,* a major subdivision of a kingdom. Two grades are usually

recognized: the *Protozoa* or one-celled animals and the *Metazoa* or many-celled animals. Man obviously belongs to the grade *Metazoa*.

(3) *Phylum* (plural: *phyla*), a subdivision of a grade. Many phyla are recognized within the *Metazoa* and man belongs to the phylum *Chordata,* which we shall describe later (see § 6).

(4) *Class,* a major subdivision of a phylum. Classes are often further divided into subclasses. Man belongs to the class of *Mammals* and to the subclass *Eutheria* or placental mammals (see § 7).

(5) *Order,* a major subdivision of a class or subclass, often further divided into suborders. Man, together with the apes, monkeys, lemurs, and tarsiers, belongs to the order of *Primates.* All but the lemurs and tarsiers, who belong to separate suborders, are grouped in the suborder *Anthropoidea.*

(6) *Family,* a subdivision of an order or suborder. All men, ancient and modern, belong to one family, called *Hominidae.* No other animals are included in this group.

(7) *Genus* (plural: *genera*), a subdivision of a family. There is some dispute as to the number of genera to be found in the family *Hominidae.* It is agreed, however, that all modern men belong to one genus, called *Homo,* which also includes a number of prehistoric forms.

(8) *Species,* a subdivision of a genus. Again there is difference of opinion as to the number of species to be recognized among men. But all modern men and some of the prehistoric types are usually placed in a single species, called *sapiens.*

(9) *Race* or *variety,* the smallest grouping generally recognized within the animal kingdom. A race or variety includes organisms possessing the greatest number of homologous traits in common. A large number of races are recognized among modern men, but there is considerable difference of opinion, both with respect to the procedure of classifying mankind into races and the content of such classifications. We shall discuss this topic in greater detail later (see Chapters 5, 6).

2. EMBRYOLOGICAL EVIDENCES OF KINSHIP AMONG ANIMALS

Structural homologies are not the only evidences of interrelationships within the animal kingdom. Further evidence may be found in the processes whereby the fertilized egg cell develops into an independent organism. Comparative embryology, which is the study of these processes among both animals and men, provides us with many other points of resemblance between the members of the animal kingdom.

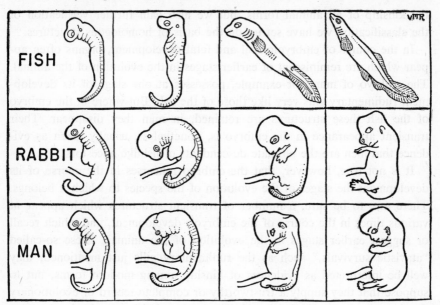

Fig. 2:3. Stages in embryological development.

The processes of reproduction are in general most similar in animals which are closely related. So, for example, all (or nearly all) mammals give birth to their young alive, all stages in the development of the embryo taking place within the body of the mother. Furthermore, the young, at birth, are in a more or less helpless condition and must be fed and otherwise taken care of until they are able to fend for themselves. Among most reptiles, on the other hand, the embryo develops in an egg laid by the mother which contains the necessary food for the growing offspring. When the young reptile emerges from the egg it is ready to care for itself. A knowledge of the processes of reproduction, then, often yields further data on the similarities and differences between the various groups within the animal kingdom.

The process of embryological development as a whole is fundamentally the same in all animals. All sexually reproduced forms begin as single cells which through a series of more or less complex processes become fully formed organisms. In the earliest stages of their development, the embryos of most animals are very much alike; in this period of growth it is often very difficult to distinguish forms which are later quite different. As the embryo continues to grow, its distinguishing traits slowly appear until at birth the offspring normally has the features which characterize its species and variety. Here, then, we not only gain evidence confirming the essential kinship of all animal forms, but we also gain further verification of the classification we have set up on the basis of homologous structures.

In the course of embryological and fetal development, organs often appear which are reminiscent of earlier stages in the evolution of the animal. The embryo of man, for example, possesses at one stage of its development rudimentary gills very like those of the fish. But where in the embryo of the fish these structures are retained, in man they disappear. Their transient appearance in the embryo is, nonetheless, usually taken as evidence that men are the ultimate descendants of fishlike ancestors.

It is not true, however, that the embryo rehearses in the course of its development the stages of the evolution of the species to which it belongs. There are, to be sure, a number of transient structures which appear at various times in the course of the embryo's development, and which recall or suggest earlier stages in the evolution of the animal. These so-called "atavistic survivals," such as the rudimentary gills just mentioned, may well be interpreted as evidences of kinship among modern forms, but to suppose that they supply a trustworthy or complete record of evolutionary development is manifestly absurd. The fetal period in man is nine months, while the evolutionary period covers millions of years. Insofar as the embryological development recapitulates evolution, it does so only in a most general way. Whole chapters of the story are omitted, while others are represented only in very sketchy fashion. Thus, while the gill structures of the fish are represented in man's fetal development, the scales, tail structures, and other organs are not.

3. DIRECT EVIDENCE OF EVOLUTION

Our classification of animals and men, as we have seen, is based upon homologies and is confirmed in many details by the data of comparative embryology. Homologies, it will be recalled, are fundamental similarities in structure. These similarities are not due to common function or environment, and are too numerous and far-reaching to be merely fortuitous. The conclusion is inevitable, then, that homologies are the result of a common ancestry. Animals which can be grouped in the same species are thus descended from a common ancestor, those belonging to a single genus are derived from a more remote common ancestor, and so on until it is evident that all animals are ultimately from one primeval source. The appearance in the embryo of atavistic survivals and the fact that the process of embryological development is fundamentally the same in all animals further confirm this conclusion.

The following questions may now be raised: Is there any direct evidence that all animals are so interrelated that they represent modern descendants of a single earlier species? What data have we to show that species change?

Data offering a partial answer to these and related questions may be found in paleontology (the study of ancient animals) and in that branch of physical anthropology which deals with the prehistoric forms of man. Prehistoric men and animals are known from skeletal materials found in the crust of the earth, from imprints of bodily structures made in soft materials which have turned to stone or fossilized, from footprints and other traces of prehistoric forms which have similarly become fossilized, and, less often, from whole animals imbedded, and so preserved more or less intact, in the ice sheets of Arctic regions. All such finds provide us with firsthand knowledge of older human and animal species. Moreover, since these evidences of prehistoric men and animals can often be dated relative to one another and to modern forms, we can sometimes provide direct evidence of the derivation of one species from another. Thus, for example, the skeletons of several horselike animals have been reconstructed for various periods in the history of the earth. Placed in their proper time relationship, these finds strikingly demonstrate the evolution of the modern horse (see Figure 2:4).

It should not be inferred from what we have just said that the paleontologist and physical anthropologist can provide us with a complete and detailed record of the evolution of modern species. This is far from being the case; fossil records of both men and animals are in general few and fragmentary. But these few and fragmentary records, taken together with the data of comparative zoology, physical anthropology, and embryology, do give us a broad picture of the phenomenon of evolution. This picture, which we shall presently examine in detail, may be summarized as follows:

(1) In the earliest periods of earth's history we find relatively few species as compared with the number that exist today. Animal species have gradually increased in numbers.

(2) The species of early prehistoric times were far less divergent than those of today. Not only has the number of species increased but so also has their variety.

(3) Some animal groups are older than others. Animals without backbones (or invertebrates, such as shellfish, insects, spiders, and so on) were in existence long before the vertebrates or backboned animals. The earliest apelike forms greatly preceded the earliest manlike forms.

(4) Many animals have changed radically in bodily structure. Thus, the earliest species of fish were quite different from those of today. Furthermore, many species of fish changed even more markedly: they became

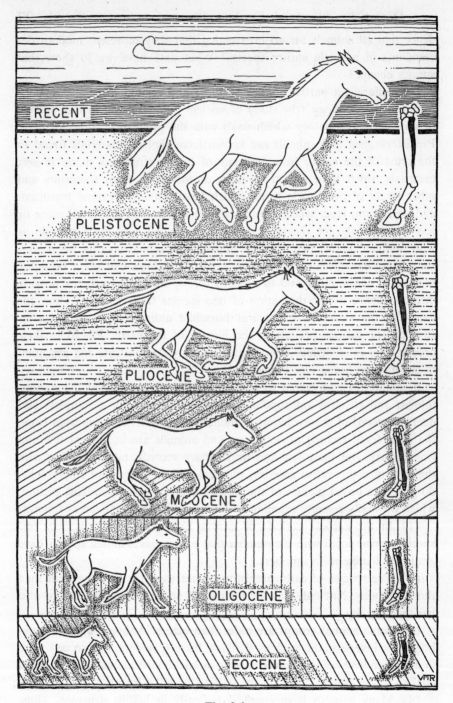

RECENT

PLEISTOCENE

PLIOCENE

MIOCENE

OLIGOCENE

EOCENE

Fig. 2:4.

28

amphibians or animals, like the frogs of today, quite different from fish. Similarly, the earliest known horse was very different from the modern horse (see Figure 2:4), and some of the men of a million years ago would scarcely be recognized as human beings if they appeared today.

(5) Other animals have changed far less in bodily structure. The ants of today are very similar to those of the remote past; ants have apparently undergone relatively little change over a very long period of time. The same is evidently true of some rare varieties of fish. A species called *latimeria,* only one specimen of which has as yet been found, is almost exactly like one that lived approximately 300 million years ago.

4. PRIMITIVE AND ADVANCED ANIMALS; SPECIALIZED AND GENERALIZED FORMS

Before we go on to describe the principal events in the evolution of man we must define one or two notions necessary to an understanding of this process. Certain animals are said to be "lower" or more "primitive" forms of life; others to be more "advanced" or "higher" forms. The difference here is simply one of structural complexity. Lower or primitive animals are those which possess a structural form characteristic of an earlier period in the history of the earth, even though such animals may actually be alive today and contemporaneous with advanced forms. The fish species *latimeria* just mentioned is obviously more primitive than most of the modern fish, and present-day fish, taken as a whole, have a much simpler bodily structure than modern man. For one reason or another the fish have evolved more slowly and along certain specialized lines, while man, a relatively generalized animal, has developed a greater structural complexity.

In distinguishing between lower and higher forms we have used the terms "specialized" and "generalized." Both these terms have to do with the development of an animal in respect to its physical environment. A specialized animal is one that has developed a number of organs which fit it particularly for one specific environment. Fish, for example, have developed streamlined bodies, gills, and other organs which are admirably suited to a marine environment but which make it impossible for fish to survive out of water. Hoofed animals have acquired a special kind of foot adapted to running and walking. Numbers of other animals have color specializations which enable them to blend with the environment and so escape detection by their enemies.

A generalized animal is one that has few specialized organs but has developed instead along broad fundamental lines. Man's brains, hands, and eyes, for example, are generalized features, even though they have developed enormously in complexity. Unlike the neck of the giraffe, the hoofs of the horse, and the long snout of the ant-eater, all of which are specialized organs, the brains, eyes, and hands of man do not give him advantages in terms of any specific environment. Man is one of the few animals that are more or less generalized throughout, and this may be one of the most important reasons for his survival and eventual domination over all other animals.

The trend of evolution is in general from simple generalized animals to more complex specialized forms. In only a few instances have highly complex animals retained the generalized form of their simpler forebears. Man is outstandingly such an exception, for though he is certainly the most complexly structured of any of the primates, he has fewer specialized organs than either the apes or the monkeys.

Specialization has both advantages and disadvantages. So long as the specialized form continues to live in the environment for which it is specialized, it is of course better fitted to survive than relatively generalized forms that have not the same equipment for adaptation. Under changing environmental circumstances, however, the generalized form can often hold its own and survive where the more specialized animal will die out. During one early period of earth's history, there existed a large number of highly specialized reptiles—the dinosaurs—which were admirably fitted to live in the warm, swampy forests of that era. Along with them were a number of generalized mammalian species, relatively small in numbers and size as compared to the giant reptiles. Gradually, however, the climate changed. As it grew slowly colder and dryer, the warm, swampy forests disappeared and with them the giant reptiles who depended upon them for food. Too well adapted to survive drastic change, the giant reptiles gradually became extinct, while the more generalized mammals were able to adjust, as a group, to the changed conditions and so survive.

5. CHRONOLOGICAL PERIODS IN THE HISTORY OF THE EARTH

Also necessary to our understanding of the evolutionary process is some knowledge of the techniques whereby geologists and paleontologists set up a time scale for world history. This is achieved by careful examination of the strata or layers of material laid down in various portions of the earth's crust in ancient times by water, wind, and volcanic action. We find that the time sequences of these strata may be determined in various ways from their positions relative to one another. To take a very simple case,

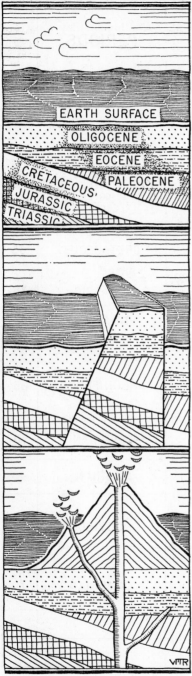

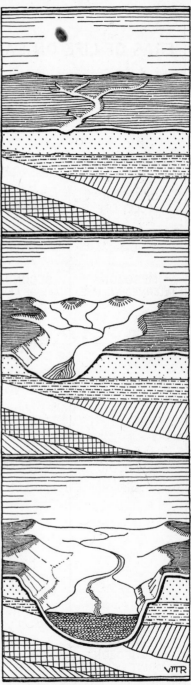

Fig. 2:5a. Top: superposition of sedimentary deposits. Middle: disturbance of sedimentary deposits by earth movements. Bottom: disturbance of deposits through volcanic action.

Fig. 2:5b. Schematic representation of river cutting. Note exposure of strata in the two upper sketches and the formation of new deposits in the bottom sketch.

31

ERAS OF LIFE ON EARTH		MILLIONS OF YEARS	PERIODS	MILLIONS OF YEARS IN EACH PERIOD
	QUATERNARY AGE OF MAN	1	HOLOCENE (RECENT)	1/50
			PLEISTOCENE	43/50
CENOZOIC RECENT LIFE	TERTIARY AGE OF MAMMALS		PLIOCENE	6
			MIOCENE	12
			OLIGOCENE	21
			EEOCENE	5
		55	PALEOCENE	10
MESOZOIC INTERMEDIATE LIFE	SECONDARY AGE OF REPTILES		CRETACEOUS	65
		120	JURASSIC	35
		155	TRIASSIC	35
		120	PERMIAN	25
	PRIMARY AGE OF AMPHIBIANS	215	CARBONIFEROUS	85
		300	DEVONIAN	50
PALEOZOIC ANCIENT LIFE	AGE OF FISHES	350	SILURIAN	40
		390	ORDOVICIAN	90
	AGE OF MARINE INVERTEBRATES	490	CAMBRIAN	70
		550		
PROTEROZOIC EARLIER LIFE				375
ARCHEOZOIC PRIMITIVE LIFE		925		575
		1500		

Fig. 2:6.

32

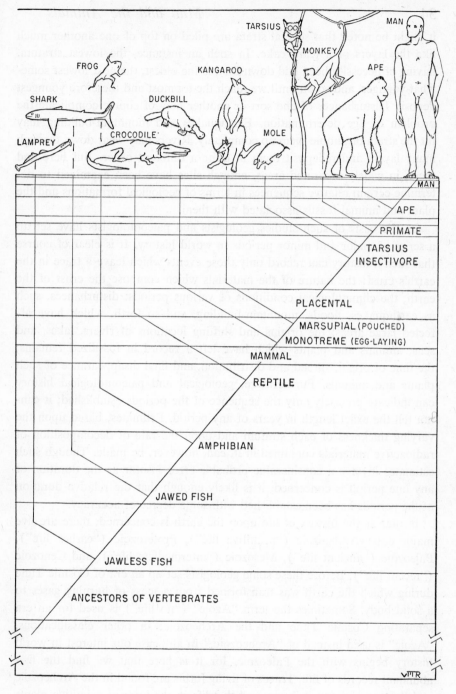

Fig. 2:6.

it might be noted that several strata are piled on top of one another much like the layers of a giant cake. In such an instance, the lowest stratum, having of necessity been laid down first, is the oldest, the next lowest somewhat younger, and so on until we reach the topmost and therefore youngest deposit. Disturbances of one sort or another may of course complicate the problem of age determination. Earthquakes and mountain-building may tilt the strata or jumble them up completely. Rivers may wear down through many layers and redeposit them in quite a different order. But here and there, in widely separated areas, enough sites have been examined to determine certain relative sequences in terms of geological formations and the plant and animal fossils associated with them.

On the basis of such studies geologists and paleontologists have set up a series of major and minor periods in world history. It is clear of course that such a history can record only those events which leave a trace in the earth's crust: the nature of the materials which compose the crust of the earth; the climatological conditions of various periods; disturbances, such as earthquakes, floods, mountain-building, and so forth, which have affected large areas; the origins and shifting locations of rivers, lakes, and seas; animals and plants which have left a record in fossilized remains; the time of origin, spread and distribution, and final disappearance of such plants and animals. Furthermore, geological and paleontological history can indicate precisely only the sequence of the periods established; it cannot tell the exact length in years of any period. Estimates, based upon the varying thickness of each stratum and upon the rate of decomposition of radioactive materials contained in it, can, however, be made. Though such estimates involve a considerable probable error insofar as the duration of any one period is concerned, it is likely enough that the relative duration of the periods has been established with some degree of accuracy.

Insofar as the history of life upon the earth is concerned, there are five major eras: Archeozoic ("primitive life"), Proterozoic ("earlier life"), Paleozoic ("ancient life"), Mesozoic ("intermediate life"), and Cenozoic ("recent life"). Before these some geologists set up an era of Cosmic Time during which the earth was transformed from a mass of burning gases to a solid body. Sometimes the term "Azoic" ("no life") is used for an era separating Cosmic Time and the Archeozoic; in other classifications, "Azoic" is used instead of "Archeozoic." In any case our interest in world history begins with the Paleozoic, for it is here that we find the first abundant records of life. Traces of living forms are found in the Archeozoic and Proterozoic, and it is assumed that life in the form of primitive plants and animals must have existed during these eras. That such forms are only rarely found is explained by the further assumption that the earliest living things were too soft to have left recognizable fossil remains. The Archeozoic probably began about 1,500 million years ago, and the Proterozoic 925 million years ago.

Beginning about 550 million years ago, the Paleozoic is divided into six periods: Cambrian, Ordovician, Silurian, Devonian, Carboniferous, and Permian. The Mesozoic began about 190 million years ago and is subdivided into three periods: Triassic, Jurassic, and Cretaceous. The Cenozoic is the last and shortest era, beginning 55 million years ago and composed of only two periods, the Tertiary and the Quaternary. In explanation of the last two terms, which mean "third" and "fourth" respectively, it may be pointed out that the Paleozoic is also called the Primary, and the Mesozoic, the Secondary.

The Cenozoic is for us the most interesting, for it was during this period that man reached his highest development. Direct evidence of man himself does not occur until the beginning of the Quaternary, a scant one million years ago. In the 1,500 or more million years of earth's history, manlike forms have existed only in the last million years. What we, somewhat egocentrically, call "civilization" is of course much younger. For, even if we date the beginnings of our western European cultures with the invention of agriculture and animal husbandry, it is at best only eight or ten thousand years old.

6. THE CHORDATES

We may now describe very briefly the evolution of life on earth with particular emphasis on man and his more or less direct antecedents. The animal kingdom, by which we refer to all animals past and present, may be divided, as we have seen, into two grades: *Protozoa* and *Metazoa*. *Protozoa* have in all probability existed since the beginnings of life on earth, and as they are today the simplest of all living animals it is probable that forms of this grade were the first animals to come into being. Man of course belongs to the grade *Metazoa*.

Metazoa are divided into ten or more phyla. The precise number of phyla, which is a matter of some dispute, need not concern us here. All but one are composed of animals differing greatly from man: for example, *Coelenterata,* such as corals, jellyfish, and sea anemones; *Porifera* or sponges; *Annelids,* segmented marine worms and earthworms; *Arthropoda,* jointed limbed animals such as insects, centipedes, and spiders; and *Mollusca,* oysters and similar animals.

Man and most of the animals figuring prominently in his cultures belong to the phylum *Chordata*. *Chordata* or chordates, as they are sometimes called, are distinguishable from other phyla by the following traits:

(1) An internal skeleton composed of bone or cartilage.

(2) A segmented backbone which encloses a spinal cord. (A few living animals classed as chordates have a stiff rod in place of a backbone and lack other features characteristic of chordates as a whole. Chordates possessing a segmented backbone are often distinguished as vertebrates. Since most chordates are also vertebrates, the two terms are often used interchangeably.)

(3) A complex organ, the brain, which centralizes the nervous system. It is usually enclosed in bone and located at the front end of the spinal cord.

(4) Bilateral symmetry: that is, one side of the body is in general a mirror replica of the other. This type of symmetry is characteristic of active animals, and chordates are excelled in mobility only by a few insects.

(5) A well-developed muscular system together with a high degree of muscular control and precisely coordinated bodily movements.

(6) Well-developed and complex sense structures such as eyes, noses, and ears.

(7) Lungs or gills by means of which oxygen is taken into the blood stream and carbon dioxide expelled.

(8) A complex circulatory system whereby blood is brought to nourish the tissues in every part of the body. The blood is pumped through this system by means of a special muscle, the heart.

There has been a great deal of discussion concerning the probable descent of the chordates, and almost every one of the other, and lower, phyla has been suggested as a probable ancestral form. The only conclusion that can be reached, however, is simply that we do not know for certain just how the transition from the lower invertebrates to the chordates took place. It is here that our paleontological evidence is scantiest. What Professor Romer says of his own hypothesis on this problem may equally well be said of all:

This discussion of the origin of vertebrates has been based solely on the comparative anatomy and embryology of the forms concerned. We have no fossil evidence to support the theory of vertebrate ancestry advocated here since the early ancestors of the vertebrates were presumably soft-bodied forms, possessing no hard parts and hence incapable of preservation under ordinary conditions. We have no certain fossil records of lower chordates or chordate ancestors, and very possibly never shall have. The oldest ancestors of the vertebrates are unknown, and may always remain unknown.[1]

Chordates comprise five major classes called, nontechnically, fish, amphibians, reptiles, birds, and mammals. Of these the fish are the simplest structurally among present-day chordates. It is not surprising, therefore, to find that they are also the first of the chordates to appear in history. The earliest traces of water-dwelling vertebrates are found in the Ordovician, the second period of the Paleozoic, but it is not until the Silurian that good skeletal remains are found. In the fourth Paleozoic period, the Devonian, fish are diversified and abundant, and we find as well the earliest amphibians, a class represented today by frogs, toads, and salamanders. The Devonian amphibians were the first land-dwelling vertebrates, and there is clear-cut evidence that they developed from the fish.

The earlier fish lacked both jaws and limbs; it was not until the Silurian that the jawed fish came into being. Limbs had their origin in paired fins which at first served only as stabilizing rudders. With, or shortly before, the coming of the amphibians, we may note two major developments: the evolution of lungs and the extension and strengthening of limbs for purposes of land travel. If we place the beginning of the Archeozoic 1,500 million years ago, it took about 1,100 million years for animals to develop to the point where life on dry land was possible.

Amphibians reached their peak of development in the Carboniferous period. Today, as a class, they are nearly extinct; frogs, toads, and salamanders represent a modern, more specialized branch of a once much larger class. Certain varieties of Carboniferous amphibians, however, gave rise to the next great class of chordates—the reptiles. A number of skeletal changes characterized this new class, particularly with respect to limbs, spine, skull, and teeth. But most important was the change in manner of reproduction. The amphibian young emerged from very small eggs which had to be laid in water, or at least in damp places, since the minute larvae were gilled and lived in water for a considerable period. Reptiles, on the other hand, laid larger eggs containing enough food to feed the embryo until it was ready to emerge as a fully equipped land animal. As a result the reptiles were freed entirely from the complete dependence upon a marine environment required by fish, as well as from the partial dependence necessary to amphibians.

As the Paleozoic drew to a close in its last or Permian period, amphibians

---

[1] A. S. Romer, *Man and the Vertebrates* (Chicago: University of Chicago Press, 1940), p. 20.

became less and less important, while the relatively new class of reptiles began rapidly to increase in number and variety. So the first 1,300 million years of animal evolution ended with the reptiles beginning to dominate the scene and rapidly to develop numerous specializations which were supremely to fit them for the climatic conditions of that day. Most of the earth during the last two or three periods of the Paleozoic was covered by warm, moist swamps, in which a rich and enormously variegated vegetation grew. Similar conditions prevailed throughout most of the Mesozoic with, toward the end, an increase of mountain-building and a gradual lowering of earth temperature.

The reptilian diversification which began in the Permian continued through the Triassic until it reached a peak in the second or Jurassic period of the Mesozoic. Reptiles grew to enormous proportions, particularly the highly specialized herbivorous ("plant-eating") types living in the swamps. In the meantime, in obscure corners here and there, the more generalized reptiles were already dividing, as early as the Triassic, into two small and relatively insignificant groups. One of these included the progenitors of present-day turtles and snakes, the other the first mammals.

Coincident with the gradual lowering of earth temperatures and the slow disappearance of the enormous swamps, occurred the extinction of the giant reptiles. It is probable that these highly specialized forms were literally killed off by the change in climate which must have drastically curtailed their food supply. Of this, however, we cannot be certain; we know only that they disappeared from the earth during the Cretaceous, and left behind them only the crocodile and the birds. Birds made their first appearance in the Jurassic, developing directly from certain forms of the giant reptiles. It should be noted that birds are not intermediate between reptiles and mammals but that both birds and mammals came from the reptile class (though of course from different subgroups within that class) in two independent and divergent lines of evolution.

At the end of the Mesozoic and after about 1,450 million years of world history, we find the earth inhabited by animals of all five classes, together of course with the many and varied descendants of the lower invertebrates. One class of vertebrates, the mammal, was just beginning to increase and diversify. The next era in world history, the Cenozoic, witnesses the gradual domination of the earth by the mammals, and especially by one of the many hundreds of mammalian species, man.

7. THE MAMMALS

Included in the class of mammals are a wide variety of earth-dwelling animals, for example, dogs, cats, cattle, horses, and man; a few marine animals, for example, whales and seals; and at least one winged creature, the bat. Despite their number and variety, however, the mammals are very much alike in basic structure. The principal characteristics by which we distinguish mammals from other classes of chordates may be summarized as follows:

(1) The young in most mammals develop within the body of the mother and are fed during this period by means of a special mechanism called a placenta.

(2) After birth the young are helpless for a period and must be fed and cared for by adults. Food is supplied by special milk-producing organs called mammary glands. It is from this trait that the class receives its name.

(3) During this period of postnatal care the young are also trained in the behavior necessary to their survival. This training is apparently made necessary by the greater complexity of the brain and nervous system.

(4) Mammals are warm-blooded, maintaining a constant, high body temperature. Hair and sweat glands are two mechanisms employed to regulate body temperature.

(5) The circulatory system is more complex and efficient in mammals than in the lower animals.

(6) The breathing apparatus is highly developed.

(7) The brain is much larger in mammals than in the lower animals. Almost all the growth has been, however, in the cerebral hemispheres, originally a small structure controlling the sense of smell. Here, in the mammals, have developed the higher brain centers which have put them so far above the lower animals in mental ability.

(8) The skulls of mammals are very different from those of the lower animals. So, for example, the nasal passage has become separate from the oral, a necessity in animals that must breathe constantly. The brain case has become much enlarged and the lower jaw is composed of a single bone instead of many.

(9) Teeth are greatly modified. Mammals have only two sets—infant or milk teeth and the second or permanent teeth—as compared to the indefinite tooth replacement in the lower animals. Mammal teeth also exhibit a greater differentiation. There are three main types: incisors for biting or cutting, canines for piercing, and premolars and molars for grinding.

(10) Eardrums are no longer on the surface as in reptiles, but are sunk into the head with an outer flap to aid in concentrating and directing the sound waves.

(11) Mammals are the most active of the chordates. Their limb development is much superior both in strength and agility. Further, the limbs are placed directly under the body so that even at rest they hold it up.

This permits all the energy expanded to go into propulsion in contrast to lower land animals who must first raise the body from the ground and then move it forward.

As we have said, the first mammals are found as early as the Triassic and continue throughout the Mesozoic. During this period, however, they are small, inconspicuous, and unimportant in relation to the gigantic and highly diversified reptilian forms. Mammals do not come into prominence and truly begin to take their present-day importance and variability until the beginning of the Cenozoic.

The first period of the Cenozoic, the Tertiary, is usually divided into five subperiods or epochs: Paleocene ("ancient recent types [i.e., mammals]"), Eocene ("dawn of recent types"), Oligocene ("few recent types"), Miocene ("minority of recent types"), and Pliocene ("majority of recent types"). In a similar fashion we may distinguish two epochs for the Quaternary, the second period of the Cenozoic: Pleistocene ("most of the recent types") and Holocene ("all of the recent types"). The last-named epoch is also called simply the Recent.

The duration of the Cenozoic is estimated at about 55 million years. Its epochs, however, are of unequal length: ten, five, twenty-one, twelve, and six million years each for the five Tertiary epochs and approximately one million years for the Quaternary. Within the Quaternary most of the time is taken up by the Pleistocene, estimated at 980,000 years, while the Holocene or Recent has lasted only 20,000 years.

Mammals of the present day are divided into three subclasses, primarily on the basis of their manner of reproduction. The first two subclasses, monotremes or egg-laying mammals and marsupials or pouched mammals, include only a few highly specialized animals. They are interesting and important, however, in that they preserve certain features intermediate between mammals and lower forms. The duckbilled platypus and the spiny ant-eater (both found only in Australia) still lay eggs and hatch them but also have a furry covering and nurse their young. These are, then, the most reptile-like of modern mammals, but because of their high degree of specialization it is impossible to regard them as truly ancestral to modern mammals. It is quite likely, in fact, that they have a separate line of descent going back to early Mesozoic times.

Pouched mammals are those who give birth to their young alive, but very small and helpless. These minute and seemingly premature offspring then crawl or are put into a pouch or marsupium on the belly of the mother. Here they are sheltered and fed until they are able to get along for themselves. Marsupials are found today in the Americas (the opossum is the most important) and in Australia. Australian marsupials include the kangaroo, the Tasmanian "wolf," the koala "bear," and the wombat, a woodchuck-like animal. Marsupials, it is quite certain, were much more common and widespread in Mesozoic times than they are now. In most places, however, they were crowded out by the later placental mammals. That they survived at all in America and flourished in Australia is due to environmental isolation which until recently protected them from destruction.

Neither monotremes nor marsupials, it is evident, are in the direct line of man's descent. They are, rather, mammalian offshoots having their own specialized historical development paralleling that of the principal mammalian subclass, the placentals. Together with a number of extinct forms known to us only from fossils, they serve to link the mammals with the more archaic reptiles from which they sprang.

All other mammals belong to the subclass *Eutheria* or placental mammals. In these animals the embryo develops within the body of the mother, food and oxygen being supplied to the embryo from an organ known as the placenta. This is a disklike organ one side of which is embedded in the walls of the uterus. On the other side, the umbilical cord connects the placenta with the embryo, and it is by means of this cord that nourishment is carried from the mother to the embryo. In this way the embryo is protected until it reaches a comparatively high stage of development. Once birth has taken place, the placenta detaches itself and is expelled.

Placental mammals are further subdivided into orders. Taxonomists disagree as to the precise number of mammalian orders, but we need not be concerned with that problem here. Man and the animals which most closely resemble him belong to the order of *Primates*. Some of the other orders are listed below.

(1) Insectivores or "insect-eaters." These are today represented by only a few rather insignificant forms such as moles, hedgehogs, and shrews. But it is quite certain that animals of this type were among the first of the mammals to appear on earth. The oldest insectivores are found in the Cretaceous and, once the great reptiles had disappeared, they spread rapidly all over the world. It is from this stock, which is now nearly extinct, that all the modern mammalian orders have developed.

(2) Carnivores or "meat-eaters." These are a large and important order including dogs, wolves, cats, lions, tigers, bears, hyenas, and marine animals such as the walrus. The order first appeared in the Paleocene. It is characterized by a high development of cutting and tearing teeth (incisors and canines), an extraordinary agility and suppleness, and sharp claws. Of this order of mammals, the dog has obviously been of most use to man. His association with man probably began at the beginning of the

Holocene or earlier, and man has used him for food, in hunting, for protection, as a pack and draft animal, and as a scavenger.

(3) Ungulates or hoofed animals. The principal characteristics of this order are the development of hoofs, a large proportion of grinding teeth (molars) in relation to cutting and tearing teeth, speed in running, the occurrence of horns (in some species), and, in a few species, an excessive specialization in tusklike canine teeth. Included in the ungulates are many animals familiar to us such as horses, rhinoceroses, deer, cattle, camels, pigs, and giraffes. There are also a number of less familiar forms; conies (small rodent-like animals found in Africa and Syria), proboscidians (elephants and many related extinct animals), and the sea cows. Many ungulates have of course played a considerable role in man's economic life. As early as the Quaternary, man hunted horses and deer for food; later he domesticated cattle, sheep, pigs, and goats; and still later the horse, camel, and certain varieties of deer were made into draft animals. Hoofed mammals first appear in the Paleocene.

(4) Rodents or gnawing animals. Familiar animals belonging to this order are rats, mice, squirrels, rabbits, beavers, and numerous others. Most of them are small and furry and possess characteristically large, chisel-like incisors which continue to grow throughout the life of the animal as they wear down from use. Rodents are almost as adaptable as man and, like him, are found in practically every region that supports life at all. One result of this wide dispersal and their relative lack of specialization is great diversification of form—there are as many varieties of rodent as of all other mammals combined. Like the ungulates, most rodents are vegetarians. Nearly all of them are terrestrial or arboreal; there are no exclusively aquatic types.

(5) Bats comprise an order by themselves. They are the only mammals who have developed true flight. Most of them live on insects. Bats are found as early as the Eocene.

(6) Whales and porpoises (*Cetaceans*), also in an order by themselves, are the only mammals who live exclusively in the water. Though they are air-breathing and, like other mammals, give birth to their young alive, they have become so adapted to marine life that they are helpless on land. *Cetaceans,* too, apparently began in the Eocene.

(7) *Edentates* or toothless mammals. A small order consisting largely of comparatively rare animals like ant-eaters, tree sloths, and armadillos. Most of these are found in South America. The order also includes a number of extinct fossil forms dating back to the Cretaceous.

8. THE PRIMATES

As we have just seen, most of the mammalian orders have names refer-ring to some outstanding trait common to its members. This is not true of the primates, for that term means merely "the first." Apart from the probability that this name was chosen because man did the naming and he is a member of the order, it would be difficult to find a structural speciali-zation which is characteristic of all primates. Indeed, it is specifically this lack of a common specialization that best distinguishes primates; they represent, as a group, the most generalized of all mammals.

We know that primates began as early as the Eocene and that they grad-ually increased in number to the present time. However, the paleontologi-cal record is far from good; fossil remains are few and fragmentary. The reason is that fossil records are best preserved in nonforested regions, and primates, until man arrived, were tree-dwellers living only in torrid rain forests.

Primates as a whole may be distinguished from other mammalian orders by the following common characteristics.

(1) Most primates are arboreal; only the baboon and man live wholly on the ground. There is good evidence that this is an archaic mode of life—the primitive placentals were tree-dwellers and the primates have continued to be so. The fact of his arboreal ancestry is important to the understanding of man, as we shall see.

(2) Primates have exceedingly mobile limbs; there is none of the re-stricted limb movement characteristic, for example, of the ungulates. This mobility is undoubtedly correlated with the primates' retention of arboreal life.

(3) Primates climb by grasping limbs of trees and so pulling them-selves up. Most other arboreal forms, such as squirrels, for example, climb by digging their sharp claws into the tree. The primate climbing technique is accompanied by other developments: flat nails instead of claws, the ability to oppose the thumb and great toe to the other digits, and a notable retention of all or most of the digits of hand and foot. In this last trait, the primates are little changed from the primitive placentals. Most of the other mammalian orders have changed radically in this respect; recall, for example, the development of hoofs among the ungulates.

(4) Arboreal life had one other important corollary. Most mammals find their way about and examine the environment in which they live primarily by means of their sense of smell. In general, we may say that the lower, ground-dwelling mammals have a very highly developed olfac-tory organ and very poor eyesight. Primates, however, are the reverse.

Eyesight is very good and the sense of smell has greatly degenerated. Further, in all primates but the lemurs, the eyes are directed forward so that both may be concentrated upon the object seen. Each eye receives an image of the object, and the two images, by means of a complex nervous mechanism, are so superimposed as to make three-dimensional or depth perception possible. This is in sharp contrast to the laterally directed eyes, independent vision, and flat perspective of the lower mammals.

(5) Mammals in general and all primates but man habitually move about on four feet. But the primate mode of climbing has resulted in a differentiation in function between fore and hind limbs. The hind limbs are primarily supporting, the fore limbs mainly grasping. As a result, there is a notable tendency among most primates toward a sitting posture while at rest, which frees the fore limbs from the necessity of supporting the body. The fore limbs and hands are then available for grasping, holding, and examining objects in the environment.

(6) The primitive long tail has been retained by some primates where it functions as a balancing device or, in others, as a grasping (prehensile) organ. In many forms, however, the external tail has been greatly reduced or lost altogether.

(7) Most primates are omnivorous—that is, they eat both meat and vegetable foods. Their dentition is therefore less specialized; they have neither the high development of canines and incisors characteristic of carnivores nor the excessive molar specialization of herbivores. The total number of teeth has been reduced from forty-four (in primitive placentals) to thirty-two. Jaws have also been reduced in length and the face has become much shorter. Most primates have projecting and interlocking canines.

(8) Relative to their body weight primates have the largest brains of all the mammals. Associated with this increased brain size is a remarkably more complex brain and nervous system, and, in general, a higher development of mental ability. It is notable that the increase in brain size has been largely in the motor areas and is probably to be correlated with the higher degree of muscular coordination required by arboreal life. Undoubtedly, too, the improved eyesight and the freeing of the fore limbs for manipulatory purposes, both of which have resulted in a wider and more detailed knowledge of the environment, have played no inconsiderable role in the development of the brain and the increase in mental ability.

(9) As a result of changes in dentition, the improvement of eyesight, the degeneration of the olfactory sense, and the increase in brain size, the skulls of primates are distinctively different in structure from those of the

lower mammals. The face is not so long, the muzzle has been greatly re-tracted, and the slope of the face from above the eyes to the mouth has become much steeper. The skull vault has enlarged to accommodate the larger brain, and the eye sockets have become a solid ring (in the higher primates, a hemisphere) of bone.

Primates are usually divided into three suborders called *Lemuroidea* ("lemur-like"), *Tarsioidea* ("tarsius-like"), and *Anthropoidea* ("man-like"). Lemurs were found during the Eocene in both the Old and New Worlds; their numer-ous and varied descendants today live only in the tropical regions of the Old World. They are the most primitive of the primates and have changed little in structure since the Eocene. Small in size, the lemur goes on all fours, lives in trees, and is nocturnal in habit. His coat is furry, his tail usually long, and his limbs of moderate length with only a slight differentiation between those fore and aft. Eyes are directed laterally and are independent of each other. Ears are pointed, and the thumb and big toe are separated from the other digits, but grasping ability is little developed. In brief, the lemur is barely a primate and is important chiefly because he is so little changed since Eocene times and so closely resembles the primitive tree shrew (an insectivore) from which all primates probably originated.

Fig. 2:7.

The suborder *Tarsioidea* contains only one genus, an animal called tarsius which today is found only in the East Indies. Structurally, tarsius falls somewhere between the lemur and the monkey, and it is quite likely that he is a somewhat specialized offshoot of one of the many varieties of Eocene tarsioids which appear to link the lemuroids to the higher primates.

About the size of a rat, tarsius is, like the lemur, arboreal and nocturnal. His eyes are enormous and point forward, and it appears that he possesses the mechanism with which to blend their images stereoscopically. The limbs are highly specialized, the fore limbs for grasping and the hind ones for the rapid hop which is his mode of locomotion when on the ground.

The suborder *Anthropoidea* includes all the rest of the primates and man. Anthropoids are, then, the most numerous and least specialized of all the primates. There are five families of anthropoids which may be grouped as follows:

MONKEY

BABOON

Fig. 2:8.

Platyrrhines ("flat-nosed") or New World anthropoids.

Cebidae, including the cebus or "organ-grinder" monkey, the spider monkey, and the howler monkey. This family is restricted to South and Central America.

Hapalidae or marmosets. South America.

Catarrhines ("downward-nosed") or Old World anthropoids.

Cercopithecidae, principally macaques and baboons. Asia and Africa. One fossil form, *Parapithecus,* an Oligocene find from Egypt, may be included in this family.

Simiidae or great apes. There are four principal modern genera: the gibbon, found in southeastern Asia, Borneo, and Sumatra; the orang from Borneo and Sumatra; the gorilla from Africa; and the chimpanzee from Africa. Fossil forms include: *Propliopithecus* from the Egyptian Oligocene; *Dryopithecus,* found during the Miocene and Pliocene in Europe, Asia, and Africa; *Pliopithecus,* a Pliocene form found in France; and *Australopithecus,* a South African form from the Pleistocene.

Hominidae. Modern men all belong to a single genus and species and are found everywhere. Prehistoric men were of several species and, until the end of the Pleistocene, were confined to the Old World. We shall list and describe them in Chapter 5.

The New World anthropoids (*Cebidae* and *Hapalidae*) are the most divergent of all the *Anthropoidea.* They are called platyrrhines because their nostrils are separated by a wide septum and are directed more to the side than downward or forward. Numerous other divergent traits—such as their prehensile tails, thick fur, dentition, and, in one species, the development of large bony resonance chambers in the throat—suggest that these monkeys are not directly ancestral to man. They represent, in all probability, a separate and parallel evolutionary line which may have branched off as early as the Eocene.

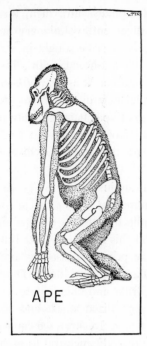

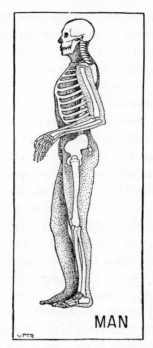

Fig. 2:9.   Fig. 2:10.

In the catarrhine anthropoids the nostrils are much closer together and are directed forward and down. Further, there is, within the group, a gradual increase in size from the *Cercopithecidae* to the chimpanzee, gorilla, and man. All the ancestral forms were probably arboreal, as the New World monkeys are today, but some catarrhines, such as men and baboons, are terrestrial, and the larger apes spend a good deal of time on the ground. Tails are shorter and never prehensile; in some forms, such as man, they are lacking entirely. It is probable that the older forms were four-footed, but in the modern species there is a tendency toward the upright posture, partial in the apes and fully developed in man. Thumbs are in all forms partially or perfectly opposable, and so is the great toe except in man. The hairy covering is light, and the face, except in certain varieties of man, without hair at all.

Anthropoids of the Old World variety go back at least to the Oligocene. In a fossil bed at the edge of an old lake near Fayum, Egypt, was found a jaw and a few other bone fragments which give us a somewhat sketchy description of an ancient monkey. This form, *Parapithecus,* is clearly an Old World monkey, indicating that the primitive catarrhine stock had already split into at least two divisions. It is very probable that the present-day Old World monkeys are descendants of this early form.

Neither the Old nor the New World monkeys are, then, directly ancestral to man. Both of them represent divergent evolutionary lines going
back to the early Tertiary. Man's ancestors must be sought in a third line
of development, beginning to the best of our knowledge with a form called
Propliopithecus found in the same place and epoch as *Parapithecus.* Here,
too, we have only the jaw, but it is sufficiently distinctive to reveal that
Propliopithecus is not a monkey but a small ape. It is probably too much
to say that *Propliopithecus* marks the point of origin of the *Simiidae* and
Hominidae, but he does, at least, indicate that apes had diverged from
monkeys as early as the Oligocene.

Other fossil finds are equally disappointing insofar as the precise history
of apes and men is concerned. The numerous *Dryopithecus* finds, uncovered chiefly in the Siwalik Hills of India but also in Europe and North
Africa, consist only of teeth and jaws. But this is enough to tell us that we
are dealing with a large Miocene-Pliocene primate possessing traits found
today only in the chimpanzee, the gorilla, and man. Some *Dryopithecus*
varieties appear to be ancestral to the gorilla and chimpanzee, others are
apparently sterile offshoots of a more generalized stock, and still others
show traits which point in the direction of man. In short, we cannot be certain that we have in *Dryopithecus* a form directly ancestral to man, gorilla,
and chimpanzee, but it does appear that *Dryopithecus* cannot be far distant from such a generalized type. A number of other late Tertiary apes,
similar to *Dryopithecus,* apparently confirm this thesis. *Pliopithecus,* uncovered in late Miocene or early Pliocene strata in France, is definitely
ancestral to the modern gibbon and so already far removed from the line
of descent which resulted in man.

Another very interesting series of fossil apes has been found in South
Africa: *Australopithecus, Plesianthropus,* and *Paranthropus.* For all of
these we have much of the face and brain case plus a number of teeth
and other bone fragments. *Australopithecus* was a child, probably equivalent in age to a human child of six or seven. The others were adults. All
three are difficult to date because they were found in a region none too
well known geologically and because the finds were made by laymen who
took no note of accompanying geological and paleontological data. Later
investigation seems to indicate, however, that none are earlier than the
Pleistocene, a time at which man had already appeared in various regions
of the Old World.

All these fossil apes are much more advanced in the direction of man
than any modern ape. This is shown by their brain size (two being definitely larger-brained than the modern ape), the shape of their faces and
jaws, the more human outline of the dental arch, a number of humanoid

traits in their teeth, and the strong probability that they walked in an erect or semierect position. Here we have, then, apelike animals which, it is quite clear, were on the road to becoming men. Because of their late date (contemporaneous with forms which were already men) they cannot be considered transitional between Tertiary apes and man. We can only conclude that these forms are probable descendants of such a transitional form which, for one reason or another, never quite succeeded in achieving human status.

9. APES AND MEN

Modern apes and men, it is now clear, are not very far removed in ancestry. Their common progenitor must clearly have been a Tertiary form, probably no earlier than the Oligocene, or about forty million years ago. The precise connecting animal (or "missing link") is lacking and may never be found, but the evidence already at hand is conclusive proof of the essential kinship of man and the higher apes. Discovery of a "missing link" is in no way necessary to this conclusion.

Further confirmation of this essential relationship may be found by comparing present-day apes and men with one another and by the fossil history of man himself. Modern apes and men differ from one another in certain specific respects but prehistoric men are often much less different from the apes in precisely the same traits. Man's prehistory will be discussed later (see Chapter 5), but in preparation for that discussion as well as to complete our picture of the *Anthropoidea* we shall describe in the following paragraphs the major points of difference between men taken as a whole and the four ape genera.

In many ways the skull offers some of the most important contrasts between apes and men. It becomes particularly important when we know that most of our data on prehistoric men are confined to the skull alone, since this part of the human skeleton is most likely to survive the ravages of time. There are two main respects in which differences of skull structure between men and apes are most marked—the shape and capacity of the brain case and the proportions of the face.

Man's brain case is largest in capacity, averaging 1,450 cc. (= cubic centimeters) as compared to averages of 500 cc. for the gorilla, 404 for the chimpanzee, 395 for the orang, and 128 for the gibbon. In other words, the skull of man has roughly three times the capacity of that of the largest-brained ape. Even more important is the fact that man's skull is highly developed in the frontal region, his forehead extending almost vertically upward for a considerable distance. In all apes this region is little developed, the head sloping sharply backward from the brow ridges. Correlated with this distinction is another: most apes possess a marked bulge of bone, called a supraorbital ridge, which extends unbroken across the region of the skull just over the eyes. This ridge is small in the orang and very small or completely absent in man. Finally, the large hole (foramen magnum) in the base of the skull through which the spinal cord goes to the brain is, in apes, to the rear of the center of the skull's base. In man it is found at or forward of this central position. As a result the ape's head hangs forward and habitually rests on his chest; it takes some effort for the ape to raise his head. The muscles employed for this purpose are large and have their line of attachment high up in the rearward portion of the skull. In contrast, man's head is balanced on his spinal column and the line of muscle attachment far lower on the back of the skull.

If we examine the profile of an ape we note that it is projected forward, the line of the face as a whole and that of the upper jaw slanting outward and downward to a point midway between the upper incisor teeth. Such forward projection is called prognathism. In man facial prognathism is practically always lacking, and alveolar prognathism (that is, the forward projection of the upper jaw) is either slight or completely absent.

The lower jaw of the ape is usually massive and lacks the bony projection which we call a chin. The muscles which control the movements of the lower jaw are large and powerful. Man's lower jaw, on the other hand, is comparatively small and his chewing muscles weak. Furthermore, all except the very earliest prehistoric men possess a well-developed chin.

Teeth in both men and apes are thirty-two in number: eight incisors, four canines, eight premolars, and twelve molars. The teeth of apes are, however, much larger than those of men and their canines project beyond the level of the other teeth. As a result, an ape's canine teeth interlock when his jaws are closed, thus obliging him to chew his food with a more or less straight up-and-down movement of the lower jaw. Man's canines are not only smaller than those of the ape, but do not project and interlock. His chewing motions are usually from side to side as well as up and down, the so-called rotary chewing. The arch in which the teeth are set also differs in men and apes. In apes the dental arch is U-shaped, in men it takes the form of a parabola.

The nose is supported by two bones, more or less rectangular in shape, which fit together along one of their long edges. From these nasal bones extends the cartilaginous nose divided by the septum into two chambers or nostrils. Apes' noses have very little or no elevation at the root and bridge (that is, where the nasal bones join together). The cartilaginous

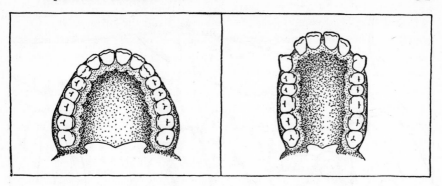

Fig. 2:11. Human dental arch (left); ape's dental arch (right).

portion is very wide, flaring, and little raised above the surface of the face. A cartilaginous tip is usually lacking so that the nostrils are prominently visible and give the impression of two large holes in the face. Man's nose, in contrast, has a slight to marked elevation at the root and bridge, and a cartilaginous portion considerably above the surface of the face. The nasal wings may be narrow or broad, but never as broad as the ape's, and the tip is always well developed. Nostrils are smaller and usually point downward.

The upper lip of the ape is very long, man's is relatively short. Membranous lips (that is, the red portion of the lips) in apes scarcely show at all when the mouth is closed. Man's lips vary from thin to very thick, but are never as thin or as mobile as those of the ape.

Apes vary in stature and weight. The gibbon is smallest, averages about 3′ 0″ in height, and weighs from fourteen to eighteen pounds. Orangs average 4′ 6″ and 165 pounds. The chimpanzee and gorilla are considerably taller, averaging about 5′ 0″ and 5′ 6″, respectively. In weight the chimpanzee averages from 88 pounds for females to 110 pounds for males. Gorillas are very much heavier, the range for males in captivity running from 293 to over 600 pounds. It is probable that wild gorillas are somewhat lighter on the average. Man's average height is about 5′ 6″, and his average weight 145 pounds. The apes have considerably longer torsos than man. Their legs are shorter than man. Their legs are shorter than their arms, whereas in man the reverse is true. The thigh bone of the ape is short, thick, and curved as compared to man's long, slender, and straight thigh bone. As a result the ape walks with a shambling gait.

Apes habitually stand in a semierect position, resting part of their weight on their hands, the knuckles of which touch the ground. Their backbones form a simple curve, not the elongated S-curve characteristic of man. Both the big toe and the thumb of the ape are imperfectly opposable to the other

GIBBON · ORANG-OUTANG · GORILLA · CHIMPANZEE · MAN

Fig. 2:12.

digits; the ape can grasp with his feet almost as well as he can with his hands. Man's thumb is perfectly opposable, but his feet have become entirely supporting organs and can no longer be used for grasping.

The gibbon is furry on head and body, the orang and gorilla are thickly haired, and the chimpanzee has a thick body hair but little head hair. Man possesses only a sparse body hair but the hair of his head is long and thick. Some varieties of man have heavy facial hair, a trait lacking among apes.

All apes have straight hair; man's varies from extremely curly to straight. In color the hair of man and the gibbon is variable. Chimpanzees are black-haired, orang hair is red-brown, and that of the gorilla is red-brown or black. Chimpanzees and man are variable in skin color; the gorilla has a brown to black skin, the orang a brown skin, and the gibbon a black skin.

The brain is the one organ in which man stands out most sharply in comparison with the great apes and the lower primates. In weight alone man's brain is more than three times as heavy as that of the largest-brained ape, the gorilla. But this is certainly not the whole story. For we find, when we compare man with the lower animals, that the growth of man's brain has been largely in one portion of it, the cerebrum or cerebral hemispheres.

In the primitive mammals the cerebrum is small and perched at the front of the brain, only slightly overlapping the two other main regions, the cerebellum and medulla oblongata. Here, as in other animals, the cerebrum controls sense perception, such as smell, sight, touch, and hearing. But in the lower mammals the area of the cerebrum devoted to the sense of smell is by far the largest, dominating all the others. This is strictly in accord with the fact that most of the lower mammals are ground-dwellers who find their way about by means of their olfactory organs, eyesight and other senses being relatively less developed.

As we pass from the lower mammals to those progressively higher, and particularly when we come to the primates, the cerebrum becomes increasingly larger until in man it covers most of the two other portions of the brain. Further, the cerebral cortex (a thin layer of gray matter covering the cerebrum) increases in area, lying in endless folds or convolutions over the entire surface of man's cerebral hemispheres. Particularly important is the fact that man's brain is not only much larger than that of the ape but it is especially highly developed in the frontal region and has a much more complex convolutionary development of the cerebral cortex.

In man the cerebrum still controls sensory perception, and certain regions of it can be assigned to each of the various senses. But where in the lower animals these sensory areas are bunched together with little or no space between them, the primates have developed the so-called "association" areas, regions of the cerebrum surrounding the sensory areas. These are the portions of the cerebrum which have increased most in size as we move from lower to higher primates, and they are of course most extensive in man. No one is as yet certain as to the precise function of the association areas. But in view of the fact that man's association areas are largest and that he also possesses the most highly developed mentality, there can be little doubt that some sort of relationship, though certainly not a simple one, exists between the size and development of the association areas and what we call mental ability.

We have now summarized, very briefly, the history of man's development and indicated the place he holds relative to other modern animals. Man, it should now be clear, is an animal, organ for organ comparable to other animals. He belongs to the grade *Metazoa,* to the phylum *Chordata,* and to the class of Mammals. Within this class he is a member of the placental subclass *(Eutheria)* and the order of Primates. Man's suborder is appropriately called *Anthropoidea* ("manlike"). Within the *Anthropoidea* are found five families, two of New World anthropoids and three of Old World anthropoids. Man's family, the *Hominidae,* together with the *Cercopithecidae* (monkeys) and the *Simiidae* or great apes, make up the Old World group. In Chapters 5 and 6 we shall take up the further problem of subdividing the *Hominidae*.

COLLATERAL READING

Ashley-Montagu, M. F. *An Introduction to Physical Anthropology.* Springfield, Illinois: C. C. Thomas, 1945. Chapters II–IV.

Hooton, Earnest A. *Up From the Ape.* Rev. Ed. New York: The Macmillan Co., 1946. Parts I, II.

———. *Man's Poor Relations.* New York: Doubleday, Doran and Co., 1943.

Howells, W. W. *Mankind So Far.* New York: Doubleday, Doran and Co., 1944. Part I.

Newman, H. H. "The Factors of Organic Evolution," *The Nature of the World and Man,* ed. H. H. Newman. Chicago: University of Chicago Press, 1926. Pp. 381–418.

Romer, Alfred S. "The Evolution of the Vertebrates," *The Nature of the World and Man,* ed. H. H. Newman. Chicago: University of Chicago Press, 1926. Pp. 304–348.

———. *Man and the Vertebrates.* Chicago: University of Chicago Press, 1941.

Simpson, George G. *The Meaning of Evolution.* New Haven: Yale University Press, 1950. Part I.

Chapter 3

HEREDITY AND GENETICS

1. HEREDITY, VARIATION, AND MUTATION

Proper understanding of the origin of man and his varieties or races and the significance of race differences depends on knowledge of heredity and its mechanisms. Our first task in this chapter is to define what we mean and what we do not mean by the term "heredity."

Most people take heredity for granted without really understanding what is implied by the term. We know that dogs give birth to dogs and not to cats or fish or birds. We are all aware that the offspring of Chinese ordinarily look like Chinese and that the offspring of Negroes ordinarily look like Negroes. It is a common observation that children tend to resemble their parents, often giving rise to discussions in which friends and relatives try to decide which parent a newborn child resembles.

All these everyday observations may really be summarized in a general statement that living things tend to reproduce their own kind. The "man in the street" might want to go further and say that living things always reproduce their own kind, but this would be inaccurate. Although heredity, meaning simply the tendency of things to reproduce their own kind, is one of the fundamental facts about living matter, it is not the only fundamental fact about organic things. Equally universal is the principle of variation and change. Although children tend to resemble their parents, almost never do children exactly resemble their parents. Brothers are never exactly alike (save possibly some identical twins); however close superficial resemblances may be, detailed differences always exist. The whole

55

technique of criminal identification with its use of fingerprints and other criteria rests on this fact. Even the same tree almost never produces two leaves that exactly resemble one another in every respect, nor are such lowly single-celled organisms as the protozoa ever exactly identical with one another. Variation, then, is quite as universal a fact in life as is heredity, and both are significant in understanding man.

Variations must never be confused with modifications. The latter are changes which take place in the organism as a result of temporary or special environmental conditions and which are not inherited. The blacksmith who develops powerful biceps muscles has experienced a modification of his body which he does not transmit directly to his offspring. Man may mutilate his body in various ways, cutting his hair, shaving, perforating the ears for ornaments, practicing head deformation or circumcision for many thousands of years, yet these modifications have no effect on each generation of infants. Men still grow hair on their faces and children's ears still have to be pierced in each generation.

Variations, on the other hand, appear in the offspring without any effort on the part of the individual or his parents. Variations represent fundamental changes in the internal organization of the individual and ultimately are to be traced to changes in the internal structure of the cells of which the body is composed. Environment has nothing to do with the production of variations directly except insofar as the environment will permit the individual to grow and develop in the direction called for by the new variation.[1] Thus, if the variation is in a direction harmful to the individual, the environment may eliminate him. A child varying in the direction of greater susceptibility to a disease common in the environment may die of the disease before he reaches maturity and has an opportunity to reproduce. Such a variation will thus disappear. On the other hand, a child varying in the direction of greater resistance to the same disease has a better chance to survive and reproduce himself than have other children, and hence the variation may be perpetuated.

Another point about variations is that they may be of two kinds. Slight changes, which constantly occur and distinguish brother from brother and child from parent, are what are usually meant by variations. Sometimes, however, striking changes occur between parent and child. Such changes are known as mutants, sports, or mutations, and represent major changes.

The significance of mutations was first pointed out by De Vries of Holland, who discovered growing in his garden a new type of primrose. De Vries, through experiment, determined that this new primrose repro-

---

[1] Indirectly, the environment may promote variations or mutations. For example, radioactive substances in an environment will stimulate a greater rate of change.

duced true to type and hence constituted a new variety which had appeared by a sudden and radical variation rather than through a series of small and successive variations (which had been Darwin's explanation of the origin of a new species). The occasional occurrence of mutations is now well established and affords another explanation for the origin of new species and varieties. Organisms of the same kind, then, resemble one another through the operations of heredity. They differ from one another as a result of inherited variations or mutations, or through the noninheritable differences or modifications developed in life as a result of different life experiences.

Probably mutations play an especially important part in the origin of those races or species which differ from one another in unimportant organs or characteristics of the body and which could hardly have arisen through the natural selection of small variations. The explanation is particularly applicable to man (although it is not the only possible explanation), for the different varieties or races of man differ from one another only in unimportant organs or characteristics.

2. MENDEL'S LAWS OF HEREDITY

Proper understanding of variation, mutation, and heredity requires some knowledge of the mechanisms of heredity. Only through investigation of the actual cell structure and the processes of reproduction can we appreciate the significance of heredity in man and discard some of the folk ideas about heredity. Such folk ideas are often very dangerous in our modern society. For example, some people talk about "purity of the blood" and "transmitting things through the blood stream." We constantly speak of people being "related by blood" or of being "blood kin." Many people, infected by these folk ideas, protested the use of Negro blood plasma to save the lives of white soldiers during World War II.

This, and all the expressions used above, are based on the medieval idea that the blood is the agency of heredity. Such ideas grew up when knowledge of the human organism was very slight. It was supposed that in the mammals and man the fetus was nourished by blood supplied by the mother through the placenta. Actually, the fetus develops its own blood stream and circulatory system. This system extends through the placenta and part of it becomes imbedded in the wall of the uterus. There is no direct connection of the veins or arteries of the fetus and those of the mother and at no time does any blood from the mother pass into the veins of the child.

All that is transmitted from mother to offspring by this circulatory system is nourishment and some influence on the environment in which the fetus develops. For example (although proof is as yet not very satisfactory), a chemical imbalance in the nourishment or surroundings of the child may affect its development, but it will not alter the heredity of the offspring.

Far from being a vague and random thing, as would be the result of inheritance through the blood, heredity operates with extraordinary precision and regularity. Whenever all the factors are understood regarding the inheritance of a particular trait, the results of various crossings and matings can be predicted with the regularity of a chemical reaction.

Discovery of the fundamental regularity of heredity was made by the monk, Gregor Mendel, who published his results in 1865. As the scientific world was, at that time, busy arguing over evolution, Mendel's results were overlooked until nearly the end of the century, when the same principles were discovered independently by three different investigators. We shall first present briefly the regularities discovered by Mendel.

Mendel for the first time discovered that the individual is not the unit of inheritance. Instead, each individual is made up of a number of characters which may be inherited separately. Such characters are called unit characters. It was with these that Mendel experimented.

Unit characters are traits which normally appear as a whole or do not appear at all and are found in contrasting pairs. Mendel experimented with varieties of peas which were either smooth or wrinkled and whose plants were either tall or short. Experiments by Mendel and others with such characters led to the discovery of two basic kinds of inheritance. These may best be illustrated by concrete examples.

The first type of inheritance is a blending of the contrasted traits in any hybrid forms (that is, forms resulting from mating of parents showing contrasted unit characters). This is illustrated by the white and red four-o'clocks.

Pure strains of white and red four-o'clocks must first be secured by breeding white four-o'clocks with each other for a number of generations in order to make sure that no other type appears. The same is also done with the red variety. The experiment is then begun by breeding white four-o'clocks with red four-o'clocks. This generation is known as the parental generation. When seeds produced by this crossing are planted, the resulting plants produce flowers which are neither red nor white but pink, resembling neither parent with respect to the character of color of flower. This group of plants is referred to as the first filial generation or

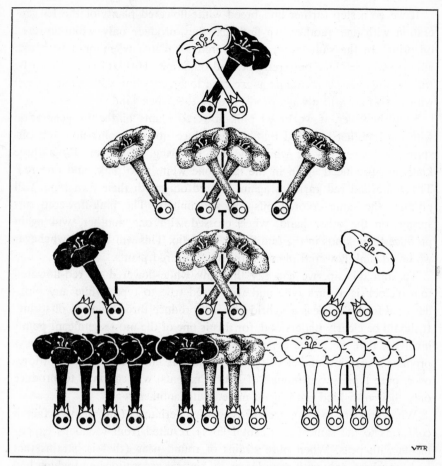

Fig. 3:1. Results of crossing pure strains of white and red four-o'clocks.

the F_1 generation. The generation, in this case, may also be called a hybrid generation.

If we now take hybrid pink-flowered plants of the F_1 generation and breed them with one another, the offspring (known as the second filial or F_2 generation) will be of three types. Some will have white flowers, some will have pink flowers, and some will have red flowers. In other words, some will resemble one member of the parental generation, some will resemble the other member, but some will resemble the F_1 generation. Moreover, if large numbers of the F_2 generation are produced, we will find that for every white-flowered plant of the F_2 generation there are two pink-flowered plants and one red-flowered plant. In brief, the three kinds of plants produced in the F_2 generation are in the ratio 1:2:1.

If we go a step further and breed white-flowered plants of the F_2 generation with one another, we find that they produce only white-flowered offspring. In the same way, red-flowered F_2 plants when bred with one another will produce only red-flowered offspring. This will continue to be true for as many generations as we care to breed white with white or red with red—they will always produce only their own kind.

Now, however, if we breed pink-flowered plants of the F_2 generation with one another, we find that they produce not only pink-flowered offspring but also red- or white-flowered offspring. Moreover, these three kinds are produced again in the ratio one white, two pink, and one red. The white and red varieties again, if bred only with their own kind, will produce the same colored offspring indefinitely. The pink-flowered offspring, on the other hand, when crossed with one another, will again produce three kinds in the familiar $1:2:1$ ratio. This will be true whenever we breed pink-flowered plants with pink-flowered plants.

To sum this up, we can say that any white-flowered or red-flowered four-o'clock is a pure type and will breed true to type, while any pink-flowered four-o'clock is a hybrid and will produce three kinds of offspring. It should be clearly understood, for this is one of the most significant points involved, that the above experiments prove that hybrid types will always produce a certain number of pure types in this kind of inheritance. Moreover, pure types, even though of hybrid parents, will continue to produce only their own kind until again mated with another type.

What appears to be a second type of inheritance (although in fact it conforms to the same fundamental laws) resulted from Mendel's experiments with peas. When pure strains of round peas (that is, strains that had been bred only with round peas for several generations and which had always produced only round offspring) were crossed with pure strains of wrinkled peas, the first filial or F_1 generation peas were all round. In the four-o'clock, be it remembered, the F_1 generation was intermediate between the parental types with respect to the trait under consideration. In the case of the peas, all the F_1 generation resembled only one parent, the round-seeded parent. Going on to the next step, that is, the F_2 generation produced by mating members of the F_1 generation with each other, the results were also different. Instead of a $1:2:1$ ratio of offspring, the F_1 peas produced offspring in the ratio of approximately three round peas to one wrinkled pea or a ratio of $3:1$. If the wrinkled peas are bred with each other or self-fertilized (the pea is especially useful for the ensuing demonstration because it is self-fertilizing), the resulting offspring will all be wrinkled. This will continue to be the case for as many generations as

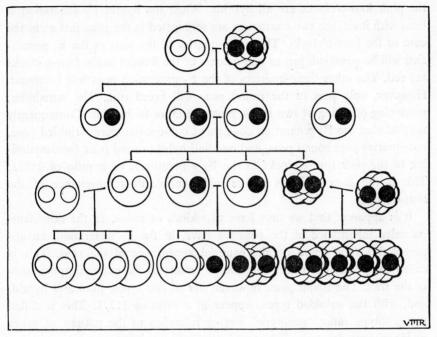

Fig. 3:2. Results of crossing pure strains of round and wrinkled peas.

wrinkled peas are self-fertilized without the introduction of a round strain. If a round strain is introduced, however, the following generation will produce only round peas again.

Turning now to the round peas of the F_2 generation, if these are self-fertilized a different result obtains. One out of every three round peas will produce only round peas, and subsequent generations of this one-third of the round peas will produce only round peas. The other two-thirds of the round peas, however, will produce offspring in the ratio of three round to one wrinkled. Moreover, if these offspring are self-fertilized, the same ratios will obtain throughout all subsequent generations. The wrinkled peas produced will, when self-fertilized, always produce only wrinkled peas. One-third of the round peas will always produce only round peas. But two-thirds of the round peas, when self-fertilized, will produce offspring in the ratio of three round peas to one wrinkled pea.

The explanation of the preceding phenomena is that the character or trait of roundness is dominant over wrinkledness. The trait of wrinkledness is therefore called recessive. Whenever two such characters are interbred, the F_1 generation will all show externally only the dominant character. Nevertheless, the members of the F_1 generation are hybrids, just as the pink four-o'clocks are all hybrids. When the hybrid F_1 generation is bred with itself, the two characters are segregated in the peas just as in the case of the four-o'clocks. Thus, one-quarter of the peas in the F_2 generation will be wrinkled, just as one-quarter of the flowers in the four-o'clocks are red. The other three-quarters of the F_2 generation peas will be round. However, only part of the round peas will breed true. The remainder, producing offspring of two types, must therefore be hybrids. Consequently we find that the F_2 generation consists of one-quarter pure wrinkled peas, one-quarter pure round peas, and one-half hybrid round peas (corresponding to the pink four-o'clocks in the F_2 generation), or a ratio of 1:2:1. This is the same ratio as occurs with the blending inheritance of the four-o'clocks.

It is apparent that we thus have two kinds of ratios. In the dominant-recessive inheritance of the peas we have, in the F_2 generation, an apparent 3:1 ratio based on the external appearance of the peas. This is called the phenotype ratio; "phenotype" refers to the external appearance of the trait. The round peas, however, are of two types, pure and hybrid, and, with the wrinkled types, appear in a ratio of 1:2:1. This is called the genotype ratio; "genotype" having reference to the pattern of genes or inheritance-determining factors in the cell.

The difference between blending inheritance (sometimes called "incomplete dominance") of the four-o'clock and the dominant-recessive inheritance of the wrinkled-round peas is thus superficial. Actually the type of inheritance is fundamentally the same. The only differences are that in blending inheritance the F_1 generation is clearly hybrid, as in the case of the pink-flowered four-o'clock, while in the case of the dominant-recessive inheritance of the peas, the hybrids of the F_1 generation all look like the dominant parent. In the F_2 generation, with blending inheritance, the pure types which are segregated out are all clearly distinguished from the hybrid pink offspring. In the case of the peas, however, only the pure recessives can be distinguished by their appearance, while the pure dominant round peas look exactly like the hybrid round peas and the two types can only be distinguished by the results of subsequent breeding.

3. CELL STRUCTURE AND DIVISION

Although at the time the structure of the cell was not well understood, Mendel showed considerable insight by attributing the phenomena of inheritance discussed above to the composition of the sex cells. The last fifty years have seen remarkable advances in knowledge of the microscopic structure of the cell and it now can be clearly shown how the phenomena occur.

Understanding of the mechanisms of inheritance really developed with the answer to the old question of which came first, the chicken or the egg. To this question the biologist answers that the chicken is merely the egg's way of taking care of other eggs. The chicken does not produce the egg but merely nourishes it and makes it possible for the egg to produce other eggs. Additional chickens are produced incidentally to the egg's opportunity to produce still other eggs.

It has long been known that living things get their start in life from a single cell. This is true of starfish, horses, and men, as well as all other living things. In complex living things, the original cell is fertilized by another cell. One of these cells is known as the egg or ovum, the other as the sperm. The cells which reproduce living things are known as reproductive cells or sex cells. It used to be thought that the reproductive cell creates a living organism and that this in turn creates more reproductive cells which incorporate characteristics of the individual. Now it is known that all sex cells are produced directly by other sex cells and are merely nourished by the body of the individual.

When an ovum or egg is fertilized by a sperm under proper conditions, the fertilized egg or zygote soon begins a process of division, producing other cells. Very early in the process of division the reproductive cells are segregated from those which develop into other parts of the organism (body cells). The primary biological function of the organism is to provide a safe place for the reproductive cells, to nourish them, and to provide opportunities for reproduction.

The processes of cell division are of considerable importance for the understanding of heredity. Although the cell is often a minute, microscopic bit of life, it actually has a complex structure. Most of these complexities do not concern us here and will not be described, but it should be remembered clearly that a cell is a more complicated thing than is indicated in the subsequent discussion.

Cells consist of protoplasm, "the material basis of life," which is made up of complex chemical substances. Among the important parts of the cell protoplasm are the cell body and the nucleus. The nucleus is usually a rounded body, somewhat denser than the rest of the cell, and surrounded by a thin membrane. It is a complex body containing various types of material. One of these is a material which readily stains with certain dyes and hence is known as chromatin. The cell body also consists of numerous substances and structures and is usually surrounded by an outer membrane or cell wall.

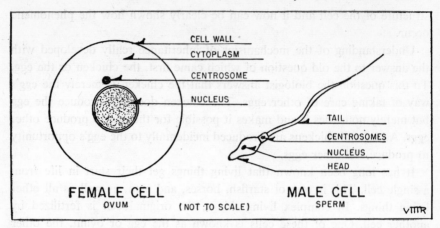

Fig. 3:3.

In a complex organism like man we find two major types of cell: reproductive or germ cells and body cells. Reproductive cells may further be divided into female sex cells (called also ova or egg cells), male sex cells (sperm cells), and zygotes, which are formed, as we have said, by a union of an ovum with a sperm. Body cells may also be subdivided into nerve cells, muscle cells, and many other specialized types.

The egg cell or ovum is usually relatively large and round in shape. It contains large amounts of nutrient substances, often known as yolk material. The egg of the hen is an unusually large female sex cell, but it is not essentially different in its major parts from any other female sex cell. The human egg is microscopic in size, about 0.2 millimeters in diameter.

The male sex cell or sperm is much smaller and, instead of being round, is long and threadlike with an enlarged head and a slender tail. The nucleus is found in the head, while the tail is lashed about to produce movement.

When a sperm cell comes in contact with a mature ovum, the head and middle part sink into the egg while the tail is usually broken off and left outside. Certain parts of the sperm appear to draw nourishment from the yolk particles of the egg and grow in size. Some of these parts remain discernible in the fertilized egg cell and may also be distinguished in all the daughter cells resulting from subsequent divisions of the zygote.

Shortly after the process of fertilization is complete, the zygote begins to divide. This process is not a simple one. First, the chromatin in the cell nucleus condenses to a number of rodlike bodies called chromosomes. Each species of animal has a certain constant number of chromosomes, which varies from two to two hundred. Man has forty-eight chromosomes.

The second step in cell division is the disappearance of the nuclear membrane. Certain parts of the nucleus move to opposite sides of the cell, while the chromosomes are arranged between them in a more or less straight line on the equator of the cell. Through a series of very complex steps, each chromosome divides lengthwise, giving rise to two daughter chromosomes. The daughter chromosomes now move to opposite sides of the cell, the cell wall constricts, and finally divides the original cell into two daughter cells, each of which is identical in structure with the parent cell.

From the standpoint of understanding heredity it is important to remember the behavior of the chromosomes. Although other structures may play some part in heredity, it is known that the major hereditary influences reside in the chromosomes. The chromosomes evidently remain in the nucleus of the cells as distinct bodies of matter at all times. When the cell divides under ordinary circumstances the chromosomes always divide in the way described, and each daughter cell contains the same number of chromosomes as did the original fertilized egg. Moreover, each chromosome of the daughter cells is part of the original chromosome from which it was created by the process of longitudinal division.

When the zygote of such a form as man begins to divide and by successive division to produce large numbers of interdependent daughter cells, these begin gradually to assume different functions. Some of them become body cells and eventually form the various portions of the body of the growing organism. Others become reproductive cells which will, when the organism becomes sexually mature, produce egg or sperm cells, depending upon the sex of the organism. Both the body cells and the

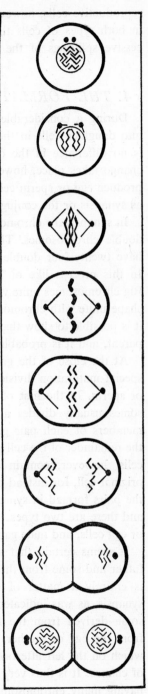

Fig. 3:4. The division of the zygote.

reproductive cells, however, have the same number of chromosomes, and in both types of cells those chromosomes have been derived from successive splittings of the chromosomes contained in the original zygote.

4. THE FORMATION OF EGG AND SPERM CELLS

During a considerable period the reproductive cells grow and divide into daughter cells in the way we have described. In other words, there is no difference in the division of reproductive cells and body cells. A change takes place, however, when a sexually mature organism begins to produce egg or sperm cells. The first step in this new procedure is known as synapsis or the conjugation of the chromosomes.

In synapsis the chromosomes of the reproductive cell unite in temporary double chromosomes. Thus in man the reproductive cells after synapsis have twenty-four double chromosomes instead of forty-eight single ones. In this process like or homologous chromosomes always pair together. Big chromosomes unite with big chromosomes, chromosomes of distinctive shape unite with chromosomes of similar shape, and so on. In some cases it is possible to show that one chromosome of each pair comes from each parent, and it is probable that this is true of all the paired chromosomes.

At the close of the growth period, the reproductive cells undergo two special maturation divisions, resulting in the formation of the mature egg or sperm. In the first of the maturation divisions, each pair of chromosomes usually divides along the junction formed in synapsis. The two members of each pair go to opposite poles of the cell, and division of the remainder of the cell proceeds as in other cases. The resulting daughter cells, however, contain only half the number of chromosomes of the original cell, for instead of each chromosome splitting longitudinally, only the pairs formed in synapsis are separated. Such cells are called gametes and there are two types: female gametes, which we have been calling ova or egg cells, and male gametes or sperm cells.

It seems certain that some of the chromosomes are derived from the father and some from the mother, but apparently the distribution of these is entirely a matter of chance. The pairs of chromosomes formed in synapsis, as was indicated, probably consist in each case of one chromosome derived from the father or sperm, and one chromosome derived from the egg or mother. Which member of a pair lies on the right and which on the left after synapsis takes place seems to be entirely a matter of chance. It is thus very unlikely (though not impossible) that in a form having many chromosomes all the chromosomes would be derived from a single parent. The second maturation division seems to be of the ordinary

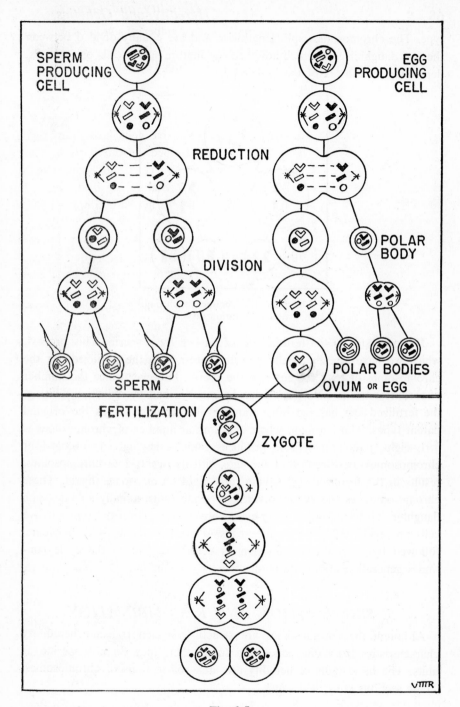

SPERM PRODUCING CELL

EGG PRODUCING CELL

REDUCTION

DIVISION

POLAR BODY

SPERM

POLAR BODIES

OVUM OR EGG

FERTILIZATION

ZYGOTE

Fig. 3:5.

type. The chromosomes split lengthwise and are equally divided between the two daughter cells which now become mature sperm cells or egg cells, depending on the sex of the individual.[2]

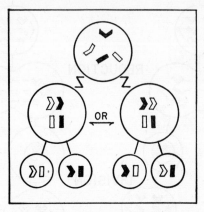

Fig. 3:6. Distribution of chromosomes after maturation division.

The next step is the fertilization of an egg by a sperm. This process, which we have already briefly described, brings to the fertilized egg the chromosomes of both the egg and the sperm. However, since the number of chromosomes in each gamete has been cut in half by reduction division, the fertilized egg has the same number of chromosomes as the original parent types. Thus in man, where the normal number of chromosomes is forty-eight, reduction division produces gametes having only twenty-four chromosomes. Fertilization of the egg, with its twenty-four chromosomes, results in the fertilized egg having forty-eight chromosomes again. These chromosomes, as the zygote divides, separate longitudinally so that each daughter cell resulting has forty-eight chromosomes until the reproductive cells are again ready to produce eggs or sperms. Synapsis then occurs, followed by the reduction division as described, and so the cycle continues generation after generation.

5. SEGREGATION AND RECOMBINATION

Although the chromosomes are structures which transmit hereditary characteristics from one generation to another, they do not operate as units. The basic units of heredity are areas or sections of chromosomes. These sections are called genes.

[2] In the case of males, the four sperm cells produced by the two maturation divisions all reach full maturity; in the case of females, only one of the four egg cells produced completes its growth. The undeveloped ova are called polar bodies; see Fig. 3:5.

The genes have often been compared to beads. Each chromosome might then be compared to a string of genes or beads. In some of the larger cells of the fruit fly *(Drosophila)* a beadlike structure has been observed, but in other forms it has been demonstrated that the chromosome is a more rodlike structure in which certain definite sections have specialized functions in heredity and may be regarded as the genes.

In various animals it has been possible to demonstrate conclusively that a particular gene influences the development of one or more characteristics of the organism. Thus, in the fruit fly, the shape of the wing may depend upon a single area or gene in a particular chromosome. Evidently there are a number of different genes, each one causing a particular form of wing in the fruit fly. However, whatever gene controls the wing development, such genes always occur in the same section of the same chromosome.

In order to explain this mechanism more clearly, a simplified hypothetical case will be discussed. Let it be assumed that there are two wing shapes found in some form such as *Drosophila* (the fruit fly), a long and a short shape. In any particular fruit fly, only one of these forms will be found, that is, the fly will have either long wings or short wings. The two characters are mutually exclusive, then, and may be regarded as alternate possibilities. Such pairs of contrasted characters are usually called allelomorphs. The factors or genes controlling these two wing shapes may be called gene l and gene s. The location of these genes is in a particular spot in a particular chromosome. However, it will be recalled that the chromosomes always come in pairs. We will call one member of this pair a and the other b. In both a and b there will be genes controlling the wing shape.

If short-winged fruit flies have been bred with each other for a number of generations and no other kinds of wings have appeared, we may assume that this strain is pure and that both a and b chromosomes have s genes in the area controlling wing shape. If the short-winged flies are crossed with a similar pure strain of long-winged flies and the long wing is dominant, the offspring of the cross, the hybrid F_1 generation, will all be long-winged. However, one of the chromosomes of the a-b pair will have come from the mother, the other from the father. If the mother was a pure short-winged type, then obviously the chromosome derived from the mother can contain only the gene s for short-wingedness, and similarly the chromosome from the father can contain only the gene l for long-wingedness. For the sake of clarity, we will assume that the a chromosome came from the mother, and the b from the father. Then the a chromosome contains the s gene, the b chromosome the l gene.

If we now cross the individual hybrids of the F_1 generation with each

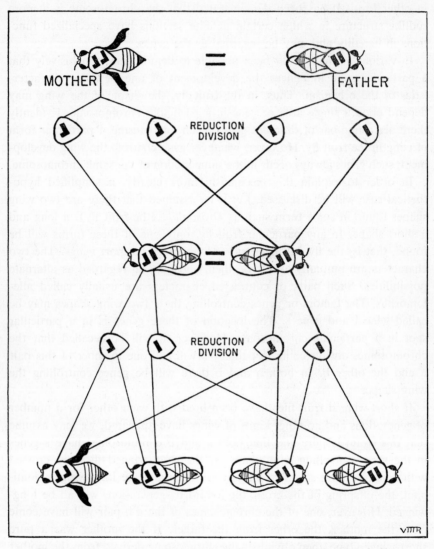

Fig. 3:7. Results of crossing pure bred short- and long-winged fruit flies.

other, certain combinations will result. In the formation of the gametes a reduction division will take place in which the a-b pair of chromosomes will be separated. Each hybrid individual will produce eggs or sperms (depending on sex) which will contain either an a chromosome or a b chromosome. Never is it possible for an egg or sperm from the F_1 hybrids to contain both, for, as in Mendel's assumptions, the gametes are pure with respect to the contrasting characters. There will obviously be as many a-bearing gametes as b-bearing gametes.

When fertilization takes place, it will be recalled, the number of chromosomes will be doubled, restoring the normal number. Thus, the fertilized egg will again contain two chromosomes, an a and a b. Note, however, that we have two kinds of eggs and sperms. In each case one kind contains an a chromosome, the other a b chromosome. Now if an egg contains an a chromosome, it may be fertilized with a sperm containing either an a chromosome or a b chromosome. It seems to be purely a matter of chance which will occur, and evidently half of the eggs containing the a chromosome are fertilized by sperms containing the a chromosome also, while the other half are fertilized by sperms containing the b chromosome. Thus, of a series of eggs containing the a chromosome, half will contain two a chromosomes after fertilization, and half will contain both an a and a b chromosome.

Similarly, the eggs containing the b chromosome also have equal chances of being fertilized by sperms containing either the a or the b chromosome. Half of the resulting fertilized eggs will contain both an a and a b chromosome in this case, just as is true if the eggs contain the a chromosome. On the other hand, half of the fertilized eggs will contain two b chromosomes and no a chromosome. The chances, in any large series, are overwhelming that zygotes will be produced in the ratio of one with two a chromosomes, one with two b chromosomes, and two containing both a and b. This may be expressed as the ratio 1aa:2ab:1bb. This ratio, it will be observed, is identical with the F_2 genotype ratio produced according to Mendel's law.

The individuals with two b chromosomes will be long-winged. Similarly, individuals with two a chromosomes will be short-winged. In the first case, only l genes are present, in the second only s genes are present. In the remaining half of the F_2 generation, however, both chromosomes are present and hence both l and s genes. As long-wingedness is dominant, however, or, to put it in other terms, the l gene is dominant over the s gene, the individuals will all be long-winged.

In further breeding, if individuals possessing only a chromosomes bearing the s gene are crossed with one another, all the offspring will also be short-winged. As these individuals have only a chromosomes, they can produce only sperms and eggs containing a chromosomes, and so obviously the fertilized egg will contain only a chromosomes. The same is true of individuals possessing only b chromosomes; their offspring can contain only b chromosomes.

On the other hand, if individuals containing both a and b chromosomes are crossed, half of the eggs and sperms produced will contain the a chromosome and half will contain the b chromosome. The offspring resulting from random fertilization will then be produced in the ratio of 1aa:2ab:1bb, just as in the case of the offspring of the F_1 generation. Fertilized egg cells or zygotes containing either aa or bb are said to be homozygous; those containing both a and b are heterozygous. It should be noted that an individual, homozygous with respect to one allelomorph, may be heterozygous with respect to another.

To sum up what the above material means, study of the actual mechanism of cell division shows that when two contrasted characters or allelomorphs are involved, the inheritance factors or genes in the cell are segregated and recombined in exactly the way necessary to produce the results observed by Mendel.

6. MENDELIAN INHERITANCE IN MAN

As far as is known, the inheritance of most if not all traits in man operates fundamentally in accordance with Mendel's law. Actually, it has been possible to demonstrate this type of inheritance in man for only a few traits. This is because man is a very complicated animal. The forty-eight chromosomes in man make study difficult. Moreover, man breeds very slowly and has few offspring, so that the mating of a single couple results in offspring showing only a few of the possible combinations of traits. In addition, man is so mixed in his ancestry that purebred lines with respect to particular traits are impossible to secure in most cases, especially as controlled breeding experiments are impossible. Finally, most human characters are not controlled by a single gene in a single chromosome. In such a characteristic as hair color it is probable that seven or eight genes are operative, very possibly located in different chromosomes. In other words, simple unit characters governed by a simple pair of contrasting genes are very rare in man.

In the case of some abnormalities, however, it is possible to demonstrate the occurrence of Mendelian inheritance in man. Thus albinism (a condition in which all pigmentation is lacking) is a recessive characteristic in man as it is in other animals. If an albino mates with a normal person, the offspring will all be normal in pigmentation. Evidently the offspring in the F_1 generation, however, bear the gene for albinism, although it is submerged by the presence of the dominant gene for normal pigmentation. If the members of the F_1 generation mate with a person one of whose parents was also an albino, there would be a strong probability that some of the offspring would also be albinos. Actually, if the number of offspring were sufficiently large, we could expect one out of every four, on the average, to be an albino.

To illustrate this situation further, let us call the chromosome bearing the gene for albinism a and the chromosome bearing the gene for normal pigmentation n. Let us assume that in the parent generation the normal parent is pure with respect to color and thus has two n chromosomes (nn). The albino parent, on the other hand, must be pure with respect to the albinism gene a, for this gene is recessive, and hence may be designated aa.

Through the mechanism of egg and sperm production and the subsequent fertilization of the eggs, the members of the F_1 generation will have one n chromosome and one a chromosome. Each member of the F_1 generation will produce both n- and a-bearing eggs, and the two types will be produced in equal numbers. If, then, an F_1 female mates with a male of normal pigmentation, eggs will be produced of both n and a types, but as the normal spouse produces only n-bearing sperms, the offspring can be either nn or na but never aa. Thus none of the subsequent generation can be albinos, although half of them may carry the gene for albinism.

Should a woman of F_1 marry a man who is also the offspring of mating between an albino and a normally pigmented person, the situation would be different. The woman would produce eggs bearing n or a in equal numbers. Similarly, the man would produce sperms bearing n or a in equal numbers. Purely as a matter of chance, one out of four times an a-bearing egg would be fertilized by an a-bearing sperm. The offspring in this case would have two a chromosomes (aa) and hence be an albino. In another fourth of the offspring the combination would be nn, while half would be na. In other words, half of the offspring would appear to be normal but would have the gene for albinism present.

So long as individuals with the a gene present mate with persons with two n genes, there will be no albino offspring. Nevertheless, one-half of the offspring will bear the a gene and will, in turn, transmit it to half of their own offspring and so on for many generations. Thus a family line with albinism in its ancestry may have had no albinos for ten or twenty or forty generations, yet whenever a member bearing the a gene mates with another individual bearing the a gene, one-fourth of the offspring may be albinos.

The number of albinos could no doubt be reduced if albinos were not permitted to reproduce themselves. However, a certain number of albino genes would continue to be produced by persons who externally have normal coloring. An interesting case in point is provided by the San Blas Indians, the so-called white Indians of Panama. In this group a strain of albinism occurs. It is reported that albinos are not permitted to marry. Nevertheless, the number of albinos in the tribe apparently remains fairly constant at about 140 in a population estimated at 20,000. Unquestionably, then, a considerable number of persons of normal pigmentation in the population actually carry genes for albinism.

A number of other abnormalities in man also appear to be simple unit characters and to be inherited according to Mendelian laws. Among those which are almost certainly carried by dominant genes are brachydactyly (abnormally short fingers and toes), syndactyly (webbed fingers and toes), polydactyly (six-fingeredness), Huntington's chorea (a nervous disorder), and defective dentin (opalescent teeth). Recessive genes, in addition to albinism, apparently carry true dwarfism, haemophilia (slow clotting of the blood), certain types of color blindness, night blindness, and certain types of deaf mutism. It may be added, however, that many defects and abnormalities said to be hereditary are only doubtfully so, or are at best the product of multiple gene combinations, and so not unit characters.

Of normal traits in man the great majority appear to be caused by a number of genes (multiple gene combinations), and their mode of inheritance is correspondingly very complex. Boyd, in a recent book, cites a number of normal Mendelian characteristics in man, including such items as skin color, hair color, hair texture, eye color, body hair, stature, and the so-called "Mongolian" eye fold (see Chapter 4, § 5). He warns, however, that these conclusions are "to the highest degree tentative and hypothetical," for all of "the characters listed belong in the category of incompletely analyzed hereditary characteristics." [3]

Eye color affords a good example of such incomplete analysis. Earlier geneticists often held that eye color is a unit character, with brown eyes dominant over blue. Recent studies reveal that the problem is not so simple: there are at least two varieties of blue eyes, numerous shades of brown eyes, and a number of types intermediate in color. Though in some cases one or perhaps all types of blue eyes appear to be recessive, this has certainly not been demonstrated beyond any doubt. An interesting apparent exception is found among the offspring of blue-eyed Europeans (or Americans) and brown-eyed Japanese, where the offspring, though

---

[3] William C. Boyd, *Genetics and the Races of Man* (Boston: Little, Brown & Co., 1950), p. 318.

displaying a number of characters like the Japanese parent, also show a surprising frequency of blue eyes.

7. VARIABILITY IN MAN

It is important to remember the mechanisms of heredity in appraising the significance of the various criteria of race. Insofar as is possible, racial criteria are based on hereditary characteristics. This means that they are based on certain specific combinations of genes. As most racial groups existing today are mixed in ancestry, many individuals in any racial group will carry genes for contrasting characters or for other combinations of characters. As a result, any group of men is highly variable and only a limited number of individuals will possess what might be termed a typical set of genes and be of typical appearance. Moreover, even such normal-appearing individuals in all probability carry a considerable number of recessive genes which, under proper circumstances (such as mating with a "typical" individual who also bears recessive genes) will produce off-spring differing noticeably from their parents. In the last analysis, then, when we describe a racial type, we are simply describing a particular combination of dominant genes occurring in a reasonable proportion of the population.

Even in matings between more or less typical individuals, it is impossible to predict accurately the character of the offspring with respect to many traits. As each individual has forty-eight chromosomes, there are 16,777,216 ways in which the reduction division can sort out the twenty-four chromosomes found in the egg or sperm. The same number of possibilities exists for the combinations produced by each member of a mating pair. The possibilities for combination occurring in the fertilization of the egg are infinitely greater, amounting to approximately 300,-000,000,000,000 possible combinations. When it is considered that each chromosome carries a number of genes, the possible combinations of genes in the offspring of any mating approach infinity.

Certain other phenomena of inheritance should be mentioned, although we still do not understand precisely how they operate in human beings. One phenomenon of possible significance is the occurrence of hybrid vigor. When crosses of markedly different strains are made in some plants and animals, the offspring are often larger and more vigorous than either parent. How long this condition persists is not certain, nor are the causes well understood. Some authorities have suggested that the phenomenon is due to the pooling of a larger number of dominant genes than existed in either parent strain. There is some evidence, for example, from some of

Boas' studies of half-breed Indians, that hybrid vigor also occurs in man.

Actually, of course, all human beings are hybrid as this term is used by geneticists, for no human is pure with respect to all the many allelomorphs occurring in our species. When a geneticist speaks of a purebred strain he means a strain that has been inbred (that is, in which matings have been between brothers and sisters or parents and children) for ten or more generations to make sure that all but one type of gene has been eliminated. Purebred strains in human beings obviously do not exist, and every human mating is between persons differing in some of their genes. All human beings consequently are hybrids in the geneticists' sense, and to some extent hybrid vigor should be a constant phenomenon. In crosses between racial types, such as the Indian-white crosses referred to above, apparently there is still greater diversity of genes and hence a measurably greater occurrence of hybrid vigor.

Another point of some significance for man is the formation of stabilized intermediate types when two different strains have been interbred in large numbers over several generations. Many present-day races of man seem to be such stabilized mixtures or intermediate types; there is, for example, considerable evidence that the American Negro is becoming such a stabilized mixture or race. However, since it is extremely unlikely that all intermixture between Negro and white will cease, the American Negro group will probably gradually modify toward the white type. This comes of the fact that there are far more whites than Negroes in the United States and so a greater number of genes for "white" characteristics. Furthermore, the American Negro population includes a large number of offspring from white-Negro matings, many of whom have as many or more white characteristics as Negro characteristics. With this preponderance of genes for white characteristics increasing in the Negro population with every Negro-white mating, there should be a gradual modification of the American Negro in the direction of the white type.

As has already been indicated, races may in some sense be considered as more or less stabilized patterns of genes occurring within a defined group or area. New genetic patterns have in part developed through mutation and the selection of variations. Where such patterns have been relatively isolated for a time, they have tended to stabilize, and racial groups have developed. Whenever groups have come in contact, they have tended to mix, and the genes of each group come to be shared to some degree. If such a mixed group again achieves relative isolation, a new pattern may develop, giving rise to a secondary or mixed race. With the breakdown of isolation resulting from modern transportation, old patterns will increasingly be broken down, and in time various genes will come to be shared more or less equally by all groups. We shall have more to say on this and related topics in Chapters 5 and 6.

8. GENETICS AND EUGENICS

Since the discovery of the laws of heredity, many people have argued in favor of improving human beings through encouraging the reproduction of "desirable" stocks and discouraging or preventing the reproduction of "undesirable" stocks. Such people argue that by preventive measures, undesirable genes will be eliminated and the general level of human welfare will rise. While there is much to be said in favor of preventing the production of offspring who will have inherited defects making the individual incapable of his own support or unable to play a useful part in society, such arguments are apt to claim too much.

It must be remembered that the majority of known inherited physical defects are recessive. Even though all persons exhibiting such defects are prevented from reproducing, the genes causing the defects occur in a certain percentage of apparently normal people. Consequently it is doubtful if any recessive defect can ever be completely eliminated. Even a substantial decrease in the number of persons showing hereditary defects would take a considerable number of generations.

More debatable are the claims of some of the more ardent eugenicists. Studies of family lines have been made in which it is pointed out that in some family lines a larger percentage of notable people occurs than in others. Conversely, it is claimed that other family lines produce a larger number of mental defectives, criminals, and other social undesirables. Control of reproduction, it is claimed, would prevent the production of undesirables and greatly improve the character of the population.

Such arguments contain many fallacies and half-truths. In the first place, the definition of what is socially desirable or undesirable is difficult. All too often it turns out that what the eugenicist means by a socially undesirable or socially inferior person is one with a low economic status, while a free-booting captain of industry will be classed as a socially desirable person. What is socially desirable or undesirable is established in terms of current social ideals. Such ideals or standards have changed many times in history and no doubt will again. Moreover, the same social ideals do not hold for all classes in society even at the same time. Thus some industrialists in our society might hold that socially desirable individuals were those willing to work the longest hours at the smallest pay. Many eugenicists, on the other hand, discovering the low economic status of such persons, would class them as undesirable and seek to limit their reproduction.

Another serious fallacy of many eugenics programs is the assumption that behavior and social status are inherited. Actually, except for types of behavior which are affected directly by deficiencies in the nervous system, such as certain nervous disorders, there is no evidence for the inheritance of behavior or social status. No one has yet discovered a gene for industriousness, cooperativeness, ruthlessness, abstention from alcohol, or church-going. The evidence for the operation of genetic inheritance involves only physical characteristics, not mental ones.

It is true, of course, that human beings, just as other organisms, show differences in behavior. It is not impossible that there may be different limits placed on behavior by genetically inherited factors, although no evidence of importance has ever been adduced for such a limitation. Nevertheless, assuming for the moment that there are genetic limitations placed on intelligence, it remains to be proven how important these limitations may be. All good geneticists today recognize that the individual's physical development is the product of hereditary possibilities plus environmental conditions. It matters not how good a genetic inheritance an individual may have, if he does not have proper care or contracts a fatal disease in infancy, he will die and not come to maturity. Even the best of genes cannot develop at all except in a certain minimal environment, while full development depends on an optimal environment. An infant may be born with genes which place an upper limit of stature at six feet, but if he has insufficient food and insufficient vitamin D he may develop rickets and a tortured, crooked body with much less than his potential limit of stature. The same applies to any inherited possibilities for behavior. A child born with an aptitude for music (and no conclusive evidence exists of the inheritance of such aptitudes) will get nowhere in an environment which forbids its use. It might, however, be best to let one of the most distinguished living geneticists in the United States, Professor T. Dobzhansky, summarize this argument. Says Professor Dobzhansky: "Heredity does not transmit skin colors or behaviors; it determines the responses, the norm of reaction, of the organism to its environment. . . . heredity is not implacable destiny to which one must submit in resignation. We should seek for ourselves, and contrive for others, environments in which our heredities respond most favorably." [4]

[4] "What is Heredity?" *Science,* Vol. 100, No. 2601 (Nov. 3, 1944), p. 406.

9. SUMMARY

It appears, then, that in living organisms physical characteristics are inherited by regular laws through the operation of rather precise mechanisms. Physical characters exist as units which are inherited independently of one another and are controlled by one or more structures known as genes occurring in the chromosomes. A particular arrangement of physical characteristics may then be considered to represent a particular combination and arrangement of genes. Most physical characteristics occur as two or more contrasted characters, each the result of a particular gene or combination of genes reproducing normally in a favorable environment. Generally these characters are either dominant or recessive, in which case hybrid forms may carry a recessive gene which is not expressed in the external physical appearance of the organism, but which may be transmitted to the offspring.

There is little or no evidence that behavior is inherited in the same way as physical traits. Although the physical basis of behavior is inherited and sets limits to behavior, the actual development of behavior is the result of the interaction of the organism with its environment. In a perhaps somewhat more limited sense this is also true of the development of physical characteristics; the exact way a particular hereditary trait develops in an organism depends on the character of the surrounding environment.

In man it is possible to demonstrate the occurrence of inheritance according to Mendelian laws in only a relatively few cases. This is because of the difficulty of studying man and the complexity of the organism. However, there is no reason to doubt that the mechanisms of human heredity are the same as those found in all other organisms reproducing by sexual means. Consequently we may regard the differences in physical characteristics between individual human beings as being due to differences in the pattern of genes, subject to the different environmental influences which have affected the development of the individuals. Races similarly may be, to quote Professor Dobzhansky again, regarded "as populations differing from each other in the incidence of certain genes." [5] Although genetic patterns may set certain limits on behavior, it is clear that in man, more even than in other animals, behavior is developed through the influence of environment.

[5] *Ibid.,* p. 406.

COLLATERAL READING

Ashley-Montagu, M. F. *An Introduction to Physical Anthropology*. Springfield, Illinois: C. C. Thomas, 1945. Chapters V, VIII.

Boyd, William C. *Genetics and the Races of Man*. Boston: Little, Brown and Co., 1950. Chapters 1–3.

Dobzhansky, Th. *Genetics and the Origin of Species*. 2nd Ed. New York: Columbia University Press, 1941.

Dunn, L. C., and Dobzhansky, Th. *Heredity, Race and Society*. Rev. Ed. New York: Mentor Books, 1952.

Hooton, Earnest A. *Up From the Ape*. Rev. Ed. New York: The Macmillan Co., 1940. Part V.

Chapter 4

THE CRITERIA OF RACE

1. THE VALIDITY OF RACIAL CRITERIA

It follows from our definition of race as populations differing from each other in the incidence of certain genes that the structural features in terms of which races are differentiated must vary in form only by reason of heredity. Variations in bodily structure due to environmental factors (such as extremes of cold or heat, moisture or dryness), the functions to which an organ is put (for example, the use of the feet as supporting organs), or cultural practices (for example, the nature and amount of food customarily taken by a people) must be ruled out. Traits which define a race must be inherited (that is, passed from one generation to the next in the germ plasm) and nonadaptive (that is, as little affected as possible by environment, function, or culture).

There has been a great deal of discussion on the question of the validity of racial criteria. As we said in Chapter 3, the problems of heredity and genetics in relation to man are still for the most part unsolved. This poses a number of difficult problems in evaluating the criteria of race. We have pointed out that, due to the presence of recessive genes, the phenotype or external appearance of the organism may not be the same as its genotype or pattern of gene assemblages. Ultimately racial classifications must be based on genotypes, yet in most cases the present criteria on which classification is based are phenotypic and not genotypic.

The reasons for this are in part historical. The beginnings of race classification antedate the beginnings of scientific genetics. Early students of race merely assumed that the criteria they chose are determined by heredity because of their relatively nonadaptive character. Today we recognize that virtually none of these criteria have been identified with specific genotypes.

Moreover, it is very significant that the one group of characters which has been identified with gene patterns (the blood types; see § 9) does not conform in distribution to conventional racial classifications. That this discrepancy has not already resulted in a serious reorganization of the customary racial classifications is probably due to the fact that blood types are not directly observable but must be determined by chemical tests. Boyd has recently pointed out that if known blood-type genes instead determined external phenotypic characters such as skin color, eye color, hair color, or stature, the usual racial classifications would soon be drastically modified.

Our discussion of racial criteria will necessarily concern itself mainly with the usual phenotypic characters. It should be kept in mind, however, that these criteria remain to be analyzed genotypically, and that, when this is finally done, the criteria of race may undergo considerable modification.

Another word of warning is pertinent at this point. The nature of the discussion of race and race criteria necessarily emphasizes the differences between men. Yet the characteristics in which men differ are relatively few and minor in importance. Actually human beings of all races are alike in hundreds, and perhaps thousands, of characteristics in contrast to the few dozens of ways in which they differ. This is particularly true of the basic physical characteristics necessary to the survival of the human organism.

The criteria of race classification used in the past were selected, as we have said, because they were believed to be inherited and nonadaptive in character. This is why so many of them are minor structural details like the shape of the nose, the degree of curliness of the hair, the thickness of the lips, the shape of the ears, and a number of others. Variation in the form of organs like these has apparently no functional significance, and where cultural standards demand the deformation of such organs for decorative or ceremonial purposes, the modifications made are easily distinguishable.

Environmental conditions, such as extremes of cold or heat, moisture or dryness, do not appear to exert any but a temporary direct effect upon bodily structure. One's hair may have a greater tendency to curl in a moist climate, and the skin may be darkened when it is constantly exposed to direct sunlight, but such effects soon disappear with a change of environment. There is no evidence at all, moreover, that such effects are passed on to one's offspring. A child born to straight-haired and light-complexioned parents whose hair form and skin color have been materially altered by long residence in the tropics inherits the hair form and skin color originally characteristic of his parents, not that which they have acquired as a result of environmental influence.

It is quite probable, however, that environment has played the role of a selective agent in determining some of man's structural characteristics. It can hardly be a mere matter of chance that most of the peoples who have the darkest skins, the widest and shortest noses, and the curliest hair are native to warm moist climates, or that Eskimos and other Arctic peoples, living where it is very cold most of the year, have very long and narrow nostrils. In such instances, climatic factors have undoubtedly favored the survival and propagation of individuals who possessed inherited variations better fitting them for survival. Individuals not inheriting such variations probably would not live to reproduce their kind.

Food supply, a function of both environment and culture, may exert considerable influence on bodily form. Stature and weight are almost wholly determined by the amount and nature of the food available, as well as by the relationship between food intake and bodily exertion. Inherited variations in stature and weight, then, are probably insignificant in relation to variations produced by environmental and cultural factors.

Cultural practices may sometimes materially alter bodily structures. Obvious variations of this sort are caused by binding infants' heads to give them a culturally required shape, the piercing of ear lobes and their artificial extension, the earlier Chinese custom of binding women's feet to prevent their growth, and various practices intended to alter the color and texture of the hair. More subtle cultural influences on bodily structure may result from a kind of artificial selection based upon specific standards of beauty prevailing in a society. Thus, in some groups, only plumper individuals are considered attractive while in others, such as our own, slender, "streamlined" figures are preferred. Such preferences, insofar as they materially affect the choice of marriage partners in a social group, may in time produce distinctive bodily forms.

The uses to which bodily organs are put during the life of the individual may sometimes greatly affect the structure of such organs. Such functionally produced modifications are apparently not inherited, but their presence in a given population may obscure inherited variations. Hands, because they are so much employed in handling objects, and feet, since they support the weight of the body, are obviously so materially conditioned by these functions as to obliterate all but the most pronounced inherited variations. Structural variations in organs of this sort are, then, essentially valueless as racial criteria.

Since man, like all other animals, is the product of a long evolutionary process, the earlier forms often possess features of structure lacking or profoundly modified in modern forms. Skull capacity, the curvature of the spine, chin development, and variations in the structure of the teeth are items of this sort. Only the most primitive humanoids have a small cranial capacity, little or no chin, a bow-shaped rather than a long, S-shaped spine, and distinctive variants in tooth structure. Modern races do not ordinarily show significant variation in these features of structure.

It must constantly be kept in mind that no single trait of structure is sufficient to define a race. This is because there is no necessary relation between the separate traits characteristic of a given race. Each structural feature, as we have seen, has its own genetic determiners and may be distributed among men quite independently of any other feature. A dark brown skin, for example, is associated with tightly curled or frizzly hair among the natives of West Africa, but in Australia it is found among people who have long, wavy hair. Straight hair is very nearly universal among American Indians and most of the peoples of central Asia, but these populations differ markedly in skin color.

Many criteria must then be used to define a racial type; the more the better. The actual number employed varies of course with the data available. Where, as in the case of prehistoric forms, our data consist only of skeletal materials, we are limited to such measurements and observations as can be taken on bones. No amount of research can tell us the skin color, nose form, eye color, or hair form of a people long dead. Similarly, in working with living peoples who have long cremated their dead, it is obviously difficult to get information on skull capacity, the shape of the nasal aperture on the skull, and similar skeletal details.

Further limitations are imposed, too, when only a small number of individuals are available for observation. Comparisons between a large living population, scores of whom have been accurately measured and described, and a prehistoric population represented by three or four fragmentary skeletons are obviously incomplete. The fewer individuals available for observation, the less accurate must be our knowledge of the structural variations characteristic of the population to which they belong.

A final set of factors which may affect the criteria by means of which races are differentiated is found in age and sex differences between individuals of the same population. It is obvious that an infant does not have the same bodily structure as a child, an adolescent, an adult, or an old person. Growth and senility not only add features of structure characteristic of certain age classes but also modify others which persist throughout the individual's life. Thus the infant, because his teeth are not fully grown and his jaws are as yet undeveloped, always has a shorter and broader face than an adult. Increasing senility, by reason of tooth loss and wear on the teeth, again tends to shorten the face. Comparisons between populations in respect to facial index (the ratio of the length of the face to its width) must then be made between individuals of the same age group.

Sexual differences in bodily structure may also affect racial criteria. Females are in general shorter in stature than males. Their bones are lighter. The female pelvis is broad and shallow, whereas that of the male is narrow and deep. Women also appear to have broader and shorter faces and a smaller cranial capacity than men. Supraorbital ridges, where these exist at all, are usually found only among males; women rarely display this characteristic. In all these traits, as in a number of others, comparisons between populations must be made between individuals of the same sex.

To summarize, then, we may set up the following specifications to be met in defining the criteria whereby racial types may be determined:

(1) Racial criteria are exclusively features of bodily structure, or such physical characters as blood types.

(2) Structural variations useful as racial criteria must be heritable and nonadaptive.

(3) No race can be defined solely in terms of a single trait. Many criteria must be employed.

(4) Whenever possible, the structural variants characteristic of a race are to be observed on a large sampling of the population concerned. Observations made on only a few individuals may not only inadequately represent the range of variation characteristic of the population to which they belong, but will also fail to indicate the degree of individual variability characteristic of the population.

(5) Since age and sex may affect racial criteria, comparisons must always be made between individuals of the same age and sex groups.

(6) Ultimately race criteria should be defined in terms of genotypes, but as yet this is possible only for a few traits such as blood types.

2. THE CRANIAL VAULT

We may now turn to the problem of defining more systematically and in some detail the measurements, indices, and observations most useful as

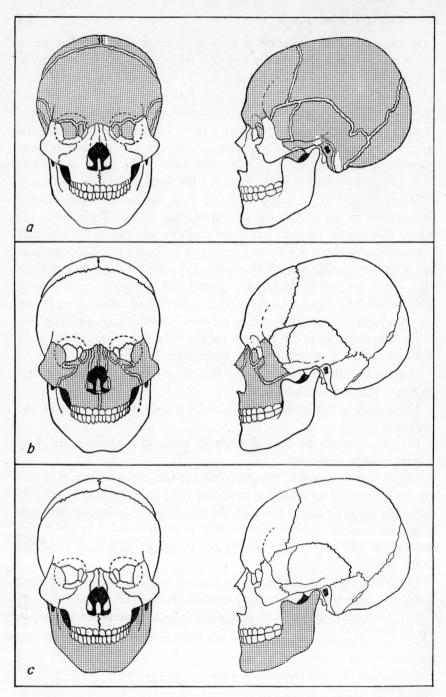

Fig. 4:1. The human skull. Shaded portions show (*a*) the cranium, (*b*) the face, and (*c*) the mandible.

racial criteria. We shall begin with the head and skull, since it is in this region of the body that many of the more distinctive inherited variations appear to be found.

The human skull may conveniently be divided into three principal portions: the cranium or cranial vault, the face, and the lower jaw or mandible. Cranium and face may be further divided; the cranium is composed of eight bones, the face of fourteen. All of these are firmly united by immovable joints called sutures. The lower jaw (a single bone) is attached by a movable joint.

The following measurements and observations may be made on the cranium: (1) capacity, (2) length and width, (3) height, (4) slope and width of forehead, (5) thickness of bones, (6) size of supraorbital ridges, and (7) position of the foramen magnum ("big hole") in the base of the skull. Significant variations are found in all these features within the family *Hominidae* as a whole. Among modern men, however, only the ratio of the width of the cranium to its length (cephalic index), cranial height, and the size of the supraorbital ridges vary significantly.

(1) Cranial capacity. This measurement, it is obvious, can only be taken on the skeleton. It is useful principally in distinguishing certain very early prehistoric forms, one or two of which are significantly low in cranial capacity. Other prehistoric forms have as large if not larger heads (in terms of capacity) as modern man.

Average capacity in modern males is about 1,450 cc.; females average about 150 cc. less. Except for the aborigines of Australia, who are said to possess a low cranial capacity, there are no significant differences among modern men in this characteristic. Individuals of the same population sometimes vary over a range as great as one-third the average for the group, such variations appearing to be roughly correlative to stature and body size.

Though brain size is obviously related to cranial capacity, it does not follow that significant correlations may be drawn between brain size and intelligence; women, for example, are not less intelligent than men. There is indeed no evidence that persons with large brains are either more or less intelligent than those with smaller brains. Still less may it be said that one race, even the relatively smaller-brained Australoid, displays an average intelligence related to brain size.

(2) Length and width of the cranium; cephalic index. On the center line of the frontal bone of the cranium and just above the point at which the two bones which form the bridge of the nose unite with the frontal bone is found a slight prominence called the glabella. On the living, glabella may usually be found between the eyebrows and directly above

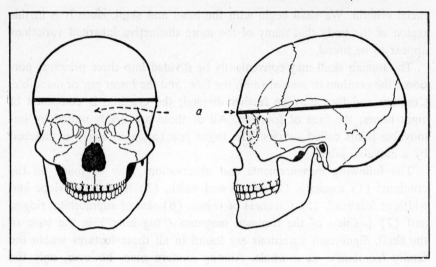

Fig. 4:2. Cranium. Heavy lines show measuring points for cranial length and width; (*a*) indicates the glabella.

the root of the nose. Cranial length is the distance from the glabella to the most distant point directly opposite the glabella on the back of the cranial vault. Cranial width is defined as the maximum distance between two directly opposite points on either side of the head.

These measurements are rarely used alone; the important characteristic is the relationship between them or the cephalic index. This is obtained by dividing the width of the head by its length and multiplying the quotient by 100. The cephalic index, then, tells us what percentage the width of the head is in relation to its length; a cephalic index of 75, for example, means that the width of the head is 75 per cent of its length. Cephalic indices are customarily grouped as follows:

Dolichocephalic (long-headed)	Below 75
Mesocephalic (intermediate)	Between 75 and 80
Brachycephalic (short-headed)	Above 80

Since ancient men are nearly all dolichocephalic, it would appear that this variation in head form is the more primitive of the three. The precise significance of this fact in the history of man's development is far from clear, however. Certainly there is no evidence that variations in head form among modern men are any more significant for their general level of development than variations in eye color.

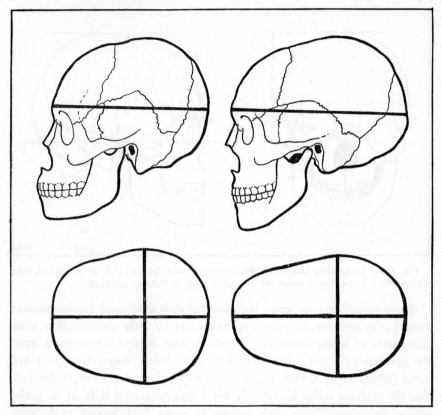

Fig. 4:3. Brachycephalic (left) and dolichocephalic skulls showing differences in relative length and width.

The question of the validity of the cephalic index as a racial criterion has been debated at some length. A given characteristic of the human body, it will be remembered, is useful in distinguishing race only if it is determined primarily by genetic factors and is not subject to radical alteration either by the physical environment or by the functions it serves.

Boas' anthropometric studies of the children of immigrants to the United States revealed that when such children were born in the United States, their cephalic indices varied significantly from those of their parents. Eastern Europeans of various nationalities but with an average cephalic index of 83 had, in the United States, children with an average index of 81. Sicilians with an average cephalic index of 78, on the other hand, had children with an average index of 80. In one case, then, the American-born descendants of European immigrants became more long-headed than their parents (83 to 81); in the other, they became more round-headed than their parents (78 to 80).

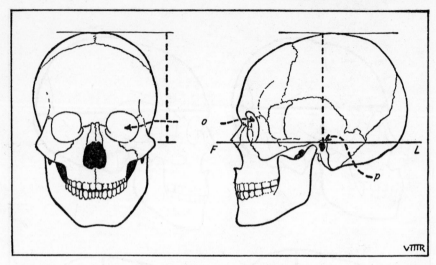

Fig. 4:4. Measuring points for determining cranial height: *F-L* = Frankfort line; *o* = orbit; *p* = porion, a point on the upper edge of the ear opening.

These variations have never been satisfactorily explained. Environmental factors may possibly be operative; there can be little question that wide differences in living conditions, nutrition, and occupation resulted from the immigrants' move from Europe to the United States. But there are other factors as well. One which may be quite important lies in the fact that the cephalic index is certainly not a unit character; it is, in all probability, determined by a large number of genes, each having to do with one or other structural feature of the bones of the head. Since these genes are inherited independently, the possibilities for individual variation approach infinity. The immigrants studied by Boas came largely from eastern and southern Europe, a region inhabited by populations extremely variable in racial type. In Europe, marriages were generally confined to individuals in the same locality, and the offspring therefore varied little in hereditary character from their parents. But in the United States, immigrants from different villages and towns came together, married, and produced offspring. Variations therefore were more likely to occur as individuals of different localities interbred.

(3) Cranial height. Cranial height is usually measured from the ear opening to the highest point on the top of the skull. To insure comparable measurements, the head is held so that a line tangential to the upper edge of the ear opening and the lower margin of the eye orbit (the so-called Frankfort line) is horizontal. Because it is difficult to obtain this measurement from the living, and because few investigators do it in the same way, the distribution of head heights among modern peoples is little known.

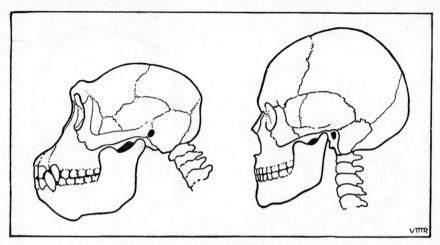

Fig. 4:5. Skulls of chimpanzee and man.

There does appear to be significant variation among modern men, however. The Australoids, for example, have markedly lower heads than most other present-day peoples.

Head height varies more markedly for some prehistoric forms, particularly those of the early Pleistocene. Here we find crania very little higher than those of modern apes. Since head height may be correlated with the size of the frontal portion of the brain, and since the development of the forebrain presumably has much to do with the development of human intelligence, it may be inferred that the markedly low-headed Pleistocene men were less human in their intellectual behavior than modern man. It is not true, however, that the minor differences in cranial height among men today are to be interpreted similarly; no test yet devised has unambiguously demonstrated significant variations in "racial intelligence." (See Chapter 7.)

(4) Slope and width of the forehead. Among the earliest prehistoric men, as well as among modern apes, the forehead slopes sharply back from the supraorbital ridges and is very narrow. Both these features, like cranial height, are related to the smaller forebrains found among apes and the earliest prehistoric men. It should be emphasized, however, that relatively few prehistoric populations possess narrow sloping foreheads—among others the forehead is as vertical and wide as it is among modern men. The minor variations in forehead slope and width observable in all modern and most prehistoric populations do not imply a significant racial variation in intellectual capacity.

(5) Thickness of the bones of the cranium. Here, again, is a trait useful only to distinguish modern from prehistoric forms. Most prehistoric forms

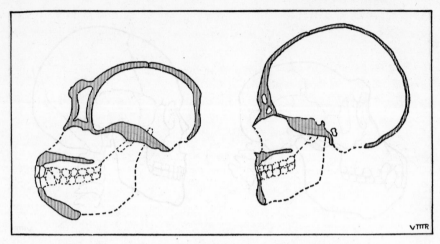

Fig. 4:6.   Thickness of cranial bones of chimpanzee and man.

appear to have thicker cranial bones than modern men, and among some
prehistoric peoples the bones of the skull are nearly as thick as those of
the anthropoid apes. Modern populations do not vary significantly in this
characteristic.

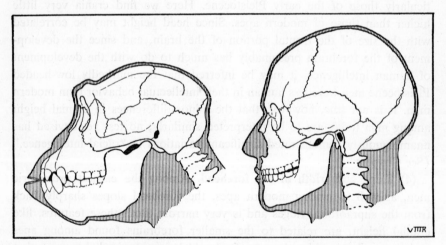

Fig. 4:7.   Position of the foramen magnum in the chimpanzee and man.

(6) Size of the supraorbital ridges. The supraorbital ridges appear to
have undergone a gradual decrease in size as man diverged more and
more from other families of *Anthropoidea*. Earlier men possess large shelf-
like brow ridges which extend unbroken across the forehead. Most modern
men lack brow ridges entirely or possess only small separate protuberances

over each eye. In only a few modern populations do we find marked supra-orbital development, and even here it is much less than among the earlier prehistoric forms.

(7) The position of the foramen magnum. The foramen magnum is the hole in the base of the skull through which the spinal cord passes to its junction with the brain. In all modern skulls the foramen magnum is situated approximately in the center of the skull's base. As a result, modern man's head is balanced on the spinal cord and habitually held clear of the chest.

Among some of the earlier prehistoric forms, however, the foramen magnum is somewhat to the rear of center. It is therefore evident that the heads of such forms projected forward with the lower jaw resting on the chest, much in the manner of the modern ape. Here again we have evidence of progressive evolutionary development; the forward projection of the head among the earlier humanoids is clearly a primitive feature.

3. THE FACE AND LOWER JAW

Man's face and lower jaw exhibit significant variations in the following features: (1) facial width and length, expressed in the facial index; (2) the shape of the malar (cheek) bones; (3) the forward projection of the face or prognathism; (4) degree of chin development; and (5) the teeth and hard palate.

(1) Facial width and length; the facial index. Face width is the maximum distance between directly opposite points on the malar or cheekbones. Face length is measured from the nasion (the point of intersection of the nasal bones and the frontal bone of the skull) to the lowest point in the center line on the upper jaw. As in the case of the head, these measures are most often expressed in terms of their relation to one another. This relation, the facial index, is calculated by dividing the length of the face by its width and multiplying the quotient by 100. Note that in this index, length is expressed as a proportion of width; in the cephalic index, width is expressed as a proportion of length. Facial indices are usually classed as follows:

	Living	*Skull*
Euryprosopic (broad-faced)	Below 85	Below 85
Mesoprosopic (intermediate)	85–88	85–90
Leptoprosopic (narrow-faced)	Above 88	Above 90

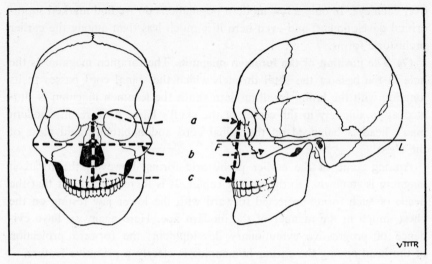

Fig. 4:8. Measuring points for determining face length and width: (*a*) nasion, (*b*) malar bones, (*c*) alveolar point, (*F-L*) Frankfort line.

There appears to be no evidence that the facial index is significantly affected by external factors. As nearly as we can determine, it is a function of heredity alone. As such it is a useful racial criterion, though, like all other single features, it must be used together with other criteria. Data on the distribution of facial indices among modern peoples are not sufficient to permit a general statement. Prehistoric forms, however, appear on the whole to have narrower and longer faces than modern races.

(2) The shape of the malar bones. Laterally and frontally projected cheekbones covered with a thick fatty layer occur with a high frequency among certain Asiatic populations, particularly those of central and eastern Asia. The trait also occurs, but less often, among populations in European Russia, the South Pacific, and native America. In other regions this feature is absent, though traces of a similar but less marked development is found in certain prehistoric forms.

(3) The forward projection of the face (prognathism). Prognathism, the degree of forward projection of the face, may be observed by noting the angle made by the line passing through the nasion and the alveolar point (in the center line of the upper jaw between the middle incisor teeth) with the Frankfort line. If this angle is 90 degrees, the face is orthognathous or straight. If, however, the angle is less than 90 degrees, the face is projecting or prognathous.

Prognathism is most marked in earlier prehistoric forms. Later forms become progressively less prognathous. Among modern men most popula-

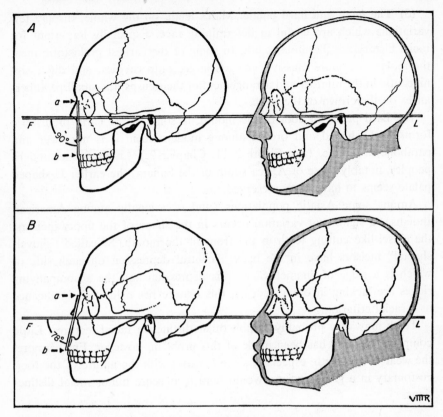

Fig. 4:9. Orthognathous (*A*) and prognathous (*B*) skulls showing measuring points: (*a*) nasion, (*F-L*) Frankfort line, (*b*) alveolar point.

tions are orthognathous; relatively few display moderate to marked prognathism. Since most modern populations are orthognathous, and since prognathism appears to disappear in the offspring of prognathous and orthognathous parents, it is evident that this feature is of little value as a racial criterion. It is useful, however, in the study of racial history.

(4) Degree of chin development. The lower jaw or mandible appears to decrease in size and change in profile as we go from the earliest forms of man to those of modern times. Like present-day apes, earlier prehistoric men have massive lower jaws which lack entirely any bony projection or chin development on their lower margins. Later prehistoric forms display a feeble chin development. Beginning with the *sapiens* races of the late Pleistocene, we find well-developed chins. All modern races possess essentially the same chin development, and display no significant variations in the size of the mandible.

(5) The teeth and hard palate. Man's teeth, on the whole, display few variations which are useful in determining race. Especially important for racial history are the molar teeth. In some of the earliest prehistoric men, the molars are more massive, possess larger pulp cavities, and differ significantly in the number and arrangement of their cusps, the small protuberances on the crown of the teeth.

The hard palate or roof of the mouth, in some of the early prehistoric forms, is U-shaped and broad; among modern men, it is narrower and parabolic in outline. (See Figure 2:11, Chapter 2.) Among some modern peoples, notably those of Africa south of the Sahara, the earlier U-shaped palate seems to have been preserved.

Among some Asiatic populations (and occasionally among American Indians), a significant variation occurs in the shape of the upper incisors, the chisel-like cutting teeth in the front of the mouth. So-called "shovel-shaped" incisors have in the back a central depression on each side of which is a ridge of enamel. Since this depression and the accompanying ridges are lacking in other peoples, this feature has a limited significance as a racial criterion.

Teeth may very probably exhibit other distinctive racial features. Little comparative study has been made of this problem, however. Furthermore, the wear on the teeth, especially since it varies with the nature of the food customary in a given society, would tend to obscure minor racial distinctions.

4. THE NOSE

The nose displays, both on the skeleton and the living, a variety of features which are not only racially variable, but are also reasonably non-adaptive. In the following discussion we shall deal only with the more important of these features.

(1) Length and width of the nose; the nasal index. The nasal index, like the cephalic index, is expressed as a proportion of width to length. The nasal index, then, is found by dividing the width of the nose by its length and multiplying the quotient by 100.

On the dry skull the length of the nose is measured from the nasion to a point at the base of the nasal spine, a bony projection between the margins of the nasal aperture. The width is the maximum distance across the nasal opening in the skull. On the living, however, length is measured from the nasion to the point at which the septum joins the upper lip, and nasal width is defined as the greatest distance across the fleshy wings of the nose. It is evident, then, that these two sets of measurements are quite

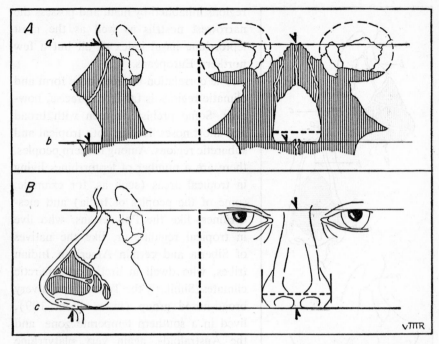

Fig. 4:10. Nose: length and width on skull (*A*) and living (*B*) showing measuring points: (*a*) nasion, (*b*) nasal margin, (*c*) juncture of septum with upper lip.

different, and, similarly, that nasal indices calculated from measures taken on the skull are not comparable to those determined from measurements on living individuals. Nasal indices, like cephalic and facial indices, are classed in three groups:

	Living	*Skull*
Leptorrhine (narrow-nosed)	Below 70	Below 47
Mesorrhine (intermediate)	70–84	47–51
Platyrrhine (wide-nosed)	Above 84	Above 51

The nasal index, like the facial index, varies with age and sex. It is higher in infants, and gradually decreases with maturity and old age. Women also tend to have broader and shorter noses than men.

It has often been suggested that there may be a correlation between nasal index and climate; narrower and longer noses, presumably more efficient in warming the air before it reaches the lungs, being more suited to colder climates. There is some justification for this view. The most distinctively broad-nosed peoples are those who live in warmer climates of Africa and the South Pacific. Eskimos, on the other hand, live in the coldest

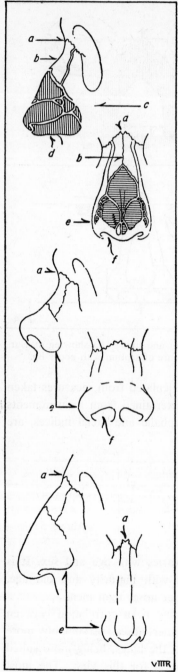

regions inhabited by man, and possess the narrowest nostrils as well as the most leptorrhine nasal index of all but a few northern Europeans.

The correlation between nose form and climatic regions is far from precise, however. Some prehistoric men with broad and short noses lived in both tropical and subarctic regions. Among modern peoples, there are a number of leptorrhines living in tropical areas (such as, for example, some of the peoples of India) and mesorrhines, like the Polynesians, who live in tropical regions, or, like the natives of Siberia and certain American Indian tribes, who dwell in arctic or subarctic climates. Similarly the Tasmanians, a very broad-nosed group (index about 109), lived in a southern temperate zone, and the Australoids, again very platyrrhine (average index 108), lived in semiarid deserts with a diurnal temperature range from 100 degrees F. at noon to below freezing at night. Temperature and humidity may have some effect on nose form, but it is evident that modifications from this source are very slow in developing. It is quite likely that hereditary factors play the most important role in the determination of nasal index.

(2) Height of nasal root and bridge. The bony portion of the nose is formed by two more or less rectangular pieces of bone which come together at an angle along one of their long sides. The nasal root is found at the junction of these bones with the frontal bone of the skull,

Fig. 4:11. Parts of the nose shown on skull above (with cartilage shaded) and on two types of nose among the living: (*a*) nasal root, (*b*) nasal bridge, (*c*) cartilages, (*d*) septum, (*e*) fleshy wings, (*f*) nostril.

and the nasal bridge is the elevation formed by the nasal bones themselves.

The nasal root varies in height from one which is level with the glabella to one just barely above the surface of the face. In a similar fashion, the nasal bridge may be high, medium, or low, and the nose may be narrow or broad at both the root and the bridge. Low and broad nasal roots and bridges are characteristic of the earlier and more primitive human forms. Among modern men similar though much less marked variations are found among Africans south of the Sahara. Other peoples, particularly those of eastern Asia, are generally intermediate in these characteristics, while Europeans often have high and narrow roots and bridges.

(3) Other observations on the cartilaginous nose. Somewhat less important observations may be made on the cartilaginous or fleshy portions of the nose. Thus, its profile may be straight, concave, or convex; the tip of the nose may be thick or thin, rounded or pointed; the lower margin of the septum may be horizontal, slanted upward, or slanted downward; the profile of the septum may be straight, concave, or convex; the fleshy wings of the nose may be thin and pinched, or wide and flaring; and the nostrils may be round or oval in diameter. For most of these observations, however, there are too few data to permit any general statement to be made of their distribution among modern races.

5. EYES, LIPS, AND EARS

Eyes, lips, and ears present a number of variations which, though rarely expressed metrically, offer useful racial criteria. It is obvious of course that features of this sort, like some we have already discussed, are only to be observed on living forms.

(1) Eyes. The most distinctive variation in eye form is found with a high frequency among Asiatic peoples, such as the Chinese, Mongols, and others, and is therefore often referred to as the Mongoloid eye. It may be described as follows:

(1) The eye opening usually has its external corner elevated so that it slants upward and outward. Non-Mongoloid eye openings are either horizontal or, less often, slanted downward and outward. A less marked upward slant is also often discernible.

(2) The Mongoloid eye is fatty with thick lids and fills the orbit completely. Often it protrudes slightly in contrast to the more or less deeply recessed non-Mongoloid eye.

(3) The Mongoloid eye usually possesses an epicanthic or so-called Mongoloid fold. This feature requires further definition since it is often confused with the trait defined in (1) above.

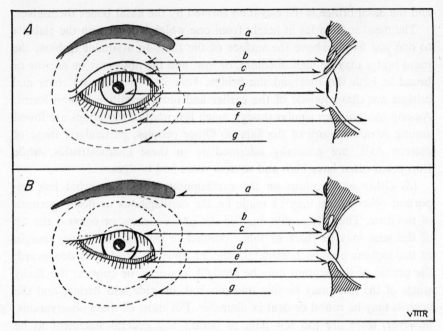

Fig. 4:12. Non-Mongoloid eye (*A*) and Mongoloid eye (*B*): (*a*) eyebrow, (*b*) fold, (*c*) upper eyelid, (*d*) iris, (*e*) lower eyelid, (*f*) eyeball, (*g*) orbit.

When the eye is open, the upper eyelid folds up upon itself much like the sections of a folding cup. In most non-Mongoloid eyes, the edge of the fold runs parallel to the edge of the eyelid so that two distinct lines may be seen along the entire length of the upper eyelid. The fold in no place overhangs the edge of the eyelid.

In other cases, however, the fold may overhang and so conceal the edge of the eyelid, either completely or at some portion of its length. When the edge of the eyelid is completely covered by the fold we have a complete Mongoloid fold. When, however, the fold covers only the inner portion of the upper eyelid we have an internal epicanthic fold. Similarly, the fold may cover only the central portion of the edge of the eyelid (median fold) or its external portion (external epicanthic or "Nordic" fold).

Characteristic of the Mongoloid eye is either the complete Mongoloid fold, or, more often perhaps, the internal epicanthic fold. The non-Mongoloid eye may display no fold at all, a median fold, or an external epicanthic fold. An inner fold may sometimes be seen in infants, regardless of race, where it is apparently associated with the infants' low nasal bridge and disappears at maturity. A low nasal bridge is not, however, the cause of the fold, since Negroids, who often possess a low nasal bridge, rarely or never have an inner epicanthic fold. Median or outer folds are found oftener in old people, presumably because of a loss of elasticity in the skin.

(2) Lips. The lip is divided into two main parts: the integumental or skin-covered lip and the lip proper or membranous lip. The latter is red in color and is sometimes separated from the integumental lip by a thin line, lighter in color than the skin, known as the lip seam.

Racial differences in the lip are manifest in the size and thickness of the membranous lip, the amount of its puffiness or protrusion, the degree to which it is everted (that is, the degree to which the red portion is visible when the lips are closed), and the visibility of the lip seam. The so-called Negroid lip, found in its most characteristic form among West African peoples, is the only really distinctive racial variant. Its membranous portion is very thick, puffy, and everted, and the lip seam is often clearly

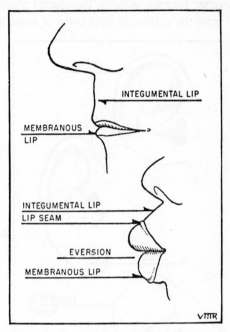

Fig. 4:13. The lips.

marked. Among other peoples the lips are much thinner, with little or no puffiness, evertedness, or lip seam.

In this connection it is interesting to recall that the lips of modern apes are not in the least puffy or everted. Furthermore, they are usually very thin and mobile, and gray rather than red in color. Judged by the degree of difference from the apes, the Negroid lip is obviously the most advanced development in this characteristic to be found among humans.

(3) Ears. Observations and measurements on the ears have not been collected in sufficient numbers to be of very great use as racial criteria. There are, however, a few gross variations in the development of the ear which appear to be distinctive. One variety of ear is small and round with little or no lobe development and a deeply rolled helix or rim. Another is longer and narrower with large free lobes and a comparatively flat or unrolled helix. Darwin's point (a small cartilaginous projection on the inner margin of the helix, said to be a vestige of the free tip of the mammalian ear) occurs most frequently in the second type.

6. SKIN, HAIR, AND EYE COLOR

Man exhibits a greater variability in skin color than is found among any other primate. Among Europeans alone we find a wide variety of shades, from the extremely light color of some Scandinavians and north Europeans to the olive and swarthy white complexions characteristic of peoples living about the Mediterranean Sea. Other peoples are somewhat less variable in skin color. They may have a yellow skin as among some Chinese, or they may be light brown or coppery red as among the Javanese and the Plains Indians of North America, respectively. Africans south of the Sahara on the whole possess the darkest skins, ranging from a dark brown to a sooty black.

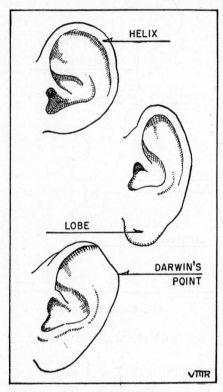

Fig. 4:14. The ear.

The color of the skin is determined by the amount of pigment it contains. This pigment or melanin varies in color from yellow to dark brown or black. It is found in the lowermost layers of the epidermis just above the true skin or dermis. Though melanin itself varies in color, the major factor which determines the color of the skin is found in the amount rather than the color of the pigment the skin contains. When the skin contains little or no melanin it is white to ruddy in color, the degree of ruddiness depending upon the thickness of the epidermis and the amount of the blood supply to the dermis. Increasing amounts of melanin in the skin bring about increasingly darker skin colors, from the swarthy white of some Mediterranean peoples to the sooty black of the East African Negroes.

The amount of melanin present in an individual's skin is apparently a constant determined in large part, if not wholly, by hereditary factors. Except for certain diseases which cause a decrease or, more often, an increase in the amount of inherited melanin, an individual does not change significantly in skin color during the course of his life. All infants, however, are lighter than their parents at birth; they do not acquire their full hereditary skin color until some time after birth. Similarly, increase in age often brings about a slight darkening of the skin.

Exposure to the sun also darkens the skin. This effect is temporary, however; an individual tanned by exposure to the sun will lose his tan when such exposure ceases. Tanning, then, apparently does not involve an increase in the amount of melanin contained in the skin. The effect of the sun's rays is rather to mass the melanin already in the skin into larger clusters or granules, the better to protect the skin from the burning effect of sunlight. Individuals possessing little or no melanin in their skin, therefore, tan slightly or not at all; exposure to sunlight only burns their skin.

Since a dark skin enables its possessor better to withstand the injurious effects of direct sunlight, and since it is quite true that the darker-skinned peoples are more or less concentrated in tropical regions, it has often been suggested that skin color is to some extent determined by environmental factors. The evidence for this view is not conclusive, however. Most dark-skinned peoples do seem to have lived in tropical regions, but the Tasmanians, also dark-skinned, lived in a temperate zone. Similarly, the tropical regions of America were inhabited by American Indians, darker, it is true, than most Europeans, but not nearly so dark as the tropical peoples of Africa. Nor have American Negroes, some of whom have lived for generations in temperate regions, undergone any significant change in skin color by reason of climatic factors alone.

Hair and eye color are due both to the amount and the color of the pigment contained in the hair and eyes, respectively. Nearly all peoples possess dark brown or black hair and eyes. Only among some Europeans do we find any considerable variation. Among these peoples, hair may be flaxen, golden, various shades of red, light brown, dark brown, or black in color. Eyes, also, may vary in color from blue through hazel to light brown, dark brown, or black. As far as we know, both hair and eye color are strictly hereditary; there are apparently no variations due to environmental factors.

7. HAIR

Among human beings hair grows most profusely on the head; there are, as far as we know, no inherently bald races.[1] Among some peoples, however, body hair also appears. Significant racial variations may be noted in regard to the form, texture, and shape in cross section of the hair in general, as well as in the amount and distribution of body hair.

[1] There is some evidence, however, that baldness is inherited. It is most frequent among Europeans, especially those of northwestern Europe.

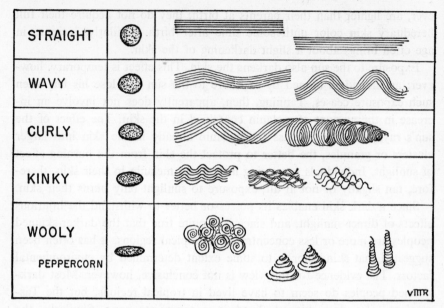

Fig. 4:15.   Hair form and texture.

(1) The form and texture of the hair; its shape in cross section. Five major categories of human hair may be distinguished. The criteria for this distinction are as follows: hair form (ranging from straight to wooly), hair texture (fine or coarse), the shape of the hair shaft in cross section (round to flat oval), and the length of the strands (long or short).

Straight hair is always circular in cross section, either fine or coarse in texture, and is usually very long and thick. It is also heavier than other kinds of hair, though in this respect there is some correlation with texture, fine hair being somewhat lighter than that which is coarse. Straight hair is found most commonly among the Mongoloids, but is also characteristic of some Caucasoids.

The strands of wavy hair are so curved as to produce regular undulations or waves. These may be long and shallow or short and deep. In cross section wavy hair is ovaloid or elliptical, the two diameters of the ellipse being nearly equal in length. Wavy hair may be quite as long as straight hair and either fine or coarse in texture. It usually weighs less.

Curly hair grows in large, loose spirals. It may be fine or relatively coarse in texture; its weight does not vary appreciably from that of wavy hair. In cross section curly hair is also elliptical, but the diameters of the ellipse differ markedly in length. Curly hair is somewhat shorter than wavy hair.

So-called kinky hair grows in very short U-shaped waves. Each hair shaft is somewhat twisted on its own axis, just enough to produce the characteristic kink, but not so much as to produce a spiral. A cross section of kinky hair reveals an elongated ellipse having one diameter considerably shorter than the other. In texture kinky hair is coarse and wiry. It is much shorter and lighter in weight than curly hair.

Wooly hair grows in short, tightly curled spirals which grow close together and intertwine, giving the hair a matted appearance. Each hair shaft is twisted corkscrew-like on its own axis and, in some cases at least, erupts at a sharp angle with the surface of the head. Wooly hair has the flattest ovaloid form in cross section and is the shortest and lightest (in weight) of all types of hair. Like kinky hair, it is coarse and wiry in texture.

A distinctive variant of wooly hair is found among the Bushmen of Southwest Africa and the Pygmies of the Congo River. This is the so-called peppercorn hair, which is like wooly hair in all respects but one. Where wooly hair grows in intertwined spirals set close together, the spirals of peppercorn hair are separated from one another by bare spaces. Each set of spiral strands forms, then, an independent conelike projection.

Moist tropical climates are sometimes said to be responsible for kinky and wooly hair, since most of the people who have such hair live or had their origin in such regions. However, there are also a number of dwellers in moist tropical regions who possess long straight hair—notably the American Indian groups of the Amazon basin and the Malays of Java, Borneo, and Malaya. It seems fairly certain that hair form is less affected by environmental factors than almost any other physical trait; it appears to be wholly a nonadaptive feature.

(2) Amount of body hair. Hair on the face, chest, arms, legs, and pubic regions varies only in amount. Relatively few populations have any considerable amount of body hair. The Ainus, a small group living in northern Japan, and the natives of Australia appear to be the hairiest of all living peoples, with some European and Near Eastern populations ranking next.

8. STATURE, WEIGHT, AND BODY BUILD

A number of variant features of the human body may be found in stature, body weight, and other measurements and observations on the trunk and limbs. As we shall see, however, most of these items are of limited value as racial criteria.

(1) Stature and body weight. Average stature for modern man is about 5' 6" with, however, a usual range of variation from 4' 3" to 6' 6" for males, and 3′ 11″ to 6′ 2″ for females. Adequate data on averages and ranges for prehistoric man are lacking, but the data available would seem to indicate that little change in stature has taken place since man's first appearance on earth.

In terms of stature human beings may be classed in five group as follows:

	Male	Female
Very short	Below 4′11″	Below 4′7″
Short	5′0″–5′3″	4′8″–4′11″
Medium	5′4″–5′7″	5′0″–5′3″
Tall	5′8″–5′11″	5′4″–5′6″
Very tall	6′0″ and above	5′7″ and above

The range of variation within most populations is very great, however, and there is considerable overlapping. It is only in a few instances, then, that stature is racially distinctive. Notable examples are the Pygmies of Africa and Oceania who fall in the "very short" category, and some East African groups, such as the Dinka and Shilluk of the upper Nile, who are classed as very tall.

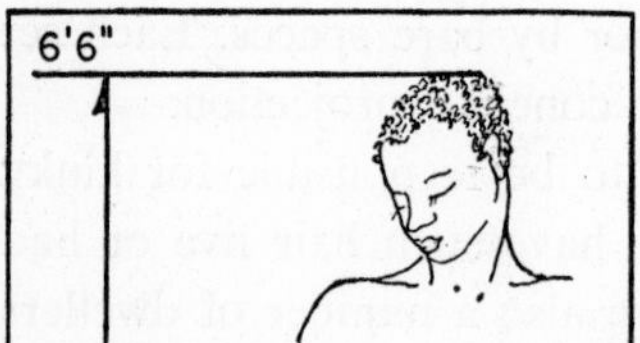

Fig. 4:16.

Stature is probably much affected by environmental conditions, particularly in regard to the kind and amount of food available. Chronic malnutrition results in considerable losses of stature, as much as 2.5 to 4 per cent when such conditions obtain over a long period. Apparently, however, an irreducible minimum may be reached below which the average stature will not descend. Similar limits seemingly exist for maximum stature under improved nutritional circumstances. It is probable that these limits are genetically determined.

Malnutrition does not necessarily mean a low average stature, however. Eskimos, Bushmen, and Pygmies—all of short or very short stature—almost certainly suffer from lacks in their diet which may affect their stature. But, in contrast to these, we find the very tall Indians of Tierra del Fuego in southern South America who are certainly no better off than the Eskimo when it comes to diet and living conditions in general.

Weight, taken alone, has no value as a racial criterion, since it is affected not only by nutritional factors but varies with stature as well. A so-called bodily fullness index relates stature and weight. It is determined by dividing weight by the cube of the stature and multiplying the quotient by 100. This index varies significantly for age and sex, apparently reflecting with fair accuracy stages of growth from infancy through adolescence and adulthood to old age. It does not, however, have any significance as a racial criterion.

(2) The curve of the spine. Among some of the earlier men the spine is only feebly curved in the lumbar region (that is, the small of the back). As a result, the spine of such forms differs distinctively from that of modern man, characterized by a decided lumbar curve. Data on this feature are lacking for other prehistoric forms, some of which may have had a simple bow-shaped spine like that of the modern ape. No distinctive variations in the curve of the spine occur among the *sapiens* races.

(3) The shape of the thigh bone. The bone of the upper leg among certain prehistoric forms is short, thick, and curved, much like that of the modern ape. Among all modern peoples, as well as in several prehistoric forms, the thigh bone is long, slender, and straight.

(4) The pelvis. As we have already seen (see Chapter 2), the semierect ape has a pelvis markedly narrower and deeper than that of the fully erect modern man. Some prehistoric humanoids also have a pelvis narrower and deeper than that of *Homo sapiens,* though it is not so narrow and deep as the ape's pelvis. This fact suggests that these earlier prehistoric forms were not so erect in posture as *Homo sapiens*—an inference which is further justified by the feebly developed lumbar curve and the rearward position of the foramen magnum in these forms. The pelvis does not vary significantly in structure among the races of *Homo sapiens.*

(5) Arm and leg length. Among some of the more primitive prehistoric men, arms are longer relative to legs than among modern races. This, again, is a primitive feature; both man and the apes are descendants of brachiating creatures (that is, animals that traveled through the forests in which they lived by swinging from one limb to another). Since man's arms and legs are no longer used for locomotion of this sort, his arms have gradually come to be shorter in proportion to his legs than is the case among apes (some of whom are still in part arboreal) and the earlier humanoids.

(6) The trunk or torso. In modern man this is shorter in relation to leg length than among apes and some prehistoric forms. Numerous other variations are also evident in the torsos of both ancient and modern humanoids. Two extreme types may be differentiated. In one, the trunk is short and thin with narrow, sloping shoulders and a narrow, flat chest. In the other, the torso is long and broad with wide, slightly sloping shoulders and a broad, deep chest. Among some prehistoric forms, as among most of the apes, the chest is deep and round (barrel-chested) rather than flattened as in most *sapiens* forms.

Some of these criteria, it is evident, have a limited value in the differentiation of prehistoric species from *Homo sapiens*. Among the races of *Homo sapiens,* however, the value of variations in the structure of the torso is somewhat more dubious. Within most modern populations the range of individual variations in torso structure is very great—only a few relatively isolated populations display any truly uniform type. Furthermore, the proportions of the trunk, like stature and weight, must seriously be affected by food intake and physical exercise. In all probability environmental and cultural factors very often tend to wipe out most if not all variations due to heredity alone.

9. BLOOD GROUPS

Human blood may be classed in four groups or types which are usually called A, B, AB, and O. Blood of the A type contains certain substances in its serum which will cause the cells of the B and AB types to clump or agglutinate. Similarly, B-type blood will agglutinate the cells of A and AB, and O-type blood will cause the cells of the A, B, and AB types to agglutinate. Blood of the AB type, however, lacks the substances causing agglutination. These differences in blood types may be tabulated as follows:

Blood type:	Agglutinates:	Does not agglutinate:
A	B, AB	A, O
B	A, AB	B, O
AB	None	A, B, AB, O
O	A, B, AB	O

Blood groups are especially useful as racial criteria because we know precisely how they are inherited. There are apparently three genes, a, b, and o, which determine an individual's blood type. Genes a and b have equal expressive value (neither is dominant over the other) but o is recessive to both a and b. The genetic determination of the four blood types may, then, be summarized as follows:

Sperm having gene:	Egg having gene:	Genotype of offspring:	Blood group of offspring:
a	a	aa	A
a	b	ab	AB
a	o	ao	A
b	a	ba	AB
b	b	bb	B
b	o	bo	B
o	a	oa	A
o	b	ob	B
o	o	oo	O

From this it is evident that there are six genotypes which, because o is recessive to both a and b, produce four phenotypes:

Genotypes aa and ao both produce phenotype A.

Genotypes bb and bo both produce phenotype B.

Genotype ab alone produces phenotype AB.

Genotype oo alone produces phenotype O.

The distribution of blood groups and blood group genes among the peoples of the world is fairly well known. Gene o is found among all the groups so far studied, and is usually far more frequent than either a or b. Genes a and b fluctuate in frequency relative to one another, but, except in a few cases, both occur in all the groups studied. It is evident, then, that populations differ, not in the presence or absence of given genes but in the frequency of occurrence of each gene. The same is also true of the blood types themselves.

Gene a occurs most commonly among the peoples of western Europe (including Americans of European origin), native Australians, and several American Indian groups, notably those of the North American Plains. It is somewhat less frequent in Africa south of the Sahara. Gene b increases in frequency as we move eastward across the Eurasiatic continent and reaches its peaks of frequency in central and southern Asia. Gene b is exceptionally rare among North American Indians; in a number of groups reported it appears to be lacking completely. Among the very few South American Indian groups so far studied, b genes appear also to be rare, with, however, two striking exceptions: the Carajas of Brazil and the Yahgans of Tierra del Fuego, both of whom are reported to show a very high percentage of b genes.

To summarize the distribution of the four blood types is not such an easy task. The following table gives a small sampling of distributions in a number of widely spread populations: [2]

[2] The data in this table are taken from a far more elaborate compilation made by William C. Boyd, "Blood Groups," *Tabulae Biologicae*, xvii, 113–240 (1939), Table I, pp. 155–229.

Population	Number	O	A	B	AB
England (eastern counties)	1,000	43.2	47.7	8.3	1.4
Copenhagen, Denmark	1,261	40.7	45.3	10.5	3.5
Detroit, U.S.A.	5,000	44.5	36.1	14.3	5.2
Berlin, Germany	1,227	40.0	39.5	15.1	5.4
Leningrad, U.S.S.R.	1,176	43.1	33.1	19.8	4.6
Buriat of Irkutsk, U.S.S.R.	1,320	32.4	20.2	39.2	8.2
Canton, China	992	45.9	22.8	25.2	6.1
United Provinces, India	2,357	30.2	24.5	37.2	8.1
Ainus of Sakhalin	1,141	25.7	28.0	34.8	11.5
Tokyo, Japan	29,799	30.1	38.4	21.9	9.7
Sundanese of Semarang (Indonesia)	682	38.7	23.2	31.0	7.3
Moros, Philippine Islands	442	41.6	23.1	30.3	5.0
Native Australians, Queensland	377	60.3	31.7	6.4	1.6
Balese, Belgian Congo	507	48.5	30.8	16.4	4.3
Pygmies, Belgian Congo	1,032	30.6	30.3	29.1	10.0
Zulus, South Africa	500	51.8	24.6	21.6	2.0
American Negroes, New York	730	44.2	30.3	21.8	3.7
Ambon, Melanesia	1,471	55.9	20.9	20.9	2.3
Bushmen, South Africa	268	60.4	28.0	7.8	3.8
Hottentots, South Africa	506	34.8	30.6	29.2	5.3
Palau, Micronesia	545	58.9	26.4	12.3	2.4
Yap, Micronesia	213	57.7	20.3	17.8	4.2
Hawaii	413	36.5	60.8	2.2	0.5
Eskimos, Greenland	607	54.2	38.5	4.8	2.0
Navahos, North America	622	69.1	30.6	0.2	0
Blackfeet, North America	235	45.5	50.6	2.1	1.8
Mayas, Central America	738	76.5	16.7	5.4	1.4
Mapuches, South America	382	75.6	17.2	6.2	0.6
Carajas, South America	61	39.0	5.0	51.0	0
Yahgans, South America	33	9.0	0	91.0	0

Blood types O and A, it is clear, are both very frequent among western Europeans and their descendants in the Americas. B is relatively rare and AB least common. Among Asiatics O is still highest in frequency, though not so high as in Europe. A and B are about equal, and AB remains relatively infrequent. Australian aborigines show a high frequency of O and a moderately high frequency of A, with both B and AB very low or lacking altogether. In Indonesia and the Philippines the distribution is like that of the Asiatic continent, but in Polynesia and Micronesia B and AB are usually very rare. Africans south of the Sahara, Melanesians, and American Negroes show a high percentage of O types, a somewhat lower percentage of A and B, and a very low proportion of AB. Most American Indians show a very high frequency of O, a moderately high percentage of A, while B and AB are rare or lacking. Those of the North American Plains, however, are more evenly divided between O and A, and in South

America we find the Carajas and Yahgans with strikingly high percentages of B.

10. SUMMARY

Our purpose in this chapter has been to clarify the concept of race by describing the more important criteria used to distinguish racial types among men. As we have seen, races are not to be viewed as isolated groups of men each of which may rigidly be distinguished from the others by averages of its phenotypic characters. The several populations which exist within the human species have not, in most cases, been isolated long enough to develop completely distinctive hereditary characters. All of them have interbred to a greater or less degree until it is probable that there are few genes which are not distributed, though in varying frequencies, throughout the whole of mankind. If this be so, it is evident that races can only be more or less temporary assemblages of genes and gene complexes, common to all of mankind but exhibited in particular populations with differing degrees of frequency.

The problem of the anthropologist, then, is not only to describe the average phenotypes of past and present races, but is also, and more importantly, to determine the distribution and relative frequency of genetic materials among human populations at different times and in different places.

In the two chapters that follow we shall review current racial descriptions, using genetic data whenever it is available. Since, however, genetic knowledge of man is still scanty and incomplete, our discussion will of necessity concern itself mainly with phenotypic descriptions.

COLLATERAL READING

Ashley-Montagu, M. F. *An Introduction to Physical Anthropology*. Springfield, Illinois: C. C. Thomas, 1945. Chapter V, Appendix.

Boyd, William C. *Genetics and the Races of Man*. Boston: Little, Brown and Co., 1950. Chapters VII–XI.

Cole, Fay-Cooper. "The Coming of Man," *The Nature of the World and Man*, ed. H. H. Newman. Chicago: University of Chicago Press, 1926. Pp. 349–380.

Hooton, Earnest A. *Up From the Ape*. Rev. Ed. New York: The Macmillan Co., 1946. Part III, V (pp. 455–568), Appendix.

Howells, W. W. *Mankind So Far*. New York: Doubleday, Doran and Co., 1944. Chapter XVIII.

Chapter 5

FOSSIL MAN AND RACIAL HISTORY

1. HUMAN ORIGINS AND THE FOSSIL RECORD

In Chapter 2 we saw that the first ape- and monkey-like forms *(Anthropoidea)* of the Old World variety were found early in the third of the four main geological epochs (the Oligocene period of the Tertiary epoch). One of these, *Parapithecus,* is considered the ancestor of the Old World monkeys, while the other, *Propliopithecus,* is clearly ancestral to the modern apes. Neither form, in all probability, stands in the direct line of man's descent. It is not unlikely, however, that *Parapithecus* is but little distant from the form ancestral to all Old World anthropoids and that *Propliopithecus* is similarly not far removed from the common ancestor of the *Simiidae* and *Hominidae.*

In the following two periods of the Tertiary (the Miocene and Pliocene) several related species (of the genus *Dryopithecus*) have been found, and these appear to be at or near the point of divergence of the higher apes and man. It is clear, then, on the basis of primate paleontology alone, that forms evolving toward man were probably in existence as early as the Pliocene and possibly before.

We do not, however, have any fossils directly linking *Dryopithecus* with the earliest hominids. The African fossil forms *(Australopithecus, Paranthropus,* and *Plesianthropus),* all of which stand structurally between the apes and man, seem to be too late to serve as connecting links. Although there is still some uncertainty as to dating, by the time these forms appear, true hominids probably were already in existence.

112

Fossil records of the earliest hominids, with one or two possible exceptions, do not occur until the Pleistocene is well under way. But, as we shall see later, the earliest of these forms are widely scattered over the Old World and are far more divergent in structure than the modern human types. Both these facts suggest that even in the Pleistocene, manlike forms had existed for some time, and that our earliest Pleistocene specimens by no means represent the first *Hominidae* to appear on earth. This conclusion of course confirms that drawn from primate paleontology, namely, that the *Hominidae* had their beginnings in the Pliocene or earlier.

We should remember, however, that there are as yet no definite records, either in skeletal or cultural materials, which incontestably prove that Pliocene man existed. This is not surprising. The first hominids were almost certainly very few in number. Like their close relatives, the apes, they probably lived in tropical regions. Possessing few or no weapons, they were at the mercy of the numerous more powerful predatory animals who shared their habitats. We may expect, then, to find little or no trace of these primeval hominids; they had no culture which could survive the ravages of time, and their bones, deposited in tropical forests or broken up by other animals, had little chance of survival.

Even our data on Pleistocene man are scanty and fragmentary. For many forms we have only partial skeletons, and in some cases only a skull or jawbone remains as proof that an entire species once existed. It is evident of course that we cannot supply detailed descriptions even of the skeletal characteristics of such scantily attested forms, nor can we give any indication of the individual variability of the species to which they belonged.

Another problem to be considered is the fact that when remains of only one individual are found, we must assume that the single specimen is representative of a whole species. At first sight, this may seem a hazardous assumption. Some early finds, indeed, were at first refused acceptance on the grounds that they represented abnormal and nontypical individuals, freaks or monstrosities. Of course this is always possible, yet a little reflection will show that the chances are overwhelmingly in favor of a surviving skeleton representing a normal individual. If we were to pick a contemporary human being at random out of the millions on earth today, the chances are we would pick one who was a normal representative of *Homo sapiens*. It is true that the single individual would not tell us all there is to know about our species. We would have no clear picture of the various races of *Homo sapiens,* nor would we be sure of the range of variation in the species. Nevertheless, we would stand a very good chance of being able to distinguish our single individual from other species of the genus *Homo,* and would find it still easier to distinguish him from other genera of the *Hominidae.* While we must always bear in mind the possibility that the remains of a single individual are not typical of a species or genus, and that in any case a single individual does not give us any idea of the range of variation within the type, nevertheless we can be fairly sure that we are dealing with a normal specimen which, in a general way, is representative of a whole group.

Despite the obvious lacks in the record, it is still possible to provide descriptions of many of the varieties of man that once inhabited the earth. And when these forms are viewed in their proper temporal sequence, and their structural characters are compared point for point with those of modern man, we can recover, at the least, the main outlines of the course of human evolution.

2. PLEISTOCENE CHRONOLOGY

As we have said, all our definitely datable finds of fossil man come from the fourth and latest geological epoch, the Quaternary. This epoch may be divided into two smaller periods: the Pleistocene, which began about one million years ago, and the Holocene or Recent, which began about ten thousand years ago. The major steps in the evolution of man took place in the Pleistocene; the men of the Holocene are essentially modern in type. It is necessary, therefore, to break the Pleistocene into still smaller time periods if we are to get any useful picture of human evolution.

Three methods are commonly employed to establish a chronology for the Pleistocene. The first of these involves the use of climatological data, the second employs paleontological data, and the third is based upon cultural change. Complete agreement between the chronologies so achieved is not yet possible, however. Because of this, and because no one of the three methods may be universally applied, it is not always possible to date relatively to one another fossil hominids found in widely separated regions.

The climate of the Pleistocene. As the Pliocene drew to a close, the earth began gradually to become cooler. The fall of earth temperatures led in turn to the extension of the polar ice caps and the gradual enlargement of glaciated areas of mountainous regions. Eventually large portions of Europe, Asia, and North America were covered by huge glaciers very like those which cover the interior of Greenland and the Antarctic continent today. The advancing glaciers affected the plant and animal life of the world as well as the rivers, lakes, and sea coasts. Plants and animals in many cases were obliged to migrate owing to drastic climatic changes, and in some cases became extinct. Because of the large amounts of water frozen in the glaciers, rivers, lakes, and seas were reduced in volume. The increasing weight on land surfaces and the reduction of weight of ocean waters caused marked changes in the interrelationships of land and sea areas. Areas of rainfall moved in toward the equator so that regions that formerly were deserts became temperate, grassy plains.

These changes took place over a very long period of time. Then, just as slowly, the earth became warm again. The glaciers retreated and in many areas disappeared entirely. Rainfall areas shifted northward and southward from the equator. Plants and animals moved back into formerly glaciated regions. Rivers, lakes, and seas rose in volume and the coast lines of islands and continents took on new forms.

Glacial advances of this sort took place four times during the Pleistocene. In Europe these major advances (there were as well a number of minor fluctuations) are known as the Günz, Mindel, Riss, and Würm, respectively. Corresponding advances in North America are the Jerseyan, Kansan, Illinoian, and Wisconsin. Between each of the European glaciations were three warmer periods, known as the first, second, and third interglacials. Four interglacial periods are recognized for North America, since the Illinoian advance had two phases, the Illinoian and the Iowan, separated by a brief interlude of warmer climate. There were also two Würm and Wisconsin advances, Würm I corresponding to the Early Wisconsin and Würm II to the Late Wisconsin. The final retreat of the Würm and Wisconsin glaciers was followed, in the European Alps at least, by a series of three minor advances and retreats of the ice, called the Buhl, Geschnitz, and Daun. At some time during this postglacial epoch—the precise time varies with the region—the Pleistocene gave way to the geological Recent or Holocene. (See Chart I.)

As we have said, the advances of ice during the Pleistocene caused the rain belts of the world to move in toward the equator. As a result, much of Africa and parts of Asia and North America received more rainfall during the glaciations than in the intervening interglacial periods. These alternating pluvial and interpluvial periods can only be tentatively correlated with the succession of glacials and interglacials. In the accompanying chart (Chart I) we have included, as an example of this kind of dating, the pluvials and interpluvials recognized by Professor Leakey for Kenya, East Africa, and have indicated their partial correspondence with the European glacial and interglacial stages.

Paleontological periods. Paleontologists customarily divide the Pleistocene into three major portions, called the Lower, Middle, and Upper Pleistocene. This division may roughly be correlated with the western European glacial epochs as follows:

Chart I. CLIMATOLOGICAL PERIODS OF THE QUATERNARY

	EUROPE	NORTH AMERICA	EAST AFRICA
HOLOCENE			
UPPER PLEISTO-CENE	Achen retreat Würm II Glacial Laufen retreat Würm I Glacial	Late Wisconsin Glacial Early Wisconsin Glacial	Second Interpluvial
			Gamblian
	Third Interglacial		
MIDDLE PLEISTO-CENE	Riss Glacial	Illinoian Iowan Glacial	Pluvial
	Second Interglacial		First Interpluvial
LOWER PLEISTO-CENE	Mindel Glacial	Kansan Glacial	Kamasian
	First Interglacial		Pluvial
	Günz Glacial	Jerseyan Glacial	
PLIOCENE			

Lower Pleistocene: from the beginning of the Günz glaciation to about the close of the Mindel glaciation.

Middle Pleistocene: from the beginning of the second interglacial to about the end of the Riss glaciation.

Upper Pleistocene: from the beginning of the third interglacial to the end of the Pleistocene.

The basis for this chronology is found in the presence or absence of certain now extinct species of animals. Though many of our modern species were already in existence at the beginning of the Pleistocene, there were a few that became extinct at various stages during this period and a few others that appeared for the first time. We may summarize a few of the more important of these changes as follows.

LOWER PLEISTOCENE

(1) The southern elephant *(Elephas meridionalis)*. This species became extinct in this period.

(2) A primitive or early form of *Elephas trogontheri,* the progenitor of the mammoth of the Upper Pleistocene.

(3) A primitive form of *Elephas antiquus,* the progenitor of the modern straight-tusked elephant. Both *trogontheri* and *antiquus* are derived from *meridionalis;* in the Lower Pleistocene this process of divergence is just beginning.

(4) *Dicerorhinus etruscus* or the Etruscan rhinoceros.

(5) *Machairodus* or the saber-tooth tiger. This species becomes extinct during the Lower Pleistocene.

(6) *Dama savini,* an older species of fallow deer.

(7) *Megaceros verticornis,* an older species of the so-called Pleistocene Irish elk.

MIDDLE PLEISTOCENE

(1) The southern elephant has now disappeared, leaving only *trogontheri* and *antiquus.* These two are now somewhat more divergent, though there still exist a large number of intermediate connecting forms.

(2) Merck's or the broad-nosed rhinoceros *(Dicerorhinus mercki)* has replaced the older Etruscan rhinoceros.

(3) *Dama clactionianus,* a new species of fallow deer, has replaced *savini.*

(4) *Megaceros germanicus* replaces the earlier *verticornis.*

UPPER PLEISTOCENE

(1) We now find two decidedly distinct elephant species, both of which go back to the Lower Pleistocene southern elephant. One of these is the mammoth *(Elephas primigenius)* and the other is a late form of *Elephas antiquus.* Both become extinct before the end of the Pleistocene.

(2) Merck's rhinoceros continues into the Upper Pleistocene. There is also, however, a new species, the so-called wooly rhinoceros *(Tichorhinus antiquatus)* which appears for the first time.

(3) *Dama dama* replaces *Dama clactonianus* as the typical fallow deer.

(4) *Megaceros giganteus,* an enormous elklike animal with a ten-foot horn spread, replaces the earlier *Megaceros germanicus.*

This method of dating is usually regarded as secondary in those regions of the earth where data on the glacial epochs are available. But in tropical regions like Java, for example, where traces of glacial action are few or nonexistent, paleontological data are often the only means of achieving a chronology.

It should be remembered, however, that chronologies based upon paleontological data are not necessarily the same for all regions of the earth. Not only did different species exist in different areas in the Pleistocene as they do today, but it seems also that the ancient animals persisted longer in some regions than in others. Many Pleistocene species apparently flourished in America, for example, long after similar forms had become extinct in Europe.

The cultures of the Pleistocene. Throughout the Pleistocene there were several varieties and species of *Hominidae* living in the Old World. (The New World was unoccupied until the very end of the Pleistocene, at which time it was invaded by peoples from Asia.) We know of the existence of these forms from their skeletal remains and from the traces of their cultures deposited in numerous places in Europe, Asia, and Africa. Since these cultural remains are often associated with specific glacial and interglacial deposits, we can date them relatively to one another. Furthermore, the remains themselves, which consist largely of stone and bone artifacts, are often deposited in more or less distinct layers or strata. This fact, plus the fact that some of the artifacts show a definite progression from simple to more complex forms, makes it possible to date, relatively to one another, even those cultures which are not specifically associated with climatological phenomena.

The cultures of the Pleistocene all fall into a single major cultural epoch, the Paleolithic or Old Stone Age. During this epoch man made his tools and weapons first of stone alone, later of stone, bone, and horn. (Other materials, such as wood, may possibly have been used, but only the artifacts made of less perishable materials have survived.) He was very evidently a nomadic hunter and food-gatherer. Toward the end of the Pleistocene (the precise time varies for different regions of the Old World) man entered a new phase of cultural development, the Neolithic or New Stone Age. This phase was marked, not only by advances in stone tools but also by the invention of agriculture and animal husbandry. The Neolithic and the subsequent metal-using periods will not concern us here, for we are primarily concerned with establishing a cultural sequence for the Pleistocene alone. (See Chart II.) [1]

Chart II. CULTURAL EPOCHS IN WESTERN EUROPE

HOLOCENE		MESOLITHIC & SUCCEEDING CULTURES	
UPPER PLEISTO- CENE	Achen retreat	Magdalenian Magdalenian Solutrean Aurignacian	Upper Paleolithic
	Würm II Glacial		
	Laufen retreat		
	Würm I Glacial	Mousterian Mousterian	Middle Paleolithic
	Third Interglacial	Acheulean	
MIDDLE PLEISTO- CENE	Riss Glacial		
	Second Interglacial	Acheulean Chellean	Lower Paleolithic
LOWER PLEISTO- CENE	Mindel Glacial		
	First Interglacial	Chellean	
	Günz Glacial		
PLIOCENE		EOLITHIC CULTURES (?)	

Paleolithic stone tools were made by chipping or flaking hard siliceous (glasslike) materials like flint, quartzite, and obsidian, which can be broken into sharply edged and pointed pieces. Broadly speaking, Paleolithic stone tools may be divided into three major categories: core tools, like hammer stones and axes, made by shaping large nodules of flint; flake tools, such as points and scrapers, made of smaller pieces knocked off a flint nodule; and blade tools, like gravers, awls, and knives, made from prismlike flakes detached from previously prepared nodules of flint. Core and flake tools occur very early (core tools, in some regions, appear to have preceded those made from flakes), but blade tools are somewhat later.

Three major stone-chipping techniques may also be recognized in Paleolithic cultures. One of the earliest is called percussion-flaking, by which

[1] Chart II, and the accompanying text discussion, presents a somewhat simplified picture of Paleolithic cultures. Prehistorians, in recent years, have added much to their knowledge of the Paleolithic, and, though there is little general agreement on terms, give us a considerably more complex presentation than is here offered. For these details, too complex to include here, we refer the student to Robert J. Braidwood, "Prehistoric Men," *Chicago Natural History Museum, Popular Series, Anthropology,* No. 37 (1948), pp. 15–54, and Grahame Clark, *From Savagery to Civilization* (London: Cobbett Press, 1946), Chapters I, II, and III.

is meant the shaping of a nodule or flake by striking it with a hammer-like stone. Later, man began to chip stone by pressing a bluntly pointed tool, such as an antler tine, against the flake to be shaped. This is called pressure-flaking. Prismatic flaking is the most recent technique. Here a flint nodule is made into a roughly conical core. Then a bluntly pointed tool is held near the edge of the base of the cone (the so-called striking platform) and struck with a hammer stone in much the same way as a carpenter strikes the butt end of a chisel with his mallet. By this means a number of long, slender, prismlike flakes may successively be detached. These, which usually have one or more sharp edges, may then be used as knives without further working, or shaped by secondary pressure-flaking into a variety of other tools.

If we apply the cultural criteria we have outlined to western Europe, archeologically the best known region of the Old World, we find that the Paleolithic of western Europe may be divided into six principal subepochs. (See Chart II.) The two earliest, called Chellean and Acheulean, respectively, are usually grouped together as the Lower Paleolithic, the third or Mousterian is sometimes called the Middle Paleolithic, and the last three, Aurignacian, Solutrean, and Magdalenian, make up the Upper Paleolithic.

The Lower Paleolithic is marked by use of core tools and percussion-flaking. The principal tool is made by shaping a nodule of flint into a roughly pear-shaped hand ax. Chellean hand axes are crudely made, but as we move into the Acheulean, the hand ax becomes smaller, thinner, and better shaped. During the Acheulean, other tools, made of large flakes, also appear, though these may have begun earlier. Chellean culture, in western Europe, is definitely associated with the first interglacial. Since it already displays a knowledge of the rudiments of stone-working, we may assume that it was preceded by an earlier period during which man learned the art of stone-chipping. This assumed period is often called the Eolithic, and there are a number of finds of what appear to be chipped stone tools which are assigned to this period. Since, however, the Eolithic can neither be defined in terms of a clearly describable cultural tradition nor definitely assigned to a given climatological period (eoliths have been found in every period from the Oligocene up to and including the Pleistocene), we need not discuss it further here.

Acheulean culture begins in the second interglacial and carries over into the third interglacial. There is no evidence that man continued to live in Europe during the Mindel or Riss glacial periods. In all probability, he was not yet able to protect himself from arctic and subarctic weather and so probably migrated to warmer areas, returning to Europe when the glaciers had retreated.

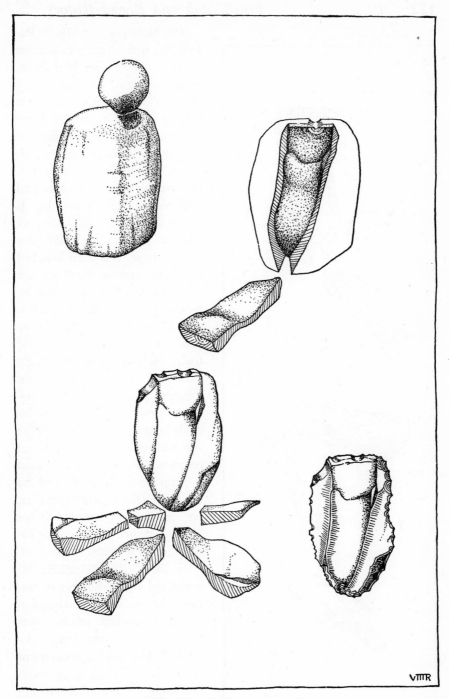

Fig. 5:1. Shaping a core tool.

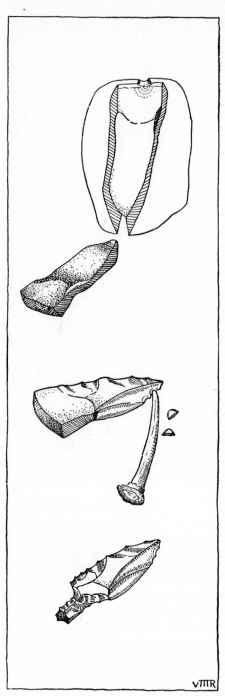

The Mousterian or Middle Paleolithic, which begins in western Europe during the third interglacial and lasts until the climax of the Würm glaciation, witnesses a large number of cultural innovations. Hand axes continue to be made, but flake tools, which began in the Acheulean or earlier, become far more numerous and important. Percussion-flaking is still employed for the hand ax and to produce the flakes for smaller tools. But once knocked off a flint nodule, the flakes are then sharpened or retouched by means of pressure-flaking. In this way Mousterian man was able to produce a wide variety of stone tools, including not only hand axes and hammer stones but scrapers, points, and perforators. Other Mousterian innovations include bone anvils and fleshers, the use of caves as dwellings, mineral colors which were probably used to paint the dead, hearths and the use of fire (fire is probably earlier, but our first evidence of it for Europe comes in the Mousterian), and the burial of the dead.

In the Upper Paleolithic we again find a large number of cultural innovations. Aurignacian culture is marked, among other things, by the introduction of prismatic flaking and a consequent variety of distinctive stone tools, the extensive use of bone and horn for tools, and the beginnings of painting, sculpturing, modeling, and engraving.

Fig. 5:2. Shaping a flake tool.

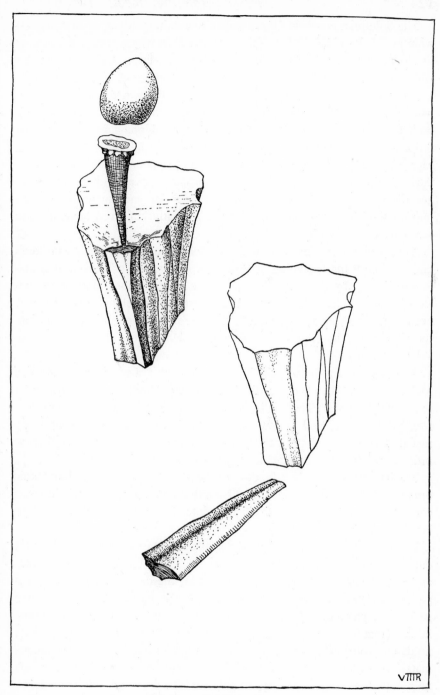

Fig. 5:3. Prismatic flaking.

The Solutrean epoch in Upper Paleolithic culture is far shorter and less widespread. Its chief distinguishing characteristic lies in the excellence of its stone work, particularly well demonstrated in large, leaf-shaped blades which are carefully chipped on both sides by pressure-flaking.

The Magdalenian continues the tradition laid down during the Aurignacian. Stone work remains at about the same level of performance; in both the Aurignacian and Magdalenian, stone-chipping is somewhat inferior to that of the Solutrean. Bone tools increase in number and variety; especially characteristic are the varieties of harpoon points and a bone device, called a spear-thrower, used to propel a spear with greater force and distance. Art work is also improved over Aurignacian times with the introduction of polychrome paintings and greatly improved techniques in sculpture and engraving.

Aurignacian culture begins with the decline of the Würm I glaciation and lasts until the beginning of Würm II. Over some of Europe it is followed directly by the Magdalenian, but in other regions, notably central Europe, the Solutrean intervenes. The Solutrean is a relatively short period occurring during the first portion of the Würm II glacial. Magdalenian culture begins at the climax of Würm II and continues through the final Würm retreat.

As the Holocene begins, the Magdalenian gives way to the Mesolithic. Many Magdalenian elements disappear in the Mesolithic, but a number of new traits appear. The dog is domesticated, the bow and arrow are used for the first time, and a new type of stone tools called microliths are made. These were apparently fastened to wooden or bone handles in order to produce a suitable cutting instrument.

The Mesolithic may best be described as a final phase of the Paleolithic driven to the wall by the incoming Neolithic cultures. It survived in some corners of Europe to a relatively late date, long after the Neolithic had become well established elsewhere.

We are now ready to examine the available data on ancient man. These data, as we shall see, are found in many regions of the Old World. Insofar as the problem of dating them is concerned, the data fall into three categories: skeletal materials which can specifically be associated with dated geological, paleontological, or cultural remains; skeletal materials found in situ (that is, in undisturbed deposits), but in regions for which few or no dated geological, paleontological, or cultural remains exist; and skeletal materials removed from their position in the earth by individuals who took no notice of associated geological, paleontological, or cultural phenomena. Finds in the first category offer few difficulties in respect to the problem of dating, but those in the second and third categories are often difficult to place with accuracy in chronological sequence. We shall discuss these chronological problems as they arise in connection with specific forms.

3. MEGANTHROPUS AND GIGANTANTHROPUS

Traces of what may well be the earliest and most primitive hominids known have recently been found in Java and south China. The form called

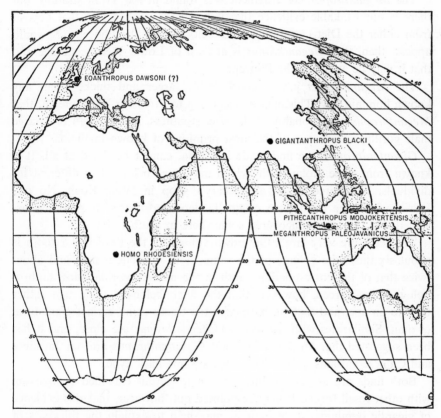

Map 5:1. Fossil men of the Lower Pleistocene. (The dating of *Eoanthropus* and *Homo rhodesiensis* is uncertain; see §§ 7, 8.)

Meganthropus paleojavanicus (the giant man of ancient Java) is known from a fragment of an enormous jaw uncovered in the fossil-bearing beds of central Java. These fossil beds, according to recent paleontological research, are stratified as follows:

(1) Deposits containing bones of recent animals.

(2) Sampoeng stratum, containing Neolithic materials and the bones of certain extinct mammals.

(3) Ngandong stratum, said to correspond roughly with the Upper Pleistocene of Europe.

(4) Trinil stratum, said to correspond roughly with the Middle Pleistocene of Europe.

(5) Djetis stratum, said to correspond roughly with the Lower Pleistocene of Europe.

(6) Three or more strata, said to contain traces of Pliocene animals.

The *Meganthropus* jaw fragment was found in the Trinil stratum, but there is unmistakable evidence that it had been washed into that deposit from either the Djetis stratum or one belonging to the Pliocene. It would appear, then, that *Meganthropus* is at least of Lower Pleistocene age and that it may be as old as the Pliocene.

The *Meganthropus* jaw is considerably larger and thicker than any known hominid jaw. This means, according to Professor Weidenreich, that *Meganthropus* was probably of the size, stoutness, and strength of a large male gorilla, and so one of the most primitive of known hominids.

Gigantanthropus, the find made in China, cannot be dated at all. It is known from three molar teeth, which may have belonged to different individuals, discovered in an apothecary's shop in Hong Kong. No one knows where the teeth were originally deposited, but it is generally assumed that they were uncovered somewhere in south China.

The teeth are very large; the crown volume of the third molar tooth is about six times the volume of the same tooth in modern man and about twice that of the corresponding tooth in the modern gorilla. Most anthropologists are agreed, however, that the teeth belonged to a man rather than to an ape, and that we have here the traces of an extinct giant form of man. Similarities with the teeth of *Meganthropus* are close, and it has been suggested that *Meganthropus* and *Gigantanthropus* are but Javanese and Chinese variants, respectively, of the same basic type.

Both finds are as yet too little known to permit extended comparison with other fossil forms. It may be pointed out, however, that this evidence of gigantic hominids, slight as it is, may help to explain the thickness of the cranial bones of other ancient forms. It is not impossible, as Weidenreich has suggested, that the earliest hominids were far larger than those of today, and that the trend of evolution in man has been toward a reduction in size and massiveness.

4. THE PITHECANTHROPUS FINDS OF JAVA

In 1891 a Dutch physician, Dr. Eugene Dubois, made a find of first importance on the banks of the Solo river in north central Java. This con-

Chart III. PREHISTORIC HOMINIDS OF THE EAST

TIME PERIOD	JAVA	AUSTRALIA	CHINA
HOLOCENE		(Modern Australoids)	
UPPER PLEISTO- CENE	*Homo sapiens* (Wadjak) *Homo soloensis*	*Homo sapiens* (Keilor and Talgai)	
MIDDLE PLEISTO- CENE	*Pithecanthropus erectus*		*Sinanthropus* *pekinensis*
LOWER PLEISTO- CENE	*Pithecanthropus modjokertensis* *Meganthropus paleojavanicus*		*Gigantanthropus blacki* (?)
PLIOCENE			

sisted of several hominid bones scattered over a distance of about forty-five feet in a water-borne deposit. The bones, which apparently belong to one or more individuals of the same species, are as follows: a skull vault, a fragment of a lower jaw, three molar teeth, and a complete left thigh bone or femur. Dubois named the find *Pithecanthropus erectus* (the erect ape-man) under the erroneous impression that it represented the form from which both modern apes and modern men were descended.

Since Dubois' discovery considerable geological and paleontological research has been carried on in this region. It is now established that the *Pithecanthropus* bones come from the Trinil stratum, which, as we have seen (§ 3), corresponds roughly to the Middle Pleistocene of Europe. It is clear, therefore, that *Pithecanthropus erectus* is too late to be the common ancestor of both man and the apes. Furthermore, there are at least three definitely *Homo sapiens* forms found in Europe which, because they are as old if not older than *Pithecanthropus erectus* (see § 11), could not have descended from *Pithecanthropus erectus*. *Pithecanthropus erectus*, then, is to be regarded as a collateral rather than a lineal ancestor of modern man.

Like most other early prehistoric forms, *Pithecanthropus erectus* is dolichocephalic, with an index of 71.2. The skull vault is very low and the forehead narrow and slanting. The brow ridges are enormous and run unbroken across the frontal bone. Similarly, the bones of the cranium are very thick; in *Pithecanthropus erectus* 16 per cent of the total skull length

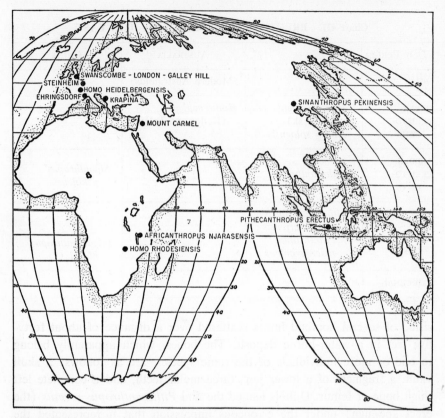

Map 5:2. Fossil men of the Middle Pleistocene. (*Homo rhodesiensis* may be earlier; see Map 5:1. The Ehringsdorf, Krapina, and Mt. Carmel finds probably belong to the early portion of the Upper Pleistocene; see § 10.)

is made up of bone as compared with 25 per cent in modern gorillas and 4 to 6 per cent in modern men. The lines of muscle attachment on the back of the skull indicate, moreover, that *Pithecanthropus erectus* held his head more in the manner of the modern ape than in that of modern man.

Studies of the endocranial cast, that is, a cast made of the interior of the skull, reveal that the frontal lobes of the brain of *Pithecanthropus erectus* are far smaller than those of modern man, though markedly larger than those of modern apes. The left frontal lobe is larger than the right, indicating right-handedness. From the development of certain parts of the brain, we may conclude that *Pithecanthropus erectus* very probably had the power of speech. The cranial capacity is estimated at about 940 cc., which is small compared to modern man, who averages 1,450 cc., but large in comparison with the modern apes, who range from 290 to 610 cc.

It is evident, then, that *Pithecanthropus erectus* had an exceedingly primitive skull and brain, intermediate in most characteristics between modern apes and modern men. His teeth are also very primitive; indeed, there are some anthropologists who maintain that the teeth belong, not to *Pithecanthropus erectus,* but to a contemporary orang-utan. Similarly, the jaw fragment is that of a very primitive hominid. The chin region is, however, more human than apelike, and the socket for the canine tooth (the tooth itself is missing) suggests that *Pithecanthropus erectus* did not have projecting and interlocking canine teeth, a trait characteristic of the great apes.

The femur of *Pithecanthropus erectus* is far more modern than his skull, jawbone, or teeth. It is straight, slender, and long, very much as among modern humans, and very different from the curved, massive, and short femora of modern apes. A ridge on the femur called the linea aspera, to which are attached the powerful extensor muscles necessary to upright posture, is as marked on the femur of *Pithecanthropus erectus* as on that of modern man. From this it is clear that *Pithecanthropus erectus* stood and walked like modern humans. The stature of *Pithecanthropus erectus* may be estimated at about 170 cm. (5' 8") and his weight at about 150 pounds. It will be noted that these characteristics are also more human than apelike.

Some anthropologists have expressed doubt that the exceedingly primitive *Pithecanthropus erectus* skull belongs with the essentially modern femur. They have attempted to resolve this

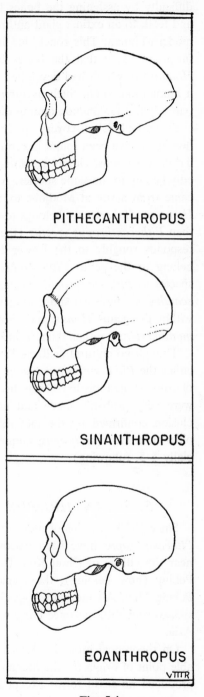

PITHECANTHROPUS

SINANTHROPUS

EOANTHROPUS

Fig. 5:4.

difficulty by assigning the bones to different animals; the skull, jawbone, and teeth to an extinct giant anthropoid, and the thigh bone to a relatively modern human. This conclusion is by no means necessary, however. It is far more likely that the bones belong to a single species—that of the *Hominidae,* which had developed a human-like posture more rapidly than a human-like skull. Such asymmetrical evolution, as we shall see, is apparently not uncommon among the *Hominidae.*

Since Dubois' discovery in 1891, several other traces of prehistoric hominids have been found in central Java. Four of these were found in the Trinil fossil beds, closely resemble *Pithecanthropus erectus,* and undoubtedly belong to the same species. A fifth, the skull of a three-year-old child, came from a site at Modjokerto, near Soerabaja, Java. This form, called *Homo modjokertensis,* belongs to the Djetis stratum and is therefore older than *Pithecanthropus erectus* (the Djetis stratum, it will be recalled, corresponds roughly to the Lower Pleistocene). *Modjokertensis* appears to belong to the genus *Pithecanthropus,* though possibly not to the same species as *Pithecanthropus erectus.* It certainly resembles the other *Pithecanthropus* finds far more than it resembles even the prehistoric species within the genus *Homo,* and should therefore be called *Pithecanthropus modjokertensis* rather than *Homo modjokertensis.*

Though no cultural artifacts have as yet been found in association with either the *Pithecanthropus erectus* or the *modjokertensis* bones, a number of crude stone tools have been discovered in the Trinil stratum. These tools were very probably made and used by *Pithecanthropus erectus;* a conclusion confirmed by the fact that other primitive forms, as old if not older than *Pithecanthropus,* unquestionably possessed a culture (see especially § 5, following).

5. SINANTHROPUS PEKINENSIS OF CHINA

Since 1929, remains of more than thirty individuals of a type similar to *Pithecanthropus* have been discovered on the mainland of Asia. Found near the village of Chou Kou Tien, forty miles from the ancient city of Peking (now Peiping), the species is called *Sinanthropus pekinensis* or Peking Man. All the known specimens come from a single cave, but the species probably was once fairly widely distributed, at least in northeastern Asia.

On theoretical grounds, Asia has long been considered the most probable point of origin for the human species. For many years, however, Asia produced no fossil forms except *Pithecanthropus.* The marginal position of the latter made it unlikely that it represented a form on the main line of human evolution, quite aside from the fact that it was too late in time.

Sinanthropus pekinensis is generally assigned to the Middle Pleistocene and hence is roughly contemporary with *Pithecanthropus*. Consequently it, too, is probably too late to form part of the main line of human evolution and, like *Pithecanthropus,* probably represents a collateral or parallel development. Nevertheless *Sinanthropus* gives added weight to the theory that the *Hominidae* originated in Asia, for it shows the presence on that continent of very early humanoid forms. No doubt when Asia is as well explored as Europe, additional forms will be discovered.

The *Sinanthropus* skulls are in general very similar to those of *Pithecanthropus,* and in some respects somewhat more advanced. The supraorbitals are not quite so heavy, the forehead is slightly higher, and the parietal bones (forming the two sides of the skull) are higher and more rounded. The foramen magnum seems slightly further forward, showing a more human-like carriage of the head. The skulls are a little broader and slightly longer, giving a cephalic index of 75. Cranial capacity ranges from 850 cc. to 1,300 cc., with an average of 1,075 cc. But *Sinanthropus* also possesses characteristics less developed than the corresponding features of the *Pithecanthropus* finds. Thus, the bones of the *Sinanthropus* skulls are definitely thicker than those of *Pithecanthropus,* and the mastoid processes, as in apes, are massive and very small and the chin region of the jaw is apelike. The teeth are also more apelike than those of *Pithecanthropus* with respect to size, proportions, and the pattern on the crown. The limb bones, however, are not fundamentally different from those of *Pithecanthropus. Sinanthropus,* like his contemporary in Java, had achieved the fully upright posture.

As we have said, the differences between *Pithecanthropus* and *Sinanthropus* are slight. Weidenreich and von Koenigswald, who have done the most work on these finds in recent years, agree that these differences are no greater than those that separate the modern races of man. Consequently the two forms, in their opinion, should be classed in the same genus and species. Since, however, our data on the two forms are still far from complete, it is probably better to class them in separate genera, as the accepted terminology implies, and leave the question of their closer relationship for future research.

Found in the same cave as the *Sinanthropus* skeletal materials and in specific association with the bones are a number of crudely chipped flake tools. These are made of quartzite and represent a tool-making tradition quite distinct from any found in Europe. They are, however, very similar to the artifacts found in the Trinil stratum of Java and so possibly provide another link between the Middle Pleistocene inhabitants of these widely separated areas.

Traces of charcoal, charred bones, and remains of ancient hearths reveal that *Sinanthropus* made use of fire. From animal and plant remains found in the caves it appears that he used both vegetable and meat foods, a conclusion further substantiated by a study of his teeth. Here, then, we have definite though not detailed evidence of a Middle Pleistocene hominid group with at least a crude cultural tradition.

6. UPPER PLEISTOCENE HOMINIDS FROM JAVA AND AUSTRALIA

In Java, as we have seen, the earliest traces of hominid forms occur in the Lower and Middle Pleistocene. These specimens, *Meganthropus* and the several *Pithecanthropus* skulls, are exceedingly primitive and must be classed in genera distinct from that of modern man.

Other fossil hominids from Java do not occur until the Upper Pleistocene. These, called *Homo soloensis* and *Homo wadjakensis,* are sufficiently advanced to be grouped with the genus *Homo,* though, as we shall see, *soloensis* at least preserves certain skeletal characteristics reminiscent of more primitive forms.

Homo soloensis was first discovered in 1931 on the Solo River near Ngandong in central Java. The initial find, a single skull lacking facial bones and teeth, was followed by the discovery of ten other crania in a similar condition and two lower leg bones (tibiae). Both finds were made in the Ngandong stratum (see § 3) and were associated with a variety of tools made of stone, bone, and horn. These paleontological and cultural associations clearly indicate an Upper Pleistocene age.

The *soloensis* skulls are all heavy with somewhat sloping foreheads and marked supraorbital ridges. Though more advanced than *Pithecanthropus,* the Solo specimens have a few structural features which suggest that the species is a descendant of Java man. The difficulty in this view is the question of time. It is unlikely that the differences which separate Solo man from *Pithecanthropus* could have evolved so rapidly. Furthermore, *Homo soloensis* resembles Neanderthal man of Europe, and in particular a Neanderthal-like form of Africa (Rhodesian man), far more than he resembles *Pithecanthropus.* It is not impossible, then, that *soloensis* may represent an early Neanderthaloid form who migrated to Java during the latter portion of the Pleistocene. His resemblances to *Pithecanthropus* may be the result of interbreeding or may derive simply from the fact of a more remote common ancestry.

Homo wadjakensis, known from two skulls discovered by Dr. Dubois at Wadjak, near Trinil, Java, is even more advanced structurally than Solo man. The find was made in an old lake bed, now filled with volcanic dust

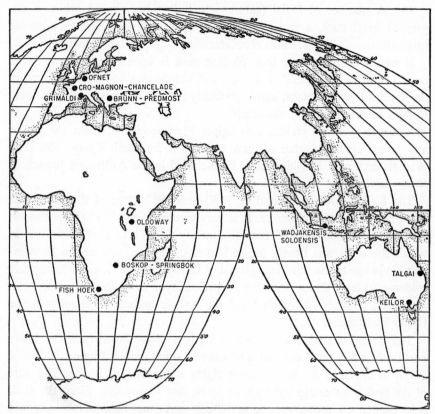

Map 5:3. Fossil men of the Upper Pleistocene.

and ashes, and has neither paleontological nor cultural associations. Dubois placed it in the Pleistocene and, though a more precise dating is still impossible, it is likely that Wadjak man belongs either to the final phases of the Pleistocene or even to the early Holocene.

Except for an unusually large cranial capacity (Wadjak I has a capacity of 1,550 cc., and Wadjak II, 1,650 cc.) the skulls are very much like those of the modern Australian aborigines. This is seen particularly in the following features:

(1) The supraorbital ridges which, though somewhat larger than those of the Australoids, are still smaller than in Solo man or *Pithecanthropus*.

(2) A weakly developed chin, similar to that of the Australoids.

(3) A forehead development much advanced over Solo man or the Neanderthaloids, but still receding in the manner of the Australoids.

(4) The area of the hard palate which in Wadjak is only four square centimeters greater than that of the Australoid, but is ten or more square centimeters greater than that of other modern *sapiens* forms.

(5) A number of facial features—including low, broad orbits, a depressed nasal root, a small and flat nasal bridge, and marked alveolar prognathism—which are also characteristic of the modern Australoid.

It would appear, then, that Wadjak man is an earlier and somewhat more primitive Australoid. This means of course that he must be placed in the species *Homo sapiens,* and is probably the first of that species to come to light in this region of the world.

Australia has also yielded two Upper Pleistocene hominids: the Keilor and Talgai skulls. Neither of these appears to be much if any older than Wadjak man and, like him, must be included in the Australoid branch of *Homo sapiens.*

The Keilor skull was found in 1940 near the village of that name ten miles northwest of Melbourne. It is very similar to the Wadjak specimens, and like them has a large cranial capacity (1,593 cc.). The deposit in which the skull was found, an ancient river terrace, appears to be comparable in age to the third interglacial of Europe. Here, then, we have small evidence at least that a primitive Australoid type came to this region from Java, and possibly ultimately from the Asiatic mainland, as early as the Upper Pleistocene.

The Talgai skull is known from a fairly well-preserved face, the lower portion of a frontal bone, and a number of small cranial fragments. It was found in northern Australia, about eighty miles from Brisbane. The date of the find is uncertain but appears to be late Pleistocene. Since the skull is so broken up, reconstruction is difficult and exact measurements cannot be made. Nevertheless, it can be said that the specimen is clearly ancestral to the modern Australoids; indeed, Keith maintains that it is closer to the Australoids than Wadjak man. This find thus would appear to be the lineal ancestor of the modern Australoid. Wadjak and Keilor, probably contemporaneous with Talgai, may represent either a collateral primitive Australoid line which eventually became extinct or, simply, variant forms of the ancestral group to which Talgai belonged.

It has been suggested that a definite line of evolution connects *Pithecanthropus* with *Homo soloensis* and Solo man with Wadjak, Keilor, and Talgai, so making the modern Australoids the ultimate descendants of *Pithecanthropus.* As we have seen, the evidence does not support the view that *Homo soloensis* evolved from *Pithecanthropus,* and there is even less evidence of an evolutionary development from Solo man to the primitive Australoids. It is probably more likely that Solo man came to Java, where he may have acquired by interbreeding a number of pithecanthropoid traits from somewhere in the great Eurasiatic continent. Later immigrants of an early *sapiens* type then arrived, and these may also have interbred with Solo man to form the type we find exemplified in Wadjak, Keilor, and Talgai, and which probably developed into the modern Australoid.

7. FOSSIL MAN IN AFRICA

While Asia is still regarded by most anthropologists as the most likely place of origin of the hominids, in recent years some have come to regard Africa as a possible place for the development of *Homo sapiens* and perhaps for the whole family of *Hominidae*. Not only does Africa today harbor two of the surviving great apes, the chimpanzee and the gorilla, but the discovery of *Australopithecus, Paranthropus,* and *Plesianthropus* (Chapter 2, § 8) also gives evidence of evolutionary developments in the general direction of man. Recent finds indeed show that at least some of these forms used fire and rudimentary tools, and hence possessed at least a crude culture. It is true that *Australopithecus, Paranthropus,* and *Plesianthropus* probably lived too late to have been directly ancestral to *Homo sapiens,* but they demonstrate a trend in the human direction. On the other hand, the mere fact of the survival of the chimpanzee and gorilla may argue that early man was absent and hence competition was less keen. The dating of *Australopithecus* and like forms has also been questioned on the grounds that these forms could not have survived human competition. Should these forms be shown to be Pliocene in age, they then would become major contenders for the role of ancestors to the hominids.

More direct evidence of the antiquity of man in Africa is not yet satisfactory. Dr. L. S. B. Leakey has found two sets of specimens which are evidently of *Homo sapiens* type and which are said to be from Middle Pleistocene deposits. If this is correct, these finds would be roughly comparable to the Galley Hill specimens (see § 11) in significance. However, the evidence so far produced has not convinced many people that the finds could not have been washed into position from later strata. For the time being, the Leakey finds and the antiquity of *Homo sapiens* should be left open.

Of more general acceptance is the rather remarkable specimen known as Rhodesian Man or *Homo rhodesiensis*. The finds come from an old cave in northern Rhodesia. As Africa has undergone few climatic changes, the associated animals are much like modern types, and it is impossible to date Rhodesian man with any accuracy. About all that can be said is that he is undoubtedly Pleistocene and may be from fairly early in the Pleistocene.

The finds consist of a complete skull lacking the lower jaw, two leg bones, one femur, and two pelves. There is some doubt whether the leg bones belong with the skull, although most people so accept them. However, parts of two individuals are certainly represented. The skull is primitive and very massive. It has a cephalic index of about 70 and a capacity in the neighborhood of 1,300 cc. The brow ridges are enormous, far larger than in any other fossil hominid. Because of this feature and because of the thick cranial walls, the brain length of Rhodesian man is only 81 per cent of his skull length, as compared with 75 per cent in modern gorillas and 92 per cent in modern man. The skull vault is low with a narrow, sloping forehead. Markings on the occiput and the position of the foramen magnum indicate that Rhodesian man held his head somewhat in the apelike position, but in this trait he is not so primitive as other fossil hominids (Neanderthal, for example; see § 10).

The face is long and large in all dimensions, the orbits are high and narrow, the upper jaw is large and projecting, and the palate is unusually broad. All these are exceedingly primitive features. The teeth, however, are essentially modern in type, and the most remarkable thing about them is their bad condition. Of fifteen teeth recovered, ten show caries or cavities. All the molars and some of the other teeth have abscessed roots. In front of the left ear lobe is a partly healed wound; it and the ear itself show abscessed conditions. Finally, the left knee shows a rheumatic condition, possibly the result of the bad teeth.

Rhodesian man stood fully erect, as is shown by his slender and straight leg bones. His height must have been about 5′ 10″ and his weight over 200 pounds. Here again we have evidence of asymmetrical evolution; Rhodesian man had essentially modern posture and tooth development linked with an exceedingly primitive skull.

The place of Rhodesian man among other fossil hominids is difficult to determine. Some class him with Solo man as an early *sapiens* type which eventually became the Australoids. Others, perhaps the majority, regard Rhodesian man as a variant of the Neanderthal species. The question must as yet be left open; until we have more precise knowledge of both Rhodesian man and his position in world history, we can only guess at his interrelationships with the other forms.

Africanthropus njarasensis (African man of Njarasa) is associated with two or three fragmentary skulls found in East Africa. The deposit in which the find was made appears to be Pleistocene in age. There is, however, no more precise indication of age, though some anthropologists, basing their conclusions on a number of associated cultural artifacts, place *Africanthropus* in the Middle Pleistocene.

The skulls are very thick, with large supraorbitals and a sloping forehead. Little is as yet known of the relationship of *Africanthropus* to other fossil hominids. Some group him with *Pithecanthropus* and *Sinanthropus;*

others consider *Africanthropus* to be an early Neanderthaloid form having close affinities with Rhodesian man. The answer to this problem, as to that raised by Rhodesian man, can only be given when the paleontology and prehistory of Africa are better known.

A number of definitely *sapiens* hominids have also been uncovered in various portions of Africa. Among these are Oldoway man from Tanganyika, East Africa, the Boskop and Springbok forms of the Transvaal, South Africa, and the Fish Hoek skull, found near Cape Town in South Africa. Three of these, Boskop, Oldoway, and Fish Hoek, have very large skulls but otherwise appear to be essentially modern in skeletal structure. The problem of their relationships to the modern men of Africa is, however, far from settled. Sir Arthur Keith believes that Oldoway is a type possibly ancestral to the modern peoples of West Africa. Boskop and Fish Hoek, according to Keith, are lineally related and possibly ancestral to the modern Bushmen of Southwest Africa. The same authority claims that Springbok, too, is a form having close affinities to the East African Negroes of present-day Africa.

8. PILTDOWN MAN OF ENGLAND

What was regarded by many as possibly the oldest fossil man from Europe has also been the center of the most controversy. Piltdown man *(Eoanthropus dawsoni)* was found in a shallow gravel pit on Piltdown common in Sussex, south of London. The gravel, which once was the bed of a river, is clearly divisible into two strata, the lower dark in color and the upper of light-colored gravels. In the lower stratum were found bones of Miocene and Pliocene animals, broken flints (possibly eoliths) believed by some to be of human manufacture, and at the very bottom, a sixteen-inch section of the femur of an extinct elephant, pointed and partly drilled. The upper stratum contained crudely chipped stone tools very similar to those of the early Chellean.

In the lower Piltdown gravels were found the right half of a lower jaw with two molar teeth in place, a canine tooth, and several large portions of the frontal, parietal, temporal, and occipital bones of the cranial vault. A second find, made about two miles away in gravels of the same sort, includes a molar tooth and parts of the frontal and occipital bones.

All of the material found was water-worn, indicating that it had been washed into the deposit by the ancient river. The age of the deposit has long been in dispute. Some assigned it to the Pliocene, but many others believed it to be Pleistocene in age and to belong either to the first or second interglacial periods. A shallow water-borne deposit of this kind is difficult to date precisely, and consequently the find long could not be placed accurately in time. Very recently, however, chemical tests of the fluorine content of the finds have convinced many that the bones are relatively late, probably no earlier than the end of the Pleistocene. If this is so, the bones were probably washed into their present position in association with materials far older.

Early controversies over the Piltdown find centered about the relationship of the skull and jaw fragments. Believing that these belonged together, Sir Arthur Keith reconstructed the skull, which resembles a slightly primitive member of *Homo sapiens*. The jaw, however, is exceedingly primitive and might be that of a chimpanzee-like form. Consequently, many anthropologists held that Piltdown was an early collateral relative of modern man, and not in the direct line of his descent. The combination of a relatively modern skull with a primitive jaw was seen as another example of asymmetrical evolution, the skull having developed far more than the jaw.

The late dating recently suggested for Piltdown makes this position untenable, and the skull fragments must be regarded as those of a relatively late *Homo sapiens* form, accidentally associated with the jaw of an older chimpanzee-like animal. This solution does not of course solve all the difficulties. It requires, for example, the acceptance of a late chimpanzee-like form in England, where no previous great apes were known. In other words, no solution so far proposed on the basis of present evidence does more than raise new problems, equally unsolvable. Consequently it seems best that the Piltdown problem be put to one side until further data produce an acceptable solution to all the problems.

9. HEIDELBERG MAN

Homo heidelbergensis or Heidelberg man is known from a single lower jaw found near the city of Heidelberg in Germany. The jaw was found in a stratum eighty-two feet below the present ground surface. Fossil associations indicate that the jaw's owner lived in either the first or second interglacial, with probabilities veering toward the first period.

The Heidelberg jaw, although very large and massive, is in almost all respects human. In actual size it is even larger than the jaw of Piltdown. The ramus (upward arm of the jaw) has some primitive features, but it is not apelike. There is no trace of chin development. In form the jaw is a parabolic curve rather than the elongated U-shape of an ape's jaw. The teeth, which are all in place, are large, but the canines are of human proportions and do not project above the level of the other teeth. The molars, too, are essentially human, although the cusp pattern shows a reduced fifth cusp, supposedly a primitive feature, though it is found as well among some of the modern Australian aborigines. A large, low pulp cavity or taurodont feature, found also in *Sinanthropus,* characterizes the Heidelberg molars. This feature has led some authorities to suggest a relationship between Heidelberg and *Sinanthropus,* but present interpretations of geological evidence indicate that *Sinanthropus* is definitely later in time than Heidelberg. However, it is clear, from the jaw alone, that Heidelberg is probably most closely related to the Neanderthal species (see § 10), and it is not unlikely that he may be ancestral to these forms. This would place Heidelberg within the genus *Homo,* though in a species different from that of modern man.

10. NEANDERTHAL MAN

Skeletal remains of Neanderthal man *(Homo neanderthalensis),* representing more than one hundred individuals, have been found in almost every country of western and central Europe, in various regions of the Soviet Union, and in Palestine. In addition, as we have seen, Neanderthaloid (that is, Neanderthal-like) forms have been found in both Africa and Java. It is probable, then, that the Neanderthal species at one time occupied much of the Old World.

Most of the European and Palestinian Neanderthalers lived during the third interglacial and the early part of the Würm glaciation. They are nearly always directly associated with cultural artifacts of the Mousterian period. There are only two exceptions to these rules: the Neanderthal type found at Steinheim, Germany, of the second interglacial age and associated with Acheulean culture, and that of Ehringsdorf, Germany, of the third interglacial age but associated with artifacts of a pre-Mousterian or late Acheulean type.

In most of the European Neanderthalers we find a more or less well-defined set of traits which we shall call the Neanderthal type, and which is quite distinct from that represented in the species *Homo sapiens.* A number of other Neanderthal specimens, however, vary markedly from this type and appear to represent either forms evolving toward *Homo sapiens* or forms which have resulted from intermixture between typical Neanderthalers and a contemporaneous variety of *Homo sapiens.*

In the Neanderthal type, the skull is large and heavy. Its elongated form and low vault give an appearance of primitiveness, as does the low, narrow, and retreating forehead. The supraorbital ridge is heavy, even in children, and the rear or occipital region is relatively large and protruding.

Chart IV. CHRONOLOGY OF NEANDERTHAL AND
NEANDERTHALOID MAN

TIME PERIODS		NEANDERTHAL TYPES	NEANDERTHALOIDS
HOLOCENE			
UPPER PLEISTO- CENE	Achen retreat Würm II Laufen retreat Würm I	Most European Neanderthalers	
	Third Interglacial	Palestine Neanderthalers Ehringsdorf Neanderthal	*Homo soloensis* (Java)
MIDDLE PLEISTO- CENE	Riss Glacial		*Africanthropus* (Africa)
	Second Interglacial	Steinheim Neanderthal	Rhodesian man (Africa) (possibly Lower Pleistocene)
			Heidelberg man (possibly First Interglacial)

The foramen magnum is farther back than in modern man, and the lower jaw must normally have rested on the chest as in the apes. The cephalic index varies from 70 to 76, while the cranial capacity varies from 1,300 to 1,600 cc. The brain is big, perhaps slightly larger on the average than the modern European brain. However, the forebrain is smaller than in modern man, and the convolutions of the brain, that is, the folds of the cortical covering, are simpler.

The face is long and projecting with large eye orbits. The nose is flat and very broad with a deeply depressed root. The upper jaw is markedly prognathous, and the lower jaw is heavy and powerful, with only the beginnings of a chin. In some specimens, however, the chin is more developed than in others.

The dental arch is intermediate in shape between that of modern man and that of the apes. The teeth are essentially human in arrangement, but in most European specimens are taurodont, like those of Heidelberg and *Sinanthropus*. The wear on the teeth shows a backward and forward chewing habit, rather than the side-to-side chewing of modern man. The incisor teeth of the upper and lower jaws ordinarily meet edge to edge, a trait found only occasionally in modern man, and in some cases the lower incisors come in front of the uppers.

The spine is massive and relatively short. Of particular interest are the neck vertebrae. In modern man the long processes or projections from the back of the vertebrae are small and turn downward. In Neanderthal they are large and horizontal to provide attachments for the heavy muscles necessary to move the massive skull, placed off balance by the rearward position of the foramen magnum. The attachments of the muscles for turning the head in the mastoid region of the skull are weakly developed, however. Neanderthal must have had a massive neck, have been incapable of turning his head freely, and probably had to tilt his head backward in order fully to open his jaws.

The curves of the neck and lumbar region which distinguish man from the apes are weakly developed. The posture was clearly a bent or stooping one. The pelvis is deep and narrow as in the apes. The arms, while relatively short, are massive with large joints and must have been very powerful. Limb and hand proportions on the whole are human, although the thumb and fingers tend to be short. The thigh bone, however, is massive and bowed forward as in the apes with a weakly developed linea aspera. Neanderthal must have been less erect than *Pithecanthropus*,

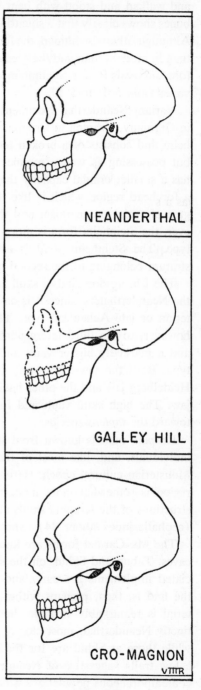

NEANDERTHAL

GALLEY HILL

CRO-MAGNON

Fig. 5:5.

and walked and stood with bent knees. The shape of the ends of the leg bones shows clearly that a squatting posture was his normal resting position. Although otherwise human, the foot has the great toe more widely separated than in modern man and the greatest weight rested on the outer edge of the foot, survivals from tree-climbing ancestors. Stature of the European forms varies from 5' 1" to 5' 5".

Variant Neanderthal specimens are found at Steinheim and Ehringsdorf in Germany, Krapina in Croatia, and Mt. Carmel in Palestine. The Steinheim find consists of a broken female skull basically Neanderthal in form but possessing as well a number of divergent traits. Thus, the specimen has a smaller cranial capacity than the Neanderthal type (1,070 cc.) and a forehead region which is like that of *Pithecanthropus*. In its lesser degree of facial prognathism and the shape of the back of the skull, however, the Steinheim form is more like *Homo sapiens* than the Neanderthal type. The Steinheim skull is associated with Acheulean artifacts in a stratum belonging to the second interglacial.

The Ehringsdorf find, a skull and two jaws, is also earlier than most of the Neanderthalers, since it is associated with implements of a pre-Mousterian or late Acheulean type. The deposit in which it is found belongs, however, to the third interglacial. The skull has a capacity of 1,450 cc. and a markedly higher vault and forehead than that of the Neanderthal type. Both the jaws, however, are rather primitive; one resembling the Heidelberg jaw and the other having points of similarity with the Piltdown jaw. The high skull vault and forehead, it may be noted, are variations toward the *sapiens* species.

Krapina man is known from the fragmentary remains of some twenty individuals, and, like most of the Neanderthalers, is associated with the Mousterian cultural epoch. Here, as in the Ehringsdorf find, the forehead region is somewhat more modern than is the Neanderthal type. Reconstructions of the Krapina skulls also reveal that the type is brachycephalic (cephalic index about 84). These are the earliest known brachycephali.

The Mt. Carmel forms are known from several skeletons found in two caves, Tabun and Skhul, on the slopes of Mt. Carmel in Palestine. Associated implements are early and middle Mousterian in type; the age of the find is, then, perhaps within the third interglacial. The skeletal material is remarkably variable, however. Thus, the Tabun forms are distinctly Neanderthal, most closely resembling perhaps the Steinheim form, while those at Skhul are for the most part like *Homo sapiens* with only a few traits suggestive of Neanderthal. Here, then, we have evidence of contemporaneous populations widely variable in physical type living within a short distance of one another.

To summarize: the Neanderthal type is customarily considered a separate species within the genus *Homo,* a view which is strongly supported by the distinctive features exhibited by a large majority of the Neanderthal species. Some anthropologists, notably Professor Weidenreich, regard Neanderthal as directly ancestral to *Homo sapiens,* at least insofar as Europe and the Near East are concerned. They justify this view by pointing out that various Neanderthal species exhibit *sapiens* features, thus suggesting an evolutionary trend toward modern man. Other anthropologists, perhaps the majority, while conceding the presence of *sapiens* features in various Neanderthal specimens, regard these as evidence of interbreeding between Neanderthal and a contemporary *sapiens* form.

The theory of Neanderthal-*Homo sapiens* intermixture is reinforced by the finds at Brünn and Predmost in Czechoslovakia. Here, in deposits of Upper Paleolithic age, were found a number of skeletons all having the same culture and presumably of the same local groups. Most of these skeletons exhibit a number of characters which suggest Neanderthal-Cro-Magnon ancestry, while others are either predominantly Neanderthal or predominantly Cro-Magnon in structure (see § 12). There seems little doubt in this instance that we have a case of hybridization between Neanderthal and *Homo sapiens.* Coon has also argued in favor of such hybridization on the basis of isolated but recurrent Neanderthaloid characteristics in modern Europeans. It seems very likely, therefore, that Neanderthal man, now extinct, added his physical characteristics to those of *Homo sapiens* at some time during the Upper Pleistocene. Neanderthal man was the last of a long line of non-*sapiens* types; the forms that lived after him, as we shall see, are all of the species *Homo sapiens.* But Neanderthal man was not exterminated by his *sapiens* neighbors and successors. He was rather absorbed by them, and so his physical characteristics remain long after his species has disappeared as such.

11. THE EARLIEST VARIETIES OF HOMO SAPIENS

It was believed until recently that *Homo sapiens* was the last species of man to evolve. The basis for this belief lay in the fact that all Lower and Middle Pleistocene forms were non-*sapiens* in type, perhaps ancestral to modern man but certainly not at his level of structural development. At this period of our knowledge, the Cro-Magnon varieties of fossil man, all of which belong to the Upper Pleistocene, were believed to represent the first of the species *Homo sapiens.*

Now, however, we have at least four distinct finds of *sapiens* or probable *sapiens* forms which contradict the earlier hypothesis: Galley Hill,

London, Swanscombe, and Fontechevade man. All of these are either contemporary with Neanderthal or earlier, so demonstrating a strong possibility that the development of *Homo sapiens,* at least in Europe, was parallel to that of the Neanderthaloids. It is perhaps significant also that many features of Mousterian culture, always associated with Neanderthal types, continue into the Aurignacian, always associated with *sapiens* types.

Galley Hill man was discovered in the hundred-foot terrace of the Thames River, just below London. Since the terrace was laid down during the second interglacial and because implements of a crude Chellean type were also found, it would appear that Galley Hill is at least second interglacial and possibly older. Because of the circumstances of the Galley Hill find, some authorities have refused to accept its antiquity. It is true that the find was made by amateurs and there is a possibility that they were misled. On the other hand the honesty of the finders seems unquestioned and their descriptions are clear and unmistakable.

Galley Hill man, if we accept his extreme age, is remarkably modern in structure. The skull, though its bones are thick, has a capacity of 1,400 cc., a high forehead, and pronounced but modern brow ridges. It is long and relatively narrow, the cephalic index being 69. Face bones are missing, but the lower jaw, though it possesses a few primitive characteristics, has a well-developed chin. The remaining bones (the skeleton was very complete) are those of a man about 5′ 3″ tall and modern in every respect. There can be no question of the fact that Galley Hill represents a primitive variety of *Homo sapiens* and probably the oldest known variety of that species.

The London skull, also definitely a *Homo sapiens* variety, is, however, less conclusive as to age. The find consists of most of one occipital bone and left parietal, plus fragments of a right parietal bone. No associated implements are found, and estimates of the age of the deposit vary from Upper Pleistocene to Middle Pleistocene, or even earlier. The skull itself, as reconstructed, has an estimated capacity of 1,250 cc. and is essentially modern in type. There are, however, a number of traits which suggest that the London skull may be a type of mixed Neanderthal and *sapiens* ancestry.

Swanscombe man, known from a left parietal and occipital bone, was found at the town of Swanscombe in Kent, England. He clearly belongs to the Middle Pleistocene and probably to the second interglacial, a date attested both by the geological evidence and the fact that implements of an Acheulean type were associated with the bones. Except for the remarkable thickness of the bones and the great width of the occiput, the bones are very little different from those of modern man. Most anthropologists accept the fact that Swanscombe man, if not already of the species *Homo sapiens,* is well advanced in that direction.

Fontechevade man was found in 1947 by Mlle. Germaine Henri-Martin, a notably careful excavator. The finds consist of parts of two individuals associated with pre-Mousterian artifacts and a third-interglacial fauna. All the material lies beneath a thick, unbroken stalagmite layer above which occur cultural materials ranging upward from Mousterian to Magdalenian. Thus there can be no question that the remains are third interglacial and pre-Mousterian, that is, pre-Neanderthal for this area at least.

The major finds are parts of two brain cases, one fairly complete, the other more fragmentary but supplying the frontal region which is missing from the first. The most complete skull is markedly dolichocephalic, rather small, with thick and robust bones, although these are apparently within the *Homo sapiens* range. The second fragment makes it clear that the supraorbital ridges were completely absent and indicates a modern forehead.

This find settles beyond dispute the pre-Neanderthal occurrence of *Homo sapiens* in Europe. It confirms the implications of the earlier Swanscombe (second-interglacial) find and presumably the London and Galley Hill finds as well, even though so far the evidence regarding early European *Homo sapiens* is confined to the skull alone. The data available make it clear that early *Homo sapiens* was contemporaneous with, or earlier than, the known *Pithecanthropus, Sinanthropus,* and Neanderthaloid types. It also seems clear that the mixed Neanderthaloid-*sapiens* forms are not, as Weidenreich and others have believed, evidence of an evolutionary development from Neanderthal to *Homo sapiens,* but are rather evidences of interbreeding between contemporaneous Neanderthaloid and *sapiens* populations. The Fontechevade finds, finally, strongly suggest that the differentiation between *Homo sapiens* and other species within the *Hominidae* began very early, perhaps as early as the Pliocene.

12. HOMO SAPIENS OF THE UPPER PLEISTOCENE

All other fossil men of the Upper Pleistocene belong unquestionably to the species *Homo sapiens,* though, as we have already noted, traces of the earlier Neanderthalers are by no means lacking in certain mixed types. It does not follow, however, that the Upper Pleistocene *sapiens* men are identical with those of today. Modern types are, to be sure, foreshadowed in some Upper Pleistocene forms, but the modern races of man do not certainly make their appearance until the beginning of the Holocene.

Homo sapiens of the Upper Pleistocene is not a uniform, homogeneous type. There is, rather, a wide diversity of forms. We cannot describe all of them in detail, however, and shall confine ourselves to five of the more important variants. These are as follows: Cro-Magnon, principally of the Aurignacian cultural epoch; Grimaldi, a variant of the early Aurignacian type; Predmost and Brünn, mixed Neanderthal-Cro-Magnon forms of the Solutrean (see § 10); Chancelade, of the Magdalenian epoch; and Ofnet, belonging to the Mesolithic.

Cro-Magnon man is known from a dozen or more skeletons, most of which are found associated with Aurignacian deposits of western Europe. The first or type find was made in 1868 near the village of Cro-Magnon in the Dordogne region of southern France.

Most of the Cro-Magnon types have large and massive skulls, with a cranial capacity as high as 1,660 cc. Cro-Magnon skulls are long and narrow with a cephalic index below 75 (dolichocephalic). Foreheads are as high as those of modern man and are broad rather than narrow. Brow ridges are only moderately developed. Faces are of the so-called disharmonic type, very short with the distance across the malar or cheekbones greater than the width of the head. Disharmonic faces, it may be noted, are also found in some modern Europeans and are said to be characteristic of the Eskimos. The Cro-Magnon nose is usually narrow and high-bridged, the jaw large but modern in form, and the chin strongly developed.

Cro-Magnon man was usually tall in stature, the type find measuring about 5' 11". He was presumably robust in build, and stood much like modern man except that his knees were bent forward in walking. Forearms tended to be long in proportion to the upper arms, the lower leg bones long in relation to the femur (thigh bone), and heel bones somewhat projecting. These features, together with certain characteristics of the pelves, are reminiscent of the modern Negroids,[2] and may be derived from mixture with a contemporaneous Negroid form, possibly Grimaldi (see below). In most other respects, however, Cro-Magnon man resembles the Caucasoids more than any other modern racial type, and he is sometimes said to be ancestral to this group. As we shall see later, however, modern Caucasoids are not to be derived in any such simple manner as this; like all modern racial types, they represent a form much more mixed in ancestry.

[2] "Negroid" is a term used of the population of Africa south of the Sahara, Melanesia, and the American Negroes of the United States and Brazil. Similarly, "Caucasoid" refers to the population of Europe and southern Asia, together with their descendants in the New World, and "Mongoloid" to those of eastern, central and northern Asia, the Malays, and the American Indians. See Chapter 6.

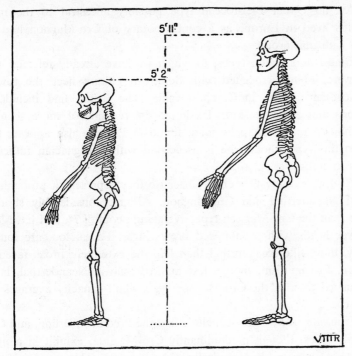

Fig. 5:6. Neanderthal man (left) and Cro-Magnon man compared.

Grimaldi man is known from two skeletons, one of a boy of sixteen and the other an adult woman, found in a grotto near the village of Grimaldi on the Riviera coast. Associated artifacts indicate that the find belongs to the early Aurignacian. The Grimaldi forms are, then, roughly of the same age as Cro-Magnon.

In general, the Grimaldi specimens are not unlike Cro-Magnon. There are, however, a number of important differences. Thus, the woman is 5′ 3″ tall, the youth 5′ ½″. In both, the lower arm and leg bones are unusually long as compared to the upper arm and thigh bone, respectively. The pelves, especially of the woman, are strikingly Negroid in form. Both skulls are long, narrow, and high-vaulted, and the cephalic indices are 68 for the female, 69 for the male. Cranial capacity in the male is 1,265 cc., in the female 1,454 cc. The noses are broad, have a low bridge, and the lower margins of the nasal opening end in gathers rather than sharp edges. Upper and lower jaws are projecting, the chin is weakly developed, orbits are low and broad, and the palate is long, high, and narrow.

It is clear, then, that the Grimaldi specimens show far more marked Negroid characteristics than the Cro-Magnons. We may conclude from this that an Upper Pleistocene type possibly ancestral to the modern Negroids lived in Europe as a contemporary of Cro-Magnon and intermixed with that group.

Predmost and Brünn types, to which we have already referred (see § 10), were found associated with Solutrean culture near the towns of Predmost and Brünn in Czechoslovakia. The Brünn find includes two skeletons and a single skull, Predmost the remains of more than forty individuals. Combe Chapelle man, found in France, also appears to belong to this type, though he is associated with Aurignacian rather than Solutrean culture.

These forms interest us chiefly because they represent a probable mixture of Neanderthal and Cro-Magnon. All are considerably shorter in stature than the Cro-Magnon type, averaging about 5' 7", and have longer, narrower heads with pronounced brow ridges. Faces, too, are long and narrow, more like Neanderthal than like the extremely broad-faced Cro-Magnon. Prognathism, though less marked than in Neanderthal, is more pronounced than in the Cro-Magnon type. Skull capacity averages about 1,590 cc.

In general, then, we may conclude that the Predmost, Brünn, and Combe Chapelle types, though predominantly Cro-Magnon, exhibit in a number of traits a considerable Neanderthaloid admixture. This means that these forms, at some period in their history, existed side by side with Neanderthal. As previously concluded (see § 10), Cro-Magnon and his contemporaries did not so much replace Neanderthal as absorb him.

Chancelade man, known from a skeleton of Magdalenian age, is a variant of the Cro-Magnon type which is said to point in the direction of the Mongoloid subspecies. He looks very much like the modern Eskimo, especially in his broad jaw and high, wide cheekbones. Other features do not bear out this impression, however. At best we can only suggest that Chancelade is again basically Cro-Magnon in structure with here and there a trait suggestive of the modern Mongoloid. Similar suggestively Mongoloid traits are found in Obercassel man, also Magdalenian in age.

It is evident, then, that we have in Europe traces of all the three major racial divisions at least as early as the beginning of the Upper Paleolithic. Moreover, the later Cro-Magnons, who are much more varied than the earlier types, have some features which suggest a mixture with the earlier Neanderthal inhabitants of Europe. These points are worth bearing in mind whenever propaganda about racial purity is bruited about. While the evidence shows that Caucasoids are of a pretty respectable antiquity, it also shows that for at least 25,000 years Caucasoids have been pretty consistently mixing with Negroids and Mongoloids. The probabilities are overwhelming that even the most lily-white European shares a few genes with the Negroids and Mongoloids, even without the abundant evidence of later intermixture.

Ofnet man is known from thirty-three skulls found in Mesolithic culture strata in Bavaria, Germany. The skulls were intentionally buried and, since neck vertebrae but no other bones accompany the skulls, the individuals had probably been beheaded. Of the skulls capable of reconstruction, eight are brachycephalic, eight are mesocephalic, and five are dolichocephalic. That the dolichocephali are not of Cro-Magnon type is indicated by the harmonic face. The importance of this group of skulls is that it represents one of the earliest occurrences of brachycephalic types in Europe; another, it will be recalled, is Krapina man (see § 10).

Chart V. FOSSIL MEN OF EUROPE

HOLOCENE		OFNET AND MODERN RACES	
UPPER PLEISTO-CENE	Achen retreat		
	Würm II		Chancelade
	Laufen retreat		Predmost and Brünn
			Cro-Magnon and Grimaldi
	Würm I	European and Palestinian Neanderthalers and Neanderthaloids	
	Third Interglacial		Fontechevade
MIDDLE PLEISTO-CENE	Riss		Swanscombe
	Second Interglacial	Steinheim	London (?)
		Heidelberg (First Interglacial?)	Galley Hill (First Interglacial?)

With the Mesolithic, and more markedly with the early Neolithic, we find evidence of the presence of most of the modern European races. In view of the cultural relationships of Europe, especially in the Neolithic, with Asia and Africa, it is difficult to avoid the conclusion that the contemporary types migrated into Europe from the east and south. In the eight to ten thousand years since the beginning of the Neolithic in Europe, there has occurred a mixture of the new types with the older Paleolithic types. There has also been a shifting of boundaries between the various forms and a progressively increasing proportion of broad-headed forms. Nevertheless, essentially modern European racial types have occupied the continent since the beginning of the Neolithic.

13. SUMMARY

The materials presented in this chapter offer a number of contradictions and problems. Many of these could be resolved with a few well-documented finds in crucial areas and time periods. There is no reason to doubt that these will occur. After all, we have been searching systematically for fossil men for only little more than half a century and the number of searchers has been few. Fossil men were never numerous and are always hard to locate. Large areas of Africa and Asia have never been well explored.

The fossil men we have discussed fall into several groups. First of all are the hominids normally not classed in the genus *Homo,* such as *Megan- thropus, Gigantanthropus, Pithecanthropus,* and *Sinanthropus.* These represent varying types of evolutionary trends, all evidently approaching modern man in some respects but not in all. They may represent collateral branches or competing genera which did not succeed in competition with the genus *Homo.* However, some profess to see the Asiatic series as ancestral to the Australoid and perhaps the Mongoloid. Others believe a form not very distant from *Sinanthropus* may have been ancestral to the Neanderthaloids, although such a form must have lived much farther back in the past than did the known *Sinanthropus* type. In this case, too, the forms are incorrectly named and should be placed in the genus *Homo.*

In the second group are the species and varieties within the genus *Homo.* These may further be divided into the several Neanderthaloid species and the species *Homo sapiens.* The Neanderthaloid species evidently did not succeed in competition with *Homo sapiens.* They include Heidelberg and Neanderthal as the best-known types, but also Solo man, Rhodesian man, and *Africanthropus.* Some believe that the Neanderthaloids developed into *Homo sapiens,* but time scales and other evidence argue strongly against this. In any case, because they are in the same genus, both Neanderthal and *Homo sapiens* must have had a common ancestor some time in the past. Finally, there is some evidence that the western Neanderthalers, at least, may have crossed with *Homo sapiens* in the closing periods of the Pleistocene and perhaps earlier.

Homo sapiens may again be divided. There are first of all finds such as Galley Hill, London, Swanscombe, and Fontechevade, which may be of Middle and even Lower Pleistocene age. Consequently they may provide evidence for the evolution of our own species in the early Pleistocene, and suggest that the separation of the *Homo sapiens* stock from other species of *Homo* and the division of the genus *Homo* from other hominids began some time in the Pliocene. Whether Galley Hill, London, Swanscombe, and Fontechevade are accepted or not, prevailing opinion today favors a Pliocene separation of the genus *Homo* from the other hominids.

The second group of *Homo sapiens* finds are unquestionably of that species and are of Upper Pleistocene age. In Europe, where the time scale is best established, these finds are clearly associated with the Upper Paleolithic and are late- or postglacial in time. The finds include such forms as Cro-Magnon, Grimaldi, Brünn, Ofnet (of the Mesolithic), Wadjak, perhaps Talgai, and the African finds of Oldoway, Springbok, Boskop, and Fish Hoek. An examination of these types suggests that the three main racial divisions of modern times—Mongoloid, Negroid, and Caucasoid—were in existence as early as the Upper Pleistocene and that the distribution of these types was not greatly unlike that of today. In the case of the Negroids, there is some indication of racial subdivision. The same is true of some European finds, such as Ofnet. Moreover, forerunners of some groups not . yet thoroughly placed and perhaps of mixed origin, such as the Australoids and Bushmen, also seem to appear in this Paleolithic group of men. In general, all *sapiens* forms of the Upper Pleistocene differ from modern types in their large size, big brains, heavy skeletons, and especially in their rugged and thick crania.

As a final summing-up, we present the following very tentative classification of fossil man. This list does not include all known finds, but only those we have discussed. It will serve as a convenient index to the forms described in this chapter.

I. *Meganthropus paleojavanicus* (See § 3.)
II. *Gigantanthropus blacki* (possibly of the same genus as *Meganthropus*) (See § 3)
III. *Pithecanthropus* (See § 4)
    A. *Modjokertensis*
    B. *Erectus* (several varieties)
IV. *Sinanthropus pekinensis* (possibly of the same genus, or even species, as *Pithecanthropus*) (See § 5)
V. *Homo*
    A. *Soloensis* (See § 6)
    B. *Africanthropus* (See § 7)
    C. *Rhodesiensis* (See § 7)

D. *Heidelbergensis* (See § 9)

E. *Neanderthalensis* (several varieties) (See § 10)

F. *Sapiens*

    1. Galley Hill, London, Swanscombe, and Fontechevade (See § 11)

    2. Cro-Magnon, Grimaldi, Predmost, Brünn, Chancelade (See § 12)

    3. Ofnet and other Mesolithic and Neolithic forms (See § 12)

    4. Wadjak, Keilor, and Talgai (See § 6)

    5. Oldoway, Boskop, Springbok, and Fish Hoek (See § 7)

COLLATERAL READING

Ashley-Montagu, M. F. *An Introduction to Physical Anthropology*. Springfield, Illinois: C. C. Thomas, 1945. Chapter IV.

Braidwood, Robert J. "Prehistoric Men," *Chicago Natural History Museum, Popular Series, Anthropology,* No. 37, 1948. Pp. 19–32.

Cole, Fay-Cooper. "The Coming of Man," *The Nature of the World and Man,* ed. H. H. Newman. Chicago: University of Chicago Press, 1926. Pp. 349–380.

Hooton, Earnest A. *Up From the Ape*. Rev. Ed. New York: The Macmillan Co., 1946. Part IV.

Howells, W. W. *Mankind So Far*. New York: Doubleday, Doran and Co., 1944. Part II.

Keith, Sir Arthur. *The Antiquity of Man*. Philadelphia: J. B. Lippincott Co., 1925.

———. *New Discoveries Relating to the Antiquity of Man*. New York: W. W. Norton Co., 1931.

Chapter 6

RACIAL TYPES AMONG
MODERN MEN

1. THE GENETIC CONCEPTION OF RACE

Among prehistoric men, as we have seen in Chapter 5, there are numerous and wide divergences in structure, which require that we group them not only into different races, but as well into different genera and species. Modern men, on the other hand, all belong to one genus and species, *Homo sapiens*. This does not mean of course that modern men are all alike, even though it is probable that the similarities among them in bodily and skeletal structure far outnumber the differences. Despite the many similarities, one need not be an anthropologist to see immediately that American Caucasoids (the so-called "white" Americans) are different in some characteristics from most American Negroes and from Americans of Japanese and Chinese ancestry.

If we examine the distribution of men in the world today we find them scattered in more or less isolated groups or populations. In some areas of the world, such as Australia and the Arctic regions, there has been until very recently a high degree of geographical isolation. Ocean and mountain barriers, as well as those imposed by climate, have very often cut off certain populations from almost all contact with peoples of other regions. Social barriers frequently have much the same effect. In the United States, for example, American Negroes are often cut off from any contact with other Americans which might lead to marriage and consequent cross-breeding.

Geographical, climatological, and social barriers, then, divide mankind into a maze of separate populations. Within any given population there is a relatively high frequency of mating between individuals of the proper age and kinship groups. Between separate populations, however, there is relatively little mating, the frequency of mating being in large part dependent upon the efficiency of the barriers which separate the populations concerned. In Los Angeles County, for example, as in many other urbanized areas, the population is divided into a considerable number of ethnic groups, that is, subdivisions differentiated from each other by some combination of physical criteria and linguistic, social, and cultural attributes. A recent study of marriages contracted in Los Angeles County from 1924 to 1933 reveals that 973 of every thousand marriages were between members of the same ethnic groups, while only 27 per thousand took place between individuals of different ethnic groups. In this area, then, for the period concerned, the barriers between Americans of European origin, Mexican Americans, American Negroes, and individuals of Japanese, Chinese, and Filipino origins were obviously very effective.

Populations may differ in racial type. This means that in one population we may find a definable set or pattern of distinctive structural features occurring oftener (that is, in more individuals) than in another population. So, for example, we note that white skins, blue or hazel or light brown eyes, long narrow noses, thin lips, and a number of other presumably inherited structural traits occur more frequently among American Caucasoids than among American Negroes. Among American Negroes, on the other hand, there is a higher frequency of dark skins, dark brown eyes, short wide noses, thick lips, and similar contrasting traits. Note that none of the traits mentioned is necessarily absent in either population. Caucasoids may be found who possess one or more of the traits frequent among American Negroes, just as there are many Negroes who possess one or several traits frequent among Caucasoids.

Note further that structural traits are frequently stated as averages, with no indication of the range of variation within the population concerned. A population described as tall in stature will include a fair percentage of very tall, medium, and short individuals, and if we plot the statures of its members, the result will be the so-called normal probability curve. This means of course that most of the population is either above or below the average stature for the group, and that some individuals may vary markedly from the average.

Similarly, a population described as of medium stature, with an average stature slightly below that of the tall population, may show a range of variation quite as wide. If the curves obtained by plotting the statures of the two populations are superimposed, it will be clear that most individuals may be included, insofar as stature is concerned, in either group.

The same is true of traits like skin color. As between Caucasoids and Negroids, for example, there is a continuous grading from the very dark-skinned peoples of East Africa to the very light-complexioned north Europeans, with no place in between at which we can draw a sharp line.

Racial differences between populations are then simply differences in the frequency of contrasting traits. Eventually, when geneticists have been able to determine more precisely the genes or gene combinations responsible for racial criteria, we shall be able to define the racial differences between populations as differences in the frequencies of these genes and gene combinations. Racial variability will then be a matter of "gene geography," in much the same fashion as we are now able to determine the distribution of the genes responsible for blood types (see Chapter 4, § 9). Such a procedure will have the further advantage of indicating clearly the degree to which recessive genes are present in the population. Finally, as progress is made, it will become possible to determine whether the traits of the aggregates now used to define racial types have any necessary linkage to each other or are merely fortuitously associated in the populations in which they occur.

At present, however, we must rely on phenotypic characters (that is, external features of bodily and skeletal structure) in the determination of racial types. It is important, however, that we use these characters with care, and treat them, not as features completely present or completely absent in a given population, but as features which occur more often (that is, with a higher frequency) in one population than another. So handled, such a designation as "the Nordic race," for example, does not refer to a particular *group of people* who possess blue eyes, fair hair, light complexions, and other similarly abstracted average traits. It refers rather to an *aggregate of traits* (phenotypic but believed to reflect a particular cluster of genes and gene combinations) which occurs with a relatively higher frequency among certain populations in Scandinavia, north Germany, and parts of the British Isles and the United States than in other populations located elsewhere.

2. CAUCASOID, MONGOLOID, AND NEGROID

Anthropologists customarily divide the populations of the world into three grand divisions or subspecies, known as Caucasoid, Mongoloid, and

Negroid. Caucasoid populations, and by this we mean of course populations which exhibit predominantly a particular aggregate of traits to be described below, are found mainly among Europeans and their descendants in the Americas, in north Africa and the Middle East, and in parts of southern Asia. Mongoloid populations include most of the peoples of central, northern, and eastern Asia, together with those of southeast Asia and Indonesia, and the Indians of North and South America. Negroid populations are found in Africa south of the Sahara (excepting of course the recent immigrants from Europe), Melanesia, and among the descendants of the Africans brought to the New World as slaves.

The traits which make up each of these larger aggregates may be summarized and contrasted as follows. It should be noted that we confine ourselves to the most important contrasts, omitting numerous details of interest only to specialists.

(1) **Head form.** Dolichocephaly or long-headedness is most common in Caucasoid populations, with however a considerable occurrence of meso- and brachycephaly. Older Caucasoid populations, known from skeletal remains, tend to show a higher frequency of dolichocephaly. In most modern populations, the head is high with a vertical forehead and little or no supraorbital development. Archaic Caucasoid populations, such as the Ainus of Japan, and some prehistoric populations have low heads, sloping foreheads, and marked supraorbital ridges.

Mongoloid populations exhibit a high frequency of brachycephaly, with occasional meso- and dolichocephalic variants. Dolichocephaly occurs most often in American Indian groups. The head is usually low relative to Caucasoid and Negroid peoples, with a vertical forehead and no supraorbital ridges.

Negroid populations are usually dolichocephalic; only a small minority are brachycephalic. The head is generally high, the forehead vertical, and there is little or no supraorbital development. In some of the more archaic Negroid groups, however, there are distinctive variations from this pattern.

(2) **Face form.** In face form Caucasoid populations are mainly narrow or leptoprosopic, though some groups may be meso- or even euryprosopic. Very long and narrow faces, rarely if ever found among Mongoloid and Negroid peoples, are also not uncommon. Neither facial nor alveolar prognathism occurs (except among some of the archaic peoples), nor are there any distinctively Caucasoid variants in the teeth.

Many Mongoloid populations exhibit a high frequency of very wide and short faces, with the malar (or cheek) bones projecting both frontally and to either side. A thick fatty layer covers the cheekbones and this, together with a characteristically square jaw, gives the face a distinctively

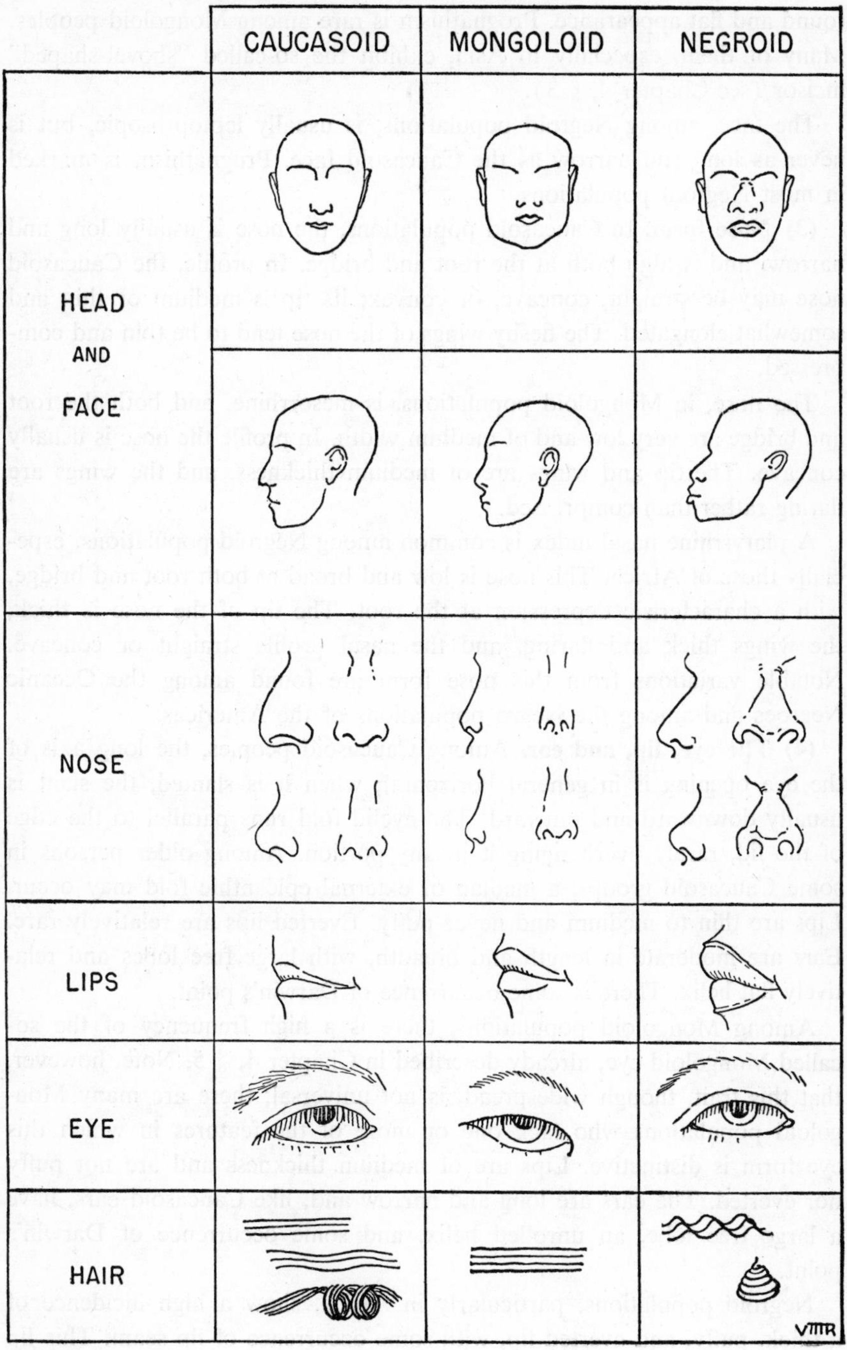

	CAUCASOID	MONGOLOID	NEGROID
HEAD AND FACE			
NOSE			
LIPS			
EYE			
HAIR			

Fig. 6:1.

round and flat appearance. Prognathism is rare among Mongoloid peoples. Many of them, especially in Asia, exhibit the so-called "shovel-shaped" incisor (see Chapter 4, § 3).

The face, among Negroid populations, is usually leptoprosopic, but is never as long and narrow as the Caucasoid face. Prognathism is marked in most Negroid populations.

(3) Nose form. In Caucasoid populations, the nose is usually long and narrow, and is high both at the root and bridge. In profile, the Caucasoid nose may be straight, concave, or convex; its tip is medium or thin and somewhat elongated. The fleshy wings of the nose tend to be thin and compressed.

The nose, in Mongoloid populations, is mesorrhine, and both the root and bridge are very low and of medium width. In profile the nose is usually concave. The tip and wings are of medium thickness, and the wings are flaring rather than compressed.

A platyrrhine nasal index is common among Negroid populations, especially those of Africa. This nose is low and broad at both root and bridge, with a characterisic depression at the root. The tip of the nose is thick, the wings thick and flaring, and the nasal profile straight or concave. Notable variations from this nose form are found among the Oceanic Negroes and among the Negro populations of the Americas.

(4) The eye, lip, and ear. Among Caucasoid peoples, the long axis of the eye opening is in general horizontal; when it is slanted, the slant is usually downward and outward. The eyelid fold runs parallel to the edge of the lid, rarely overhanging it in any portion. Among older persons in some Caucasoid groups, a median or external epicanthic fold may occur. Lips are thin to medium and never puffy. Everted lips are relatively rare. Ears are moderate in length and breadth, with large free lobes and relatively flat helix. There is some occurrence of Darwin's point.

Among Mongoloid populations, there is a high frequency of the so-called Mongoloid eye, already described in Chapter 4, § 5. Note, however, that this trait, though widespread, is not universal; there are many Mongoloid populations who lack one or more of the features in which this eye form is distinctive. Lips are of medium thickness and are not puffy nor everted. The ears are long and narrow and, like Caucasoid ears, have a large free lobe, an unrolled helix, and some occurrence of Darwin's point.

Negroid populations, particularly in Africa, show a high incidence of a thick, puffy, and everted lip, with some occurrence of lip seam. This lip form occurs much less often among Oceanic Negroes and those of the

Americas. The ear, among many Negroid peoples, is short and wide, with small, often attached, lobes, a deeply rolled helix, and no Darwin's point. Eyes, among Negroid peoples, are much the same as among Caucasoid groups.

(5) Hair, skin, and eye color. With a majority of Caucasoid populations, the hair and eyes are light- to dark-brown. Among others, however, there is considerable variation in both features. Hair may be flaxen, golden, or various shades of red; the eyes blue, gray, hazel, or an indeterminate blue- or gray-green. Skin color is similarly variable. A few populations show a high incidence of white skins; the others may be ruddy, swarthy white, or light- to dark-brown in skin color.

Both hair and eyes are dark brown to black in color among nearly all Mongoloid populations. The skin varies from light yellow to a yellowish brown, light brown, and, in some cases, a coppery brown.

Among Negroid populations, hair and eyes are dark brown to black. The skin, however, is in general much darker than in the other two divisions; it varies from brown to sooty black.

(6) Hair texture and body hair. Among Caucasoid populations, the hair may be fine or coarse, and varies in form from straight to curly. In cross section it is usually ovaloid. The hair of both head and face is usually abundant and long. There is also a considerable amount of body hair, much more than is found among peoples of the other grand divisions.

Head hair is straight, long, and coarse among nearly all Mongoloid populations. In cross section the hair shaft is round. Both face and body hair is scanty or lacking altogether.

Among most African Negroes, the head hair is frizzly or wooly, with a rare occurrence of the peppercorn variety. It is short to very short and coarse and wiry in texture. In cross section the hair shaft forms a very flat oval. Among Oceanic Negroes, the head hair is longer, and in the Americas, there is considerable variation. African and Oceanic Negroes have little or no face and body hair; it is more frequent among the Negroes of the Americas.

(7) Stature and body build. Stature varies widely among Caucasoid populations. There are, however, no very short or very tall peoples, though such variants may occur with individuals within some Caucasoid groups. The trunk, too, varies widely in form, with almost every variant from the short, slender extreme to that which is long and broad. Arms are usually of medium length (in some populations they tend to be short and thick) and legs are more often long than short.

Stature varies from medium to short in most Mongoloid groups, but

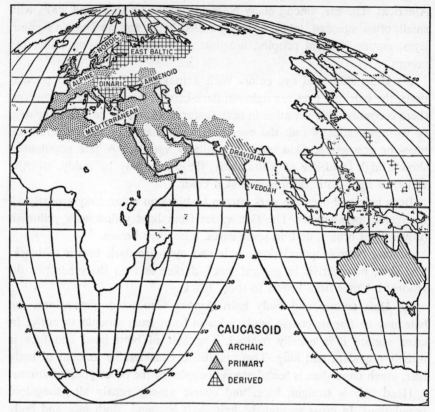

Map 6:1a. Distribution of Caucasoid races: Old World.

some small groups (e.g., among the American Indians) may be tall or very tall. The torso tends to be long with broad shoulders. Arms are of medium length and legs are short.

Negroid populations vary more in stature than those of either of the two other divisions. The bulk of them are, however, medium to tall in stature, with some very tall groups and other very short ones. Trunk form is also variable, long, broad types contrasting with the short, slender bodies of the East African Negroes and the narrow-shouldered and infantile torsos of the Pygmies of the Congo Forest. Arms are usually long, the legs short to long, and, among some Negroid populations, the forearm is notably long relative to the arm.

3. CAUCASOID RACIAL TYPES

A closer examination of the populations characterized as Caucasoid makes it amply clear that these exhibit a variety of racial types. To take

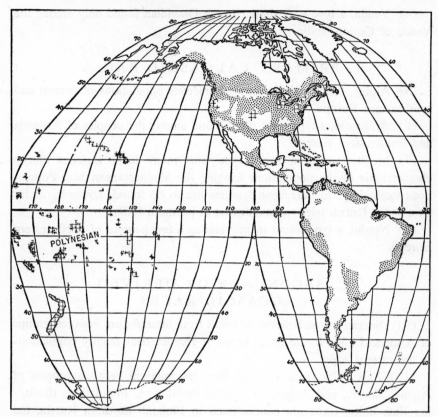

Map 6:1b. Distribution of Caucasoid races: New World. (For key, see Map 6:1a.)

an extreme example, it is obvious that the populations found in some portions of northwestern Europe show a high percentage of tall, fair-haired, blue-eyed, and light-complexioned individuals who stand in decided contrast to the shorter and more darkly pigmented individuals so numerous in the populations of northern India.

Though extremes like the one cited are easily distinguished, it is not so easy to characterize as clearly all the racial types within the Caucasoid subspecies. There are eleven such types, which may be grouped as follows:

A. ARCHAIC CAUCASOID RACES

(1) Ainu, found only among the people of the same name living in northern Japan.

(2) Australoid, the racial type of the natives of Australia.

(3) Dravidian, a type found chiefly among the Dravidian-speaking peoples of central and southern India.

(4) Vedda, a type very similar to the Dravidian found only among the Vedda of Ceylon, India.

B. PRIMARY CAUCASOID RACES

(5) Alpine, found chiefly among numerous populations of central and southeastern Europe.

(6) Armenoid, a type most often found among the peoples of Armenia and southeastern Europe.

(7) Mediterranean, a racial type with many local varieties chiefly characteristic of the populations fringing the Mediterranean Sea. Populations exhibiting Mediterranean features are to be found, however, as far west as the British Isles and as far east as northern India.

(8) Nordic, a type found mainly among a few peoples of northwestern Europe.

C. SECONDARY OR DERIVED CAUCASOID RACES

(9) Dinaric, a type believed to result from intermixture between groups of Armenoid and Nordic racial types. It characterizes mainly populations in the eastern Alps.

(10) East Baltic, said to result from intermixture between peoples of Alpine, Nordic, and Asiatic Mongoloid racial type. Populations displaying East Baltic traits are concentrated in Finland, northern Russia, the Baltic states, and parts of north Germany.

(11) Polynesian, the result apparently of intermixture between peoples of early Mediterranean, Asiatic Mongoloid, and Oceanic Negro racial type. Groups exhibiting Polynesian structural features are scattered today throughout Micronesia and Polynesia in the South Pacific.

4. ARCHAIC CAUCASOID RACES

The four races of this group are briefly compared in Chart VI. It will be seen that the four are very similar and that all of them have a number of primitive structural features. Note, for example, the extreme dolichocephaly of the Vedda, the low cranial capacity of both the Australoid and the Vedda, and the abundant body hair of the Ainu and the Australoid. These primitive features may well indicate that the archaic Caucasoid races are the fragmentary survivals of some very early Caucasoid variety. This conclusion is borne out by the fact that the populations exhibiting these features have long been geographically isolated.

Chart VI. ARCHAIC CAUCASOID RACES

TRAITS	AINU	AUSTRALOID	DRAVIDIAN	VEDDA
Headform	Dolicho- to mesocephalic	Dolichocephalic	Dolichocephalic	Very dolichocephalic
Cranial Capacity	Average	Low	Average	Very low
Forehead	Slight or no slant	Low, slanting	Slightly sloping	Slightly sloping
Brow ridges	Large	Very large	Slight or none	Moderate to large
Face index	Mesoprosopic	Euryprosopic	Meso- to leptoprosopic	Euryprosopic
Prognathism	Moderate	Marked	Little or none	Little or none
Nose index	Mesorrhine	Platyrrhine	Usually mesorrhine or platyrrhine	Platyrrhine
Nasal root	Depressed	Greatly depressed	Depressed	Depressed
Nasal bridge	Low, broad	Low, broad	Medium to low height and width	Low, broad
Nasal profile	Concave	Concave or straight	Usually straight	Straight
Lips	Medium, thin	Medium	Medium to thick	Medium
Eye color	Light brown	Dark brown	Dark brown	Dark brown, black
Hair color	Dark brown, black	Dark brown, black	Black	Black
Hair form	Wavy	Wavy or curly	Wavy or curly	Wavy or curly
Body hair	Very abundant	Abundant	Scanty	Very little
Skin color	Swarthy white	Dark brown	Dark brown	Dark brown
Stature	Av. 5′ 2″	Av. 5′ 6″	Av. 5′ 2″	Av. 5′ 0″
Torso	Thickset	Slender, short	Slender	Slender

Negroid features may also be noted in the Australoid, Dravidian, and Vedda races. These are seen particularly in the dark brown to black skins of all three types, the platyrrhine nasal index of the Australoid and Vedda, the low and broad nasal roots and bridges of all three races, and the marked prognathism of the Australoid. It is not impossible that an early Negroid population, possibly the antecedents of the modern Negrito or of the Oceanic Negro, was also among the ancestors of these archaic Caucasoid peoples as we find them today. However, the unpublished work of Joseph Birdsell clearly shows the basically Caucasoid character of the Australoid; offspring of Australoid-European crosses are usually indistinguishable from European types.

5. THE PRIMARY CAUCASOID RACES

As nearly as we can tell, the four racial types composing this group are not to be derived from one another, but represent probably more or less parallel developments from some common ancestral variety. The four types are briefly described and compared in Chart VII.

Chart VII. PRIMARY CAUCASOID RACES

TRAITS	ALPINE	ARMENOID	MEDITERRANEAN	NORDIC
Head form	Brachycephalic	Brachycephalic	Dolichocephalic	Mesocephalic
Head height	High	Very high	Low, medium	High
Forehead	Vertical	Some slope	Vertical	Vertical or slight slope
Brow ridges	Small or none	None	Small	Small
Face index	Eury- to mesoprosopic	Lepto- to mesoprosopic	Leptoprosopic	Leptoprosopic
Nose index	Meso- or leptorrhine	Leptorrhine	Very leptorrhine	Leptorrhine
Nasal root	Medium high	Very high	High	High
Nasal bridge	Medium height and width	Very high, narrow	Moderate to high, narrow	High, narrow
Nasal profile	Straight	Convex	Straight or concave	Straight
Lips	Medium to thin	Full, lower lip everted	Medium	Thin to very thin
Eye color	Medium to dark brown	Brown	Light to dark brown	Blue, gray, hazel
Hair color	Medium· to dark brown or black	Brown to black	Dark brown to black	Blond, yellow, or light brown
Hair form	Usually straight	Straight, wavy, curly	Wavy or curly	Straight or wavy
Body hair	Abundant	Abundant	Moderate to scanty	Moderate
Skin color	Brunet white or olive	Swarthy white, olive	Olive to brown	White, ruddy
Stature	Av. 5' 5"	Av. 5' 6"	Av. 5' 4"	Av. 5' 8"
Torso	Thickset	Commonly heavy and broad	Slender, medium	Slender, short

Archeological evidence makes it quite clear that the Mediterranean is the oldest of the primary Caucasoid races. We cannot say for certain when it first appeared, but forms as ancient as Galley Hill, Swanscombe, and even Piltdown have features suggestive of the Mediterranean type. At the beginning of the Neolithic, populations mainly Mediterranean in type already dominated Europe, North Africa, and the Near East, and had begun as well to spread south into Ethiopia and the region of the upper Nile, and east to India and southeastern Asia. Invasions of Europe and Asia by peoples of other racial types have, however, considerably reduced the territory they now occupy.

We shall not attempt to describe in detail the Mediterranean race in all its present and prehistoric varieties. The brief description contained in Chart VII lists only those traits characteristic of Mediterranean populations as a whole; present-day populations which best illustrate this description are found in Spain, Portugal, southern Italy, and among some of the Egyptian, Arabic, and Berber-speaking peoples of North Africa.

More nonsense has been written on the origin and history of the Nordic race than about any other in the world. Not only have the structural traits of peoples said to be Nordic in race been exalted and exaggerated, but Nordic populations have been assigned, on the basis of no valid evidence whatsoever, unusual mental abilities, rare spiritual qualities, and a special genius for the development of civilization. Race propagandists have even assigned languages of the "Aryan" variety to nonliterate prehistoric Nordic peoples, though it is well known that unwritten idioms are not preserved in archeological deposits.

The facts of Nordic racial history are few and prosaic. We do not know where the type originated; it appears for the first time in eastern Russia. Populations possessing Nordic characters then apparently spread west and south, mixing as they went with Mediterranean populations. There is also some reason to believe that they moved eastward and added their features to some of the early peoples of northern Asia.

Today peoples of relatively unmixed Nordic type are found for the most part only in Scandinavia, the Baltic countries, and northern Germany. A population combining Nordic and Mediterranean features is found in northern France and the British Isles. Less important Nordic elements may be noted among populations predominantly East Baltic and Dinaric in race, and among some of the peoples of North Africa whose racial characteristics are mainly of the Mediterranean variety. It is worth noting that, except for stature and pigmentation, the Nordic type is very like the Mediterranean. Some students, indeed, regard the Nordic type as secondary, that is, as a tall, partially depigmented Mediterranean variety.

The Alpine race is best illustrated today among certain populations of central and eastern Europe, notably the Czechs and Bavarians. The type also occurs sporadically in other regions of Europe, Asia Minor, and among the Caucasoids of the Western Hemisphere. Its origins are unknown. Some anthropologists connect the Alpine race with the Asiatic Mongoloid and place its point of origin in central Asia, while others regard the characteristic Alpine features as survivals from some European upper Paleolithic population, somewhat reduced in size.

The earliest known center of development for Armenoid populations appears to be in Asia Minor. Here we find the type represented in the sculptured remains and monuments of the Sumerians of the third and fourth millennia B.C. Similar Armenoid traces are found among the later Babylonians, Assyrians, and Hittites.

From Asia Minor, Armenoid populations apparently spread southeastward to Arabia and India. Their invasion of Europe, however, did not occur until the Iron Age, when they came in great numbers to the Balkans, Greece, and Italy. The later dispersal of the Ashkenazim Jews (many of whom have Armenoid features) again brought individuals of Armenoid racial type to eastern and central Europe.

Today Armenoid populations are concentrated in Turkey, Syria, and Persia. Many are found as well in Greece and Bulgaria, and in the cities of central and eastern Europe and the United States.

6. DERIVED CAUCASOID RACES

The races of this group, briefly described and compared in Chart VIII, are all the result of relatively recent intermixture between populations of diverse racial types. In all three, however, Caucasoid traits are dominant; the Mongoloid features of the East Baltic race and the Mongoloid plus Negroid characteristics of the Polynesians are relatively few.

The Dinaric race, as we have said, includes both Nordic and Armenoid features and so must be regarded as more recent than either. It is perhaps most similar to the Armenoid race; only in the shape of the face, eye color, and body build do we find traits suggestive of the Nordic.

Like the Dinaric, the East Baltic race is a mixture of traits from diverse sources. Nordic and Alpine traits appear to be dominant; in addition to these there are a few features, particularly in the face, nose, and eyes, suggestive of an Asiatic Mongoloid race. Traits suggestive of the Nordic race are found in hair, skin, and eye color, and in the form and distribution of the hair. Head form, forehead, stature, and body build may have been derived from various Alpine populations.

There are two quite different hypotheses concerning the origin of the peoples of Polynesia and Micronesia. According to the first of these, the islanders are the descendants of an early Mediterranean population which moved down the Malay Peninsula into Indonesia. In the course of this migration they encountered both Negroid and Mongoloid groups and acquired some characteristics from both. As a trihybrid mixture, then, they moved on through Melanesia (where they may have picked up more Negroid characteristics) and out into the widely spaced island archipelagoes of their present home.

Chart VIII. DERIVED CAUCASOID RACES

Trait	Dinaric	East Baltic	Polynesian
Head form	Brachycephalic	Brachycephalic	Usually brachycephalic with many meso- and dolichocephalic variants
Head height	High	High	High
Forehead	Sloping or straight	Vertical	Slightly sloping
Brow ridges	None	Moderate	Little or none
Face index	Leptoprosopic	Euryprosopic	Mesoprosopic to leptoprosopic
Prognathism	None	None	Little or none
Nose index	Leptorrhine	Mesorrhine	Usually mesorrhine but also lepto- or platyrrhine
Nasal root	High	Medium to low	High
Nasal bridge	High, narrow	Medium high and broad	High, broad
Nasal profile	Usually convex	Concave	Concave, straight
Lips	Moderately full	Medium, thin	Moderately thick
Eye color	Brown or black, hazel or blue	Gray or blue	Dark brown
Hair color	Brown to black	Tow-colored	Dark brown to black
Hair form	Straight or wavy to curly	Straight	Wavy; rarely curly or frizzly
Body hair	Abundant	Usually scanty	Scanty
Skin color	Olive to brunet	Tawny white	Yellow brown
Stature	Av. 5′ 8″	Av. 5′ 2″	Av. 5′ 8″
Torso	Slender	Heavy, broad	Well proportioned

The second hypothesis appears to be somewhat preferred. According to this, a Mediterranean population having taken on a few Mongoloid traits during its wanderings in Asia, moved from the coasts of China to the islands of Micronesia and Polynesia, without encountering the Negroid populations farther to the south. Its Negroid traits were acquired by later contacts with Melanesians. Support for this hypothesis is found in the fact that the Micronesians appear to display mostly Mediterranean and Mongoloid traits and few of Negroid origin. Polynesians with marked Negroid characteristics appear mainly in the southern areas of Polynesia, and such characteristics are most marked among peoples, such as the Samoans and Tongans, who live nearest to Melanesian groups.

In any case, it seems evident that the Polynesians and Micronesians are a much mixed group racially and that they have lived in their present territory for only a relatively short time. It is not likely that much, if any, of Polynesia and Micronesia was occupied at all until well into the Neolithic.

7. CAUCASOID RACES IN THE AMERICAS

Since the beginning of the sixteenth century, Caucasoid peoples from every region of Europe have emigrated to the Americas. To America north of Mexico came groups of every one of the primary and derived Caucasoid races. The bulk of the earlier migrants were probably Mediterranean, Alpine, and Nordic in racial type; later, however, many peoples of Armenoid, Dinaric, East Baltic, and even Polynesian racial type came as well. In many, perhaps a majority of, cases, racial lines were ignored, and peoples of diverse racial type intermarried. As a result, the bulk of the present-day inhabitants of America north of Mexico are fairly well mixed in racial type; certainly it is impossible to characterize the population, except perhaps in a few of the more remote rural areas, in respect to one or other of the Caucasoid races.

Interbreeding, in America north of Mexico, between peoples of Caucasoid racial type and American Indians (basically Mongoloid in race) occurred relatively rarely. But the importation of Negroid slaves from West Africa did result in comparatively large-scale, though extralegal, Caucasoid-Negroid admixture. Today the American Negro, as we shall see later, is often less Negroid than Caucasoid in racial type.

South of the Rio Grande, the European immigrants were far more homogeneous racially and much fewer in numbers. Reliable estimates reveal that from the time of the conquest of Mexico by Cortes (1520) to 1820, the year in which Mexico gained independent status as a nation, there were no more than 300,000 Europeans entering that country. All of these were Mediterranean in type and most of them from Spain. Since the Indian population of Mexico is estimated from five to ten million, it is obvious that these migrations had much less effect racially than those to America north of Mexico. Large numbers of Negro slaves (in excess of 300,000) were also brought to Mexico. These, however, had relatively little effect on the racial type of the Mexican, since the average life expectancy of a slave in Mexico during Spanish domination was about nine years.

Today the bulk of the Mexican population is of the so-called "mestizo" type racially. Mestizos are predominantly American Indian in race with many Mediterranean features and, in some regions, a very few Negroid traits. About three-fourths of modern Mexicans are of this type; the remaining one-fourth display mostly Mediterranean traits (this is a very small group) or are indistinguishable from American Indians.

The same thing is true in general of most of the other Latin-American countries. In some of them (for example, Peru and Bolivia) there are perhaps more people of the Indian type and fewer mestizos; in others, these proportions may be reversed. Only in Costa Rica, Uruguay, Argentina, and portions of Chile is the population predominantly Caucasoid; in these countries, as in America north of Mexico, Caucasoid-Indian mixtures are numerically small. In Brazil, the presence of a large Negroid population and the relative absence of anti-Negro prejudice has resulted in a larger percentage of trihybrids.

8. MONGOLOID RACES

We include within the Mongoloid subspecies three major races; the Asiatic Mongoloid, the Indonesian-Malay, and the American Indian. The first of these is the least mixed; both the Indonesian-Malay and the American Indian races, though predominantly Mongoloid, show numerous traits of Caucasoid and Negroid origin. These three racial types are briefly described in Chart IX.

Little is known of the history of the Mongoloid subspecies. From the distribution of the relatively unmixed Mongoloid populations of Asia, it would appear that the type had its origins somewhere in the vast steppe lands of central Asia. The time of origin is probably later than that of the other two subspecies, since Mongoloids everywhere except in central and eastern Asia appear to overlay earlier Caucasoid or Negroid populations.

From central Asia Mongoloid peoples apparently spread northeast, east, southwest, and west. The northeastern branch, in relatively late prehistoric times, eventually crossed Bering Strait into America and there mixed with an earlier long-headed population, probably of archaic Caucasoid affinities, to form the mixed groups today known as the American Indians.

The southeastern migrants found that both an archaic Caucasoid and an archaic Negroid people had preceded them into southeastern Asia and the islands of Indonesia and Melanesia. The Mongoloid migrants interbred with these already mixed groups, so forming the modern trihybrid populations of Indonesia, which are predominantly Mongoloid, with the Caucasoid-Negroid groups found only in the more isolated regions.

Only in Asia north of Persia, Afghanistan, and India, and east of the Ural Mountains and the Caspian Sea do we find today relatively unmixed Mongoloid peoples. Some of these peoples moved at various times into

Europe, where remnants, such as the Lapps of northern Scandinavia, may still be found. Traces of Mongoloid intermixture may also be noted in at least one eastern European race, the East Baltic.

Chart IX. MONGOLOID RACES

TRAIT	ASIATIC MONGOLOID	INDONESIAN-MALAY	AMERICAN INDIAN
Head form	Brachycephalic	Meso- to brachy-cephalic; some dolichocephaly	Markedly variable but in the main brachycephalic
Head height	Low	Low	Low to medium
Forehead	Vertical	Vertical	Usually vertical
Brow ridges	None	None	Little or none
Face index	Eury- to mesoprosopic	Eury- to mesoprosopic; some leptoprosopic	Eury- to mesoprosopic
Prognathism	None	None	Slight to medium
Nose index	Mesorrhine	Meso- to platyrrhine	Usually mesorrhine, less often platy- or leptorrhine
Nasal root	Very low	Low	High, some medium or low
Nasal bridge	Very low	Low	High, some medium or low
Nasal profile	Concave	Concave	Straight or convex
Lips	Medium thick	Medium thick	Thin to medium thick
Eye fold	Frequent inner and complete fold	Some occurrence of eye fold	Rare
Eye color	Brown to dark brown	Dark brown	Medium to dark brown
Hair color	Black	Black	Black
Hair form	Straight	Straight; some wavy variants	Straight; some wavy variants
Body hair	Scanty	Scanty	Scanty
Skin color	Yellow, yellow brown	Brown to yellow brown	Yellow- to red-brown
Stature	Short	Short	Tribal averages vary from 5' 0" to 5' 8"
Torso	Long, heavy, broad	Long, broad	Usually broad and heavy

The Asiatic Mongoloid race is said to be more or less uniformly dominant among all of the numerous populations of central, eastern, and northern Asia. Very little is known, however, of the racial characteristics of these populations. It is not unlikely, therefore, that future research may uncover several races in this area. Such subdivision has already been suggested; Hooton, for example, refers to Mongol-speaking peoples such as the Tungus, Buriat, and Kalmuck as more typically Mongoloid than the

Chinese, Koreans, Manchurians, and Japanese. The physical traits which are characteristic of the Asiatic Mongoloid race listed in Chart IX do not differ very much from those which characterize the Mongoloid subspecies as a whole.

The Indonesian-Malay race is found widely distributed in portions of Tibet and southern China, northeastern India, Burma, Indo-China, the Malay Peninsula, and the islands of Indonesia. Mongoloid traits are dominant on the mainland but become less so in the remoter island areas, such as the interior of Java, Borneo, and Luzon.

At one time, presumably, all or most of southwest Asia and Indonesia was occupied by a thinly scattered Caucasoid-Negroid population having few or no Mongoloid traits. More recent migrations of relatively unmixed Mongoloid peoples to this region have resulted in the Indonesian-Malay populations on the continent and along the coasts of the island region. Scattered remnants of the earlier population are still found in the interiors of the larger islands, however. These differ from the Indonesian-Malay in possessing longer heads and faces, slightly wavy hair, a taller stature, and more slender bodies.

The New World was undoubtedly populated from Asia, the migrants moving slowly into the Americas over the Bering Strait route. As nearly as we can tell, this migration began some 25,000 years ago or more, during the retreat of the Wisconsin glaciation. The earliest migrants were apparently of a type not very different from that which first populated Malaysia, though with considerably fewer Negroid characteristics. Later migrants, however, were much closer to the Asiatic Mongoloid in race, and today the majority of American Indian groups, though far more variable than either Asiatic Mongoloid or Indonesian-Malay populations, are clearly Mongoloid in racial type.

9. NEGROID RACIAL TYPES

Lack of detailed knowledge prevents us from classifying Negroid racial types with as much detail as those of the Caucasoid subspecies. The following is only a tentative classification, based upon the somewhat inadequate data available.

A. PRIMARY NEGROID RACES

(1) Forest Negro, found chiefly among the native populations of West Africa and the Congo basin.

(2) Negrito, the racial type of numerous small populations in the Congo

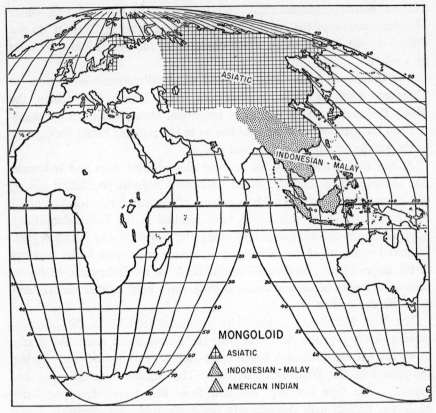

Map 6:2a. Distribution of Mongoloid races: Old World.

basin of Africa, the Andaman Islands, several portions of Indonesia, and the remote highlands of New Guinea.

B. DERIVED NEGROID RACES

(3) Bushman-Hottentot, the racial type of a few small populations living in and about the Kalahari desert of southwestern Africa. It is said to be an old, relatively stabilized combination of traits from an early Negroid variety, perhaps the Negrito, and some Mongoloid-like race.

(4) Nilotic Negro, apparently a combination of traits from an early Mediterranean variety and a Negroid race, possibly like the Forest Negro. The Nilotic Negro race is often divided into a number of subvarieties; apparently the populations of East Africa which exhibit this type vary considerably in the relative numbers of their Negroid and Mediterranean traits.

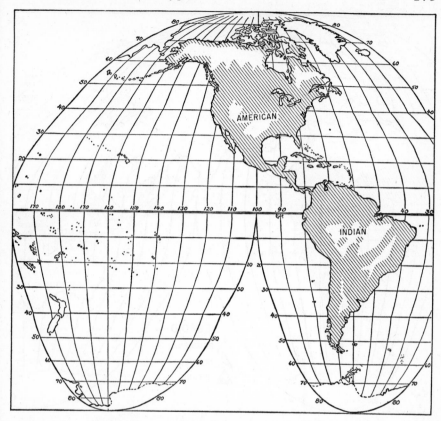

Map 6:2b. Distribution of Mongoloid races: New World. (For key, see Map 6:2a.)

(5) Oceanic Negro, apparently a relatively archaic Negroid variety plus a number of Mongoloid traits. It is found chiefly among the modern peoples of New Guinea and Melanesia.

The place and time of Negroid origins are still very much in doubt. Present-day distribution of Negroid populations suggests a point of origin somewhere between Africa and Oceania. Little is known, however, of the populations of this region and less of their racial history. Modern Dravidian-speaking peoples of India and the Australian aborigines, both of whom show strong Negroid admixture, point possibly to an early Negroid substratum in southern and southeastern Asia. Further evidence for this is found in the Negroid element manifest in the Indonesian-Malay race and in the remoter Tasmanian group, who may have been the last relatively unmixed survivors of this substratum.

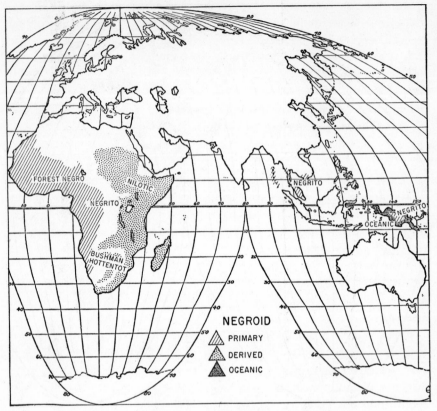

Map 6:3. Distribution of Negroid races: Old World.

The earliest traces of Negroid racial traits are found in Grimaldi man of the Italian Aurignacian and in skeletons belonging to the upper Aurignacian of Kenya, Africa (see Chapter 5, §§ 7, 12). The latter are regarded as similar to Oldoway, a late Pleistocene form of South Africa, said by Keith to manifest unmistakable Negroid traces. Keith also maintains that Springbok man of South Africa, another late Pleistocene form, is an early Negroid, having his closest affiliations with the modern Nilotic Negro.

Further but less direct evidences of Negroids in antiquity are supplied by the Negrito groups. The wide and scattered dispersal of these peoples, plus their primitive cultures, suggests that they have lived long in the Old World. Some anthropologists, indeed, identify them as descendants of an early south Asiatic Negroid substratum. Furthermore, the Bushman-Hottentot peoples of southwest Africa are apparently a mixture of an early Negrito group and some unknown group presumably of the Mongoloid subspecies. Bushman-Hottentot peoples presumably originated in Africa. Keith ties them in with the earlier Strandloopers and Boskop man, thus giving them an unbroken line of descent in Africa extending from late Pleistocene times to the present. If this is correct, it would mean that Negrito peoples, too, are of late Pleistocene age or earlier in Africa.

It is clear, then, that Negroid types probably appeared early in human history and that forms ancestral to modern Tasmanian, Negrito, and Bushman-Hottentot peoples were probably among the first to appear. Other modern Negroid races are probably later in origin and development, though no precise time sequence can be established.

10. PRIMARY NEGROID RACES

The Forest Negro race is characteristic of populations living in western Africa, from the Sahara on the north to the southern edge of the great tropical forest of equatorial Africa. The eastern boundary of their territory is roughly a line running north and south through Lake Chad. On the northern edge of this region there are found peoples displaying both Negroid and Caucasoid traits, while along the southern and eastern boundaries are found peoples combining Forest Negro and Nilotic Negro characteristics.

Forest Negro populations have apparently lived in this region for a long time, perhaps since the beginning of the Neolithic. There is, however, no direct archeological evidence on the point, just as there is no evidence of any non-Forest Negro population in this area. Since Forest Negro traits are found in no other population in the world (except among the recently formed Negroids of the New World), we must conclude that the race originated in West Africa. See Chart x.

The Negrito race is found both in Africa and the South Pacific. Negrito peoples of Africa are today a numerically small group who live in scattered bands deep in the Congo forests. They are believed to have lived here a long time and to have been one of the first of modern peoples to occupy the dark continent. Like the Bushman-Hottentot populations, whom they resemble in many respects, they may, in prehistoric times, have occupied more territory than they do today. Later invasions of the culturally more advanced West African and Nilotic peoples probably reduced the Negrito groups in numbers and drove them to more inaccessible retreats within the tropical forest.

Oceanic Negrito populations live in the Andaman Islands, the interior of the Malay peninsula, on several islands of the Philippines, and in the remoter highlands of New Guinea. Here, too, it is probable that they were early migrants and, at one time, were to be found throughout southeastern Asia and Indonesia. As in Africa, later invasions of culturally more advanced peoples (in this case, peoples of Oceanic Negro and Mongoloid type) forced them back into the less favorable and more isolated regions they now occupy.

Chart X. PRIMARY NEGROID RACES

TRAIT	FOREST NEGRO	NEGRITOS
Head form	Dolichocephalic	Meso- to brachycephalic
Head height	High	Medium
Forehead	Vertical or slightly sloping	Bulging
Brow ridges	Little or none	None
Face index	Leptoprosopic	Medium length and width
Prognathism	Marked	Marked
Nose index	Platyrrhine	Very platyrrhine
Nasal root	Low	Low
Nasal bridge	Low, broad	Low, broad
Nasal profile	Concave or straight	Straight or concave
Lips	Thick, everted	Medium thickness
Eye color	Dark brown to black	Dark brown
Hair color	Black	Black
Hair form	Wooly	Wooly or peppercorn
Body hair	Scanty	Scanty
Skin color	Dark brown to black	Dark brown to black
Stature	Av. 5′ 8″	Av. 4′ 8″
Torso	Broad and heavy	Slender, infantile

There has been much speculation on the problem of Negrito origins and racial history. Little is known, however, apart from the present-day distribution of Negrito groups, which suggests a point of origin somewhere in Asia between the two areas now occupied.

Despite the fact that the African and Oceanic Negrito populations have been separated a long period of time, they are essentially the same in physical type. This type is described in Chart x.

11. DERIVED NEGROID RACES

In and about the Kalahari desert of southwestern Africa are found two numerically small and isolated populations, the Bushman and the Hottentot. As we noted in § 9, these may at one time have occupied all of South Africa and be the descendants of the Strandloopers and Boskop man, both of mid- or late Pleistocene age. With the invasion of Africa by peoples of Nilotic racial type, the Bushmen were gradually forced back to their present homeland while, as a result of interbreeding between Bushmen and Nilotic peoples, there developed a racially mixed or intermediate group, now known as the Hottentots. Hottentots, however, are far more like the Bushmen than the Nilotic people and so are generally linked with the Bushmen.

The physical characteristics of the Bushman-Hottentot, listed in Chart XI, are said to be reminiscent of the Negrito race on the one hand and of an early Mongoloid variety on the other.

Chart XI. DERIVED NEGROID RACES

TRAITS	BUSHMAN-HOTTENTOT	NILOTIC NEGRO	OCEANIC NEGRO
Head form	Dolicho- to mesocephalic	Dolichocephalic	Usually dolicho- but sometimes brachycephalic
Head height	Medium to low	High	High
Forehead	Slightly sloping	Sloping	Rounded or sloping
Brow ridges	Slightly developed	Little or none	Small to prominent
Face index	Triangular, short; euryprosopic	Leptoprosopic	Lepto- to mesoprosopic
Prognathism	Moderate to slight	Slight or none	Marked
Nose index	Very platyrrhine	Platyrrhine	Platyrrhine
Nasal root	Very low	Low	Depressed
Nasal bridge	Very low, broad	Low, broad	High, broad
Nasal profile	Concave	Straight, sometimes concave	Concave or straight; sometimes convex
Lips	Full, everted	Thick, everted	Medium to thick
Eye fold	Inner fold frequent	None	None
Eye color	Dark brown	Dark brown	Dark brown, black
Hair color	Black	Black	Black
Hair form	Peppercorn	Wooly	Frizzly, rarely curly
Body hair	Scanty	Scanty	Scanty
Skin color	Yellow to yellow brown	Very black to dark brown	Black or dark brown
Stature	Av. 4′ 9″ to 5′ 0″	Av. 5′ 10″ or more	Av. 5′ 6″
Torso	Slender; steatopygous	Short, slender	Well proportioned

As we said earlier in this chapter (§ 5), there is good evidence that some of the prehistoric Mediterranean populations moved south into Ethiopia and the regions about the headwaters of the Nile. Here they encountered and were absorbed by Negroid peoples. These mixed peoples then moved farther south, dispossessing the Bushman-Hottentot groups who formerly occupied most of South Africa. In northeastern Africa (that is, the eastern Sudan, Ethiopia, and Somaliland), Nilotic Negro populations, though basically Negroid in type, display marked Mediterranean characteristics. Farther to the south in the lakes region, Angola, Rhodesia, and other areas in South Africa, the Mediterranean traits gradually become less evident until in some regions there is little real difference between so-called Nilotic peoples and those of West Africa and the Congo.

The Oceanic Negro race has more primitive physical traits than either the Forest Negro or the Nilotic Negro. In Oceania, however, Oceanic Negro populations appear to have followed those of Negrito type since, in New Guinea, where both are found, the Negrito groups inhabit the remoter interior highlands. Two Oceanic Negro subraces are sometimes distinguished. One of these is found among speakers of Papuan languages who live only in the interior of New Guinea and presumably represents a less mixed type. The other is found among the Melanesian peoples who occupy the coast of New Guinea and the remaining islands of the Melanesian group. These peoples differ from the Papuans in certain minor details which suggest a slight, and probably recent, Mongoloid admixture.

The former inhabitants of the island of Tasmania are the least known of the Negroid peoples, since they became extinct soon after European colonization began on their island (1879). Our information suggests, however, that their racial type, like the Negrito, belongs to the most primitive stratum of the Negroid stock, and that they entered Oceania very early. Dixon has suggested that they are a divergent Negrito race, somewhat altered by a few Caucasoid traits like those more prominent in the Australoids. Others group them with the Australians.

The little data available on the Tasmanian physical type may be summarized as follows. The head is dolichocephalic, with some tendencies toward brachycephaly. It will be remembered that the Negrito is brachycephalic. Faces are very short and broad. Prognathism is moderate. The nose is very broad and short, with an index of 109. Lips are of medium thickness. The skin is dark brown to black, the hair black, and the eyes dark brown or black. Head hair is wooly or frizzly. Face and body hair is scanty.

12. THE AMERICAN NEGRO

The slave trade brought large numbers of Africans to the New World. Most if not all of these were taken in West Africa. They were used principally on the vast plantations of the West Indies, southern United States, and in various Latin-American countries. Many lived only a short time under the harsh conditions of slavery; in Mexico, for example, the majority of the slaves survived only about nine years and had little opportunity to add their racial characteristics to the mixed Caucasoid-Mongoloid populations then coming into existence. The few that remained in Mexico after slavery was abolished were soon absorbed into the general population.

The fate of the West Indian Negro, however, was quite different. In some regions, as for example Haiti, the Negro became for a time politically and socially dominant and is still numerically dominant; in others he remains as a large and important minority group. The extent of his mixture with non-Negroid peoples is unknown and we can say little of the racial character of the present-day West Indian Negro.

In Brazil, too, the Negro survived the period of slavery. Here, however, there were few or no social barriers between Negro and non-Negro peoples, the latter principally Mediterranean in type. As a result, the modern population of Brazil displays, to a large extent, both Mediterranean and Forest Negro traits, with traces of American Indian characteristics. A recent study dealing in the main with the city of Bahia, Brazil, states as a "hypothesis for further testing" the following:

. . . Although probably more Africans were imported into Brazil than into the United States, or into any other region of the New World, the Brazilian Negro, as a racial unit, like the Brazilian Indian before him, is gradually but to all appearances inevitably disappearing, being biologically absorbed into the predominantly European population. . . .

. . . There is now growing up a relatively permanent mixed racial stock . . . The Brazilian mixed bloods are absorbing the blacks and are themselves in turn being absorbed by the predominantly European population.[1]

There are no accurate data as to the relative frequency of Negro and Caucasoid traits today present among the peoples of Brazil. Nor do we have any detailed racial descriptions of these groups. But it is evident that neither the Brazilian Negroes nor the mixed groups are to be identified wholly as Forest Negro populations, and it is certain that the Brazilians who will eventually emerge as a result of this process of absorption will be neither Mediterranean nor Forest Negro in physical type.

More is known of the physical characteristics of Negro peoples of the United States. Recent researches have conclusively demonstrated that our popular conception of the Negro in the United States as merely a transplanted Forest Negro population is wholly erroneous. Interbreeding between groups of African origin, American Indians, and Caucasoid peoples in the United States began during the period of slavery and continued for a long time afterward. Even today, despite many social and legal barriers, intermixture continues, though perhaps on a much less extensive scale than formerly. More important, however, for our consideration, is the fact that numerous persons with only a few Negroid traits annually "pass over" and are absorbed into the dominant Caucasoid population.

This long-continued period of interbreeding in the United States has

[1] Donald Pierson, *Negroes in Brazil* (Chicago: University of Chicago Press, 1942), p. 345.

considerably modified the racial type of the Negro. Professor Herskovits, who has studied the United States Negro in some detail, concluded that "from as diverse racial stocks as it is humanly possible to assemble—Caucasian, Negro and Mongoloid—has come a type which is homogeneous and little variable—a veritable New Negro, the American Negro." [2] Similar conclusions have been expressed by other competent scholars. It is evident, then, that in the United States at least (and probably in Brazil and the West Indies as well) the bulk of those who are called Negroes represent a complexly mixed and wholly new racial type which is in no sense to be confused with the Forest Negro of Africa.

The characteristics of this new race are known only for the United States; studies of American Negro populations in other regions of the New World are only fragmentary. The few data available on the Negro populations of the West Indies and Brazil suggest, however, that these do not depart too radically from those of the United States. West Indian Negro groups on the whole are probably somewhat less mixed than those of the United States, while in Brazil it is likely that the process of mixture has been somewhat more complete. In both the West Indies and Brazil, Caucasoid traits have been largely of Mediterranean origin in contrast to the highly diverse Caucasoid strains that have entered into the United States mixture. In all three regions, American Indian traits are relatively few.

The racial type of the American Negro, then, may be described in the following terms, if we keep in mind the fact that this description applies primarily to the Negro populations of the United States.

In head form the American Negro populations, like the majority of the peoples which have combined to produce them, are dolichocephalic. They are, however, somewhat more low-headed than the Forest Negro populations. Brow ridges are usually small, though they tend to increase in size with a greater Caucasoid admixture.

The face is somewhat longer than among Forest Negro populations, but about the same width. American Indian admixture does not seem to have increased facial width or the prominence of the cheekbones. The majority of American Negro populations appear to display little or no prognathism.

The nose appears on the whole to be intermediate between that of the Forest Negro and that of the Caucasoid. It is higher and narrower at root and bridge than among the Forest Negro, concave in profile, and possesses a somewhat thinner tip and wings.

Lips decrease in thickness and evertedness with an increase of Caucasoid

[2] Melville J. Herskovits, *The American Negro* (New York: Alfred Knopf, 1928), p. 33.

admixture. Ears are somewhat longer than among Forest Negro populations and have a less deeply rolled helix. Eyes are not distinctive.

The hair is usually black or dark brown, with lighter shades in groups having many Caucasoid traits. Eyes are usually dark brown or light brown. Skin color varies from olive to dark brown, and appears to become, in general, lighter as the amount of Caucasoid mixture increases. This does not mean, however, that skin color alone is a reliable guide to intermixture; a given shade of pigment may occur in many groups, from those with only a few Caucasoid traits to those whose traits are nearly all Caucasoid.

Hair, too, appears to become longer and less curly as Caucasoid and American Indian admixture is increased. Body and face hair is more abundant among Negro peoples of the Americas than among those of West Africa.

American Negro groups appear to be taller on the average than those of West Africa. Legs are somewhat longer in proportion to arm length; the latter measurement appears to decrease with increasing amounts of Caucasoid admixture.

13. SUMMARY

We may best summarize the data presented on modern races by examining each of the larger areas of the world in respect to the racial composition of its populations.

Europe. The races represented in Europe are the Armenoid, Alpine, East Baltic, Dinaric, Mediterranean, and Nordic. Relatively unmixed populations of these are very hard to find, however. The bulk of the populations of modern Europe display features of two, three, or even more of the races listed. In general, however, we may say that Nordic traits are most common among the populations of northern Europe, Mediterranean traits occur most frequently in the Iberian Peninsula and the areas bordering the Mediterranean Sea, and Alpine racial features are widely distributed in central and eastern Europe. Armenoid traits are most often seen in the Balkan region, together with and often combined with both Alpine and Dinaric features. East Baltic types are found most commonly in Finland, North Russia, and the regions bordering the Baltic Sea.

It is very probable that, in the cities of Europe at least, several new racial types are developing as a result of recent intermixtures. There is certainly no truth in the statement frequently heard to the effect that some populations of Europe are racially "pure." All European populations are racially heterogeneous; they differ only in degree of intermixture and in respect to the racial strains which have entered into a given intermixture. It would be wholly false, then, to conceive of Europe as divisible into distinctive racial areas, each characterized by a single relatively unmixed racial type. More accurately, each of the racial features found in Europe has its own unique distribution; the racial types we have listed are nothing more than temporary combinations of some of these contained in a given population at the present time.

North Africa, the Near East, and southern Asia. The broad racial type extending throughout this region is, in the main, Mediterranean. There are, however, other types as well, found either in small isolated groups or in combination with the traits of the dominant Mediterranean race. Thus, Nordic elements are discernible in North Africa, Armenoid traits in several areas of the Near East, and in northern India a variety of Caucasoid racial types exist alone or in combination with traits of the darker Mediterranean races. Here, too, then, populations mixed in racial type are the rule, not the exception. As in Europe, the Near East has been racially a melting pot since times immemorial, and there is no possibility today of drawing sharp lines between one race and another.

Central and South Africa. Here we find four distinctive types: the Forest Negro, centered in the western Sudan and the Congo basin; the Nilotic Negro, centered in the lakes region of East Africa; the Negrito, found in small scattered groups in the Congo forests; and the Bushman-Hottentot, in and about the Kalahari desert of southwest Africa. Mixed populations combining traits from these four are not uncommon—indeed, they are found wherever peoples of contrasting racial type meet. The Sahara is a vast region of mixed types; here Forest Negro and Nilotic traits have combined endlessly with one another and with the Mediterranean traits of the northern groups. Forest and Nilotic Negro characteristics are also found combined over much of South Africa. And, finally, the invasion of Africa by Europeans of many racial stocks has in recent years added a new element to the mixtures already present in the aboriginal period.

Central and eastern Asia. Throughout this vast territory, excepting only the tiny Ainu minority of northern Japan, the racial type is the one we have called Asiatic Mongoloid. Many variations in this population have been noted by travelers, explorers, and others, and it is highly probable that we have, in this region too, a population more mixed than homogeneous. At the present time, however, there is little that we can say about the races and subraces of Asia—it is truly an area racially unexplored.

The Indian Peninsula, southeastern Asia, and the islands of the South Pacific. In various isolated regions within this area are found small exotic ethnic units, apparently survivors of earlier and more widespread populations pushed to the wall by later invaders. There are the Vedda of Ceylon, the Australian aborigines, the Tasmanians, the Negrito groups of Malaysia and New Guinea, and the Oceanic Negro populations. The Vedda and the Australians apparently represent an early Caucasoid-Negroid intermixture which by reason of isolation and environmental selection has become a distinctive and unique type. Negrito groups are also isolated but have remained almost identical with their racial brethren of Africa. They, too, are apparently old in this region and are very possibly the descendants of the Negroid populations which entered into the Vedda-Australoid type. Tasmanians, again, display archaic Negroid characteristics, possibly related to those of the Negrito, while the Oceanic Negro is a third Negroid race, retaining some archaic features, but very different from both the Negrito and the Tasmanian.

Elsewhere in this region are found only mixed populations. Central and southern India is, as we have seen, inhabited by populations displaying Vedda-like elements with those of several Mediterranean subraces. Malaysia is today occupied largely by the predominantly Mongoloid Malay, with here and there traces of populations exhibiting archaic Caucasoid and Negroid traits. And in Micronesia and Polynesia, the populations are trihybrid, combining Caucasoid, Mongoloid, and Negroid traits in varying degrees.

The New World (North and South America). The aboriginal population of the New World is basically Mongoloid in type. There are, however, a number of rather distinctive local varieties; the Indians of the Pacific Coast of British Columbia, the Eskimos, the Plains Indians of North America, and the Gê-speaking population of the Amazon valley illustrate some of the more striking of these varieties. In the Americas, then, as in Polynesia, the racial type is highly variable.

The invasion of the New World by Europeans introduced new racial features. In America north of Mexico, the Indians were in large part replaced by Caucasoid populations of every European variety and a large number of West Africans brought here as slaves. Consequent intermixture between these populations is bringing into existence at least two distinctively new races: the North American Caucasoid, a highly variable type combining traits from most European Caucasoid races with some from the American Indian and Negro, and the American Negro, again a complexly mixed type which unites Forest Negro traits, those of various Caucasoid races, and a relatively few American Indian characteristics.

In Mexico, the West Indies, Central America, and South America, European invaders were apparently less diverse in racial type and, except in Brazil, Negro populations played little or no role in the resulting intermixtures. Much of Latin-America today is racially a composite of various American Indian traits and those of Mediterranean origin. Relatively unmixed Mediterranean and American Indian populations are comparatively rare. In Brazil, a considerable Negroid population is creating still a newer type, composed of Mediterranean Caucasoid, Negroid, and American Indian elements.

It should now be amply clear that there are no racially "pure" populations anywhere in the world. All populations are mixed to some degree, and the majority of present-day peoples are greatly mixed. Whatever homogeneity may have existed in the first men to appear on earth has long since disappeared—there is no stock on earth today which has not, many times in its history, been subject to mixture. Furthermore the evidences available indicate clearly that when populations of different racial type interbreed, the separate characters are distributed independently throughout both populations. There is no necessary linkage between race criteria; any one of them may be combined now with one set, and again with quite a different set.

Since human populations have from their earliest beginnings been subject to a more or less continuous intermixture, it is evident that all, except for a few long-isolated groups such as the Australians, have been and are in a state of slow but constant change. At any given time in history, provided that we have the requisite data, we may set up a racial classification of populations based upon the then observable distribution of racial criteria. Such a classification must always, however, be solely descriptive; it does not imply that any particular set of criteria, at that time combined in a single population, has any necessary permanence as such. "In short," to quote from Professor Ashley-Montagu's recent study of race, "the so-called 'races' merely represent different kinds of temporary mixtures of genetic materials common to all mankind." [3]

COLLATERAL READING

Ashley-Montagu, M. F. *An Introduction to Physical Anthropology*. Springfield, Illinois: C. C. Thomas, 1945. Chapter VI.

Boas, Franz. *Race, Language and Culture*. New York: The Macmillan Co., 1940. Pp. 18–27, 28–59, 60–75, 138–148.

Coon, Carleton S. *The Races of Europe*. New York: The Macmillan Co., 1939.

Herskovits, Melville J. *The American Negro*. New York: Alfred A. Knopf, 1928.

[3] M. F. Ashley-Montagu, *Man's Most Dangerous Myth: The Fallacy of Race* (New York: Columbia University Press, 1942), p. 14.

Hooton, Earnest A. *Up From the Ape*. Rev. Ed. New York: The Macmillan Co., 1946. Part V, pp. 568–662.

Howells, W. W. *Mankind So Far*. New York: Doubleday, Doran and Co., 1944. Part III.

Klineberg, Otto. *Characteristics of the American Negro*. New York: Harper and Bros., 1944.

Krogman, Wilton M., "The Concept of Race," *The Science of Man in the World Crisis,* ed. Ralph Linton. New York: Columbia University Press, 1945. Pp. 38–62.

Chapter 7

RACE PROBLEMS

1. RACE AND LANGUAGE, CULTURE, AND NATIONALITY

Race differences, as we have seen, consist of variations in bodily structure which are determined primarily by the genes. Each such variation has its own distinctive distribution among human groups which is independent of that of any other variation. In one population, for example, we may find wavy hair associated with a dark brown skin while in other populations it may be associated with lighter complexions. Variations in hair texture are inherited independently of variation in skin color, stature, or other bodily characteristics.

Among individual populations in different regions of the world, however, there may exist, more or less temporarily, unique combinations of genetically determined features. A given population, then, is racially distinctive if its inherited variations, taken as a whole, differ from those of other populations. The Australoid race, to take only one example, is unique by virtue of the high frequency of occurrence among native Australians of such genetically determined structural characters as dark skin color, marked prognathism, long, black, and curly hair, short, broad noses, extreme dolichocephaly, large brow ridges, and relatively short, slender bodies. Most of these separate traits are found also in other populations, but the particular complex of traits temporarily and fortuitously associated among Australian aborigines is unique to them.

It is obvious, however, that human populations do not differ in bodily

186

structure alone. They may also be distinguished by the languages they speak. So, for example, do the people of France differ from those of Germany, or the people of China from those of Japan. Within most speech communities we may find smaller linguistic differences such as those which separate mid-Westerners in the United States from people born and reared in the deep South. It is possible, then, to set up linguistic divisions among men, the boundaries between such groups being determined by differences in speech habits.

In much the same manner peoples may be differentiated in terms of their cultures taken as a whole, the total complex of behavior patterns learned by men as a result of their membership in a social group. Even among Europeans it is obvious that differences of this kind exist. Englishmen and Italians, for example, may differ markedly in their favorite foods, modes of dress, religious beliefs, as well as in many other aspects of culture. Among American Indians we find even more divergent cultural practices. The Indians of California, for example, live primarily on acorns, other wild vegetable foods, and the animals found in their habitat. Their neighbors, the Pueblo Indians of New Mexico and Arizona, depend mainly on maize, beans, and squash, foods which they cultivate on small farms. These two Indian groups contrast sharply in almost every detail of their cultures.

Among many of the modern peoples of the world we find still another commonly employed criterion of difference, which to a certain extent overlaps differences determined by linguistic and cultural barriers. This is the criterion of nationality. Strictly speaking, nationality is determined by legal residence; an individual belongs to the nation in which he has his permanent legal home. Since people living in the same nation are often in close contact with one another they may also share a common language and culture. But this is not necessarily true; in the United States, for example, we may find numerous linguistic and cultural differences among those who are legally citizens of the same nation. The same is obviously also true of such European and Asiatic nations as Switzerland, Jugoslavia, the Soviet Union, China, and Japan.

Linguistic and cultural differences among peoples, as well as differences in nationality, are very often confused with racial differences. We frequently hear and read of the "Slavic race," the "Latin race," or the "Semitic race." Since the terms "Slavic," "Latin," and "Semitic" can properly only be used of languages, the association with the word "race" is obviously erroneous and misleading. Peoples who speak Slavic languages (such as Russian, Polish, and Serbian) belong to many different races, and the same thing is obviously true of speakers of Spanish, Italian, and

French (the so-called "Latin" peoples) or those whose native tongues are Arabic, Hebrew, or Aramaic of the Semitic group. Furthermore, it is amply clear that language is not genetically determined but acquired rather by training and education. In the United States, for example, there are thousands of Mongoloids and millions of Negroids who, because they were born and reared in English-speaking communities, know no other tongue but English. They have nothing in common linguistically with Mongoloid and Negroid populations elsewhere.

The confusion of cultural groups with races is almost equally common. Terms like "Negro culture" or "Jewish race" illustrate this confusion. There is of course no culture common to all Negroids. Those who live in Africa exhibit considerable variation in culture, and even more marked differences exist among African Negroids, Oceanic Negroids, and those of the Western Hemisphere. Similarly, it is arrant nonsense to speak of a "Jewish race." Jewish groups, who at most share only relatively few cultural traits, may exhibit Mongoloid racial features, Negroid racial features, or almost any one of the specific combinations of racial characters listed under the Caucasoid subspecies. Culture, like language, is learned, not determined by the genes.

Finally, in terms like "French race," "German race," or "Japanese race," we find a double confusion. The words "French," "German," and "Japanese" may refer either to languages or to nationalities. In either meaning they obviously cannot be coupled with the concept of race as it is defined by science. Nationality, like language and culture, has no genetic determiners as is made perfectly clear by the fact that no nation, either of modern times or of antiquity, has ever been made up exclusively of a racially homogeneous population.

It is evident, then, that features of race, language, culture, and nationality have no necessary connection. Racial features are in large part genetically determined and biologically transmitted. Features of language and culture are learned and transmitted by the processes of training and education. Nationality is acquired by the fact of birth in a certain locality or by legal processes set up by a nation for the determination of citizenship. We may share the racial type of our parents and grandparents by virtue of our genealogical relationship to them but we share their language, their culture, and their nationality only if we have been subjected to the same training, education, and citizenship requirements.

2. RACE AND INTELLIGENCE

The problem to be discussed in this section may briefly be stated as follows: Do populations different in racial type also differ in inherited intelligence? Before discussing this problem, however, it will be necessary to know just what is meant by inherited intelligence and how it can be measured.

As we have already seen (Chapter 3, § 9), the genes do not transmit any trait; they merely determine the responses of the organism to the environment in which it develops. The fully developed organism, then, is a result of its heredity plus the effects of environment. We do not know that intelligence has any genetic determiners, but if it does, the development of these, too, must be affected by the environment. In view of the fact that human beings are subjected to constant training and education from birth onward, it appears likely that intelligence, more than any other human trait, is largely the product of the cultural environment.

A large number of tests purporting to measure intelligence have been devised and widely used, particularly in the United States. When these have been given to individuals of essentially the same cultural background, the subjects usually show significant variations in scores. Such variations have been taken as evidence that the individuals tested differ in inherited intelligence, it being assumed that the environmental factors affecting intelligence are essentially the same for all the subjects.

Results of intelligence tests given to identical twins reared in widely different environments appear to confirm this conclusion, for such twins resemble each other very closely in their performance in intelligence tests. Here, then, the inference is drawn that because identical twins have the same genes, their inherited intelligence is so much alike that even widely differing environments cannot alter it greatly. According to Professor Klineberg, the facts cited above "argue strongly in favor of an hereditary basis for part of the differences in intelligence between individuals and family lines." [1]

The fact that there may be individual variations in intelligence which have a hereditary basis does not necessarily mean that whole populations, alike or different in racial type, also differ in inherited intelligence. It may very well be that the range of individual variation in intelligence is basically the same for all groups, or that such group differences as may be observed can readily be accounted for by other factors.

Scores in intelligence tests often differ markedly for racially contrasting groups. An important and widely quoted difference of this sort was disclosed by tests given by a group of psychologists to army draftees during World War I. Tests were given to 93,973 Americans of widely varying European antecedents and to 18,891 American Negroes. The grades of those who made D— and higher, arranged on a seven-point distribution curve (from a low point of D— to a high of A) are as follows, with the

[1] Otto Klineberg, *Race Differences* (New York: Harper and Bros., 1935), p. 154.

figures representing the percentages of each group who made the grade indicated:

	D−	D	C−	C	C+	B	A
European-Americans	7.0	17.1	23.8	25.0	15.0	8.0	4.1
American Negroes	9.0	29.7	12.9	5.7	2.0	0.6	0.1

Expressed another way, the results revealed an average "mental age" for American Negroes of 10.4 years as compared to 13.1 years for Americans of European extraction.

If we accept this test as truly measuring inherited intelligence, it is obvious that we have here a very important example of racial difference in intelligence. But there are many reasons why we cannot accept this conclusion. These have largely to do with two factors: (1) the purpose of the army tests and the techniques employed in giving them and (2) the differing social environment and educational background of the men tested.

The purpose in giving the tests was to facilitate the selection of men for higher positions in the service. Since only about 5 per cent of the total number of draftees were required for such positions, the tests were so timed that 5 per cent or less of any average group examined would finish in the time allowed. But not so many Negroes as non-Negroes were "needed" by the army for these higher positions. The examiners were then instructed to act accordingly; that is, to select fewer Negroes than non-Negroes.

One means employed to achieve this end was to re-examine less than 20 per cent of the Negroes who made scores of D and below despite the fact that of the Negroes who made D or less on the Alpha test (designed for English-speaking literates) and who were re-examined, 86.9 per cent made higher scores. Non-Negroes were re-examined in much larger numbers in order not to lose human material of potential value to the army.

A second way of reducing the selection of Negroes is found in the fact that 65.5 per cent of the Negro draftees as against 24.7 per cent of the non-Negroes were given the Beta test, designed for illiterates and those who did not speak English. Since the rate of illiteracy of the Negro draftees was only twice that of the non-Negroes, it is obvious that in many cases there was no attempt to separate literates from illiterates among the Negroes. This arbitrary procedure, when coupled with the fact, admitted even by the examiners, that Negroes were at a disadvantage in the Beta test, further makes suspect the validity of the army tests as genuine measures of intelligence. We may then conclude with Reuter that these procedures "certainly raise some questions as to the finality and scientific reputability of any conclusions derived directly from the relative racial ratings." [2] Indeed, we may go even further and point up a more significant fact: that prejudice against Negroes in higher army positions most certainly affected not only the procedures employed but also the conclusions that may be drawn from the tests.

But even if we overlook the somewhat questionable procedures used in the army tests, it is still doubtful that they reveal any real difference in inherited intelligence between American Negroes and Americans of Caucasoid racial type. It may be noted, for example, that there are marked differences between northern and southern Negroes, as shown in the following table:

	D−	*D*	*C−*	*C*	*C+*	*B*	*A*
Northern Negroes	19.6	27.6	22.1	21.4	6.7	2.3	0.6
Southern Negroes	55.7	26.4	9.8	6.2	1.4	0.4	0.1

These differences, it is clear, cannot be due to race. But it is not difficult to account for them, at least in part. The northern Negroes among the draftees had an average of 4.9 years in school, while those from the South averaged only 2.6 school years. Seven per cent of the northerners had no schooling, 50 per cent had completed the fifth grade, and 25 per cent had finished the eighth grade. Among the southern Negroes, however, 19 per cent had no schooling, more than 50 per cent had finished only the third grade, and only 7 per cent had completed the eighth grade.

These differences in education are still more impressive when we compare the quality of education available to Negroes in the North and South. During the decade in which these tests were given (1910–1920), southern states spent far less for the education of Negro children than was spent in the North. Thus, for example, Louisiana spent only $1.31 per year per child as compared to New York's $45.32 per year per child. South Carolina expended $1.44 per year per child while Pennsylvania spent $36.20. Furthermore, the Negro children in the South had to go to segregated schools, far less well equipped than the schools for non-Negroes, while the Negroes in the North went to the same schools as their fellow countrymen of Caucasoid racial type.

We may add, parenthetically, that this situation has not changed remarkably since the decade 1910–1920. Recent reports of the American Council on Education indicate that the average expenditure per classroom per year is only $477 in southern Negro schools, as compared to $1,166 in southern white schools and $2,199 in northern schools. Similarly, the National Education Association, on the basis of the 1940 census, reveals

[2] E. B. Reuter, *The American Race Problem* (New York: Thomas Y. Crowell Co., 1927), p. 78.

that teachers in the South received average salaries of $917 per year as compared with an average of $1,607 for teachers in non-southern states. These figures make amply clear the fact that southern education for both Negroes and whites, but especially for Negroes, is far below national standards.

It seems that these differences in educational opportunity might wholly explain. the differences in performance between northern and southern Negroes, quite aside from the many other social disadvantages suffered by the Negro. But if this is true, then perhaps the differences between American Negroes and American Caucasoids shown in the same tests are not racial at all but the result of social and educational background. The following figures classified with respect both to racial type and locality give evidence on this point.

American Negroes		American Caucasoids	
State	Median	State	Median
Pennsylvania	42.00	Georgia	42.12
New York	45.02	Arkansas	41.55
Illinois	47.35	Kentucky	41.50
Ohio	49.50	Mississippi	41.25

It will be noted that the lowest median score for northern Negroes (42.00) is only slightly below the highest score for southern Caucasoids (42.12). All the other northern Negro groups score materially higher than the southern Caucasoids. Since education for non-Negroes in the South is very little better than that provided for Negroes, these differences are probably to be explained by differences in educational opportunity. Certainly they have nothing to do with differences in "racial intelligence."

We have confined our discussion so far mainly to the army tests made in World War I. We have done this partly because few of the results of tests in World War II are available and also because most of the ideas current about intelligence differences are based on World War I data.

It is significant that most of the tests used by the army in World War II were not considered intelligence tests; rather they were again considered devices quickly to isolate those individuals who had special capacities or limitations with respect to the needs of the service.

One interesting study has been made of the distribution of persons rejected by the armed forces because of "insufficient intellectual capacity." This phrase is an ambiguous one and the individuals rejected were often simply functionally illiterate, that is, unable to meet average fourth-grade reading standards. An attempt was made to correlate the percentage of rejections (of draftees, both Negro and white, from particular states) made for this cause with the average amount of educational expenditures made by the states. The correlation is almost perfect; the lower the expenditure, the larger the percentage of rejections. When Negro draftees are segregated from white draftees, it is apparent that in the southern states, where less is spent on Negro schools, the percentage of Negroes rejected is much higher than the percentage of whites rejected. To a lesser degree this is also true of northern and western states where there has been a large-scale recent migration from the South. In a few states, however, such as Ohio, New York, and Illinois, where there have been fairly large Negro populations for some time and where educational facilities for Negroes are nearly the equal of those for whites, the percentage of Negroes rejected is only insignificantly greater than the percentage of whites rejected. It is further of significance that in these northern states the percentage of Negroes rejected is far lower than the percentage of whites rejected in southern states with low educational expenditures.

Many of the individuals rejected for army service were, as we have indicated, functional illiterates. Beginning in 1943, the army began to send such illiterates, as well as those who had made scores below sixty on the Army General Classification Test, to special training centers. In a little over two years, 218,000 illiterates and 69,000 men with scores of less than sixty on the Army General Classification Test were sent to these centers. In from three to four months, 83 per cent of these had learned enough to be acceptable for normal army training.

It was also discovered, in these centers, that many functional illiterates are slow learners, while those who made high scores on the Army General Classification Test are rapid learners, a difference which is not ordinarily considered a matter of innate intelligence. Of the rapid learners, many had successfully completed college, but there were also nearly a million men who had not even completed high school. The majority of these had not continued their education for economic reasons, despite the fact that as a group they would probably have succeeded as well in college as those who actually enrolled and graduated.

In any type of intelligence test which in any way reflects educational background, however, the rapid learners without a college education would probably make lower scores than the college graduates. And because Negroes and members of other minority groups are usually kept from higher education for economic reasons, they would as a group be even more likely to make lower scores in such test.

The conclusions we may draw from our analysis of these tests are quite clear. Either the army tests measure only educational opportunity, or education so markedly affects the results of the tests as to make them practically useless for comparative studies of racial intelligence.

The same criticisms may be made of all other tests so far devised to measure the relative intelligence of human groups. None of these tests demonstrates that racial differences in intelligence exist. This does not mean of course that racial differences in intelligence cannot exist; when our techniques have been further improved, it may well be that such differences will be found. Many anthropologists would agree that there is no good reason to expect that populations which differ widely in structural features do not also differ to some extent in intelligence, special aptitudes, or other psychological characteristics. But until significant differences of this sort are actually demonstrated to exist we may well be highly critical of any attempt to evaluate a people's intellectual abilities solely on racial grounds. It is more than likely that inherited differences in intelligence, if these exist at all, are so small as to make no real difference to the developed intelligence of the group.

3. RACE, CHARACTER, PERSONALITY, AND SPECIAL APTITUDES

Most popular references to race include traits descriptive of character, personality, and special aptitudes. One "race" may be said to be impulsive, improvident, or even immoral. Others are described as cruel, inherently vicious, childlike in emotional response, shiftless, or unreliable. Less often, a "race" may be characterized as inherently honorable, sensitive, or rational. Crime is said often to be natural to some people, while others are believed to be innately artistic or particularly endowed with musical ability. The catalog of vices, virtues, and endowments attributed to racially contrasting groups includes nearly every characteristic ever assigned to human beings.

It is worth noting, however, that the traits used in this fashion fall into two major classes. In one are found only laudatory or neutral terms; in the other, forms having a derogatory or patronizing tone. It is very often, if not always true, that the laudatory or neutral terms are applied by the speaker to his own group, while he employs the derogatory or patronizing terms for others. Madison Grant, for example, who fancied himself a "Nordic," describes the Nordics as a race of rulers, aristocrats, adventurers, and explorers. Nordics possess chivalry, generosity, and other traits of noble character upon which our great civilizations are founded. Other races, according to Grant, are devoid of these traits of inherent nobility; of the "races" in the United States, Alpines are described as a "race of peasants," while Mediterraneans, though superior to Alpines in intellect and superior even to the "noble" Nordics in the field of art, are restless, frivolous, and have less sense of honor and truth than Nordics.

It goes without saying that there is no scientific basis whatsoever for using traits of this sort in racial descriptions. A number of attempts have been made to devise tests of personality, character, and special aptitudes, and to apply such tests to the study of racial differences. None of these has been successful. Professor Klineberg, after reviewing much of the literature concludes:

This review is far from complete, but it is doubtful whether even a more exhaustive survey would reveal any significant racial differences [in character, personality, and special aptitudes]. The problem is of especial importance, but there are in the meantime no satisfactory methods for its solution . . . There is no doubt that tests of personality require a great deal of improvement before they may be applied with profit to the problem of racial psychology.[3]

It is not without interest, however, to note that views like those of Grant and a host of lesser imitators can be explained in other terms. It is no accident that writers like these invariably ascribe "noble" traits of character and personality, as well as superiority in intellect, to races they denominate variously as Nordics or Aryans. Nor is it from scientific research that such men learn that non-Nordic races do not measure up to Nordics in intellect, character, and personality. Quite the contrary is true; the racist is always biased in favor of one race and anxious to "demonstrate" the inferiority of another. He falls, then, into the obvious error of assuming what he proposes to prove, as is strikingly revealed by a writer who asks, "What is the psychological explanation of the impulsiveness, improvidence, and immorality which the Negro everywhere manifests?"

Until bias is replaced by scientific objectivity, it is clear that we have no evidence that racially contrasting populations are truly different in character, personality, and the possession of special aptitudes. We may actually go further, for it is clear that these traits, like those relating to intelligence, are in all probability greatly if not wholly determined by the social environment. It may well be that inherited variations in character, personality, and special aptitudes are wholly insignificant as compared to those imposed by differences of training, education, and culture.

4. RACE AND CULTURAL ACHIEVEMENT

A favorite argument of those who would demonstrate inherited differences in mentality between racially contrasting populations is based upon

[3] Otto Klineberg, *Race Differences*, pp. 207–208.

the very real differences in degree of cultural achievement that exist between the peoples of the world. It is frequently pointed out, for example, that the peoples of Europe and their descendants in other regions of the world are the "creators" of the greatest civilizations known in human history. The civilizations of European peoples far surpass those of Africa south of the Sahara, the American Indians, and most if not all of the peoples of Asia. Such cultural superiority, it is maintained, demonstrates the higher intelligence of European peoples, who are largely of the Caucasoid subspecies.

Some racists have gone even further and attempted to show that even Caucasoids may differ in cultural achievement. Nordics or the so-called Aryans have frequently been mentioned as having been solely responsible for European civilization. Madison Grant argues in this fashion that Nordic peoples (his "great race") fashioned the principles upon which our great civilizations are based, and views with alarm the "passing of the great race" through intermixture with inferior peoples (other Caucasoids, as well as Negroids and Mongoloids), an intermixture which Grant maintains will cause this great civilization to decline and eventually to perish.

Arguments such as these are admittedly impressive. It is so easy to show that European machines and manufactures are superior to those of Asiatics, Africans, and American Indians. It is also easy to believe that our political systems are superior (haven't Europeans conquered most of the world?), that we have a "higher" standard of living, and that our religious beliefs are both aesthetically and morally superior to "pagan superstitions." On this basis it seems almost self-evident that peoples of Negroid and Mongoloid races have achieved less in the way of culture; even when peoples of this sort live with us they are apparently unable to assume any but an "inferior" position as compared with their neighbors of Caucasoid racial type.

At the same time, however, we must remember that cultural traits are not acquired in the same manner as racial characters. We have already seen that culture is transmitted by training and education, not by the genes. We have shown, furthermore, that no one has yet been able to demonstrate any real differences in inherited intelligence between the races. In the face of these findings, it is readily apparent that other means must be found to account for differences in cultural achievement. If cultural traits are not genetically determined and if no inherited differences in intellectual ability can be shown to exist between races, it is entirely clear that differences in cultural achievement cannot be regarded as significant for the determination of race.

An examination of the facts of cultural history soon dispels the illusion that one race or subrace holds a monopoly on cultural achievement. When the predecessors of Madison Grant's "great race" had only a rude stone-age culture, the Sumerians and Egyptians had already developed a civilization as much in advance of theirs as today the civilizations of Europe surpass those of Africa south of the Sahara. Indeed, there were advanced civilizations among the Negroid peoples of West Africa when Europe was still an area of relatively undeveloped cultures. And the civilizations centering in China in the days of Marco Polo overshadowed those of Europe of the same period in much the same fashion as the civilization of Europe overshadowed that of the American frontier at the close of the eighteenth century.

It is evident, then, that centers of civilization shift from one region to another and from one people to another. Today when we speak of "civilized" peoples we generally refer to the modern European and American nations. But in 3000 B. C., the region of higher civilization lay entirely outside Europe in the valleys of the Nile in Egypt, the Tigris and Euphrates of Mesopotamia, and the Indus in India. Here the Egyptians, Sumerians, and ancient Indians already had metal tools, a system of writing, great cities, agriculture, domestic animals, and many other appurtenances of a complex culture. The Europe of that day was still in the Stone Age, a region of relatively simple cultures. We may be sure that if the Egyptians and Sumerians knew of the Europeans at all, they spoke of them as rude primitives of an inferior race who were wholly incapable of developing a true civilization.

From Egypt and the Near East the center of civilization moved slowly to Crete, Greece, and finally into western Europe itself. In each of these areas, great civilizations developed and eventually gave way to others. In no single one of these early centers of civilization do we find a completely homogeneous racial type, nor do we find today that a single racial type characterizes the so-called "civilized" peoples of the world. Indeed, quite the contrary is true. The great centers of civilization today, as in the past, are in regions of numerous contacts between peoples of widely different origins, and it is far more likely than not that the peoples of such regions are racially quite heterogeneous.

Moreover, regardless of the racial type of the population, the more complex cultures are invariably made up in large part of traits having their origins elsewhere. This may especially well be demonstrated in the civilizations of Europe and America today. Thus, for example, linen and wool were first used in the Near East, while cotton came originally from India and silk from China. Our common foods have similarly disparate origins: canteloupes from Persia, coffee from Abyssinia, sugar from India, and maize, tomatoes, and potatoes from the American Indians. Indeed, few of our food plants and animals were originally domesticated in Europe; in most instances we borrowed them from other, less "civilized" peoples. The same is of course true of other traits; our "great civilization," upon analysis, turns out to be, like all other cultures, a mosaic made up of hundreds of historically diverse elements.

5. RACE PREJUDICE

It is now quite clear that there is no scientific basis for the myth that one race is superior to another, or for the related fallacy that certain races suffer under the handicap of an inherited inferiority. We have reviewed all the scientific data available to us and have found that:

(1) No modern race, taken as a whole, is structurally more primitive than another. Differences in bodily structure do exist, but there are often none but subjective and irrational reasons for regarding these variations as inferior. All modern races are primitive in some characters and advanced in others. The important fact is that all are more or less evenly balanced in respect to primitivity.

(2) There is no significant relation between racial type, language, culture, and nationality. To confuse these different ways of classifying men is wholly unscientific.

(3) No scientific evidence exists that racially contrasting populations differ significantly in intelligence, character, personality, or the possession of special aptitudes.

(4) The level of cultural achievement reached by a people has no necessary relation to their racial type.

In spite of these wholly sound scientific conclusions, however, so-called race prejudice does actually exist. We find that groups of people very often possess attitudes and opinions about other groups which are not in the least justified by objective analysis. As examples, we may cite the customary attitudes of many Americans toward Negroes, Jews, Asiatics, and individuals whose parents or grandparents came from Mexico. In many communities, prejudices of this sort lead to discrimination and segregation of the group in question to the extent that such groups may actually suffer a considerable loss of social status, economic freedom, and political equality.

It is worth noting, however, that so-called race prejudice is only rarely directed against people actually different in racial type from their persecutors. In the United States, the Jews are an amalgam of several Caucasoid racial strains, just as non-Jews are. The differences between Jews and non-Jews are cultural and religious, never obviously and rarely in any sense racial. Many who are called American Negroes are not actually Negroid in racial type. Some of them certainly exhibit more Caucasoid traits than Negroid traits, and, to all but the very careful observer, may be wholly indistinguishable from the darker Caucasoid varieties. Nevertheless, such mixed types are subject to the same amount and degree of prejudice as their more Negroid fellows.

Finally, we may sometimes note that prejudice exists where the differences between the groups concerned are neither racial nor cultural. During the economic depression of the early 1930's, many people of Caucasoid racial type migrated to California from Arkansas and Oklahoma. These were poverty-stricken farmers who had lost their property and came to recoup as migratory workers on the great farms of California. They were met with considerable suspicion and hostility from older residents of California, including many who had originally come from the same areas in the United States. The kind of prejudice, discrimination, and segregation directed against these migrants from Oklahoma and Arkansas was very much the same as that directed toward Negroes.

Race prejudice, then, has little to do with what we have called race. It is certainly not caused by actual differences in racial type. Nor is it caused by some "natural" or "instinctive" aversion for peoples who differ markedly from ourselves. So-called race prejudice is merely a set of stereotyped opinions and attitudes, wholly false and irrational, held by one group of people about another group. The opinions and attitudes making up this prejudice are learned by the individual as a result of his education and training in the group to which he belongs. Very young children have no prejudices of this kind; if they acquire them later it is because they have been taught them by their parents, teachers, and associates.

Sanford and Levinson, two professors at the University of California, recently devised a scale to measure the intensity of anti-Semitism among their students. In the course of this task, they made a number of interesting discoveries about the nature of anti-Semitism and the stereotyped opinions and attitudes with which it is associated. Thus, for example, they found that the items included in the stereotype are invariably false. All or nearly all of these items were statements about Jews taken as a whole or suggestions as to the treatment of Jews as a group. These were accepted as true by the more prejudiced of the subjects, though the construction of the test was such as to make it logically impossible that statements like "*all* Jews are clannish and conceited" could be accepted as true. Thus it was discovered that the stereotype of the Jew included definitely contradictory statements, both of which could not possibly be true of the same group. The more anti-Semitic of the subjects, however, accepted as true such contradictory statements as "Jews are seclusive and non-participative" and "Jews are over-assimilative, tend to push in where they are not wanted"; or "Jews are rich and powerful" and "Jews accept lower standards of living by doing menial work." [4]

Finally, it was found that the stereotype of the Jew was destructive and implicitly vicious. All of the items included in the test, which were accepted as true by the prejudiced, were mildly or markedly derogatory; there were no items in praise of or even neutral toward Jews as a group. Those subjects who showed even a slight degree of prejudice agreed with at least some of these statements; they believed, in part at least, that a group of people could be stigmatized as inferior because of their membership in the group.

These discoveries enable us to see quite clearly the nature of prejudice. Prejudices or stereotypes are beliefs and opinions which the holder has never examined objectively in the light of sound evidence. They are similar to other beliefs derived from one's social group in that they are accepted and often acted upon without much if any question.

6. THE BASIS OF RACE PREJUDICE

What brings about race prejudice? If the opinions and attitudes held by a group about another group are usually false, contradictory, and destructive, what brings them into existence and keeps them alive? This question is especially important in view of the fact that prejudiced peoples only rarely lose their prejudices when they learn of their false and contradictory nature. We have all met the individual who agrees with all we have said about the nature of prejudice but still insists that the "mixture" of "races," whether socially or biologically, leads only to the moral degradation of the dominant group.

One very interesting approach to this problem has been suggested by Gunnar Myrdal in *An American Dilemma,*[5] a study of anti-Negro attitudes in the United States. Dr. Myrdal outlines a "theory of cumulative causation." According to this hypothesis, race prejudice arises when an initial fear, suspicion, or economic advantage leads one group to discriminate against and segregate another. Discrimination and segregation, if it continues over a period of time, brings about actual social and economic inferiorities in the group toward which it is directed. Members of such groups are unable to get decent housing or to get the education and training neces-

[4] Daniel Levinson and R. Nevitt Sanford, "A Scale for the Measurement of Anti-Semitism," *Journal of Psychology,* 17 (April, 1944), 339–370.

[5] New York: Harper and Brothers, 1944.

sary to fit them for better-paid positions. As a result they are obliged to live in overcrowded slums and to work at menial and low-paid jobs, and poverty, disease, and crime become commonplace among them. These effects of discrimination and segregation are then taken by the group on top as evidence to support their initial fears and suspicions, and they proceed to tighten restrictions and discriminate even more against the group so feared and despised.

To exemplify this process, we shall describe very briefly the history of the Negro in the United States. As is well known, Negroes were first brought to this country as slaves, and treated in about the same way as domestic animals. Indeed, during the earlier phases of slavery, the Negro was treated with far less consideration than a domestic animal; slaves were numerous and cheap and it was less expensive to replace those who died from overwork and ill treatment than it was to take proper care of them. In brief, the Negroes were initially regarded as animals, sources of profit, not entitled to human treatment. For these reasons it was felt that Negroes had to be kept apart or segregated, like other domestic animals. Even where segregation was not practiced, as in the case of Negroes who were house servants or nurses, the attitudes toward such individuals were more like those we direct toward house dogs or cats than like those employed toward humans. In one of his stories, Mark Twain makes the interesting observation that a dog named Jack might be called Jack Harrison, but a slave named Jack would be referred to as Harrison's Jack.

As a result of this treatment, the Negro remained ignorant and uneducated. He was very often obliged to live in crowded and filthy quarters. Not permitted access to job training, he was fit only for the simpler menial occupations. Furthermore, when the Civil War brought about the abolition of slavery, the Negro was released from many of the controls exerted over him by the slave-owners. The obvious inferiorities of Negroes as a group when compared to non-Negroes, plus the increased fear that free Negro voters would revenge themselves on their former owners, brought about an enormous increase in the restrictions on the Negroes' freedom of action. It is necessary to emphasize that the Negroes' inferiority was brought about by the dominant group; it was not an "innate" or "inherited" inferiority. Further restriction, segregation, and discrimination, then, served only the purpose of increasing these signs of inferiority which in turn led to increased efforts at segregation.

It is evident that the Negro can do little to escape this cycle of cumulative discrimination. Whatever he does, however skilled he may become, he is still visibly a Negro, linked to his group by a stereotyped complex of false attitudes and erroneous beliefs. The discrimination can only be ended by the dominant group. When restrictions are lifted and segregation is discontinued, the response made by the Negro group in terms of improved living and higher status will gradually dissipate prejudice.

It is interesting to note that this has actually happened to some minority groups. Irish immigrants, at an earlier period in our history, also suffered discrimination and segregation. They, too, came in under a cloud of suspicion and hostility which led to measures designed to "keep them in their place." Such measures kept them in poverty and ignorance, so bolstering the initial fears and suspicions. But the Irish immigrant did not long remain visibly different from other Americans. As his children learned American ways and lost their foreignness, they could and did manage to escape the restrictions imposed on those more visibly Irish. Today, little anti-Irish sentiment remains; freed from discriminatory practices and segregation, the Irish-Americans have shown themselves the equals of any other group.

Negroes and many other segregated minorities do not of course have this relatively easy way out. They stand out too visibly from the majority population. They can only be freed from the bonds of discrimination by those who understand the causes of race prejudice and work hard to release them. Once the Negro has educational, political, and social opportunities equivalent to those available to the majority, he may well prove himself as valuable a citizen as anyone else. In this respect, it is interesting and perhaps significant that many American Negroes have succeeded, despite their many economic and social handicaps, in reaching positions of honor and service to their community and country. The greatest cost of race prejudice may indeed lie in the possibility that those who practice and maintain it thereby rob their communities of much potentially valuable human material.

COLLATERAL READING

Ashley-Montagu, M. F. *Man's Most Dangerous Myth: The Fallacy of Race.* Rev. Ed. New York: Columbia University Press, 1945.

————. *An Introduction to Physical Anthropology.* Springfield, Illinois: C. C. Thomas, 1945. Chapter VII.

Benedict, Ruth. *Race: Science and Politics.* Rev. Ed. New York: the Viking Press, 1945.

Boas, Franz. *The Mind of Primitive Man.* Rev. Ed. New York: The Macmillan Co., 1938.

————. "Race," *Encyclopedia of the Social Sciences.* New York: The Macmillan Co., 1934. XIII, 25–34.

————. *Race, Language and Culture.* New York: The Macmillan Co., 1940. Pp. 191–195.

Huxley, J. S. and Haddon, A. C. *We Europeans*. New York: Harper and Bros., 1936.

Klineberg, Otto. *Race Differences*. New York: Harper and Bros., 1935.

———. "Race Psychology," *The Science of Man in the World Crisis,* ed. Ralph Linton. New York: Columbia University Press, 1945. Pp. 63–77.

Myrdal, Gunnar S. *An American Dilemma*. New York: Harper and Bros., 1944.

Chapter 8

THE NATURE OF CULTURE

1. THE DIVERSITY OF HUMAN BEHAVIOR

In contrast to physical anthropology which, as we have seen, is concerned mainly with man's bodily structure, cultural anthropology deals with man's behavior and specifically with the ways in which human beings carry out the activities involved in daily living. Where most animals, including the anthropoid apes, reveal within a given species essentially the same patterns of behavior, man does not. On the contrary the species *Homo sapiens,* though its members function physiologically in much the same ways and have essentially similar bodily structures and psychological mechanisms, demonstrates a truly remarkable variation in patterns of behavior. These variations, as we have noted before, are wholly independent of racial differences; the divisions of mankind based upon their ways of behaving both cut across and subdivide groupings based on race.

The diversity of human behavior may be illustrated in almost every activity in which men engage. Food habits, for instance, vary endlessly. The Eskimos of the Arctic live almost exclusively upon meat and fish in contrast to many Mexican Indian peoples whose diet is based for the most part on cereals and vegetables. Milk and its products are regarded as luxury foods among the Baganda of East Africa, while the peoples of West Africa regard them as inedible and probably poisonous. Fish is used as a food by many American Indian tribes, but the Navahos and Apaches of New Mexico and Arizona consider it nauseating and unfit for human consumption. Dog meat is eaten by many peoples (among some Mexican In-
204

dians a variety of dog was especially bred for food), but there are many others who, like ourselves, look with horror upon dog meat as food.

There are variations as well in the manner in which foods may be combined. Orthodox Jews do not combine meat and dairy products in the same meal but take them separately. A similar custom obtains among the Eskimos, who require that sea foods be kept quite distinct from foods obtained from land animals, and who even serve these in different containers. Special observances of this sort may extend to the very processes of eating: witness not only the Polynesian custom of reserving certain utensils for the eating of human flesh but also the rigid formality of our own table etiquette in respect to the proper use of knives, forks, and spoons.

Habits of dress and ornament are similarly variable. Many peoples, like the native Australians and the Indians of Tierra del Fuego, go about nearly naked, while others, for example the Baganda of East Africa, must be fully clothed from neck to ankles. Ornaments include such varied devices as earrings, nose and lip plugs, and combs and other articles worn in the hair. The body may be decorated with paint or clay, or tattooed in intricate designs. Some peoples, whose skins are too dark to be tattooed effectively, make designs on their bodies by raising long scars.

The ways which govern the behavior of men toward each other also show considerable divergence. Among the Navahos and numerous other peoples, a man must not speak to or even look at his wife's mother. Among the Crows of the North American Plains a man is required to joke with certain of his relatives and may not show anger when these relatives humiliate him in public. The Trobrianders of Melanesia do not require a man to support, educate, or discipline his children; these functions belong to the children's uncle, specifically the mother's brother. In the Kariera tribe of Australia, an individual can marry only one related to him as cross cousin, that is, as cousin through his mother's brother or his father's sister.

The catalog of behavioral differences is a long one and we shall examine it more systematically in later chapters. The examples we have given sufficiently illustrate the fact that human beings differ in their ways of behaving, that there are few or no ways of behaving which hold for all men at all places and times. What are the reasons for these differences? Why are men so variable in behavior despite the fact that they belong to one species?

2. THE CONCEPT OF CULTURE

A partial answer to these questions is found in the fact that man learns a far greater proportion of his behavior than any other animal. Man comes into the world a helpless infant possessing no really developed inherited mechanisms for behavior. He must be taught to eat, to speak, to walk, and to perform nearly all the overt actions required for living. Even when, as an infant, he performs certain actions, such as swallowing or elimination, these are often profoundly modified by experience and learning. During his relatively long period of infancy and childhood, man is ceaselessly subjected to a learning process which eventually provides him with certain ways of living appropriate to the society into which he is born and in which he is educated.

Men, like animals, live in more or less organized clusters which we shall call societies. Members of human societies always share a number of distinctive modes or ways of behaving which, taken as a whole, constitute their culture. Each human society has its own culture, distinct in its entirety from that of any other society. The Navahos, to take an example, form a society of some 60,000 individuals who today live on a large reservation in New Mexico and Arizona. Navaho culture includes a large number of distinctive ways of behavior very different from those of the other Indians living near them, the Spanish-speaking peoples of the same area, and the so-called Anglo-Americans of New Mexico and Arizona. Some of these distinctive items of Navaho culture are: their language, which is wholly unrelated in any way to English or Spanish; their ways of dressing and ornamenting themselves; their houses, a kind of log structure covered with earth; the fact that they are divided into large family units called clans in which descent is traced through the mother; their possession of an extraordinarily complex set of rituals for the curing of disease; their belief that some people may on occasion practice black magic or witchcraft and by so doing make others ill or even kill them; and their belief in a rather complex hierarchy of gods and supernaturals with whom the Navahos must maintain harmonious relations in order to retain health and prosperity. Here, then, is a society—the 60,000 Navahos living together in a common territory—and a culture—Navaho culture, the ways of behaving characteristic of all or most of the members of this society.

The concept of culture, which Kluckhohn has defined as all the "historically created designs for living, explicit and implicit, rational, irrational, and non-rational, which exist at any given time as potential guides for the behavior of men," [1] helps to understand human behavior. The diversity of human behavior is also clarified by this concept when we realize that

---

[1] Clyde Kluckhohn and William Kelly, "The Concept of Culture," *The Science of Man in the World Crisis,* ed. Ralph Linton (New York: Columbia University Press, 1945, pp. 78–106), p. 97.

each human society has a distinctive culture, or to quote Kluckhohn again, "a historically derived system of explicit and implicit designs for living, which tend to be shared by all or specifically designated members of a group [that is, a society]." [2] These definitions, which serve only as a starting point to a discussion of culture, will become clearer as we go on.

3. OTHER MEANINGS OF CULTURE

To begin with, it is clear that the anthropological definition of culture is far more comprehensive than that of the word as it is ordinarily employed. Many people hold that culture is synonymous with development or improvement by training and education. A "cultured," more properly, "cultivated," individual is one who has acquired a command of certain specialized fields of knowledge, usually art, music, and literature, and who has good manners. Persons not so well educated in these fields, or persons whose manners were learned in the streets rather than in polite society, are often called uncultured.

In anthropological usage, however, this distinction is not significant. Culture is not restricted to certain special fields of knowledge; it includes ways of behaving derived from the whole range of human activity. The designs for living evident in the behavior of the Eskimos, the natives of Australia, or the Navahos are as much a part of culture as those of cultivated Europeans and Americans. Culture includes, not only the techniques and methods of art, music, and literature, but also those used to make pottery, sew clothing, or build houses. Among the products of culture we find comic books and popular street songs along with the art of a Leonardo da Vinci and the music of a Johann Bach. The anthropologist does not employ the contrast "cultured versus uncultured," for this distinction of popular usage represents only a difference in culture, not its absence or presence.

Historians often use "culture" to denote special developments in artistic and intellectual fields. To many such scholars, the phrase "Greek culture" applies only to the activities of learned Greeks, skilled in art and literature, or, even more narrowly, to the learned Greeks of the Golden Age of Greek intellectual development. It has no reference, as the anthropological concept has, to the many other activities characteristic of Greek society, nor is it usually applied to peoples like the American Indians or the Africans south of the Sahara who lack a written history. Here again the anthropological concept is broader and more comprehensive.

Culture, finally, also includes civilization. No modern anthropologist

2 *Ibid.*, p. 98.

regards civilization as qualitatively different from culture, nor does he make a distinction between the civilized and the uncivilized. All civilizations, including the great ones of today and ancient times, are but special instances of culture, distinctive in the quantity of their content and the complexity of their patterning, but not qualitatively different from the cultures of so-called uncivilized peoples. The common habit of using the term "culture" only for peoples whose ways of life strike us as quaint or exotic is decidedly unanthropological. Culture prevails in New York, London, and Paris just as it does among the Eskimos and Navahos, and the customs and manners of Christian missionaries are just as much a part of culture as those of the Indians, the South Sea Islanders, or the Hottentots they are attempting to missionize.

4. CULTURES AND SUBCULTURES

Though it is quite correct to say that each human society has its own culture, different in its entirety from the culture of any other society, it is also true that anthropologists frequently apply the term "culture" to groups both larger and smaller than a single society. On the Plains of North America, for example, there lived during the aboriginal period no less than thirty-one American Indian societies. Each of these had its own tribal name (examples are the Crow, Cheyenne, and Omaha), each had a culture and language which taken as a whole was different from the cultures and languages of all the rest, and each was politically independent. Nevertheless, the thirty-one Plains cultures did have a large number of characteristics in common. In all the tribes, buffalo were hunted for food; dwellings (called tipis) were built of poles covered with skins; the dog (and later the horse) was used as a pack animal and to pull a kind of land sledge (travois) made of poles; clothing was made of buffalo hide and deer skin; hides were worked with a high degree of artistry and skill; art works of a geometric type were common; men were organized into a number of warrior clubs; dwellings were usually set up in a distinctive order called the camp circle; a complex ritual (the sun dance) was practiced; and men were graded in terms of their success in warfare in accordance with a system of honors. These ways of behaving, together with a number of others, are collectively called Plains culture to distinguish them from similarly broad complexes of cultural items found among other groups of American Indian tribes, such as those of the eastern woodlands, the North Pacific coast, or the California area.

In terms like "Plains culture," "North Pacific coast culture," or "Eastern Woodlands culture," then, the term "culture" applies to ways of behaving common to a number of societies, not to one alone. Societies which share certain aspects of culture in this way have presumably had some degree of contact with each other, though not so intensive a contact as occurs among the members of any one society. By reason of intersocietal contacts, certain aspects of culture may spread beyond the borders of a single society and become common to several societies.

In a similar fashion, particularly in the larger and more complexly organized societies of the world, it is often possible to distinguish areas of culture which are restricted to some portion of a society's membership. The great Quechua nation, which centered in ancient times in Peru and included at its height several millions of people, was divided into three major classes. At the top were the Incas, an aristocratic class composed of individuals related by blood and common interest to the emperor's family. Next came a class of provincial nobility, the Curaca, composed for the most part of kings, chiefs, and other officials of conquered nations and tribes. The great mass of common people made up the third and largest class.

Differences in culture between these classes of Quechua society were marked. The Incas wore clothing of the finest fabrics; ornamented themselves with gold, silver, feathers, and precious stones made into symbols distinctive of their class; occupied massive dwellings of stone or adobe; educated their children at a special college at Cuzco, the capital city; took over the top positions in the government, the army and the priesthood; and were even said to employ a special language. The Curaca class shared some of these ways of behaving but not all. Their clothing and ornaments were less elaborate, their positions in the army and government were not so near the top of the hierarchy, and they probably did not share in the religious rituals peculiar to the Incas nor in the special Inca language. Commoners could wear only coarse garments of wool and were forbidden all ornaments. They were obliged to till the soil and do other menial labor, but owned no land and occupied no positions of significance in either the government or the army. It is quite probable that they spoke a variety of languages and dialects and that their religious beliefs and practices were not only different from those of the Inca and Curaca but also varied from region to region.

In Quechua society, then, we find at least three subcultures dependent upon class affiliation and probably a number more dependent upon local variation. This is quite a common phenomenon and one which may readily be illustrated among both the modern and ancient societies of Europe and Asia.

To summarize: "culture," as the term is used by the anthropologist, may be applied (1) to the ways of life or "designs for living" common at any one time to all mankind, (2) to the ways of living peculiar to a group of societies between which there is a greater or less degree of inter-action, (3) to the patterns of behavior peculiar to a given society, and (4) to special ways of behaving characteristic of the segments of a large and complexly organized society.

5. CULTURE AND BEHAVIOR

It should now be clear that culture is an abstraction from behavior and not to be confused with acts of behavior or with material artifacts, such as tools, containers, works of art, and other artifacts that people make and use. The anthropologist cannot observe culture directly; he can only ob-serve what people do and say and the processes and techniques they em-ploy in the manufacture and use of material artifacts. As Redfield has said, culture is "manifest in act and artifact"; it does not consist of acts and artifacts. Baskets, pottery, weapons, paintings, sculptures, and many other items of the same sort are collected and studied because they repre-sent the end products of ways of behaving current in a given society. Similarly, many varieties of human actions are studied, not as isolated items of behavior, but for the light they may throw on the ways in which human beings are taught to behave in the societies in which they live.

This point may be illustrated from a study of Chiricahua Apache culture made by Morris E. Opler. The Chiricahuas are a society of some six hundred people who now live in eastern New Mexico. One of them re-counted the following incident which took place when as a young un-married man he went to visit an old lady, the grandmother of a marriage-able girl.

I went to her place that night. I had heard the old lady had some *tiswin* [a fermented liquor made of corn]. When I got there she told me to have a drink. As we talked she told me that I was single and needed a wife. She mentioned this girl [her grandchild] and said it was worth two horses to get her. I had never seen the girl before. When I got home I started to think about it seriously. I talked it over with my relatives. An uncle of mine gave me a mule, and a cousin gave me a horse.

The next day I went to the home of a certain woman, a middle-aged woman. She was eating when I arrived. I called her outside and hired her to speak for me to this girl's grandmother. This woman lived just on the other side of a stream from the girl and her grandmother. The next day my go-between went to the old woman and asked her to give me the girl. The old woman demanded two good horses. My go-between thanked the grandmother and came to tell me what had been said. I gave her the horse and the mule to lead to the old woman, and the next day I went to the girl.[3]

In the course of his work among the Chiricahuas, Opler collected scores of incidents which, like the one quoted, had to do with getting a wife. When all of these were brought together and analyzed, it was possible to abstract from them certain common procedures relating to marriage in this society. So, for example, Opler discovered that the initiative in proposing marriage could be taken by the girl's relatives, the boy's family, or less often, by the young people themselves. In the account quoted, the first of these procedures is followed: the girl's grandmother suggests to a likely young man whom she knows that her granddaughter would make him a good wife.

Once a young man decides to marry he must consult his relatives, both to gain their consent to the marriage and their help in raising the necessary bride-price, a gift made by the boy's family to the family of the girl. Note that the young man quoted talked it over with his relatives and was successful in obtaining a horse and a mule from them.

Next, a go-between must be selected to make the necessary arrangements for the marriage; a young man cannot with propriety do this himself. The go-between, according to Opler, is usually an older relative or friend, preferably one who is known for his ability in matters of this sort. The young man quoted chose a friend of his, a middle-aged woman. She then went to the girl's grandmother, made the proposal on behalf of the young man, was told the bride-price required, and carried this information back to the young man. He in turn gave the go-between the horse and mule to lead to the girl's grandmother and went on the next day to claim his bride.

6. PATTERNS OF CULTURE

The ways of behaving which compose the culture of any society represent generalizations of the behavior of all or some of the members of that society; they do not precisely describe the personal habit system of any one individual. In our society, for example, it is customary for a man to raise his hat when greeting a woman on the street. But not all men perform this action in the same way. One may lift his hat with a sweeping gesture, another may only lift his hat slightly, and a third may just barely touch his hat. Each individual, in the performance of this simple action, reveals an individual or idiosyncratic variation of a common cultural procedure.

[3] Morris E. Opler, *An Apache Life-Way* (Chicago: copyright 1941 by University of Chicago Press), p. 157.

Such variations are found in all societies; it is a mistake to believe that any culture prescribes precisely the same behavior for each of its participants. To say, therefore, that in our society it is customary for a man to raise his hat when greeting a lady is to generalize on the behavior of men greeting women; we are describing a pattern of our culture and not attempting the endless task of summarizing the totality of individual actions current in our society.

The term "pattern," as we shall use it, refers to a specific way of behaving which is part of a given culture. A little reflection soon makes it evident, however, that cultural patterns are not all of the same sort. An observer in our society might note, for example, that some Christian members of our communities, while they profess the ideal of the Golden Rule, at the same time behave very differently in the conduct of their business and personal affairs. Or he might note that many city people would state unequivocally that certain traffic signs require a driver to stop his car at an intersection and look carefully both ways before proceeding. But an observation "on the behavior of 1,541 automobile drivers in the presence of [a] boulevard stop sign" made by Fearing and Krise [4] gave the following interesting results: 5.1 per cent actually stopped their cars at or beyond the stop line, 11.5 per cent slowed to one to three miles per hour, 45.1 per cent slowed to three to six miles per hour, 35.0 per cent slowed to six plus miles per hour, and 3.2 per cent ignored the signal entirely.

These illustrations point up the fact that cultures include two major types of pattern: ideal patterns and behavioral patterns. Kluckhohn has said that ideal patterns define what the people of a society would do or say in particular situations if they conformed completely to the standards set up by their culture.[5] Behavioral patterns, on the other hand, are derived from observations of how people actually behave in particular situations. The Golden Rule and the statement of the meaning of a stop sign are ideal patterns of our culture, while the actual behavior of Christians in relation to others and the actual behavior of drivers at stop signs represent behavioral patterns of our culture.

Similar differences between ideal and behavioral patterns are found in every culture. Among the Chiricahuas, Opler tells us that a man who discovers that his wife is unfaithful is expected to take drastic action.

A wronged husband who does not show some rancor is considered unmanly

---

[4] "Conforming Behavior and the J-Curve Hypothesis," *Journal of Social Psychology,* 14 (1941), pp. 109–118.

[5] Clyde Kluckhohn, "Patterning in Navaho Culture," *Language, Culture and Personality,* ed. Leslie Spier (Menasha, Wisconsin: Sapir Memorial Publication Fund, 1941), pp. 109–130.

. . . The woman, since she is close at hand, is likely to be the first to feel the husband's wrath. A beating is the least punishment she suffers. If there is no one to intercede for her, her very life may be forfeit, or she may be subjected to mutilation. . . . The husband is just as insistent that the man who has disrupted his home be punished: [quoting an Apache] "After the husband has punished or killed his wife, he will go after the man and kill him." [6]

But actual examples of infidelity reveal that affronted husbands do not always take such extreme steps. In one account given by Opler, the husband, though he pretended great fury, "didn't care. He married right away to a Comanche." [7]

Ideal patterns represent the "musts" and "shoulds" of a particular culture as expressed in the acts and speech of its participants. But not all ideal patterns define only one acceptable means of meeting a given situation. Many and perhaps most of them indicate several procedures, though these need not be equally acceptable. Kluckhohn in the paper previously referred to has suggested that ideal patterns may be classed in five categories:

(1) Compulsory, where the culture provides but one acceptable means of meeting certain situations.

(2) Preferred, where several ways of behaving are acceptable, but one is more highly valued than the rest.

(3) Typical, where several ways of behaving are more or less equally acceptable, but one is more often expressed than the rest.

(4) Alternative, where several ways of behaving are acceptable and there is no difference either in value or frequency of expression.

(5) Restricted, ways of behaving which are acceptable only for some members of a society, not for the society as a whole.

These differences may be illustrated by a description of what Opler has called the avoidance relationships in Apache society. Among these people, a man when he marries must establish certain well-defined relations with his wife's relatives. There are three possible relationships: (1) total avoidance, which means that the man and his relatives-in-law may not have any direct contact whatsoever; (2) partial avoidance, where direct contact may occur but only along strictly formal lines; and (3) no avoidance, where the man and his relatives-in-law ignore all special usages.

Total avoidance is obligatory between a man and his wife's mother, father, mother's mother, and mother's father. "With these persons," writes Opler, "[total] avoidance is the unalterable rule and no choice is per-

[6] Morris E. Opler, *An Apache Life-Way* (Chicago: copyright 1941 by University of Chicago Press), pp. 409–410.

[7] *Ibid.*, p. 409.

mitted." [8] The sisters of the wife's mother, however, do have a choice between total and partial avoidance. Total avoidance is preferred, especially when the relative concerned takes a lively interest in her niece. Partial avoidance, on the other hand, is not so highly valued and would only be chosen by an aunt who had little contact with her niece and so was not directly concerned with her marriage.

Male relatives of the wife, excepting those for whom total avoidance is obligatory, may regard all three procedures as nearly alike in value; their typical pattern is partial avoidance. Most female cousins of the wife, and sometimes her sisters as well, regard the three possible procedures as alternatives and may choose the one most in keeping with their convenience.

Restricted ideal patterns, which are not illustrated above, are frequent in the culture of the Quechua Indians of the pre-Conquest period. In this society, as we have seen, a sharp distinction was made between the ruling Inca and Curaca classes and the common people (the *purics* or householders) over whom they exercised sovereignty. This distinction was marked by many ways of behaving which were proper to the rulers alone. Members of the ruling classes wore clothing made of fine fabrics, the use of which was prohibited to the *purics*. Only an Inca and a Curaca could be army officers, government officials, church dignitaries, and *amautas,* wise men or teachers; the *puric* was limited to the humbler occupations of farming, herding, mining, army service in the ranks, and service as a laborer. An Inca or a Curaca could have more than one wife and take concubines as well from the *puric* class, but a *puric* was restricted to one wife who must also be a *puric*. All of these and many other patterns were restricted, and functioned in this society to mark the boundary between the rulers and the ruled.

Ideal patterns, to summarize our discussion in this section, represent ways of behaving held to be desirable by the members of a given society. They are the imperatives (musts) and optatives (shoulds) of a particular culture, and they differ to a greater or less extent from behavioral patterns, derived from the observation of what people actually do in meeting particular situations.

7. THE INTEGRATION OF CULTURE: BENEDICT'S ANALYSIS

When we examine and compare the ways of behaving which form the content of a given culture, it soon becomes evident that these hang to-

8 *Ibid.,* p. 164.

gether in some distinctive fashion or fashions; they are not mere random assemblages of traits or patterns. In recent years a number of anthropologists have attacked this problem, and we shall attempt in this and the following section to summarize the more important results of their researches.

The late Professor Ruth Benedict was one of the first to attempt a solution of the problem of describing a culture in terms of a unified and integrated plan. In her *Patterns of Culture* she states:

A culture, like an individual, is a more or less consistent pattern of thought and action. Within each culture there come into being characteristic purposes not necessarily shared by other types of society. In obedience to these purposes, each people further and further consolidates its experience, and in proportion to the urgency of these drives the heterogeneous items of behavior take more and more congruous shape.[9]

Cultures which achieve this subordination of all or most of their heterogeneous ways of behaving to "characteristic purposes" or "drives" are said, in Benedict's terms, to be integrated. She adds, however, that "some cultures . . . fail of such integration, and about many others we know too little to understand the motives that activate them. But cultures at every level of complexity, even the simplest, have achieved it." [10]

Benedict illustrates her concept of cultural integration by reference to the Zuñi and neighboring Pueblo Indians of New Mexico. These cultures are integrated, she says, about an Apollonian ideal, described, in contrast with its opposite, the Dionysian, in the following terms:

The basic contrast between the Pueblos and the other cultures of North America is the contrast that is named and described by Nietzsche in his studies of Greek tragedy. He discusses two diametrically opposed ways of arriving at the values of existence. The Dionysian pursues them through "the annihilation of the ordinary bounds and limits of existence"; he seeks to attain in his most valued moments escape from the boundaries imposed upon him by his five senses, to break through to another order of experience. The desire of the Dionysian, in personal experience or in ritual, is to press through it toward a certain psychological state, to achieve success. The closest analogy to the emotions he seeks is drunkenness, and he values the illuminations of frenzy. With Blake, he believes "the path of excess leads to the palace of wisdom." The Apollonian distrusts all this, and has often little idea of the nature of such experiences. He finds means to outlaw them from his conscious life. He "knows

[9] Ruth Benedict, *Patterns of Culture* (Boston and London: copyright 1934 by Houghton-Mifflin Co. and Routledge and Kegan Paul Ltd.), p. 46.
[10] *Ibid.,* p. 48.

but one law, measure in the Hellenic sense." He keeps the middle of the road, stays within the known map, does not meddle with disruptive psychological states.[11]

In contrast to their neighbors, predominantly Dionysian in their cultures, the southern Pueblo cultures are Apollonian, according to Benedict. The search for supernatural power, for example, is common to both the Pueblos and their neighbors. But while the non-Pueblo peoples achieve such power through vision experiences induced by fasting, self-torture, the use of drugs and alcohol, and similar excesses, the Pueblo peoples avoid visions and gain access to supernatural power by membership in a cult. Such membership is purchased and requires only that the candidate learn by rote an extensive ritual. He is not to indulge in excess in preparing himself for membership, in his efforts to be promoted to higher grades, or in any aspect of the practice of his religious rites. Benedict notes further that, though the objective details of the search for religious experience (the vision quest) are much the same among the Pueblo Indians as among their Dionysian neighbors, the Pueblo experience explicitly avoids Dionysian excess and becomes a mechanical, Apollonian routine.

In this way, then, the Pueblos tend to bend all the miscellaneous patterns of their culture to a single summative principle or configuration, defined by Benedict as Apollonian. Not all cultures achieve the same high degree of integration; some, indeed, are set apart by the very fact that no single integrative principle may be discovered for them. In brief, integration to Benedict is a matter of degree, and may presumably be estimated in a given culture by the extent to which a single dominant drive is evident in the multitudinous ways of behaving which form its content.

8. THE INTEGRATION OF CULTURE: THEMES

As Morris Opler has pointed out, "there are a number of gaps and inadequacies in Dr. Benedict's position which have never been properly explained." [12] He notes that many cultures, perhaps even a majority, appear to be unintegrated in Benedict's terms; integration, in the sense of a whole culture dominated by a central summative principle, appears to occur with relative rareness. If Benedict's concept is to be useful in the description and comparison of cultures, it should be more broadly applicable. In Opler's words:

---

[11] *Ibid.*, pp. 78–79.

[12] "Some Recently Developed Concepts Relating to Culture," *Southwestern Journal of Anthropology*, 4, 107–122 (1948), p. 111.

To many it appears that the dominant drive-configuration analysis is at best applicable to selected cultures rather than to culture as such and that it is therefore not the even-handed conceptual tool for which we are seeking. And whenever a theory can cope with only a part of the evidence, it usually is found to be inadequate, and is finally either rejected or becomes absorbed in some more comprehensive viewpoint.[13]

Opler has himself proposed a theory of culture which he believes meets the objections cited. He suggests that the content of a culture may best be organized about a number of summative principles, called themes. A theme is defined as "a postulate or position, declared or implied, and usually controlling behavior or stimulating activity, which is tacitly approved or openly promoted in a society." [14] A theme is known by its expressions, these corresponding to what we have called the patterns of a culture. Themes are therefore abstracted from the ways of behaving which prevail in a society or, in Opler's terms, a theme "is identified by and directly related to behavior by its expressions, 'the activities, prohibition of activities, or references which result from the acceptance or affirmation of a theme in a society.' " [15]

An excellent example of a theme and its expressions in a culture is given by Opler in a recent article. Describing Chiricahua Apache culture, Opler says that one of its themes may be stated as follows: "men are physically, mentally, and morally superior to women." [16] Evidence for this theme, according to Opler, is found in the following widely different patterns of Chiricahua Apache culture:

. . . predictions concerning an unborn child are guided by this theme, for, if a fetus has "lots of life," it is assumed that the child will be a boy. The value given to prenatal movement derives from the fact that, in this society, success depends largely on activity and participation. There are many other clues. Chiricahua women are charged with being more excitable and unstable than men and more likely to say or do things that cause domestic or inter-family strife. They also are credited with less will power than men and are said to be more easily "tempted," in regard both to sorcery and to irregular sexual conduct. It must be remembered that this is not the judgment of the men only but an appraisal which the Chiricahua women accept and help to perpetuate.

There are constant reminders of the same theme in political life and in social forms. The tribal leaders are all men, and all posts of importance are formally

[13] *Ibid.,* p. 112.
[14] *Ibid.,* p. 120.
[15] *Ibid.,* p. 120.
[16] Morris E. Opler, "Themes as Dynamic Forces in Culture," *American Journal of Sociology,* LI, No. 3 (copyright November, 1945, by University of Chicago Press), 192–206, p. 199.

assumed by men. In council it is ordinarily the oldest active male who speaks for the extended family. In social etiquette the same deference to men is evident. Men must be allowed to precede women along paths. At feasts a special place is arranged for the men; the women eat wherever they can find a place. If guests are present, the male guests are served first and the women of the entertaining household last of all.

In ceremonial life, too, women suffer some restrictions. For instance, they may not use the sweat lodge or impersonate important supernaturals called "mountain spirits." A menstruating woman is particularly dangerous. Her condition may endanger the health of men with whom she comes in contact at this time and may even "spoil" good male horses. While the thoughtless acts of individual men can bring misfortune, males are not contaminating because of sex-linked natural functions.

Even recreation is not free from the influence of this theme. Thus, women are not expected to sing social dance songs, and the grounds of the hoop and pole game, where men gather daily, are strictly forbidden to women under the supernatural sanction of blindness. Women have no comparable sanctuary.[17]

Unlike Benedict's dominant drives, themes are not necessarily all-pervasive. Though in some cultures (such as that of the Zuñi) it is conceivable that a single theme may govern the whole of the culture, this is the exception, not the rule. In most instances cultures exhibit many themes. Some of these may reinforce each other, but many will serve as limiting factors. To Opler integration in culture consists of a balancing and interplay of themes, not the subordination of all the patterns in a culture to a single summative principle.

To illustrate the interplay of themes in a culture, Opler considers the Chiricahua theme expressed in the words: "Long life and old age are important goals." The significance and importance of this theme are evidenced by its many expressions running through all of Chiricahua culture. In customs relating to childbirth, in the ceremonies performed when the child begins to walk and is given his first haircut, in the elaborate puberty rite conducted for girls, and in the many patterns of deference shown by young people to the old, there are endless repetitions of the theme of long life.

But this concern for long life and the resulting respect paid to the old has not given the aged anything like a complete control over Chiricahua society. Leaders for the most part are middle-aged men of experience and wisdom who are still physically fit and active. Here, then, enters a second theme, "validation by participation," which severely limits and balances the first. Opler points out:

[17] *Ibid.*, p. 199.

As long as a man is physically fit and active, age is an asset, for it denotes experience and wisdom in addition to the other virtues. But when a leader can no longer keep pace with the strenuous young man, his years and knowledge do not prevent his retirement. [18]

It is this relation of the theme of old age to the requirement of "validation by participation" that shapes that part of Chiricahua culture which governs these people's political and social behavior.

9. EXPLICIT AND IMPLICIT CULTURE

To review what we have now discovered of culture, it may be helpful to summarize the salient points so far discussed and illustrated.

(1) Culture, in its most general application, refers to the ways of life common at any one time to all mankind. It applies specifically to ways of behaving characteristic of a group of more or less interacting societies (e.g., the Plains Indians), to the patterns of living peculiar to a given society (e.g., the Chiricahua Apaches), or to special ways of behaving prevailing in a segment of a large and complexly organized society (e.g., regional variations as between South, North, and West in the United States or class variations as between Inca, Curaca, and common people of the ancient Indian empire of Peru).

(2) Culture is an abstraction from behavior which is not to be confused with individual actions or with so-called "material culture," the artifacts resulting from certain kinds of behavior.

(3) Ways of behaving abstracted directly from observation of behavior in a given society are called patterns. Patterns may be ideal (the "musts" and "shoulds" of behavior) or behavioral, summary statements of how individuals in a given society react to particular situations. In general the anthropologist is concerned for the most part with ideal patterns. Some anthropologists have maintained that behavioral patterns are irrelevant to a science of culture, while others feel that the difference between ideal and behavioral patterns is of little significance and that "when precept [ideal patterns] and activity [behavioral patterns] draw too far apart, a modification of one or the other is likely to take place to close up the gap." [19]

(4) To most modern anthropologists, the patterns of a culture are held together or integrated in terms of abstractions variously known as

---

[18] *Ibid.,* p. 204.
[19] Morris E. Opler, "Some Recently Developed Concepts Relating to Culture," *Southwestern Journal of Anthropology,* p. 116.

themes, configurations, drives, or postulates. Kluckhohn summarizes this view in the following words:

> Every group's way of life, then, is a structure—not a haphazard collection of all the different physically possible and functionally effective patterns of belief and action. A culture is an interdependent system based on linked premises and categories whose influence is greater, rather than less, because they are seldom put in words.[20]

Kluckhohn and others have noted a point we have not yet discussed, namely, that the patterns and themes which make up a culture range from an extreme called explicit or overt to the opposite extreme of implicit or covert. Patterns in general belong to explicit culture in that they are readily abstracted from behavior and are more or less easily verbalized by the participants in the culture. Themes, on the other hand, tend to be implicit in behavior; they must usually be dissected out by an intensive analysis of the overt patterns which carry or express them. Participants in a culture often find themes difficult to verbalize; the themes tend to operate very largely on the unconscious level.

Though the distinction between overt and covert culture is perhaps of little theoretical significance, it does serve to call attention to the fact that much of our daily activity is controlled by patterns and themes of which we are only dimly aware, if indeed we know of them at all. This unconscious nature of much of culturally governed behavior has its advantages; much of the routine of daily living is performed without thinking about it at all. It is because normal human beings are so thoroughly trained in the patterns of their culture that they are free to devote their conscious thinking to new situations and problems. It is hardly likely that men would have moved so far toward an understanding of the world about them had they not developed as culture-bearing animals.

But the unconscious nature of much of cultural behavior has disadvantages as well. The better adjusted we become to our native culture, the less can we adapt to one which is new and strange, or even understand the behavior of peoples whose cultures diverge widely from our own. The need for intercultural understandings in the world of today underscores this point and indicates one of the many ways in which the comparative science of culture, even in its present undeveloped state, can contribute to the solution of modern problems.

[20] Clyde Kluckhohn, *Mirror for Man* (New York: McGraw-Hill Book Co., 1949), p. 35.

10. *CULTURE IS LEARNED*

It will be recalled that in an earlier section (§ 2) we accepted Kluck-hohn's definition of culture as all the *"historically created* designs for living . . . which exist at any given time as potential guides for the behavior of men" and also his definition of a culture as "an *historically derived* system of explicit and implicit designs for living, which tend to be shared by all or specifically designated members of a group" (italics added). So far, however, we have paid little attention to the fact that culture and specific cultures are historically created or historically derived, a fact about culture that deserves further attention.

As we have emphasized before (see Chapter 7), cultures are learned; they are not, like racial characteristics, genetically transmitted. Differences in culture do not arise because different peoples have different inherited capabilities, but because they are brought up differently. We learn to speak, think, and act the way we do because of our daily associations, and when these change, our habits of speaking, thinking, and acting also change. Children have no culturally based ways of behaving at birth, they only acquire these as they grow up and as the result of a long and complicated process of learning.

We must not let the fact that cultures are learned lead us to the conclusion that all learned behavior is culture. Animals also learn, but few, if any, anthropologists would credit them with culture. The difference between the learned behavior of animals and the culturally based behavior of man is an important one, not only for an understanding of the genesis of culture but as well for an appreciation of the nature of culture.

Experiments with chimpanzees seem to demonstrate that their mental powers, by which we mean such operations as memory, imagination, and reasoning, are in many respects very similar to those of human beings. Chimpanzees, when confronted with a problem, appear to solve it by much the same processes we use; they differ only in that the problems they are capable of solving are far simpler than those which men must handle in the course of their everyday affairs.

To illustrate the problem-solving abilities of the chimpanzee, let us review an experiment performed by Dr. Wolfe of Yale University. Dr. Wolfe constructed a number of slot machines in which chips could be inserted to obtain food. The chimpanzees learned to operate the machines by imitating their human instructors and each other. Once the association between chips, machines, and food was firmly established, the animals worked and fought as hard to get chips as they did to get food. When chips (including some that would not operate the machines) were scattered about their cages, where there were no machines, the chimpanzees carefully picked them up, rejected those that were valueless, and preserved the rest until they had a chance to use them.

The Kelloggs performed an even more interesting and instructive experiment. To reveal the essential differences (and similarities) in learning behavior between men and animals, they secured a very young chimpanzee of the same age as their own child and reared the two together. As much as possible the two infants were treated in the same way. They played together, ate together, and they were given the same food, clothing, and instruction. Gua, the chimpanzee, learned quite as readily as the child. In some respects, because of her more rapid physical maturation, she learned more quickly, as, for example, in games requiring strength, agility, and muscular coordination.

The noises made by the two infants were also similar; both employed essentially the same sounds to indicate hunger, thirst, physical discomfort, and a desire for toys, utensils, and other objects. But when the child began to acquire language, the chimpanzee was soon outdistanced. With the acquisition of language, the child began to participate in his human environment in a way that was forever barred to the chimpanzee. The child began learning ways of behaving that could not be taught to the languageless animal.

We may summarize the results of these and many other similar experiments as follows: animals, at least those of the so-called higher orders, are capable of some kinds of learning. Common observation of domestic animals confirms this conclusion. Dogs, cats, and horses learn from both their human caretakers and from each other. Animals may even respond to human language; a dog, for example, can be taught to respond appropriately to a large number of spoken commands. Gua not only responded to oral commands in much the same way as the preverbal child, but also used sounds to communicate with humans.

Despite these similarities between animal and human learning, it still remains true that no animal species has ever developed a culture. Animal tool-using, for example, is nonprogressive; animals learn to use and even to make simple tools, but no animal society develops its techniques beyond a very rudimentary level. Research into the prehistory of men and animals reveals that apes have existed as long or longer than man (see Chapter 5). But where man's techniques have progressed from an early use of crude stone tools to the complex machine technology of today, apes still remain on the crudest levels, far below even the primitive hominids of the Paleolithic. Similarly, though many animals can be taught to respond to the spoken word, and though in some animal societies sounds are employed to stimulate action by the group as a whole, there is no animal society in which speech has developed to the point where one individual can communicate his own private experiences to another. In even the most primitive of human societies, men regularly not only stimulate group action by spoken words, but also share each other's experiences by means of language and even create new experiences in myth, legend, and fiction for their amusement and instruction.

The reason for these differences lies in the fact that the origin and development of culture are dependent upon the creation and use of symbols. Leslie White expresses it in the following words:

All human behavior originates in the use of symbols. It was the symbol which transformed our anthropoid ancestors into man and made them human. All civilizations have been generated, and are perpetuated, only by the use of symbols. It is the symbol which transforms an infant of *Homo sapiens* into a human being . . . All human behavior consists of, or is dependent upon, the use of symbols. Human behavior is symbolic behavior; symbolic behavior is human behavior.[21]

11. THE ROLE OF SYMBOLIC BEHAVIOR IN CULTURE

To understand the role played by symbolic behavior in the origin and perpetuation of culture, it is necessary to be clear about the nature of symbols. Briefly, a symbol may be defined as a physical phenomenon (such as, for example, an object, artifact, or sequence of sounds) which has a meaning bestowed upon it by those who use it. This meaning is arbitrary in the sense that it has no necessary relation to the physical properties of the phenomenon which bears it. To take a simple example, there is no necessary relation between the physical properties of a cross and the symbolic values attached to it by Christians. A non-Christian unaware of these symbolic values cannot discover them by an examination of the cross itself; he must be told of them or infer them from observing the behavior of Christians toward the cross.

In the same way the meaning of a linguistic symbol such as the word "horse" is in no physical sense linked to the sequence of sounds which make up the word. Put another way, there is nothing horselike about the word "horse," nor houselike about the word "house." The meanings of words are bestowed upon them by the society which uses them; a stranger to

---

[21] "The Symbol: The Origin and Basis of Human Behavior," *Philosophy of Science,* 7 (1940), p. 451.

that society must be told what the words mean or infer their meaning from a careful observation of the situations in which they are used.

Once a symbol comes into being it may be used as a sign. The meaning of a sign may be determined by observation of the contexts in which it is used. Thus, a person who knows no English may in time and by dint of careful observation perceive the relation between words like "horse" and "house" and the physical phenomena for which they stand. In Wolfe's experiments described earlier, the chimpanzees were taught to use chips to obtain food from a machine. As a result of this teaching, the chips became signs of food to the apes to the extent that they struggled to obtain chips just as they struggled to obtain food. But neither the non-English speaker nor the apes bestowed upon words and chips, respectively, the meanings they possessed; they simply learned that these meanings existed.

In the same way, Gua the chimpanzee learned that a relationship existed between the noises she made and certain desirable attentions from the humans about her. One noise brought food, another relief from discomfort or pain, and still another brought comforting or affection. Again we emphasize that Gua did not bestow these values upon her "words"; she merely learned that they existed.

Men symbolize, that is, bestow meanings upon physical phenomena, in almost every aspect of their daily lives. The color "red" may stand for danger or for the stop signal at an intersection, or it may be the symbol of a political party. An elephant symbolizes the Republican party in the United States, a donkey the Democratic party. A motion-picture studio uses a lion as its symbol or trademark, and many animals have been employed to symbolize football or baseball teams. Mathematics is replete with symbolizing, and the same is true of many other sciences and disciplines.

But animals never learn to symbolize. Their learning is confined to the manipulation of signs, to perceiving through experience that values bestowed by someone else (usually their human caretakers) belong to physical phenomena of one kind or another. This difference between men and animals is a difference of kind, not of degree. Symbolizing is either learned or not learned; there is no intermediate stage between learning to use signs and acquiring the technique of symbolizing. Once the Kellogg child learned to symbolize, he rapidly outdistanced Gua both in the amount he learned and in the complexity of the problems he became able to solve.

There are two principal ways in which symbolizing is necessary to the development of culture. Symbolizing enables man to transmit his learning more effectively than the animals, and symbolizing makes it possible for man to bridge the gap between discrete physical experiences and so make his experiencing continuous.

Animals learn, as we have noted, by direct experience and by observing and imitating the actions of others. Wolfe's chimpanzees learned to use the machines by imitating their human associates and each other. Koehler cites many instances of apes learning by a process of trial and error, and he notes as well that this process is speeded if the ape has the opportunity of observing another in the solution of the same problem. But men learn, not only by experience, observation, and imitation, but also by having an experience recreated for them in symbols, usually linguistic symbols. Once a human being has solved a problem or perfected a procedure, he can summarize it in words, omitting all his false starts and fumblings, for the benefit of others. In this fashion all the experiences and observations made by one member of a society can eventually be made available to the rest.

But this is not all. Language and other techniques of symbolizing also enable men to summarize and transmit their learned ways of behaving to each new generation. The human child is not limited to procedures acquired through his own experiences and observations; he may receive, as soon as he commands the symbols of his society, more or less continuous instruction in the accumulated ways of behaving of the entire society. The results of years of experience and observation, made by many generations of men, are given to him in a relatively short time, a time far shorter than it would take to acquire all this through individual experience and observation. The young human begins his adult life in possession of much of the knowledge accumulated by the society in which he lives and ready to add to its store.

The creation and use of symbols also enable man to make his experiences continuous. Physical experiences, for both men and animals, are necessarily discontinuous. Each has a beginning and an end, and a longer or shorter time span separates one experience from another. Most experimenters agree that apes are not concerned with problems which are no longer before them; once a problem situation has been removed, it is forgotten until its physical reappearance stirs memories of the previous occurrence. Chimpanzees, for example, are apparently much concerned if one of their number is sick or very much hurt. But when the ailing animal is moved out of sight and hearing, their concern disappears, not to return unless and until they are again in the presence of the sick animal.

Wolfe's apes, to be sure, did react to the chips even when the machines were not present. But this means only that the chips, which the apes had learned to connect as signs with the machines and food, revived their memories of the machines and their function. There is no evidence that Wolfe's apes were "thinking" about either machines or chips when both of these were physically absent.

This is not true of man. His habit of symbolizing permits him to keep a problem in mind even though it is not physically before him. We know this because human beings discuss their problems with others and with themselves, recreating the problem in words and testing possible solutions in conversation or imagination. In brief, though man's physical experiences, like those of the animals, are discrete and discontinuous, he achieves continuity of experience and learning by symbolizing his experiences in words, by means of written records, and by numerous other devices of the same order.

Man accordingly not only learns more rapidly than the animals, but he can also bring to bear upon a particular problem all the procedures acquired from similar or analogous experiences he has undergone or has heard of in the past. It is this faculty that enables man to solve increasingly more complex problems. An ape's ceiling of achievement is limited by the fact that it depends essentially on procedures derived from his own experiences and observations. Man's ceiling is much higher, since he has available as well ways of behaving accumulated from the experiences and observations of his associates present and past. A complicated device like an automobile motor is not the achievement of one man; it is the result of separate inventions and discoveries accumulated by many individuals through several generations.

To summarize: culture consists not only of learned ways of behaving; it is a body of learned ways of behaving accumulated by many men over many generations. Accumulation of learned ways of behaving is made possible by the creation and use of symbols; without this facility, learning is static or nonprogressive as among the animals. As far as we know, man is the only animal capable of symbolic behavior; other animals learn to use signs but they do not create symbols. Culture, in essence an accumulation of learned patterns of behavior originated and developed by means of symbols, came into being when man learned to symbolize.

12. SUMMARY

In this chapter we have introduced the reader to the concept of culture and have explored the more important of the many ramifications of this concept. Culture, as we have seen, is a complex network of patterns and themes which represents in general the pooled learning of mankind. Because man symbolizes and may therefore transmit culture, this pooled learning includes not only what is presently known but also much of what has been discovered by the men of the past. Separate cultures represent special instances of accumulated and learned ways of behaving.

In the chapters that follow we shall review briefly the content of culture in its several substantive divisions. The categories of culture recognized for this purpose are those commonly used by anthropologists, and may roughly be defined as follows.

(1) Technology: the ways of behaving by means of which men utilize natural resources for the purpose of securing food, and to manufacture tools, weapons, clothing, shelters, containers, and the many other artifacts necessary to their ways of life. See Chapters 9–11.

(2) Economics: the patterns of behaving and resultant organization of society relative to the production, distribution, and consumption of goods and services. See Chapter 12.

(3) Social organization: the ways of behaving and resultant organization of society relative to the maintenance of orderly relations between individuals and groups within a society and between a society or its segments and other societies. See Chapters 13–15.

(4) Religion: the patterns of behaving relative to man's relations to unknown forces and the resultant systems of belief and ritual in respect to such forces. See Chapter 16.

(5) Symbolic culture: systems of symbols and the techniques of using them relative to the acquisition, ordering, and transferring of knowledge. Language is clearly the most important of these systems of symbols, but there are also others, such as the arts (e.g., drama, painting, music, and literature). See Chapters 17–18.

In later chapters, after we have gained some knowledge of the variety of cultural content, we shall discuss how the individual acquires his culture (Chapter 19), problems of cultural change (Chapters 20, 21), and the possible applications of our knowledge of culture (Chapter 21).

COLLATERAL READING

Benedict, Ruth. *Patterns of Culture.* New York: Houghton-Mifflin Co., 1934.

Kluckhohn, Clyde. "Patterning as Exemplified in Navaho Culture," *Language, Culture and Personality,* ed. Leslie Spier. Menasha, Wisconsin: the Sapir Memorial Publication Fund, 1941. Pp. 109–130.

Kluckhohn, Clyde, and Kelly, W. "The Concept of Culture," *The Science of Man in the World Crisis,* ed. Ralph Linton. New York: Columbia University Press, 1945. Pp. 78–106.

Opler, Morris E. "Themes as Dynamic Forces in Culture," *American Journal of Sociology,* LI, 198–206, 1945.

———. "An Application of the Theory of Themes in Culture," *Journal of the Washington Academy of Sciences,* 36, 137–166, 1946.

———. "Some Recently Developed Concepts Relating to Culture," *Southwestern Journal of Anthropology,* 4, 107–122, 1948.

White, Leslie A. *The Science of Culture.* New York: Farrar, Straus and Co., 1949. Part I.

ETHNOGRAPHIC REFERENCES

Chiricahua Apaches: Opler, 1937, 1941.
Navahos: Kluckhohn and Leighton, 1946.
Plains (Crows): Lowie, 1935.
Quechuas (Incas): Means, 1931; Murdock, 1935, Chap. XIV.

Chapter 9

TOOLS AND CONTAINERS

1. TECHNOLOGY AND MATERIAL CULTURE

With this chapter we begin the study of technology and material culture, two aspects of culture which are often confused. By a technology, we refer to the sum total of the techniques possessed by the members of a society, that is, the totality of their ways of behaving in respect to collecting raw materials from the environment and processing these to make tools, containers, foods, clothing, shelters, means of transportation, and many other material necessities. Material culture, on the other hand, is applied to the sum of the artifacts (manufactured goods and devices of all sorts) which are the result of a technology. Such artifacts include tools and containers of all kinds, processed foods, shelters (from rude huts to elaborate temples), items of clothing, and any other material object or device used by members of the society.

In a strict sense, according to our definition of culture as a set of patterns and themes for the guidance of human behavior, material culture is of course not a part of culture at all but only a result or product of it. Nevertheless, these results of technology are important to the anthropologist, for it is by the careful study of material culture, as well as by the study of human activities, that we may abstract the patterns and themes that make up culture itself.

Technology, it is evident, is a cultural screen that man sets up between himself and his environment. Where most other animals simply utilize the natural environment as such for food and shelter, changing it relatively

229

little in the process, man alters or transforms his environment to a greater or less extent. He makes tools of wood, stone, and metals to increase his efficiency in working the environment, he builds shelters and manufactures clothing to protect himself from the weather, and he not infrequently causes food plants to grow or keeps food animals under domestication, the better to supply his needs. As a result, though men, like the apes, are by nature tropical animals, man is able to live almost anywhere on the earth's surface. Human societies are found in the Arctic, in deserts and semiarid regions, in tropical rain forests, in grasslands and subarctic tundras, and the great temperate zones of the world. In contrast, man's closest relatives anatomically, the anthropoid apes, are restricted to the moist tropical regions of Africa and Asia; lacking man's technologies, they cannot survive elsewhere.

Peoples differ widely in the complexity and efficiency of their technologies, and hence in the degree to which they may fully exploit environmental resources. A society with a very simple technology and lacking any means of transportation save human carriers is confined to the resources of a single area, and unless this is unusually rich in easily obtained food plants and animals, the society may achieve only a bare subsistence. There are many examples of such societies, even in recent times—the desert-dwelling Indians of Nevada and southeastern California, the Eskimos of the Arctic coasts, and the Pygmies, tropical forest-dwellers of Africa.

Then, too, many societies are restricted by their technology to a single use of their environment, even though other uses are possible. The Plains Indians of North America, for example, obtained much of their food from the buffalo, which also supplied skins for clothing and shelters and numerous other needs. Lacking efficient devices for cultivation, the Plains Indians made practically no use of the agricultural potentialities of their environment, which today is one of the best farming areas in the world.

Societies with more advanced technologies exploit their environments more fully—the Iroquois Indians, for example, practiced hunting, fishing, food-collecting, and horticulture. In our own western European societies, technological advance permits an almost exhaustive exploitation of environmental resources. Further, efficient transportation has made it possible for us to use the resources of many environments, so that even some of our common foods are imported regularly from widely diverse regions. Conversely, modern technology and transportation enable men to live comfortably even in waterless deserts, or, as Admiral Byrd and his men did, on the Antarctic continent, an area which, in the winter, is almost totally devoid of food resources.

If we examine all human societies, we find that certain broad categories of technology are universal. All men have some techniques for the gathering or production of food, for the building of shelters and the making of clothing, for manufacturing tools and containers, and for transporting their belongings. This does not mean of course that these categories are equally developed in all societies. Food-gathering and production include techniques as disparate as berry-picking and modern agriculture, the latter a series of highly complicated, machine-aided techniques. Tool-making includes, not only the chipping of flint to make arrow- or spear-points, but also the intricate techniques of the modern machine shop. Building techniques show a similarly wide range, from the simplicity of constructing a lean-to to the complexity and multiplicity of techniques involved in the construction of a skyscraper. In short, technologies vary obviously from one culture to another; and the range of variation is great, from the crude, stone-tool technology of the Australian aborigine to the complex, industrial technology of modern Europe and America. In this and succeeding chapters, we shall examine the broad categories we have named in some detail, beginning with tools and containers. In each case we shall examine both the character of the objects produced and used (the material culture) and the means employed in producing or using the artifacts (the technology).

2. CUTTING TOOLS: CLASSIFICATION AND USE

A tool, broadly defined, is any material device employed by man to transform raw materials into a more usable form or to construct other and more elaborate tools. In this chapter, however, we shall confine ourselves very largely to cutting tools, such as knives, scrapers, drills, and choppers, to mention only the simpler types. Other tools will be treated later, in relation to the special techniques in which they are employed.

Cutting tools assume primary importance over others in all technologies. This is because the efficiency with which a society exploits its environment and provides other tools and devices depends very largely on the kinds of cutting tools it makes and uses. It is said today that the industrial potential of a modern nation (that is, its ability to produce goods and services) rests largely on its capacity to produce machine tools, the more elaborate power-driven cutting tools of our society. Similarly it appears that the technological development of simpler societies may in large part be measured in terms of the cutting tools they possess. The archeologist, for example, not infrequently divides prehistory into periods determined for the most part by the kinds of cutting tools used. Thus in the Old World, we note three broad periods of cultural development: the Paleolithic (or

Old Stone Age), in which cutting tools were chipped from flint and other similar materials; the Neolithic (or New Stone Age), in which ground or polished stone tools were added to the earlier chipped implements; and the Metal Ages, in which first bronze and later iron came to be used in the manufacture of cutting tools. (See Chart XII, p. 269.)

Cutting tools may be classified in three major ways: by their function or use, by the materials of which they are made, and by the techniques used to manufacture them. Other classifications, by shape, size, and other criteria, are also used in special researches but may be ignored in this general discussion.

In terms of their function or use, we may distinguish the following broad categories of cutting tools: knives, choppers, chisels or gravers, scrapers, and borers. (Points might also be added, though these find their chief use in weapons such as arrows, spears, and the like.) Knives, tools having at least one sharpened edge, are used by all peoples to cut or sever softer materials by drawing the sharp edge across the material to be cut, by whittling away small bits, or by splitting the material. Choppers—such as axes and adzes—have also a sharpened cutting edge, but are both heavier and more bulky than knives. Cuts are made by striking the heavy chopper forcefully against the material to be severed—as when a woodsman chops down a tree or a carpenter smooths the rough surface of a beam or plank with an adze.

Chisels and gravers are generally long, slender tools with a sharp cutting edge at one end. Cuts are made by exerting pressure on the tool, and so gouging out small bits of material. Scrapers, like knives, have a long cutting edge, but this is designed, not to sever materials but rather to reduce uniformly the surface of the material being worked. Scrapers are often used to prepare skins, or to smooth wood surfaces; in our own society, both planing and sanding machines illustrate the type. Borers are usually long and cylindrical tools with a sharp cutting edge about one end, or, in the more elaborate metal drill, extending spirally up the implement. Borers are used of course to produce holes or indentations in materials, usually by rotating the tool on the material while exerting pressure.

It does not follow from the above classification that single tool types found in a given society have but one function. In many societies, there may be only a few types of tools, each of which serves, more or less efficiently, in two or more functions. The Igorot of the Philippines, for example, often strikes the pointed butt of his head ax (primarily a weapon to chop off the heads of enemies) in the ground and uses the blade as a knife, just as we may sometimes use the point of a knife to drill a hole. In the early periods of the Paleolithic, it is probable that the chipped-flint hand ax (a

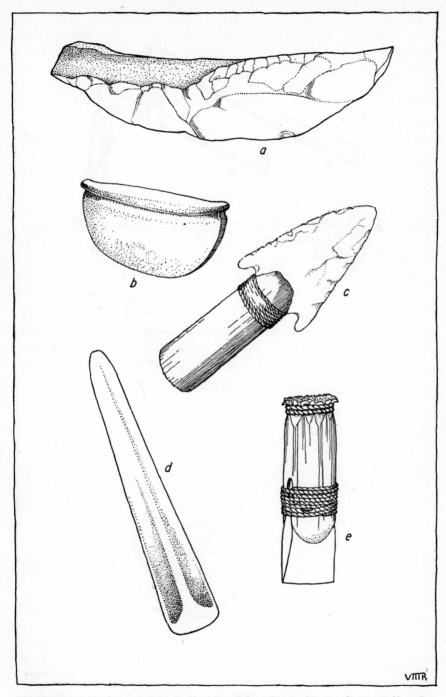

Fig. 9:1. (*a*) Curved flake knife, after Moorehead; (*b*) semilunar knife, after Willoughby; (*c*) hafted flint knife, after Willoughby; (*d*) copper chisel, after Moorehead; (*e*) chisel, after Goddard.

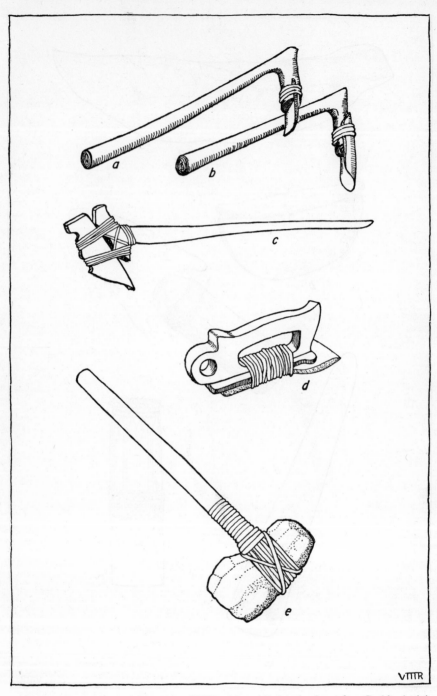

Fig. 9:2. (*a, b, c*) Adzes, after Willoughby; (*d*) hand adze, after Goddard; (*e*) ax, after Moorehead.

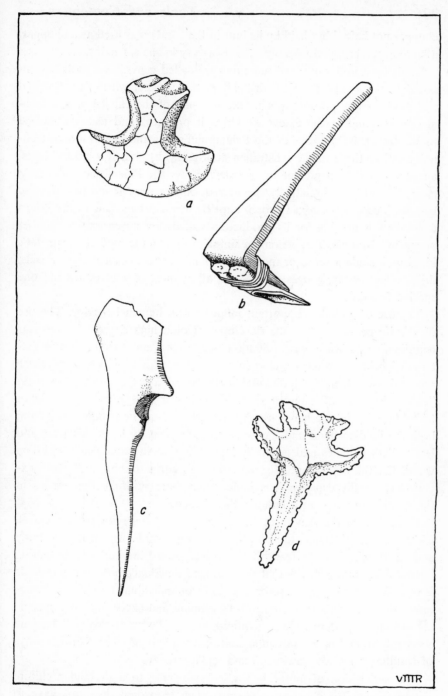

Fig. 9:3. (a) Chipped flake scraper, after Moorehead; (b) elk-rib scraper, after Holling; (c) bone awl, after James; (d) stone drill, after Moorehead.

chopper not hafted but held by its butt in the hand) was used as a chopper, a knife, a scraper, and possibly even as a very inefficient borer.

Tools used in a variety of functions are called generalized tools, as opposed to those, like the steel drill bit in our society, which are designed and used for one purpose alone. One measure of the efficiency of a technology is found in the extent to which it produces and uses specialized tools. Earlier technologies of the Paleolithic, and some more modern technologies like those of the Australian aborigines, use but few cutting tools, all generalized to a greater or less degree. As the Paleolithic came to a close, the number of relatively specialized tools increased, and this increase has continued, in western Europe, until the present day. Our own modern technology is notable for its production and use of an enormous number of specialized tools. To give only a simple example, the modern carpenter's kit must include a score or more tools: hammers of various sizes, chisels, drills, planes, saws, gouges, and so on, all or most of which have but one specific function.

The use of tools has important influences on human behavior. The use of a knife or ax requires the development of a high degree of muscular coordination as well as coordination with vision and touch. Special patterns of behavior often develop in connection with tool-using, and these are so imposed on the individual members of a society that they seem "natural" or "right." Thus, at an early age in our society, most males learn to hold a stick in one hand, usually the left, and cut or whittle away from both the holding hand and the body. Females usually learn this later and less well than males and generally have less skill in cutting and whittling wood. On the other hand, females, through early training and more experience, usually can handle a knife much more skillfully than males in the multifarious uses of a knife in the kitchen.

If we turn to the American Indian, a different behavior pattern exists. Most American Indians hold a stick with one hand away from the body and cut or whittle away from the hand but toward the body. Examination of tool-using shows clearly that the average individual's behavior with tools is not any inherent response or the result of individual thought or "common sense," but is rather the result of training and experience in a specific set of culture patterns. Once acquired, such patterns or "habits" become so deeply rooted in the muscular and nervous systems that all other ways of handling tools seem awkward and unnatural.

The acquisition of motor habits in conformity to a particular culture pattern makes for a certain efficiency. The individual does not have to think about the best way to hold each stick he whittles, and can begin work at once. To employ a useful term commonly employed in other connections, the individual acquires a "stereotype" regarding the use of his knife or other tool. The use of new tools designed to take advantage of existing motor habits is easily learned. On the other hand, the acquisition of such habits inhibits experimentation to discover better techniques. Even should an individual discover a better way of doing a job, his fellows with fixed habits are apt to think it queer, awkward, and unnatural, and so may ridicule the discoverer. New tools which involve marked changes in cultural patterns of tool-handling may find only slow acceptance in a society or even be rejected entirely.

Practical recognition that tool-using and other work techniques follow more or less rigid patterns is found in many so-called "time and motion" studies carried on by engineers. These studies, however, frequently ignore the factor of culture. Thus, while modern engineering schools sometimes employ physiologists to aid in designing machines best adapted to man's physiological capacities, they have not as yet studied the influence of the culture in the formation of motor and work habits. While this neglect probably makes little difference where designers and users of tools and machines are participants in the same culture, the cultural factor may certainly become significant when American- and European-designed machines are exported to peoples of non-Euro-American cultures.

Cutting tools may also be classified in terms of the materials of which they are made. The most important materials are stone and metals, but we find in addition, or as substitutes where stone is lacking, bone, shell, animals' teeth, and even special woods such as bamboo or ironwood. Stone is widely used among modern nonliterate peoples, and was used almost everywhere in the world during the Paleolithic and Neolithic. Metal cutting tools are found, in general, only among peoples with relatively advanced technologies, or among others who have trading contacts with them. Metal occurs late in human history; its use for cutting tools is probably no more than four or five thousand years old.

The manufacture of cutting tools requires a variety of techniques, too long and complex to summarize here. We shall describe the more important of these in the sections that follow.

3. STONE CUTTING TOOLS: PERCUSSION- AND PRESSURE-FLAKING

The manufacture of stone cutting tools involves four major techniques, as practiced by known prehistoric and modern peoples: percussion-flaking, pressure-flaking, striking blades from prepared cores, and grinding or polishing. Percussion-flaking, that is, the fracturing of stones by smashing them together or by striking them with a heavy hammer stone, is the earliest known technique, and appears at the very beginning of the Paleolithic. Later, about the mid-Paleolithic or before, pressure-flaking appears, the technique of removing small bits of stone by applying pressure with a pointed awl-like tool made of bone or antler tines. Blade tools are still later, toward the end of the Paleolithic, and are made by splitting slender prisms of stone from a prepared core. A pointed tool, similar to that used in pressure-flaking, is struck with a hammer stone in much the same way as a carpenter splits wood with a chisel and mallet. Grinding or polishing —the shaping of a stone into a tool by rubbing it with an abrasive-like sand or a harder, rougher stone—does not make its appearance until the end of the Paleolithic or shortly thereafter.

The first three of the techniques mentioned above require stones with definite lines of cleavage. All, or virtually all, such stones have a high silica content and hence a glasslike quality. The most desirable materials are flint and obsidian or volcanic glass. Modern stone-using peoples sometimes obtain, by trade, certain varieties of industrial glass which are excellent materials with which to chip cutting tools. Less desirable materials are cherts, quartzites, silicified shales and slates, and some relatively rare stones, such as jasper. Polishing and grinding require quite different materials—in general, fine-grained homogeneous stones without definite planes of cleavage, like granite, diorite, serpentine, jade, and many others. Stones suitable for ground cutting tools are far more abundantly distributed throughout the earth's surface than those which may be chipped or fractured.

The manufacture of even the crudest stone tools clearly requires a considerable knowledge of the environment (to find the appropriate materials) and of the properties of the materials to be cut and shaped. There is good evidence, both among modern peoples and those of prehistoric times, that men of simple cultures must often travel considerable distances and engage in extensive trade to obtain suitable stones for tools. Obsidian from the Rocky Mountains has been found in archeological deposits of the Ohio Valley, and the best flint deposits of France evidently served wide areas in Europe during the Paleolithic. Indeed, the distribution of flint tools in Paleolithic Europe, as compared with that of known sources of flint, indicates a widespread trade both in raw materials and in finished tools among those people of very simple cultures.

Tools made by percussion and pressure are both the oldest and the most widespread types, and probably are the first cutting tools to be made by man. It is possible, of course, that early man made crude and inefficient cutting tools of wood and other perishable materials before he used stone, but no evidence survives to this effect. In the few stoneless areas of the world, such as the Amazon basin, there are modern peoples who use bamboo, ironwood, shell, and animals' teeth for tools, but such technologies, if they existed in prehistoric times, have left no traces in the archeological record. As far as we can tell, then, man's first cutting tools were made of stone.

Percussion, as we have said, is a basic technique for fracturing and flaking stone, and is as well the oldest known technique. (See Figure 5:1, p. 121.) In very early times, man may have smashed nodules of flint by throwing them against other stones, and then selected as tools those of the fragments which possessed sharp edges or points. Later, it is evident, nodules of flint were dressed down by percussion-flaking to produce suitably edged and pointed tools. One example of this process is the so-called *coup de poing* or fist ax, found so commonly throughout western Europe in the Chellean and Acheulian periods of the Paleolithic. Sometimes, however, a large flake would be knocked off the nodule, to be used as a tool without further shaping or to be shaped with a hammer stone to produce a smaller and more specialized implement.

It is clear, however, that the percussion technique alone is a poor one for the making of any but rather large and crudely shaped stone tools. Hammering flint or other easily fractured stones is quite likely to break a nearly completed implement; the craftsman has little control over the lines of fracture. There is, in the remains of ancient flint-working places in western Europe, much evidence to the effect that Paleolithic craftsmen had numerous failures in chipping by percussion, and that even their successful implements were only crudely fashioned, with uneven cutting edges and inadequate points.

Pressure-flaking solved some of these problems and brought into existence much more refined, delicate, and specialized tools. (See Figure 5:2, p. 122.) In this technique, as we have said, small flakes are removed by pressing with a pointed implement against a particular place on the material being worked. Here, obviously, the craftsman has greater control over the fracturing of stone; knowing the lines of cleavage through experiment, he can take off as little or as much as he needs and at the same time place his fractures in precisely the right spot. Pressure-flaking did not, however, replace the percussion technique; it was added to it, not substituted for it. The Paleolithic craftsman still produced the major outlines of his tool by percussion-flaking, and then added the finer details by pressure-flaking. In particular, pressure-flaking was used to sharpen and straighten the edges of axes, knives, scrapers, and other tools, and sometimes as well to smooth the surfaces of these and other implements.

The introduction of pressure-flaking greatly increased both the number and variety of tools produced. It made smaller tools possible, for pressure-flaking could be applied on small flakes that would be broken if worked by percussion. With the increase in the variety of tools, there was also a greater specialization of function in the implements made. Where the older percussion-made core and flake tools were used for a number of purposes, the later pressure-flaked implements tended to be restricted, as knives, points, scrapers, or borers, to particular uses. Pressure-flaking, finally, also marked a decided advance in man's skill in handling stone, and one of the earliest clearly attested improvements in human technology.

Both percussion- and pressure-flaking are known to all stone-using peoples of historic times, and are used, as a matter of fact, even among peoples who also possess metals. Pressure-flaking became a highly developed art among the Solutrean peoples of western Europe, who made exceptionally fine implements, carefully pressure-flaked over the entire surface. Some of these implements—in particular the long, very thin laurel leaf spear-points—were apparently made as objects of art, for they are too fragile to have served as tools or weapons. Similarly, fine pressure-flaking is found in the Neolithic, after the beginning of stone-polishing, and among the early metal-using Egyptians.

Many American Indian groups also made unusual pressure-flaked implements. One of the oldest cultures of the New World produced the Folsom point, a dart or spearhead which is finely pressure-flaked all over its surface in a manner reminiscent of the European Solutrean. In addition, the Folsom point has two long, longitudinal grooves, one on each side, made by removing two long, slender flakes. Extraordinary skill was required to do this successfully. Of more recent Indian groups, the Mayas of Central America and the Indians of California, especially those around San Francisco Bay, were outstanding in their skill and the variety of implements produced. Unique among these implements are the enormous ceremonial blades made by the Yuroks of northern California and their neighbors.

4. BLADE TOOLS AND POLISHED STONE TOOLS

Though blade tools were apparently not made in Europe until the late or upper Paleolithic, it is probable, from recent finds in the Near East, that the technique was invented much earlier. (See Figure 5:3, p. 123.) In Europe, a suitable flint nodule was shaped by percussion and flattened at one end to provide a striking platform. Blades were then rapidly and easily split off from the prepared core by setting a pointed tool at the

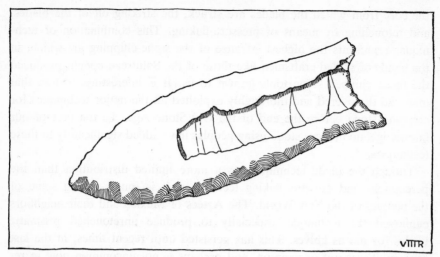

Fig. 9:4. Outline of Folsom point, emphasizing longitudinal grooving, after Fischel, Figgins.

proper place and angle and striking its base sharply with a hammer stone. The prismatic blades so produced had a straight or nearly straight cutting edge of great sharpness, and therefore required no retouching by means of pressure-flaking. So rapid and efficient was this technique of making blade tools that it was easier to produce new blades than to sharpen old ones by pressure-flaking.

Prismatic blades served also, however, as blanks for the manufacture of other tools, made by pressure-flaking. Braidwood lists seven special types of tools made from blades: (1) the backed blade, a knife with one edge blunted, probably to protect the user's fingers; (2) the burin or graver, a chisel-like tool; (3) the shouldered point, an arrow- or spear-point with one or two "shoulders" or incipient barbs; (4) the notched blade, used to smooth arrow- or spear-shafts and similar to the modern draw knife or spokeshave; (5) the borer or awl, probably used to make holes or indentations; (6) the blade with one or both ends sharpened to give a good scraping edge, and used possibly to hollow out wood or bone or to scrape hides; and (7) the fine laurel- or willow-leaf Solutrean points that we mentioned in the preceding section and which were made, according to Braidwood, of blades carefully retouched over both surfaces by pressure-flaking.[1]

The manufacture of tools from blades, it is evident, requires all three of the stone-chipping techniques we have described: percussion to shape

[1] Robert J. Braidwood, "Prehistoric Men," *Chicago National History Museum, Popular Series, Anthropology,* No. 37 (1948), pp. 62–65.

the core from which the blades are struck, the striking off of the blades, and retouching by means of pressure-flaking. This combination of techniques represents the highest advance of the stone-chipping art which, in the hands of skilled craftsmen like those of the Solutrean epoch, produced the finest chipped stone tools known to us. It is interesting to note that man had discovered and thoroughly exploited all the major techniques for chipping stone before the end of the Old Stone Age. To the best of our knowledge, no modern stone-using peoples have added significantly to these techniques.

Though the blade technique has a more limited distribution than the percussion- and pressure-flaking techniques, it is found among some of the peoples of the New World. The Aztecs of Mexico and their neighbors employed the technique, especially to produce unretouched prismatic blades for use as knives. This has persisted until recent times; in the last century, it was not uncommon, and perhaps is not uncommon now in remote areas of Mexico, for a barber in rural villages to use a prismatic blade of obsidian as a razor, chipping off a new blade for each customer. Similarly in Europe, nineteenth-century English craftsman, making flint-lock guns to be sold in the African trade, chipped their flints by a technique called flint-knapping, very like the prismatic blade technique of the upper Paleolithic.

The technique of grinding or polishing stone appeared in the Old World some eight or ten thousand years ago; the date varies considerably in various regions. It spread rapidly until it reached ultimately all but very few peoples. Only the Tasmanians of Oceania lacked the technique in the Old World, and though some of the earliest cultures of the Americas show no evidence of stone-polishing, all the modern peoples of the New World either practice the technique or, as in the case of the aborigines of the stoneless Amazon basin, secure polished stone implements by trade.

As we have noted earlier, the technique of grinding stone tools permits the use of much material unsuited to stone-chipping and far more abundantly distributed than flint or other easily fractured stones. It is this factor that makes the technique important, for as we shall see, grinding is much more laborious than chipping and produces only a few tools that cannot be made as well by chipping techniques. In making polished stone tools, a hammer stone or chisel of hard stone is first used to peck or abrade (but not to chip) the raw material to the general shape of the article desired, which is then given a smooth surface and a cutting edge by rubbing with abrasive material. The process is extremely time-consuming and laborious as compared with stone-chipping. Where a skilled craftsman can chip out a flint knife, ax, or arrow-point in a half-hour or less, it takes many days of hard labor to produce even a small polished stone tool. It is for this reason, perhaps, that stone-chipping persists even among peoples who know the grinding technique, provided of course that they have access to flint or other appropriate material.

Tools made by polishing are chiefly axes, adzes, mauls, and heavy seed- or grain-grinding equipment like the quern, the mano and metate, and the mortar and pestle. Ground stone axes and other heavy edged tools, while only a little more efficient than their chipped counterparts, are apparently more durable. This is because chipped tools, made of easily fractured materials, are likely to be broken under hard usage, while ground stone tools are not so easily fractured. Tools used for lighter cutting, such as knives and scrapers, are quite satisfactory when made of flint or obsidian, though there are some people, like the Eskimos, who make polished knives of slate and other materials.

It is of some interest to note that the grinding of stone, though a later technique, actually requires somewhat less skill and knowledge of materials than does flaking or chipping. In other words, grinding is not a technique

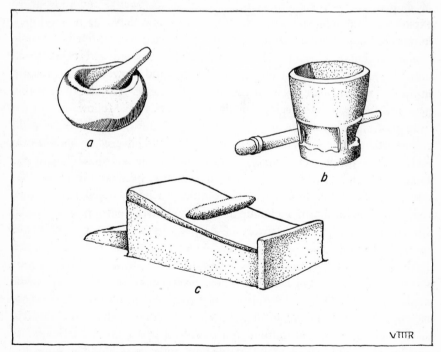

Fig. 9:5. (*a*) Stone mortar and pestle from Santa Cruz Island; (*b*) Mohegan mortar and pestle of wood, after Willoughby; (*c*) Pueblo metate and mano.

developed from an earlier knowledge of chipping techniques, but an entirely separate method of making stone tools. Though its sources are obscure, it is not improbable that the grinding of stone stems from the far earlier techniques of shaping tools from bone and horn. These materials cannot be chipped but must be split, cut, or polished.

Though in some areas of the Old World, polished stone tools appear to be coincident in time, or nearly so, with techniques of horticulture, it does not follow that only food-producing peoples possess polished stone tools. There are many peoples in the world who make and use polished stone tools but lack any food-producing techniques whatsoever. Examples are found among the Eskimos of the Arctic, the Plains Indian buffalo-hunters, and the food-gathering aborigines of California and the Great Basin. It is true, however, that land cultivation is probably aided by polishing techniques, useful in producing axes to clear away forest growth and brush, smooth sharp stones to serve as tips for digging-sticks, hoes and rude plows, and grain-crushing devices like grinding-stones and mortars.

The grinding or polishing of stone is the last of the major stone-shaping techniques to be invented by man. With it, all or nearly all the ways of shaping stones for cutting tools have been discovered and thoroughly exploited, excepting only such refinements as may have been developed in our own industrial civilization. Many peoples never developed any tool-making techniques beyond this point, and have continued using stone until the present day. In a few areas of the world, however, and notably in the Near East, man began to use metals for tools. We shall discuss this new and far-reaching development in the sections that follow.

In passing, however, it may be well to elucidate further a point made earlier—that stone is by no means the only material used by prehistoric and modern peoples of simple cultures for the making of cutting tools. Bone and horn retouching tools, as we have noted, were used in the middle and late Paleolithic. In the late Paleolithic, we find as well many other tools of bone or horn, including fishhooks, knives, pins, needles, awls, spear-points, and many varieties of harpoon-heads, some of which are exceedingly well made and elaborate. Among contemporary peoples, the Eskimos are notable for their extensive use of bone and ivory, used to manufacture lance- and harpoon-heads, prongs for fish spears, knives of many sorts, needles, and scrapers. The Witotos of the Amazon basin, lacking stone, use animal teeth for awls and scrapers, and make knives, spearheads, swords, and mortars and pestles of ironwood and other hardwoods. Their only stone tool, obtained in trade, is a polished stone ax. The Semang of the Malay Peninsula, except for occasional stone and metal tools obtained in trade, are similarly dependent on bamboo for cutting tools. Sharp slivers of bamboo are used for spear-points, arrowheads, blow-gun darts, and knives. In short, though few if any peoples of simple culture are entirely lacking in stone implements, these are universally supplemented by tools of other materials, and, in a few cases, where stone is lacking and stone tools come only through trade, the substitute materials assume primary importance for the making of cutting tools.

5. THE DISCOVERY AND SPREAD OF METAL-WORKING

Though metal tools are today obviously superior to those made of stone, especially for such operations as cutting, chopping, boring, and scraping, this was not true at the dawn of the Metal Age. The metals were rare and hard to find, techniques of smelting (that is, of freeing the metal by heat from its ores and other impurities) were crude and cumbersome, and the techniques of forging, casting, and otherwise working metals were imperfectly known and time-consuming. Hence the resulting artifacts were few and crude, and the cutting implements often less efficient than stone tools. Even the people who knew metal-using techniques continued to use stone tools for most purposes and to reserve their metals for special weapons, tools, and ornaments. This was true, for example, among the ancient Egyptians and the late Mayas of Yucatan, for though both these peoples used metals, the great pyramids of Egypt and the impressive temples of Yucatan were alike made of stone quarried and shaped by stone chisels and hammers.

The earliest and most primitive metal tools were made of materials like copper, gold, and meteoric iron, found in relatively pure form and requiring no smelting to make them usable. Metals of this sort were cold-hammered into tools and ornaments by peoples like the Badarians of Neolithic Egypt, a number of American Indian tribes who lived where free copper was available, and the Eskimos who used bits of meteoric iron to make tools. Neither copper nor gold, however, is very useful for cutting tools because of its softness; stone tools are far superior to those made of copper, even when the latter is hardened by cold-hammering or by subjecting it to moderate heat (annealing). Meteoric iron, a much more useful material for cutting tools, is too rare to afford a basis for an extensive technology.

Properly speaking, then, the age of metals does not begin until the discovery of metallurgy, that is, the technique of separating metals from their ores by smelting, and the associated techniques of alloying, forging, and casting. These techniques do not appear until relatively late in human history; the first smelting probably occurred some time about 3500 B.C. in the Near East. Because metal tools are today so commonplace, we often forget both their recency and the fact that many nonliterate peoples lack any metal-working techniques whatsoever, and obtain metal tools, if they use them at all, only by virtue of trade and contact with peoples of more advanced technologies.

The first metal used extensively for cutting tools, apart from the earlier use of free copper and meteoric iron, was bronze, an alloy of copper and tin. Bronze was apparently first developed in the Near East, some time before 3500 B.C., and came into general use in Egypt and Mesopotamia about 3100 B.C. ($\pm$150 years.) By 3000 B.C., bronze had diffused to Syria and other areas of the eastern Mediterranean. It then moved slowly into Europe, reaching central Europe between 1900 and 1800 B.C. and the Scandinavian peninsula about 1500 B.C.

The Indus Valley of India, the center of a complex culture roughly co-incident in time with those of the Near East, had two kinds of bronze, one a tin-copper alloy and the other of arsenic and copper, as early as 2700 B.C. or even before. Bronze came relatively late to China, however, for we do not find it until the Shang period, roughly from 1540 to 1300 B.C. Bronze did not spread into Negro Africa, nor does the technique of making it occur anywhere in southeastern Asia or Oceania.

Bronze was discovered independently in the New World, probably in Bolivia, but this did not occur until a few centuries before the coming of the Europeans. Among American aborigines, bronze is used only by the Indians of Peru and Bolivia (the so-called Incas) and by the Aztecs of Mexico, who either developed it independently of the Andean peoples or learned it through indirect contacts with them. Neither of these groups, however, made extensive use of bronze (though both the Incas and the Aztecs did expert gold and silverwork); at the time of the Spanish conquest of Mexico and Peru, early in the sixteenth century, both groups were still largely dependent on tools of stone. Another metal alloy called *tumbaga,* made of copper, silver, and gold, and equal to bronze in hardness, was made by the Indians of Colombia.

Iron-smelting came later than bronze, even though iron ores are some-what easier to reduce than those containing copper and require less heat (about 700 to 800 degrees centigrade) in the process. The first occurrence of iron-working took place apparently on the Anatolian plateau, the region of modern Armenia, somewhere about 1400 B.C. Since by that time metallurgical techniques were well known in much of the Old World—from previous experience with bronze—the making and use of iron spread rapidly. It reached the Greeks and upper Italy as early as 1000 B.C., cen-

tral Europe about 800 B.C., and areas as remote as England and Scandinavia between 600 and 500 B.C. The Chinese, to the east, learned the
use of iron at about the same time as the Britons, though there is some
evidence of a wide domestic use of iron in China as early as 700 B.C.

Nearly all the peoples of Negro Africa use iron and have apparently
known iron-working techniques for a long time. However, the origins of
iron-working in Africa are obscure. Some scholars have claimed that the
Negroes of Africa developed iron independently of the Near East, but this
appears unlikely. It is more probable that the iron-working of Negro
Africa, like that of Europe and Asia, came from the Near East, for the
oldest dated evidence of iron tools is found at Meroë in Nubia (700 B.C.),
no great distance from Egypt. Other African specialists, however, believe
that iron-working reached Negro Africa at a relatively late date as a result of contacts with Arabia or India along the eastern coast of the continent.

In India, particularly the Indus Valley, iron-working techniques apparently began by 1000 B.C. or earlier, probably diffused from centers in
the Near East. From India, iron and iron-working diffused slowly into
parts of southeastern Asia and Indonesia, but it did not reach the latter
region until some 2,000 years ago. Furthermore, the bulk of the peoples
of Indonesia never acquired the technique of smelting iron but only the
art of forging pure iron, which is obtained by trade from technologically
more advanced groups. Both iron tools and the working of iron are lacking in Melanesia, Polynesia, and the cultures of the New World.

6. TECHNIQUES OF METAL-WORKING

From what has been said, it is evident that metal-working requires a
far greater knowledge of the environment and its resources than stone-
working. In a stone-using society, almost any adult individual can recognize and find the raw materials used for tools, for stones may be taken as
they occur in nature and chipped or ground to the required shape. The
same is true, of course, of free copper and meteoric iron, which are probably regarded by many peoples as particular varieties of stone.

But making tools of metals imbedded in ores is not so easy. Neither
copper or tin ores nor iron-bearing sands or ores look at all like the metals
that may be abstracted from them; they are, rather, raw materials which
must first radically be altered in form and appearance to be made into
tools. Metal-working, then, requires the development of numerous techniques, each of which is of equal or greater complexity than the finding
and shaping of stone. Among the more important of these are: (1) min-

ing, that is, the discovery and collection of suitable ores or metal-bearing sands; (2) smelting, the abstraction of pure metals from ores or sands; (3) alloying, the mixing of different metals to produce others which are harder or otherwise more useful; and (4) forging and casting, the techniques whereby metals are finally shaped into tools and artifacts. In order to practice these techniques, a people must also be able to build adequate furnaces and other devices to produce the heat necessary both to the smelting of ores and the forging or casting of metals. Finally, anvils, hammers, tongs, molds, and other tools are needed to complete the process of shaping metal artifacts.

Cold-hammering, the shaping of metals by beating without first heating them, was undoubtedly the first metal-working technique to be discovered. It was applied, we know, by all peoples who had ready access to free copper or meteoric iron. Thus, the Indians living about Lake Superior, where free copper is found, hammered this into crude knives and other cutting tools, and the Eskimos, as we have noted, hacked off bits of meteoric iron to use as knives, lance-heads, and scrapers.

We may also suspect that free copper was cast or at least liquefied before smelting was known; once man had discovered that native copper would melt under heat, it was probably no great step to the heating of ores and the discovery that this process would smelt out the pure metal. However this may be, it is apparent that smelting was first applied to copper, gold, silver, and lead ores, and that the metals so obtained were cast into various tools and implements. Finely cast copper is found in southern Mesopotamia in the late Neolithic. The Incas of Peru similarly cast beautiful gold and silver artifacts, many thousands of which were taken by the Spanish conquerors, melted down into ingots, and shipped back to Spain.

The finest casting technique is the *cire perdu* or "lost-wax" method. The object to be cast is first modeled in wax and this model is then covered with a coating of clay, or more commonly, with a mixture of clay and other materials. One or more openings are left in the clay envelope, which is then hardened by baking, and the wax, melted by the heat, is "lost" and runs out of the openings. Molten metal is finally poured into the clay mold so prepared, thus producing in metal the artifact originally modeled in wax. Objects of great complexity and intricacy of design may be made by this method, but each is unique, for the model is destroyed in the process.

The next metal-working technique to be discovered was alloying—first applied to the making of bronzes. Several types of bronze are found in prehistory, each of which consists mainly of copper hardened by a small admixture of tin, phosphorus, arsenic, or gold and silver. Copper-tin mixtures are, however, the most widespread, and the alloy so formed—of 90 per cent copper plus 10 per cent tin as the optimum mixture—makes far more serviceable cutting tools than copper alone, and is in addition an ideal metal for casting. We do not know just how man first discovered bronze, but it may have been accidental, owing to the smelting of copper ores mixed in nature with other ores.

There is a similar mystery in the discovery of iron and its smelting, for iron ores and iron-bearing sands give little or no clue to the metal that may be obtained from them. Here again we may lay it to accident or, possibly, to a deliberate search, once man had discovered the technique of smelting, for other metal-bearing ores.

Smelting, forging, and casting require of course the use of furnaces and devices to increase the heat of fires by supplying them with plenty of air. Most primitive furnaces are made of clay, and the most commonly used fuel is charcoal. Many techniques are employed to supply a forced draft: the Aztecs of Mexico had a number of men blow on the fire through hollow reeds, the Incas of Peru set their furnaces on mountain ridges swept by strong winds, and many Old World peoples devised bellows of one sort or another.

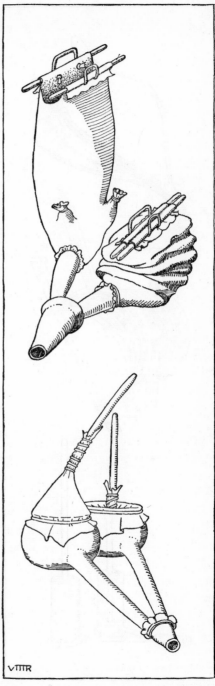

Fig. 9:6. Leather and pottery bellows.

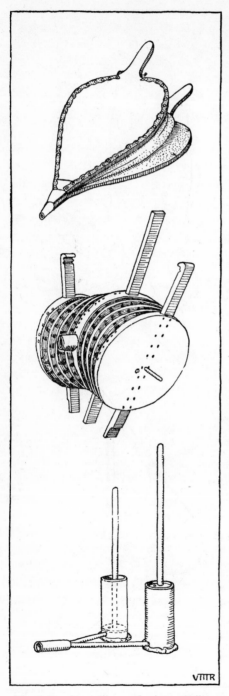

Fig. 9:7. Accordion and piston bellows.

In Africa two principal types of bellows are employed. One is a large leather bag which is opened as it is lifted. The upper opening is closed and the bag is then compressed, the air escaping through a nozzle or tube directed at the fire. Since two bags are used, each alternately raised and compressed, the draft is made continuous. The second type is a solid chamber of wood or pottery fitted on top with a loose diaphragm of leather, and at the bottom with a nozzle (often of clay) leading into the fire. By alternately raising and lowering the diaphragms of two such drum bellows, a continuous draft is forced through a common nozzle at the fire.

The Europeans, until the recent introduction of the rotary blower, used an accordion-like bellows, now familiar for its use in many households with a fireplace. There is also an African accordion bellows—possibly a compromise, recently developed, between the native drum bellows and the European accordion bellows.

In Indonesia, we find a quite different bellows, the so-called piston type. It consists of two hollow cylinders, made of bamboo, each of which is fitted with a close-fitting piston or plunger. Nozzles from each cylinder are joined into one which leads into the fire. The operator pumps the pistons alternately, thus directing a continuous stream of air into the fire.

To make the process of primitive metal-working more vivid, let us turn to the Akikuyus, a Bantu-speaking people of East Africa, well known for their skill in the smelting and forging of iron. We should note, however, that Akikuyu iron-working is primitive only in contrast to our highly mechanized techniques; the Akikuyus, though lacking the machines and extensive knowledge of our culture, do possess all the major techniques of iron-working and produce by hand extremely well-made and efficient tools and artifacts.

The Akikuyus obtain their ores in open quarries from decomposed iron-bearing rocks. These quarries are in gorges where streams have broken down the rocks and washed out iron-bearing sands. Sometimes the Akikuyus hasten this process by directing a stream against the rocky sides of a gorge and so increasing the supply of sands. The ferriferous sand is gathered in bags and carried to the lower portion of the stream, where women and children pan and wash it much in the same way as gold miners pan out gold dust from river sands. Large quantities of sand are heaped in the pans, and water is poured on it to remove, by continuous washing, the lighter particles and leave behind the heavier iron-bearing sand. After repeated washings of this sort, the last of which takes place in small gourds, the residue is made up largely of quartz grains, magnetite, and ilmenite ores, with a high iron content. The process is laborious and the yield about one pint of well-cleaned ore per one hour of labor.

The ore is then taken to a furnace for smelting. The furnace is a hole in the ground lined with clay and so constructed that the clay lining is brought well over the edge of the hole in a convex, everted border around the entire oval mouth of the furnace. The bellows is a cone of sewn goatskins, four feet long and six inches in diameter at the large end. A wooden tube, six inches long, is set into the small end of the cone. When in use, the cone is pegged to the ground, and the nozzle set toward the fire. Over the mouth of the nozzle is fitted a pipe of pottery which runs over the everted lip of the furnace and down into it just above the fire. Two straight slabs of wood, with thongs at their top ends, are attached to each side of the cone. Two such bellows are employed so as to produce a continuous stream of air. To work the bellows, one thong is caught by the thumb, the other by the fingers and palm. The operator then closes his hand, so bringing the slabs of wood together to compress the goatskin cone. As his hand closes, he also pushes the cone over against itself and so increases the air pressure directed into the fire. One operator works both bellows, squeezing each alternately.

The furnace is filled with alternating layers of charcoal and ore, and allowed to burn, under draft from the bellows, all day long. As the charcoal is consumed and the furnace contents sink to the bottom, more charcoal and ore are added, a little at a time. Finally, when all the ore has been added, and all the charcoal burned, the slag is left overnight to cool. In the morning it is removed and knocked to pieces, and the pure iron removed in small lumps from the slag. These are again heated and beaten together into ingots or blooms weighing about two pounds each.

The iron blooms are then taken by the smiths, the most skilled of the iron-workers, who forge the pure iron into a variety of tools. The smith uses a smooth river boulder as an anvil, and a hammer, tongs, chisel, and other tools which he makes himself of iron. Other tools and artifacts made include spearheads, arrowheads, swords, axes, adzes, knives, razors, tweezers, branding irons, bells, rattles, earrings, and rings. Akikuyu smiths make wire by beating iron into a long, thin rod and drawing this through a hole in another piece of iron. They also make chains, among the most difficult of the smithing arts, which require a high degree of skill. There is, in fact, no forging technique, possible by hand, that is unknown to the Akikuyu smiths. They do not, however, cast iron; all their artifacts are made by forging.

7. METAL-WORKING: ITS EFFECT UPON SOCIETY

It is quite often erroneously assumed that the acquisition of metalworking techniques by itself raises a society to a new stage of culture, superior in every respect to that of earlier and contemporaneous stone-users. That this is not necessarily the case is demonstrated by the fact that some metal-using societies are not very different in their total technologies and cultures from some stone-users.

The Ifugao of the Philippines, for example, make excellent iron axes and other tools but, from the standpoint of technology, their culture as a whole is not greatly different from nor superior to that of the Neolithic lake-dwellers of Europe. Nor is it superior, even in technology, to the cultures of such contemporaneous peoples as the aboriginal Hawaiians and Maoris of Polynesia, who lack iron. Similarly, though the Negroes of the Congo have highly developed iron-working techniques, their lack of massive architecture, the wheel, and urban communities makes them inferior in these respects to the Bronze Age Egyptians. In brief, one cannot adequately rate cultures solely by the presence or absence of tool-making techniques, for these do not necessarily accompany other cultural advances of equal and even greater importance.

Nevertheless, the introduction of metal-working does often affect materially the rest of culture. Stone-using peoples nearly always are food-collectors (gatherers, hunters, or fishermen) or live in small isolated villages as farmers. Most such communities tend to be isolated, to engage in relatively little trade or other forms of contact with others, and to practice few or no specialized crafts.

With metal-working, this picture often changes. Metals, unlike stones, have a limited distribution, and the use of them stimulates trade, both in raw materials and finished artifacts, over considerable areas. Trade leads of course to wider contacts between disparate peoples and as well to the wider diffusion of cultural innovations. Metal-working, too, because it requires the development of many complex techniques, tends to develop specialized crafts, a feature of economic organization often lacking among stone-users. Thus the Akikuyus have at least two specializations related to metal-working—some people spend all their labor in collecting and smelting ores, while others are smiths whose task it is to forge iron into tools and artifacts. This leads of course to internal trade: the smelters sell their iron to the smiths, and these sell the completed tools to others.

It follows, then, that the onset of metal-working is not infrequently associated with increased specialization of labor, intensified internal and external trade, the growth of urban centers, the beginnings of written records, improved transportation, and a more complex development of social and political organization. It is not asserted that any of these changes stand in a causal relationship to each other, and least of all that metal-working itself brings them about. But it is clear that these cultural changes have occurred together, notably in the Near East, and they may quite possibly result from a single cause, or complex of causes, as yet undiscovered. We shall return to this topic in later chapters, especially in that devoted to economics (Chapter 12).

We have noted that metal-working originated, as far as we can tell, only once in the Old World, probably in the Near East, and that it spread slowly from this center to other Old World areas. The same is true in the New World, where bronze at least seems to have been first discovered in Bolivia, from where it may have spread, indirectly and by devious routes, as far north as the Mexico of the Aztecs.

This history of metal-working—its spread or diffusion from one or two centers of origin—is paralleled by many other important cultural innovations. Writing is a good example, for it, too, presumably developed but once in the Old World and once in the New. In the Old World it spread far and in many variant forms (see Chapter 17, § 10 for details), while in the New World it occurred later and had a far more restricted diffusion. Despite the distinctiveness of individual cultures, then, many fundamental ideas and techniques appear to have been invented only once or a few times and to have diffused from the place of discovery to many other peoples. An individual culture, including its technology, is never the creation of its possessors alone, but is rather a historical accumulation of techniques, patterns, and ways of living derived from a great variety of sources. Invention, indeed, tends to be rare among all peoples; a culture is rich not so much by reason of the superior inventiveness of its participants as by their greater opportunities to share in the inventions of many other peoples. The distinctiveness of separate cultures tends to be reflected more in their ways of ordering and integrating their patterns of behaving than in the content of these patterns. We shall discuss this point in more detail in the chapters that follow; see especially Chapter 20.

8. SIMPLE CONTAINERS

Containers and techniques for making them are as universal as cutting tools, and as necessary apparently for human activities, even in societies with the simplest of cultures. Among some peoples, for example the Aruntas of Australia, we find only a few rather crude containers: troughs or basins, from one to three feet in length, hollowed out of wood, and poorly woven bags of vegetable fibers. In contrast we may instance the numerous elaborately woven baskets of some California Indians, the finely carved wooden bowls of many Polynesians, and the enormous variety of containers made of wood, china, pottery, and metals by western European peoples.

Containers function everywhere as means of transporting and storing foods, artifacts, and other material possessions. In addition, containers are widely used in cooking, and particularly in the boiling of both liquid and solid foods.

Though many nonliterate folk never boil their foods, others do so quite consistently even when they lack containers that may be set on a fire or other hot surface. Thus, the California Indians weave watertight baskets for this purpose, and boil foods in them by dropping hot stones into the mixture to be cooked. The same technique is employed, using wooden boxes, by the Indians of the North Pacific coast, and by the Indians of the Plains, who use containers of hide. Among some Basque-speaking peoples of the Pyrenees, stone boiling was until very recently regarded as the only proper way to cook milk, despite the presence of pottery and metal containers.

Containers may also be employed to preserve foods, as witness our own techniques of canning meats, fruits, and vegetables. Among the Plains Indians, dried meat is pounded to a powder and mixed with fat to make pemmican. This is kept in a leather bag with melted fat poured over it to preserve it until it is eaten. The Eskimos, according to Freuchen, preserve birds (little auks) by stuffing them into a bag or poke made by skinning a seal through the mouth so as not to split or tear the skin. Once the bag, oily inside from the blubber left on the skin, is full, it is tied tightly and stored out of the sunlight so that the meat may cure. The resulting food, eaten in the winter long after the spring bird-hunting season is over, is regarded as a delicacy by the Eskimos.

We may classify containers, roughly, into two major groups: (1) simple containers, that is, those which may be used as found in nature (e.g., shells) or those which may be made by very simple processing techniques (e.g., gourds), and (2) processed containers, those which require more or less elaborate techniques to manufacture. Containers of the second category may be subdivided in terms of the materials used to make them into wood, leather, fiber, clay, and metal containers.

Little is known of the earliest containers made by man (they leave few or no traces in archeological deposits), but it is likely that these were simple containers made of netting, leaves, wood, or bark. Paleolithic hunters may also have made containers of hide or leather. Certain evidence of basketry occurs early in the Neolithic (for example, among the Swiss lake-dwellers), though it may well have existed earlier. The first evidences of pottery occur also with the beginning of the Neolithic, but metal containers are not found in wide use until metallurgy is relatively far advanced. (See Chart XII, p. 269.)

The only simple container, widely used and requiring no processing, is that made of large mollusc shells. These are used whenever such shells are easily available, even sometimes by peoples who make more elaborate containers. A very few peoples, like the Onas of Tierra del Fuego, apparently have no other containers for heating water or other liquids, though such poverty is rare. Among others, like the Navaho, Hopi, and Zuñi Indians, abalone shells are used only to hold sacred objects and substances in ceremonials; other more elaborate containers of basketry and pottery are used for more casual, everyday functions. This use in a sacred function, plus the rarity of abalone shells in their desert environment, gives the abalone shell a high value to these peoples.

The most common simple container is the gourd *(Lagenaria),* found in a wild state in all continents and on many islands. The techniques of processing gourds vary widely from those which involve only a simple hollowing of the gourd to those which require careful shaping and elaborate decoration. Some farming peoples cultivate the gourd, and among these the growing gourd is not infrequently shaped by binding to produce certain specialized containers. Even today, farmers in some parts of Mexico

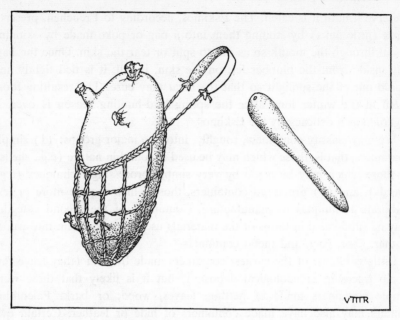

Fig. 9:8. Skin container (left) and gourd for collecting maguey sap.

produce specially lengthened gourds for use in collecting the sap of the century plant or maguey to make a fermented drink called *pulque*. Gourds, however, are so extensively used as water bottles, cups, dippers, and other devices that we cannot begin to exhaust the subject. Indeed, so various and curious are the uses of gourds that a special society has been organized just for their study.

Other simple containers appear to be employed only casually, or else are restricted to particular peoples. Polynesians and others who dwell in tropical forests not infrequently make casual use of large leaves, particularly to wrap foods to be baked in the fire or in ovens. Bark is widely used for casual purposes—and sometimes, as among the Indians of the eastern woodlands area of North America, we find rather elaborate bark containers. The Bushmen of Africa blow out ostrich eggshells to make containers for transporting water—a rare commodity in their desert environment. In some tropical areas, particularly southeast Asia and Indonesia, sections of the giant bamboo are made into containers by cutting a large stalk just below two adjacent nodes. These bamboo buckets are efficient for carrying water and even for boiling foods over a fire, for the green bamboo does not burn readily. Where bamboo is easily obtainable, new containers, to replace those too badly charred by fire, can soon be prepared.

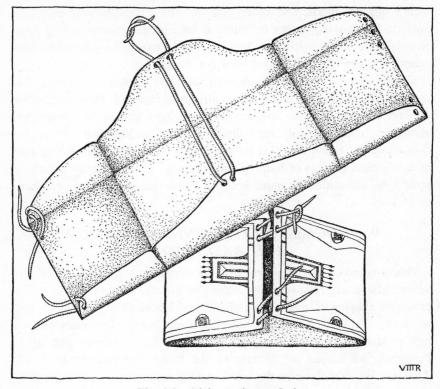

Fig. 9:9. Plains Indian parfleche.

Some simple containers are made of stone, netting, hides, and wood. Soft steatite (soapstone) and sandstone are made into bowls by the Indians of the Santa Barbara channel region in California and by the Eskimos, and there is evidence of shallow bowls of soapstone in the late Paleolithic of Europe. Net bags are widespread, especially among the Australian aborigines. Cord of vegetable fibers or animal hair is made by rolling the fibers on the thigh and then knotting the cords together. Often a shuttle of wood or bone is used to carry the cord, and a gauge may be employed to space the knots at equal distances.

Hide containers are especially important for hunting and pastoral peoples insofar as their flexibility makes them easy to transport without breakage. By removing the hide whole except for the feet and head and by tying the openings, a large water or other container can be made. Such containers, slung on burros, are still widely used in parts of Latin America, Asia, and Africa. Wallets or envelopes of rawhide or leather may similarly be used for storage or transport. An excellent example is the Plains Indian parfleche, a large envelope of hide used to store and carry personal possessions, sacred objects, foods, and other objects. The Plains Indians even use rawhide for cooking, either by lining a hole in the ground with a large piece of hide or by supporting the hide on sticks to make a bowllike container. The contents are heated with hot stones.

Simple containers of wood are relatively rare among nonliterates, except for the use of bark and bamboo already mentioned. Nevertheless, we do find wooden troughs and traylike containers among the Australian aborigines, used primarily for collecting wild vegetable food. Many Indian groups of South America hollow out large troughs from tree trunks by a laborious process of burning and scraping. These are used mainly to brew large quantities of maize beer for important ceremonial occasions.

9. PROCESSED CONTAINERS OF WOOD AND BASKETRY

Processed wooden containers, like the simple containers of wood described above, are relatively rare among nonliterate peoples, probably because the shaping of wood is a difficult and laborious process in the absence of metal tools. There are, however, a number of stone-using peoples who produce rather elaborately processed wooden containers, notably in Polynesia and among the Indians of the North Pacific coast of North America. We shall describe the woodworking techniques of the latter peoples in some detail; their work is probably the best to be found among stone-users.

The North Pacific coast peoples do all their woodworking with cutting tools of stone or horn. Their tools include hafted hammers, adzes, and axes of ground basalt, jadeite, dolerite, and other similarly hard stones, together with chisels of stone or horn and wedges made of wood. With these, they cut down large cedar trees, numerous in the area, and split off planks so smoothly and evenly that they apear to be sawn. Planks are also split from standing trees, so avoiding the labor of first felling them. The tree trunks and planks so obtained are used for many purposes: to build large houses (on the average forty feet long, thirty feet wide, six feet high at the eaves, and ten feet high at the ridge), to construct seagoing boats (some of which are seventy feet long and capable of carrying thirty men and a load of three tons), to make elaborately carved poles (the so-called totem poles), and to make paddles, serving-trays dug out of cedar, bowls, ladles, water buckets, and boxes.

The boxes, which are made in many sizes and capacities, well illustrate the Indians' skill in handling wood. A cedar plank is first given cross-

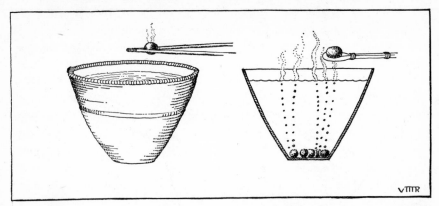

Fig. 9:10. Heating water in a cooking basket using hot stones. Note the hinged stick to lift stones from fire and the looped stick to remove stones from the basket. After Holmes.

grain grooves to mark off the ends and sides of the finished box. The grooved areas are then steamed and the plank so bent into the required shape. A series of holes is next drilled at the ends of the planks, and these ends are tightly laced with a four-ply rope made of cedar twigs twisted together. Finally, another piece of wood is shaped to form the bottom of the box and grooved to fit the sides tightly without lacing. Boxes so made serve many purposes, including the storage of both dry and liquid foods. They are also used for boiling food by dropping hot stones into the mixture to be cooked.

Carved or dug-out bowls and other containers are of course far more common than the boxes just described. Some of the best examples are to be found in Polynesia, where wooden containers, often very elaborately decorated, are carefully and laboriously carved out with cutting tools of stone, bone, and shell. The Northwest coast Indians also make finely carved containers of cedar wood, yew, and alder or maple knots, and square water buckets hollowed out of a solid piece of cedar. Some of the carved bowls and ladles of this region are shaped like miniature boats, or have tiny animal figures carved at either end.

Basketry is much more widely distributed than woodworking; indeed, there are probably few peoples anywhere who do not possess some basket-making technique, and archeological researches suggest that baskets were among the earliest containers to be employed by man. There are two major types of basket-making techniques: coiling or sewing and weaving. Both are widespread; many peoples possess techniques belonging to both categories. Coiling is found in the Mediterranean area, Africa, eastern Asia,

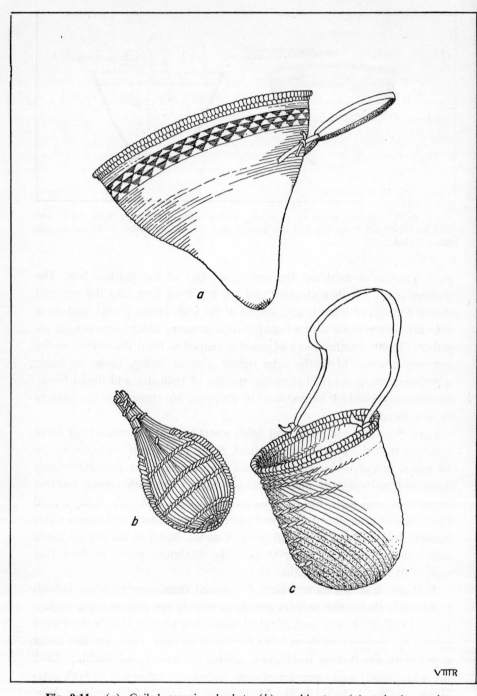

VIIIR

Fig. 9:11. (*a*) Coiled carrying basket; (*b*) seed-beater; (*c*) twined carrying basket. After Mason.

Indonesia, Australia, and many parts of the Americas. Weaving similarly is found in many parts of the Americas, and in Asia, the East Indies, and Africa.

Coiled basketry has a continuous foundation made of a single rod, a bundle of fibers or splints, or even two or three rods or bundles bound together. This foundation is built up by coiling the element spirally, beginning in the center of the bottom of the container, and each coil is sewn to the one next to it by means of a continuous sewing element or weft (see Figure 9:12). An awl or needle is used in sewing. By the use of differently colored sewing elements, designs of varying degrees of complexity may be made as the container is gradually built up to the desired shape.

Woven baskets (together with numerous other artifacts like mats, bags, wallets, and the like) are made by a wide variety of techniques. The commonest and most widespread is twilling, where the warp and weft are flat fibers (often made from split cane or bamboo) of equal thickness and pliability. The simplest twilling, called checkerwork, is done by passing each weft element over and under alternate warp fibers, so producing a checkerboard effect. Variations of many kinds may be introduced, however, by passing the weft fibers over two or more warps and by so staggering this process as to secure a diagonal twill. Similarly, by using differently colored elements, the weaver may quite simply introduce any number of geometric designs over

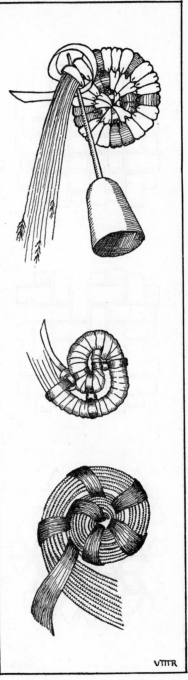

Fig. 9:12. Basketry coiling.

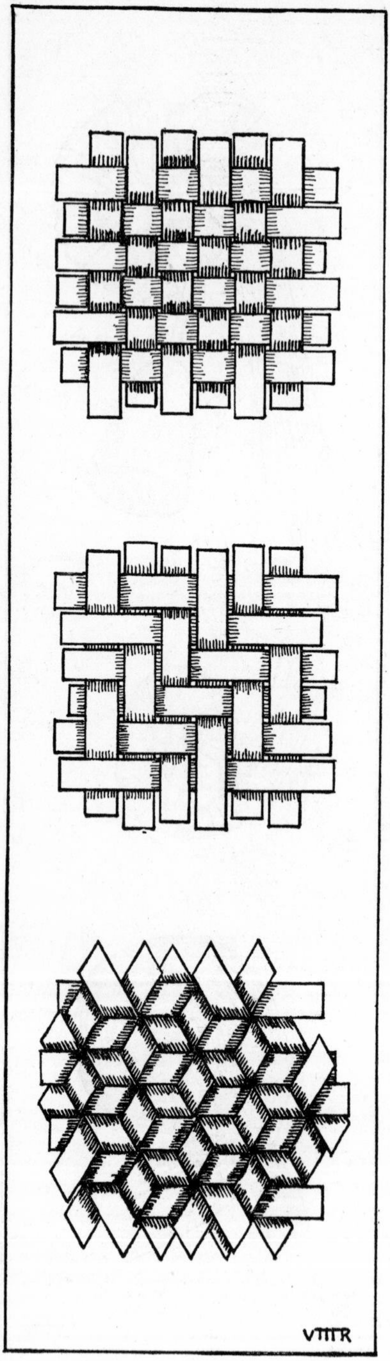

Fig. 9:13. Basketry twilling.

the completed surface. Wickerwork is another twilling technique, in which the warp is made of a wide and rigid material whereas the weft elements are slender and pliable.

In twined basketry the warp is either flexible or rigid, and the weft elements, often of twine, are pliable. Each weft element is then wrapped around successive warps to build up the completed container. There are, however, numerous variations in this technique: sometimes two wefts are passed through the warp together so that one goes under and the other over each successive warp and the two are crossed between each warp. Similarly, two or more warps may be bound together by the weft element and this process staggered for successive wefts in such a way as to produce various designs.

The above description by no means exhausts the variety of basket-making techniques, though it does note the principal ones. Otis Mason, in his classical *Aboriginal American Basketry* (U. S. National Museum Report for 1902, published in 1904) describes five principal weaving techniques (checkerwork, twilled work, wickerwork, wrapped work, and twined work), one of which, twining, is subdivided into five categories. He also lists no less than ten variations in coiled or sewn basketry, depending on the kind of foundation used and the technique of sewing.

Among some peoples, such as the Indians of California, basket-work is both a practical and a fine art. In addition to numerous baskets made for storage and transportation, these Indians frequently demonstrate their skill in weaving by making tiny baskets, some less than a quarter of an inch in diameter, and made of weft materials finer than those of coarse pongee. The Pomos also demonstrate a fine artistic ability in decorating baskets —both by geometric designs produced in the weaving and by introducing colored feathers into the weft. At the other extreme, the Pomos often make enormous storage baskets of coarse materials, with a capacity of several bushels, and baskets so tightly woven that they may be used for cooking by the hot-stone method.

10. POTTERY AND METAL CONTAINERS

Basketry and hide containers, because of their flexibility and strength, are especially well suited to nomadic food-gatherers, peoples who must often travel far and wide to gain their sustenance. Pottery containers, on the other hand, are too heavy and fragile to be used widely by nomads, and are consequently found most often among sedentary farming peoples. Indeed there is good reason to believe that pottery was first invented in the Neolithic, when farming, too, first came into existence. Nevertheless, there are modern nomads who make and use pottery— such as the western Eskimos and the Navaho and Apache Indians of southwestern United States—though nearly all such peoples make but a few small pieces which are used mainly for cook-

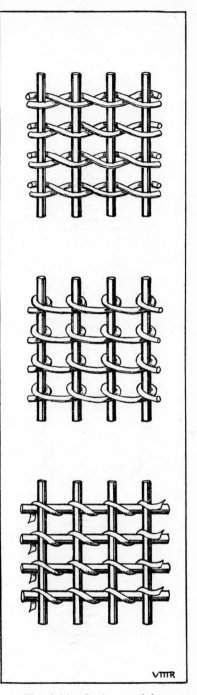

Fig. 9:14. Basketry twining.

Fig. 9:15. Coiled pottery.

ing. There are also farmers who lack pottery; a notable instance is the Polynesians who live in an area where the proper clays are also lacking.

The manufacture of pottery is no simple matter of taking any convenient clay, shaping it, and baking the vessel so formed in the fire. Rather, pottery-making requires a detailed knowledge of suitable materials; of the processes of mixing these materials to secure the optimum strength and durability; of the ways of shaping clay so that internal stresses will not cause cracks or other damage; of proper methods of drying and finishing clay vessels; and of techniques of firing that will produce just the right amount of heat.

Clay suitable for pottery-making consists mainly of silica and aluminum oxide. Because the proportions of these substances vary in natural clays, it usually is necessary to mix in other materials to make the clay either more plastic or less sticky and apt to crack in drying. Such materials, called tempers, include sand, mica, pulverized fragments of broken pottery (sherd temper), quartz, lime, or feldspar. Organic materials such as straw are also added at times, although such tempers are usually less satisfactory. The process of modeling the clay also sets up stresses in the finished vessel which may cause breakage during firing or make the completed pottery very fragile. Many of these stresses may be avoided by the use of special techniques for shaping. Among most nonliterate peoples the coiling method is used, that is, the vessel is built up by pinching on successive rolls of clay (see Figure

9:15). A smooth surface is then produced by scraping or rubbing, although sometimes the coils are left as an ornament on the exterior. Pottery vessels also may be modeled from a lump of clay or clay may be forced into a mold.

The most efficient method of shaping pottery is by rotating a lump of clay on a turntable or potter's wheel. With the hand or an implement, the rotating clay is quickly shaped into the desired form. Usually a pedal arrangement is added so that the wheel may be rotated with the foot and both hands left free for manipulation of the clay. Generally the potter's wheel is limited to advanced cultures in which the wheel is also used in transportation and in other devices. The earliest wheel-made pottery appears to be in the Tigris-Euphrates region of the Near East, where it is found in sites slightly earlier than the first use of bronze. By 3000 B.C. the wheel was widely used in the Near East, although not employed by everyone, and it seems to have spread with the use of bronze. Today the wheel is employed mainly by metal-using peoples in the Old World; its use never developed among the aborigines of the Western Hemisphere.

After shaping, clay vessels must be thoroughly dried, for an excess of moisture in the clay will cause breakage in firing. Firing must also be carefully done; temperatures of 400 degrees centigrade or higher are best to ensure the transformation of the material into pottery. If subjected to lesser heat, the material will revert to clay when wet. On the other hand, firing at excessive heats will fuse the materials and the

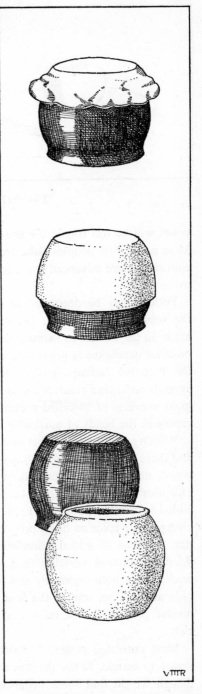

Fig. 9:16. Forming body of pottery over mold. The shoulder and rim are formed by hand.

Fig. 9:17. Potter's wheel.

vessel will be too fragile for use if it does not simply melt out of shape. Most nonliterate peoples bake their clay vessels in open fires, but peoples culturally more advanced use enclosed heating chambers, such as kilns or ovens.

Pottery may be decorated in various ways. Most frequently, perhaps, the vessels are decorated, before firing, by incised or engraved designs made on the surface in various ways, or by adding special rims, legs, bases, or other details made separately and fastened to the finished pots. Among the Peruvian Indians, pots were not infrequently shaped to represent animals and other creatures, and in some regions of Peru there are found great numbers of so-called portrait pots, shaped, it has been suggested, to represent the heads of particular individuals.

Painting, however, is the most common form of pottery decoration, and there are literally thousands of painted designs, geometric, representational, and abstract, found among the nonliterate peoples of the world (for illustration, see Chapter 18, "The Arts"). Painted designs are usually added before the pottery is fired, and the pigments used not infrequently change their color as firing progresses. Some pottery may also be slipped, that is, given an added smoothness or a particular color by coating the dried but unfired vessel with a very thin clay. Painted pottery designs tend to vary both regionally and in time, and so form, where written records are lacking, one of the best indicators of cultural contacts between diverse peoples and of cultural change within the history of a single society.

Most untreated pottery is more or less porous and so permits liquids slowly to escape. Many peoples make no effort to remedy this condition, though we do find some instances of resin-coated pottery. In the Near East, however, the discovery of glass led to the technique called glazing, where materials similar to glass were applied to pottery to make it water-proof and to give it a smooth and highly polished finish. Some American Indians apparently developed a similar glazing technique independently of the Old World. The ultimate discovery in the use of glaze was made by the Chinese who, after several centuries of experimentation, learned to mix glaze materials with the clay to produce porcelain or "china." The technique of making porcelain spread to Europe several centuries later and is today a very important industrial process in our culture, with many applications in chemistry, medicine, and sanitation. In medical biology, for example, a filterable virus is an organism sufficiently small to pass through a porcelain filter.

The possession of pottery not only makes the storage and transportation of liquids easier, it can also be used for the storage of small grains, seeds, and other materials. Foods can be boiled directly over the fire rather than by the stone-boiling technique. Pottery is also used for pipes, ornaments, ladles, lamps, and other objects, and some peoples use large pottery vessels for burial of the dead. Except where the use of metal has become cheap and common, pottery still provides one of the most important sources of containers for most of mankind. Even in many areas of Western civilization pottery is extensively used for cooking and the transportation of liquids, and in the United States we still employ pottery or china dishes for eating and baking.

Metal containers are obviously used only by peoples who know metal-working or who are able to secure metal containers in trade. Early in the Metal Age, and even today in many metal-working societies, metal containers tend to be rare and are used only for ceremonial occasions or for certain special types of cooking. The Greeks and Romans, for example, made fine metal containers for their temples and as decorative pieces; metal was still too rare and expensive to be used for everyday needs. A similar situation exists today among the African metal-using peoples, where iron is used almost exclusively for tools and weapons, while metal containers, except as they may be secured in trade, are rare or lacking.

In the New World, only the Peruvian Indians made metal containers, usually of silver and gold, and none of these was used for cooking or eating. Most of them, apparently, were considered objects of art or had ceremonial significance, though there is some evidence that silver cups, numerous and widespread, may have been used for drinking, at least on ceremonial occasions.

Metal containers, then, did not become abundant until the development of Western industrial civilization, when the increased cheapness of metals and improved techniques of mass production made wide distribution possible. Our western European cultures are unique in their wide use of metals for all sorts of containers, together of course with the continued use of wood, baskets, pottery, and china. The wide use of metals—in cutting tools as in containers—is comparatively a recent innovation, and metal artifacts are still rare and expensive in many parts of our modern world.

11. SUMMARY

All living peoples make use of tools and containers, although often they may be very simple and crude. With tools other implements may be made and the environment manipulated to some degree, while containers permit the storage and transport of food and other goods to an extent impossible without them. Without knives, lathes, drill-presses, gas tanks, water tanks, and other tools and containers, our own culture would disintegrate almost overnight. All prehistoric peoples also used tools, but because of the perishable nature of some materials, we do not always have evidence of containers unless stone, pottery, or metal was used.

The most fundamental tools are those used for cutting. Early cutting tools were made of stone, chipped or polished by a variety of techniques, many of which are still in use among contemporary nonliterate peoples. Metal tools, first of copper-bronze, then of iron or steel, are relatively late. In the last few centuries there has been a great elaboration of power-driven cutting tools in western European civilization. Cutting tools permit the more efficient utilization of power and are necessary either to perform elementary industrial processes or to make tools and implements for more complex industrial techniques.

It is probable that the earliest containers were natural products such as shells, bark, and leaves. Netting and basketry are so universal among modern nonliterates that we suspect them also to be very old, although no evidence for them exists from the European Paleolithic. In a number of arid regions, such as Egypt and the American Southwest, there is evidence that basketry preceded pottery. Pottery containers are used primarily by relatively sedentary farming peoples. Peoples such as the nomadic Plains Indians or the pastoral people of Asia and Africa generally use basketry or leather, although metal containers are also valued if obtainable. Wide use of metal containers seems confined to highly industrialized cultures.

Containers are essential for the storage of food supplies for most people. Perhaps a still more important function is to increase the efficiency of transportation. Food may be more easily transported in quantity from the field to camp, or from one residence to another. The shortage of common containers such as paper bags during World War II is evidence of how our own complex culture is dependent on containers for such a simple process as getting food from store to home. In later chapters we shall frequently have occasion to refer to this use of containers.

Chart XII. CHRONOLOGY OF TOOLS AND CONTAINERS

(Dates: Approximate Earliest Appearance)

Culture Periods	Techniques of Major Cutting Tools	Types of Container
Iron Age (1500 B.C.)	Steel (1000 B.C.) Wrought iron	Cast iron (1500 A.D. in Europe, earlier in China)
Bronze Age (3000 B.C.)	Cast, sometimes hammered	Cast or hammered bronze (rare)
Copper Age (4000 B.C.)	Cast or cold-hammered	
Neolithic (10,000 B.C.)	Ground stone (earlier in Asia)	Pottery (possibly late Paleolithic in Near East)
Upper Paleolithic (25,000 B.C.)	Chipped stone— "blade" techniques	
Middle Paleolithic (50,000 B.C.)	Chipped stone— pressure-flaking	Presumable use of basketry, netting, hide, and other simple containers of perishable materials
Lower Paleolithic (1,000,000 B.C.)	Chipped stone— percussion-flaking	

COLLATERAL READING

Braidwood, Robert J. "Prehistoric Men," *Chicago Natural History Museum, Popular Series, Anthropology,* No. 37, 1948, pp. 47–85.

Childe, V. Gordon. *Man Makes Himself.* New York: Oxford University Press, 1939. Chapters IV–VII.

———. *The Dawn of European Civilization.* London: Kegan Paul, 1948.

Cline, Walter. *Mining and Metallurgy in Negro Africa.* Menasha, Wisconsin: General Series in Anthropology, No. 5, 1937.

McCurdy, George G. *Human Origins.* New York: D. Appleton and Co., 1924. Vol. 2, Chapters XII–XIV.

Martin, Paul; Quimby, George; and Collier, Donald. *Indians Before Columbus.* Chicago: University of Chicago Press, 1947. Part II.

Mason, Otis. "Types of Basket Weaves," *Source Book in Anthropology,* eds. A. L. Kroeber and T. T. Waterman. Harcourt, Brace and Co., 1931. Chapter 26.

O'Neale, Lila. "Basketry," *Handbook of South American Indians,* ed. Julian H. Steward. Bulletin 143, Bureau of American Ethnology, Washington, D. C., 1949. Vol. 5, pp. 69–96.

Root, William C. "Metallurgy," *Handbook of South American Indians,* ed. Julian H. Steward. Bulletin 143, Bureau of American Ethnology, Washington, D. C., 1949. Vol. 5, pp. 205–226.

Willey, Gordon. "Ceramics," *Handbook of South American Indians,* ed. Julian H. Steward. Bulletin 143, Bureau of American Ethnology, Washington, D. C., 1949. Vol. 5, pp. 139–204.

Wissler, Clark. *The American Indian.* New York: Oxford University Press, 1938. Chapters III, IV, VII, XV.

Chapter 10

THE GATHERING AND PRODUCTION
OF FOOD

1. THE BASIC TECHNIQUES

Essential to the existence of any society is a technology for securing sufficient food to satisfy the wants of its members. The term "wants" seems preferable to the term "needs," for although a society must provide sufficient food to maintain a degree of health and vigor in its population, culturally patterned behavior nevertheless tends frequently to create wants for particular kinds of edible substances and to suppress or minimize others. The staple articles of diet may be pretty well determined by the resources of the environment and the available technology, but in nearly all societies people make efforts to secure some foods out of proportion to their nutritive value, while often rejecting or forbidding foods highly prized in other societies or possessing high nutritive values. Some Plains Indians, for example, spend much time seeking certain kinds of berries which form only a minor part of their diet, while at the same time forbidding the eating of fish. Similarly, we will go to some lengths to collect arthropods such as shrimps, but look with horror on the eating of another, the grasshopper, although this is regarded as a delicacy in many other societies.

The techniques for securing food are almost infinitely varied, but fall into two major divisions, gathering and production. Gathering techniques involve utilization of the resources of the environment as "given," without any methods to improve or increase the available supply. The production

271

of food, on the other hand, involves such techniques as farming and caring for domesticated animals, and results in a much greater food supply from a given area than can be secured by gathering. Nevertheless, the two divisions are not mutually exclusive. Although a number of purely gathering technologies exist, most production technologies also make use of gathering for part of the food supply. In our culture, for example, such things as fish, wild rice, piñon nuts, brazil nuts, and other minor foods may be secured by gathering techniques and form part of what our economists call extractive industries.

Gathering technologies may be further subdivided, according to the dominant techniques, into hunting, fishing, and collecting. No culture relies exclusively upon one of these methods, but generally the greater part of the diet is provided by one means or the other. Often the dominant techniques are partly determined by the character of the environment. Thus many California Indians have good hunting techniques, but secure most of their food by collecting seeds and fruits, supplemented by roots, tubers, bulbs, and berries. This orientation is partly determined by the Mediterranean climate of much of California, which results in the presence of many plants rich in starch.

Production technologies are likewise of many kinds. In one category, illustrated by the technologies of many nonliterate societies, are the farmers who depend wholly on man power to cultivate their land—the so-called gardeners or horticulturists. Even when such peoples possess domestic animals, these are used only as additional food resources, as indicators of status, or for similar functions, but not as aids in land cultivation. Our second category of food-producers is the agriculturalists, that is, those peoples who use animal power (e.g., horses or oxen) or mechanical devices (such as power-driven plows and reapers) to work the land. Finally, we find a third major category, the pastoral peoples, who devote their primary attention to animal husbandry, and who do little or no raising of food plants.

Within each of these categories—food-gatherers, horticulturists, agriculturalists, and pastoralists—there are of course numerous variations, due to environment, tool-making technologies, and historical circumstances. We shall review and discuss these in the sections that follow.

2. FOOD-GATHERERS: GENERAL CHARACTERISTICS

It is sometimes forgotten that man, who today quite often possesses extraordinary skills in the production of food, was a food-gatherer throughout most of his history, that is, for the several hundred thousand years of the Paleolithic. Not until the Neolithic—some eight to ten thousand years ago—did any human society develop food production. As a gatherer man evolved, dispersed over much of the inhabited world, and laid the broad foundations for human culture.

Archeological evidence suggests that the earliest men depended primarily on vegetable foods, supplementing this diet with eggs, insects, and such small game as might be captured without weapons. This is because the people of the early Paleolithic probably had no weapons for hunting other than stones, clubs, crude hand axes, throwing sticks, and spears with wooden points. With such inadequate tools, it is unlikely that men secured any large amounts of meat, except as they might have scavenged the kills of other animals or recovered the bodies of animals who died of natural causes. Like their anthropoid relatives, the great apes, early men lived almost wholly by collecting wild vegetable foods, and were probably less often hunters than hunted.

By the Mousterian epoch of the mid-Paleolithic, however, man added a handle to his crude stone ax and apparently used this implement to hunt some of the largest and most ferocious animals of his time. Near Trieste, for example, has been found a hafted ax, sunk into the skull of a cave bear, an animal which was larger and probably more dangerous than the North American grizzly. There is of course no evidence of the fate of the hunter, nor is there proof that Mousterian hunters regularly sought out the cave bear. Nevertheless, it is perhaps significant that California Indians sometimes enter caves to kill hibernating black bears and that they also goad bears into charging from a cave and so kill them with spears. It is not impossible, then, that mid-Paleolithic man had become a hunter, whose weapons, though still crude, enabled him occasionally to secure animal food, or at least to defend himself against the larger animals.

By the Upper Paleolithic, man was in possession of numerous missile weapons, among them the spear, harpoon, and spear-thrower. These weapons, the existence of great herds of ruminants such as the reindeer and the horse, and the finding of great piles of animal bones near man's dwellings prove beyond doubt that late Paleolithic man lived primarily by hunting. Fishing was also important, as is evidenced by harpoons, fish-hooks, and fish bones found in archeological deposits. Later, in the Meso-lithic, the bow and arrow further increased man's efficiency as a hunter, and emphasizes the fact that man had moved, albeit very slowly, from a primitive food-collector little advanced over other anthropoids to a hunter and fisherman well able to gain support from his environment.

There are today no peoples so primitive as to be dependent upon wild vegetable foods alone. All nonhorticultural peoples possess adequate tools and weapons for both hunting and fishing, though, as we have noted, the relative emphasis on collecting, hunting, and fishing may vary considerably from one society to the next. Though food-gathering societies are by no means identical in other aspects of their cultures, there are certain general characteristics common to all or most of them. These may be summarized as follows; details will appear in the succeeding sections.

(1) Population density is usually low in food-gathering societies. Exceptions to this rule occur only in societies, like those of the North Pacific coast or the Great Plains of America, that live in areas especially favorable to collecting, hunting, or fishing.

(2) Food-gathering societies are usually small and isolated, and often move continuously or at frequent intervals from place to place in search of wild plants and animals. They tend, in brief, to be nomadic, in contrast to the more sedentary food-producers.

(3) Food-gatherers are organized primarily as self-sufficient family groups or, more often, as loose confederations of families. Accordingly, their mechanisms of social control and interaction are based more on kinship than on political organization.

(4) Finally, the food-gatherers of today are found, for the most part, in remote or marginal areas, to which, presumably, they have been driven by the larger and more powerful food-producing societies. As a result, the food-gathering societies of the world tend to be slow to change and so to retain certain patterns of culture which have long disappeared elsewhere.

It should not be assumed, however, that food-gathering peoples are intrinsically inferior to others, or less able intellectually to achieve more advanced cultures. Food production, as we shall see later, developed in only a few places, especially favored with a suitable environment and proper animal and plant species for domestication. Arising late in human history, food-production techniques have not spread to all parts of the world—at least not until very recent historical times. Gathering peoples are those who, more venturesome or unlucky than the food-producers, wandered early to remote and undesirable locations and so did not receive the benefits of later food-producing inventions.

3. HUNTING

Hunting technologies depend upon game for the bulk of the food supply, yet within this category great differences may exist. The Australian centers his attention on the kangaroo and other marsupials, while the Ona of Tierra del Fuego concentrates on the guanaco, a camel-like animal. Both of these peoples move about from place to place as the supply of game in one area becomes scarce. The Plains Indian, on the other hand, depends mainly on the bison (buffalo) and must either kill large numbers at certain times of the year and preserve the meat, or must follow the bison herds in their seasonal migrations. Many of the Eskimos depend primarily upon sea mammals such as the seal and walrus in winter time, but move inland in summer to hunt the caribou. In each case techniques differ noticeably.

A study of the implements and techniques of hunting clearly refutes any notion that nonliterate peoples are always mystical or nonlogical in their thinking. Instead, it becomes obvious that within the limits of their knowledge they are both practical and ingenious. Supernatural aid may be sought for the hunt, and failure may be attributed to supernatural intervention or to the violation of taboos. Nevertheless, the usual attitude of the hunter, whatever the nature of the culture in which he participates, is quite like that expressed in the classical phrase: "Trust in God and keep your powder dry."

Among the most important missile weapons employed in hunting are the spear, harpoon, and bow and arrow. Of more limited occurrence are such implements as the sling, bola, boomerang, spear-thrower, and others. These are best described by the illustrations in Figures 10:1 to 10:6.

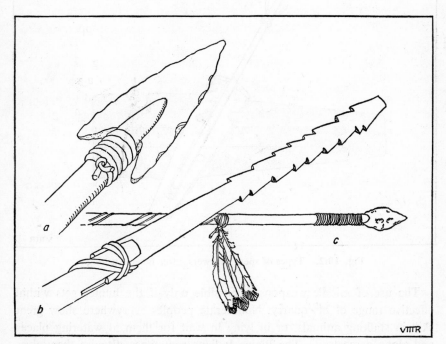

Fig. 10:1. (*a*) Southwest lance point, after Holling; (*b*) Early Aleut spearhead, after Martin, et al.; (*c*) Nez Percé spearhead, after Wissler.

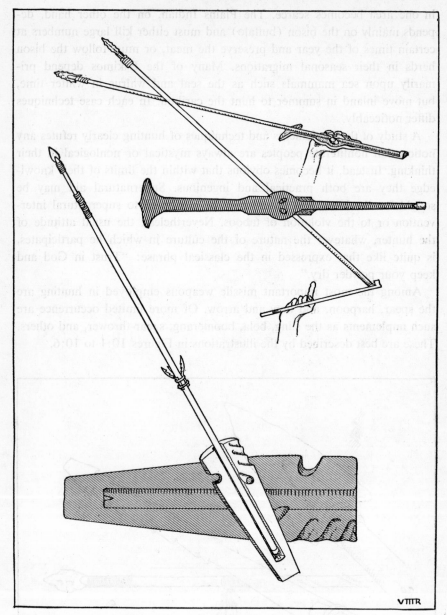

Fig. 10:2.   Types of spear throwers, after Boas, Cushing.

The use of missile weapons is possible only if the hunter gets within effective range of his quarry. Nonliterate peoples everywhere show great skill in stalking animals, or in lying in wait for them at watering places and along game trails. The Plains Indians sometimes disguise themselves

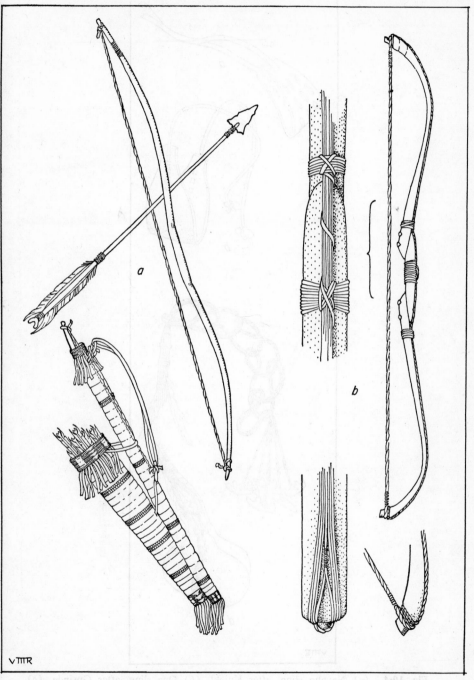

Fig. 10:3. (*a*) Dakota selfbow and stone-tipped arrow with flaring nock (above), quiver and bow case of dressed buffalo hide (below); (*b*) Eskimo compound bow backed with sinew. After Mason.

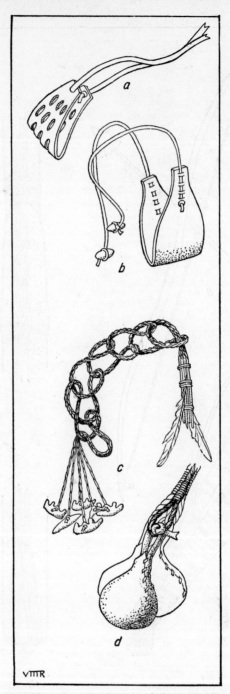

Fig. 10:4. (*a*) Navaho sling, after Knight. (*b*) Ona sling, after Gusinde. (*c*) Eskimo bird bola, knotted for carrying; note ivory weights shaped like bear, seal, and bird. The handle is quilled to guide it in flight. After Nelson. (*d*) Argentine bola; weights of clay or stone covered with leather. After Knight.

278

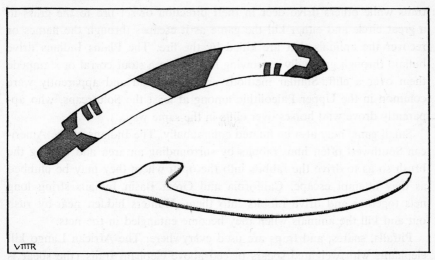

Fig. 10:5. Hopi throwing stick (top), after Hough; Baganda throwing stick (bottom).

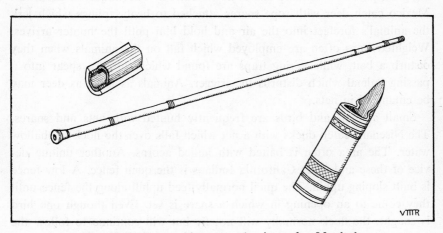

Fig. 10:6. Semang blowgun and quiver, after Murdock.

as wolves to approach buffalo herds, while the California Indians wear a deer head and deer skin to approach grazing deer. The Bushmen of South Africa similarly impersonate the ostrich. The Eskimos stalk seals on the ice by covering themselves with a white cloak, or waiting for hours beside a breathing hole in the ice. Mating calls are often simulated to attract animals, and the Eskimos imitate the sound of a seal scratching on the ice.

Group activities are often more effective than individual effort. Among the Nisenans of California several hunters station themselves beside game trails while others drive deer in their direction or set fire to the grass in a great circle and either kill the game as it escapes through the flames or recover the animals that are killed by the fire. The Plains Indians drive buffalo through gradually narrowing fences into a stout corral or stampede them over a cliff. Similar methods are widespread and apparently were common in the Upper Paleolithic among at least the Solutreans, who apparently drove wild horses over cliffs in the same way.

Small game may also be hunted communally. The Indians of the American Southwest often hunt rabbits by surrounding an area and beating the brush so as to drive the rabbits into the open where they may be clubbed as they attempt escape. California and Great Basin Indians string long nets together and drive rabbits into them. Hunters hidden near-by rush out and kill the animals when they become entangled in the nets.

Pitfalls, snares, and traps are used everywhere. The African Lango kill elephants with weighted spears placed above elephant trails (the spear is released as the animal, passing along the trail, trips a cord set there), or dig great pitfalls with sharp stakes at the bottom. The Yaquis of northwest Mexico catch deer with rope snares attached to bent saplings which jerk the animal's forefeet into the air and hold him until the hunter arrives. Weighted traps often are employed which fall on the animals when they disturb a bait, while spring traps are found which throw a spear into a passing animal which disturbs the trigger. Animals as large as deer may be entangled in nets.

Small animals and birds are frequently hunted with nets and snares. The Nisenans catch ducks with a net which falls over the flock in shallow water. The area often is baited with hulled acorns. Another unique device of these and other California Indians is the quail fence. A low fence is built sloping uphill. The quail normally feed uphill along the fence until they come to an opening in which a snare is set. Even though one bird is caught, the flock normally will not fly but will continue to follow the fence and be caught one by one at successive openings.

A number of peoples on the shores of the North Pacific, both in Asia and America, engage in whale-hunting. Hunting is carried on from boats with the use of the harpoon and a long line. Some of these peoples also apparently use a poison, aconitine, successfully. Whale-hunting is a very dangerous occupation, and usually only specialists who have secret supernatural powers and perhaps secret techniques engage in this activity. Other coastal peoples prize the flesh of the whale but do not hunt it, utilizing only the occasional animals stranded on the shore.

Although most hunting peoples have dogs, not all employ them in hunting, while others raise specially trained hunting dogs which are highly

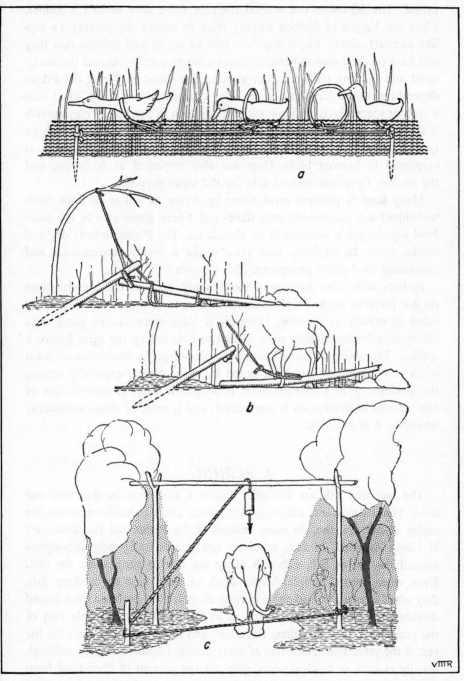

Fig. 10:7. (a) Eskimo duck snare, after Nelson; (b) Bushman animal trap; (c) East African elephant trap, after Lindblom.

prized. The Nisenans use trained dogs to drive deer toward a hunter, while the Yaquis of Mexico employ them to corner the peccary (a pig-like animal). Some Yaqui dogs are said to be so well trained that they will hunt on their own initiative, driving a single peccary toward the settlement and barking until a hunter comes. The Onas of Tierra del Fuego depend on trained hunting dogs to bring guanaco at bay to be killed with a club or spear. Even a widow without any men in her family may survive if she has a good hunting dog. In parts of southern Asia, the cheetah (a type of leopard) is trained for hunting, while in Central Asia the falcon is employed in hunting birds. Dogs are also employed as retrievers, and the ancient Egyptians trained cats for the same purpose.

Many hunters preserve meat either by drying or salting or both. Such techniques are particularly well developed where game affords the main food supply, yet is seasonal in its abundance. The Plains Indians dry and smoke meat. In addition, they often make a highly concentrated and nourishing food called pemmican. (See Chapter 9, § 8.)

Peoples with other sources of food supply, such as the Yaquis, often do not preserve meat. As the climate in Sonora is warm, the meat is all eaten as rapidly as possible. Formerly if large quantities of game were taken, neighboring villages were invited to help eat up the meat before it spoiled. The ability of some hunting peoples to gorge themselves on meat when it is abundant has been noted in many places, especially among the Eskimos. Where transportation is simple or lacking, conservation of any amount of meat often is impractical, and it must be eaten abundantly whenever it is available.

4. FISHING

The fact that fish are available does not always mean that they are used. The Tasmanians, although they collect and eat molluscs, taboo the eating of fish. So, too, do many Indians of the Plains and the Southwest in North America. In fact, relatively few people build their subsistence around the use of fish, although many use fish to supplement the diet. Even when coastal people devote much of their time to catching fish, they often secure a considerable portion of their food by trade from inland dwellers in return for fish. Others, as in California, eat fish only part of the year, when they live along the coast, and move inland to hunt for the rest of the year. The inhabitants of many Pacific Islands, however, although usually classed as horticulturists, gain a large portion of their food from the sea. In some cases, as among the Gilbert and Marshall Islanders of Micronesia, several hundred people per square mile are concentrated on islands offering very poor opportunities for farming. Only fishing keeps such large populations alive.

Among the peoples most dependent on fish are those of the northern Pacific, especially in areas where salmon occur. In British Columbia and southern Alaska such groups as the Haida, Tlingit, and others, gain their major food supply by fishing and hunting sea mammals such as whale and seal. Land-hunting and collecting are resorted to only to add variety and interest to the diet. Among these peoples, salmon are available in large numbers during part of the year, when the fish move from the sea and up the river to spawn. During this period (about three months), the Indians work as many as twenty hours a day catching and smoking salmon. The rest of the year, however, is far less strenuous—cod, halibut, and other fish are caught by deep-sea fishing and various sea mammals are hunted from boats. The regularity and abundance of the salmon supply permit these Indians to live in large and closely spaced permanent villages, and develop cultures exceptional for their arts, crafts, and ceremonialism. Unlike hunting peoples, then, fishermen often do not have to change their hunting grounds and can live most of the year in one spot occupied for a long time.

The gathering of shellfish or molluscs affords an important source of food for many coastal peoples and involves the simplest technology. A hardwood chisel to pry the molluscs off the rocks is virtually the only tool needed, and often women do most of the work. Fishing, on the other hand, usually involves a complex and varied technology and is commonly carried on by men.

Spears and harpoons are extensively used for fishing in many parts of the world. The fisherman spears or harpoons fish from a canoe or raft, a rocky point over deep water, or a platform built out over the water. Such locations may also serve for dip or cast nets and, in shallower waters, for shooting fish with a bow and arrow.

Nets, traps, and weirs, however, are the devices most used by fishermen. Long nets with floats on one side and weights or sinkers on the other are used to surround schools of fish feeding near the surface, while cast nets and dip nets are employed in shallow water. Small traps made of withes or basketry are employed mainly in streams, while weirs are used most often in shallow tidal waters.

Hook and line fishing, with some exceptions, seems confined to the peoples of Oceania and the shores of the North Pacific, who indulge in deep-sea fishing, and to those of more complex civilizations. Set lines, that is, lines with several hooks with a weight at one end and the other fastened to a stake on shore, are widely used along both beaches and

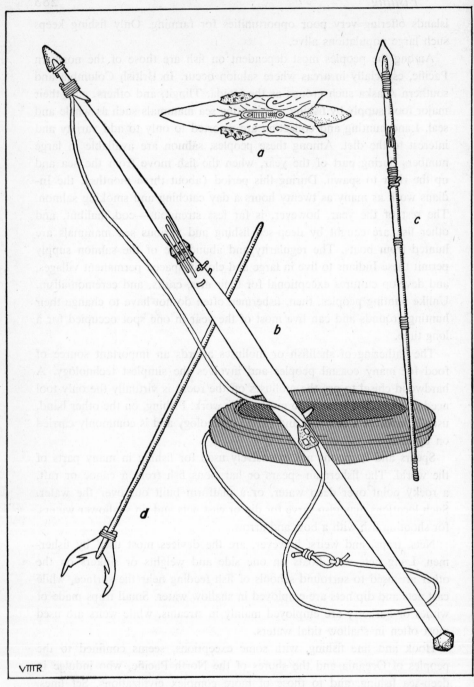

Fig. 10:8. (a) Decorated harpoon head of ivory with side blades of chipped stone, after Martin, et al.; (b) composite harpoon, after Boas; (c) whale lance, after Holling; (d) California Indian fish spear with prongs of antler, after Martin, et al.

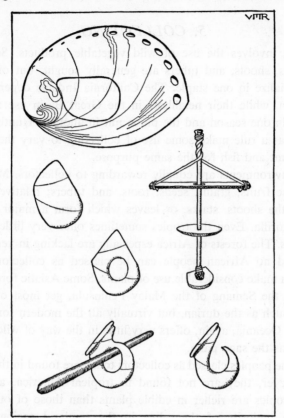

Fig. 10:9. California Indian fish hooks, showing steps in manufacture. Courtesy, Museum of Natural History of Santa Barbara, California.

streams. The Haidas of British Columbia use a variety of hooks, and fish either with a single hook or with long lines with large numbers of hooks, depending on the type of fish sought.

One of the most widespread methods of fishing is with the use of poisons or stupefacients, that is, substances which stun or paralyze the fish. Employed primarily in quiet pools in streams or in tidal lagoons or pools, this method produces large quantities of fish with relatively little effort but usually calls for the cooperation of several people. Fish-poisoning is very widely distributed throughout the tropics and is nearly as common in the temperate zones of America and Asia. The poisons or stupefacients are usually harmless to humans, and the wide variety of plants employed suggests extensive and thorough experimentation with the environment.

5. COLLECTING

Collecting involves the use of wild vegetable products. Seeds, fruits, berries, roots, shoots, and tubers are generally sought, but often peoples tend to specialize in one staple. The California Indians depend primarily on the acorn, while their neighbors in the Great Basin use a variety of small seeds in one season and the piñon nut in another. Hunting and fishing peoples as a rule make some use of collecting to vary the diet, while collectors hunt and fish for the same purpose.

Not all environments are equally rewarding to collectors. Most modern collectors use fruits, grains, seeds, roots, and tubers; relatively little use is made of the shoots, stalks, or leaves which form a major part of the diet of the gorilla. Even the tropics sometimes offer very little in the way of wild foods. The forests of Africa especially are lacking in vegetable food supplies, and no African people can be classed as collectors, although the Bushmen make considerable use of plants. Some Asiatic forest-dwellers, for example the Semang of the Malay Peninsula, get most of their food from fruits such as the durian, but virtually all the modern forest-dwellers are farmers. Oceania, again, offers very little in the way of wild foods save such plants as the sago palm.

Most of the peoples classed as collectors today are found in the Americas. Again, however, they are not found in tropical America, although the American tropics are richer in edible plants than those of other regions. Instead, the majority of them live in the semiarid regions of North America, that is, the Southwest, the Great Basin, and California.

The collectors of these regions do not have a simple technology. Actually, collecting involves not only great knowledge of the environment and the characteristics of the plants that grow in it, but it requires as well special implements and methods of preparing wild foods. Often plants of great importance are inedible without special treatment or are too difficult to gather without special tools. If lower Paleolithic Europeans were primarily collectors, they probably relied on a limited number of plants, for they apparently lacked most of the special devices of contemporary collectors.

To illustrate, the gathering by hand of large quantities of small seeds, grasses, or other plants is practically impossible. The Great Basin peoples use for this purpose a seed-beater, an artifact that much resembles our old-fashioned carpet beater. With this, they flail or thresh the seed-bearing plants and catch the seeds in a tightly woven basket tray made especially for this purpose. Then they grind the seeds into a flour or meal on a metate, a trough-shaped stone, by rubbing a smaller mano or milling stone back

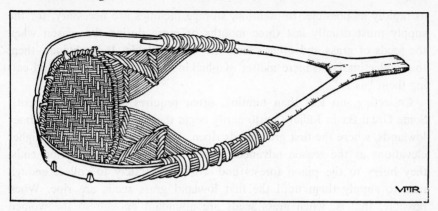

Fig. 10:10. Seed-beater.

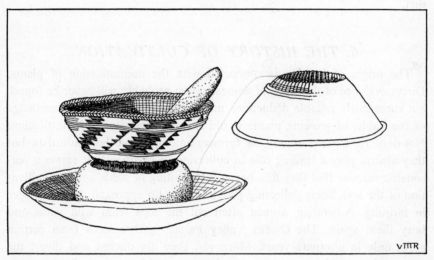

Fig. 10:11. California Indian acorn-grinder, set in a shallow basket to catch the meal. After Mason.

and forth over the seeds. Some seeds, like the acorn, contain tannic acid or other elements which make them inedible; these must be removed by a complex leaching process before the meal can be used for food. Acorns are customarily pounded in a mortar and when the flour is prepared, it is mixed with water and boiled into a mush in baskets by the hot-stone method, or it is molded into loaves or cakes to be baked in hot ashes.

Piñon nuts, the other Great Basin mainstay, must be collected by knocking down the mature but still green cones and roasting them in a fire. Once the cones open naturally, the nuts cannot be collected efficiently. Consequently collecting must begin at just the proper season and proceed as rapidly as possible. In addition, storage facilities are necessary, for the supply must usually last three months or more during the season when the seeds of grass and other plants are not available. It is obvious, then, that collecting is no mere matter of plucking the fruits of nature and eating them "as is."

Collecting, no less than hunting, often requires seasonal movements. Some Great Basin Indians customarily begin their collecting in the warmer lowlands, where the first grass seeds ripen, and move gradually into higher elevations as the season advances. When the seed-ripening season ends, they hurry to the piñon forests and work desperately to collect enough nuts to supply them until the first lowland grass seeds are ripe. When possible, that is, when grass seeds are abundant enough so the women alone can provide the supply, the men hunt game to augment and vary the diet.

6. THE HISTORY OF CULTIVATION

The origin of farming is connected with the domestication of plants. Direct evidence of the mode of domestication probably will never be found, but some fairly reliable deductions may be made. An intimate knowledge of the habits of growing plants would seem a necessity to domestication. Not only are women usually the farmers among simple horticulturists, but they always play a leading role in collecting; consequently it seems a reasonable surmise that they first began the planting of seeds and the cultivation of the soil. Some collecting peoples today do approach the first stages in farming. Australian women often cut the tops from wild yams and bury them again. The Owens Valley Paiutes gather seeds from certain areas only in alternate years. Moreover, they dig ditches and divert the waters of mountain streams to spread out over wider areas and so promote the growth of a good crop of wild grasses. In some cases, the Indians even scatter seeds over the irrigated areas. Both the Australians and the Paiutes, then, are but a step removed from farming, in that they employ with wild plants techniques of irrigation, casual sowing, and crop conservation.

For many years the theory was held that domestication had taken place in only two or three areas, Egypt or some near-by region, southeastern Asia, and Middle America. Generally it was believed that irrigation in arid regions first gave early man the idea of planting seeds, and as the Nile Valley affords an excellent example of natural flooding or irrigation of large areas, many claimed that farming first originated in Egypt. However, no wild relatives of any of the early domesticated plants are to be found in Egypt, and as a result of the work of modern botanists and geneticists, particularly of the Russian Institute of Plant Genetics when headed by Vavilov, an entirely different view now prevails. Within a few years we should have a fairly complete and accurate history of all the domesticated plants.

Recent evidence, uncovered by these researches, suggests that plant domestication was undertaken in many areas and in relation to numerous plants. This fact was long obscured because certain domesticated plants (such as wheat and maize) have spread so widely throughout the world as to eliminate or restrict the use of others of lesser value. Moreover, it is by no means certain that domestication first occurred in desert oases such as the Nile Valley of Egypt, where periodic floods provide a kind of natural irrigation. Indeed, the technique of irrigation itself may have developed first in mountain valleys and sprung from practices not unlike those we have noted for the Paiutes of the Great Basin.

Three major areas of domestication are now recognized: the highlands of Ethiopia, Anatolia, Iran, and Afghanistan; a less clearly localized area in southern or southeastern Asia; and the New World. It is also possible that there was a fourth area for the development of the root and tuber crops of the Old World tropics.

Old World areas of domestication may be divided into several special regions, as follows:

(1) Southwest Asia (that is, northwest India, Afghanistan, Iran, Transcaucasia, and eastern and central Anatolia), the home of soft wheat, rye, small-seeded flax, small-seeded peas, lentils, apples, pears, plums, and many other of the temperate zone fruits. Here are found numerous well-watered mountain valleys of moderate elevation with temperate and even climates. The valleys are protected from too easy incursions from the outside, have limited natural food resources, yet will quickly repay efforts to increase yields. Finally, it is a region of great botanical diversity, offering many different species of plants for experimentation.

(2) The Mediterranean area, the home of the olive, fig, and the broadbean.

(3) Ethiopia, the home of hard wheat, some of the barleys, and the large-seeded peas.

(4) Mountainous China and near-by sections, the home of the soya bean, millet, numerous herbs, and perhaps hemp.

(5) Central and southern India, Burma, and Indo-China, the home of rice, sugar cane, and Asiatic cotton.

The banana is certainly Asiatic in origin, but for this, as well as such crops as coconut, taro, yam, breadfruit, and others, evidence still seems indecisive.

The New World was the source of many of our most important domesti-

cated plants. Three-fifths of the world's agricultural wealth today is estimated to derive from plants unknown to Europe before Columbus. As in
the Old World, domestication took place in many different places, but the
most important areas of origin seem to have been in Central America and
the northern part of South America. The following partial list of American
cultivated plants shows the large number of American domesticated plants
and that many peoples contributed to their development:

Agave or maguey (three species), amaranth, arracacha, arrowroot, avo-
cado, beans (five species), cacao, canna, cherimoya, chia, chile pepper,
Chilean tarweed, cotton (two species at least), custard apple, guava,
Jerusalem artichoke, lupine, maize (many varieties developed under domestication), mango grain, manioc (two species), papaya, passion fruit,
peanut, pineapple, pumpkin and squash (four species, some with independently domesticated varieties), potato (unknown number of species),
quinoa, sapodilla, soursop, spondias, star apple, sunflower, sweet potato,
tobacco (at least two species), tomato (two species).

Places of domestication mentioned for various species include: eastern
United States, northwest Mexico and Arizona, central Mexico, Chiapas,
Guatemala, Central America, the Antilles, Colombia, Venezuela, Ecuador,
Peru, Chile, Brazil, and possibly Paraguay. Others can be less closely
identified as to modern national boundaries and can only be assigned to
broad areas such as the Amazon-Orinoco, Andean highlands, temperate
Andean valleys, warm humid Andean valleys, and so on.[1]

It is evident from the fact that so many peoples contributed to the
domestication of our stock of plants that the process is less difficult than
was once supposed. Evidently once a certain stage of culture was reached,
opportunity was the most important factor. Aside from general environmental conditions, the presence of many different wild species and varieties
seems to have been of major importance. In this connection, almost any
of the small Central American countries or the south of Mexico possesses
more species of wild plants than can be found in the entire area of the
United States.

Once domestication occurred, other plants might be domesticated more
easily. However, in each case, successful transition from a gathering technology seems associated with the presence of an adequate starch-producing plant. For this purpose the grains are clearly superior except in some
tropical areas. Not only do they give greater return for the effort involved
but they are more easily stored for considerable periods of time. Grains
superior in yield and storing qualities tended to spread to other peoples,

[1] We are indebted to Mr. Joseph Hester for permission to summarize from an
unpublished compilation prepared by him.

even though the latter already had a domesticated starch-producing plant; less desirable plants, on the other hand, tended to have restricted distributions.

About the production of grains often cluster other plants. Sometimes these evidently have developed accidentally as secondary grain crops. Thus rye and oats apparently first appeared as weeds in wheat. As it was difficult with primitive methods to eliminate the weed seeds, they persisted until it was found that for some purposes they had advantages of their own. In America, squash and beans usually accompany maize.

The shift to a grain diet caused a much greater demand for salt, and this in turn resulted in a development of trade. Salt-working was carried on in some sections as a specialty, and in the early metal ages the salt mines of central Europe were one of the most important centers of industry and trade. It is probable also that the shift to a grain diet had effects upon the physique of Neolithic man, perhaps resulting in a lightening of the bony structure and other changes. This aspect of anthropology, however, is as yet little explored.

A recent writer has suggested that there are three major phases in farming. One, typified by early horticultural techniques, results in soil exhaustion and is often called "soil robbery." A second phase is one in which conservation practices are followed to prevent the erosion and destruction of the soil. The third phase is where efforts are made to enrich and develop the soil. Much of Europe has been in the last of these three phases for some time. In the Americas, however, only the Peruvians and perhaps some Mexican tribes had reached the third phase, and their practices were abandoned after the coming of the Spanish. As a result, Peru is probably less productive today than it was in aboriginal times, despite the introduction of better farming tools. Most of America is still in the stage of soil robbery. Only here and there have tentative efforts been made at conservation; in the United States extensive efforts are little more than a decade old. The third stage is almost completely lacking, and while here and there in the United States individual farmers practice soil building and restoring methods, these cannot be said to be at all general.

7. HORTICULTURE

Horticulture is the term usually applied to the cultivation of domesticated plants for food and other purposes without the use of the plow. Although the term "horticulture" implies the use of the hoe, actually the major implement employed is the dibble or digging stick, supplemented at times by the hoe or spade. Only metal-using peoples have hoes or spades

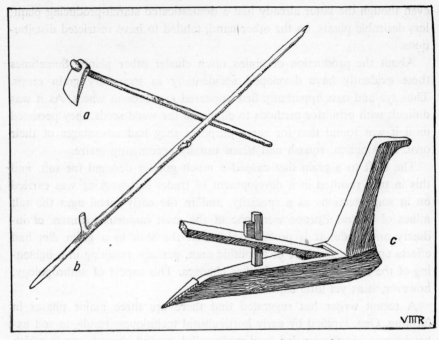

Fig. 10:12. (*a*) Hoe; (*b*) digging stick; (*c*) plow.

adequate to turning over the soil sufficiently for farming; other peoples, with hoes or spades of wood, shell, bone, or other materials, use them only for light cultivation.

Like many other classificatory terms, the word "horticulture" is applied to a number of widely different farming complexes. Farming techniques not only vary greatly, but often quite different assemblages of plants are cultivated.

African horticulture is of particular interest, for it is almost entirely a borrowed technique. As mentioned above, the forest regions of Africa possess few food plants, and virtually the only native plants which almost certainly were domesticated in Africa are the sorghums. The cultivated yam of Africa may have been locally domesticated also, but it is equally possible that it was borrowed, and while barley may be of Ethiopian origin, it is little used in Africa. The banana, a mainstay of many African tribes, is of Asiatic derivation and is propagated by transplanting side shoots growing up beside the stalk. Indeed, the plant has been cultivated so long that its seeds no longer will germinate. The wild bananas present in Africa lack side shoots, are large-seeded, and are virtually inedible. Bananas take relatively little attention after a grove is once established. Yams are propagated by cutting off the heads and replanting them. The sorghums and an imported plant, millet, are grown to some extent in parts of Africa, but only in a few cases do they form an important part of the diet. Millet, indeed, is often grown only for the purpose of making beer.

As the Negro peoples of Africa were long in contact with Egypt, it is sometimes asked why more elements of Egyptian culture, such as wheat-growing, were not adopted. The answer seems to be that much of the Egyptian farming complex was unsuited to the African climate. Wheat, for example, does not do well in tropical areas. That the African Negro was not unreceptive to new additions to his farming techniques is shown by the great rapidity with which New World plants were adopted when they became available. Today the staple plants of many African groups are maize, peanuts, and manioc derived from the American tropics.

In the Oceanian region are found not only the yam and banana, but the coconut, breadfruit, taro, and sugar cane. In the poorer coral islands of the Pacific, the coconut is often the principal plant grown. Techniques of growing these plants vary considerably. Coconuts can be laid on the surface and, if given protection from animals, and the underbrush is cut away periodically, will sprout and grow with no further care. Breadfruit trees, once established, produce for many years without cultivation. Sugar cane, on the other hand, is propagated by burying cuttings of the stalk containing joints, while the taro is a tuberous plant which must be grown in swamplike conditions.

In parts of Indonesia and southeast Asia, rice is an important plant among horticulturists. Both dry and irrigated rice are cultivated with no other tool than the digging stick. Often such horticulture is elaborate and intensive as in the case of the Ifugao of the Philippines, who construct large-scale irrigation systems and terrace entire mountainsides for rice cultivation.

In the New World, a number of tubers and roots are cultivated in tropical areas, including the peanut, manioc, and sweet potato. Manioc is of special interest, for the preferred type, and apparently the earliest one domesticated, is the so-called bitter manioc containing prussic acid. Special procedures of grating the flesh and extracting the juice are required to make the plant edible. Manioc produces the year round and thrives in moist, humid lowlands where other crops can be grown only with difficulty.

The sweet potato has been more adaptable and is grown also in temperate zones such as the eastern United States and the highlands of Central America. In highland South America another tuber, the potato, is the staple food at elevations too high to grow maize.

In the Old World the major grain-cultivating peoples use the plow and are classed as agriculturists. Nevertheless, probably all the grains were originally grown by horticulturists, as is still the case with some rice-growers. Early Chinese farmers grew millet without the plow, while the earliest wheat farmers of Europe were horticulturists. With the exception of rice, however, the Old World grains do not lend themselves well to horticultural techniques.

The major New World grain, maize, on the other hand, thrives under horticultural methods. So, too, do the usual accompaniments of maize cultivation, squash and beans. The Old World grains such as millet, wheat, barley, and rye, on the other hand, grow best when sown broadcast in fairly large plots of prepared ground, difficult to prepare with simple tools. Rice is usually sprouted in seed beds, and the young plants are transplanted one at a time to a prepared and flooded plot of ground. Maize, on the other hand, is planted in hills by most primitive farmers. A jab of the digging stick in the earth opens a hole for several kernels of corn. Often beans and squash are planted in the same hole, which is then covered with earth and pressed down with the foot. Another hill is planted eighteen inches or more away. As the plants grow, the earth is heaped up about them and the weeds are cut away. None of these tasks has to be done over a large area in a short time, and the yield is quite high in proportion to the labor.

The advantages of maize-growing permit the development of intensive types of farming even with horticultural methods. Although many farming peoples of the Americas were relatively simple in culture, those of Middle America and the highland regions of South America developed advanced cultures of great complexity, as did some African and East Asiatic horticulturists.

The techniques of horticulture, as practiced by most people, are not greatly different in many respects from those of collectors. The most widely used horticultural tool, the digging stick, is the same as that used by such collectors as the Australians to dig out wild plants. Most simple horticulture is done by women, and only when horticulture comes to provide the main food supply does it become men's work.

Very often people classed as horticulturists secure only a portion of their food supply from farming. The Yumas at the mouth of the Colorado river are always classed as horticulturists, yet probably not more than 40 per cent of the food supply comes from farm products; the rest is provided by mesquite beans, game, and fish. This contrasts markedly with the neighboring Pueblo Indians who gain the greater portion of their food from farming. In the eastern part of the United States, again a fair proportion of the food supply is from game and wild plants. In general, however, the peoples south of the United States rely heavily upon gardening, especially in the more complex cultures. In Oceania, too, gardening is very important, though on some islands it is outranked by fish as a source of food. The horticulturists of Africa and Asia again rely primarily on garden produce.

Often horticulture is carried on by very inefficient methods. In regions of heavy rainfall the minerals in the soil leach away rapidly and fields are quickly exhausted. Cultivation by all horticulturists is very shallow, and usually farmers must clear and cultivate new fields every few years. When the near-by land is exhausted, the village is moved to a new spot; consequently many horticulturists are as migratory as gathering peoples, although their movements may be slower and extend over many years.

Only in a few areas do more advanced techniques involving fertilization exist. In Peru, where irrigation and terracing existed, fertilizing was common in pre-Spanish times. This is also true of horticultural rice-growers such as the Ifugao. Most Africans, however, are migratory farmers, as are most of the peoples of tropical America and eastern United States.

Certain domestic animals are associated with various types of horticulture, although not used as draft animals or even as important sources of food. The dog seems present almost everywhere, and in a few areas, such as pre-Spanish Mexico, the dog was specially fed and bred for food. In Africa, chickens, pigs, cattle, sheep, and goats are variously present among horticulturists. The chicken is often used primarily for divination and sacrifice, while the pig, goat, and sheep are little used. Cattle likewise are rarely slaughtered for their flesh, although eaten after sacrifices. Nevertheless, among many of the eastern and southern Bantu-speaking tribes, dairy products are an important supplement to the food supply.

In southeast Asia and Oceania the pig and chicken are the main animals of the horticulturists. Here again they are eaten only on special occasions. The fowl especially is primarily a sacrificial animal. In a few instances water buffalo are present to a minor extent; but again they are eaten only on special occasions.

New World horticulturists had even fewer animals; for many the dog alone is present. The Pueblo Indians raise domesticated turkeys for their feathers but do not eat them. In Mexico, however, the turkey is sometimes eaten. Peru possesses the llama and the guinea pig. The former is utilized as a beast of burden, as a source of wool, and is sometimes eaten, but the humble guinea pig is perhaps a more important source of meat for most poor Peruvians.

Associations of other cultural elements with horticulture may likewise be noted. Pottery, which because of its fragility and weight is of little use to non-farming peoples, is found among most horticulturists. Weaving also is mainly confined to farming peoples, both horticulturists and agriculturists, while the true loom is not found among nonfarmers. In part this may be due to the fact that the principal fibers used extensively for weaving are the product of domesticated animals or plants, flax in Europe and western Asia, hemp in eastern and central Asia, cotton in India, and cotton and henequen in the Americas. Wool, widely used in the Old World, is important only in Peru in the Americas. Housing likewise tends to be more substantial among farmers, particularly among nonmigratory farmers such as the Pueblo Indians. And as noted before, farming communities and tribes tend to be larger, more stable, and more complex in organization. On the negative side, however, it should be noted that horticulturists usually lack writing and the wheel, while metal-working occurs only in the more advanced horticultural civilizations.

8. AGRICULTURE

True agriculture involves use of the plow and draft animals. The practice is confined to the Old World and particularly to Europe, North Africa, Asia, and some adjoining parts of Indonesia. In the wheat-growing areas, moreover, there is considerable use of either flesh or dairy products to supplement the diet. Nevertheless, agriculturists apparently have added very little to the number of either domesticated plants or animals.

Until fairly recent times, of course, the plow was a much cruder implement than we are accustomed to. It lacked any moldboard to turn the soil, and the share was simply a heavy piece of pointed wood, sometimes tipped with metal, attached to a pole fastened to a yoke or harness on the draft animals. Such a plow does little more than stir the ground five or six inches down. This early plow still is used in many parts of the world.

Poor as it is by modern standards, the plow cultivates the soil much more efficiently than can be done with digging-stick or spade. Moreover, heavier soils can be cultivated as well as many of the grasslands. Finally, larger areas can be prepared and planted at one time, and the growing of wheat, barley, rye, and millet is much more profitable. The forest lands preferred by horticulturists are shunned, for the tree roots pose great difficulties for the plow.

Two great agricultural areas may be distinguished. One is characterized by wheat as the dominant plant, and extends from Europe, North Africa, and the Near East across central Asia to North China. Associated with wheat in this area is a variety of other plants, especially barley and rye, with emphasis on cattle, sheep, horses, goats, and pigs, and, except in

China, dairying. The second area is the great rice-growing region of Japan, South China, southeast Asia, Indonesia, and India. Here the typically associated animal is the water buffalo, supplemented by the pig and chicken. Cattle and horses, although sometimes present, are of little importance. Dairying techniques are found in India but not elsewhere, while the eating of flesh from domesticated animals is reserved for special occasions or is absent. In China, draft animals are usually too valuable to be slaughtered, even though no taboos exist on their flesh as in India.

The agricultural areas are also associated with other culture elements. Metal-working is general, the wheel is in use, writing is common, architecture tends to be larger and more substantial. Large public architecture and urban centers are confined mainly to agricultural peoples except in Mexico and Peru. Political units tend to be of greater size and complexity of organization; there is greater specialization of function and often more marked class differentiation. Some of these last features, however, are also to be found among intensive horticulturists. Nevertheless, again with the exception of Mexico and Peru, all of the great and complex civilizations known now or in the past rest or have rested on an agricultural basis.

9. THE HISTORY OF DOMESTICATED ANIMALS

The number of domesticated animals is far smaller than that of domesticated plants. In the Old World, horses, donkeys, cattle, sheep, goats, swine, reindeer, camels, cats, and dogs are the only mammals (if we classify the yak and water buffalo as members of the cattle family). Other forms, such as elephants, are not classed as domesticated animals, for they are merely tamed and do not breed freely in captivity.

The origins of animal domestication, like the origins of plant domestication, may only be surmised. Cattle and other animals were in full use in Egypt, Mesopotamia, and northwest India by 3000 B.C. or before. The earliest levels at the archeological site of Anau near the southern end of the Caspian Sea, however, reveal a horticultural people who apparently were in contact with cattle-breeders but did not themselves have cattle. While the age of this site is not certain, it probably is older than any site with evidence of domesticated animals in Egypt or Mesopotamia. More recent excavations by Carleton Coon in Belt cave near the Caspian Sea show a sequence of occupation, first by people who hunted animals, then apparently herded sheep and goats for their flesh, and still later began to farm, to make pottery, to milk sheep and goats and use their wool for weaving, and perhaps slightly later to raise pigs and oxen. The last period is dated about 6000 B.C. Interestingly enough, the skeletal remains from the first period just before domestication again show a type intermediate between Neanderthal and modern man. (See Chapter 5, § 10.)

It is far from certain, therefore, that the first animal domestication was carried on by farmers. Indeed, this almost certainly was not the case with the dog. Theories attributing the origin of domestication to farmers assume that hunters have neither the patience nor the fixed habitations necessary to domestication. This is not necessarily true; many hunters keep the young of various animals as pets and some have relatively sedentary habits for at least part of the time. For animals psychologically fitted for domestication—and there is evidence that many animals are psychologically unsuited—the process of domestication may not have been a very long one.

The first domesticated animal was the dog. The earliest evidence of the domesticated dog is from the Mesolithic in the Baltic region of Europe about 10,000 years ago. However, the dog seems to be derived from the Asiatic wolf, and hence the first actual domestication must have taken place somewhat earlier. A further evidence of the priority and antiquity of the dog is found in its wide distribution. Although some peoples do not have the dog, usually this seems to be because of climatic reasons. Only the Tasmanians and Andamanese almost certainly never had the dog, while the Australian dog is only partly domesticated. Even the inhabitants of Tierra del Fuego make significant use of the dog, and it seems certain from this and from the numerous varieties of dog found in the Americas that the animal must have been a companion of some of the earlier (but not the first) immigrants to the continent.

Despite new evidence we are not entirely certain which animal was the second to be domesticated. The sequence at Belt cave may not hold for other areas. Sheep, goats, cattle, pigs, and donkeys are all well established in Egypt by 3000 B.C., and all but the donkey are known from the Egyptian Neolithic. The domestic camel likewise appears fairly early in northwestern India. Even less certain are the motivations which led to the first domestication of animals. Sheep were almost certainly kept before they were bred for wool, and goats, commoner than sheep in the European Neolithic, were probably domesticated long before they were used for either milk or meat. Milking, whether applied to cattle, goats, sheep, or mares, appears to be a later development than animal husbandry, and is even today absent among many peoples who keep the animals.

Domestication for meat seems a likely early motivation, even though many peoples of today eat their domestic animals only on rare ceremonial occasions. This fact suggests that animals may in part have been domesticated as religious offerings. In most of southeast Asia and Africa today, chickens are kept solely as sacrifices and for use in divination; they are never eaten. This is also true of pigs in most of Oceania and of the water buffalo in parts of Indonesia. Finally, it is well known that Near Eastern peoples regularly sacrificed animals even in early times and that this practice continued well into the Roman period.

The place of animal domestication is likewise uncertain. Donkeys seem very likely to have been developed first in North Africa where wild relatives occur. Cattle, on the other hand, while they may have been domesticated in North Africa, could equally well have been domesticated in southwest Asia. Such forms as the zebu or humped cattle and the water buffalo were domesticated in India, either through copying the domestication of regular cattle or as an independent discovery.

Sheep and goats come from the highlands of western Asia between Anatolia and the Hindu Kush where three wild forms occur, all of which seem to form part of the ancestry of domestic sheep and goats. The history of the horse is somewhat less clear. Evidently it is a later domestication, perhaps copied from that of the donkey. However, there is no evidence of wild horses south of the Asiatic highlands, and the grasslands of Central Asia seem the most likely home. It is true that there were small wild horses in Europe, but there is little reason to believe that they were domesticated, although they may form part of the ancestry of the modern horse through interbreeding with wild forms. The origin of the pig is somewhat less certain. It appears in the early Neolithic of both Egypt and China. Most opinion favors southeast Asia for a home, although it is possible that more than one domestication occurred. Cats seem to have been fairly late except in Egypt. They did not spread into Europe until much later than the other animals and still were not common in medieval England.

Reindeer are considered by many to be the last major animal to be domesticated. The earliest evidence for their domestication is from Chinese sources nearly five centuries before the beginning of the Christian era. Moreover, all the techniques of using reindeer seem derived from techniques applied to other animals as well. It is interesting also that the Eskimo and American Indian did not domesticate the closely related caribou. The reindeer now found in Alaska and Canada were imported by the respective governments in the hope of improving the economic status of the native peoples.

In addition to mammals, several birds and at least two insects, bees and silkworms, were domesticated. Chickens are certainly native to southeastern Asia where their domestication no doubt first occurred. Both ducks and geese seem to have been domesticated at least twice, in Egypt and in China. The Egyptian goose seems to have disappeared from modern cultures, for all modern domesticated geese are derived from Chinese sources.

The American Indians in general have many fewer domesticated animals than Old World peoples. For one thing, the number of animals amenable to domestication is much smaller. Bison (or buffalo), the closest American relative of cattle, seem unsuitable; at least all recent attempts to domesticate them have been unsuccessful. No horselike animals were present in recent times. Consequently, the list is very small—the llama, alpaca, vicuña, guinea pig, and muscovy duck in Peru, the turkey in Mexico and the Southwest, a stingless American bee in Mexico and Central America, and, of course, the dog derived presumably from Asia.

The small number and inferior quality of domesticated animals in America were a severe handicap to the development of American Indian cultures. None of the animals the Indian possessed were suitable for draft animals except the dog, which was used only in the Arctic. The llama is a somewhat inferior pack animal, and the dog is used for the same purpose in parts of North America. Ritualistic purposes often were important in the New World as in the Old, and may again have been a prime motivation for the original domestication.

The antiquity of domesticated animals in America is unknown. The turkey was present in Arizona and New Mexico by at least 700 A.D. and the llama and guinea pig probably were used in Peru by the beginning of the Christian era. The dog, of course, is probably much older.

10. PASTORALISM

Pastoral peoples depend upon domesticated animals for most of their food supply. Normally they do little or no farming, and any vegetable products in their diet are gained by gathering or by trading with farming peoples. Pastoral peoples make use of sheep, goats, cattle, horses, camels, reindeer, or some combination of these. The pig, a very common animal among farmers, is unsuited for a true pastoral life, for it does not travel readily. The water buffalo is likewise restricted in use, for it must spend part of each day in mud or water to be healthy. Dogs and cats, if present, are of minor importance for food and afford no basis for pastoral life.

All pastoral peoples are found in the Old World, mainly in the great grassland and desert belt extending from the boundaries of China on the east through Mongolia and southern Siberia to the plains of eastern Russia. From central Asia this belt swings southward across the highlands of Iran and Anatolia into Arabia, thence across North Africa and the Sudan on the one hand and southward along the east African highlands on the other. This great stretch of country is, with few exceptions, a region of light or deficient rainfall. In some areas, such as parts of the Sudan and east Africa, it is park land, that is, grassland interspersed with clumps or belts of trees. In the Sahara, Arabia, and parts of Mongolia it is desert. In the great Central Asiatic and east Russian plains it is steppe—fairly dry grassland areas with trees found only along the permanent streams. In this latter area are found the classical examples of pastoralism among such peoples as the Kirghiz and Kazak.

The Kazaks utilize virtually all the domesticated animals suitable for pastoral life except the reindeer. In mountain areas they even use the yak, but cattle and sheep are the animals of primary economic importance. Goats are herded with the sheep and little distinction is made between them. Both the two-humped Bactrian camel and the single-humped dromedary are prized pack animals and have a semisacred character. Dogs and cats are kept also. But the most prized animal among the Kazaks, although of secondary economic importance, is the horse. Children often learn to ride before they walk. It is proper to inquire about a man's horse before inquiring about his family, and an attractive woman is often described as a handsome filly.

Horses are reserved primarily for riding. Cattle and camels (and in mountain areas the yak) are packed when moving camp. The flesh of sheep, cattle, and horses is eaten, and all suitable animals are milked, including mares. A variety of milk products is manufactured, the most unusual being *kumiss,* a slightly fermented mare's milk which affords almost the only food eaten by the wealthy during the summer.

Pastoral peoples are often described as nomads because they must frequently change location to obtain the best pastures for their animals. Contrary to popular opinion, however, they do not move about at random. A Kazak family may cover several hundred miles in a year, and different herds belonging to a family may at times be two or three hundred miles apart. The routes followed are nevertheless about the same each year and the group always returns to the same winter quarters.

The severe winter climates of Central Asia make sheltered locations a necessity. Winter quarters are in river or mountain valleys with trees and a good supply of grass. Here permanent houses are maintained. The winter pastures are privately owned, although summer pastures are used communally by the tribe. The number of livestock and the size of the population are limited, not by the amount of pasture available in summer, but by the number of good winter pastures.

In Africa below the Sahara the pastoral peoples concentrate on cattle. Horses and sheep, if present, are of secondary importance. Sheep may be a major source of food, it is true, but wealth is measured in cattle, even though little economic use is made of them. Such characteristic cattle-breeders as the Masai of East Africa use no horses and always travel on foot. Above all else, cattle ownership expresses social position. Among some tribes cattle are named, and the owners develop such deep emotional attachments to favorite animals that suicides sometimes follow the death of a beloved animal.

Among some of the horticultural peoples of South and East Africa, cattle play a similar role in determining social prestige. Usually dairying is a little more important among the horticulturists, but while men devote themselves to cattle-raising, much of the food supply is the product of the women's gardens.

In the Sahara and southwest Asia the major animals are camels, sheep, goats, and horses. Sheep and goats are less numerous or absent among some of the people in the region, but even if of primary economic importance, they are regarded less highly than camels and horses. Great care is expended upon the latter and careful breeding has been carried on for centuries. The excellence of Arabian horses is proverbial. Camels are likewise specially bred, and there is a vast difference between fast riding camels, which may cover a hundred miles a day, and a plodding baggage camel which may cover only twenty.

Life again centers about the needs of animals. Migration may be necessary in certain seasons, but usually the group has a permanent headquarters in an oasis. Here a special type of horticulture or even agriculture may be carried on. Dates, wheat, millet, and sometimes olives are grown in the oases and are an important part of the diet of some groups. Elsewhere the town-dwellers carry on the farming, and trade with groups which are entirely pastoral. In Syria the camel is even adapted to such uses as plowing. Dairying, too, is carried on with the camel; camel wool is important in weaving, and camel meat is eaten.

In a number of areas dairying is carried on by peoples not ordinarily classed as pastoral, but who are equally dependent on their livestock. In many parts of Europe sections of the population or entire districts gain their livelihood primarily from animals; they farm only to produce food for the animals. Residence shifts seasonally according to the needs of the animals, the higher mountain pastures being used in summer, the valley locations in winter. Scandinavia, Switzerland, Spain, and Albania are countries where such groups still exist.

Another special example of a dairying people is the Toda of the Nilgiri hills in India. Here dairying has been transferred to the buffalo. The animals are sacred and the flesh is not eaten except on rare occasions. Most of the food supply is obtained from dairy products, part of which are traded to neighboring peoples for grain. Social life and religion center about the herds. Although a pastoral people, the Todas are in no sense nomads, for they live in permanent villages and do not have even seasonal changes of residence.

Of special interest are pastoral peoples dependent primarily on reindeer. Reindeer-breeding extends in a belt across northern Asia and Europe, in or close to the arctic regions. The reindeer was probably domesticated at a fairly late date, and evidently most of the techniques are adaptations from the uses of other animals. Although a few technical traits are found universally among reindeer-breeders, others are found sporadically. Fairly general is the use of reindeer as draft animals in winter. The animals are hitched to sledges in ways which suggest adaptation from the use of the dog for traction, a more widespread circumpolar trait. A few peoples, however, such as the Tungus, have developed special breeds of reindeer to use as riding rather than as draft animals. The Tungus, indeed, are essentially a hunting people who use reindeer to extend the range of their hunting and make little other use of the animals. Many others use reindeer as pack animals. Dairying is limited in occurrence and evidently was adapted at a late date from practices used with cattle. The Lapps in northern Scandinavia are the principal example of dairying in connection with reindeer.

Pastoral peoples, except for such dairying groups as the Toda and the European dairying peoples, often are in conflict with farming peoples. Herdsmen frequently despise both farming and the farmers. Although farmers sometimes are tolerated, provided they do not infringe on pasture lands, open conflict often occurs. Conflicts between cattlemen and nesters (farmers) characterized the expansion of our own western frontier. The superior mobility of pastoral peoples often enables relatively small numbers to raid, dominate, or conquer relatively large numbers of settled farmers.

The Mongols of the thirteenth century afford an outstanding example of the ability of pastoral peoples with dynamic leadership to dominate their neighbors. Under Genghis Khan the Mongols conquered China, India, and most of western Asia, as well as eastern and central Europe. The Mongols, however, lacked both sufficient numbers and sufficient administrative experience to retain their conquests. Despite the most efficient communications system developed up to that time, contacts with remote parts of the empire were too feeble and distant regions soon broke away. In India the Mongol leaders became independent local kings, the Moguls, a word now passed into English to designate a rich and powerful person. In China it was necessary for the Mongols to retain the bureaucratic officialdom of the previous Chinese government, and within two generations the Mongols had become completely acculturated, that is, they had adopted Chinese culture and merely formed a ruling dynasty.

Out of the conflict of pastoral and farming peoples, however, political states have frequently arisen. In Africa many of the large kingdoms seem to have resulted from the conquest of farmers by cattle-breeders who established themselves as a ruling caste. The desert people of Arabia in early times frequently overran the farming cultures of Mesopotamia and developed new and often more powerful states after a period of acculturation.

11. THE SIGNIFICANCE OF FOOD PRODUCTION

Of all the various steps in the development of civilization, the discovery of methods of food production is probably the most important. For the first time man was able to augment the productivity of his environment and to gain some degree of control over his food supply. Foresight and long-range planning became increasingly profitable, while under favorable circumstances greater leisure was possible.

The early effect of what Childe has called the first great revolution in human affairs was not spectacular. Restricted by crude tools to forests or other poorly productive lands, quickly exhausted, the farmer was still seminomadic. The best farmers of the northeastern United States, the Iroquois, apparently move their villages about every ten years. In such a fashion, apparently, farming crept into Europe through the forests, unheralded and probably spurned by many of the inhabitants who, for a long time, preferred their accustomed way of life dependent upon game, supplemented in some places by fish. Even when farming was accepted by many peoples, it seems to have been done so grudgingly, with the focus of interest remaining on the gradually less productive pursuit of game.

Thus some of the Plains Indians farm half-heartedly, and even the most intensive farmers regularly take up a nomadic life part of the year in pursuit of the bison. East of the Mississippi most native groups hunt extensively. In both areas farming is carried on exclusively by women, save for a few small plots cultivated for ritualistic purposes by the men of a few tribes.

As we have seen, the Paleolithic world was one of relatively discontinuous bands of hunters and fishermen. At first sight the early Neolithic (the Neolithic period begins approximately with farming) showed little difference. Yet the changes were highly significant. A given area supported a larger population through farming, and though the villages which developed were still small and isolated, they nevertheless were closer together, and contacts might be maintained between villages over considerable periods of time. As the village might be occupied for many years, there was some point to sturdier and more permanent housing. With moves infrequent, pottery became practicable. The true loom seems generally to accompany even relatively simple farming and cloth-weaving, and the wearing of garments of cloth rather than skin was adopted by many farmers.

Although apparently the peoples of Europe and perhaps parts of Asia achieved relatively little advance in the early days of horticulture, the technique had great possibilities when properly organized. The fairly complex civilizations of the Mayas, Aztecs, Incas, and others in the Americas, are one example of what organization can accomplish on even a horticultural basis. Southeast Asia and the Negro kingdoms of Africa furnish other examples. In Europe and much of Asia, however, the dependence on wheat apparently offered fewer potentialities for horticulturists than did the maize of the American Indian, the rice of southeast Asia, or the banana of Africa. Not until the invention of the plow and the adaptation of animals for draft purposes did the wheat-growing peoples realize the full potentialities of farming.

Exactly where and how the plow was invented and animals trained to draw it is relatively unimportant. The event probably took place somewhere in the Near East, perhaps first by pulling a crude wooden hoe through the ground by man power, and later with oxen. What is important are the associated effects of this discovery when it really began to be widely adopted. Large areas could be quickly prepared for sowing and could be planted in a short time. The productivity of the individual laborer increased greatly, while more fertile soils hitherto too difficult to farm became accessible.

Apparently population grew enormously with the adoption of agriculture. Land shortages quickly appeared, and the rapid diffusion of the plow was accelerated by major movements of peoples in search of new lands. Where horticulture had crept into Europe, agriculture swept across the continent in a surging tide.

With the adoption of agriculture, the village became more stable. Lands could now be cultivated for generations. Villages were close together, and in areas such as Mesopotamia and Egypt, where collective irrigation works were necessary for the fullest utilization of the farming resources, villages began to be linked together into political units. Specialization and trading were accelerated as well as the growth of a town-dwelling class with greater leisure. It is no surprise, therefore, that a host of new inventions tread on the heels of the expanding agricultural technique. Dairying, the wheel for land transport, the horizontal wheel for pottery-turning, and finally writing and metallurgy.

The last two inventions were particularly important. Writing made possible communication at a distance and the more accurate preservation of records and knowledge. It is true that in the early days writing seems to have been too complex for more than a privileged class—the priest and the merchant—to learn and use, and hence its full possibilities were not realized until the invention of the alphabet roughly a thousand years before Christ (see Chapter 17, § 10). Metallurgy, on the other hand, quickly ushered in the second major revolution in human affairs.

So long as man got his food by farming, wove his own cloth, and made his own tools of wood and stone, the family or the village was relatively self-sufficient. Once the superiority of metal tools became evident, however, this was no longer true, for the necessary raw materials are less abundant and less evenly distributed. The farmer for the first time became dependent on the specialist and he in turn on the trader and the miner. The town was converted into the city, and organized military forces, armed with the superior metal weapons, were required to protect both the wealth of the city and its dependent territory and to ensure the control of trade routes and natural resources.

The earliest effective metal tools and weapons were of bronze, an alloy of tin and copper. Consequently it is no surprise that the first consistent foreign policy we know, that of Egypt, was concerned with the control of the copper mines of the peninsula of Sinai. This policy was the core of Egyptian statecraft throughout its independent history, and the most ambitious imperial enterprises into Asia seem to have had the primary purpose of protecting the northern approaches not only to Egypt but to the Sinai Peninsula.

The downfall of Egyptian power and its ultimate loss of independence, first to Assyria, then to Persia, and successively to Rome, the Saracens, the Turks, and the British, are due to many complex causes. Nevertheless, a great part was no doubt played by the discovery of the superior metal, iron, about 1500 B.C., and the fact that Egypt neither had deposits of iron within its borders nor any near enough to be controlled. This circumstance, together with the virtual exhaustion of the copper mines of Sinai, meant that Egypt became wholly dependent for her arms and essential tools upon other nations.

In another of the great early centers of civilization, Mesopotamia, we find the Kings of Ur and Lagash and other early cities of Sumer in southern Mesopotamia boasting of their irrigation works and of their punitive expeditions to the north to protect trading posts and keep the trade routes open. Traders from early Sumer reached the Black Sea and perhaps southern Russia some 3,000 years before the Romans landed in Britain.

By 3000 B.C., then, in Egypt and Mesopotamia, and perhaps almost as early in the Indus Valley in north India, the foundations of all the great Old World civilizations including our own were laid. The wheel, basis of most mechanical devices, was in common use, as was the application of power from other sources than the human body. Metal was fairly abundant. Political organizations and highly differentiated societies of urban type were in existence. And all rested on an agricultural base.

It is true that enormous refinements and complexities have been added since, that the city has had its vicissitudes as it well may have again with the threat of atomic bombing. New metals, new tools and techniques, new types of organization, and new sources of power have been added, some of them with revolutionary effects on society, such as the use of coal and the attendant industrial revolution. The potentialities of modern civilization, however, seem all to have been established in the period between the invention of agriculture and the effective use of metallurgy.

12. SUMMARY

All societies must have techniques which provide sufficient food to permit survival of its members. Food techniques of simpler peoples depend on the gathering of food existing naturally in the environment in contrast to the more efficient techniques of food production. Peoples relying on gathering are classified, according to the dominant source of food, as hunters, fishermen, and collectors. Food-producers are classified as horticulturists, pastoralists, and agriculturists.

Hunters depend primarily on game for food and generally have a relatively elaborate technology. Missile weapons are important, as are traps and communal game drives. Although all hunting weapons are widespread, only the spear is universal. Methods of hunting are both individual and group, the latter involving cooperation and often special social organization. Marked differences in methods and technology exist depending on the type of game hunted. Hunting buffalo is a different problem from hunting rabbits, jungle animals, or sea mammals.

Fishing likewise requires a fairly elaborate technology. Nets, weirs, and traps are the most common instruments, but the use of stupefacients is widespread. The fish spear and bow and arrow are often used, while hooks and lines are usually associated with deep-sea fishing. The latter also requires boats, canoes, or rafts. Group effort again is common. Molluscs are often important to people who do relatively little fishing. Where fish or molluscs are abundant, relatively permanent settlements are often possible in contrast to the usual tendency of hunters and collectors to change residence frequently.

Collectors generally have a simpler technology, although often complex techniques are necessary both to collect food and to make it edible. Environments differ widely in the possibilities they offer collectors. In some cases collectors must move frequently, often following a cycle of seasonal changes. In other regions relatively stable settlement is possible but requires adequate storage techniques.

In general, food-gatherers show keen observation and an intimate knowledge of their environment. On the other hand, they are often "anchored" to an environment because movement to a new environment would require many inventions or even the adoption of a new technology.

The domestication of plants took place mainly in the mountain valleys from Ethiopia to northern India, in southeast Asia, and in the highlands from Mexico to Chile. The domestication of most animals took place in much the same areas, but probably was at first more ceremonial than utilitarian in nature. Early farming made no use of draft animals, even when accompanied by stock-breeding.

Horticulturists practice gardening with the digging-stick as the main tool. Hoes and spades, if known, are too feebly constructed in most cases to permit deep cultivation. The inadequacy of tools often prevents use of most fertile clay or grassland soils. Forest areas or sandy soils are usually preferred. Lack of fertilization and crop rotation lead to rapid soil exhaustion, and horticultural peoples usually are slowly migratory. Exceptions are found in Peru, Indonesia, and a few other places where permanent cultivation occurs.

Widely different plants are often cultivated. Cultivation of coconuts, breadfruit, bananas, and roots and tubers differs markedly from cultivation of grains. The former are mainly confined to tropical areas, the potato of Peru being the most important exception.

Grain cultivation is of three different types centering around either rice, wheat, or maize. The first is found in southeast Asia and Indonesia, often associated with the coconut-breadfruit-banana-tuber type of cultivation. Wheat is mainly cultivated in the remainder of Asia, Europe, and North Africa, while maize is confined to parts of the New World.

Domesticated animals other than the dog are often found among horticulturists, but are not commonly used in farming; neither are they always important as food. Ceremonial and religious uses predominate. New World horticulturists variously use the turkey, guinea pig, and llama. Old World horticulturists mainly use the pig and chicken, although some have sheep, cattle, or water buffalo.

Pastoral peoples derive their food from domesticated animals, either relying directly upon them for most of their diet or using meat and dairy products for trade. Pastoral peoples are confined to the Old World, mostly in desert, steppe, or grassland environments. The principal animals are cattle, horses, sheep, goats, camels, and reindeer, but the importance of each varies from one area to another. Pastoral peoples must shift residence according to the needs of the animals, but usually within prescribed limits with seasonal return to the same localities.

Conflicts between pastoral peoples and their farming neighbors is common, with the latter often occupying a subordinate position. In many cases pastoral peoples form a dominant caste, and in numerous historical instances the merger of pastoral and farming peoples has resulted in the establishment of large and usually aggressive political units. Nevertheless, few, if any, stable political groupings have developed among pastoralists.

Agriculture involves the use of the plow drawn by domesticated animals, and is confined to the Old World where it is usually associated with wheat cultivation and less frequently with rice cultivation. Although fairly complex cultures developed on a horticultural base in Mexico, Peru, Indonesia, and parts of Africa, most of the great historic urban civilizations have depended on agriculture.

Gatherers necessarily live in small, discontinuous groups, and invention and diffusion are very slow. Early horticulture ushered in village life; although tribal units remained relatively small, much denser populations were possible. The earliest spread of horticulture was slow and irregular, however, for plants had to be adapted to new environments and many fertile soils could not be cultivated without the plow.

With the application of animal power to drawing the plow, agriculture spread rapidly in Europe and parts of Asia. Increased efficiency permitted the beginnings of urban life and specialization. True cities, however, did not usually appear until the invention and spread of metallurgy. The uneven distribution of metallic ores and the dependency of the farmer on the smith broke down the self-sufficient village economy and gave rise to political units of increasing size.

We may trace, then, several revolutionary events in human history, revolutionary in the sense that they greatly altered the way of human life. First was the beginning of culture itself—communication and the first tools. Second was the invention of food production. Third was the discovery of metallurgy. The fourth is the application of mechanical power to the processes of production, that is, the industrial revolution, with its accompanying development of scientific methods.

COLLATERAL READING

Childe, V. Gordon. *Man Makes Himself*. New York: Oxford University Press, 1939. Chapters IV–VII.

———. *The Dawn of European Civilization*. London: Kegan Paul, 1948.

Forde, C. Daryll. *Habitat, Society and Economy*. New York: E. P. Dutton, 1950. Part IV.

Linton, Ralph. "Crops, Soil, and Culture in America," *The Maya and Their Neighbors*, eds. Clarence L. Hay and others. New York: D. Appleton-Century Co., 1940. Pp. 32–40.

Sauer, Carl. "American Agricultural Origins: A Consideration of Nature and Culture," *Essays in Anthropology Presented to A. L. Kroeber*, ed. Robert H. Lowie. Berkeley: University of California Press, 1936. Pp. 279–298.

Spinden, Herbert J. "The Origin and Distribution of Agriculture in America," *Source Book in Anthropology*, eds. A. L. Kroeber and T. T. Waterman. New York: Harcourt, Brace and Co., 1931. Chapter 23.

Wissler, Clark. *The American Indian*. New York: Oxford University Press, 1938. Chapters I, II.

Chapter 11

CLOTHING, SHELTER,
AND TRANSPORTATION

1. THE FUNCTIONS OF CLOTHING

While clothing is perhaps less fundamental to human needs than such artifacts as tools and containers, it appears true that no human society lacks it entirely. It is indeed man's ability to protect himself in this way from weather and other environmental vicissitudes that has made it possible for him to live almost anywhere on the earth's surface. Were it not for clothing, and the added protection afforded by shelters, it is probable that man, like the anthropoid apes, would still be confined to tropical rain forests and their environs.

A comparative study of clothing soon reveals, however, that it is rarely, and perhaps never, worn only for protection against the weather. Nearly all clothing has as well some function as adornment, and it is frequently difficult to draw a sharp line between protective clothing and articles worn primarily as bodily ornaments. Nor is this all, for in most societies clothing functions also to cover certain parts of the body it is considered improper or immodest to reveal. The functions of clothing, then, are many rather than one; in addition to those already named there are others, such as the indication of social, political, economic, or occupational status, or the simpler function of protecting parts of the body from insect bites, rough ground, thorns, and other similar hazards.

The role of modesty in the wearing of clothing varies enormously from one society to the next. The Eskimo, for example, is dressed from head to foot in carefully tailored fur garments when he works outside in the winter. But in his well-warmed house, whether or not guests are present, he usually goes about naked to the waist and he may even, without indecency, wear nothing but a breech cloth or a piece of string about his waist. The Naskapi Indians of Labrador, on the other hand, who are neighbors of the Eskimo and wear much the same clothing, consider it highly indecent for either sex to expose any part of the body save the hands and face under any circumstances. The equatorial Baganda of East Africa goes about covered from neck to ankles, but the Witoto of the Amazon habitually goes naked or wears only a cord or band about the waist and one or more ornaments such as necklaces and plaited bracelets. Only on ceremonial occasions does the Witoto wear what we should consider moderately adequate clothing, and even this may be discarded should perspiration from dancing threaten to injure a valued ceremonial garment.

Standards of modesty obviously vary as well. Among the Haida Indians, a woman is rarely disconcerted at most bodily exposure but will blush violently if seen without her labret (a lip ornament). So, also, in parts of Mohammedan Africa, a woman may expose her breasts but not her face, for this must be veiled against all but her closest relatives. In our own society the degree of bodily exposure considered proper varies with the occasion. A bathing suit or evening dress may well be considered immodest in a classroom though quite proper on the beach or in a ballroom. The University professor, similarly, customarily wears a collar, tie, and coat while lecturing; to omit these, or to appear in garments more suited to the beach than the classroom, would certainly be regarded as both improper and immodest. Modesty, then, appears to be a culturally determined function of clothing, and very likely not a fundamental or original purpose.

Clothing for purposes of protection is undoubtedly necessary for effective occupation of severe climates, including most of the temperate zone with its harsh winters. Tropical peoples are very apt to wear little or no clothing, at least on some occasions. Most occupants of temperate and arctic environments wear some protective garments. Often, however, the degree of clothing is minimal and does not offer really adequate protection. The Onas of Tierra del Fuego, where frost may occur any day of the year, wear only a loose cape of fur, and smear a mixture of grease and clay on their bodies to keep themselves warm while working. The Indians about San Francisco Bay seem to have resorted to coatings of mud for the same purpose. The Athapaskan-speaking Indians of the Mackenzie River, although they wear tailored garments covering most of the body during cold weather, make their garments of tanned skins rather than em-

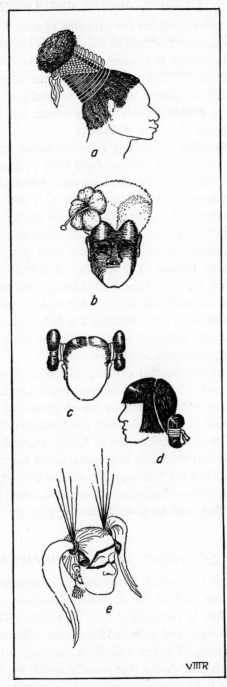

Fig. 11:1. (*a*) New Guinea (Papuan) hairdress; (*b*) Melanesian (Solomon Islands) hairdress; (*c*) hairdress of unmarried Hopi girl; (*d*) Hopi man's clubbed hairdress; (*e*) hairdress of a priest (Rio Grande Pueblos).

ploying the much more adequate fur garments of their Eskimo neighbors. And when fashion demands, women of northeastern United States will wear short skirts and sheer hose in subzero weather. It is clear again that the kind of clothing worn may achieve only a minimal adaptation to an environment. Not only do people cling to a culturally established type of clothing if it meets minimal needs for protection but they may be influenced heavily by the demands of fashion.

An important function of clothing is to symbolize status. Among the Aztecs of Mexico only certain classes could wear particular feather-decorated garments or certain kinds of ornaments. Although most Peruvian Indians appear to have worn ear ornaments, only the Inca ruling class could wear the enormous ear plugs which caused the Spanish to call them *orejones,* "big ears." Only warriors who had accomplished certain deeds could wear the feather war bonnet that for most people has become a symbol of the Plains Indians. The wearing of a crown is a symbol of royalty in much of Europe, Asia, and Africa. The term "white-collar worker" is familiar to every American, while overalls are a mark of the man who works with his hands. Wearing top hat, white tie, and tails, on formal occasions, is the badge of a restricted class, while varied uniforms mark soldier, sailor, policeman, cook, and nurse.

It is important to observe that clothing, like other products of culture, is not to be explained in terms of biological needs alone. Clothing serves many functions other than the obvious one of protecting the wearer from weather, troublesome insects, and other environmental hazards. Some—perhaps most—of these functions are to satisfy culturally created needs, as is seen from the fact that their expression varies enormously from one society to the next. Even the biological function of clothing is strongly conditioned by the culture—sometimes, as we have seen, to the extent of rendering the clothing inadequate protection against the weather.

2. CLOTHING AND ADORNMENT

As we have noted, clothing is frequently adornment, even when it serves other functions such as the demands of modesty or protection. In our own society, this is particularly true of women's clothing. Buttons, brooches, pleats, sashes, and other additions are often made which lack any utilitarian purpose whatever, and there are even articles of clothing (for example, high-heeled shoes) that actually inhibit the wearer's freedom of action. Clothing is likewise supplemented, in nearly all societies, with many articles solely for adornment, such as hair ribbons, necklaces, ear and nose plugs, bracelets and anklets, rings, combs, and numerous other devices.

In many societies, particularly in tropical or mild climates, adornment may be wholly divorced from clothing and far more important. Not only do such peoples wear various ornaments, but they decorate the body as well by painting, tattooing, scarification, and other techniques. Painting is often restricted to ceremonial occasions, when sacred designs of one kind or another are made on the body. It is also used for secular occasions (as when women in our society paint their faces and nails), either to beautify the body or, sometimes, to indicate status or class. Tattooing is widespread, especially in parts of Oceania, where a Polynesian of high rank may literally be tattooed from head to foot. Where tattooing is ineffective—as among dark-skinned peoples like the Australian aborigines on whom tattooed designs are not readily visible—designs are made on the body by scarification. The skin is cut with a sharp knife, and soot or other material is rubbed in so as to raise large scars or welts, often in intricate designs.

Teeth are often blackened, or chipped or filed into special shapes. Among some peoples of Oceania, white teeth are considered ugly and doglike, and every self-respecting adult chews betel nuts that his teeth may be black. Shaping the teeth by filing or chipping is a regular procedure among many Indonesian peoples, where this operation is part of the ceremonies marking

Fig. 11:2. Zuñi head ornaments (top and bottom) and mask (center). After Stevenson.

the transition from boyhood to manhood. Among some Mexican Indians, such as the Mayas, valued stones, such as jade or turquoise, are set into the teeth. Heads are often shaped in infancy into culturally desirable forms, by binding and other techniques. Thus the Mayas flatten their foreheads, while other peoples flatten the back of the head, and still others bind it so that it rises to an almost conelike shape. Other ornamentation of the body includes cutting and dressing the hair, shaving, growing and trimming mustaches and beards, plucking the eyebrows, allowing fingernails to grow very long and shaping these in various ways, and adding colors, permanent or temporary, to the hair, skin, or nails.

Obviously, not all of the techniques mentioned above are used by a single people. Nevertheless, there are few if any peoples who do not in some way shape or embellish parts of the body for purposes of adornment. And there are many who undergo extreme discomfort or pain to achieve these effects—tattooing in the tenderer regions of the body, scarification, tooth-filing, and many other similar techniques are painful to the subject. The motivation in each case is of course similar to that among ourselves when we cut our hair, shave, pluck our eyebrows, or undergo plastic surgery —namely, to shape or embellish body parts to culturally determined standards of beauty or attractiveness.

For purposes of adornment, human beings employ an enormous variety of materials. Wood, stone, bone, and shell are used by many peoples to make beads, bracelets, collars, and ornaments for the ear, nose, lips, and hair. More complex cultures employ metals, and in recent years our culture has added plastics and other synthetic materials. Colored seeds may be used for beads, and strips of fur for anklets or waistbands. Plaited hair or fiber ornaments often are used in many ways, while feathers are either simply stuck into the hair, attached to elaborate headdresses or hats, or fastened to netting and woven materials to make cloaks. Indeed, man throughout the world perhaps exploits his environment more thoroughly in discovering materials for adornment than for any other purpose, and he is extraordinarily ingenious in discovering ways of utilizing these materials.

Many groups go to great labor in preparing ornaments for the body. One burial in Arizona yielded 60,000 beads so tiny that they fill less than a quart jar, while another burial from the same graveyard gave up 40,000 similar beads. Some South American Indians have discovered that by feeding parrots a special diet, the color of the feathers may be changed and new types of ornaments made. With the most simple tools, often utilizing only abrasive sands and wooden drills, hard stones are carved into elaborate ornaments. Before the beginning of the Christian era, the Stone

Age inhabitants of southern Vera Cruz in Mexico were producing exquisite ornaments of jade and other hard stones. With more efficient implements, craftsmen in our own society expend great effort to make ornaments of the hardest stone, the diamond.

When clothing is worn, ornament often is applied to the garments. Plains Indian buckskin shirts are frequently decorated with fringes of human hair or with designs made by sewing on dyed porcupine quills. Women's dresses are often loaded with hundreds of elk teeth, which present a problem to the modern museum curator because of the value placed on these ornaments as insignia of a fraternal order; the teeth sometimes disappear from even the best-guarded garments. Decoration is often made a part of fabrics, either through weaving, dyeing, or painting. Although in our society women make most use of adornment applied to clothing in the form of sequins, buttons, and other objects, men also employ functionless buttons and useless pocket flaps for the same purpose.

Even garments we are apt to regard as essentially utilitarian, such as men's hats, often are not so. (No one, of course, could consider women's hats as utilitarian.) In-

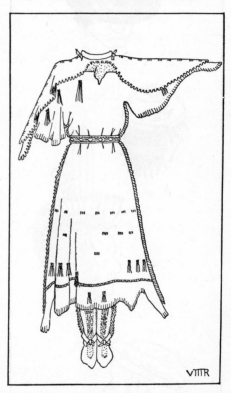

Fig. 11:3. Plains Indian woman's dress.

deed, most nonliterate peoples habitually go without any headgear. Groups such as the Eskimos who live in very cold climates may wear hoods or caps of hide or fur, while dwellers in tropic environments such as southeast Asia may use hats as sunshades. Others wear hoods of light materials, for example, the Bedouins of Africa. Some hunters wearing long hair may wear a net or cap when passing through the woods. The women of the Hupa and their neighbors in northwest California wear a tight-fitting basketry skullcap at times. This headgear apparently was developed to protect the head when carrying weights with the aid of the tumpline. Nevertheless, many peoples wear headgear only while participating in dances or other ceremonies or to indicate rank or status. Plains Indian warriors, for ex-

ample, ordinarily go without a head covering (the hair is worn long and is often carefully dressed); only privileged persons are entitled to the feather war bonnet and then it is worn only on special occasions.

3. CLOTHING MATERIALS

Both animal and vegetable products are extensively used in the manufacture of clothing. The simplest article of clothing—and perhaps the first to be used by men —is probably the robe or untailored cloak made from the skin of a large animal. Even this simple garment, however, requires considerable processing, for an untreated or raw hide becomes stiff and hard as soon as it dries. The skin must first be thoroughly scraped to remove the fat and flesh which adhere to it. Then it must be softened. Among some peoples, the hide is softened only by mechanical techniques, such as alternately wetting and beating the hide until it is flexible. The Eskimos soften even large hides by chewing them bit by bit until they are suitable for clothing. Mechanically softened hides, however, are not permanently cured, for if they become wet again the whole process must be repeated or the hide dries as stiff and hard as one which has not been treated.

Better curing is achieved by rubbing the hide with fatty or oily sub-

Fig. 11:4. (*a*) Wooden hat; (*b*) Pomo head basket; (*c*) headdress of northeast forest Indian; (*d*) Albanian mountain man's head covering; (*e*) Lapp's cap.

stances while it is being manipulated mechanically. Animal fats, such as brains and marrow, are widely used for this purpose, though urine and dung may also be employed. The result is, of course, a pliable but very oily skin, which remains soft only as long as the oil remains. Nevertheless, many hunting peoples possess no better technique for curing hides, and still manage to produce cured skins quite effective for the making of clothing.

The best curing technique—called tanning—is to treat the hide with vegetable substances that contain tannic acid. The bark of oak or willow trees, soaked in water, is adequate for this purpose; hides thoroughly worked in such solutions are quite unaffected by water and remain pliable even after repeated wettings. True tanning, as opposed to curing with animal fats, is limited to the Old World and to the technologically more advanced cultures of Europe, North Africa, and parts of Asia.

In cold climates, robes made from the skin of a large animal may be improved by cutting, sewing, and shaping the skin so that it conforms more closely to the body. It seems probable that the first fitted garments were made of skins or furs by people living in a cold climate. At least tailored garments of skin were worn by nonliterate peoples throughout most of the northern hemisphere long before peoples of more complex cultures began to cut and fit garments of either skin or cloth. It is possible, too, that Paleolithic peoples living at the borders of the great glaciers made tailored skin clothing at least as early as the Solutrean, though there is of course no direct evidence of clothing remaining in archeological deposits.

Where only small animals are available, the production of clothing requires ways of combining the skins of several animals to make a single garment. Often the best and warmest furs come from relatively small mammals. In most places the solution is to sew skins together, but many North American Indians use a weaving technique. This is especially common in areas such as Utah and Nevada where the only numerous animals are rabbits. Rabbit furs are cut in strips and either twisted by themselves into a long furry rope or twisted about a cord. Cords are then strung on a framework or back and forth between two poles to form a warp, and the fur strings or fur-covered cords are used as a weft in a simple weaving technique. The result is a soft, warm robe or blanket rather than a fitted garment.

Another way of utilizing animal materials for clothing is to employ the hair or wool. A central Asiatic people, probably the ancestors of the present Mongols, developed the technique of felting. In one method, wool or hair is combed out and placed in layers on a mat. Water is sprinkled on the material and the mat rolled up as tightly as possible. It then may be beaten with a stick, but more commonly is rolled back and forth for several hours between two lines of women. At the end of this time the hairs or wool fibers have become thoroughly matted. After patting, stretching, and sometimes repeated rolling, the resulting felt is light, warm, and durable. It may be cut and sewn, and is employed not only for garments and head-gear but for boots, tent covers, and rugs. The first technologically advanced people to use felt were apparently the Chinese. Today we employ felt mainly for hats, but considerable credit for the success of the Russian winter campaigns against the Germans in World War II must be attributed to the Russian use of felt boots or inner boots which provided an ideal protection against frostbitten feet.

The hair of dogs, buffalo, goats, and other long-haired animals is used by some nonliterate peoples to make woven garments. The hair is usually twisted into a cord by rolling it on the thigh with the palm of the hand, and then is woven into blankets, robes, and other articles of clothing. The Indians of British Columbia made the famous Chilkat blanket from the hair of the mountain goat. Plains Indians sometimes use dog or buffalo hair to produce small fabrics. Usually, though, peoples who use hair do little weaving or possess only primitive weaving techniques. Wool is the only really satisfactory animal fiber for weaving.

Wool-using is mainly confined to Old World peoples who possess do-mesticated sheep. The first employment of wool seems to have occurred in the Neolithic period, but, as early sheep had little wool, extensive use of the material did not come until varieties of sheep had been developed with more abundant coats. In the New World the Peruvian Indians secure wool from several types of native American camels, the llama, the alpaca, and the vicuña. Often wool is used to embroider designs upon a cotton fabric rather than for weaving itself. In the Old World, camel hair is some-times woven, but our so-called camel's hair coats are usually made of llama wool. Wool-weaving requires of course the possession of the loom, but we shall discuss this artifact and the techniques of weaving in the next section (§ 4).

Simple clothing of unprocessed vegetable fibers is illustrated by the grass skirt made in certain parts of Oceania. This garment consists only of long grasses tied to a waistband or cord. Similar garments are also made of willow bark which has been beaten to produce long bunches of fibers.

In most cases, however, vegetable materials, like those derived from animals, require considerable processing before they can be made into clothing. An example is found in bark cloth, which is probably the most widespread of all vegetable materials used for clothing. A suitable spongy bark—that of fig and paper mulberry trees is best—is stripped off in layers and soaked in water to make it pliable. Then three layers of bark are laid out on top of each other on a flat anvil—often of stone—with the grain of the center layer lying at right angles to that of the other two. A mallet is then used to pound the bark until the fibers are matted tightly together. The pounding also thins out and widens the bark and makes it soft and pliable. Large pieces of bark cloth are made by pounding separate sections together or even by gluing them as we should glue separate sheets of paper into a single larger piece. Designs may be added to bark cloth by employing mallets that have carved designs on their pounding surfaces. Bark cloth is often oiled or painted to preserve it.

Bark cloth was widely used in Oceania before the introduction of European trade cloth, and it is said that many Oceanic peoples revived the technique of making bark cloth—called *tapa* in the Malayo-Polynesian languages—when World War II prevented trade in European and American clothing materials. *Tapa* was so important to the aboriginal Oceanic peoples that they domesticated the paper mulberry tree, the bark of which produces an exceptionally fine fabric. Trees were planted in clumps so that they might grow with straight trunks and few branches. A special form of bark cloth, made of reeds pounded into flat strips and joined together, is the papyrus of ancient Egypt, which was used as a writing material.

Bark cloth is not very good material for cutting and sewing, and hence is found most often in relatively warm climates where close-fitting garments are not required. Bark cloth garments are usually made from a single rectangular piece of material, which is wrapped around the waist or chest as a sarong.

All other vegetable fiber clothing involves the technique of weaving. Bark fibers, such as those obtained from cedar bark by some American Indians, are occasionally woven into cloth. Extensive weaving, however, appears to be confined to relatively few vegetable fibers—flax, two kinds of hemp, and cotton in the Old World, and henequen (agave fiber or sisal hemp) and cotton in the New World. Peoples who use those fibers to weave cloth almost invariably cultivate the plant as well; weaving on an intensive level is found almost always among peoples who have domesticated plants. Nomadic gathering peoples, probably because weaving is a lengthy process that requires bulky and heavy equipment, only rarely make their clothing of woven fabrics.

4. SPINNING AND WEAVING

Fibers, whether of animal or vegetable materials, must first be spun into long threads before they can be woven into fabrics. We have already noted one technique for spinning—the twisting of fibers into cord or thread by rolling them on the thigh. This technique, however, is both crude (in that the thread produced is apt to be lumpy or uneven in diameter) and slow. Where a great deal of weaving is done, threads must be made by a better and faster technique.

The most widespread tool for spinning, in societies where the wheel is lacking, is the spindle. This is a slender rod, usually of wood, which is furnished with a weight or whorl made of wood or clay. The whorl functions as a flywheel to keep the rod turning once it is given a sharp twist.

There are two major spinning techniques—one found mainly in the Old World and the other used principally by the American Indians. In both techniques, the spinner begins by taking a bit of fiber and twisting it by hand into a short length of thread or yarn. This is then fastened to the spindle. In the Old World technique, the spindle is next twisted to start it turning and allowed to fall toward the ground while the spinner elongates the thread or yarn by adding bits of fiber to it. When the spindle reaches the ground and stops turning, the spinner picks it up, winds the finished thread or yarn on it, and repeats the process. In the New World technique, the spindle often rests on the ground or in a pottery bowl and is continuously twisted with the fingers as the spinner adds fibers to elongate the thread or yarn. Sometimes, too, the spindle may be revolved by rolling it against the thigh.

Whatever technique is employed, the process of spinning by a spindle, though far slower than the spinning wheel or modern machine-spinning, produces excellent threads and yarns. Indeed, some of the finest threads and yarns known have been made by the spindle. This was especially true among the ancient Peruvian Indians, whose cotton and wool threads, used in their most elaborate tapestries, are among the best to be found anywhere in the world.

The simplest form of weaving, which is done with the fingers alone and requires no implements, is essentially the same as that employed in making woven baskets, except of course that the fineness and pliability of the warp and weft threads complicate the process. Finger-weaving is very slow and is used only for small fabrics, such as those used by the Witoto Indians of Brazil to make arm and leg bands.

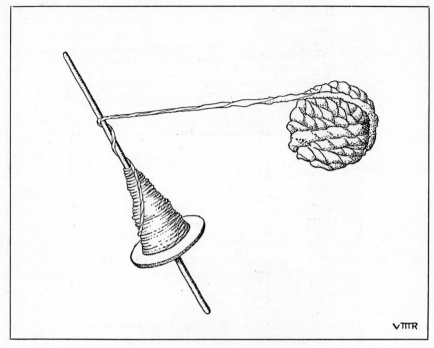

Fig. 11:5. Spindle and spindle whorl.

Another simple form of weaving requires a crossbar resting on two posts (the so-called false or one-bar loom) to suspend the warp. The other ends of the warp threads are unattached, though sometimes these loose ends are weighted, the better to keep each thread in its proper place. Once the warp has been hung, the weft threads are inserted by the fingers, over and under each warp thread in turn. Though this is a slow and laborious process, and the resulting fabric, because of the suspended warp, tends to be loosely woven, some peoples use the technique to produce quite good fabrics. An excellent example is the so-called Chilkat blanket, made on the one-bar loom by a Tlingit tribe on the coast of British Columbia. Some Plains Indian groups also make occasional use of the one-bar loom, though their fabrics are inferior both in workmanship and decoration to the Chilkat blanket.

Finger weaving may also be done on a two-bar loom, where the warp threads are stretched between two crossbars which are part of a rectangular frame. This method is also slow, though it does produce a more tightly woven fabric than the one-bar method. Finger-weaving, then, whether it is done without a loom, with the suspended warp, or with the weaving

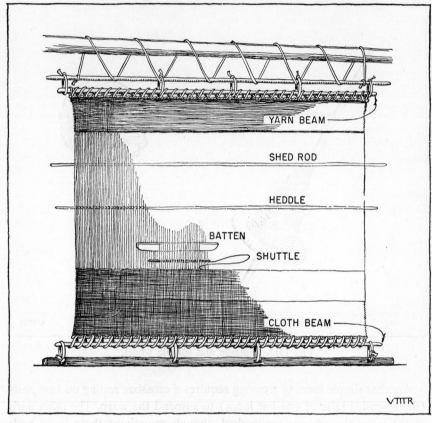

Fig. 11:6. Hopi loom.

frame, is found only where textiles are relatively rare and unimportant.

The true loom is an improvement on the weaving frame by the addition of one or both of two implements, the heddle and the shuttle, which enormously increase the speed of weaving. The heddle is a slender rod set into the warp by attaching it with yarns to alternate warp threads. When the heddle is raised, the attached warp threads are also raised, so permitting the weaver to pass his weft thread through at one stroke instead of weaving it alternately over and under each warp thread. A second heddle similarly opens a passage for the return of the weft. The shuttle, a small implement containing a bobbin on which the weft thread is wound, further speeds the weaving. As the heddles open the warp, the shuttle is thrown through and the weft inserted with a single movement. In making more complexly decorated fabrics, several sets of heddles—each opening a section of the warp—may be used, so that differently colored yarns, each on a separate shuttle, may be inserted.

Further improvements include: a set of foot pedals so arranged that the weaver can manipulate the heddles with his foot, a batten or comblike implement set into the warp to pack the wefts firmly into place, and revolving beams in place of fixed crossbars. In looms with revolving beams in place of fixed crossbars, the completed fabric is rolled up on the lower beam while the upper one contains as much warp thread as may be required, to be fed out as needed. Thus, while the two-bar loom permits only the weaving of fabrics of a fixed size, the revolving-beam loom limits only the width of the fabric, not its length as well. Today, of course, our machine-age technology permits power looms, which are, however, essentially the revolving-beam loom plus devices to make the process of wefting wholly automatic. Fabrics woven on hand looms, for example the excellent tapestries woven by the Peruvian Indians of pre-Conquest times, are quite equal and often superior to modern machine-age fabrics.

In the New World, the true loom is found only in Mexico, Central America, and Peru, with a less well developed form in the Pueblo area of southwestern United States. These areas, it may be noted, are also areas in which henequen is widely used for fibers, or in which cotton is grown. Weaving on the true loom is apparently much older in the Old World, but there, too, though the association is less precise, the true loom occurred, before the industrial revolution, mainly in areas where cotton, flax, or hemp were also grown.

Loom-woven fabrics directly condition, to a large extent, the kind of clothing made and used. This is because loom-made fabrics are made only in rectangular shapes, hence, until relatively recent times, textile garments have retained this essentially rectangular character. Rectangles of fabric were knotted over one shoulder, worn as capes or wrap-around skirts, and similarly employed without extensive cutting or fitting. Sometimes, as even today among many Latin American peoples, rectangular fabrics are folded and sewn part way up the sides, with a hole cut in the folded edge to allow for the head and arm holes left in either side. Sleeves are occasionally added, but these too are folded rectangular pieces sewn into the arm holes in such a way that the entire garment, laid out flat, is nothing more than a series of rectangular forms. Indeed, fitted garments of cloth are made even today only by the Europeans, Americans (of European ancestry), and the Chinese; all others employ fabrics only for loose wrap-around clothing.

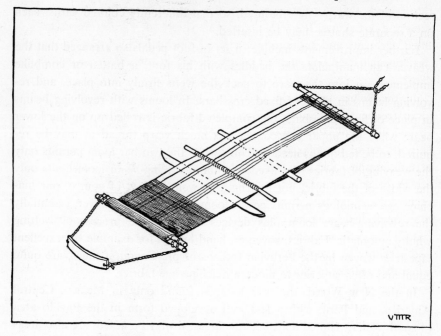

Fig. 11:7. Belt loom used in Middle America.

5. THE ORIGINS OF CLOTHING

As we noted earlier in this chapter, the origins of both clothing and adornment are obscure; clothing and ornaments, unlike stone tools, do not survive in archeological deposits. From the fact that chimpanzees, at least in captivity, will deck themselves with strings and rags and smear paint on themselves, it has been suggested that adornment was employed early in human history. However, the first hint of such adornment does not occur until the mid-Paleolithic, where ochre, a pigment, is found frequently in Neanderthal burials.

Indirect evidence of clothing in the Mousterian epoch is found in the fact that Mousterian man lived in Europe during part of the Würm glaciation, and hence must have had some covering to protect himself from the cold. He also made scrapers of bone which may have been used, as non-literates do today, to clean hides of fat and flesh and so prepare them for use as clothing.

In the Aurignacian period, the evidence for clothing is still stronger, for here are found the first eyed bone needles. These may well be taken as evidence of sewing and probably that skins were cut and shaped into garments. It is even likely, given the cold climate of parts of Europe during this period, that Aurignacian garments were tailored, like those of the present-day Eskimo. If so, this represents surely the earliest appearance of fitted garments and supports our earlier conclusion that tailored clothing developed first among hunting peoples living in the colder regions of the earth.

In the Solutrean and Magdalenian epochs, bone needles become far more frequent, and other artifacts of bone, such as a possible fastener shaped like a collar button, appear as well. All of this makes it fairly certain, despite the complete absences of any actual garments in archeological deposits, that Paleolithic man had achieved clothing possibly as early as the Mousterian and certainly by the Magdalenian, when the wearing of clothing must have been general.

Textile garments, however, are not known until the Neolithic, with the appearance of weaving. Remains from the Swiss lake dwellings afford positive evidence that flax was domesticated and its fibers used in weaving, and we find numerous examples of actual fabrics demonstrating a high technical skill. This clothing is not tailored, however, as was probably the case with at least some of the earlier Paleolithic skin garments. Positive evidence of tailored textile garments occurs first among the Chinese, who evidently acquired their clothing styles and techniques from their nomadic Mongol neighbors. During Roman times, tailored clothing was reported for the so-called "barbarians" of northern Europe, but it did not come into general

Fig. 11:8. Untailored woman's dress (Pueblo area).

use in Europe until well after the beginning of the Christian era. Indeed, we know that the Romans resisted this innovation—at one time they even decreed the death penalty for those who wore trousers.

6. EARLY SHELTERS AND DWELLINGS

As in the case of clothing, both the form and function of shelters reveal an enormous diversity. Shelters range in form from simple lean-tos of brush or skins, set up in fifteen or twenty minutes, to colossal structures of steel and concrete that require, even with a modern machine technology, months in the building. In some societies, such as our own, shelters serve as genuine dwelling and working places, to the extent that an individual may spend nearly all his time within one structure or another. In contrast, many nonliterate peoples use their shelters only for sleeping; their waking hours, whether engaged in play, work, or gossip, are spent largely in the open.

Though shelters of some sort are today universal among men, we do not know just how they began nor when in human history man first used them. It is often supposed that natural shelters, like caves, were the first to be used, and that constructed shelters came later. There is no certain evidence to support this view, however. It is true, of course, that men lived in caves during the middle and late Paleolithic in Europe, and that a very few peoples, like the Veddas of Ceylon, used caves well into modern times. But there is no evidence of shelters, natural or constructed, during the earlier Chellean and Acheulian periods of the European Paleolithic, and it must be supposed that the people of this time either lived without shelters or built simple structures of which we have no trace. The latter is certainly a possible conclusion, for the Australian aborigines of the historical period, together with many other nonliterate peoples, did actually build simple brush or skin lean-tos which fall apart soon after abandonment and leave no visible traces whatsoever. It is indeed quite likely that the earliest hominids constructed some sort of sleeping places at least, as a protection against the colder night weather, occasional rains, and the raids of predatory animals. Even the apes provide this much protection for themselves.

Cave shelters came into use in Europe in the Mousterian, probably as a protection against the cold of that period. They were used widely in western Europe until the end of the Paleolithic, as is shown by deposits of tools and implements laid down over the cave floors. Other shelters were also used, however, especially during the Magdalenian. Evidence for these is found in the so-called tectiform drawings on cave walls—these drawings almost certainly represent crude constructed dwellings. Recently archeologists have also found traces of Magdalenian semisubterranean houses in southern Russia, the earliest certain evidence so far uncovered of constructed dwellings.

The south Russian houses built by the Magdalenians evidently consisted of a pit dug down two or three feet into the ground. Over this was erected a roof of poles, supported by posts and covered with brush and probably earth. Such semisubterranean houses have a wide distribution in the northern hemisphere. Elaborate semisubterranean houses are the customary shelters of some Siberian peoples, and are also used by some of the western Eskimos and some of the Indians of the northwestern part of North America. In California large semisubterranean structures, sometimes fifty or sixty feet in diameter, are used for men's club houses or ceremonial chambers. Similar structures, known as pit houses, were widely used in the Southwest by the early Pueblo peoples and their predecessors, the Basket Makers. Today they survive among some Pueblo Indians as ceremonial chambers or kivas. It seems likely that the semisubterranean house is the oldest type of complex shelter and that it represents a single invention which has spread through a considerable portion of the northern hemisphere. Recently pit houses have also been reported from the Chaco region of South America. Whether these represent a separate invention or are the result of some migration of pit-house-using peoples from the north in early times is still in question, although the Chaco people show many striking similarities in their culture to the Indians of North America and particularly California. Pit houses seem generally to be lacking in tropical areas and in the southern hemisphere with the exception of this instance in the Chaco.

With the Neolithic and the succeeding metal ages we find many evidences of constructed dwellings that are widely diverse in type. Some, like the Swiss lake dwellings, were built of wood and set on long piers, extending into the water. Others were even more elaborate structures made of stone, of sun-dried brick, or of walls of interlaced branches covered with a daub of mud or clay. In the Near East, in late Neolithic or early Bronze Age times, we find huge stone structures, which were used, however, as temples, tombs, or palaces rather than as dwellings. Large stone tombs of many varieties—the so-called dolmens—also diffused widely into Mediterranean Europe and even as far north as the Scandinavian peninsula. Needless to say, not all peoples developed elaborate dwellings; earlier types persisted, especially among the more nomadic food-gathering peoples, many of whom possessed neither the materials nor the need to build elaborate and permanent dwellings.

7. SIMPLE AND MOVABLE DWELLINGS

Among nonliterate peoples who do not possess transportation facilities which enable them to import large quantities of building materials, dwellings are conditioned for the most part by two factors: the kinds of building material easily available in the environment, and the degree to which the food quest requires the people concerned to move from one place to another. Nomadic peoples in general construct only simple shelters which may be abandoned on moving without great loss, or else they possess dwellings that are easily transported. Sedentary peoples, on the other hand, often build more or less elaborate structures which they expect to use for some time. This rule is of course not invariable. Thus, the Polar Eskimos, a nomadic folk, build rather elaborate winter houses of stone, to which they return year after year after the summer's wanderings. The snow house, in these regions, is used only for temporary shelter during winter hunts away from home, and a movable skin tent serves a similar function during the summer hunting season.

There are some nomadic peoples, however, who live much of the time in the open and build only very simple structures as sleeping places. This is true, for example, of many Australian bands, in particular those who live in arid regions and so not only lack building materials, but are forced to travel far and wide to find the wild animals and plants on which they live. The camps of these bands are made up of crude lean-tos of poles and brush, set up against the prevailing wind and warmed by a fire built near the open side. Similarly, the Onas of Tierra del Fuego, despite their cold and rainy climate, build only simple windbreaks of guanaco skins supported by poles to protect them from the weather. Shelters of this sort can be built very quickly and easily, and abandoned if necessary when the band moves.

Other peoples, who live in more favored environments and who need not move so often, may construct more elaborate houses. A good example is the Apache wickiup, a dome-shaped structure of poles, grass, and skins. The poles are set into the ground and bent in toward the center where their tops are lashed together. This framework is then thatched with long bunches of grass, often covered with hides to make the house impervious to cold and rain. The wickiup, which requires about three days to construct, may be used for some time, and is easily patched should wind or rain damage it. When the band moves, the wickiup is usually abandoned, for it is not transportable. The poles and hides may be saved, however, to be used in the construction of a new house.

Movable dwellings are also widespread among nomadic nonliterates. The most common of these is undoubtedly the conical skin tent, a simple structure of poles covered with skins. It can be set up very quickly and is just as easily taken down to be packed for transport. Many Eskimos, as we have noted, use such a tent for their summer hunts, though, for the lack of wood, poles are replaced with the rib bones of large animals. The Indians of the Mackenzie area in northwestern Canada use the movable skin tent all the year round, despite its inadequacy in the cold weather. Dwellings of this type may also be made of poles covered with bark, in areas where this material is plentiful.

In some regions, such as the North American Plains and central Asia, movable dwellings are excellently contrived and very efficient. The Plains Indians, nomadic buffalo-hunters, use the tipi, an elaborate skin tent which is both carefully built and easily moved. Among the Crows, the tipi is twenty-five feet high and accommodates as many as twenty people. It is built, like the skin tent, of poles covered with hides, and a large number of buffalo skins must be sewn together to produce an adequate cover. The tipi cover is held down at the bottom by stones and is fitted with a ventilating device at the top, so that the smoke from the central tipi fire may escape. Skins and furs cover the floor, which is used as a sleeping and lounging place. The structure is so well built as to be warm and comfortable even in the cold Plains winter. In moving, the tipi cover is removed, folded, and packed on a pair of parallel poles. These poles are then hitched, like the shafts of a cart, to a dog or horse, and the whole dwelling is in this way easily transported.

A similarly elaborate movable dwelling is the yurt, used by the pastoral nomads of central Asia, and probably the finest portable dwelling ever devised. The yurt—as made by the Kazak—consists of a light wooden framework covered with felt, in the shape of a cylinder with a dome on top. The framework has three parts: a circular, vertical wall of wattle which is from four to five feet high, a ring of wood supported by a center pole which forms the top of the dome, and a set of slats fixed to the ring and running down to the top of the wall where each slat is lashed with cord. The ring is left open to let out the smoke from the central fire, but it may be closed with felt in bad weather. Some yurts have wooden doors set into a frame; in others the door is just a strip of felt. The floor of the yurt is of beaten earth covered with carpets, and the interior of the yurt is divided into separate rooms by means of screens made of rush. Despite its elaborate construction, the yurt can be taken down or reassembled in about a half an hour. It can also be transported quite easily on oxen, horses, or camels.

It is evident, then, that nomadism, of itself, does not prevent the construction of comfortable or efficient dwellings. The houses of a people are determined by other factors as well, notably the status of their technology —which affords a rough measure of the efficiency with which they may process the raw materials of their environment—and the resources of the region in which they live. Simple structures are found where the environment is poor in building materials and the technology is crude and inefficient. In other areas, peoples with an adequate technology can and do produce dwellings which, even though they are portable, are not necessarily crude, uncomfortable, or inefficient.

8. FIXED OR IMMOVABLE DWELLINGS

Though farming peoples, who in general lead a more sedentary life than food-gatherers or pastoralists, often construct immovable and more elaborate dwellings, it does not follow that such dwellings are unknown among food-gatherers. Indeed, we have already noted (§ 6) that some California Indians—all of whom are food-gatherers—build large semisubterranean structures, certainly as elaborate and immovable as the pit houses or semisubterranean dwellings of the early Pueblo Indian farmers. Exceptions of this sort are frequent among food-gatherers who live in areas which are exceptionally well supplied with quantities of easily secured wild foods. This is the case among many California Indians, who depend mainly on acorns and other wild foods found in profusion at no great distance from their permanent villages. Again we note (see preceding section) that house types are not determined alone by a single factor, even one of such great importance as the manner of securing food.

To further illustrate this point, let us turn to the Indians of the coast of British Columbia. These peoples live mainly by fishing and hunting, and are fortunate enough to live on rivers in which, at certain times of the year, there are almost endless streams of salmon. In a few weeks of hard work, enough food may be secured to provide for the whole year, and this without extensive travel. Since the salmon runs occur yearly, the peoples of this region, though food-gatherers, live just as sedentary a life as any farming society. Note also that this region is exceptionally well supplied with wood, and that the Indians, though their cutting tools are made of stone, shell, and bone, have developed an extremely skilled and efficient set of woodworking techniques.

Accordingly, the houses built in this area are not only immovable, they are also large, elaborate, and well constructed. A house of average size among the Haidas of Queen Charlotte Island is thirty feet wide, forty long, and has a sloping roof measuring ten feet high at the ridge and about six at the eaves. The roof is supported by six to ten massive posts sunk into the ground along the center and at the corners, and the walls are constructed of perpendicular planks split from cedar trunks. The houses are tightly constructed, though neither nails nor pegs are used in the building; all the elements are either lashed together with stout vegetable fibers or "sewn" by an elaborate technique of inserting vegetable fibers in previously drilled holes in the ends of the planks. At the front of the house there is usually a massive and elaborately carved "totem pole" made from a single cedar trunk, and often as much as sixty feet in height. These houses, it is evident, are well built and substantial, and will last, with proper care, for fifty years or more. They are of course exceptional among peoples with only a stone-using technology; there are few other nonliterate peoples who have an equal command of woodworking techniques coupled with an environment so rich in workable woods.

Immovable structures of wood are usually less elaborate than those of British Columbia. The Indians of the eastern woodlands of North America, even though in part horticultural, usually build rather simple "wigwams" of poles and bark, no better in actual fact than the Plains Indian tipi. But the Iroquois of this region, using the same materials, build larger structures, the so-called "long houses." These are communal dwellings, rectangular in shape, measuring twenty to thirty feet in width, about the same in height, and from fifty to 150 feet in length. The house has a long central corridor from which opens, on either side, a number of separate apartments. Long houses, built of bark laid on a solid framework of poles, are substantial structures, which offer ample protection against the severe winters of upper New York and the adjacent regions of Canada.

In New Mexico and Arizona, where wood is not so easily secured, the Pueblo Indians build houses of stone laid in adobe mortar or of adobe clay bricks, dried in the sun. Walls are made of the stone or adobe alone, covered, inside and out, with an adobe plaster. Roofs, also of stone or adobe, are supported by log beams. These houses, like the Iroquois long house, are communal dwellings, but the tiers of apartments are built in stepped stories, sometimes as many as four or five stories high. Except that occasional heavy rains wash off the outside plaster, which then must be replaced, the Pueblo structures are built to last. At Acoma, a Pueblo village near the Rio Grande in New Mexico, there are structures of this sort which have probably been continuously occupied since 1540, when they were first seen by the Coronado Expedition.

There are of course many other varieties of immovable or semipermanent houses built by nonliterate peoples, and we cannot begin to describe them all. Some of the more widespread are the wooden structures built on piles in southeast Asia, Indonesia, and Melanesia; the lighter and less substantial bamboo houses of the same region; the earth-covered, semisubterranean huts of the Navaho and other American Indians; and the huge beehive-shaped thatched houses that are so common in tropical Africa. Many of these houses, and even the more elaborate clay and adobe structures, strike us as unusually small, as compared with our own roomier dwellings. The reason for this is obvious; for a great many nonliterates, houses are used primarily as places to sleep; living, working, and playing are done in the open. Moreover, a small house, with tiny entrances and no windows is easier to keep warm, a factor of some importance among peoples who have no other way of producing heat except by an open fire.

As we encounter the more complex cultures of nonliterates and literates, we find of course more elaborate constructions, built of stone and mortar. Among most non-European peoples, however, these are temples, altars, or palaces, rather than dwelling places. The ancient Egyptians, as is well known, built huge monuments, exemplified by their great pyramidal tombs. So also did the Mayas of Central America, the Aztecs of Mexico, and the Incas of Peru. Many of these exhibit great architectural and engineering skill, especially when we remember that they were often built without machines or draft animals, and with cutting tools of stone. The labor of building such monuments was available only to large semiurbanized societies, who possessed an economic organization that permitted a great deal of specialization and true division of labor.

9. TYPES OF TRANSPORTATION AND THEIR HISTORICAL DEVELOPMENT

If the modern use of air travel be excepted, transportation techniques fall into two main categories: land transport and water transport. Each of these in turn may be considered in terms of motive power, devices and techniques employed, and the function of transportation. We will consider only the so-called primitive aspects of transportation in use up to a little more than a century ago, omitting consideration of such very recent types of motive power as steam, electricity, and the internal combustion engine.

Of the two main categories of transportation, land transportation seems the more widespread; all known peoples have some form of transportation on land, but a number lack water transport. Nevertheless, the functions of the two categories are essentially the same, the transport of goods and persons from one place to another.

Transportation of some sort apparently is essential to all human societies. The simplest form of transport theoretically is that effected by use of human hands, backs, and legs without the use of any cultural devices. All known peoples, however, make use of cords and containers to increase their carrying capacity, even though the motive power may still be human labor. Some idea of the significance of transportation in human culture may be gained by comparing simple human groups with the apes, who lack any transportation devices. The gorilla, for example, has no means of conveying food except in his hands. As a result, the gorilla spends most of his life slowly moving from place to place securing food which he eats on the spot. While he may return to the same location repeatedly to spend the night, he does not accumulate any possessions. Even if gorillas desire possessions (and there is no evidence that they do), they are unable to transport more than they can carry in their hands when they change location. Only small infants are transported, usually clinging to their mothers by their own efforts.

In contrast to the gorilla and other apes, human groups of even the simplest culture establish camps or locations which they may occupy for several days or weeks. The economically productive members of the group leave the camp in search of food, and while they may eat part of the food on the spot, some is transported back to the camp to be eaten over a period of time or to feed the aged or young who may have been left in camp or to be stored for a period of scarcity. When the near-by food supply is exhausted, the camp may be moved to a more convenient location, but a certain number of possessions are also transported from one camp to another. Thus a skin shelter or tent cover may be preserved for many years, being moved from one camp to another. Extra clothing and ornament, tools, weapons, containers, and ceremonial objects are similarly transported.

If techniques of transportation are very simple, the number of objects preserved is small. Moreover, the size of the group is also limited unless food supplies are very abundant. As a rule a large group will exhaust food supplies in the vicinity of a camp so rapidly that the group will have to move too frequently. Thus the size of the group tends to conform to the amount of food available and the efficiency of transportation techniques.

Obviously good transportation also makes a much wider variety of raw materials available to a given people. It further encourages specialization of occupation with a resulting increase in interdependence of groups occupying larger areas. Yet, while good transportation usually is related to advanced techniques and improved motive power, much evidently can be done by proper organization of simple kinds of transport. The great Negro kingdoms of Africa and the complex and extended cultures of Mexico,

Central America, and Peru depended mainly on the efficient organization of man power for transportation and communication.

No direct evidence of transportation exists for the Paleolithic. While it is probable that late Paleolithic man had means of crossing smaller streams by swimming or using floats or rafts, there is no certainty that he did so. The sole exception known is from the Maglemose culture of Scandinavia in the Mesolithic. The Maglemose people may have lived on floating rafts on lakes and apparently possessed simple dugout canoes hewn or burned from a single log. On the other hand, by analogy with modern nonliterates, we may be fairly confident that most Paleolithic men had simple transportation techniques involving human motive power and the use of crude containers. Such a conclusion is suggested by the fact that even Chellean men evidently occupied the same camps for some time and so may have transported food to these camps. Upper Paleolithic man sought or traded desirable stone materials over considerable distances, and inland dwellers used shells and fish from the sea, such facts again arguing some simple means of transport.

Animal transport introduces a new source of power and allows the use of resources over a wider area. Greater size of the social group is also permitted. As yet, however, we lack historical evidence of the beginnings of animal transport. Domestic animals certainly existed in the Neolithic. They may have been used to draw the plow, but even for this certain evidence is lacking. The first positive evidence of the use of animals for transport by packing is the wide use of the pack ass in the Near East in Copper Age times.

The simplest type of land vehicle, the sledge, was indeed in use by the Mesolithic of Finland. This earliest known vehicle was for use on ice or snow, but it was usable also on the plains of the Near East, where it probably existed before 4000 B.C. Again, we may guess that Neolithic people harnessed oxen to the sledge.

If evidence of Neolithic land transport is mostly inferential, evidence for water transport is certain. Not only was the dugout canoe known in Mesolithic times, but actual examples are known from Swiss lake-dwelling cultures. Moreover, most contemporary nonliterates possess some type of water transportation if their environment is suitable.

The Copper Age provides the earliest definite use of draft animals from Nearer Asia where two- and four-wheeled carts were in general use before 3000 B.C. By 1000 B.C. wheeled vehicles were used from western Europe to China. In many regions, though, their use was limited until the invention of ironshod wheels and the development of roads and bridges. Pack animals consequently continue to be used in parts of Europe up to the present time and in most sections were superseded only with the advent of railroads and automobiles. In some regions such as rural China, for example, human motive power still is the major type of transportation. More detailed treatment of the various types of land transportation is given later.

In the New World, human motive power supplied the only land transportation before European discovery with two exceptions. In Peru the domesticated llama was employed to carry packs, while in some parts of North America the dog was used similarly. The wheel, although apparently used on toys in Mexico, never served for transportation before the coming of Europeans.

Early water transportation probably was confined to canoes and rafts or floats. The first evidence of larger boats comes with the Copper Age cultures of Egypt, where evidently some sort of seagoing craft was in use perhaps as early as 3500 or 4000 B.C. Human motive power was in the main employed, though sails are represented on Egyptian vases dated shortly before 3000 B.C. Navigation techniques were poor, and long-distance ocean voyages, except along coasts or in such enclosed seas as the Mediterranean, were rare and hazardous undertakings. Not until after the discovery of America were there any real improvements in ocean navigation. Columbus used essentially the same navigation and sailing techniques as were employed by the Egyptians and the Phoenicians.

10. LAND TRANSPORT: FOOTWEAR, CARRYING DEVICES, AND CONTAINERS

Simple land transport depends upon human motive power. Consequently part of the technology of transport in such cases includes footgear to facilitate human travel. Devices in this category include not only shoes, boots, sandals, and moccasins, but also snowshoes and skis.

In many environments people apparently get along quite well without any footgear whatever. In environments with abundant rocks or spines, however, some type of footgear seems necessary for any significant amount of travel. Throughout much of the tropical and temperate zones, the only footgear worn is the sandal, the distribution being similar to that of weaving in both hemispheres. Sandals consist of a sole, held to the foot by cords or thongs or, in some cases, straps. Soles may be of hide or leather but in some localities are woven or braided from vegetable fibers. Thus in the American Southwest, where game was relatively scarce, sandal soles were

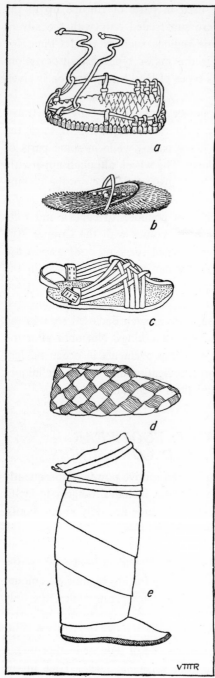

Fig. 11:9. Sandals and moccasins: (*a*) Japan; (*b*) Peru; (*c*) Afghanistan; (*d*) Finland; (*e*) Zuñi. After Mason.

made of yucca fiber. Styles and techniques of manufacture differ in various time periods. The shape of the sole and the technique of attaching sandals to the feet also vary for time and place.

Moccasins are a shoelike footgear. As in the case of sandals, the style of cut differs in time and place. Some of the North American Indians, for example, made the moccasin top out of a single piece of soft leather to which a sole was sewn. Moccasins are confined to the northern hemisphere (except for a moccasin-like boot worn by the Patagonians), and Hatt has shown that they are closely identified with arctic cultures. In the Pueblo and Plains regions of North America, moccasins are often hard-soled, but elsewhere the sole is usually soft. A correlation has been suggested between the soft-soled moccasin and the use of the snow-shoe.

Boots seem an invention of horse-riding people and are not related to foot travel. Apparently the Chinese borrowed the riding boot from their pastoral northern neighbors. The Chinese account of this event is perhaps the earliest record of the use of boots. Shoes are a relatively late type of footgear and are modified hard-soled moccasins to which a heel has been added.

The snowshoe, an oval, circular, or flounder-shaped framework of wood with a webbing of cords, is attached by thongs to the foot and is used to travel in soft snow. It is particularly valuable in the snowy regions of the northern hemisphere to which it is mainly confined. The distribution extends southward in the Americas to central California, but it is known throughout the arctic and subarctic areas of North America, Asia, and Europe, suggesting a diffusion from a common source. In these regions successful winter travel and hunting would be almost impossible without snowshoes.

The ski is also associated with regions of heavy winter snow, but is confined to northern Asia and Europe. The ski is a long, narrow piece of wood attached loosely to the foot. With a pair of skis, a skilled traveler may keep up with a herd of reindeer and travel as many as seventy miles a day with a heavy pack.

All these devices assist humans to travel more easily or protect their feet in inhospitable environments. Such devices would be of little assistance for transportation without aids to carry objects. Except for small purses or pouches of limited capacity, most people carry heavy loads either on the head or on the back.

The majority of Africans tend to carry loads on the head. For loads of more than sixty or seventy pounds a wooden frame is often used to contain the load. This is supported with one hand, while a staff in the other often aids the bal-

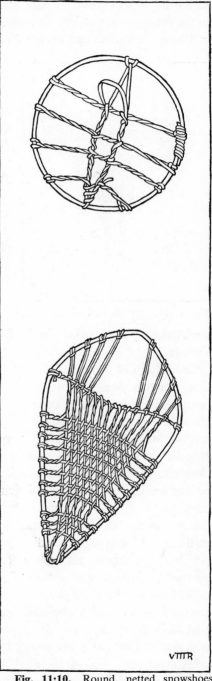

Fig. 11:10. Round, netted snowshoes (top); oval, netted snowshoes (bottom). After Mason.

ance if the load is heavy. In Asia, too, loads are often carried on the head. In the Americas apparently only women normally carry loads on the head, as among the Pueblo and many Central American peoples. A ring of fiber or fabric sometimes aids in the support of the object carried. The women of the Pueblo region are noted for their carriage as a result of carrying large pottery water vessels balanced on their heads without support from the hands.

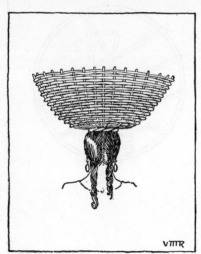

Fig. 11:11. Basket carried on head.

Carrying on the back involves some form of support. The most common device is the tumpline, a band attached to the burden by cords, and passing either over the chest or the forehead. This method of supporting the load seems to have considerable advantage over the shoulder straps common on the knapsacks used in European cultures, for the tumpline is sometimes used today by backpackers in the frontier areas of the United States and Canada.

Some form of container is used by most people for human transportation (see Chapter 9). In most cases the containers are especially designed for the purpose. For small objects, bags are often carried. Many Mexican Indians carry a rectangular woven bag suspended over one shoulder. Men among the Huichol Indians of that country have gone further and wear considerable numbers of small ornamented pouches as part of their costume. Although at times used to contain small objects, the pouches have become primarily a decorative part of the costume and a mark of a wife's esteem for her husband. Purselike pouches are used by Australian aborigines to transport their scanty stock of small possessions, and similar containers are found in many other areas.

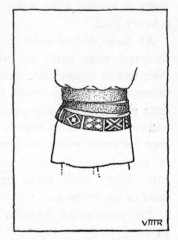

Fig. 11:12. Huichol Indian pouches.

For larger objects, bags, nets, blankets, and crates are used. The American Indian usually carries these on his back with the tumpline. One of the

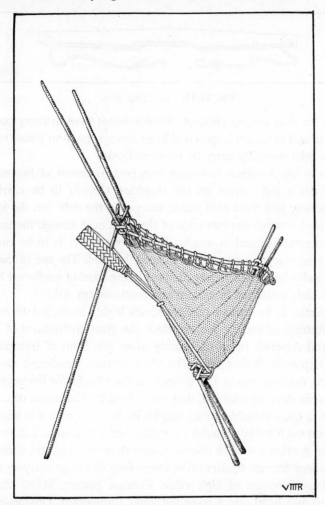

Fig. 11:13. Papago carrying net and frame. After Mason.

most common Mexican devices is the *huacal,* a crate made of sticks tied together. Often these crates are highly specialized; the Mixe Indians of Oaxaca, for example, carry pottery in a crate which is partitioned to keep the individual pieces apart and hence reduce breakage.

Another common container in Mexico is a large cylindrical basket. Baskets are used in other parts of the Americas but often are conical in shape, as in California. Perhaps the most striking human carrying device in North America, however, is the carrying net used by the Pimas and Papagos of southern Arizona, which is supported by a special frame.

In South America some special devices may be noted. Many tribes use carrying bands, slung bandolier fashion around the body and over one

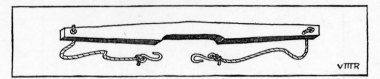

Fig. 11:14. Carrying pole.

shoulder, for transporting children. Similar bands used to carry goods are widespread and often are improvised in an emergency from pieces of fabric by people who normally carry by other methods.

Unique in the Americas is human transport by means of two nets suspended from a rod carried on the shoulder. Objects to be carried, including pottery jars filled with water, are put in the nets, but the load has to be divided between the two ends of the pole, even though the two parts are not necessarily equal in weight. If only one object is to be carried, a stone may be placed in one net to balance the load. The use of the carrying pole in aboriginal America is confined to the coast of northwest Mexico, but it is widely employed in eastern and southwestern Asia.

Transportation by human carriers seems highly inefficient to members of an industrialized society. Nevertheless, the great civilizations of Mexico and Central America relied exclusively upon this form of transport, and it is still important in that area. The Mixe Indians, mentioned above, export coffee, carrying nearly 150 pounds on their backs for journeys lasting as long as six days. In addition, they carry food for the round trip. Coffee, of course, is quite valuable for its weight; in the same area it is impractical to transport such bulky material as maize, and when crops fail the entire population is often forced to migrate rather than try to import corn.

In southern Mexico traders often cover long distances carrying specialized or local products of high value. Fabrics, pottery, skins, chocolate, wood, and metalwork are among the items transported. Obviously, then, even a considerable degree of specialization is possible using only human motive power in transportation, but the only goods which may be transported any distance are those of high value in proportion to their weight.

11. LAND TRANSPORT: ANIMALS AND VEHICLES

The use of domesticated animals for motive power effects a great improvement in land transportation, even though many methods are crude. Larger groupings of people are possible because food can be transported over longer distances. At the same time, face-to-face interaction becomes possible among more widely separated peoples. Trade can be over longer distances and in bulkier goods. Migratory people may own more possessions. All these factors apparently contribute to the formation of larger social units and the development of politically organized groups.

The least efficient use of animal power is by packing or riding. The Peruvian Indians of South America utilize the llama for packing and are thus somewhat more advanced than most other American Indians. The llama is a relatively poor beast of burden; it can carry only about forty pounds of weight, and it travels slowly, grazing along the trail, and so covers only about ten miles a day. Nevertheless, one man can pack and drive a considerable number of llamas and thus transport far more goods than he can by himself.

Some of the Plains Indians of North America use the dog as a pack animal. It is even less satisfactory than the llama, but it is still an improvement over human transportation. The Eskimos likewise use their dogs in this fashion in summer.

In the Old World a variety of animals are used for packing. Cattle, horses, donkeys, and camels are so employed over fairly wide areas, while the yak, elephant, and reindeer have a more limited distribution. Cattle may carry as much as 500 pounds but can travel only about ten miles a day with this load. Camels, on the other hand, can carry 1,500 pounds as far as twenty miles a day. Both animals are thus more efficient than the horse, and peoples who possess all three, like the Kazaks of central Asia, customarily use the horse mainly for riding. In the Mediterranean area the donkey seems to have been the principal beast of burden for a very long time, while the camel is the main animal employed in the deserts of North Africa and southwest Asia. In central Europe, however, the principal pack animal is the horse.

In the extreme north many European and Asiatic peoples use reindeer as pack animals. The Lapps of northern Scandinavia and many people in Siberia pack reindeer during the summer season. Each animal can carry about eighty pounds, divided between two bags or pouches slung on each side, and a herd so loaded is capable of covering long distances.

The riding of animals apparently developed first among the herding people of Central Asia, who used both the horse and the camel. Horse-riding, rare or absent in the early Mesopotamian cultures, becomes far more common after contact with migrants from central Asia. Evidence of camel-riding, however, is found in the Indus valley of India as early as 2500 B.C. Saddles are generally used with both animals, but the horse requires as well a special bridle.

Some reindeer breeders, like the Tungus, applied the techniques of horse-riding to reindeer, developing for this purpose a larger and sturdier breed of reindeer. Even these, however, must be ridden on the shoulders, for the reindeer cannot carry much weight on its back. Elsewhere such animals as cattle, yaks, elephants, and water buffalo are ridden, but the practice is not extensive and often it is confined to women and children, or to herdsmen caring for animals at pasture. It is perhaps notable that the American Indians, some of whom became excellent horsemen after European contact, had no riding animals at all in the aboriginal period.

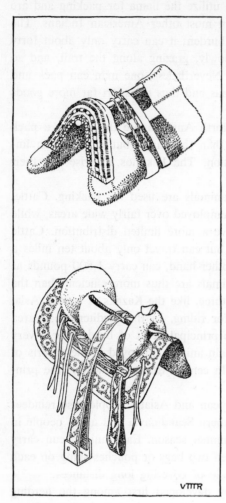

Fig. 11:15. Tungus saddle (top), after McCreery; Charro saddle (bottom), after Toor.

Most animals can pull greater loads than they can carry, and devices for this purpose mark a considerable technological improvement. The simplest of such arrangements is the travois used by the Plains Indians of North America. The load is placed on a small platform fastened to two poles. At one end the poles drag on the ground, while at the other they are fastened to a harness over the animal's back or else cross over the back of the animal. In aboriginal times the travois was used with dogs, but after the Indians acquired the horse, the device was also applied to the new animal. Even infants may be entrusted to the travois, enclosed in a cage of withes. In the Old World the same device is reported in fairly recent times from Russia, but there is no evidence that it was ever widespread.

Throughout the arctic regions of both the Old and New Worlds, the sled or sledge is extensively employed. In regions of soft snow, such as the forest belts of North America, the toboggan, essentially a flat-bottomed, runnerless sled, is employed; but elsewhere runners are more efficient, for they reduce the amount of friction. Dogs trained for this purpose are hitched to the sled in teams, either by a system of double traces in which

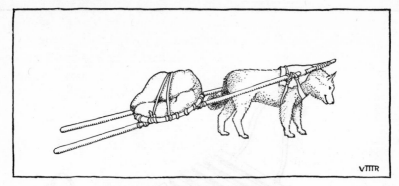

Fig. 11:16. Plains Indian dog travois.

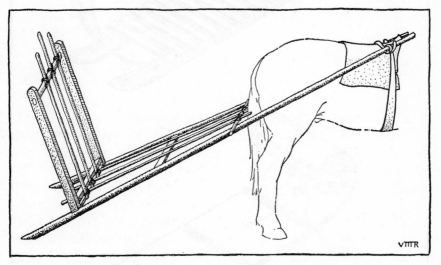

Fig. 11:17. Horse-drawn travois, Central Asia. After Clark.

the dogs travel single file, or by a number of single traces with the dogs fanned out in front of the sled. Under good snow conditions, long distances can be covered with the use of dogs and sleds, and large loads of game and other materials may be carried. Without some such efficient means of transportation, life in the arctic would be difficult if not impossible, for arctic cultures require the use of many bulky objects which can hardly be carried on the human back. Moreover, frequent movement is necessary owing to the seasonal nature and scattered distribution of the game animals.

The techniques of dog traction apparently were transferred to the reindeer when this animal was domesticated. Instead of several dogs, one or two reindeer suffice to draw a large sledge over long distances in a day, in some cases as many as a hundred miles. A number of reindeer teams, each drawing a sledge, may be handled by a single driver by tying a lead

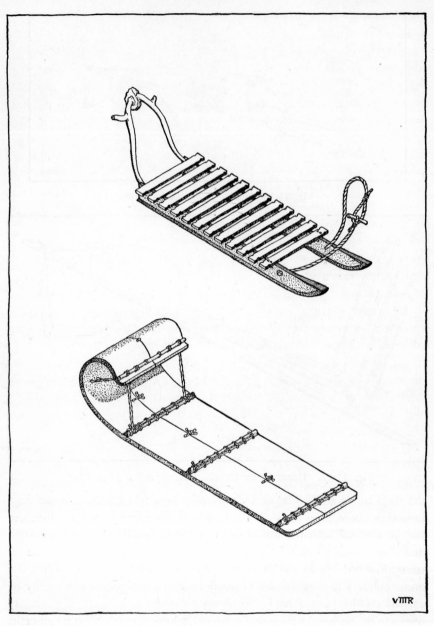

Fig. 11:18. Eskimo sled (top), after Boas, Indian toboggan (bottom), after Mason.

rope from one team to the sledge of a team in front. The driver rides in the leading sledge.

Although the sledge is employed mainly in regions of severe winters and heavy snowfall, its use has long been known in warmer climates. The Egyptians evidently used the sledge to drag building materials and other heavy objects as early as the pyramid-building days. The sledge is sometimes used by our own farmers for special purposes, such as bringing firewood out of the woods when the country is too rough for wheeled vehicles and roads are lacking. Although far from efficient in snowless regions, the sledge nevertheless is superior to packing when the distances to be covered are short and the terrain is not too rocky.

The greatest advance in land transportation came with the invention of the wheel. The wheel in our culture is such a commonplace device that we are apt to ignore its importance. Actually it is a triumph in applied physics on which most of our machines depend. Basically it is a way of converting straight-line force or movement into rotary movement. Applied to transportation, it greatly minimizes friction so that the same amount of force may move a much larger weight. The same physical principle, moreover, is inherent in the reciprocating steam engine and the internal combustion engine. Virtually no significant machine in our culture fails to make use of the principle of the wheel in some form or other. The discovery of the wheel is, then, a basic invention which must rank with such other basic inventions as fire-making, metal-smelting, writing, and the true arch. Like these, the wheel was first devised by some unknown "primitive" of the remote past.

Early wheeled vehicles seem to have been two-wheeled carts in which the two wheels and the axle were hewn out of a single large log. The wheels and the axle rotated together, the point of friction occurring between the axle and the bed of the cart. At an early date, however, the wheels and axle were made separately. The axle was then fastened rigidly to the bed of the cart and the wheels turned on the axle. Nevertheless, wheels were heavy and clumsy, usually being made of a single piece of wood, or, if more than one piece was used, still being solid. Such two-wheeled carts were usually drawn by a single pole fastened to a yoke resting on the necks of a pair of animals, either oxen or, at a later date, horses. Clumsy carts of this type are still employed in parts of Asia, Europe, and Latin America.

Lighter, spoked wheels were developed in Mesopotamia, where they were employed in war chariots as early as 2300 B.C. Such wheels were of little use in a rocky terrain, however, until they were protected by a metal tire. Apparently this step was not taken until iron became fairly abundant.

The effective use of wheeled vehicles depends on improved roads. Al-

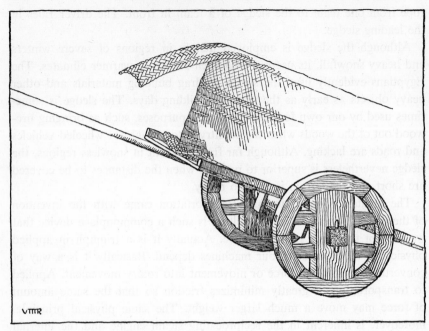

Fig. 11:19. Chinese two-wheeled cart with stationary axle and large basket on platform to carry freight. After Clark.

though some of the peoples of the great plains of eastern Europe and Asia were able to use four-wheeled carts without roads because of the open level terrain, the use of the wheel long was limited. In the great cities of Mesopotamia, narrow streets prohibited wheeled traffic inside the city limits, and donkeys or human porters carried goods inside the city. The great roads of the Persians were for post-riders on horseback, but not for wheeled vehicles. Similarly the Romans, in spite of the fact that they were the first great road-builders of Europe, designed most of their roads to facilitate the marching of foot soldiers and not for wheeled traffic. Long-distance land travel or transportation was mainly by riding or pack animal. In America, the Peruvian Indians built roads many hundreds of miles in length and spanned deep gorges with suspension bridges, but only foot travelers and llama herds used these routes. The Mayas of Yucatan built an extensive system of roads which were evidently used solely for ceremonial pilgrimages and processions on foot. The Baganda of East Africa similarly have a very elaborate road system, but do all their travel on foot and use only human motive power for transportation.

After Roman times, road-building was virtually abandoned in Europe. People traveled on foot or on horseback and used pack animals to transport goods. Carriage or wagon travel was limited in extent and continued to be difficult almost until modern times. Even though efforts were made at road improvement, and bridges were built in increasing numbers, eighteenth- and nineteenth-century travel was slow, difficult, and uncomfortable even in the most developed countries of Europe. Not until the invention of the steam engine and its application to the locomotive did land transportation become relatively fast, cheap, and comfortable, while road-building, except in and around cities, was not extensive until the automobile came into general use after the beginning of the present century. When confronted with the difficulties of travel in so-called backward parts of the world, it is well to remember that a century or a century and a half ago, most of Europe and America was no better off. Vivid descriptions of such travel difficulties are found in many books and novels of the period, as, for example, Mark Twain's *Roughing It,* or any of Dickens' novels.

12. WATER TRANSPORT

As mentioned in § 9, water transport probably did not develop until the Mesolithic and in most areas not until the Neolithic, although some simple means of crossing streams may have existed earlier. Logs, gourds, or inflated skins as floats to support swimmers or to convey goods are rather widely known and may have been used at a very early date. Such devices are obviously unsuited to long-distance travel or transport.

The use of the *balsa,* a raft made by fastening together bundles of dry reeds, exemplifies one type of raft. Like other rafts and floats, the *balsa* depends upon the natural buoyancy of the materials of which it is made (boats depend for support upon the displacement of water by a hollow air space in the hull). Reed rafts occur sporadically in a number of areas. The Indians of California about San Francisco Bay and in the lakes of the interior of the state use such devices, as do the Indians of the Gulf of California. Farther south, on the elevated lake of Titicaca in Bolivia, large *balsas* are employed even today and are equipped with sails. The Tasmanians also used rafts of this type. Reed boats have been used by the Egyptians of the Nile delta for thousands of years, though these soon become waterlogged, thus limiting their utility.

Log rafts are often made for short trips on streams, but are rarely used on a significant scale. On the Balsas River of Mexico, additional buoyancy is provided by fastening large gourds underneath the raft. Inflated skins as supports for swimmers in crossing streams are used in Europe by the Albanians as well as others.

The simplest transportation depending for buoyancy upon the displacement of water is the coracle, so named from a Welsh boat consisting of a

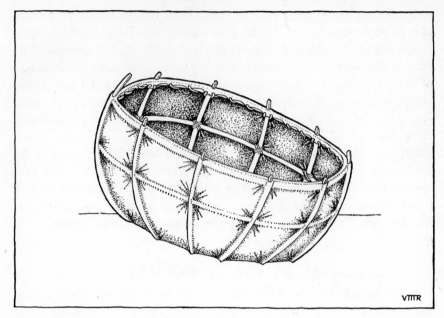

Fig. 11:20. Plains Indian coracle.

circular frame covered with skin. Such craft are clumsy and unmanageable but serve well enough for crossing streams. The Mandans of the Missouri River use a similar craft, which led one early writer to assert their Welsh origin. Coracles occur among other Plains Indians and also in Patagonia. Travelers on the Tigris-Euphrates rivers sometimes use similarly shaped vessels of basketry coated with pitch to travel downstream.

Widespread is the use of dugout canoes made by hollowing out a single log. When adequate cutting tools are lacking, such a canoe may be made by heaping hot coals on the part to be removed, scraping out the charred sections, and repeating the process until the task is completed. Dugout canoes of this type are widely known among nonliterate peoples who have access to proper trees. The size and adequacy of such canoes varies greatly, however. The Ainus of northern Japan make a narrow, shallow canoe barely large enough to support two people, which they handle with great dexterity. Often the two passengers will stand upright in such a canoe, one poling or paddling, the other poised to spear fish. On the other hand, the Indians of the coast of British Columbia make canoes from the trunks of the giant cedar trees capable of carrying sixty or seventy men and two or three tons of freight.

In Asia and in the forested parts of North America, birch bark is sewn carefully over a wooden frame and the joints calked with vegetable gum.

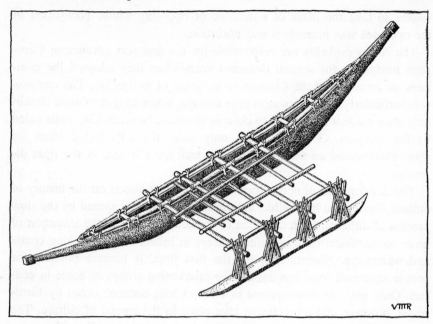

Fig. 11:22. Outrigger canoe, Melanesia. After Haddon, Hornell.

coast on canoes, the New World made little use of sails. Canoes are too unstable to use wind power safely. In any case, the craft must generally sail straight before the wind or it is in danger of capsizing. In this respect the Oceanians had a great advantage; with the outrigger not only was danger of capsizing reduced to nil except in high winds, but the craft could tack, that is, sail into the wind at an angle, an art unknown to Europeans at the time of Columbus.

By all odds the greatest navigators until after the voyage of Columbus were the Polynesians. Not only had they mastered the art of sailing into the wind, but they had developed crude navigation devices for determining latitude. Planned voyages of over 2,000 miles are known to have occurred, and the Polynesians discovered and occupied most of the habitable islands in the vast expanse of the central Pacific at a time when European sailors dreaded leaving sight of land.

While there is evidence that Egyptian and Phoenician sailors may have circumnavigated Africa before the beginning of the Christian era, such voyages were in short stages within sight of land. Sails were employed early, but lacking the knowledge of sailing into the wind, oars remained important, particularly in the relatively calm waters of the Mediterranean. In Roman times and after, vessels designed for speedy travel or for warfare, where continuous mobility was essential, relied on large numbers of rowers to take the place of unreliable or opposing winds. Navigation in the open sea was precarious and uncertain.

The Arabs probably are responsible for the first real advance in European navigation for several thousand years when they adapted the compass, an invention of the Chinese, to purposes of navigation. The compass was particularly useful in waters near Europe, where long-continued cloudiness often made it impossible to observe the stars. Nevertheless, while aided by the compass, Columbus could only order the sails furled when his ships encountered an adverse wind and wait for a breeze in the right direction.

The development of ocean travel had important effects on the history of culture. During the Paleolithic, culture traits could only spread by the slow process of diffusion from one tribe to the next. Even with the invention of boats, communication was limited except in inland seas and along coasts and waterways. Nevertheless, for the first time, it became possible for people separated from one another by intervening groups to come in contact. Only with the development of efficient long-distance travel by Europeans, however, did a revolution take place in the spread of culture. The earlier voyagers, except for the Polynesians, were generally either very limited in their range or made long voyages so infrequently that these had little or no effect on the transmission of culture. Even the Polynesians seem to have had little or no effect on the cultures of the Americas, although it seems very likely that they reached the American coast more than once.

The social conditions existing in Europe after the discovery of America, coupled with rapid improvement in navigation and boat design, resulted in radical changes of culture in widely separated areas of the world. Trade introduced European ideas throughout the world, and in turn brought Europeans in contact with myriad new ideas, concepts, and culture elements. Europeans also settled many portions of the globe. The result not only was the enormous flowering and enrichment of European cultures as old habits and mental barriers were broken, but also the wide diffusion of European culture patterns to many parts of the globe and to peoples who had long lived in almost complete isolation.

13. SUMMARY

We have reviewed in this chapter a wide variety of cultural products and techniques related to clothing, shelter, and transportation. We have noted that no peoples are wholly lacking in these products and techniques, though in some societies clothing, shelter, and transportation are reduced to the bare minimum necessary to survival. It is also clear that the techniques of nonliterate peoples—and the products of these techniques—though sometimes crude are not necessarily so. Even societies having cutting tools far inferior to our own may produce excellent and efficient clothing, shelters, and transportation devices. This is particularly well illustrated by the clothing of the Eskimos, the elaborate houses of the Indians of British Columbia, and the outrigger canoes of many Oceanic peoples.

Clothing, though it probably first developed as a protection from the environment, also serves many other functions—such as adornment, the needs (as conceived in particular societies) of modesty and good taste, and the symbolizing of status and occupation. Adornment, we have noted, is more varied and widespread than clothing, and may indeed have preceded it historically.

The types of clothing worn are conditioned by technology, the resources of the environment, the need for protection against the weather, and historical traditions and contacts with other peoples. Tropical peoples, especially those living in forests, commonly use bast or bark materials such as bark cloth or *tapa*. Tailored clothing apparently was first developed by a people who lived in a cold climate. The application of tailoring to textile garments is relatively a recent development.

Textiles are later in time as clothing materials than animal skins or the use of wild vegetable products. Together with textiles, or possibly preceding their use, are the techniques of spinning and weaving, which probably did not come until the Neolithic. Sewing, however, is an earlier technique—used on skins—as is evidenced by the bone needle of late Paleolithic cultures.

Shelters, like clothing, apparently developed first as a protection against the weather, even though some peoples, like the Tierra del Fuegians, have shelters which are only barely adequate for this purpose. Nomadic peoples, on the whole, build either temporary shelters which may be abandoned without great loss or else shelters that are readily movable. Among sedentary peoples—and even with some nomads who return to certain areas year after year—we find more elaborate, permanent structures. Shelters, like clothing, exhibit an enormous diversity, both in materials and construction. The types depend very largely on the cutting tools available, environmental resources, facilities for importing building materials, the exigencies of the food quest, and historical contacts.

Transportation devices are broadly of two sorts—those usable on land and watercraft. Land transport of some sort is apparently universal, while water transportation, though widespread, is lacking in a few societies. A great many nonliterate folk are wholly dependent on human carriers for land transportation, and we find a great variety of devices—including such items as footwear, containers, tumplines, and the like—to aid in this function. The use of animals for transport is relatively recent, and the development of wheeled vehicles even more recent. Sleds and sledges are, however, quite old, and especially in regions like the Arctic, well suited to their use.

The earliest water transport was apparently accomplished by floats and rafts. True boats are relatively recent. Human motive power for watercraft is old and widespread; sails are only occasionally employed by nonliterates. Except for the Polynesians, who made long ocean voyages, watercraft, until recently, was used only on inland waters for coastwise travel.

As transportation devices, whether for land or water travel, improved, there occurred as well many important changes in cultures generally. Trade was stimulated and interactions between peoples of diverse cultures broke down much cultural isolation. The world today, by reason of its rapid transportation and easy means of communication, becomes more and more a single community, the destinies of its still widely divergent peoples inextricably intertwined.

COLLATERAL READING

Beals, Ralph; Carrasco, Pedro; and McCorkle, T. *Houses and House-Use of the Sierra Tarascans.* Washington, D. C.: Smithsonian Institution, Institute of Social Anthropology, 1944.

Bennett, Wendell. "Architecture and Engineering," *Handbook of South American Indians,* ed. Julian H. Steward. Bulletin 143, Bureau of American Ethnology, Washington, D. C., 1949. Vol. 5, pp. 1–66.

Crawford, M. D. C. "Peruvian Textiles," *Anthropological Papers of the American Museum of Natural History,* Vol. XII, New York, 1915.

———. "Peruvian Fabrics," *Anthropological Papers of the American Museum of Natural History,* Vol. XII, New York, 1916.

Hatt, Gudmund. "Moccasins and Their Relation to Arctic Footwear," *Memoirs, American Anthropological Association,* Vol. 3, No. 3, 1916.

McCurdy, George C. *Human Origins.* New York: D. Appleton and Co., 1924. Vol. 2, Chapters XII–XIV.

Martin, Paul; Quimby, George; and Collier, Donald. *Indians before Columbus.* Chicago: University of Chicago Press, 1947. Chapter 8.

Morgan, Lewis H. "Houses and House-Life of the American Aborigines," *Contributions to North American Ethnology,* Vol. 4, Washington, D. C., 1881.

O'Neale, Lila. "Weaving," *Handbook of South American Indians,* ed. Julian H. Steward. Bulletin 143, Bureau of American Ethnology, Washington, D. C., 1949. Vol. 5, pp. 97–138.

Wissler, Clark. *The American Indian.* New York: Oxford University Press, 1938. Chapters II, III, VI.

Chapter 12

ECONOMICS

1. FUNDAMENTAL ECONOMIC PROBLEMS

The study of economics, broadly defined, centers its interest on three fundamental questions:

(1) How are the goods and services needed by human societies produced? Here of course economics is not concerned principally with technology, the means by which raw materials are converted into usable foods and artifacts, but rather with the patterns which govern the human activities and interactions involved in the production of goods and services. It seeks to discover how the work of production is divided among members of human societies and whether or not individuals or groups within a society specialize in particular occupations. In our society, for example, there are a large number of specialized trades, crafts, and professions, many of which require years of apprenticeship or learning. In contrast, smaller and more homogeneous societies, like those of the Australian aborigines, have few or no specialized occupations; every individual of the same age and sex group performs or is capable of performing the same tasks, most of which are learned in youth as part of the process of growing up.

(2) How are the goods and services that are produced distributed among the members of human societies? Here again the emphasis lies on the patterns of human interaction which govern the processes of distribution, not on the techniques employed to achieve this end. Is distribution, as in many of the simpler societies, merely a family concern, in the sense

that members of the family produce all that is necessary to meet their needs? Or is the family part of a larger unit, within which goods and services are distributed by some system of barter or trade? In modern world societies, of course, the organization for distribution is exceedingly complex; nearly all the needs for daily living must be obtained by trade, and many of them come from distant places and go through many hands before reaching the ultimate consumer.

(3) How are the goods and services that are produced and distributed in human societies eventually put to use and consumed, and what patterns of behavior govern this process? In many societies, where the techniques of production and distribution are extremely simple, production, distribution, and consumption take place within one small group, the members of which live in daily face-to-face contact with each other. Such societies, because they produce little above their daily needs, do not face the problem of accumulated wealth and the question of the ownership and control of such wealth. The situation is very different in modern world societies, where highly developed techniques of production result in large surpluses. Here the question arises as to the ownership and control of surplus production, a question which involves ultimately not only economic power but also political control.

In the sections that follow we shall examine each of these questions in some detail in an attempt to learn how a comparative study of human societies may result in a better understanding of the economic aspects of human culture.

2. TECHNOLOGY AND THE DIVISION OF LABOR

The problem of the division of labor, to be properly understood, must be examined in relation to the complexity of techniques. Certain techniques, like the manufacture of stone tools, require relatively little skill and the labors of only a single individual. In an area where proper materials are easily found—and such areas are numerous on the earth's surface—almost anyone can soon be taught to select the right stones and to chip or grind them into useful cutting tools and other artifacts. Accordingly, in societies which have only cutting tools made of stone, the art of tool-making is usually known to every adult male, each of whom has learned it in a relatively short time from his father, older brother, or other male companion. Moreover, since the entire process of stone tool-making is usually too simple to require division into separate operations, one individual can search out the necessary raw material and shape it in a few minutes to the required tool.

Other techniques, such as the manufacture of iron tools, are far more complicated and not so quickly learned. It requires considerable experience to find iron-bearing sands or ores and to recognize that such deposits, which are not at all similar in appearance to pure iron, contain the required material. Training is also necessary to learn the process of smelting iron ores and so separating the pure metal from the foreign substances in which it is embedded. Finally, the individual must be taught how to shape iron into tools and artifacts, whether by heating or hammering or by the somewhat more complex process of liquefying the iron and pouring it into prepared molds.

As techniques increase in complexity, two tendencies often emerge:

(1) The technique, because it requires skills which take some time to learn, may become specialized to a particular segment of the society and is not learned as a generalized craft by all of a given age and sex group. Among the Baganda of East Africa we find a number of specialized artisan groups, adult males who spend all or most of their working time as iron-workers, carpenters, canoe-builders, leather-workers, drum-makers, potters, house-thatchers, or floor-makers.

(2) The technique, because of its complexity, may be segmented into a number of distinct operations, each of which then becomes the specialty of a group of artisans. We note above, for example, that Baganda specialists may either be concerned with a whole technique (such as canoe-building or leather-working) or with some particular operation, such as house-thatching, which is only a part of the technique of house-building. In some instances, indeed, a society may know only one operation pertinent to a technique and have no idea of operations which necessarily precede it. Some African tribes are adept at forging iron tools, but know nothing of mining the ores or smelting; they purchase lumps of pure iron from others. Similarly the Homeric Greeks imported pure iron by sea; their specialists knew only the arts of casting and forging. In modern American society, of course, this process of dividing techniques into smaller operations has been carried to an extreme. Whole factories of men are employed, for example, to build motor cars, where the finished vehicle is the result, not of one craftsman's efforts, but of the efforts of several score, each of whom performs only one simple operation repeatedly as a machine moves the material to his station on the assembly line.

3. DIVISION OF LABOR BY AGE AND SEX

We must not infer from the preceding discussion that division of labor occurs only in societies which have complex technologies. Actually it is important to recognize two kinds of division of labor: that based on age and sex, which is found in all societies, and that based on specialization (often called true division of labor) which is lacking or only incipient in societies possessing relatively simple technologies.

Division of labor by age results from the obvious biological fact that human beings undergo three major periods of development. In childhood, the period of growth and maturation, the human is in large part dependent upon adults for food, shelter, and other necessities; he has neither the strength nor the skills to provide for himself. Children, in most societies, have only light tasks as helpers to adults or none at all, and when duties are assigned, these are often regarded as educational, to prepare the child for his adult occupations.

Adulthood, the second major period of growth, is ordinarily the period of greatest vigor and ability. The adult man or woman, in nearly all societies, takes on full responsibility for the duties of his sex and special occupation. In many societies, in particular those in which the technology requires physical strength and stamina, the adult in the prime of life assumes a most important position and is often assigned the more responsible positions in the group.

Old age, since it inevitably brings about a loss in muscular vigor and a decline in sight, hearing, and coordination, again results in a change in occupational status. This does not necessarily mean that the old lose prestige; many societies make full use of their older members' experience and wisdom and employ them to direct the efforts of the more vigorous but not so experienced adults.

Sex division of labor is more difficult to account for in strictly biological terms. For though it is true that women, by reason of the fact that they bear the children and in most societies must be available to feed them during infancy, are therefore more restricted in occupation than men, very little sexual division of labor is explainable on this basis alone. We may note, for example, that the Hopis of northern Arizona assign to men the spinning of cotton, the weaving of cloth, and the making of all clothing, that intended for women as well as their own. But their immediate neighbors, the Navahos, who probably learned to spin and weave from the Hopis, consider these to be female occupations almost exclusively; men only weave the ceremonial fabrics. Again, house-building and repairing, male occupations in our society, are, except for the heavy labor of raising roof beams and handling large stones, female occupations among the Hopis.

A careful survey of the division of labor by sex lends little support to the oft-repeated assertion that women are fit only for occupations that require relatively little skill or intelligence. The history of our own society amply disproves this assertion; in recent years women, freed from economic bondage to their fathers and husbands, have shown themselves fully capable in nearly all professions, arts, trades, and crafts in which they have been given the opportunity to participate. The fact that women must, in many societies, take over occupations which can be carried on successfully together with the care and feeding of children is no proof of their incapacity in other occupations. Man's wider range of occupation and the fact that he very often occupies the more important positions of leadership in human societies, is probably less due to his allegedly superior intelligence than to his greater freedom from the biological function of childbirth and the necessarily feminine duties in the care of infants.

4. TRUE DIVISION OF LABOR

Among many peoples, and in particular among those who possess only crude tools and live in areas poor in natural resources, there is no true division of labor but only that which is determined by the factors of age and sex. An example is found among the Hopis of northern Arizona, who live on a semiarid plateau, some 6,000 feet in elevation, which has only a scanty rainfall and no permanent rivers.

Despite this scarcity of water, the Hopis are a horticultural people who raise, by dint of arduous labor, corn, beans, squash, pumpkins, sunflowers, and cotton. Additional foods are secured by hunting and gathering, but the animals and plants so supplied are definitely secondary food resources. Tools and weapons are made by hand of wood, stone, and bone; containers of pottery and basketry. All the techniques employed, whether in food production or the making of tools and artifacts, are relatively uncomplicated and may be learned in a short time. More important, Hopi productive capacity is small, resulting only in enough food to support a few hundred people more or less successfully throughout the year. There is little surplus over immediate needs; if Hopi society is to survive, nearly every able-bodied individual must spend most of his working time in actually producing food.

In keeping with these facts, Hopi society possesses no full-time specialists; and only a few adults, and these the older men, can be spared some of the labors of food production. These men are priests and governors; the men who, by virtue of age and experience, conduct the long and complicated rites performed for the most part in winter to assure the success of the next year's crop. Aside from these part-time specialists in ritual and ceremony, the division of labor is entirely in terms of age and sex. Men carry on all horticultural operations, hunt, go to war, spin and weave cotton cloth, make clothing, make their tools and weapons, and gather fuel and house-building materials. Women gather wild vegetable foods, perform all household tasks, care for the children, build and repair houses, make baskets and pottery, and conduct the very occasional trade whereby the Hopis, when they have a successful year, exchange their small surplus for foods and artifacts they themselves do not produce.

Though we have said that an incipient specialization of labor occurs among the Hopis, it is important to note that the Hopi priests and governmental functionaries are not paid for these services; their reward comes only in an enhancement of prestige. If a priest is able-bodied and capable, he may well work in the fields as other men do; if not, he is supported, but in this he possesses no advantage not given to others in the same plight who are not priests. In brief, the specializations that exist in societies of this type are performed as added duties and not as means of making a living.

True specialization and division of labor occurs only when the society is so organized that some individuals may devote part or all of their time to particular occupations which serve as their means of making a living. The iron-workers among the Baganda may serve as an example. They spend all their time in mining, smelting, and forging iron, and exchange the artifacts so made for food and other necessities. The existence of such specialists in Baganda society means of course that Baganda techniques of food production and the natural resources of the area in which they live are such as to produce enough food for all the population even though only a part of the working force engages directly in food-producing activities. The Baganda horticulturist, unlike his Hopi counterpart, produces a surplus over his immediate needs and employs that surplus to purchase the tools and artifacts made by the specialist. Were it not for this exchangeable surplus, obviously the specialist could not exist.

Apparently, then, specialization and true division of labor are dependent, not alone on the development of a more complex technology, but as well on the production of an exchangeable surplus. This point appears to be demonstrated in the archeological records of Old World cultural history. Horticultural techniques, invented probably somewhere in the Near East toward the end of the Pleistocene gave rise, in the fertile and well-watered oases of the Tigris, Nile, and Euphrates valleys, to extremely productive societies. Because their food production increased so rapidly, these societies not only grew in population but, as the archeological record shows, made marked and rapid improvement in technology. This led to expansion, an application of new techniques to wider areas, and began a cycle of economic development which led ultimately to the western European civilizations.

5. TECHNOLOGY AND THE ORGANIZATION OF LABOR

Technology also exerts an influence on the ways in which human societies organize their working groups. Certain techniques can best be performed by one individual working independently; these techniques are not suited to coordinated group effort. The Eskimo hunter, for example, must creep up on his prey as quietly as possible in order to get close enough to use his bow and arrow, spear, or harpoon without frightening the animal into flight. Such still hunting or stalking is obviously performed more efficiently alone, for the presence of others may actually contribute more to failure than to success. Similarly, though for the sake of company a group of Eskimos may go together to gather wild foods, each member of the party works independently; there is no need for them to coordinate their activities.

Other techniques may require highly coordinated group effort. An excellent example is the Plains Indian buffalo hunt, which often involves every able-bodied male and female in the tribe. Once a large herd is located, the men begin to construct a stout corral and, extending from its entrance, a pair of diverging fences. Near the corral these fences are strongly built, but as they move outward and become wider apart, the construction is lighter. During this building operation, great care is taken not to disturb the buffalo, and any individual who, by independent hunting or other activity unrelated to the common effort, causes the buffalo to stampede and to move far from the enclosure under construction is severely punished.

When the corral and the fences converging upon it are completed, a group of men go out to stampede the buffalo in the direction of the corral. As the herd moves between the converging lines of fence, other men, stationed along the way, urge it along and attempt to keep it from escaping through the weaker portions of the fence. Eventually, if the run is successful, the herd of buffalo pours into the corral where, unable to escape, the animals are killed by men standing outside the enclosure. Once the killing is done, the women skin and butcher the fallen buffalo, preparing choice bits of meat for immediate consumption and drying the rest for storage and later eating. The food so obtained is divided among all the families who participated in the hunt.

Techniques like these, it is evident, require careful organization and precise timing. Each individual must coordinate his own efforts with those of the rest or the project will fail. Among the Plains Indians this coordination is achieved by a buffalo chief, aided by one of the men's clubs that function as his messengers and police force. For the duration of the hunt, the word of the buffalo chief is law, and anyone who disobeys is promptly punished by being stripped of his possessions and publicly whipped.

In a society where techniques are predominantly individualistic, there is little organization of the labor force; each adult works as he pleases, spurred only by the need, which is often very great, to produce the necessities of life for himself and his dependents. The working unit is usually the family (a man, his wife, and their children), and this unit is frequently self-sustaining. In seasons of the year when food is plentiful and easy to secure, many families may live together and enjoy relative freedom from the food quest. But when food is scarce and hard to find, each family or set of two or three families will forage alone, and spend the bulk of their time in just getting enough to eat.

When a society has even one technique requiring the coordinated efforts of several families, this demand for a large and carefully organized labor force imposes obligations on the individual over and above his responsibilities to his family. It is to his advantage to become a member of this larger group and, in return for his allegiance and cooperation with them, to share in their greater productivity. The Plains Indian has both a more plentiful and more regular supply of meat and skins because of the communal buffalo hunt than he could provide by his own unaided efforts.

In modern world societies like our own, technology requires even more careful coordination and organization of labor. Almost everyone has a place in a labor force so large and so complexly organized that it is difficult to comprehend it as a whole or understand all its workings in detail. During World War II, people in the United States lacked tires and other rubber goods because the Japanese had invaded Malaya, and the local economy of the United States was profoundly disturbed by the necessity for providing and supporting an army of many millions of men. These happenings vividly illustrate the economic interdependence of modern nations. Any disruption in the working force affects, to a greater or less degree, almost every member of the society, however remote he may be from the source of the disturbance.

6. DISTRIBUTION IN SUBSISTENCE ECONOMIES

Patterns of culture which govern the distribution of goods and services in human societies tend, like patterns which guide the division of labor, to be influenced by the degree to which a society produces an exchangeable surplus. In societies where little or no such surplus is produced, the means of distributing goods and services are simple: the unit which produces goods and services also makes use of them. Where surplus production is possible, and where such production allows a true division of labor, some more elaborate means of distribution, such as a system of markets, is generally found.

The Hopi will serve to illustrate the first of these types. Hopi technology, as we have seen, because it operates in an environment none too rich in resources, ordinarily produces little or no exchangeable surplus. The Hopi primary family (a man, his wife, and their children) is the basic producing-consuming unit. The family lives in a house that its members have built, eats the food produced by the work of its members, makes its own clothing, and makes all the tools and artifacts necessary to its producing activities. The land which is used for hunting and gathering is owned by no one; there is ample space for all in the society to exercise use rights without denying such rights to others. Farming land is owned by clans (groups of primary families linked in the maternal line) and assigned equitably to each of its members who heads a primary family. Even here, however, there is no sharp competition for farming lands, since the supply is well in excess of the demand.

When, by reason of crop failure or lack of success in hunting or gathering, a family is unable to sustain itself, food and other necessities are provided by related families as gifts, these imposing on the recipients the obligation to give similar aid when it may be required. No family may hoard food or other necessities when others are in want, for such action would violate every canon of Hopi behavior. Generosity and a "good heart" are among the highest Hopi ideals; stinginess a mortal sin. As a result, the Hopi village, an independent political unit composed of families and clans, achieves a distribution of the goods it produces without any of the mechanisms of internal trade and commerce. Indeed, since Hopi society lacks a true division of labor and its accompaniment in an exchangeable surplus, there can be no internal trade.

Systems of distribution like that of the Hopi, though they may differ in detail, are relatively common among so-called primitive peoples, only a few of which have developed their technologies to a point where exchangeable surpluses can be produced. These systems, characteristic of subsistence economies, are often lumped together under the term "primitive communism," largely because the communities which live under them, lacking true division of labor and internal trade, share their goods and services. This term is misleading, however, in that it mistakenly links subsistence economies with modern communism, which only came into existence, as a political-economic theory of government, with the industrial revolution. The essence of the Hopi system of distribution lies, not in its sharing features, but in the fact that each family, since it possesses in its members all the productive techniques available to the society as a whole, is capable of sustaining itself. The Hopi pattern of sharing in case of need is only a form of insurance against the failure of the food supply and has none of the political overtones characteristic of modern communism.

7. TRADING IN SOCIETIES WITH SUBSISTENCE ECONOMIES

While, as we have seen, the lack of an exchangeable surplus and an internal division of labor inhibits trade within societies having only subsistence economies, it does not follow that such societies have no external or intersocietal trade. The Hopis, for example, engage in a little trade with the several tribes that surround them, exchanging farm products and cotton textiles for piñon nuts, mescal, red ochre, shell beads, and tanned deerskins. Similarly, the Australian Aruntas, whose productive facilities are even less than those of the Hopis, obtain a number of goods by trade, notably *pituri,* a narcotic, which appears to come from tribes in Queensland, some two hundred miles from the Arunta territory.

Much of intersocietal trade on this level results from the fact that certain raw materials, used by all the societies living in a given region, are not equally available to all of them. Accordingly some of the societies must acquire these materials by trade, and regular routes, often involving a series of intertribal contacts, may be established to achieve this end. The procedures governing such trade, especially when it occurs between societies relatively poor in productive capacities, are not very complicated. They involve only a simple exchange of one kind of goods for another, with exchange values calculated by rough rule-of-thumb methods. Since the goods exchanged are usually few in number and no great quantities of material are involved, neither markets nor other elaborate trading procedures are necessary. Trading contacts usually occur between individuals who meet at irregular intervals for this purpose and whose exchanges are more in the nature of mutual gift-giving than trade as we know it.

Intersocietal trade of this character is also stimulated where the several societies occupying adjoining areas have markedly different technologies, especially when the techniques of food-gathering or production are diverse. As a result, while these tribes may possess no true internal division of labor, each society as a whole specializes in some form of hunting, gathering, horticulture, or animal husbandry. Such specialization often makes it possible to reserve some of the produce obtained for trade and so provide a more varied diet and supply of materials than would otherwise be possible. Thus, the Plains Indians, who devoted nearly all their primary productive efforts to hunting the buffalo, exchanged, where possible, a portion of the meat and hides so obtained with neighboring tribes, in particular the Pueblo Indians bordering the Plains, for farm products and textiles. After the annual buffalo hunt was finished, parties of Plains Indians traveled to the nearest Pueblo group, there to conduct their trade before returning to winter quarters.

A similar trading relationship has been noted between the inland Chukchee of Siberia and the maritime Chukchee. The inland people specialize as a group on raising large herds of reindeer, pastured in the forests and tundras of northeastern Siberia, while the maritime Chukchee specialize in fishing and the hunting of sea mammals. The inlanders accordingly exchange some of their reindeer meat and hides for sea mammal meat, far richer in fats than reindeer meat, and the hides of seals and walruses which, because these are thicker and tougher than reindeer hides, are better suited for thongs and boot soles.

To conclude this section, it is notable that intersocietal trade is apparently universal; there are few if any societies that are so isolated as to be dependent alone on their own resources. Trade between societies with subsistence economies varies considerably in importance, depending upon the distribution of raw materials and the frequency of contact between the societies concerned. The amount of exchangeable surplus available also affects the amount and importance of trade at this level of cultural development.

8. SYMBIOTIC TRADE RELATIONS

The phrase "symbiotic trade relations" is usually applied when two more or less independent societies establish a special trading relationship whereby a larger and economically more advanced society is linked by trade to a society which has no internal division of labor and is unable, without the aid of its trading partner, to produce an exchangeable surplus. An outstanding example of this phenomenon is found in the Ituri Forest of Congo Africa, occupied both by Bantu-speaking Negroes and Pygmies, the latter a dwarfed people of quite a different racial classification than their Negro neighbors (see Chapter 6, §§ 9–11).

The Negroes of Congo Africa are primarily a horticultural people who live in large villages, produce a considerable exchangeable surplus, and have both a true division of labor and an extensive internal trade conducted through large market systems. In contrast, the Pygmies are hunters and food-gatherers who roam in small nomadic bands throughout the more inaccessible portions of the Ituri Forest. They have no true division of labor, no internal trade, and their tool- and weapon-making techniques are simple and crude. Each Negro society controls a large territory in which they have cleared sections of the forest for their villages and farms. Within the territory but outside the Negro villages are found the Pygmy bands, each of which ordinarily maintains trade relations only with the Negro society in control of the area in which it lives.

Despite the simplicity of their technology, we find the Pygmies eating domesticated plantains along with game and wild vegetable foods, and using well-made tools and weapons of iron, as well as manufactured articles which are clearly beyond their ability to make. All these domesticated foods and advanced artifacts are obtained from the Negro societies by trade. In return, the Pygmies supply the Negro villages with meat, hides, wild honey, forest fruits, roofing leaves for houses, and rattans and fibers for mat-making. The Pygmies also serve as scouts and spies for the Negroes of the territory in which they live, giving warning at the approach of raiding parties from adjacent areas.

Trading takes place at regular intervals but involves a minimum of face-to-face contact. Bunches of plantains and other articles are left in agreed upon places in and about the Negro villages where the Pygmies come to pick them up and leave their own products in return. This form of trading—often called silent trade or dumb barter—occurs in other portions of the world and most often in connection with symbiotic trade relations. In some regions, it is conducted secretly, in the sense that one party to the trade goes at night to a designated spot to pick up articles and leave others, which are then taken up later by the second party. Despite the lack of contact and bargaining by the traders, neither side can afford to cheat the other if it is desirable to continue the relationship. For example, should the Pygmies fail to bring enough meat or forest products to pay for the plantains and manufactured articles left for them by the Negroes, the latter would reduce their offerings in later exchanges. Similarly, if the Negroes proved to be stingy in their offerings, the Pygmies might well decide to take their meat to another village or even to leave the territory for that of a more generous Negro tribe.

Symbiotic trade, though not taking place between economic equals, has obvious advantages to both sides. The Negroes gain the services of forest peoples skilled in hunting and warfare, while the Pygmies share in the advanced Negro technology. In one sense, however, the Negroes dominate the relationship, for the Pygmies have no choice but to trade with one or other of the stronger and more advanced Negro tribes, unless of course they choose to isolate themselves completely.

Here, then, we have what appears to be the beginning of a system of economic classes: the Pygmies may develop into a group of hereditary hunters and gatherers, a functioning part of Negro society but much lower in status. According to Putnam, the Pygmies "consider themselves inseparably attached to their hosts and think it their duty to provide them with meat," but it is a duty "regarded as something of a nuisance" and performed grudgingly.[1] The Negroes, on the other hand, consider the Pygmies "a species apart, neither human nor animal, but in between. The main point of distinction lies not in their size or physique, but in the fact that the Pygmies do no cultivation." [2]

It is interesting to note that similar economic relationships occurred during the period of American expansion to the west. In the Great Plains, for example, when the enormous buffalo herds of this region still existed, American traders furnished guns and other equipment to the Indians, who provided buffalo meat and skins in return. In this fashion the traders were able to employ whole tribes of Indian hunters to exploit a given territory and to increase the efficiency of this exploitation by improving the Indians' technology. The arrangement was short-lived, since the area was soon denuded of its buffalo. Similar arrangements, some of which still continue, are found between the fur traders and the Indians of the subarctic regions of Canada, and between urban and folk peoples in many parts of Latin America.

9. THE KULA RING OF THE TROBRIANDS

As we move on to societies with true division of labor and exchangeable surpluses, intersocietal trade becomes more complicated and formalized. In general, such trade takes one of three forms: trading partnerships, a system of traveling merchants or peddlers, and market systems. The *kula* ring of the Trobriand Islanders of Melanesia offers an excellent example of the first of these forms.

In the Trobriand Islands, which lie directly north of the eastern tip of New Guinea, we find a number of Melanesian communities, most of which are separated by sea from each other. Technologically, these communities are well advanced, for though their cutting tools are made of stone and shell, the people are expert horticulturists and fishermen, as well as boatbuilders and navigators. The area in which they live is so well suited to gardening and fishing that food production is large; Trobriand communities customarily produce far more food than can be consumed, even though portions of the available labor force are employed in specialties, like

---

[1] Patrick Putnam, "The Pygmies of the Ituri Forest," *A Reader in General Anthropology* by Carleton S. Coon (New York: Henry Holt and Co., 1948, pp. 322–342), p. 324.
[2] *Ibid.*

boat-building, which are not directly productive of food. Accordingly, all Trobriand communities possess a true division of labor and considerable exchangeable surpluses. Moreover, many of the specialized occupations pursued, whether they relate to food production or to manufacturing, are localized on particular islands. Therefore, though the foods and artifacts used are much the same in all Trobriand communities, no one of these has both the raw materials and the skills to produce all the commodities consumed. It follows, then, that each community depends on trade to supply some portion of its wants.

The *kula* rings of this area appear at first sight to be elaborate systems of rites and ceremonies involving the exchange of certain highly valued ritual objects. Members of communities belonging to a given ring are united by *kula* partnerships, linking some of the members of a given community to individuals dwelling on two islands in opposite directions from their own. Figure 12:1 represents a schematic map of such a ring, highly

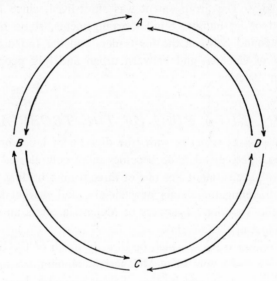

Fig. 12:1. Scheme of the *kula* ring.

simplified and containing only four interlinked communities, designated by the letters A, B, C, and D. The curved arrows represent lines of contact between *kula* partners; thus, members of A will have *kula* partners in B and D, B has *kula* relations with A and C, and so on round the ring. Note, however, that no lines connect A with C, or B with D. *Kula* contacts between such communities are always through one or more intervening communities and are never direct.

Two types of ritual objects move incessantly from one community to another within the closed circuit of the ring. Long necklaces made of red shell move in a clockwise direction along the arrows connecting A, D, C, and B, while bracelets of white shell move counterclockwise from A to B, C, and D. Thus, when a man of community A receives a necklace from his *kula* partner on B, he must within a reasonable time present this to one of his partners in community D. In return, the partner in D must, either when he receives the necklace or as soon as possible later, give a bracelet of equal value to his *kula* partner in A. The values of these ceremonial gifts, calculated in terms of the length of time they have been circulating in the ring, must be carefully matched in every exchange if the *kula* relationship is to endure. Bound up with these exchanges is an endless series of rites, ceremonies, and formalities, all of which are regarded as necessary to the maintenance of the *kula* relationship.

Despite this enormously complex ritual detail, it is amply clear that the *kula* ring functions mainly as a vehicle for trade. As a member of the ring sets off to visit his partners in either direction, he loads his watercraft with as much of the locally produced foods and artifacts as he believes he can dispose of. After the formalities incident to the exchanges of *kula* gifts are completed, these commodities are traded for others, the special products of the island being visited. As in the case of the gift exchanges, close attention is paid to exchange values, and though no standardized media of exchange are employed, it is always desirable that both traders be satisfied with their bargain. An individual who engages in sharp practice, attempting to gain more than he gives, is very likely to find himself excluded from further *kula* trading.

By this elaborate and somewhat cumbersome procedure, the Trobrianders eventually succeed in distributing goods locally produced throughout the islands belonging to the ring. Since rings often interlock by the fact that a single island community may participate in more than one, goods may be distributed over considerable areas. Though trading partnerships are rarely so complicated and burdened by rite and ceremony as that of the Trobrianders, it is well to note that few trading procedures are entirely free from ways of behaving only indirectly related to commercial functions. Even in our own society, the important buyer may be subjected to elaborate entertainment by those who desire his custom, and even the casual customer may find himself receiving more deference and attention than his simple purchases may seem to warrant.

10. AZTEC MARKETS AND TRAVELING MERCHANTS

Though the *kula* ring is an extraordinarily complex trading device, it is basically a system of barter whereby communities specializing in certain foods and artifacts are enabled to exchange their products. It involves, as we have noted, no media of exchange nor any commercial procedures much more complex than may be observed in the simpler societies previously discussed.

Among the Aztecs of the Valley of Mexico, however, we encounter a system of distributing goods and services which is far more sophisticated economically. The Aztecs, though they had only stone tools and no beasts of burden or machines, managed, as horticulturists in an extremely favorable environment, to support a large population while using only a portion of the working force directly in food production. The rest engaged in a large number of specialized crafts and professions, as priests, merchants, government and court officials, carpenters, fishermen, wood-carvers, masons, stone-cutters, goldsmiths, silversmiths, jewelers, weavers, tanners, and many others. In brief, the machinery of production was complex rather than simple, characterized by a high degree of specialization of labor and large exchangeable surpluses. Further stimulus to trade was provided by marked differences in natural resources through the close proximity of environments ranging from the tropical lowland to the temperate and even arctic highland.

The Aztec Empire was a loose organization of city-states held in subjection by force of arms to the great capital, Tenochtitlan, situated where Mexico City stands today. Each subject city and locality—and these extended at the time of the Conquest in 1521 through most of central Mexico —paid tribute to Tenochtitlan and acknowledged its sovereignty. Throughout the empire there existed, in each city, large markets for the local distribution of goods. These were connected to each other and Tenochtitlan by a system of traveling merchants who had their headquarters in the capital.

At Tenochtitlan local markets were held daily in various portions of the city for the sale of provisions. In addition a great market, located in an outlying suburb, took place every fifth day. To this came artisans, producers, and purchasers for miles around. Each kind of merchandise had its special place in the great market square, an arrangement very similar to that which exists in many Mexican markets of today. Great varieties of goods were offered. Bernal Diaz, the historian of the Cortes expedition in the 1520's, notes, among many other things: gold, silver, jewels, feathers, clothing, chocolate, tobacco, tanned and raw hides, footwear, slaves, meats of many varieties, vegetables and fruits, salt, bread, honey, tools, pottery, and household furnishings. The market was under the direction of special officers who maintained order, supervised weights and measures, and adjudicated disputes.

Though many of the market transactions were simple exchanges of one kind of goods for another, certain articles, such as cacao beans, squares of cotton cloth, copper ax blades, and quills of gold dust, served as media of exchange. Details are lacking as to the standards of exchange values, but there is no doubt that such standards existed, at least in rudimentary form. There was also a system of credit whereby loans were made on good security but without interest. The penalty for failure to pay a debt was extremely severe—the debtor was enslaved until his obligation was discharged.

Linking the market of Tenochtitlan with others within and outside the empire was the function of the traveling merchants. These formed a special, closed guild centered in the capital, with hereditary membership and its own insignia, officials, gods, ceremonies, and system of justice. Merchants traveled together in strongly armed bands, their goods carried by retinues of porters. They moved from one market area to another, distributing local specialties throughout the empire and beyond, and bringing back to the capital goods from outlying regions. It is also of interest to note that the merchant bands functioned as spies, informing the home government of important military and political matters. They were protected by the Aztec government, for any injury to a merchant was in itself a cause for war.

In Aztec society, then, we find a developed system of commerce and trade, based on a complex specialization of labor and an efficient system of production. Each Aztec community depended in part upon trade for the fulfillment of its wants; unlike the societies with subsistence economies, local production was not organized to meet all these needs. In short, as increased production made possible the development of specialization, and as specialization provided surpluses for exchange, there arose a system of distributing goods and services through trade to a widely spread group of interlinked communities.

11. PROPERTY AND WEALTH
IN SUBSISTENCE SOCIETIES

It follows from what we have said of production and distribution in subsistence societies that in such societies the goods produced are consumed very largely by their own members. A subsistence society normally produces only enough to supply its members with a bare living; no individual or group within the society can accumulate any considerable surplus or gain exclusive control over the means of production. Accordingly, in such societies we do not find the same concepts of wealth and property we are accustomed to in our own.

Eskimo culture well illustrates this situation. The Eskimos live by hunting and fishing in a rigorous arctic climate. Since their tools and artifacts
are made of stone, bone, wood, and skins, and since neither fish nor game
are consistently plentiful, the Eskimo level of production is low and the
population thinly scattered. Each primary family must be economically
self-sufficient, for it often travels alone and lives only during the winter
in communities of more than eight or ten families. The man hunts and
fishes, and makes the tools and weapons used in these pursuits; the woman
cares for the house and children, makes and repairs clothing, and does
such gathering as is possible near the dwelling. Between them, and by continuous and arduous labor, a man and his wife can manage to support
themselves and their children. Beyond this they cannot go. If children come
too closely, one must be exposed to die for lack of means to feed it, and
if an adult, by reason of age or illness, cannot support himself, he must,
for the same reason, be abandoned to perish of cold and hunger.

In such a community there is obviously no wealth nor property as we
know it. Food is shared within the community in accordance with complicated rules which govern its distribution. Each adult, male or female,
makes his own tools and retains ownership as long as he uses them. Food
stored in caches may be used by anyone who needs it, and even a house
belongs to the family that built it only as long as they continue to live in
it. Since all an individual's time is required to support himself and his
family, he has no means of accumulating property nor the means to retain
exclusive control over a hunting or fishing area. In short, the means of
production are open to all who can make use of them, and no individual
or group is technically equipped to build up a surplus of privately controlled wealth.

Not all subsistence societies live so close to the edge of starvation as the
Eskimo. Among the Hopis, for example, the village usually produces
enough to support all of its members, including the aged, the sick, and
all the children born. In good years, as we have seen, it may even have
a small surplus for trade. Furthermore, though most Hopi adults are directly engaged in food production, there are always a few older men who
are in large measure exempt from these activities and who devote their
time to governing the village, settling disputes, and conducting the elaborate
ceremonies so necessary to the Hopi way of life.

But it should be emphasized that these men do not form a propertied
class living on the income from invested capital. They are rather salaried
officials, paid in maintenance for their valued services. Their status is high
because of age and specialized knowledge, not because of their wealth.

In Hopi society, land, the chief source of production, is owned by the clan, an enlarged family, and is distributed among clan members for their use. It cannot be sold nor can it go by inheritance to one outside the clan. Houses, tools, weapons, and other artifacts are owned by those who make and use them, as among the Eskimos, and since all who need such equipment can make it, there is no market for a surplus. Here too, then, it is the right to use property that is possessed; there is no ownership unaccompanied by use and consequently no wealth which enables an individual to live from the labor of others.

12. WEALTH AND STATUS AMONG THE HAIDAS

Though the patterns of production, distribution, and consumption illustrated by the Hopis are in general common to societies of this technological level, there are a number of interesting divergences. One of these, that found among the Haida Indians of the Queen Charlotte Islands off the coast of British Columbia, may be summarized here for the light it throws on the development of economic systems.

The region in which the Haidas live is mild and equable in climate throughout the year. Rainfall is very heavy, averaging some sixty inches a year, and the area is accordingly well forested. Both land and marine fauna are exceptionally rich, including land- and sea-fowl, bear, deer, shellfish, whales, seals, sea lions, and many other food and fur-bearing animals. Coastal waters and rivers teem with fish: halibut, cod, herring, and salmon, among others. The potential food supply is consistent and dependable, for though it is less in winter than in summer, there is no season when food is really difficult to obtain.

Haida technology is based exclusively on hunting, fishing, and gathering; the Haidas have no domestic animal but the dog and grow no crop except a little tobacco. Tools and weapons are all of shell, stone, bone, and wood; containers of wood and basketry. Despite their crude tools, however, the Haidas are exceptionally able woodworkers. They build elaborate houses, large, sea-going boats, and many kinds of wooden artifacts, including dishes, bowls, elaborately carved paddles, watertight boxes, tall and intricately carved totem poles, and ceremonial masks. Clothing is made of furs, skins, and vegetable fibers, and blankets are woven on a false loom from the wool of mountain sheep.

The Haidas, though geographically distributed in a number of villages, are as a whole divided into halves or moieties. An individual belongs to the moiety of his mother, but must take his spouse from the opposite moiety. Each moiety includes about twenty clans, and these are further subdivided into a varying number of households, each of which may have as many as thirty members living in one large dwelling. The clan controls the major sources of production, since each clan has recognized and exclusive rights to hunting grounds, salmon streams, village and house sites, berry patches, and strips of beach from which sea-hunting and fishing may be done. None of these rights can ordinarily be alienated from the clan. The clan also owns important intangible property, such as personal names, ceremonial titles to houses and boats, rights to perform songs, dances, and ceremonies, and rights to carve and display a number of crests, symbolic of both the clan and the moiety to which it belongs.

The household is the producing unit and usually can find among its members all or most of the skills and labor it requires. Property is accumulated, not only by hunting, fishing, collecting, and manufacturing, but also by an elaborate technique of lending at 100 per cent interest and by trade and warfare with neighboring tribes on the mainland. Each household, despite the ease of making a living in this rich environment, works very hard to accumulate as large a surplus as possible, especially in storable foods, oils, furs, blankets, slaves, and shields made of native copper. The accumulations so made are not for trade, however. Indeed, since there is little true division of labor as between Haida households, such internal trade is not required; each household can amply supply its own wants.

Instead the surplus accumulated by a household is consumed in lavish feasts and elaborate entertainments called potlatches. Feasts involve only the consumption of food. A household, after working hard to accumulate great stores of food, invites guests, always from the opposite moiety, and not only feeds them well but also sends them away with all that remains after the feast is done. Potlatches are far more elaborate and function in several ways: to celebrate the accession of an heir to the position of his deceased predecessor (the funeral potlatch), to initiate the building of a new house, to restore dignity after public humiliation (the face-saving potlatch), and to remove the stigma of insult or other infringement of honor (the vengeance potlatch).

On occasions of funeral and house-building potlatches, guests are fed and given enormous quantities of furs, copper shields, blankets, carved dishes, and other property, until the host household is completely destitute. The amount of goods so distributed may be gauged from the fact that a house-building potlatch may require many years of labor to accumulate the gifts. Face-saving and vengeance potlatches involve, not the giving, but the destruction of property. Thus, a man publicly insulted will hold a potlatch to destroy as much of durable goods as may be accumulated, so disgracing his opponent for life unless the latter immediately destroys an equal amount.

To understand the functioning of this system of consumption, we must know something of Haida conceptions of social status. Members of Haida society differ in status, ranging from the highest "nobles" or individuals of top status to the lowest "commoners" or those of little status, with many gradations in between. Status cannot be inherited or gained for oneself; only those individuals whose parents have potlatched rise in status. As a result, potlatching is necessary to all households according to their economic ability; those of high status to retain it for their children and those of low status to improve the social standing of their offspring. Potlatching of the face-saving and vengeance kinds is also related to status, in that it protects the individual and household from loss. Finally, accession to political position requires potlatching; no one may inherit rank, found a household, or otherwise acquire rank without giving an elaborate potlatch.

It is clear, then, that the potlatch provides an enormous incentive to hard work and the accumulation of property among the Haidas, even though such accumulations are not really necessary to survival and have no outlet in trade. The patterns of the potlatch and its associated economic activities find their own logic in the total framework of Haida culture.

13. CONSUMPTION OF WEALTH AMONG THE AZTECS OF MEXICO

In § 10 of this chapter we outlined the system of trade and markets which prevailed among the Aztecs of Mexico in pre-Conquest times. As a result of this system, the Aztecs of Tenochtitlan, the dominant city-state, became enormously wealthy, for it was the concentration point of most of the surplus production garnered throughout the empire by the far-flung Aztec network of trade and conquest. We may now complete the picture and learn how the wealth was consumed by the population at Tenochtitlan.

At the time of the Conquest (1521), Aztec society was divided into three major classes: a large middle class composed of members of the *calpulli* (land-owning units which may have been clans), a smaller but increasingly important upper class (*tecutin* or honorary lords), and a small but growing lower class composed of those who had lost *calpulli* membership for various reasons. There was as well a class of slaves who, except for the fact that they had no choice of employers, may for our purposes be included in the lower class.

The *calpulli* were twenty in number. Each owned large tracts of land, which were distributed among its members for as long as they or their descendants put the land to use. *Calpulli* lands could not be alienated and, if abandoned by the grantees, reverted to the *calpulli*. One member of each *calpulli* represented the group in the minor council, a governing unit which declared war, made peace, decided disputes between *calpulli,* and carried on ordinary administrative duties. The *calpulli* were also represented in the great council, which met every eighty days to decide matters of larger importance to the empire and which also elected a new emperor at the death of the incumbent.

It is evident, then, that *calpulli* members were on the whole well off. They had direct access to land, the major source of wealth, which could not be taken from them. They also had a part in government, and some of them at least had opportunity to gain fame and fortune as war leaders, merchants, minor political figures, and craftsmen.

Calpulli members whose services to the state in trade, warfare, politics, or religion were exceptionally meritorious were elevated by the emperor to the status of *tecutin* or honorary lords. By such elevation they not only retained their rights in the *calpulli* but they received in addition freedom from all but nominal taxes, a share as individuals in the rich tribute that flowed into Tenochtitlan from conquered city-states, and individual grants of land made from conquered territories at the disposal of the emperor. They were also members of the great council along with *calpulli* representatives and other officials, and so had a share, as appointees of the emperor, in the government of the nation. Though *tecutin* were in theory appointed only for life and so could not pass either their titles or their privately owned lands to their sons, it had become increasingly common, at the time of the Conquest, to appoint sons of *tecutin* to the offices and statuses of their fathers. Thus in actual fact, if not in legal theory, the *tecutin* were on the way to becoming hereditary lords and a small but powerful class of wealthy land-owners.

Members of the lower class included, as we have noted, individuals expelled from the *calpulli,* aliens who had never had *calpulli* membership, serfs attached to the lands of the *tecutin,* and slaves—war captives, debtors who failed to meet their obligations, and those who sold themselves into slavery and/or were so sold by their parents by reason of poverty. These underprivileged folk had of course no access to land, tribute, or public office; they made their living as farm laborers for wealthy *calpulli* members and *tecutin,* or as porters for merchants. There was little hope for them to rise in status, for *calpulli* expulsion was seldom if ever reversed and there was usually no way in which they could acquire land nor the free time to learn and practice a craft or profession.

Among the Aztecs, then, the consumption of goods and services was not uniform throughout the society. The *tecutin* class, together with the emperor and his family, wealthy merchants, and *calpulli* members who held high governmental positions, were marked by conspicuous consumption; they lived in large houses, wore fine clothing, ate the best foods, and provided the best in education and training for their children. Members of the middle class, though secure in economic position by virtue of *calpulli* membership, had less to do with than the upper class. Most numerous, they formed the solid backbone of the empire, furnishing its farmers, craftsmen, merchants, soldiers, minor military leaders, and the bulk of its political officers. Finally, the lower class, lacking property and direct access to the land, consumed least. For their services as unskilled laborers, the freemen among them earned only a bare living and, when this was lost through disability or misfortune, had only themselves or their children to sell in return for subsistence.

14. SUMMARY

While the examples given in the preceding sections by no means exhaust observed variations in the production, distribution, and consumption of goods and services, they are perhaps sufficient to illustrate the more important characteristics of economic systems. To summarize this chapter, it may be useful to review these briefly.

(1) No society exists which lacks division of labor, but it is important to distinguish so-called natural division of labor, based on age and sex, from true division of labor. Natural division of labor is universal, but true division of labor is dependent upon a technology advanced enough and an environment suited to the production of an exchangeable surplus.

(2) Where no true division of labor is found, internal and external trade is ordinarily only feebly developed, usually as one or other form of gift exchange. However, societies living in environments favorable to food production may engage in extensive external trade even without true division of labor. Such trade occurs under two sets of circumstances: (a) where a subsistence economy has established, by reason of certain special skills in hunting or gathering, a symbiotic trade relationship with a more advanced and politically dominant society, and (b) where a number of societies, each producing surpluses in food and artifacts more or less exclusive to itself, establish a system of external trade for the purpose of exchanging these surpluses.

Extensive internal trade is clearly linked with true division of labor; the two increase in complexity together. Among some societies with complex internal trade but isolated from others of equally high economic development, there is little external trading merely for lack of opportunity.

When external trade can develop, it apparently leads, by reason of improved technology, to an intensification of internal trade and an increased division and specialization of labor.

(3) In societies lacking true division of labor and any considerable internal or external trade, patterns of consumption are ordinarily uniform throughout the society. Each unit of the society has about as much as its neighbors and no group achieves either material wealth or any patterns of conspicuous consumption. Note, however, that some societies, favored by environments rich in resources, may be able to produce large surpluses, even with a simple technology and no important true division of labor. This may lead to external trade, as we have noted, but it may also lead to exceptional patterns of conspicuous consumption, marked by lavish hospitality and even the wanton waste or destruction of goods.

Where we find an efficient technology, a complex true division of labor, and both internal and external trade, the society, perhaps inevitably, reveals class divisions marked, among other things, by differential patterns of consumption. The Aztec and our own society furnish examples. But class division and differential patterns of consumption may also be found in societies lacking both internal and external trade. An outstanding example is found among the Quechuas of Peru, an Indian empire ruled by an aristocracy of nobles called the Incas. The Incas held all the surplus wealth provided by the empire, consumed much of it lavishly and conspicuously, and distributed the rest, by a rigid system of governmental controls, to the great mass of the population, who were only allowed enough to give them an adequate living. Here a political system controlled all distribution of goods, both internal and external, for the Incas did not trade with their neighbors but conquered and absorbed them.

COLLATERAL READING

Childe, V. Gordon. *Man Makes Himself.* New York: Oxford University Press, 1939.

Firth, Raymond. *Primitive Polynesian Economy.* London: Routledge, 1939.

Forde, C. Daryll. *Habitat, Society and Economy.* New York: E. P. Dutton, 1950. Part IV.

Herskovits, Melville J. *Economic Anthropology.* New York: Alfred A. Knopf, 1952.

Lowie, Robert H. *Social Organization.* New York: Rinehart and Co., 1948. Chapters 6, 12.

Thurnwald, Richard. *Economics in Primitive Communities.* Oxford: Oxford University Press, 1932.

ETHNOGRAPHIC REFERENCES

Aztecs: Coon, 1948, Chap. 15; Murdock, 1935, Chap. XIII; Thompson, 1933; Vaillant, 1941.

Baganda: Murdock, 1935, Chap. XVII; Roscoe, 1911.

Chukchee: Bogoras, 1904–09.

Eskimos: Birket-Smith, 1936; Coon, 1948, Chap. 4; Murdock, 1935, Chap. XIII; Rasmussen, 1908, 1931.

Haidas: Murdock, 1935, Chap. IX; Swanton, 1909.

Hopis: Eggan, 1950, Chaps. II, III; Murdock, 1935, Chap. XII; Titiev, 1944.

Nisenans: Beals, 1933.

Plains Indians (Crows): Lowie, 1935.

Pygmies: Coon, 1948, Chap. 11; Schebesta, 1933.

Quechuas (Incas): Means, 1931; Murdock, 1935, Chap. XIV.

Trobrianders: Coon, 1948, Chap. 10; Malinowski, 1932.

Chapter 13

THE FAMILY

1. THE NATURE AND VARIETY
OF FAMILY GROUPINGS

The family may briefly be defined as a social grouping the members of which are united by bonds of kinship. In its simplest form, the primary or elementary family, it consists of two mature adults of opposite sex, who live together in a union (marriage) recognized by other members of their society, and their children. The kinship ties which unite these individuals are three: that which exists between the married pair (the husband-wife relationship), that which exists between the married pair and their children (the parent-child relationship), and that which exists between the children of the married pair (the sibling relationship).

It should be emphasized, however, that these ties, though they often involve certain physiological interactions between the individuals concerned, are in large part culturally determined. As Lowie has pointed out:

Kinship is differently conceived by different societies, . . . biological relationships merely serve as a starting point for the development of sociological conceptions of kinship. Society may ignore or restrict the natural blood tie, it may artificially create a bond of kinship, and again it may expand a natural bond to an indefinite extent.[1]

[1] Robert H. Lowie, *Social Organization* (New York: copyright 1948 by Rinehart & Co., Inc.), p. 57.

To illustrate this point, it is only necessary to remember that the children of a primary family need not include only those born to the parents; some of them may be adopted. Similarly, in many societies, bonds of kinship are frequently extended to individuals with whom no genealogical relationship exists nor is even claimed. Thus, in our society, we frequently use the terms "uncle" or "aunt" to old family friends or to the spouses of actual uncles or aunts not in the least related to us genealogically. Among the Baganda of East Africa, genealogically unrelated males of the same generation may undergo a ceremony before witnesses which makes them brothers, a kinship tie which thereafter governs their interactions just as if they had been born members of the same family.

Even within the primary family, then, we often find individuals not related genealogically. Nevertheless, a tie of kinship exists between them, for kinship is a set of culturally determined relationships contingent upon membership in the same family, however this may be attained. It is this factor that distinguishes the family among human beings from the superficially similar breeding groups of the animals.

In many societies the family itself is extended to include kin we do not ordinarily regard as family members. Such extension gives rise to quite different family structures, the more important of which may be outlined here for later discussion. Roughly, extended families belong to three major categories, as follows:

(1) Extensions of the primary family. Primary families are found in two principal extended forms: the polygynous primary family consisting of an adult male, his two or more wives, and their children, and the polyandrous primary family, composed of an adult female, her two or more husbands, and their children. Another much rarer form is illustrated by the Marquesans of Polynesia. Here a man of means, the head of a household, will seek to marry a woman who has many lovers, trusting that some or all of these will join his household as secondary husbands, so forming a polyandrous primary family. Later, however, he may marry other women and even bring their admirers, if he can, into the household. The result is a combined polygynous-polyandrous primary family, headed by the household chief and his principal wife, but including as well a number of secondary wives and husbands. All of these, in theory at least, enjoy equal conjugal rights with each other.

(2) Joint families. These are built up as a result of common residence as between primary families linked either through the paternal or maternal lines. In the patrilocal joint family, the male offspring at marriage continue to reside in the family dwelling (or else in a new dwelling close to that of their fathers) and add their wives and children to the group. Female offspring, correspondingly, leave the paternal residence at marriage and go to live with their husbands' joint family, though in some cases, at least, they do not entirely lose touch with the father's family but are regarded as possessing dual family membership. The matrilocal joint family reverses this procedure: female offspring remain in the family of the mother after marriage and male offspring leave to join the joint family of the wife. Here, too, we may find dual family membership, for the males do not always sever ties completely with the family of their birth.

(3) **Clans.** The clan still further extends family membership, though here, unlike the joint family, kinship alone, rather than kinship plus residence, is the determining factor of family affiliation. Clans are of two sorts: patrilineal, where the individual belongs to the clan of his father, and matrilineal, where an individual's clan affiliation is the same as that of his mother. Clan ties are not affected by either marriage or residence, nor is there any instance of dual clan membership; an individual obtains his clan affiliation by birth or adoption and retains this unchanged throughout his life. Clans differ most markedly from primary and joint families in that their members need not live together in the same residential unit nor even in neighboring residential units. Because the clan is exogamous (that is, its members must marry someone not of their own clan), both the primary and the joint family, in a society having clans, necessarily include individuals belonging to different clans.

Clans are often very large groupings, as contrasted to primary and joint families, and often include individuals who rarely if ever come into actual contact with each other. Their genealogical relationships, then, are not a matter of record; it is merely assumed, usually, that all the members of a given clan are descended from a common ancestor, who is often symbolized by a mythical figure of one kind or another.

Clans are frequently both subdivided and included in still larger kinship groupings. Clan subdivisions are called lineages (paternal or maternal, for patrilineal and matrilineal clans, respectively), by which we mean the members of a clan who live in the same locality and who are recognized, by one means or another, as a formal grouping. Larger groupings including clans are called phratries; these are recognized social groupings built up on the supposition that certain clans are, in origin, descended from a common mythological ancestor. The term "moiety," where it refers to a kinship grouping, may apply to a society which has but two clans or to one in which a number of clans are classed in only two phratries.

It must not be assumed that primary and extended families are necessarily mutually exclusive; more often than not, we shall find a given society with family groupings of several different sorts. Our purpose in this chap-

would be disastrous, for under the severe conditions of Eskimo life, neither a man nor a woman can successfully live alone; the skills and labor of both are necessary. A man or woman without a spouse is quite literally under sentence of death.

It is equally clear that the family must be limited in size to a group that can be supported by the labors of its adult members. Accordingly, if babies come too quickly, some must be exposed to die in order to allow the others to live. And though occasionally an unattached adult may be taken into a primary family, sometimes as a second wife or husband, this too can only be successful if the added member is fully capable. The old and the sick among the Eskimos cannot long be supported by their children and relatives, and must ultimately go off to die alone of cold and exposure.

Note, finally, that relationships between primary families take place along kinship lines. Villages and hunting groups are often made up of families whose adult members are siblings to each other, or if no genealogical ties are found between them, who are linked by ties of comradeship quite as strong. According to Rasmussen, one of our foremost authorities on the Eskimos, the people who hunt together feel strongly attached. Alone there is insecurity and fear; together they gain confidence and strength and provide a refuge for each other.

In summary, Eskimo social organization, based on the primary family and patterns of kinship and comradeship, is a result of simple and direct personal contacts between individuals who, in small face-to-face groups, must work together in a difficult environment to secure a bare living. These contacts are both limited and reinforced by economic necessity; the rigors of the arctic environment do not permit larger groupings and the development of impersonal relationships while, at the same time, the need to survive imposes on the Eskimos a social organization based on mutual congeniality and cooperation.

3. THE CHIRICAHUA APACHE FAMILY

Relatively few societies provide so narrow a scope for kinship and so simple a family organization as is found among the Eskimos. On the contrary, in most societies outside the influence of western European culture, the family tends to be far larger and more complexly structured, and the scope of kinship in the patterning of social interactions much wider. This is achieved, not by replacing the primary family by another form, but by including it in some fashion in a larger kinship grouping. In this section we shall examine one such extended family, that found among the Chiricahua Apaches of southwestern United States.

The Chiricahuas, like the Eskimos, are a nomadic people who make their living by hunting and gathering. But the region in which they live, though a semiarid territory not overly stocked with resources, supports larger concentrations of population than the Arctic. Accordingly, the Chiricahuas are found in three bands, each composed of a number of local groups or communities. Each band has a defined territory over which its constituent local groups range in the course of their search for food. But the band is an amorphous social unit held together only by reason of common culture and language; it is in no sense politically organized and exerts no authority over its members. The local group, though it has a leader (usually the most respected family head within it), is also weak, and the separate families which compose it are free to leave at any time. The leader has no authority save that which results from his status as an older, abler, and more experienced man. Accordingly, local group membership is constantly in flux; a given family, in the course of a lifetime, may be affiliated, at different times, with as many as three or four local groups.

This leaves the family as the

social unit to which a Chiricahua's attachments are anything but casual. To each of its members he stands in a definite relationship—a relationship which defines his obligations to them and his requirements of them. This group is immediately and intensely interested in him. It supervises his early training. It tests his manhood. It governs whom he may or may not marry. It passes on his marriage choice, if it does not, indeed, choose for him in respect to a mate. If he falls into disgrace, he disgraces this unit. If he is killed, this unit is bound to avenge his death. When he dies, members of this unit . . . accompany his body to a suitable cave or rocky crevice for disposal.[2]

This unit is a matrilocal joint family (see Figure 13:1), for it is made up of several primary families united by kinship and common residence. When a new primary family is founded by marriage, it belongs to and resides with the joint family of the wife.

As we have noted, the Apache joint family looms large in the life of the individual; it is no exaggeration to say that an Apache spends most of his life in the company of relatives. But the joint family is also very significant in the economic life of the Apache. It produces all its members' wants in food, clothing, shelters, and other necessities. The labor and skills necessary to this production are found within the joint family, divided by age and sex, and the goods produced are distributed and consumed within the

[2] Morris E. Opler, "An Outline of Chiricahua Apache Social Organization," *Social Anthropology of North American Tribes,* ed. Fred Eggan (Chicago: copyright 1937 by University of Chicago Press), p. 183.

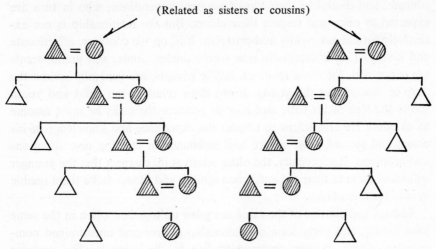

Fig. 13:1. The Chiricahua joint family.

KEY

An equals sign (=) indicates marriage, a vertical line the parent-child relationship, and a horizontal line the sibling relationship. ▨ indicates males who have become members of the joint family by marriage, ◉ females born or adopted and reared in the joint family, and △ males born and reared in the joint family but who leave it at marriage. Each symbol ▨ , △ , and ◉ stands for all possible individuals in the given relationship.

same group. Though the joint family always lives in a local group in more or less close association with other joint families, it is subject to no authority but its own, adminstered by its older and more experienced members. In short, social control within the joint family as well as the orderly conduct of relations between different joint families is achieved very largely through kinship, the customs by which the behavior of relatives is regulated in their social interactions. It is, therefore, very important to understand these customs and to see how they function in Apache life.

Apache kinship usages fall roughly into four major groups: (1) those which prevail between consanguine kin of different generations (that is, parents and children, uncles or aunts and nephews or nieces, grandparents and grandchildren), (2) those between siblings and cousins of the same sex, (3) those between siblings and cousins of opposite sex, and (4) those between a man and his affinal kin (that is, his relatives by marriage).

It is the duty of parents, uncles, aunts, and grandparents to care for, educate, and discipline their kin of younger generations, who in turn are expected to obey and respect their elders. But the relationship is not excessively formal nor rigidly authoritarian; it is, on the contrary, affectionate and kindly. This is especially true where uncles, aunts, and grandparents are concerned, for these relatives, unlike parents, are generally spared the duty of disciplining the young. From these relatives the child and youth learns the lore of his tribe and how to perform the tasks he must assume as an adult. He also learns to respect the experience and knowledge of his elders and to seek their advice and assistance in meeting new situations and problems. Reciprocally, the older relatives may expect that the younger will assist them in their old age, when senility and illness make them unable to care for themselves.

Siblings and cousins of the same sex grow up together, often in the same joint family, and early form a relationship of free and unrestrained comradeship which, if they continue to live in the same locality, endures throughout life. Brothers and male cousins are boon companions, always ready to help each other and free to call for such help when it is needed, even though, after marriage, they may live in separate communities. Sisters and female cousins usually live in the same joint family and characteristically work together as adults in the endless routine of household tasks. There is no relationship in all of Apache culture so sincerely cordial as this one; the Apache finds in his siblings and cousins of the same sex all his best friends and most trusted companions.

In contrast to the closeness and warmth between siblings and cousins of the same sex, that between those of the opposite sex is rigidly formal and restrained. Early in the life of the child, as soon as he begins to learn the tasks appropriate to his sex, he learns as well to avoid siblings and cousins of the opposite sex and, where such contacts are necessary, as within the primary and joint family, to handle these with gravity and reserve. For these relatives must never be alone together and, even when others are present, must not speak together unless this is necessary. It goes without saying that sexual relations between such relatives, however remotely they are akin, are absolutely forbidden; indeed, should even a mild allusion to sex be made in their presence, both are expected to leave immediately.

Between a man and his affinal relatives, who live in the same joint family with him, there exists an even more formal relationship. This is expressed in two ways: by the so-called polite form and by total avoidance. The polite form requires that affinal kin be reserved and grave in each other's presence and indulge in no profanity, coarseness, or joking. Any reference to sex, even by a third person, is forbidden in their presence. Both must avoid being put in an awkward or embarrassing position when together, and neither should, under any circumstances, do anything to humiliate the other. Total avoidance has all the implications of the polite form plus the obligation never to have face-to-face contact with the avoided relative; all necessary intercourse between kin who avoid each other must be conducted through a third person. Total avoidance is required between a man and his wife's immediate relatives, principally her parents, while either total avoidance or the polite form is necessary with all or most of the others.

The function of these techniques of social control is clearly to affirm the solidarity of the joint family and to regulate the social interactions of kin so as to provide for cooperation and harmony both within and between joint families. This function is attested by the following facts:

(1) An effort is made to care for and instruct the young to assume the adult roles in the joint family. Children are economic assets to the joint family, for female children will not only remain within it but will also replace, with their husbands, the loss of the males who marry and leave the joint family.

(2) Cooperation and a sense of comradeship are encouraged between siblings and cousins of the same sex. This is particularly important for female siblings and cousins, who live in the joint family all their lives in close association with each other. Should they be divided by competition and ill feeling, the whole family suffers disharmony. Male siblings and cousins, though they live as married adults in different joint families, are nevertheless often within the same local group and always in the same band. The ties of comradeship and mutual affection established between them in their formative years go far to make for harmonious relations between separate joint families.

(3) Sexual relations between siblings and cousins of the opposite sex are prohibited. The formality and restraint of this relationship require the youth of the joint family to seek their spouses among nonrelatives and so unite unrelated joint families by ties of kinship. Such ties are essential to harmony within the local group, the group which wages warfare, a significant economic activity, and organizes its constituent families for defense against alien raiders.

(4) Males entering the joint family as husbands are required to avoid or maintain only the most formal relations with their wives' consanguine kin. The reason for this is evident: a woman, when married, leaves her parents' wickiup and goes to live in another with her husband, but remains within the encampment of the joint family. Preoccupation with her husband and later with her children considerably alters her formerly in-

timate association with her parents and other consanguine kin within the joint family. This disruption, if unprovided for, may lead to trouble and a consequent loss of the husband, an economic asset to the joint family. To prevent potentially disruptive relations between a married man and the affinal kin he is expected to live with and serve, Chiricahua culture strictly limits their social interactions and so helps to insure the harmony of the joint family.

4. THE TANALA JOINT FAMILY

Joint families are rather frequent among nonliterate peoples, and especially so in societies small enough to be adequately governed by kinship ties alone. Another example, the patrilocal joint family among the Tanala of Madagascar, is worth examining briefly, since it provides a contrast, both in structure and functioning, to the joint family of the Chiricahua Apaches.

The Tanala live in a mountainous region which is covered by a dense jungle or rain forest. Wild food is scarce and difficult to secure, horticulture (the principal economic resource of the Tanala) involves much heavy labor in cutting and burning the forest cover, and, though the Tanala keep cattle, the grazing is poor and the animals do not thrive. The farming techniques of the Tanala (rice is their staple crop) require that the land lie fallow five to ten years between plantings; as a result, new lands must be cleared each year. Thus, because of this combination of environmental and technological factors, Tanala villages tend to be isolated from each other and more or less independent politically.

Villages, because of the need for defense, are located in easily protected areas and are usually fortified. A village includes some fifty to eighty primary families, divided among two to ten or more joint families, each of which occupies a section or ward within the village. The village is governed by an informal council composed of family heads, one of whom assumes the position of chief or headman. But he exercises no authority other than that derived from status and prestige; his functions are to advise and lead, to arbitrate intravillage disputes brought to his attention, to coordinate communal activities, and to represent the village in dealings with other villages. Together with the informal council, the headman assigns land under the control of the village to its constituent joint families.

A joint family can be founded by any man who has enough male descendants to form its working force and who has accumulated enough wealth in cattle to acquire or build a house in the village. Such a family may consist, in addition to the founder and his wife, of his sons and their wives, and his grandchildren. Daughters and granddaughters, at marriage, go to their husbands' joint families and, though these women still owe obedience to the founder of the joint family in which they were born and may be called upon for various services, their children are completely under the control of the founder and head of the husbands' joint families (see Figure 13:2).

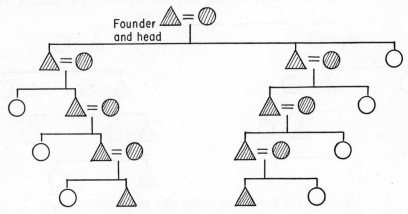

Fig. 13:2. The Tanala joint family.

KEY

: males born in the joint family.

: females married into the joint family.

: females born in joint family but leaving it at marriage.

(Compare Fig. 13:1)

As long as the founder and head is alive, he remains (with rare exceptions) in supreme control of the joint family. He organizes and directs its activities (principally in respect to farming), settles disputes between its members, and receives the obedience and respect of all its members. Most important, he retains all the profits derived from the family's farming, though he is obligated to support the family and pay the bride-price for his sons' wives, and he occasionally presents gifts to various of his descendants. But as long as the founder is in control, none of his sons can accumulate enough wealth to found their own families; they are obliged, for the lack of the necessary wealth, to remain with the father and work for him.

When the founder dies, his position and the bulk of his property go to his eldest son. But now control over the family's profits is no longer exclusive to the family head; he is obliged to share these with his brothers. Since it is usually economically more rewarding to keep the joint family together, and since the brothers are used to working together, the death of the founder does not usually break up the joint family. It continues as before, but with the eldest son as head, and with the prospect, depending on circumstances, of each of the brothers accumulating wealth (see Figure 13:3). But when the eldest brother dies and his eldest son inherits the

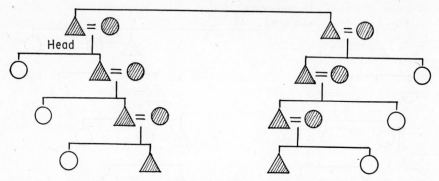

Fig. 13:3.   The Tanala joint family after the founder's death.

KEY: See Fig. 13:2.

position of head, the joint family is very likely to break up, for by this time the remaining brothers will in all likelihood have enough property and descendants to establish their own independent households. There is, more-over, a strong noneconomic incentive to do so, in that the founder of a joint family not only has prestige during his lifetime but is also honored after death (the Tanala practice a form of ancestor worship) by all his de-scendants in the male line; while a man who does not found a joint family is honored only by his sons and grandsons.

Though our data are not so detailed for the Tanala as for the Chiri-cahuas, it may be noted that the Tanala joint family is also governed wholly in terms of kinship relations. The founder or head, as father or grand-father, receives the utmost in respect and obedience from his sons, daugh-ters (even though these live elsewhere), grandsons, and the women who marry into the group. Relations between brothers appear to be friendly and cooperative, though the eldest brother, especially if he becomes head, shares in the respect accorded the father. In short, the patterns of behavior regulating the social interactions of kin are designed, as among the Chiri-cahuas, to bolster the solidarity of the joint family and make it an efficient working unit.

5. ECONOMIC FACTORS AND THE JOINT FAMILY

We have noted, in discussing the Polar Eskimos, that their simple type of family organization is in large part a result of the environment in which they live and the ways in which they exploit this environment for food and other necessities. Among the Chiricahuas and the Tanala, as we have seen, larger concentrations of population are possible, with a consequent increase in both the size and the complexity of their family structures, here as among the Eskimos responsible for the bulk of economic activities. The next question that emerges from our study as it has so far progressed concerns the difference between patrilocal and matrilocal joint families. Is this difference to be correlated with economic differences between societies? Let us review the Chiricahua and Tanala data with this question in mind.

First, it is clear that both the Chiricahua and the Tanala joint families are economically self-sufficient in large part; both produce nearly all the goods their members require. The labor of production is in both cases divided within the family by age and sex, and kinship so regulates the social interactions of members as to make the family a harmonious and efficient producing, distributing, and consuming unit.

In Chiricahua society, men engage primarily in hunting and warfare, two principal productive techniques, while women take over the equally important tasks of maintaining the household, building and repairing dwellings, caring for children, preparing food, making clothing, and gathering wild plants. Men's occupations take them away from the encampment at frequent intervals and, especially when on raids, for considerable periods of time. Women's tasks, on the other hand, are centered in and near the encampment, for even their foraging expeditions in search of wild foods, for reasons of safety, rarely take them very far or keep them away for more than a portion of a single day.

Chiricahua hunting does not involve coordinated group activity; the men of the joint family go out alone or in twos or threes to stalk and kill the game on which they depend. War and raiding parties are larger; they may include as many as ten men. But these are not men drawn from one joint family alone, but from the local group as a whole. Moreover, raiding parties are transitory units; their membership varies from one time to the next. In short, the economic activities of Chiricahua men do not result in permanent working groups composed of men from the same joint family, but rather in small and more or less transitory units made up of men from the local group generally.

Women, on the other hand, by the nature of their occupations both before and after marriage, work in more or less constant association with others within the joint family. Where the boy, from puberty on, has frequent occasion to leave the family encampment, the girl stays home, constantly under the supervision of and working with her female relatives. Her identification with the joint family of her birth and orientation is strengthened as she grows up, while that of the boy is gradually weakened by his increasing preoccupations outside the encampment. Where she is drawn more and more into a complex of activities centering in and about the family encampment, her brothers find themselves drawn out of the family into the local group. Chiricahua economy, dependent for its functioning on the unity of the joint family, requires in it a nucleus of women who are accustomed to living together, while, since the men of the joint family need not cooperate closely in economic activities, harmonious adjustment between them, though important, is not so necessary. It is this factor, in all probability, that tips the scales in favor of matrilocal residence.

The Tanala, on the other hand, are horticulturists who grow rice on small farms laboriously cleared each year from the jungle. This work is done by men and is far more efficient and profitable if it is done by gangs of fifteen to twenty men working under the direction of an experienced leader. Indeed, it is doubtful if one man, or even a group of three or four, could clear enough land to produce a crop. Moreover, since Tanala farms are often at some distance from a village and hence exposed to enemy raids, a larger force is necessary for purposes of defense.

Accordingly, among the Tanala, the men of the joint family customarily work together, year after year, under the direction of the founder or head. In a society governed by kinship usages, this is the only practicable plan, for who, except an older and respected relative, can exercise the necessary authority to weld these men into an efficient working force? A family that lacks an adequate number of men, or whose men are torn by dissensions and bickering, will soon disintegrate, its constituent primary families aligning themselves with other, more successful, joint families. Success, wealth, and prestige come only to those families who are able to hold together and so produce, not only their own subsistence, but also the surplus necessary to achieve these ends.

It follows that a Tanala male, as soon as he learns anything, learns to work with his brothers and male cousins under the direction of the family head. In contrast to the Chiricahua male, he is drawn into the life of the family and encouraged to strengthen his identification with it. Patrilocal residence merely operates to reinforce this association and so maintain, within the joint family, the integrated working force it so urgently requires, a force which could obviously not be built of men drawn, as adults, from numerous outside families. The loss of women born and reared in the joint family is, in comparison, less important.

6. THE CLAN AMONG THE CROW INDIANS

The Crow Indians live on the Great Plains of the United States, in northern Wyoming and in Montana, south and east of the Missouri River. Not an agricultural people and possessing no domesticated animal but the dog, the Crows live mainly by hunting and collecting. The large buffalo herds that roam the Plains supply their principal food resource, and supply as well the dried dung used as fuel, skins for clothing and shelters, horn for various household utensils, and material for bags and water vessels. Though buffalo and other game animals are often hunted individually, the more common method, and the most productive, is the communal drive, which involves the cooperative and coordinated effort of a large number of men and women.

The term "Crow" applies equally to three large bands, similar in language and culture, and recognizing each other as comrades and kin. But each band is politically independent of the others, for there is no governmental apparatus that links them into a single tribal unit. Band government is informal: the group, consisting of a thousand individuals or more, is ruled by a council made up of most of the adult men. But the important men in this council are those honored for their deeds of valor in warfare, one of whom is chosen as headman. Except during the annual buffalo hunt and other occasions requiring group action, the headman has no way of enforcing his authority, which rests rather on his status as an experienced military leader and his age and wisdom.

Cross-cutting the bands is an organization into thirteen exogamous, matrilineal clans. Members of these clans regard each other as kin and interact accordingly. Note, therefore, that a Crow has kin in all three bands, despite the fact that these are politically independent. This means that a Crow can visit a neighboring band and, by reason of his clan affiliation, be treated as a relative, even by people he has never met before. Clan membership, then, functions here as a means of identification, as between individuals who, living in different local groups, have ordinarily little or no contact with each other.

Clan members, especially those living in the same band, constitute a truly unified body of kindred. As such, they frequently camp and feast together and exchange gifts. They are always expected to help each other in case of need, and especially to avenge the death of one of their members. This duty holds even within the band, for clan loyalty, as Lowie puts

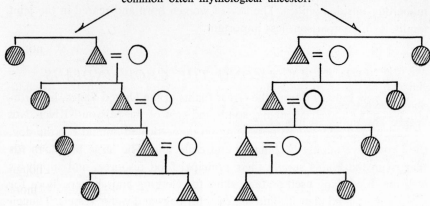

Sets of siblings related or said to be related through a common often mythological ancestor.

Fig. 13:4. Scheme of a patrilineal clan.

KEY

△ ⊘ : male and female clan members.

○ : females not clan members.

Compare Figs. 13:1, 13:2, and 13:3. Note that where the joint family includes sets of spouses related by common residence and excludes either married male siblings or married female siblings, the clan includes sets of siblings related in the paternal or maternal lines and does not require residence as a condition of membership.

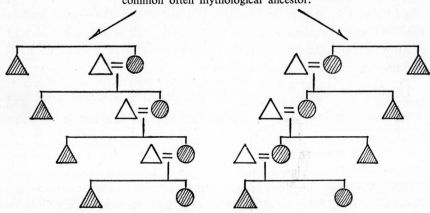

Sets of siblings related or said to be related through a common often mythological ancestor.

Fig. 13:5. Scheme of a matrilineal clan.

KEY

△ ⊘ : male and female clan members.

△ : males not clan members.

Compare Fig. 13:4.

it "characteristically overrode their sense of duty to any larger group." [3] Thus, should a man be murdered by someone not of his clan, the clansmen of the victim take immediate steps to avenge his death. It is interesting to note that such revenge need not be visited upon the actual murderer, but can be achieved by killing any adult male of the murderer's clan. In short, each member of a clan may expect, not only that his clansmen will regard any injury to him as an injury to the clan, but also that they will take responsibility, as a group, for his actions in respect to persons outside the clan.

The clan, like the band, is governed by its older and more experienced men, one of whom is regarded as chief or headman. Any disputes between members of the same clan are settled in terms of this machinery; the band leader has no authority to interfere in a clan's internal affairs. But disputes between clans must be settled by the band council and headman, if continued blood feuds are not to result. According to Lowie:

Under normal circumstances the clans were *not* warring against each other, but expected to form a united front against hostile aliens. It is on behalf of such union that the police society [an association of men chosen to assist the headman of the band] pacified aggrieved tribesmen and that neutral clans [in a particular dispute] repeatedly strove for reconciliation.[4]

The thirteen Crow clans are grouped into six nameless and somewhat amorphous phratries. These apparently have little function other than to recognize a remote kinship tie between groups of clans. In some cases, the clans included in a single phratry are forbidden to intermarry, but this is not true of all.

To summarize: Crow clans represent named matrilineal kinship groupings which function (1) to extend kinship ties and usages through all three bands and so provide a means of interband contact, (2) to prohibit marriage within the clan and occasionally within the phratry, and (3) to provide assistance and protection to its members and represent them before the band council. Note especially that the clan, among the Crows as elsewhere, is considerably larger than either the primary family or the joint family and that, since it is not a local or residential unit, it includes many members whose knowledge of each other is derived, not from frequent interpersonal contacts, but only from their common membership in a large and scattered body of kindred. But clans have other functions than those illustrated by the Crows, and we shall examine the more important of these in the sections that follow.

[3] Robert H. Lowie, *The Crow Indians* (New York: copyright 1935 by Rinehart & Co., Inc.), p. 9.
[4] *Ibid.*, pp. 10–11.

7. TOTEMISM AND THE CLAN

Among a number of nonliterate peoples, we find a phenomenon of culture called totemism, best defined perhaps in Radcliffe-Brown's words as a set of "customs and beliefs by which there is set up a special system of relations between the society and the animals and plants and other natural objects that are important in the social life." [5] Such relations, where they exist, are usually divided between various social groupings of the society in such a way that each grouping maintains a systematic relationship with a particular species of animal or plant or with a given class of natural object. These animals, plants, or natural objects are then designated the totems of the social grouping.

It is important to note, first, that totems are not universally associated with clans; there are many instances of clan division which have no totemic implications whatsoever. Second, it must be added that totemism is used to refer to a wide variety of special relationships between a society or its segments and the so-called totems. In many instances, as among the Iroquois Indians of New York, clans are totemic only in the sense that they are named after animals, such as the bear, snipe, turtle, and eel. No other relationship between the animal species and the clan is implied by these names.

Among the Haidas of the northwest coast of America, clans have also been described as totemic, and much has been made of the fact that so-called totemic crests, highly conventionalized representations of animals, are tattooed on the bodies of clan members, displayed on their clothing, and carved, painted, or otherwise marked on all of their belongings. Careful investigation discloses, however, that these crests—and a given clan may lay claim to several, some of which may also be shared by other clans —do not even represent the name of the clan. Actually, according to Professor Murdock, totemic crests function only as symbols of the clan; they indicate the clan of the individual who displays them and nothing more.

Among the Hopi Indians is found still another variant of totemism. Here, as with the Iroquois, clans have animal or plant names (Bear, Snake, Reed, and Mustard are examples) or may even be named after a class of artifacts, as is true of the Carrying Strap clan. In most cases these names have no further implications, though it has been observed that members of the Butterfly and Coyote clans do not kill these animals. Significantly, however, this prohibition does not apply to the Rabbit clan, where the animal concerned is an important source of food. In any case, Hopi totem-

[5] A. R. Radcliffe-Brown, *Social Organization of Australian Tribes,* the "Oceania" Monographs, No. 1 (Melbourne: Macmillan and Co., 1931), p. 29.

ism is best understood in the light of the fact that the Hopis divide every-thing in their universe—men, animals, plants, natural objects, and artifacts—into certain classes. The relation of a clan to animals, plants, or other natural or manufactured objects is, then, merely a result of the fact that they are classed together, and has, apparently, no further significance.

A somewhat more complex totemic relation may be observed among the Baganda of East Africa. Here we find thirty-six exogamic patrilineal clans, each of which traces its descent from a common ancestor, whose name must be borne by the clan chief. Each clan also has a stock of names, re-served for its own members, a distinctive drum beat, and two totems. The name of the clan (examples are the Lion, Leopard, Monkey, Otter, Rat, and Mushroom clans) is taken from the more important of these totems, most of which are mammals. In addition, clan members are strictly for-bidden to eat the animals or plants after which they are named, though others in the society are not similarly bound. Note, however, that the clan ancestor is not identified (any more than are his modern descendants) with the totem, and that clan ceremonies are directed, not to the worship of the totem, but rather to the honoring of the clan's dead and various non-totemic supernatural beings associated with the clan.

It is in Australia, apparently, that we find the most complex development of totemism, though even here it is not consistently associated with clans as such. Our best data on Australian totemism comes from the Aruntas, a desert people of north central Australia. Arunta local groups, essentially patrilocal joint families, each occupy a given territory over which they ex-ercise complete control and from which they hunt the wild animals and collect the plants on which they live. Included in each territory is a number of sacred places or totem centers, where the mythological ancestors and creators of the present inhabitants are believed to have died, their bodies descending into the ground and leaving behind certain *churinga* or sacred objects. Totem centers are marked by special trees or rocks and the pres-ence of the *churinga* of the ancestors. The twin souls of the ancestors also reside in the totem centers, one remaining always with the *churinga* and the other awaiting its opportunity to enter the body of a passing married woman to be reborn into modern Arunta society. Thus it is that a totem group or cult is made up of those within the local group who were con-ceived from a given totem center. Each member born in the local group belongs to such a cult but, since the territory of a local group includes a number of totem centers, there are an equal number of totem cults.

Totem centers are also centers for various animals or plants important in Arunta culture, for it is believed that the ancestors who died at the totem center were associated with a particular animal or plant. It is clear, then, that these are totems by reason of their association with human beings born of the center, the members of the totem cult.

Each cult has a chief, who presides over its rites. Totem cult members may eat only sparingly of their totem animal or plant, and must leave the choice bits to others. Rites are held at the totem center from time to time for the purpose of increasing the number of the animal or plant species with which the cult is totemically associated. The totem cult is thus believed to be responsible for the maintenance of the food supply, or that portion of it represented by their totem species. Accordingly, they exercise certain controls over the killing and eating of their totem animals; thus, though non-cult members may eat as much as they like of a cult's totem animal, they must not do so outside the camp, but must bring it in. Failure to observe this and other like regulations will anger the cult members and so result in a failure of that portion of the food supply.

This rather complicated set of totemic observances is a far cry from the simple Iroquois custom of naming clans after certain animals, also referred to as totemism. It is evident, then, that simply to call clans—or other social segments—totemic does not mean much; we must, in each case, specify the particular observances denoted by the term.

Totemism, where it involves, as among the Aruntas, a more or less complex body of myth and ritual, obviously functions both to enhance the solidarity of the social segment through its members' common participation in certain beliefs and ceremonies, and to link the social segment with that portion of the universe which has significance to the society as a whole, and so to relate it as well to other social segments in the same society. But where so-called totemic clans are merely clans designated by names of various animals and plants, it is doubtful that we have anything more than a means of identifying the clan. Linton has observed this variety of "totemism" among ourselves, where members of football and baseball teams refer to themselves as Bears, Tigers, Wildcats, and other more or less ferocious animals. Since names like Dogs, Horses, Cows, and Chickens are not similarly used, there may be, in addition to the function of identification, some belief that naming a team appropriately may improve its athletic ability.

8. RELIGIOUS FUNCTIONS OF THE CLAN: THE HOPI INDIANS

Clan function in religion and ritual is by no means confined to the relatively rare instances where the clan may be identified with a totemic cult. In some societies, of which the Hopis are an outstanding example, the clan may play a principal role in the religious life of the people.

We have discussed the Hopis earlier (Chapter 12, §§ 4, 6) in respect to their location and economic life. The tribe, made up of six politically autonomous villages, is divided into a large number of matrilineal, exogamous clans, loosely grouped into twelve exogamous phratries. Clans are named for the most part after plants or animals, but phratries have no special names. Essentially the same clans are found in all six villages, thus providing here, as among the Crows, a means of social interaction governed by kinship usages between politically independent groupings. Apart from real property, each clan possesses certain rights in shrines, ceremonial objects, and kivas or ceremonial chambers, and, most important of all, owns one or more ceremonies, in the sense that it has the exclusive right to present these ceremonies. It is by virtue of this ceremonial property that the clan holds title to its lands, for, according to Hopi mythology, each clan agreed, when it joined the village, to have its ceremony performed at appropriate intervals in return for rights of cultivation on lands surrounding the village.

Paralleling the clans are a large number of religious fraternities or cults, which ordinarily bear the same names as clans, though they are not identical in membership. But, since each religious fraternity has as its principal function the performance of a given ceremony owned by a clan of the same name, the clan head is always the chief priest of the corresponding fraternity and his clan members make up a large proportion of the membership of the fraternity. Thus, the Snake clan owns the Snake Dance (an important summer ceremony designed to bring rain to the growing crops) and the Snake Fraternity, including as its chief priest the head of the Snake clan as well as, among others, a large proportion of the Snake clan's membership, performs this ceremony.

Hopi religion and ceremonial practice center about the need for rain, vital among a horticultural people living in a semiarid region and associated in Hopi thought with the well-being, physical and spiritual, of all the people. The winter ceremonies, a continuous round spread through nearly every month of this season, represent in effect a ritual growing of crops in the kivas, a necessary preparation, to the Hopis, for the summer's work in the fields. Summer ceremonies, less elaborate and frequent because of the accompanying hard labor on the farms, are chiefly a series of elaborate prayers for rain needed for the growing crops. Every ceremony, then, is conceived in essence as a more or less direct aid to the primary economic activities of the Hopis, and as a means of maintaining a good and fruitful life in the community as a whole.

The role of the clan in this economic and ceremonial round is very important. Each clan includes, not only its living kin, but also a large number of *kachinas,* metamorphosed spirits of the clan's deceased members.

These do not represent specific individuals but rather a generalized class of clan ancestors. Included also in the clan is a species of animal or plant after which it is named, akin to both living clansmen and *kachinas,* and certain supernaturals and anthropomorphized natural phenomena linked to this species and worshiped alike by the clan and its *kachinas. Kachinas* reside in an underworld, living much as human beings do, except that their seasons are reversed: summers among the Hopis are winters to the *kachinas* and the *kachina* summers, winters to the Hopis. Once a year, during the Hopi winter, the *kachinas* return to the villages and participate, through personification by masked dancers, in elaborate rites, in which the Hopis plead with them to use their supernatural powers and their influence with the gods to bring rain and other benefits to the living. In this manner, then, the clans, by reason of their kinship with the dead, provide a bridge to the world of the supernaturals, both to establish and maintain the harmony with the universe and all it contains that is so necessary, in Hopi belief, to successful living.

We should not conclude from this single example, of course, that rite and ceremony are necessary functions of the clan; there are many instances, as among the Crows, where the clan plays little or no role in religious life. The Hopis supply only an additional example of the way in which patterns of kinship as formalized in the clan may be integrated into the total culture of a people, especially in those societies in which the clan is a dominant factor in the maintenance of social control.

9. CLAN IN GOVERNMENT:
THE LEAGUE OF THE IROQUOIS

Though clans are frequently found in societies like the Crow and Hopi, where political organization is at best only feebly developed, this does not mean that the clan is necessarily absent from social organizations marked by a more complex political development. Quite the contrary may be true; just as organizations based on kinship may have significant ceremonial functions in societies like the Hopi, where religion plays a dominant role in everyday affairs, so may the clan and other kinship groupings take on governmental functions in societies distinguished by more or less complex political development.

We have already noted that clans characteristically play a large role in social control and even function as subdivisions within simple political units such as the band and the village. Among the Crows, it will be remembered, the band, a political unit, is in essence a confederation of clans, held together only by the need for maintaining a "united front against hostile aliens"—a need which is often strong enough to override clan loyalties and force the clans to remain at peace with each other. Similarly, the Hopi village is made up of clans that have yielded control over some of their affairs, when these concern the village as a whole, to the council of clan chiefs which constitutes the ruling body of the village. The Iroquois, whose clan system will concern us in this section, only exemplify a more elaborate development of the same kind of interclan relation.

The Iroquois live in the well-watered woodlands of northern New York, and gain their living from horticulture, hunting, fishing, and collecting. The region is well stocked in game, fish, and edible wild plants, besides being easily cultivated even with relatively crude stone, bone, and wood implements. As a result, it supports a fairly high density of population, and the six Iroquois tribes live, not too far from each other, in a number of relatively large stockaded villages. Each tribe has its own well-defined territory, within which its villages are distributed and its members hunt, fish, and raise their crops. Hunting and fishing grounds are open to all, but farms are owned by those who work them, the separate lineages of the clans included within the tribe. Certain fields are excepted; these are owned by the village as a whole and used to provide food for the community festivals and other affairs involving the entire village.

Division of labor is strictly along sexual lines. Men go to war and do all the hunting, fishing, house-building, the manufacturing of canoes, paddles, and other artifacts, and assist the women in the heavier horticultural activities, such as clearing the land and harvesting. But the main bulk of the farming activities, caring for the children, maintaining the household, weaving and basketry, collecting wild vegetable foods, and cultivation and care of the crops is done by the women of the maternal lineage working together in gangs under the direction of the head woman on the lands owned by the lineage.

The residential family unit among the Iroquois is made up of women belonging to a single maternal lineage, their husbands (who, since the lineage and clan are exogamous, come from other lineages), and their unmarried sons. This group usually occupies one great house (the long house), with each primary family within the group having a room to itself. The men who have married into the long house, though they work for it and spend much of their time there, have all their political and religious rights in the houses of their mothers and maintain considerable interaction with members of their maternal households.

Lineages related in the maternal line make up a clan. Though the number of clans varies from tribe to tribe, there are usually eight, divided into two exogamous phratries. Marriage, then, must in all cases be outside lineage, clan, and phratry. It should also be noted that here, as among the Crows and Hopis, members of the same clan and phratry, even though they belong to different tribes, interact as kin, and so the clan provides a means of peaceful contact between separate political entities.

The Iroquois tribes, however, are not united alone by kinship ties and a similar cultural tradition, but are organized into a strong confederacy or league. This organization (initially including five, but later six, tribes) is ruled by a council of fifty sachems, unevenly divided among the constituent tribes. The sachems, who meet annually, but who can also be called into special session in emergencies, are charged with the duty of maintaining peace between the tribes, of representing the tribes as a whole to outsiders, and of coordinating tribal activities in a common warfare against non-Iroquois. No one tribe dominates the league, despite the unequal distribution of sachems, for all league decisions must be unanimous. Note, also, that the council of sachems conducts all its meetings publicly and even permits all to speak who wish to do so, though voting is confined to council members. Sachems who consistently misrepresent their tribe, or who fail to support the best interests of the league, can be deposed.

To illustrate the functioning of kinship groupings in the Iroquois governmental system, it will be sufficient perhaps to describe how sachems are selected and how, if they prove unworthy, a tribe may recall its sachems.

First, then, it should be made clear that only certain lineages have the right to provide candidates for the office of sachem, though these are usually so distributed that each clan contains at least one lineage which has this right. When a sachem dies, the head woman of his lineage, in consultation with the older women of the same lineage, selects a candidate to replace him. A man belonging to the lineage is always chosen and, if possible, a younger brother or sister's son of the previous sachem. A meeting of the lineage is then called, which may be attended by other members of the clan, to have the lineage council (the child-bearing women of the lineage) ratify this choice. If this is done, the head woman then notifies the chiefs of all the clans in her phratry and the one opposite. On confirmation of the candidate by both moiety councils, a meeting of the league is called. The sachems after approving the candidate and holding a ceremony of mourning for his predecessor, install the new sachem who, dropping his own name, assumes that appropriate to the office he now occupies.

Lineage, clan, and tribe observe their incumbent sachems very closely to see that they represent them properly in the council of the league. Should a sachem compromise his constituents in any way, the head woman of his lineage warns him publicly of his errors. If, after two such warnings, the sachem persists in his misdeeds, impeachment proceedings are initiated by the head woman, first in the lineage, then to the clan council, the two phratry councils, and eventually to the league. The league council can also dismiss an unworthy sachem, or refuse confirmation to one they do not believe fit to hold office.

Though the election and impeachment of sachems is one of the more important political duties of the lineage, clan and phratry councils, it is not the only one. They are, in a very real sense, the guardians of law and order within their respective jurisdictions, even to the extent of trying and punishing criminals among their members. These family units, then, by reason of the particular political structure of the Iroquois tribes, formally implement, by means not dissimilar to, though far less elaborate than, those employed by our cities, states, and nations, rules for peaceful and orderly relations between their members.

10. PATRILINEAL VS. MATRILINEAL CLANS

Though our examples have all been drawn from societies divided into matrilineal clans, it must not be assumed that patrilineal clans are rare or that they do not share in functions very similar to those described for the others. The two forms of the clan are, indeed, very similar in both structure and functioning; they differ only in the line of kinship that serves as the criterion for membership. (See Figures 13:4, 13:5, p. 398.)

The reason for this difference has been much discussed, without, however, yielding much in the nature of a really convincing conclusion. Much of the discussion has, indeed, confused rather than clarified the issue, which deals, not with whether men or women dominate in a given society, but solely with the relative emphasis of one line of descent over the other. Maternal clans do not necessarily imply that women rule a society, any more than the existence of paternal clans carries the implication that women are regarded as slaves or chattels. Matriarchy (absolute rule by women) and patriarchy (absolute rule by men) are exceedingly rare extremes; in most societies, nonliterate or otherwise, the differences in the status of men and women are relatively slight.

As we saw in discussing patrilocal and matrilocal joint families, these differences in residence are probably to be interpreted in the light of the degree to which men or women must learn to cooperate in performing the essential economic functions of a society. Where cooperation between men is customary in a society dominated by joint families, it is not surprising that the society makes use of the habitual association of males in the family to create a functioning work force and so, as among the Tanala, emphasizes patrilocal residence. But where, as among the Iroquois, the women ordinarily work together in cooperative enterprises (and the men do not), the matrilocal joint family (the Iroquois long house and its residents) probably fits in best with this custom.

But it is not necessary that the paternal clan be associated always with patrilocal families, nor the maternal clan with matrilocal families, even though this correlation may be frequent. The Trobriand Islanders of Melanesia are one illustration of an opposite association, for here, though residence is patrilocal, clans are matrilineal. Thus, children, though by birth members of their mother's clan, are born in the household and village of their father's clan and reared there until adolescence. To be sure, both support and education come, not from their father but from the mother's brother, who belongs of course to their clan, who lives in his own clan village, and only visits them at intervals to bring food and see to their education and discipline. At marriage, a woman goes to her husband's village, but a man goes to that of his mother's brother, there to assume his appropriate position in the clan of his ancestors. Clan membership, since it is never dependent on residence, cannot be determined alone by the same factors that apparently play so large a role in the difference between patrilocal and matrilocal joint families.

It seems probable, however, that the difference between patriliny and matriliny may be correlated with other cultural views as to the relative value of men and women to the society concerned. Among the Iroquois, the women of the maternal lineage form the core of the household and are alone responsible for the production of its principal foods—corn, beans, and squash. These foods, and consequently the activities involved in producing them, are held far higher than those derived from hunting and fishing, uncertainly rewarded activities, even in a richly stocked area, by virtue of the fact that continuous raiding, with its need for eternal vigilance and defense, makes it difficult for men to provide a dependable supply. The farm crops, in contrast, yield a much more regular supply of food, for the farms are both near at hand and more easily guarded. Women, then, possess an authority backed by their services to the community and attested in nearly every phase of Iroquois life, familial, economic, political, and religious.

In contrast, let us consider the Baganda of East Africa, where, despite the fact that women are, as among the Iroquois, mainly responsible for the principal food supply, the clans are patrilineal. Women among the Baganda do nearly all the farm work, excepting only the heavier tasks of clearing the land, which is done by men. Men, while they supply some food by hunting and fishing, on the whole provide only a much less important portion, for the ordinary Baganda household is very largely supported by its plantains; meat and fish, when available, are but added luxuries.

But there is one other activity, also economic, in which men make a better showing. The Baganda have a highly developed social and political organization, including about one million people organized into a monarchial state, governed by a hereditary king and a large number of court officials, chiefs, and subchiefs appointed by the king. Warfare is a most important activity and one which requires many men to carry it on successfully, for women never go on war expeditions except as menials. When the date of the annual war expedition against their hereditary foes is decided upon by the king and his counselors, great levies of men are raised and the army moves out beyond the borders to establish a base of operations. From here, smaller groups are sent forth to raid and pillage. But since the enemy is prepared for defense, pitched battles between large armies frequently ensue, with considerable loss of life. Warriors are pledged to act bravely and to die if necessary in fighting for their king—a pledge enforced by the fact that failure to meet it brings complete disgrace and confiscation of the culprit's property. Success in warfare, on the other hand, brings both honors and prestige, not to mention considerable rewards in property. Large numbers of women are frequently taken as spoils of war and distributed among successful warriors as a reward for their bravery. Half of the material rewards of a successful campaign goes to the king, for warfare is one of the chief sources of support for the royal family and their government.

Similarly, men are the artisans among the Baganda—the house-builders, iron-workers, carpenters, boat-builders, leather-workers, potters, and the like. All these goods, together with the crop surpluses, are periodically brought to great markets for trade. The markets are controlled by an official appointed by the king to keep order and to collect a 10 per cent tax on all transactions, another important source of funds for the royal treasury.

In view of this economy, it is not surprising that men are highly valued among the Baganda, and especially by the state, whereas women have a much lower status. But there is yet another factor to be considered. Though we know little of Baganda history, it does seem clear that the kingdom is relatively recent and that it was founded by a cattle-keeping people, who moved into this territory before the period of recorded history and imposed their rule on a less aggressive horticultural people who lived under a simpler political system in which matrilineal clans were dominant social groupings. The cattle people, in consonance with the fact that their cattle, their chief support, were exclusively tended by males, had, in all probability, a political system dominated by paternal clans. As a result of this conquest, the whole of the social organization of the conquered was made over to fit the patterns of organization held by the conquerors. Moreover, the ownership and care of cattle became a mark of prestige (as a symbol of the ruling group), while horticulture, the work of the dominated people, became degraded. Today among the Baganda, even though the main body of the people live almost wholly on farm products and the cattle are rarely used for food, it is only the possession of cattle that marks a wealthy and powerful family; ownership of land, however extensive, has little or no prestige value. It is this historical factor, with its reversal of the original values in a society, plus the increasing importance of men as warriors and defenders of the state, that probably accounts for this particular patrilineal clan organization.

It is evident from the preceding discussion that we cannot account for the emphasis on one line or another in clan organization wholly in terms of contemporaneous cultural factors. In every society, there may be peculiar historical factors which must also be taken into account to make the present culture wholly understandable. On the other hand, historical events, whatever their initial impact, do not alter the fact that the several elements of a culture have a significant and determining effect on each other. The change from maternal to paternal clans among the Baganda would not have been accomplished had not the new state of affairs created by the conquest also brought about important changes in the total economic patterns of the group.

11. SUMMARY

The data presented in this chapter may be summarized in the following statements:

(1) Groupings based upon kinship, though universal in human societies, assume widely variant forms because they are shaped, not by biological needs common to all men, but by the cultures of the societies in which they are found. A family, whatever its structure may be, is a body of kin who interact according to certain culturally defined patterns or kinship usages.

(2) The more important kinship groupings are the primary family and its several extended forms, the joint family (patrilocal or matrilocal), and the clan (patrilineal or matrilineal) plus lineages, subdivisions of clans, and phratries, larger groupings linking clans in a more remote kinship relationship.

(3) Kinship groupings assume many functions in addition to the nearly

universal function of providing for the care and rearing of children. These functions are determined in large part by the cultures of which the kinship grouping is a product and may be economic, political, or religious.

(4) Patrilocal or matrilocal residence tends to be linked in any society with the ways in which men or women customarily work as cooperating units in the performance of essential economic functions. Patrilocal residence, encouraging the habitual cooperation of male kin, is found in societies where men ordinarily work together in integrated labor forces, while matrilocal residence is found where women's work is similarly integrated. Where joint families exist in societies having no economic pursuits requiring the cooperative labor of either men or women, they tend to be matrilocal by virtue of the fact that women's activities tend, in all societies, to center about the household.

(5) Patriliny or matriliny, though also conditioned by historical factors, are in the large associated with other cultural patterns emphasizing the value of men's work over that of women or the reverse, respectively.

We have also noted that many nonliterate societies are organized wholly or in large part in terms of kinship usages and so are characterized by the fact that kinship groupings play a dominant role in their social organization. The size and inclusiveness of kinship groupings in such societies appear to be conditioned in large part by the following considerations.

Where, as among the Eskimos, a population must remain thinly scattered for most of the year in order to maintain itself, the primary family plus transitory communities made up of relatively few primary families are the dominant social units. Because Eskimo communities are both transitory and unstable, and because the contacts of a primary family with others are few and more or less evenly divided as between related and unrelated primary families, there is little opportunity for the development of larger kinship groups.

A next step is illustrated by the Chiricahuas where the transitory and unstable local group is, by virtue of an environment richer in resources, made up of joint rather than primary families. Here again, however, the contacts of a joint family are more or less evenly divided as between related and nonrelated joint families, so, together with the instability of the local group, inhibiting any larger kinship grouping.

Clans and phratries will develop, then, only when environmental circumstances and technology permit either (1) the more or less continuous living together of relatively large groups of people or (2) a high frequency of contact between the same nomadic joint families. The first of these conditions is illustrated by the Crows and Iroquois, where the band and tribe, respectively, are permanent local units with a high degree of stability. Note also that the three Crow bands and the six Iroquois tribes live sufficiently in touch with each other to permit the clan and phratry to cut across the boundaries of these autonomous political units. The second condition is illustrated in Australia, where, though environment and technology require a thinly spread population, the small nomadic bands (always equivalent to a joint family) move year after year through the same territory and frequently gather, during seasons of relative plenty, with similar bands on the borders of their territory. These repeated gatherings of the same bands lead, in some areas at least, to the formation of clans.

When we turn now to still larger societies, it soon becomes evident that kinship groupings break down, with their functions in the maintenance of social control increasingly taken over by social units whose members are bound together by factors other than kinship. The Baganda represent an approach to this situation, for though the clan still persists, much of social control rests, not with it, but with the state. Among the Incas of Peru, this development seems to have gone much farther. Here we find a powerful empire, ruled by an absolute monarch and divided politically into numerous subdivisions, among which we find the *ayllu,* possibly the remnant of an older clan. But whatever the basis of *ayllu* structure may have been in the past, it is now only a division of the empire, ruled by impersonal administrators whose authority derives not from their status as kin but from their status as nobles and their appointment to office by the monarch.

Similarly, in our society, family groupings play a conspicuously small role in the social life of the individual; at best, their only remaining function lies in the care of children during infancy and early childhood, and in the support of children until they are able to establish themselves. Parents are no longer exclusively responsible for the education of their children; this function must be shared with the state and parents may even be prosecuted for not sending their children to school. The family, with rare exceptions, no longer provides its children with a career in a family enterprise; the child must go outside to find his job and living. Religious exercises, except for rare family prayers at meals and other occasions, now belong to the church, which has, in large part, assumed control over religious education as well. And it is obvious that the family plays no role at all as a unit of government, nor is it exclusively responsible for the good behavior of its members, for even minors must be disciplined by the courts if they offend seriously against the laws of their community.

In brief, as societies, by virtue of increasingly improved technological development, become larger and more concentrated in population, the social organization changes from an earlier dependence on kinship usages for the maintenance of social control to a social order based on the rule of law and its enforcement by complex and impersonal political bodies. Kinship and the usages associated with it no longer retain the significance they previously held and still hold in nonliterate societies. Apart from immediate relatives within the primary family, individuals in our society react toward their relatives, not in terms of their kinship status, but in terms of their feelings for them as individuals. As Lowie puts it, "a congenial outsider may mean incomparably more to us and evoke acts of friendship denied to an unattractive kinsman." [6] The primary family in modern western European society is not, as among the Eskimos, the result of minimum population density, but represents a kinship grouping shorn of its former importance and numerous functions by the rise of other more inclusive social groupings.

COLLATERAL READING

Lowie, Robert H. *Social Organization*. New York: Rinehart and Co., 1948. Chapters 1, 4, 10, 11.

Murdock, George P. *Social Structure*. New York: The Macmillan Co., 1948. Chapters 1–5.

Stern, B. J., ed. *The Family, Past and Present*. New York: Harcourt, Brace and Co., 1938.

ETHNOGRAPHIC REFERENCES

Aruntas: Coon, 1948, Chap. 7; Murdock, 1935, Chap. II; Radcliffe-Brown, 1931, Part I; Spencer and Gillen, 1927.

Chiricahua Apaches: Opler, 1937, 1941.

Crows: Murdock, 1935, Chap. X; Lowie, 1935.

Eskimos: Birket-Smith, 1936; Murdock, 1935, Chap. VIII; Rasmussen, 1908, 1931.

Hopis: Eggan, 1950, Chaps. II, III; Murdock, 1935, Chap. XII; Titiev, 1944.

Iroquois: Morgan, 1901; Murdock, 1935, Chap. XI.

Tanala: Linton, 1933, 1939.

[6] Robert H. Lowie, *Social Organization* (New York: copyright 1948 by Rinehart & Co., Inc.), p. 60.

Chapter 14

MARRIAGE

1. MARRIAGE AND MATING

As a preliminary to the discussion of marriage, it is important to distinguish it from mating, by which we refer to unions of men and women, entered into primarily for purposes of sexual gratification. Such unions are nearly always transitory, or even casual, and they ordinarily impose no familial obligations or responsibilities upon the participants. Nearly all societies provide for matings in one fashion or another, and in some societies it is considered necessary that young adults engage in a number of casual and transitory matings before undertaking the serious business of marriage.

Marriage, while it is obviously, like mating, a means of sexual gratification, has other and more important social functions. Married couples, among all peoples, live together in a union recognized and publicly approved by other members of the society. Moreover, they are expected to cooperate with each other and sometimes with other relatives in the maintenance of a household. They are similarly expected to produce children —in some societies, a marriage is not valid until the first child is born. When children do come, the married couple must acknowledge them as their own and provide for their care and rearing. Though most cultures provide means for the dissolution of marriage, it is ordinarily expected that those who marry intend the union to be lifelong and not just a transitory affair to be broken off at the whim of one or the other partner.

In sum, marriage is everywhere a set of cultural patterns to sanction parenthood and to provide a stable background for the care and rearing of children. It is, in effect, the major cultural mechanism to insure the continuation of the family and other groupings based on kinship.

The distinction we have drawn between marriage and mating finds exemplification in our own society. To be sure, we do not, in terms of our ideal cultural patterns, explicitly approve of nonmarital matings, even though, in behavioral terms, there is no question but that they take place. In our society, individuals are expected to remain chaste until marriage, and after marriage to confine their sexual intimacies to their wives or husbands. But our culture provides, nevertheless, for nonmarital matings in a variety of ways, so condoning a set of behavioral patterns not explicitly sanctioned by the themes and ideal patterns of our culture.

Quite a different situation is found among the Samoans of Polynesia. In this society, young men and women are expected to engage in a number of matings before marriage, none of which need necessarily result in marriage. These affairs take place clandestinely; couples do not live together openly but meet at night on the beach or in the palm groves. If a girl is afraid to venture out at night, her sweetheart may even slip into her house. Both boys and girls ordinarily participate in many such affairs, and it is not unusual for an individual to carry on several at one time. The Samoans do not share our romantic ideal that love is lifelong or is necessarily centered upon one particular person.

Eventually, however, the Samoan youth must marry and settle down to the serious business of establishing a family. When a young man makes this decision, he must initiate formal and public courtship of the girl of his choice. With his *soa* or go-between, he calls upon her, bringing with him a ceremonial gift of food for her family. If they approve the affair, the gift is accepted and the young man and his *soa* invited to dine and spend the evening. While the young man sits watching, his *soa* pays elaborate court to the girl, urging her to accept the suitor as her husband. Several such calls may be necessary, for Samoan girls are understandably reluctant to give up the pleasant and easy life of an unmarried girl for the serious responsibilities and the hard work of marriage. Once the suitor is accepted, he goes to live with his bride-to-be, though the marriage ceremony may not take place until all the necessary arrangements have been made some months later.

An even more explicit approval of premarital mating occurs among the Masai, a people of Kenya in East Africa. Masai young men, after a series of ceremonies marking the end of boyhood, leave their native village and go to live in a near-by warriors' encampment or kraal. Here they learn the arts of war from older men and take part in occasional raids for cattle and other booty. Ordinarily a Masai male spends from ten to fifteen years as a warrior, during which he accumulates property in cattle, turned over to his father for safe-keeping.

Masai warriors are not permitted to marry, but this does not mean that they must remain celibate during their years in the warriors' kraal. Young unmarried girls also live in the kraal, to serve as the warriors' sweethearts and sexual partners, a relationship openly maintained and approved in Masai society. As with the Samoans, these matings are explicitly transitory and solely for purposes of sexual gratification; the men and girls involved are not considered married. Living with the warriors places no stigma on the girl, for every normal Masai girl has this experience in her youth. Should a girl become pregnant, she returns to the village to be married. Having a child out of wedlock stigmatizes neither the girl nor the child. Indeed, it aids a girl to secure a husband, for the Masai welcome children and regard barrenness as a principal cause for divorce.

When a man completes his service as a warrior, he returns to the village, takes charge of the property he has accumulated, and marries. He has now acquired the status of a household head and leaves the free life of a youth to assume the burdens and responsibilities of establishing a family.

It is evident from these examples, which may be multiplied endlessly, that the human need for sexual gratification, though served by marriage, is in no sense wholly responsible for it. Marriage in every human society that we know is a complex cultural phenomenon, in which the purely biological function of mating plays but a small role in comparison to such sociological functions as the care of children, the maintenance of the household, and other culturally imposed needs of the family.

2. MARRIAGE AND KINSHIP: INCEST REGULATIONS

Though marriage itself results in kinship ties, these differ from kinship relationships, usually described as consanguine, which link individuals to the families in which they are born and reared. Marriage relates individuals affinally, a term which describes not only the tie between husbands and wives but also the so-called in-law relationships between their respective sets of consanguine kin.

All societies provide, in their cultures, some means of regulating marriage in respect to consanguine relationships already in existence, presumably so that the marriages of members of family groupings will disturb intrafamilial harmony and cooperation as little as possible. Such devices are known as incest regulations, that is, the forbidding of marriage between designated categories of consanguine kin, or, less often, the requirement that marriages may be contracted only between members of certain kin groupings.

We cannot too strongly emphasize the fact that incest regulations are wholly cultural in nature, and have nothing to do with biological considerations. While it may be quite true that long-continued inbreeding often has deleterious biological effects, it is certain that this fact is not responsible for the prohibition of marriage between consanguine kin. For it can easily be shown that incest regulations frequently do not prohibit such marriages, but may even tend to promote them. Moreover, the same set of incest regulations may prohibit marriage between one group of kin while actually requiring others, biologically just as closely related, to marry.

This point is very nicely illustrated by the incest regulations of the Karieras, an aboriginal people of western Australia. In this society, an individual (hereafter called "ego") has four sets of kin in his own generation: (1) his brothers and the sons of his father's brothers and of his mother's sisters (technically called male parallel cousins), (2) his sisters and female parallel cousins, (3) the sons of his father's sisters and of his mother's brothers (technically called male cross-cousins), and (4) his female cross-cousins. We should keep in mind that, among the Kariera, kinship is indefinitely extended to include all the people with whom an individual has any social dealings whatsoever. This means that the term "cousin" (as used in the foregoing) includes individuals very remotely related to ego as well as those who are first cousins.

The rule of Kariera marriage is very simple: an individual can only marry someone classed as a cross-cousin; marriage, or indeed any interaction remotely suggestive of sex, is strictly prohibited with siblings, parallel cousins, or individuals in generations above or below that to which ego belongs. This means, of course, that a male Kariera may well marry the daughter of his father's sister or of his mother's brother, a first cousin as we reckon kin, but is forbidden to marry the daughter of his father's brother or of his mother's sister, also a first cousin. Biologically, these two relatives are related to ego in precisely the same degree; sociologically, in terms of Kariera culture, they are worlds apart, at least for purposes of marriage.

Though cross-cousin marriage, a form of what is often called preferential mating, is fairly widespread among nonliterate peoples, it is by no means universal. Among the Chiricahua Apaches, for example, marriage is forbidden, not only between cross-cousins, but between any man and woman genealogically related, no matter how remote the relationship may be. Opler illustrates this point by the following anecdote:

The . . . case involved two distant relatives, connected through their fathers, who . . . have the right to call each other cousin. The woman was legitimately married. While her husband was away on some work, she disobeyed the time-honored Chiricahua injunction and went to cook for her cousin. The incest relationship followed. The husband, disgusted and outraged, has remained away, which amounts to a divorce for the Chiricahua. The couple have put a bold face on things. The woman divorced her husband, and she and her cousin have become formally married with the agent's permission.

The old man who first told me of this case was unable to trace the exact genealogical relationship of the two, although he was unusually well versed in such matters. Despite the extreme remoteness of the connection, he was decidedly incensed at the parties to the incest. "He couldn't pull this off when I was young," he said grimly. "A man could be killed for such a thing then. But now we are under the white law." [1]

Chiricahua incest regulations, it is evident, are far more rigid than our own. Though we do not prefer cousin marriages, and though some communities may forbid first-cousin marriage, there is certainly no universal feeling that such marriages are incestuous. In our culture, incest refers primarily to marriages or matings between individuals of the same primary family.

The only truly general rule of incest is that which prohibits marriages of fathers and daughters, mothers and sons, and brothers and sisters. To be sure, there are societies in which certain individuals may be required to marry their siblings. This was true, for example, of highly placed nobles among the Incas of Peru, the ancient Egyptians, and in the old kingdom of Hawaii. But these exceptions—for even in these societies only a few were permitted to marry siblings—only serve to emphasize the rule. The individuals required to marry siblings were very special people, often divine personages, whose mating for purposes of obtaining an heir worthy to succeed them could take place only with one of equal rank or divinity, that is, a sibling.

It is clear, then, that while all human societies define incest and prohibit it, neither the definition nor the prohibitions are precisely alike in every culture. It is this fact which negates the hypothesis that the concept of incest has its basis in biological considerations. But it also suggests that incest regulations are, like other aspects of culture, definable patterns guiding human behavior which persist because they in some way serve the basic needs of human societies. The essential problem posed by the ex-

---

[1] Morris E. Opler, "An Outline of Chiricahua Apache Social Organization," *Social Anthropology of North American Tribes,* ed. Fred Eggan (Chicago: copyright 1937 by University of Chicago Press, pp. 173–242), p. 195.

istence of incest regulations lies, therefore, not in determining their origins, but in ascertaining their function.

3. THE FUNCTION OF INCEST REGULATIONS

Incest regulations, because they prohibit marriage or mating between designated categories of consanguine kin, often result in the formation of exogamous kinship groupings, that is, in primary families, joint families, or clans, whose members must find their spouses or sexual partners outside the group. Among ourselves, the primary family is exogamous, as it is, with few and unimportant exceptions, in all societies. With the Kariera, exogamy resides in the patrilocal joint family, for a Kariera's cross-cousins always belong to another such group. Among the Navahos, and many other people, the clan, which may include scores or even hundreds of individuals, is exogamous, for one is forbidden to marry within one's clan of birth.

One frequently advanced explanation of exogamy based on incest regulations emphasizes the psychological nature of kinship ties, especially those between individuals born and reared within the same family grouping. It is pointed out that when children are born or adopted into a family unit, two new kinship ties appear: that between parents (and others who care for the children) and the infants they care for, and that between siblings who are reared by the same parents. Both these relationships are ordinarily asexual, since they begin to form long before the children are sexually mature, and are therefore psychologically incompatible with affinal relationships, like those established by marriage or mating, which involve sexual intimacies. The so-called "dread of incest" is apparently a result of this incompatibility: a normal individual is said to be unable, psychologically, to engage in sexual intimacies either with a parent (or some other adult who has functioned in that capacity) or a sibling (or a person one has been taught to regard as a sibling).

The difficulty with this hypothesis lies in the fact that constant association within a family unit does not automatically produce an aversion to sexual intimacies between those so associated. If it did, no incest regulations would be necessary as between, for example, the members of the primary family. Yet it is a stubborn fact that such regulations are all but universal—nearly all societies strictly prohibit father-daughter, mother-son, and brother-sister marriage or mating. Furthermore, it is universal also that the severest punishments are meted out to those who break these rules.

Moreover, as Freud and others have pointed out, many psychological disturbances have their roots in unconscious but rigidly suppressed erotic desires formed by children for their parents or their siblings. The fact that members of family groups may live in close daily association has of itself no tendency to inhibit sexual attraction. Indeed it may increase it; White points out, for example:

> As a consequence of proximity and satisfaction [in persons close to him], the child fixates his sexual desires upon his immediate associates, his parents and his siblings, just as he fixates his food hungers upon familiar foods that have given satisfaction.[2]

Finally, it should not be overlooked that incest regulations are frequently enforced between relatives not living in close association, and even between relatives who are strangers to each other. As we have noted in § 2, the Chiricahua Apaches regard a marriage between remote cousins as incestuous as one between brother and sister. So also do the Navahos prohibit marriage and mating between all the members of a clan, regardless of whether or not they were born and reared in the same primary or joint family. Kluckhohn illustrates this point in an anecdote of a reservation teacher, annoyed by two young Navahos at a social gathering who flatly refused to dance together. The teacher failed to realize, in Kluckhohn's words, that the two were

> from the same clan, and the thought of having the type of physical contact involved in white dancing gives Navahos the same uncomfortableness the teacher would feel if the manager of a crowded hotel demanded that she and her adult brother share the same bed.[3]

Psychological factors obviously do not explain incest prohibitions of this nature.

Nearly all anthropologists agree, then, that neither biological factors nor psychological factors sufficiently account for incest regulations. Linton puts the matter succinctly in the following passage:

> The causes which underlie . . . incest regulations are very imperfectly understood. Since these regulations are of universal occurrence, it seems safe to assume that their causes are everywhere present, but biological factors can be ruled out at once. Close inbreeding is not necessarily injurious. Even where hereditary defects in the strain may make it so, its deleterious results require a long time to manifest themselves. . . . Neither are purely social explanations

[2] Leslie A. White, "The Definition and Prohibition of Incest," *American Anthropologist*, 50, 416–435 (1948), p. 424.

[3] Clyde Kluckhohn and Dorothea C. Leighton, *The Navaho* (Cambridge: Harvard University Press, 1946), p. 233.

of incest regulations altogether satisfactory, since the forms which these regulations assume are extremely varied. . . . It seems possible that there are certain psychological factors involved, but these can hardly be strong enough or constant enough to account for the institutionalization of incest regulations. . . . Incest regulations, once developed, are a valuable tool for preventing conflicts in the statuses held by individuals, but it is a little hard to imagine their invention for this purpose. They have probably originated from a combination of all these factors.[4]

4. CULTURAL FACTORS IN INCEST REGULATIONS

Earlier, in our chapter on the family, we repeatedly urged the fact that families, whatever their structure, are highly integrated groupings, whose members cooperate closely in the all-important tasks of rearing and educating children and making an adequate living. In so-called primitive societies we noted as well that the family and kinship served often as the most important means of social control, that is, as the most important means of maintaining orderly and cooperative relations between members of the society.

Now, as Malinowski has made clear:

The sexual impulse is in general a very upsetting and socially disruptive force, [it] cannot enter into a previously existing sentiment without producing a revolutionary change in it. Sexual interest is therefore incompatible with any family relationship, whether parental or between brothers and sisters . . . If erotic passions were allowed to invade the precincts of the home it would not merely establish jealousies and competitive elements and disorganize the family but it would also subvert the most fundamental bonds of kinship on which the further development of all social relations is based. . . . A society which allowed incest could not develop a stable family; it would therefore be deprived of the strongest foundations for kinship, and this in a primitive community would mean an absence of social order.[5]

Incest regulations apparently serve, then, as one means of maintaining the family grouping, and they differ in nature and extent depending on the structure of the family. But it is important to note that incest regulations have a further and even more important function, that of establishing ties between families and so uniting them into a larger cooperating whole.

[4] Ralph Linton, *The Study of Man* (New York: copyright 1936 by Appleton-Century-Crofts, Inc.), pp. 125–126.

[5] Bronislaw Malinowski, "Culture," *Encyclopaedia of the Social Sciences* (New York: copyright 1930 by The Macmillan Company), Vol. IV, p. 630. Used by permission.

Human beings, unlike most anthropoid species, do not live in isolated reproductive clusters. They live rather in communities, organized territorial assemblages including many reproductive units and often many families, primary and extended. The members of such communities, by means of culture, cooperate rather than compete in the struggle for existence. For man to become the master rather than the victim of his environment, cooperation between families is necessary, and incest regulations are one means to this end. To quote White on this point:

> If persons were forbidden to marry their parents or siblings they would be compelled to marry into some other family group—or remain celibate, which is contrary to the nature of primates. The leap was taken; a way was found to unite families with one another, and social evolution as a *human* affair was launched upon its career.[6]

We cannot of course verify this conclusion in historical terms; the origins of incest regulations lie far back in the unrecorded past. But we can illustrate the fact that incest regulations today provide for harmonious and cooperative relations between families. For this purpose, let us turn again to the Chiricahua Apaches where, as we have noted, the ban on marriage and mating extends to all known consanguine relatives, however remote the relationship may be.

In this society, the individual begins his life in the wickiup of a primary family, tended as an infant by his parents and older siblings, and sometimes as well by his maternal grandparents and mother's sisters. As soon as he is able to move about for himself, his social world enlarges to include other children in the encampment of the joint family (his cousins), their parents (his aunts and uncles), and older maternal relatives. Less often, he has contact with the joint family of his father where he learns to know his paternal cousins, aunts, uncles, and grandparents.

Boys and girls are early taught to separate for play and amusement, and this separation becomes more rigid as they grow older. Gradually they learn to behave with restraint and formality to siblings and cousins of the opposite sex, whether these live in their own encampment or in that of a related joint family. This attitude is encouraged by differences in training and occupation, for boys must learn to hunt, to make weapons, and to practice other manly arts, while girls work with their mothers and other female relatives at endless household tasks. As Opler says: "This dichotomy tends to draw the child's interest away from situations which involve the

---

[6] Leslie A. White, "The Definition and Prohibition of Incest," *American Anthropologist,* 50, 416–435 (1948), p. 425.

opposite sex and to seek recognition, rather, in those outlets unequivocally masculine or unequivocally feminine." [7]

Up to adolescence, then, Chiricahua boys and girls associate principally with relatives of the same sex, and are most at home within the joint family of orientation. Here they form lasting consanguine ties and prepare for the time when, by reason of sexual maturity, they must enter a new and broader social milieu.

Adolescence brings a heightened round of activities for both sexes. At or soon after their first menstruation, girls undergo a complex four-day ceremony, designed to prepare them ritually for womanhood and to symbolize their readiness for marriage. These ceremonies are attended by all the joint families of the local group and may even see visitors from other local groups within the band. Social dances take place at the same time and offer many opportunities for unmarried youths to meet, even though under the watchful eyes of the girls' elderly female chaperons.

Boys mark their advance to manhood by participating as novices in four successive raiding parties. Under the supervision and protection of older and experienced warriors, they learn the techniques of raiding and warfare. During these trips, the novices must carefully observe certain ritual procedures, speak only when addressed and even then answer only in a special war-path language, and perform all the petty and menial tasks incident upon camping and traveling away from home. When the four raids are done, the boys, if they have proved their ability, are welcomed as men, free to marry and assume all the responsibilities of adult status.

As a result of their training in the joint family, capped by the puberty rites, youths of both sexes are directed to seek their wives and husbands outside the bonds of consanguine kinship. They have learned, under threat of severe penalties, to avoid all siblings and cousins of the opposite sex, or to treat them, when contact is inevitable, with extreme formality and respect. But the joint family and the local group also provide, on numerous social occasions, opportunities to meet nonrelatives of the opposite sex, and older members of the joint family not infrequently arrange appropriate marriages for their offspring.

Such marriages link joint families, as well as the bride and groom, in affinal ties not easily dissolved. The importance of these is evident when we remember that the Chiricahua local group is not a highly organized body held together by a tight political apparatus. It is, rather, a more or less unstable confederation of joint families, united by mutual compatibility and a common respect for an outstandingly able and experienced leader.

[7] Morris Edward Opler, *An Apache Life-Way* (Chicago: copyright 1941 by University of Chicago Press), p. 78.

When the joint families of such a group are also united by intermarriage, the unity and permanence of the local group are further insured. And since the local group is a principal agency of offense and defense in a society which spends much of its time in raiding and warfare, its preservation is important to the security of all its constituent families.

To summarize this section, it seems clear that incest regulations function in at least two important ways: (1) to maintain a stable and cooperative family unit for the care and training of children, and often for economic purposes as well, and (2) to insure that the sexual impulses of men and women are directed to the end of establishing essential relations between families. Though these social functions of incest regulations may not throw much light on their origins, they do illuminate their relation, as patterns, to the rest of the culture.

5. PREFERENTIAL MATING

The data presented in the preceding section suggest that marriage involves, not only a contract between individuals, but also one between families. Marriages are frequently so arranged, by means of incest regulations, as to cement alliances between families and larger exogamic units and so provide a wider base for intrasocietal cooperation than would otherwise be possible.

Even in our own society, where, as we have seen, the family plays a relatively small role in social control, marriage may still involve the family as much as the individual. Many a man or woman has discovered, before or after marriage, that he or she has acquired not only a spouse but also a number of new relatives whose claims are difficult if not impossible to ignore. Moreover, families not seldom contrive to have their offspring marry individuals not unlike themselves in religious faith, racial or ethnic group membership, and socioeconomic status. In a broad sense, all such limitations on the choice of a spouse may be defined as preferential mating —the preference or even requirement that a spouse be found among individuals of a certain defined subgroup within the society.

In other societies, and especially in those very largely governed by kinship usages, preferential mating may be more precisely defined and more rigidly enforced. Thus, as we noted in § 2, the Australian Karieras require that an individual marry his cross-cousin, near or remote; the spouse may come from no other group. This practice often results in two patrilocal joint families more or less regularly exchanging marriageable women; the daughters of one family marrying the sons of another, and vice versa.

An arrangement like this has certain obvious advantages, both to the stability of the family itself and to the maintenance of interfamilial cooperation. The women coming into the family at marriage are known to it as relatives of the women already there; their coming has been anticipated and they have already begun to adjust to their future in-laws. Accordingly, when these women actually take up residence with their spouses, there is little disturbance of intrafamilial harmony and cooperation. Similarly, two joint families, united by many affinal ties and the promise of more to come, have increasingly more in common and every incentive to cooperative effort.

Cross-cousin marriage is widespread among the peoples of the world, but it is not always as uniformly and as rigidly enforced as among the Karieras. In many regions of China, for example, cross-cousins, though preferred as spouses, are not required; individuals not infrequently marry nonrelatives. Here, too, however, cross-cousin marriage, in those areas where it is preferred, enables the newly made bride to adjust to her husband's joint family with a minimum of difficulty and friction, and, further, gives families united by many marriages a firmer basis of cooperation than would otherwise be possible.

Another but far rarer form of preferential mating is found in parallel-cousin marriage, illustrated by the Arab camel nomads (the Bedouins) of northern Arabia. These people live in a desert environment, moving from place to place in search of water and pasturage for their camels, their most important means of livelihood. To care for their camels, and to protect them against the raids of enemy groups, the Bedouin bands require a strong force of men, united in close bonds of kinship, since kinship usages are the principal means of social control. It is therefore desirable that a young male not leave the band at marriage but remain in it and either bring his bride to his paternal band or find one within that band. Marriage outside the band would, however, divide the male's loyalties between the band of his birth and that of his bride, a contingency hardly in keeping with the extreme hostility between bands as a result of an intense competition for the little water and pasturage available. Bedouin bands tend, therefore, to be endogamous—that is, marriages take place within the band—and the preferred marriage is with the father's brother's daughter, a parallel cousin, born and reared in the same band. By this means young males are not only kept in the band but also have their relation to the father's brothers, already a strong one, further reinforced by the affinal tie.

Preferential mating, then, may be viewed as a further technique of reinforcing social solidarity and broadening the cooperative base within a society. It takes on particular importance in societies governed largely by kinship usages—in societies where cooperation between distinct familial groupings is essential to survival. In the history of our own society, as it moves from an earlier preindustrial stage with emphasis on familial ties and kinship usages to the modern industrial civilization in which the family is small and kinship usages play but a small role in social control, preferential mating—and indeed the whole role of the family in respect to marriage—has decreased in importance. In the earlier period, the family played a large role in selecting the spouses of its offspring, even to the point of arranging preferred marriages for their children without consulting them or taking their feelings into account. Today, though the family undoubtedly plays some role in the marriages of its young, arranged marriages are obsolete.

6. LEVIRATE AND SORORATE

In most societies, it is probable that ideal patterns of culture hold marriage to be a more or less permanent tie, one not to be dissolved easily at the whim of either partner. More than this, however, is the fact that marriages, once begun, establish enduring ties between families in many societies; ties that outlive even the principals to the marriage. The expression of this fact in cultural terms is found in the levirate and sororate, two patterns of culture widespread among nonliterate peoples. According to the levirate, a man is required to marry the wife or (in a polygynous society) the wives of his deceased brother. The sororate, in turn, requires that a widower ordinarily accept an unmarried sister as successor to his deceased wife. The precise manner in which these customs operate to maintain once established marital relations between families is nicely illustrated by the Chiricahua Apaches, who practice both the levirate and the sororate.

Among the Chiricahuas, as we have noted, the functioning social and economic unit is the joint family with matrilocal residence. Young men become members of their wives' families, taking the place, in an economic sense, of the sons who leave the joint family upon marriage. Should these sons-in-law turn out to be economic assets to the joint family, it is obvious that they must be encouraged to stay and, indeed, that their contract to marry assumes that they will stay.

To effect this permanence of residence is the function of the levirate and the sororate. If a man's wife dies while he is still of an age to marry again, he may not do so until his deceased wife's sisters (or those of her cousins resident in the joint family) have had the opportunity to claim him as husband. Should one of them make such a claim, he is required to marry her, and such marriage may take place very soon after his wife's death.

Only if no eligible women exist, or if those eligible do not press their claim, may the widower seek a spouse outside his deceased wife's family. Even then, he cannot properly marry until the deceased wife's family have given him permission to do so, and such permission may not be given until the appropriate period of mourning—a year or more—has passed. It should be noted, too, that a widower who is not claimed by members of his deceased wife's family eligible to do so, may find it quite difficult to find another spouse outside. It is more or less assumed, in such cases, that the widower remains unclaimed because he was more a liability than an asset to his deceased wife's family. Accordingly, few if any other families may be found who are willing to take him in.

When a woman's husband dies while she is still marriageable, she is under the same obligation to her deceased husband's brothers and male cousins, provided, of course, these are unmarried. Should one of these ask to marry her, and so take the place of her deceased husband in the economic life of her family, she has no recourse but to accept. Of course, if none of those eligible to claim her do so for a period of a year or more, she is then permitted to take another husband, if one offers himself.

The import of these patterns of conduct is clear. Marriage, in the view of the Chiricahuas, establishes a bond between joint families which is not dissolved by the death of either man or wife. The wife's family, even after her death, retains an indissoluble claim on her husband which, should they choose to exercise it, may not be declined by him or by his family. The family of a deceased married man hold a similar claim over his wife, in the sense that they may, at their discretion, provide her with a husband she is bound to accept. In these instances, not at all uncommon among nonliterate peoples, it will be noted that the family interest in a marriage of one of their number takes considerable precedence over that of the individual concerned.

7. MONOGAMY AND POLYGAMY

Anthropologists commonly distinguish three forms of marriage: monogamy, the marriage of one man to one woman, polygyny, the marriage of one man to two or more women, and polyandry, the marriage of one woman to two or more men. Polygyny and polyandry are often linked under the single term "polygamy," a marriage of one individual to two or more spouses. Very rarely, a fourth marriage form is found, a combination of polygyny and polyandry where sets of men and women enjoy more or less equal conjugal rights over each other. This form, often called "group marriage," will be discussed in § 8.

Though there are many societies which permit, or even encourage, polygamous marriages, it does not follow, in such societies, that every married
individual, or even that a majority of them, has more than one spouse.
Quite the contrary is true, for in most, if not all, of so-called polygamous
societies monogamy is statistically the prevailing form. The reason for this
is clear: the proportion of male to female births in any human society is
roughly the same, and if this proportion is maintained among the sexually
mature, a preponderance of plural marriages means that a considerable
number of either men or women must remain unmarried. No society can
maintain itself under such conditions; the emotional stresses would be too
great to be survived. Accordingly, even where the cultural ideals do not
prohibit plural marriages, these may occur on any notable scale only in
societies where, for one reason or another, one sex markedly outnumbers
the other. In short, monogamy not only prevails in most of the world's
societies, either as the only approved form of marriage or as the only
feasible form, but it may also prevail within a polygamous society where,
very often, only a minority of the population can actually secure more
than one spouse.

To illustrate polygamous marriage, let us turn to the Baganda, a society
numbering about one million members living in Uganda, East Africa. The
Baganda are a cattle-raising and horticultural people living in a region
extremely favorable to both these pursuits. Their political system is an
autocratic monarchy, and the king, aided in governing by a large number
of chiefs and subchiefs appointed by himself, has almost absolute political
powers. As the supreme ruler and the wealthiest man in the kingdom, the
monarch has hundreds of wives. Chiefs and petty chiefs may have ten or
more wives, depending upon their wealth and political status. Farmers,
petty officials, and artisans, the lower strata in the population, work very
hard to secure at least two wives (as a symbol of their status and wealth),
and some of the more fortunate may have three or even four. But the poorer
peasants often have but one wife, largely because they are unable to raise
the rather high bride price necessary to the acquisition of a second. Though
accurate figures are unavailable, it appears that the Baganda are among
the few peoples of the world among whom plural marriages form a large
percentage, perhaps even a majority, of the whole.

In a polygynous household, the husband must supply a house and garden
for each of his wives. The wives live with him in turn, cooking and serving
for him during the period of their visit. Though they come only at his invitation, and though the husband may actually prefer one to the rest, he
must also be careful not to arouse jealousies and resentments that may
destroy the peace and harmony of the household. The first wife takes preced-

ence over the others and has charge of the household fetishes, objects in which ghosts or spirits are believed to reside and which are important in Baganda religious rites. The second wife, too, has important duties: she shaves her husband's head and trims his nails, occupations which gain their significance from the fact that hair and nail clippings must carefully be protected against the machinations of enemies, who might use them to injure or even kill the husband.

The wide dispersal of polygyny among the Baganda is made possible by the high mortality rate among Baganda males. In chiefly families, male children are often killed at birth; the princes of the royal house, once the successor to the throne has been chosen, are put to death; the king arbitrarily kills off male retainers and servants who displease him; males, never females, must be sacrificed in great numbers to the gods at appropriate ceremonies; and great numbers of men are killed in the annual wars the Baganda conduct with their neighbors. As a result of these factors, plus the fact that large numbers of women are taken as booty in war expeditions, the women outnumber the men by three to one. It is this disparity in the relative numbers of men and women that makes polygyny on so wide a scale possible.

Polyandry is much rarer than polygyny; a typical example is found among the Todas, a people of southern India who live largely on the dairy produce of their great herds of water buffalo. The ideal pattern of marriage in Toda culture is fraternal polyandry, which dictates that when a woman marries a man she becomes, in theory at least, the wife of all his brothers, both the living and those as yet unborn. Frequently such marriages occur in fact as well as in theory, and a set of brothers (or clan brothers) with but one wife may live together in a single hut. There is little jealousy or friction. When one of the brothers is with the wife, he places his mantle and staff outside the hut as a warning to the rest not to come in. During the wife's first pregnancy, one of the brothers performs a ceremony over her known as "giving the bow" and so becomes the recognized (or legal) father to her children. The remaining brothers are only fathers in a secondary sense.

Occasionally polyandry may be nonfraternal (the men belonging to different clans). When these live in different villages, the wife customarily spends about one month with each in turn. The men "give the bow" in turn, so that the first is father to the first two or three children and the others, in sequence, fathers to the rest. Since, however, these arrangements frequently lead to much dispute and bickering, fraternal polyandry tends to be a preferred form.

As with the Baganda, Toda polyandry is undoubtedly the result of a disproportion in the ratio of men to women; in a population of 800 there are about 100 more men than women. This disproportion arose through the pattern of female infanticide. Single girl babies are frequently killed at birth and when twins are born of different sexes, the female twin is always killed. Since twins are believed "unnatural," one is killed even if both are boys, and if the twins are girls, both are killed.

It is of interest to note, however, that polyandry is still a preferred form of marriage, even though infanticide has greatly decreased and the proportion of males to females is approaching normal equality. The practice of polyandry obviously takes a somewhat different form: thus a set of brothers may take two or even more wives instead of just one. But the persistence of the older cultural form is indicated even where each brother has a wife, for these wives are clearly considered to be held in common by all the brothers.

It should now be clear that polygamy is not, as so frequently indicated, universally a result of human immorality. It is simply not true, in this aspect of culture as in many others, that people who follow patterns of culture deemed immoral in our society are thereby lacking in morality. Our ideal and compulsory pattern of marriage, which holds that monogamy is the only appropriate form of marriage, is not shared by all peoples, even by some of those who regularly practice monogamy. In a great many societies, monogamy is only one possible form of marriage, with polygyny or polyandry as perfectly possible, though less frequent, alternatives. And in some societies, as among the Baganda, monogamy may be regarded as a poor substitute for polygyny, symbolic of a low status both economically and socially.

8. "GROUP" MARRIAGE

Some of the earlier theories as to the origins and ancient history of human cultures have postulated that man, in his primeval state, had no marriage forms at all but lived in a state of promiscuity. Later there developed, according to these theories, a kind of "group" marriage, whereby sets of males and females shared more or less equal conjugal rights over each other. Still later, it was supposed, came polygyny and polyandry, while monogamy represented the latest and highest form of marriage.

Evidence for this hypothesis was sought in "primitive" cultures, on the assumption that these preserved ancient forms relatively unchanged. But, as we have noted, polygamy is by no means general among so-called primitives. Rather, monogamy occurs far more often if only for the reason that polygamy is impossible except under rare and special circumstances. Moreover, polygamy, or at least polygyny, occurs not seldom among peoples who are by no means primitive in culture; for example, among such peoples as the modern Mohammedans, the Chinese, and the ancient Incas of Peru. Polygamy, as we have seen, is conditioned, not by primitivity in culture, but by particular conditions affecting the ratio of men to women in a given society.

No evidence of a state of promiscuity has ever been recorded, whether among primitives or others. Every human society known has rigid rules of marriage, similar in kind and complexity to those we have illustrated. And group marriage, while it occurs, is so rare as to be notable, and, like polygamy, is not confined to primitives. We have already mentioned one instance among the Todas, where a set of brothers may possess a number of wives in common, and here it is obviously a recent development from an earlier polyandry, caused by a decrease in female infanticide. Another instance of group marriage is reported by Linton for the Marquesans of Polynesia. We shall examine this in some detail for the light it throws on this unusual form of marriage.

The Marquesans are a fishing and agricultural people, by no means "primitive," who live in isolated villages along the coasts of the larger islands of the Marquesas group. Each village is made up of large extended families, and each family has a head man and a small cluster of buildings set on a platform. The platform, by its size and elaborateness, symbolizes the family's wealth and prestige; the larger and finer it is, the higher is the socioeconomic status of the family. To gain such status and to retain it, the family requires, above all, a large supply of man power. It takes much human labor to build a family center and to cultivate and collect the food and other resources necessary to maintain it. The chief of the village has the largest and wealthiest household, and from there the households in the village grade down to the small families of little status who occupy the lowest stratum of the class structure.

The headship of a household is inherited by the first born child, who acquires this title as soon as he is born. Active control, of course, is not achieved until maturity and marriage; in the meantime, the former head acts as regent for the child. Younger children have no position at all in their family of birth, but at marriage will attach themselves to the households of their spouses.

Girls among the Marquesans are encouraged to take many lovers, since by this means their chances of a good marriage are improved. This is because a young household head seeks by marriage, not only to gain a wife suitable to his station in life, but also to add to his house as many young men as possible in the capacity of secondary husbands. Secondary husbands of course are younger sons, not eligible to the headship of their households of birth, who must seek their fortune by attaching themselves in this way to a wealthy and powerful house.

When a young household head marries, then, he attempts to set up a polyandrous family. But he may, if he is wealthy enough, marry more than one woman and so add even more secondary husbands to his house. In this situation, the result is a kind of group marriage, with the head and the secondary husbands having equal conjugal rights over the wives. The head and the first wife rule the household, which also includes the older relatives of the head and the children born of these marriages.

It should not be assumed that the secondary husbands lack any means of enforcing their rights. To keep them there, and so to retain the man power necessary to maintain the family's status, the household head must treat the secondary husbands fairly. Should he fail to do so, they are under no compulsion to stay, but may well seek to attach themselves to another household where they have the promise of better treatment.

Linton indicates that only the wealthier Marquesan households have more than one wife, while most of the rest tend to be polyandrous to a greater or less degree. In only the poorest households is there but one husband and one wife; in these cases, apparently, the head is unable to attract secondary husbands to his group. Frequently such a household head may even fail to find a wife and be therefore obliged to abandon his heritage and join another household as secondary husband.

The prevalence of polyandry among the Marquesans, as among the Todas, arises through a scarcity of women due to the practice of female infanticide. Group marriage, where it exists in the Marquesas, is obviously an extension of the polyandrous family by adding to it one or more wives. It derives, not from any excessive primitivity of Marquesan culture, but from socioeconomic circumstances peculiar to it.

9. BRIDE PRICE AND DOWRY

The customs of bride price and dowry, so frequently associated with marriage, are much misunderstood, especially in societies like our own where these patterns of culture are lacking. Bride price is often conceived as reducing women to the status of chattels to be bought and sold, and dowry as a means of securing husbands by purchase. Neither conception is accurate; there is no necessary implication in either bride price or dowry that spouses may be bartered as insensate pieces of property.

Bride price may roughly be defined as a marriage payment made by a prospective husband, or more often by his family, to the family of the bride. This payment serves many functions, among which are: that of symbolizing the socioeconomic statuses of the families to be united affinally, that of establishing an economic tie between the families of the bride and groom to insure further the stability of the marriage, and that of providing the family of the bride with a means of replacing her by daughters-in-law. To illustrate these points, let us turn to the Baganda of East Africa, where, as in so many African societies, bride price is a highly developed pattern of culture.

Among the Baganda, men may marry as early as sixteen, and girls at fourteen. A young man wishing to marry must ordinarily accumulate enough property to pay the bride price and to supply the numerous other gifts necessary to a somewhat complex marriage ritual. He may, however, secure wives by other means: by inheritance from a deceased older brother (the levirate), as a reward for meritorious service from a superior, as a gift from a subordinate who desires to curry favor, or as part of his share of loot from a raiding expedition. But the most frequent and preferred way of securing a bride, especially in the case of a first marriage, is through negotiation and the payment of a bride price.

Since the task of accumulating a bride price is likely to be long continued, and to require as well the assistance of his family, a Baganda young man learns to choose his wife with care. Good health, the ability to bear children, skill in gardening and household arts, and a reputation for industry and obedience are qualities to be desired in a bride; relative to these, other considerations, such as good looks, are minor. Having found a girl to his liking, and one who can meet the critical scrutiny of his family, the young man initiates negotiations with her older brother and paternal uncle, whose duty it is to arrange the marriages of the girls in their family. If the young man gains their consent, he brings several gourds of native beer, and swears before witnesses (the usual form of contract among the nonliterate Baganda) to be a good husband. At this point, the girl must also signify her assent by serving the beer to those present; if she refuses to do this, negotiations are thereby broken off and the young man must go elsewhere for a bride.

If the girl consents, however, the couple are considered betrothed, and the clansmen of the girl proceed to set the bride price. The customary base price is 2,500 cowry shells (roughly the equivalent of a single head of cattle), to which may be added an amount in domestic animals, beer, bark cloth, and other materials in keeping with the status of the girl's family and with the ability of the young man to pay. To set too small a bride price may lower the family status, while too high a bride price may discourage the prospective husband. The girl's family must steer a middle course, both to preserve their social position and to make the best marriage possible for their offspring.

The marriage does not take place until the bride price has been paid. For a poor man, this may require some time; for one better endowed with worldly goods, the interval between betrothal and marriage may be shorter. During this interval, the girl is carefully fed and groomed by her family, that she may become plump and attractive to her husband. The sisters of the young man visit the prospective bride frequently, to bathe her and to examine her critically for physical defects.

The whole tenor of these arrangements reflects the concern of both families that the marriage be successful. The bride price insures that the girl, once married, becomes mistress of her husband's household, to engage in gardening and other gainful occupations for him; her labor power may no longer be claimed by her family of birth. Similarly, her children belong to her husband's clan, though here it is interesting to note that every third child belongs to the wife's clan unless redeemed by further payment by the father or his clansmen. If the wife runs away from her husband, her clansmen must send her back or return the bride price. But where a marriage is successful, the bride price is ordinarily used by a family to secure wives for their young sons and so replace the daughters who marry out with daughters-in-law, whose labor power and children will add to the resources of the clan.

Though the pattern of providing brides with a dowry has often degenerated into one of permitting noble but impoverished families to recoup their fortunes by marrying wealthy commoners, dowry, it is evident, has originally a function not dissimilar to that of bride price. As the custom existed in Europe (and to some extent is still practiced) the dowry represented a gift in money, goods, or both made by the bride's family toward the establishment of her household. Because the husband was head of the family, and because it was considered unfitting that a woman handle business affairs, the dowry usually became the property of the husband, with the understanding that it be used to the best advantage of both himself and his wife. It did not represent a payment for an agreement to marry, but simply a means of assisting a young man (who was often similarly assisted as well by his own family) to begin the expensive business of establishing a home for his wife and the children to come. Like bride price, dowry united the families of the bride and groom in an endeavor to provide the best possible economic base for marriage, and so to insure its permanence and success.

Dowry appears to be a rarer cultural form than bride price. It was apparently very common in Europe, at least among the upper economic strata, but is scarcely represented at all among so-called primitives. The custom has now largely disappeared even in Europe, though the modern custom of providing a bride with household equipment and a stock of new clothing possibly represents a survival of the older cultural pattern.

Many peoples lack both bride price and dowry, though among some of these, gift-giving is considered a necessary prerequisite to marriage. A typical example is found among the Chiricahua Apaches, where according to one of Opler's informants: "A man must give a present to his wife's relatives or be disgraced; the woman is disgraced too if this is not done." [8] But there is no limit to the number of such gifts, nor does the size of the gift affect the status of the principals. The gifts are not a bride price; they "do not entitle the husband or his family to any extraordinary control over the wife or her property. . . . Moreover, these gifts or their equivalents are never returned, not even in cases of unfaithfulness on the part of the woman or of dissolution of the marriage tie." [9]

But it is of interest to note that the marriage gift "functions as initial evidence of the economic support, cooperation, and generosity which a man owes to his wife's close relatives. The promise of future assistance can even take the place of a gift on occasion. . . ." [10] This correlates with what we already know of the Chiricahua family—the young man joins his wife's joint family at marriage and becomes one of its economic supports. It is obvious that his gifts cannot be interpreted as a compensation to the girl's family for the loss of her services and children. The marriage gifts, divided among the wife's kin, serve only to cement ties between the families of husbands and wives and to symbolize their economic parity.

10. DIVORCE

Though we have emphasized the fact that marriage is universally conceived as a permanent tie and have illustrated many cultural patterns designed to secure this end, there are few if any societies that do not provide some means, easy or difficult, of terminating unsuccessful marriages. No society known approves of divorce in principle—to do so would of course be tantamount to denying the permanence of the marriage tie—and no society encourages divorce. But nearly all societies, in practice, recognize that certain conditions, diversely defined, make it better to terminate a

---

[8] Morris Edward Opler, *An Apache Life-Way* (Chicago: copyright 1941 by University of Chicago Press), pp. 161–162.

[9] *Ibid.*

[10] *Ibid.*

marriage than have it continue as a failure, and perhaps as a deterrent to others approaching marriage.

Recognized causes for divorce vary widely from one society to the next and even from one period to another in the history of a single society. In a recent study of divorce in forty non-European societies, Murdock gives a table, listing the more commonly recognized grounds for divorce and indicating opposite each the number of societies which permit or forbid divorce for this reason.

REASONS FOR DIVORCE *

(Forty Sample Societies)

	Permitted				Forbidden			
	Definitely		Inferentially		Definitely		Inferentially	
Reasons	To Man	To Wife	To Man	To Wife	To Man	To Wife	To Man	To Wife
Any grounds, however trivial	9	6	5	6	14	13	12	15
Incompatibility without more specific grounds	17	17	10	10	6	7	7	6
Common adultery or infidelity	19	11	8	12	8	10	5	7
Repeated or exaggerated infidelity	27	23	8	10	5	5	0	2
Childlessness or sterility	12	4	15	18	7	7	6	11
Sexual impotence or unwillingness	9	12	24	21	3	4	4	3
Laziness, nonsupport, economic incapacity	23	22	11	9	4	5	2	4
Quarrelsomeness or nagging	20	7	7	12	6	11	7	15
Mistreatment or cruelty	7	25	19	9	3	4	11	2

* G. P. Murdock, "Family Stability in Non-European Societies," copyright November, 1950, by *Annals of the American Academy of Political and Social Science,* 272, 195–201, p. 200.

It will be noted that this table also emphasizes the fact that, in most of the societies studied, divorce is as easy for women to secure as it is for men. According to Murdock, "In thirty of the forty cultures surveyed it was impossible to detect any substantial difference in the rights of men and women to terminate an unsatisfactory alliance." [11] Men hold superior rights to divorce "in only six societies" [12]—the Moslem Kurds of Iraq, the Siwans of Egypt, the Japanese, the Baganda, the Siriono Indians of Bolivia, and the Guaycuru Indians of the Gran Chaco. "In four societies," Murdock continues, ". . . women actually possess superior privileges as regards divorce." [13] These are the Kwomas of New Guinea, the Dahomeans of West Africa (when the marriage is the "stable" form "characterized by patrilocal residence and the payment of a bride price" [14]), the Yurok Indians of California, and the Witotos of Brazil.

The suggestion has been made, from time to time, that sexual rights in initiating divorce are related, roughly at least, to the relative status of men and women in the society concerned. Among the Aruntas of Australia, for example, divorce is made very easy for the man, who can send his wife away on the slightest pretext, while the woman has no right to a divorce at all. If she is badly treated or her marriage is otherwise made intolerable, her only recourse is to run away, and even then she is subject to recapture and may be made to return to her husband.

A similar differentiation between the rights of men and women in divorce is found among the Baganda of East Africa. Here a man may also divorce his wife at will, sending her back to her family and demanding the return of the bride price. He is almost sure to do this if she is barren, for barrenness is not only a great misfortune but a positive danger to the fruitfulness of his gardens. However, since a barren woman has practically no chance for remarriage, her husband may simply neglect her, reducing her to the status of a household drudge and near-slave.

The Baganda woman cannot divorce her husband, though if she is badly treated, she may run away and claim the aid of her clansmen. These individuals seek a meeting with the husband and attempt to mend matters but if, for good reasons, the woman persists in running away, she will be given sanctuary by her kinsfolk and all or part of the bride price returned to the husband.

Among both the Aruntas and the Baganda, the ease of divorce for men

[11] G. P. Murdock, "Family Stability in Non-European Societies," copyright November, 1950, by *Annals of the American Academy of Political and Social Science,* 272, 195–201, p. 196.

[12] *Ibid.*

[13] *Ibid.*

[14] *Ibid.*

and the corresponding difficulty of divorce for women appear to be correlated with the relatively low status of womanhood. An Arunta woman, though she is hard-working and contributes considerably to the economic resources of the household, lives in the joint family of her husband and is subject to the rule of men. She has no political rights and holds no position of importance in the band, nor is she permitted to participate in sacred ceremonies. Similarly, the Baganda woman lives among her husband's clansmen and is often only one of several wives. Her work is gardening, an occupation important to Baganda well-being but despised by the upper ruling class, who are hereditary cattle-keepers. Women do not participate in politics, hold no important positions, are often forbidden to partake in religious rites, and are forbidden even to approach the cattle. Among both the Aruntas and Baganda, then, it is not surprising to find that the woman's right to dissolve a marriage is nearly nonexistent, while a man may divorce his wife whenever he sees fit, with or without cause.

Quite a different situation exists among the Chiricahua Apaches. Here men and women have almost equal rights to a separation and on similar grounds. Unfaithfulness, barrenness or impotence, brutality, nagging, laziness, or even incompatibility may result in divorce, and a woman may initiate such proceedings just as easily as a man. When a divorce takes place, the couple simply separate, each retaining his own property, and the man leaves his wife's joint family to return to his own or remarry. Unless she is the guilty party—being divorced, for example, for ill temper, barrenness, or laziness—a divorced woman has no difficulty in remarrying, and the same applies to men. This equality of opportunity for divorce is again probably related to the status of women, which in Apache society is quite high. Woman's work is not despised, and though women do not hold important positions of leadership in Apache society, they do play a considerable role in influencing their husbands. Moreover, the woman lives in her family of orientation after marriage, the joint family is matrilocal, and it is the husband who must prove his worth to critical in-laws.

An even better situation for women is found among the Iroquois of upper New York. Here also the joint family is matrilocal. The newly married couple live in a room of the long house, owned by the wife's clan, and ruled very largely by her older female relatives. The men have neither political nor economic rights in their wives' long house; these they exercise only in their houses of birth. Consequently a wife may put her husband out whenever she decides it is necessary, with no more formality than putting his belongings outside the house. But the man has equal access to an easy divorce; he need only stay away.

Murdock's data do not explicitly deny the hypothesis suggested and illustrated above, though they do emphasize the fact that equality in initiating divorce as between the sexes is very widespread, and may even be found in societies where men appear to be dominant.

It is . . . surprising to encounter an equal facility in divorce among patrilocal and even patriarchal peoples like the Mongols, who see no reason for moral censure in divorce and say in a perfectly matter-of-fact manner that two individuals who cannot get along harmoniously together had better live apart.[15]

On the relative frequency of divorce as between different societies, Murdock finds only sixteen societies in which

the stability of marital unions is noticeably greater than in our society. . . . In the remaining twenty-four societies, constituting sixty per cent of the total, the divorce rate manifestly exceeds that among ourselves. Despite the widespread alarm about increasing "family disorganization" in our own society, the comparative evidence makes it clear that we still remain well within the limits which human experience has shown that societies can tolerate with safety.[16]

Neither Murdock's data, nor any other, are evidence that most societies regard the marriage relationship as casual. On the contrary, as even our brief survey of marriage forms has shown, there is, in nearly all societies, a constant effort toward the end of encouraging and rewarding permanent unions, not to dissolving them. The general attitude toward divorce, as Murdock says,

is clearly that it is regrettable, but often necessary. It represents more of a practical concession to the frailty of mankind, caught in a web of social relationships and cultural expectations that often impose intolerable pressure on the individual personality. That most social systems work as well as they do, despite concessions to the individual that appear excessive to us, is a tribute to human ingenuity and resiliency.[17]

11. SUMMARY

The material presented in this chapter may be summarized in the following general statements:

(1) Marriage is everywhere a set of cultural patterns devised, among other things, to guide the individual in the choice of a spouse. Though

15 *Ibid.*, p. 199.
16 *Ibid.*, p. 197.
17 *Ibid.*, p. 201.

marriage customarily serves the function of providing sexual gratification, it is not always the only cultural pattern to serve this end, and it does not derive from this purpose alone. Rather, the function of marriage lies primarily in the social sanction it supplies for parenthood and in the fact that it supplies a stable background for the care and rearing of children. It is in this sense that marriage may be defined as a major cultural mechanism to insure the continuance of the family and other groupings based on kinship.

(2) Incest regulations are an inevitable accompaniment of marriage and are found in all societies. Because of the diversity of consanguine kin proscribed as spouses, it is evident that incest regulations are not designed to prevent close inbreeding. Nor are incest regulations wholly to be explained in psychological terms; there appears to be no inherent psychological distaste for incestuous unions, and those psychological disorders which may result from incest seem to be an effect rather than a cause of incest regulations.

(3) Probably more important to the origin and persistence of incest regulations are factors which are cultural in nature. Among other functions, marriage serves that of preserving intrafamilial harmony and widening the social basis for cooperation among men to include more than one familial unit. To achieve this end, incest regulations direct the sex impulses of individuals outside the family and use them to establish affinal ties between families.

(4) In many societies, and in particular among those whose techniques of social control rest primarily in kinship usages, certain marriages may be preferred or even required. By this means, some of the possible intra- and interfamilial disruptions at marriage may be avoided; for preferential mating, by anticipating certain unions, makes it possible to prepare individuals and their consanguine kin for the affinal ties and obligations they must later assume.

(5) The levirate and sororate, in addition to serving some of the functions attributed to preferential mating, also illuminate the fact that marriage ties impose interfamilial obligations as well as individual ones. By reason of the levirate and sororate, families united by marriages of their offspring continue this alliance even after the death of the individuals actually married, if such continuance is possible and to the mutual benefit of both families.

(6) Not all societies practice the same forms of marriage: we find monogamy, polygyny, polyandry, and various combinations of polygyny and polyandry often designated as group marriage. Monogamy appears to be by far the commonest accepted marriage form and the prevailing form even in societies which permit polygamous unions. This results from the

fact that extensive polygamy is inoperable unless there is a considerable disproportion in the relative number of men and women in a given society, a condition which arises only rarely.

(7) It does not appear that polygamous marriage, of whatever form, is more primitive than monogamy. Older theories proposing a development from primeval promiscuity through group marriage, polyandry, and polygyny to monogamy, do not appear to be supported by either historical fact or by the conditions under which polygamous marriages take place.

(8) Bride price is seen, not as a custom whereby women are purchased as chattels, but as a cultural pattern enabling a family to compensate the loss of a daughter by securing brides for their sons. Dowry, similarly, is not to be conceived as an inducement to marriage but as a device whereby the bride's family seek to aid their daughter's husband set up an economically stable household. Both of these customs again emphasize the fact that marriage is very largely a family concern, and not only of interest to the bride and groom.

(9) Just as marriage exists in all societies, so do all societies provide some technique whereby marriages may be dissolved. Divorce, however, is universally a cultural practice admitted by necessity, for no society appears to recognize in principle that marriage is not a permanent union. Both causes for divorce and the ease with which it may be obtained vary widely in different societies. In some societies divorce is difficult and may be secured, especially by women, only under the stress of intolerable conditions; in others, divorce, for both men and women, is relatively easy to achieve. Nevertheless there are universally techniques whereby pressures of one sort or another may be brought to bear upon those dissatisfied with married life. Even in divorce, then, we find support for the ideal, probably universal in human societies, that marriage, once contracted, should be a permanent tie.

COLLATERAL READING

Lowie, Robert H. *Social Organization.* New York: Rinehart and Co., 1948. Chapter 5.

Murdock, George P. *Social Structure.* New York: The Macmillan Co., 1949. Chapters 9–11.

ETHNOGRAPHIC REFERENCES

Baganda: Murdock, 1935, Chap. XVII; Roscoe, 1911.

Bedouins: Coon, 1948, Chap. 13; Forde, 1950, Chap. XV.

Chiricahua Apaches: Opler, 1937, 1941.

Karieras: Radcliffe-Brown, 1931, Part I.

Marquesans: Linton, 1939.
Masai: Forde, 1950, Chap. XIV; Hollis, 1905.
Samoans: Murdock, 1935, Chap. III; Turner, 1884.
Todas: Murdock, 1935, Chap. V; Rivers, 1906.

Chapter 15

POLITICAL ORGANIZATION

1. THE NATURE AND FORMS
OF POLITICAL ORGANIZATION

As we have seen in Chapter 13, kinship plays an important role in social organization, particularly in nonliterate societies lacking an industrialized economy. Kinship, however, is not the only principle whereby such societies are organized. Equally important is coresidence, the habitual association of human beings in communities or local groups. It is this principle that apparently underlies all forms of politico-territorial grouping, from the informal and amorphous local group to the highly organized modern state.

The local group may briefly be defined as an aggregate of human beings characterized by (1) common residence within a continuous and more or less well defined territory, (2) the possession of a common culture and language, (3) a certain "like-mindedness" or esprit de corps by which its members distinguish themselves from outsiders, and (4) a long tradition of friendly association between its members. While members of some local groups may also be linked by kinship, this is not universally the case. Many, and perhaps most, local groups are made up of several kinship units not all of which need be related either by marriage or by kinship.

Though the local group forms a starting point for the study of political organization, it is not itself necessarily a political unit. Political groups, even where they are identical in membership with a local group, are more explicitly organized into a functioning whole. This organization is accom-

443

plished through a leader or set of leaders who command the respect and allegiance of the members of the group. These leaders (1) maintain peace within the political group, (2) organize and direct community enterprises, and (3) conduct group activities, such as warfare, directed against neighboring units of the same order.

The introduction of political organization into the local group, it is evident, gives rise to a unity between its members which stands over and above that imposed by kinship. Many political units, as we shall see in the following sections, are in essence voluntary alliances of families and clans who not only acknowledge the same political leaders, but who also, through the medium of this leadership, habitually work together in economic enterprises, social and ceremonial affairs, and in the conduct of offensive and defensive warfare. It is, indeed, extremely likely that true political organization begins only with the development of cooperation between distinct and unrelated kinship groups. As long as, in a particular society, kinship units are relatively self-sufficient economically and require no aid in defending themselves against hostile aliens, political organization has little opportunity to develop.

Among many nonliterate peoples, the local group actually does lack political organization, or is at best only incipiently or intermittently a political group. The simplest form of true political organization appears to be the band, essentially a local group plus a system of leaders. A second type occurs when neighboring bands organize into tribes or confederacies, so extending band organization to cover a number of locally autonomous units. Bands, tribes, and confederacies appear to represent the most frequent types of political organization found among nonliterate peoples, and it is of interest to note that these political forms are perhaps universal among peoples who have never developed warfare for conquest. The warfare that does exist in such societies is generally a matter of petty raiding for small economic gain or for purposes of vengeance and prestige. Where warfare is more highly developed in such societies, it is often directed to the extermination or expulsion of enemy groups, not to their subjugation for purposes of political and economic exploitation.

Warfare for conquest and economic exploitation brings us to still another type of political organization, the state, or better, the conquest state. In contrast to bands, tribes, and confederacies, which are characteristically linked to subsistence economies, the conquest state is nearly always associated with a surplus-producing economy. In general, such a state develops when a well-organized tribe, often in league with others, and possessed of a highly productive economy, is thereby enabled to extend its sway by force of arms over neighboring tribes. Instead of expelling or exterminating them, however, the conquerors retain them as subjects for economic exploitation. Accordingly, the conquest state requires force to attain its ends and to maintain itself intact; it is not, like the band, tribe, or confederacy, a more or less voluntary organization of smaller kinship or local units. The conquest state is, therefore, distinguished by the fact that its leadership, however selected, has an acknowledged and exclusive right to exercise force in both internal and external affairs. As Lowie puts it:

> We conceive [the state] as the association corresponding to law, both sharing as their diagnostic feature the monopoly of legitimate physical force, i.e., of force which the community concerned recognizes as properly exercised. An Eskimo group in which a bully can wrest away from a fellow resident any possession he craves, maiming him with impunity . . . has neither law nor statehood because the exhibition of force, though accepted unresistingly, is not acknowledged as proper. On the contrary, when the king of Uganda orders a chief to be executed at his pleasure, this is wholly "constitutional," hence a sign of how the people define acceptable coercion. The state, then, embraces the inhabitants of a definite area who acknowledge the legitimacy of force when applied by the individuals whom they accept as rulers or governors.[1]

As a guide to our study of political organization, we may set up the following provisional categories:

(1) Societies in which there is no true political organization, that is, where the local group has no continuous or well-defined system of leaders over and above those who head the individual families which make it up. Societies of this sort tend also to be small and widely dispersed, to have economies which yield only a bare subsistence, and to lack any form of organized warfare.

(2) Societies organized politically as bands, tribes, or confederacies, in which the population tends to be somewhat more concentrated, the economy yields a richer subsistence but no exchangeable surplus, and warfare, though frequent and often of great importance, is usually a matter of ceaseless raiding between neighboring political units. Where wars are more decisive, they result only in the extermination or expulsion of enemy units, not in their conquest and economic exploitation.

(3) Societies organized as conquest states, established by dint of offensive wars, in which conquered peoples are not usually destroyed but are held as tributaries or incorporated as inferior classes into the conquest state. Populations are large and highly concentrated, the economy produces an exchangeable surplus, and ruling power, in most instances, tends to be centered in a small hereditary elite.

It should not be assumed of course that these categories exhaust the

[1] Robert H. Lowie, *Social Organization* (New York: copyright 1948 by Rinehart & Co., Inc.), p. 317.

almost infinite variety of current and past political forms. They represent, rather, only broad divisions, each of which might be greatly subdivided. Nor should it be assumed that sharp lines may be drawn between the three; as with other social phenomena, each category shades into the next and there are numerous transitional forms.

2. THE ESKIMOS AND WESTERN SHOSHONI

Societies lacking political organization are found today principally in the marginal areas of the world, where a difficult environment, a simple technology, and a lack of adequate food resources keep the human population small and thinly scattered. An excellent example of such a society is found among the Polar Eskimos of northern Greenland. Among these Eskimos, as we noted in Chapter 13, § 2, there are but two social units: the primary family, a small but autonomous kinship group, and the winter village, an intermittent and unstable association of primary families who are not necessarily linked by kinship ties. The winter village is only an incipient political grouping; its member families have neither the constancy of association nor the common enterprises necessary to the development of a stable leadership or a well-defined system of political controls. Ordinarily the families in a winter village, though temporarily united by common residence, act independently of each other; their technology, whether in food-gathering or house-building, requires no high degree of cooperative labor. In times of stress, when a storm or lack of game reduces food stores to the danger point, a shaman, well known and respected for his supernatural powers, may call the families together to participate in a ceremony intended to restore the food supply. But the shaman's authority is limited to just such occasions; at other times he has no right or occasion to direct or command.

Similarly, though a strong and aggressive man may, by his achievements as a hunter, gain the esteem and respect of his fellows, there are few or no occasions when he may capitalize on this to assume a position of leadership. In short, the winter village has literally little need for leadership, for not even warfare exists to combine its primary families for offensive or defensive action. Leadership resides only within the primary family where it is shared by husband and wife, each in his or her own sphere of activity. The family maintains itself largely through its own efforts and is linked to other families only through intermarriage, remote kinship, or ties of mutual affection and regard.

A very similar social organization occurs among the Western Shoshoni, Indians who live by hunting and collecting in the arid deserts of Nevada. Here also we find but two major social units: the primary family and the winter village, the latter a seasonal aggregate of from two to eight or ten primary families. During the summer, families travel alone or in groups of two or three related families to collect wild vegetable foods and store them for winter use. In the fall, numbers of families, often from different winter villages, combine at some favorable place to conduct a rabbit drive under a competent leader. But these community hunts rarely last more than two or three weeks, when the families disperse to return to the village and settle down for the winter. It should be noted, too, that the hunts only rarely involve the same families year after year; they are actually groups formed almost by chance, and they include families who happen to be near the same good hunting area at the end of their summer's wanderings.

The winter village, alone and sometimes together with neighboring villages, has only a few community enterprises. These, mainly ceremonial affairs, are guided by a headman, esteemed for his age and experience in this role. But here, as among the Eskimos, the association of families in the winter village is too brief, and its common enterprises too few, to do more than establish an incipient political unity. The headman has no well-defined authority—only that accorded him on certain occasions by those who respect and defer to him—and any family is free to leave the village at will or to join another as it sees fit.

Among both the Eskimos and the Western Shoshoni, then, there is no true political organization. The reason for this appears to lie in ecological factors, that is, in the modes of behavior whereby these people adjust to their environments. For both peoples, the environment furnishes but sparse and widely scattered food resources which, together with a crude technology, force them to wander great distances to maintain themselves. This enforced nomadism and the physical impossibility of maintaining, except temporarily, social units larger than one or two primary families, effectively inhibit political organization. No stable and well-defined system of leadership can develop, and social control is maintained largely through kinship usages. The "tribe" is actually a local group, that is, an aggregate of smaller kinship units, bound together by geographical contiguity and the habit of associating, albeit intermittently, on a basis of friendship and mutual esteem.

3. THE KARIERA HORDE AND THE ANDAMANESE VILLAGE

On a somewhat more advanced level in respect to social organization are the Karieras of Australia and the people of the Andaman Islands in the Bay of Bengal. The functioning Kariera local unit is usually called a horde, while that of the Andamanese is customarily referred to as a village.

The Kariera horde is ordinarily very small, rarely numbering more than seventy-five individuals of all ages. It is also—and this is unusual—coincident in membership with one of the Kariera kin groups, for the horde is actually a patrilocal joint family, made up of a number of primary families related in the paternal line. Note, however, that by no means all of a Kariera's kin live in his horde; he has many in other, neighboring hordes, and some of these are quite as closely related to him as his relatives within the horde.

Each Kariera horde owns a certain territory over which it roams in search of food. No other horde may enter or hunt in this territory without first gaining the consent of its owners; to violate this rule may cause ill feeling and even quarrels between hordes. Neither do horde members permanently leave their home country, for to do so, in Kariera belief, is to risk eternal destruction. The Kariera who dies at home may soon be reborn into his horde, but should he die far from his native country, his soul may not return to be reincarnated.

The horde is led by its older male members, the fathers and grandfathers of the younger males. These old men are esteemed for their age and experience, as well as for their status as elderly relatives. Meeting informally, they decide when and where the horde is to move, conduct negotiations with neighboring hordes, and direct other matters affecting the horde as a whole. Since the horde is very small, order is maintained largely through the force of public opinion; the fear of ridicule and consequent loss of prestige are ordinarily quite sufficient deterrents to antisocial behavior. In extreme cases, an offender runs the risk of death through private vengeance or expulsion from the horde, and the latter, in view of the Kariera's attachment to his native country, is as severe a punishment as may be meted out.

Contacts between adjacent hordes are frequent, since, as we have noted, these are related, more or less closely, as kin. Many adjacent hordes are linked through marriage (hordes, being patrilocal joint families, are exogamous), and this, too, promotes friendly intercourse between hordes. Quarrels are frequent, but only rarely lead to warfare; they generally resolve into a test of arms between the individuals actually involved. At most, hostile relations between hordes consist of petty, sporadic raids, and even these are often more noisy and vituperative than actual displays of violence.

The Kariera horde, then, is actually an enlarged kinship unit which possesses certain functions which in many other societies are associated with political units. The leaders of the Kariera horde act much as family heads, exercising authority both by reason of their age and experience and because of their status as older kin. Nevertheless, the Kariera horde is a permanent organization of primary families, not intermittent as with the Eskimo and Western Shoshoni, and does have control over a given territory recognized as its own. In these characteristics, then, plus a stable leadership, it certainly approaches, if it does not achieve, the status of an independent political entity.

The Andaman village is perhaps a better example of a rudimentary political unit, since here we find a number of primary families linked, not necessarily by kinship, but by common and habitual association. Like the Kariera horde, the Andaman village is very small, averaging some forty to fifty individuals of all age groups.

Again like the Kariera, each Andaman village group ranges a given territory, recognized as its own, and permits no other group to exploit its resources. Contacts with neighboring villages, when these are on a friendly footing, may occur frequently. Individuals and families may visit back and forth, and even decide to move permanently from one village to another. When food is plentiful, one or more village groups may come together for a time to feast, dance, and exchange gifts. But these contacts do not result in larger political groupings, nor in any but short-lived alliances. The Andaman village, like its Kariera counterpart, never becomes part of a larger political structure, tribal in scope.

Leadership, among the Andamanese, rests with men who are respected for their skills in hunting and warfare and who are kind, generous, and even-tempered. Such men attract followers among the young who seek the good will of the leaders by giving them gifts, helping them in their work, and accompanying them on hunting or war expeditions. Contrariwise, men who are violent, stingy, and bad-tempered are feared and avoided by their fellows.

Social control among the Andamanese is largely a matter of public opinion. The lazy individual, or one who is lacking in respect to the elders, may be punished by ridicule and contempt. Quarrelsome persons are avoided and, if they inflict serious bodily harm, may be subjected to personal vengeance from the friends and relatives of their victims. An especially violent and quarrelsome individual, or one who has committed a murder, may eventually be forced out of the group or killed by those he has injured.

When violent quarrels occur at intervillage meetings, these may lead to warfare between neighboring villages. In such situations, a recognized leader gathers a few followers and plans an attack on the enemy encampment. The raiders seek to surprise their foes, attacking in the evening when all are busy with the evening meal, or early in the morning before anyone is awake. If the surprise is successful, the raiders rush in to kill as many as possible before the defenders melt away into the surrounding forest. However, should the defenders be prepared for the attack, or manage to kill one of the raiders, the latter will retreat at once. Wars—or better, feuds—of this sort are customarily terminated by an offer of peace after the foes have exchanged a few raids.

The Andaman village, it is evident, is organized much like the Kariera horde, differing only in that its constituent primary families are not all united by kinship. For both peoples, leadership exists only in a minimal sense, since the crude technology, based largely on individual rather than group labor, does not afford much opportunity for concerted and coordinated activity. The limitations on the size of the Kariera and Andaman social units are again ecological: the environment, particularly in respect to food resources, does not permit larger permanent assemblages to form. Tribal unity, here as among the Eskimos and Western Shoshoni, is based on geographical contiguity, intermittent meetings between local groups for festivals and trade, a common language, remote kinship ties, and a tradition of more or less friendly intergroup relations.

4. THE CROW INDIANS

The peoples so far discussed, it is evident, lack true political organization; they live in small local groups whose member families only rarely work together as a unified force. As a result, leadership outside the family either does not exist at all, as among the Eskimos, or is evidenced only rarely, when some able and esteemed member of the community takes charge during a crisis. Ecological circumstances, because they effectively prohibit large and permanent assemblages of people, account in part for this situation. Equally important, perhaps, is the fact that the technologies of the societies described emphasize, as a whole, individual rather than group effort. In the relative absence of cooperative community enterprises, there is little chance for a system of leadership to emerge outside the family. As Steward makes clear for the Western Shoshoni:

> The village headman or "talker" was little more than a family leader or village adviser. Inter-family and inter-village alliances for cooperative enterprises were of limited scope and brief duration, occurring only at communal hunts or festivals, each of which had a special director. Because, however, of the erratic occurrences of wild seeds and the frequent variation of terrain covered, alliance did not always bring together the same families or village members. Habitual cooperation of the same people and therefore the development of fixed if limited political allegiances and controls was impossible.[2]

[2] Julian H. Steward, *Basin-Plateau Aboriginal Sociopolitical Groups,* Bulletin 120, Bureau of American Ethnology (Washington, D. C., 1938), p. 257.

Let us turn now to the Crow Indians, discussed earlier in this book (Chapter 13, § 6) in respect to their kinship groupings. The Crow live in local groups considerably larger than those of the peoples just discussed and, more important, characterized by a truly political organization. There are three such units among the Crow, each having a population numbered in the hundreds rather than by scores, as among the Kariera and Andamanese. Because they possess political organization, we shall refer to the Crow local groups as bands, the simplest of our several forms of political grouping.

Crow bands, though wholly autonomous politically, nevertheless recognize a common unity with each other based on remote kinship (the same clans are found in each of the three bands), a common language and culture, and intermittent friendly contacts. Warfare is practically unknown between the bands and, at least on rare occasions, bands have united temporarily for purposes of defense against a common enemy.

In common with other Plains tribes, the Crows are continually on hostile terms with their neighbors, and any non-Crow is automatically an enemy. Warfare, however, is largely a matter of small-scale raiding, either to steal horses from an enemy encampment or to avenge the death of a tribesman in some previous raid. Horse-stealing parties seek to take as many horses as they can without disturbing the enemy camp; they fight only when necessary to defend themselves. When revenge is the object of a war party, however, they try to surprise the enemy and, having succeeded, to kill as many as possible without losing any of their own men. A war leader, whether he sets out to capture horses or to get revenge, is not considered successful unless he brings his own party home intact.

Success in warfare is of enormous importance, for it is through the slow accumulation of war honors that Crow men achieve reputation and prestige. War honors are clearly defined; they are awarded for (1) leading a successful war party, (2) capturing an enemy's weapon in actual combat, (3) being first to strike an enemy, living or dead, in the course of a fight, and (4) driving off a horse tethered in an enemy encampment. A man who achieves one of each of these deeds becomes, in Crow terms, a "good and valiant man," or a chief, and his status as chief increases as the number of his earned war honors increases. Contrariwise, one who has not yet attained the minimum of four honors necessary to chieftainship is regarded as not yet a man, but only an untried youth.

The chiefs form a kind of military aristocracy that makes up the band council. One of their number, usually an older man with many war honors, is recognized as head chief. He decides when the band is to move or settle down in its yearly wanderings in search of food, when war parties are to be sent out and when they are to be restrained, and he conducts the annual buffalo hunt, a cooperative endeavor in which the whole band unites to secure a store of winter food. To aid him in these duties, the band chief has a herald or crier to announce his decisions and to inform the band members of important news. Each spring, the head chief also appoints one of the men's clubs (there are several such within the band) to act as police, and particularly to aid the head chief in the conduct of the buffalo hunt.

Note, however, that the head chief's authority is by no means absolute; he is, as Lowie says, "neither a ruler nor a judge." In effect, the head chief is a leader rather than a ruler; it is his function to persuade and influence rather than to command.

This point is well illustrated by the procedure employed among the Crows to settle internal disputes, apparently of frequent occurrence within the band. When quarrels and violence occur between members of the same clan, these are resolved by the older kin, acting as clan heads. But when a feud threatens between clans, the head chief, his police, and influential chiefs belonging to neutral clans exert all their powers to prevent further hostilities and restore peace. These efforts are often successful, for the Crows, continually at war with their neighbors, fully realize the values of band solidarity. As Lowie makes clear:

Under normal conditions the clans were *not* warring against each other, but expected to form a united front against hostile aliens. It is on behalf of such union that the police society pacified aggrieved tribesmen and that neutral clans repeatedly strove for reconciliation. . . . [In one feud] outsiders figure as vainly pleading with the combatants: "It is bad, don't do it, *we are one people;* all our children are related to one another, don't do it." [3]

But there are other occasions, mainly the annual buffalo hunt, when the head chief and his police may resort to force rather than persuasion to maintain order. In such instances, the police "severely whipped any one who prematurely attacked the herd, broke his weapons, and confiscated the game he had illegally killed." [4] Here the need for a winter's supply of food and the fact that this need cannot be adequately served without the closest coordination of effort within the band more than justify, in Crow eyes, the head chief's authority over his tribesmen. It should be noted, however, that such displays of authority are rare; apart from such special occasions as the community buffalo hunt, bandsmen are allowed to act pretty much as they please, subject only to the discipline of public opinion. Among the

[3] Robert H. Lowie, *The Crow Indians* (New York: copyright 1935 by Rinehart & Co., Inc.), pp. 10–11.
[4] *Ibid.,* p. 5.

Crows, as among the others we have described, the threat of ridicule and the obligations imposed by kinship are normally sufficient deterrents to antisocial behavior.

To conclude: the Crow band is a union of localized clans who (1) habitually live and travel together within a well-defined territory, (2) have the same enemies against whom they wage continual though petty warfare, and (3) regularly engage in at least one large community enterprise, the annual buffalo hunt. The clans, though autonomous in their own internal affairs, acknowledge the authority of the head chief, his police, and the band council in matters affecting the welfare of the band as a whole. This authority may only occasionally be backed by force—as in the conduct of the annual buffalo hunt; more often, it rests on the ability of the chiefs to persuade and influence their followers. And this ability rests, not on any impersonal authority vested by law in the chiefs, but rather on their personal achievements as warriors and on the respect and esteem in which they are held by band members as a whole.

5. THE SAMOANS OF POLYNESIA

Band organizations similar to that of the Crow are widespread among nonliterate peoples. Frequently, too, we find two or more bands living in adjacent territories, sharing a common language and culture, and enjoying friendly though sporadic contacts with each other, as in the case of the three Crow bands we have just described. Such bands are often referred to as forming a "tribe," though, as we have noted with the Crow, the tribe, so defined, is not a political, but rather a social entity.

It occasionally happens, however, that local groups organized as bands are combined into larger political units. For an example of such an organization, let us turn now to the Samoans of Polynesia.

The Samoans live on a small group of fourteen volcanic islands lying just north of 180 degrees east longitude and 20 degrees south latitude. Their territory, some 1,200 square miles in extent, supports a population estimated at more than 50,000. Samoan technology includes both horticulture and fishing and is sufficiently productive to enable the relatively sedentary Samoan villages to be closely spaced on the several islands. As expert navigators and boat-builders, the Samoans make frequent interisland voyages, so permitting a high degree of interaction, not only between villages on the same island, but also between those separated by the sea.

The principal kinship unit among the Samoans is the household, a large joint family whose members, often numbering fifty or more, live in several adjacent houses. It is governed by a head man, who has charge of family ceremony and ritual and who organizes and directs its economic activities. This head is chosen by the family from among the older men and retains his position only so long as he maintains the respect and esteem of his kin.

Households are further grouped into villages, each of which numbers ten or more households, not all of which are related as kin. The village is a locally autonomous political unit, and owns, as a corporation, a certain bounded territory (on which its members build their houses and grow their crops), communal fishing grounds, and a large community house for meetings, ceremonies, and the entertainment of visitors. It is governed by a village chief, chosen by the group, who is aided by a council or *fono,* composed of titled men or so-called "nobles." The village chief and council both legislate and judge for the village as a whole, and, as well, direct and control all community enterprises. Their decisions, however, are not made by voting; instead, each noble has, as part of the prerogatives of his title, the right to make decisions on certain matters. Once these decisions are made and backed by the council, they are strictly enforced. A villager who disobeys or ignores legislation or judgments by the council may have his property confiscated or destroyed and, in extreme cases, suffer banishment as well.

A man's position and role in a Samoan village depend on whether or not he possesses a title, or, having one, on the rating of his title. Titles are of two kinds: those which make one a sacred chief and those which designate orators or talking chiefs. Both categories are elaborately subdivided, for there are numerous grades of both sacred and talking chiefs. Sacred chiefs are believed to radiate supernatural power harmful to untitled commoners, and this power increases with the rank of the chief. Thus, the higher sacred chiefs must never be touched by commoners, must be addressed in a special ceremonial language, and must in general be treated with great circumspection. In public the sacred chief remains silent, allowing his orator or talking chief to speak for him when necessary. At feasts and ceremonies, the sacred chief sits in a specially favorable position, is served first with the best food, and is privileged to eat foods forbidden to others.

Talking chiefs, on the other hand, have no such supernatural powers; they are the executive officers, the custodians of tradition, the masters of ceremony, and the judges of etiquette. They must accordingly have a wide and detailed knowledge of custom and ritual, and be especially skillful as orators. Very often, by reason of their association with high ranking sacred chiefs, the orators wield great power, and are in fact more influential in everyday affairs than the sacred chiefs they represent.

Titles and the powers that go with them are not hereditary among the Samoans, but must be acquired by long and arduous preparation. Depending on their importance, titles are awarded by households, villages, or districts to men having courage, charm, integrity, skill, and demonstrated capacity for leadership. Birth in a family possessing high titles, while it helps a young man achieve one, does not insure it; he must, like others not so fortunate, prove himself worthy of a title. Young men compete vigorously for titles, each seeking to outdo the rest in warfare and economic pursuits, and to cultivate, as best he can, proper deportment, oratorical ability, ceremonial knowledge and skills, and numerous similar prerequisites of rank. Few men acquire their first titles, usually minor ones, until they are thirty or over, and the higher titles usually go to older men, mature and experienced. When a man becomes very old, he resigns most of his titles, so making them available to others, and retains only the lesser titles necessary to hold his place in the village council.

Though the Samoan village is locally autonomous, it is usually associated with other villages in a larger political entity called a district. This is governed much in the same way as the village, that is, by a district chief and a district council. The district chief is the sacred chief with the highest title in the district, and his village is regarded as the capital of the district. The district council is composed of other high-titled chiefs from the villages within the district.

The district chief and council function principally to adjudicate disputes between the member villages and to prevent warfare between them. The association of villages in a district is wholly voluntary, for any village may decide to leave one district and join another, or even to remain independent. However, the wide prevalence of warfare between villages and districts makes it almost mandatory for a village to have allies that it may not be destroyed by its enemies.

Villages, whether or not they belong to the same district, come together often for trade, ceremonies, and feasting, as long as friendly relations obtain between them. But these friendly associations are frequently interrupted by intervillage and interdistrict warfare. Such hostilities may arise from many causes, including disputes over boundaries and the awarding of titles, insults offered to sacred chiefs and other high personalities, revenge for the murder of a chief, and sometimes simply through a desire for increased prestige and status.

Ordinarily, warfare is conducted by small raiding parties, composed of young men anxious to prove their worth to titles, whose objectives are to secure the heads of enemy warriors as trophies and to make slaves of the women. In some cases, however, when serious provocation has been offered, the victors may destroy an enemy village or force the survivors to pay heavy indemnities.

The district appears to be the largest political grouping extant among the Samoans; there is no record of a government holding sway over the entire Samoan "nation." But it does happen, very rarely, that a single man may acquire the highest chiefly titles in the four major districts—those on Upolu and Savaii, the two largest islands of the group. Such an individual possesses enormous status as a sacred chief and is potentially the "king" of all Samoa, since the smaller districts are necessarily unable to produce one of equal stature. In actual fact, however, the "king" has no power to rule the entire archipelago, nor is there any "national" political machinery to effect this end. And since such an accumulation of titles is necessarily acquired late in life, the kingship is short-lived. When the incumbent dies, his titles, which like others are not hereditary, are usually divided among others.

Samoan political organization, it is evident, is a step toward a larger political unity, whereby localized bandlike organizations (the villages) are combined into larger districts. The district is, however, an unstable unit, subject to serious disruption by intervillage warfare and apparently incapable of exerting any considerable control over its member villages. It is, indeed, primarily a defensive alliance, contrived to preserve at least a measure of peace among its members, the better to withstand attacks from the outside. In this respect, of course, it resembles the Crow band which, as we have noted, combines clans in a voluntary organization expected to form a united front against hostile aliens. But the Crow clans have another motivation toward unity, their cooperation in the annual buffalo hunt, while no similar economic factor appears to strengthen the Samoan district.

Finally, the wider scope and larger population of the Samoan district are apparently due to ecological factors: the Samoan technology and environment permit a higher concentration of population than is physically possible among the Crow. It is this higher density of population, permitting frequent and continual contact between villages, that leads to the district and even to a potential "national" or "tribal" unity. These fail to develop, except in the unstable district, for the lack of any compelling motivation (other than defense) to cooperation between villages.

6. THE LEAGUE OF THE IROQUOIS

The Iroquois-speaking Indians of northern New York and Canada, whose clan system and political functions were discussed previously (see Chapter 13, § 9), offer an excellent example of tribal government and of the formation, under stress of warfare, of an intertribal confederacy. The League of the Iroquois, formed under the legendary heroes Hiawatha and

Dekanawida about 1570, is one of the most elaborate forms of government developed by the American Indians north of Mexico.

Archeological and historical researches indicate that the Iroquois tribes moved into northeastern United States and the adjacent areas of Canada from an earlier homeland centering near the mouth of the Ohio River. They probably came as separate tribes, though closely related in language and culture. Nothing is known of their earlier government except for the fact, as stated above, that the League—a tight union of five tribes (the Mohawk, Seneca, Oneida, Onondaga, and Cayuga)—came into existence in 1570, apparently in a move to preserve peace between these tribes and so unite them against their common enemies, their Algonkin-speaking neighbors. Later, in 1715, the Tuscarora, also Iroquois-speaking, were admitted as the sixth "nation," following the League's expressed ideal of eventually combining all Indian "nations" into a union to preserve peace.

Each Iroquois tribe is made up of several villages, varying in population from 300 to 3,000 individuals. These local groups are closely spaced within a well-defined territory and, though probably autonomous in village affairs (largely governed through kinship usages), owe a common allegiance to a tribal council. Fishing and hunting rights belong to the tribe as a whole and are available to all without restriction. Farming lands, however, are owned by the lineages who cultivate them. The villages move from time to time in search of virgin lands, since Iroquois methods of cultivation lack any techniques for fertilizing and restoring the soil. Iroquois economy, then, is based on horticulture, fishing, and hunting, and, while it produces no exchangeable surplus, it does provide a good living for a relatively high concentration of population.

Each Iroquois clan is represented on the tribal council, the ruling body for the tribe and its court of highest appeal. Council members, always men, are chosen for their personal achievements and ability by the councils of the clans they represent, and can be removed by the same body, should they fail in their duty to clan or tribe. All council meetings, whether of the clan or the tribe, are public affairs, well attended, and the actions of its members are accordingly under continuous and close observation. In a very literal sense, then, the Iroquois tribal leaders work only under the eyes of their constituents and are held directly responsible for their acts and rulings.

As with the Crows, Iroquois warfare is normally a matter of small-scale raiding, and the organization and direction of war parties is generally left to the initiative of ambitious young men, eager to gain honors and prestige. In theory the Iroquois tribe is at war with all peoples with whom it has no definite treaty of peace. But warriors may sometimes be restrained, by either the tribal or the League council, should these feel it desirable to prevent open hostilities with a neighbor. In other instances, though these are rare, the tribes within the League may unite their forces in a general war directed against an enemy common to all. In all warfare and raiding, however, the objective is either to destroy an enemy or to gain personal glory and prestige, for the Iroquois do not engage in warfare for conquest and economic exploitation.

The League council consists of fifty sachems, unequally distributed among the five member tribes. These are chosen, as we have described in Chapter 13, by a complex procedure from specified lineages in which the position is hereditary. The League council meets once a year in regular session, though special sessions may also be called, if needed, by any member tribe. It has primary jurisdiction, both executive and judicial, over any intertribal matter, that is, over disputes or decisions which affect relations between member tribes or require their cooperation. Each matter is discussed exhaustively, usually in the presence of a large number of visitors from all the tribes, for League councils are great occasions and well attended. After everyone, including both sachems and others, have had their say, the sachems vote. To go into effect, the decisions of the League council must be unanimous; any matter on which unanimity cannot be obtained must be dropped. It is significant, however, that the council rarely fails to reach agreement; evidently the need for intertribal harmony far outweighs, in most instances, the special interests of member tribes. Note, too, that the rule of unanimity gives each tribe equality in the League council, despite the fact that some tribes have more sachems than others.

It is evident that the League developed mainly as a defensive alliance between autonomous tribes faced with a common enemy. But it is probable that such an alliance was made easier by the fact that the Iroquois tribes, even before their alliance, were similar in language, culture, and tradition, and the further fact that Iroquois tribal structure lends itself readily to expansion. The League council, like the tribal council, is formed of representatives from its constituent bodies, its deliberations are public and subject to the immediate pressure of public opinion, and, finally, the League council is limited to intertribal matters, just as the tribal council confines itself to interclan matters.

As a confederation, the League directs and coordinates the voluntary activities of its member tribes; it does not function, as a state, to coerce these into specified lines of action. This is evidenced by the rule of unanimity in the League council: the League never acts until all its members have agreed on a course of action. Given the subsistence economy of the Iroquois, it it is not difficult to see why a statelike organization did not emerge among them. There could be no central authority or elite sufficiently strong to dominate the tribes either politically or economically. The League thus differs no whit in principle from the Crow band or the Samoan village or district, for it is governed, as these are, by leaders chosen for their personal qualities and achievements, and who govern, not by force or the threat of force, but rather by persuasion and influence.

7. THE AZTECS OF MEXICO

We turn now to political organizations illustrative of the state, the last of our major categories. States differ from bands, tribes, and confederacies in many respects, but most importantly in the fact that the state possesses a centralized authority with power—backed by armed force if necessary —to enforce its decrees. Such power is rare if not nonexistent in the forms of government previously discussed, where persuasion and influence, as we have seen, are the principal governing techniques.

The so-called Aztec Empire provides an excellent example of the state, especially since it is, in part at least, a transitional form, revealing in its structure the traces of an earlier tribal order. To the best of our knowledge, the Aztec Empire had its beginnings with a small tribal unit confined to the Valley of Mexico. These people evidently had a horticultural economy which produced far in excess of their immediate needs. With the exchangeable surplus so formed, there soon developed both a complex specialization of labor and an extensive trade which, in an area of high concentration of population, brought the Aztecs in frequent and profitable contact with neighboring groups of much the same economic and political development. Early in the fifteenth century, the Aztec city of Tenochtitlan, in league with two neighboring cities, Tezcoco and Tlacopan, embarked on a series of military conquests which led ultimately to their economic and political control over most of central and southern Mexico. The conquered cities and states were not destroyed; on the contrary, the Aztecs permitted them to retain local autonomy, demanding only political allegiance to Tenochtitlan, a yearly tribute in goods and services to the Aztec emperor, and exclusive trading rights. It was this economic empire—politically a loose aggregate of city-states controlled from Tenochtitlan—that was conquered by the Spaniards under Cortes in 1521.

The city of Tenochtitlan, at the time of the Conquest, was divided into twenty *calpulli,* small groups not unlike the Iroquois clans, composed of primary families said to be related in the paternal line. Each *calpulli* owned a tract of arable land, a council house, and a temple. The land was allotted in small farms to each family within the *calpulli,* to hold as long as the family continued its cultivation. Families could cultivate their own land, retaining the proceeds for their own support, or rent it to others, but it could not be sold or otherwise alienated from the *calpulli*. On the death of a family head, the land went to his oldest son, or in the absence of such an heir, to another relative within the *calpulli*. Should the family line die out, or a family fail to cultivate its land for two successive years, the land reverted to the *calpulli* for reallotment. Each *calpulli* retained a reserve of land for assignment to younger sons and to be cultivated in common for the support of *calpulli* officials, the temple, and the warriors belonging to the *calpulli*.

Calpulli were governed by a council of family heads. This council was headed by the *calpullec,* who also was in charge of land distribution and who kept a record of land holdings. Together with the council, the *calpullec* adjudicated property disputes and other conflicts between *calpulli* members, administered the public stores, and carried on various other administrative and judicial duties. The *calpullec* was elected by the council but, unless he was demonstrably incompetent, the successor to the position was customarily chosen from one of the sons or other near relatives of his predecessor in office. With other *calpulli* officials, the *calpullec* was exempt from the need to cultivate his own lands; all full-time *calpulli* officers were supported from the *calpulli's* land reserve.

Each *calpulli* had two other elected officers. The *achcacautli* or war chief led *calpulli* warriors in battle, instructed young men in the arts of war, and acted as the police chief of the *calpulli,* preserving internal peace and executing the orders of the *calpullec* and council. The *tlatoani* or speaker represented the *calpulli* in the state council.

The *calpulli* were grouped into four larger divisions of five *calpulli* each, headed by a captain-general who led its forces in battle. The four captains-general formed a military council to advise the king and together were responsible for the maintenance of order within the city.

The state council consisted of the twenty *tlatoani* or speakers, who met at frequent intervals to administer affairs of state, declare war, make peace, and to judge disputes between *calpulli*. In addition, there was also a great council, which included the twenty *calpullec,* the *tlatoani,* the *achcacautli,* the captains-general, the ranking priests, and a number of other state officials. This council judged exceptional legal cases submitted to it by the state council, and, at the death of the king, selected a successor. The king or *tlacatecutli* was always chosen from a single royal lineage, and was usually a younger son or nephew of the deceased king. The king was the supreme military commander and collector and distributor of tribute from the conquered city-states.

It is evident that Aztec political organization, though more complicated and of broader scope than those we have previously described, still retains a measure of democratic procedure. In essence, the center of the Aztec empire was ruled by its citizens, the members of the *calpulli,* who formed the largest single group in Tenochtitlan. To be sure, the positions of *calpullec,* king, and other leaders were in part hereditary, since these were customarily chosen from particular lineages, but we note as well that the choice of a leader depended also upon reputation and ability. Similarly, though the king had great power as a military leader in a state more or less continuously at war, and as the distributor of tribute, this power was, in law at least, controlled by the two councils and so ultimately by the *calpulli* members.

But as Tenochtitlan grew in wealth from its numerous conquests and its ever-widening control of trade, the political pattern gradually underwent a change. Most important, there developed a class division in Tenochtitlan society along socioeconomic lines, as follows:

(1) An upper class, composed of *tecutin* or honorary lords: These were men, *calpulli* members, who were given titles for outstanding services to the state as warriors, merchants, public officials, or priests. *Tecutin* were universally honored and esteemed, had many privileges including certain exemptions from taxation, were preferred for high governmental and military positions, and, most important, were given large estates and shares of tribute by the king, to be held as private property during their lifetime. These rewards clearly made the *tecutin* economically independent of the *calpulli* and, moreover, allied them with the king, from whom their honors and rewards came and who could also withdraw them. *Tecutin,* by virtue of their governmental, military, and priestly posts, were generally members of both councils.

(2) A middle class, composed of *calpulli* members who were not *tecutin.* These formed the bulk of the population of Tenochtitlan, self-supporting through their membership in the *calpulli,* and with a voice in the government through their representatives in the state and great councils.

(3) A lower class, divided into propertyless freemen and slaves. The former were men exiled from the *calpulli* for various crimes and so had no way of making a living except by hiring themselves out to wealthy *tecutin* as agricultural laborers or as porters in the caravans of the merchants. Slaves were similarly dependent for a living on their labor. Neither had a voice in the government. Though initially small, the lower class increased in numbers with increasing conquests, and was of course the more in demand as the *tecutin* class continued to expand.

As these socioeconomic classes emerged and class lines became more sharply drawn, Aztec government moved inevitably in the direction of an absolute, hereditary monarchy. *Tecutin* clearly supported this tendency to their advantage, and increasingly, by various devices, managed to pass on their titles and private property to their heirs, and so move slowly to the formation of a hereditary nobility. At the time of the Conquest, it is probably no exaggeration to say that Aztec government was essentially in the hands of an emergent feudal order, with political power increasingly centered in the king and his *tecutin* rather than in the elected representatives of the *calpulli*.

8. THE INCA EMPIRE OF PERU

Progress toward a hereditary feudal aristocracy was much further advanced among the peoples of Peru, whose empire, conquered by the Spaniards in 1531, represents one of the best examples of this form of government to be found among nonliterate peoples. The Inca Empire developed on the west coast of South America, presumably as the result of a long series of conquests by a people originally limited to the Cuzco Valley in the highlands of southern Peru. At the time of the Spanish Conquest, the Incas held absolute control over a vast territory, extending from southern Colombia to the center of Chile, and from the Pacific Ocean to the western borders of Amazonia in Brazil.

The Peruvian Indians were a horticultural people who, despite a technology based on stone and bronze implements, managed by intensive land cultivation and well-developed irrigation and drainage systems to produce with a high degree of efficiency. As a result, there was in Peru and the neighboring areas of Ecuador, Bolivia, and northern Chile, a considerable concentration of population. Archeological and historical evidence indicates that this region had long experienced large and populous cities, many of which were, from time to time, organized into statelike governments, ruled by kings and emperors. The empire of the Incas represents the latest of these great kingdoms, built by force of arms through the successive conquest of neighboring peoples. It reached the height of its development shortly before the Spanish Conquest; the small Spanish army under Pizarro succeeded largely because the Inca Empire itself had begun, through internal dissension and civil war, to fall apart.

The ancient Peruvian society, at the height of its development, was divided into four major classes: the ruling Inca nobility, composed of the emperor and his relatives, who were said to be more or less directly descended from the sun god; the Curacas, composed of the nobles of conquered states and their descendants; the *puric* class, made up of men between the ages of twenty-five and fifty, their wives, and their relatives older than fifty and younger than twenty-five; and the *yanacuna* (men) and *acllacuna* (women), a class of hereditary craftsmen and servitors to the Inca aristocracy. Membership in these classes was determined almost entirely by birth; exceptions occurred only when sons of Curaca were made Incas by adoption and when sons or daughters of *purics* were selected to enter the ranks of the *yanacuna* and *acllacuna,* respectively.

All political and economic power was vested in the Incas and Curacas, the members of which assumed positions appropriate to their rank in the governmental hierarchy. At the top of this hierarchy stood the emperor, the Inca who was the eldest son of the previous emperor and who was believed to be the direct lineal descendant of the sun god. The emperor was not only the supreme political authority, he also owned all the property in the empire, had the power of life and death over all his subjects, and served as general of the armies, supreme judge, and chief priest. Indeed, there is good evidence to the effect that the emperor was himself believed to be a god, before whom all others, regardless of rank, were obliged to exhibit the utmost deference and respect.

Four viceroys, each having charge of one of the quarters into which the empire was divided, formed an imperial council to advise the emperor. These were chosen from the emperor's closest relatives, usually his brothers and uncles. The choice was made by the emperor and, like all officials, the viceroys' term of office continued only at the pleasure of the emperor.

The quarters of the empire were divided into provinces of 40,000 households, each ruled by an Inca governor. Provinces, in turn, consisted of four tribes of 10,000 households each, and the rulers of these could be either Incas or Curacas. Tribes were subdivided into ten units of 1,000 households and each of these into halves composed of five centuries, each century numbering 100 households. Like the provinces, the centuries and units of 500 and 1,000 households were governed by Inca or Curaca nobles, depending on whether they were located in originally Inca-ruled areas or in provinces gained by conquest. Finally, the century was divided into halves composed of five decuries each, and a decury was made up of ten households. The heads of decuries and units of five decuries were usually *purics,* but these officials had little power; they functioned merely as aides to the centurion, the Inca or Curaca in charge of the century.

All the officials in this hierarchy, from the centurion up to the emperor, functioned both as administrators and as judges. But no official had a great deal of independent authority; in general, he functioned only on orders sent down from the emperor, and he was required to report his actions periodically to the officials above him and through these to the emperor. To insure the efficient functioning of this system, the emperor had at his command a corps of extra-hierarchial officials, who constantly traveled through the empire and reported any irregularities directly to their chief. The emperor, too, made periodic tours of inspection, during which he held court and considered appeals from the rulings of his subordinates. To enforce his authority, the emperor could, if the occasion demanded, quickly raise an army to put down any official who might attempt to defy the authority of the supreme ruler.

The *purics* or householders were the largest of the four classes in the empire and the economic mainstay of the government. Their actions—indeed their lives—were carefully controlled by law. Each man married at the appropriate time and, on his marriage, was assigned land enough to support himself and his wife. As his family increased, so did his land assignment, changed each year to meet his needs. When his children grew up and married, the land assignment was decreased proportionately and at fifty or shortly thereafter, the *puric* retired from active labor to be supported by the community in which he lived.

Taxes were paid in labor; each *puric* was obliged to spend part of his time working for the state as an artisan, craftsman, soldier, laborer, or in any other capacity in which he could serve. Part of this reservoir of labor power went to support the state religion, part for public works (i.e., irrigation projects, buildings, bridges, or roads), part for army service, part to support the members of the *puric's* own community who were prevented from supporting themselves by old age, sickness, or disability, and part to the support of the families of *purics* absent on government service.

No *puric* could leave his community except by order of the state; the clothing he wore, designed by state officials, symbolized not only his social status but his native community as well. Similarly, though no law-abiding *puric* was allowed to suffer hunger or other basic deprivation, he was also not allowed to accumulate land or other forms of wealth, or in any way to become economically independent of the state. Local markets, where they existed, dealt only in minor exchanges; the bulk of exchangeable surplus, in food, tools, weapons, minerals, cloth, and other products, was stored by the government to be issued as needed to various portions of the empire. All of the finer goods went to embellish and adorn the temples and the palaces of the nobles; it is in these places that the Spaniards found the incredibly rich treasures in gold and silver at the time of the Conquest.

To keep this governmental system functioning and to provide for the needs of the population, the Incas took a complete census of both property and human resources each year. Excess population was drained off by taking young men and women from *puric* households into the *yanacuna* and *acllacuna,* respectively, or by moving whole groups of *purics* to under-populated areas or unfavored regions made habitable by irrigation or other land-conserving techniques. The excess wealth of the empire was used for public buildings, temples, roads, bridges, and many similar benefits, and to extend the conquests of the Incas far beyond their original borders. In effect, the Inca state maintained its rigid authoritarianism largely through being constantly at war. It began to fall apart only when it had succeeded in conquering all who could seriously oppose it. The Spanish Conquest did not initiate the fall of the Inca empire; it merely completed, perhaps prematurely, a decline which had already begun.

9. SUMMARY

The contrasts drawn in the preceding sections suggest that the following factors are important to an understanding of the growth and development of political structures.

(1) Ecology, or the patterns of culture whereby a people adjust to their environment, undoubtedly plays a large role in the initiation of political systems and in some aspects of their further development. Where, as with the Eskimos or Western Shoshoni, ecological factors make for a thinly spread and nomadic population, true political groupings are essentially impossible. Political structures appear only when ecological factors permit permanent groupings larger than the family, as with societies like the Crow. Further, there is good evidence that political structures are more complex and wider in scope in areas where food resources are such as to permit a people, given an adequate technology, to achieve a high concentration of population.

(2) Economic patterns of culture seem also to be linked to political patterns, at least in part. In subsistence economies, political groupings tend to be of the band, tribe, or confederacy type, while, with surplus-producing economies, as among the Aztecs and Incas, we find states or statelike political systems. Linton emphasizes this correlation especially for the conquest state, formed by the subjugation of weaker groups by stronger ones. Conquest states, according to Linton, "are nearly always associated with patterns of settled life and a degree of technological advance which makes it possible for a population to produce an economic surplus." [5]

It should be noted, however, that these statements do not imply that political systems are invariably determined by economic factors alone. A correlation of economic patterns of culture with political patterns does not

[5] Ralph Linton, *The Study of Man* (New York: copyright 1936 by Appleton-Century-Crofts, Inc.), p. 243.

mean that these necessarily stand in a cause-effect relationship. It suggests merely that some common factor possibly underlies both economic and political development.

(3) Patterns of warfare, like economic patterns of culture, appear to be linked with the development of political systems. It is notable, for example, that warfare is rare or lacking among peoples like the Eskimos and Western Shoshoni, where no true political organization exists. Similarly, in the cultures of the Crows, Samoans, and Iroquois, warfare appears to be continuous, and directed toward the end of raiding for small economic gains, the achievement of personal glory and status, and, less often, the extermination or expulsion of enemy groups. In no case, however, does warfare, at this level of political development, lead to conquest and economic exploitation. Such warfare occurs only with the larger and more complex conquest states, illustrated by the Aztecs and Incas.

We need not conclude from this of course that warfare and conquest are essential to the maintenance of the state, as it exists among the present-day peoples of the world. There is much in modern history which suggests that the conquest state is slowly giving way to one in which warfare, if only for its increasing threat of total destruction, must disappear.

Our study of political systems among nonliterate peoples also helps clarify certain widespread misconceptions such as so-called "primitive communism" and the supposed "anarchy" of allegedly primitive societies. The simpler political systems, as we have seen, are in essence democratic —small communities governed very largely through chiefs and councils selected by the group for their age, wisdom, and demonstrated capacity as leaders. These leaders tend to govern more by persuasion than by force; indeed, in most cases, they lack any power but that of directing and co-ordinating the voluntary activities of the subordinate units making up the political structure.

The investment of leaders with the exclusive right to employ force or coercion in government occurs only with the formation of the conquest state. As our survey illustrates, the conquest state, among nonliterates, is characteristically a monarchy with political power and often economic power as well, concentrated in a small hereditary elite. Modern representative government, as illustrated by European and American democracies, is unknown to nonliterate societies. This becomes understandable when we realize that representative government is recent even in Europe, dating back no earlier than 1789 with the breakdown of the earlier European monarchies. Associated with the development of representative government is the so-called industrial revolution, whereby an earlier agricultural economy slowly gave way to one based on power-driven machinery, mass production, and the extensive development of business and trade. In effect, this important economic development appears to be a necessary correlate to representative government in all of its present forms. And since non-literate societies obviously lack a machine-age technology and its economic correlates, it is not difficult to understand the corresponding lack of modern representative government.

Finally, we may say with Linton that, despite the long history of man's experiments in government, the problems of governing and being governed have not yet been perfectly solved. Linton goes on to say:

The modern world, with the whole experience of history to draw upon, still attacks these problems in many different ways and with indifferent success. One thing seems certain. The most successful states are those in which the attitudes of the individual toward the state most nearly approximate the attitudes of the uncivilized individual toward his tribe. If the members of a state have common interests and a common culture, with the unity of will which these give, almost any type of formal governmental organization will function efficiently. If the members lack this feeling of unity, no elaboration of formal governmental patterns or multiplication of laws will produce an efficient state or contented citizens. How such unity may be created and maintained in great populations and especially in fluid ones where the individual's close, personal contacts are reduced to a minimum is probably the most important problem which confronts us today.[6]

COLLATERAL READING

Fortes, M. and Evans-Pritchard, E. E., eds. *African Political Systems.* London: Oxford University Press, 1940. Introduction.

Hogbin, H. I. *Law and Order in Polynesia: A Study of Primitive Legal Institutions.* New York: Harcourt, Brace and Co., 1934.

Lowie, Robert H. *The Origin of the State.* New York: Harcourt, Brace and Co., 1927.

————. *Social Organization.* New York: Rinehart and Co., 1948. Chapters 7, 14.

Steward, Julian H. "The Economic and Social Basis of Primitive Bands," *Essays in Anthropology Presented to A. L. Kroeber,* ed. Robert H. Lowie. Berkeley: University of California Press, 1936. Pp. 331–350.

————. *Basin-Plateau Aboriginal Sociopolitical Groups.* Bulletin 126, Bureau of American Ethnology, Washington, D. C., 1938. Pp. 230–262.

[6] Ralph Linton, *The Study of Man* (New York: copyright 1936 by Appleton-Century-Crofts, Inc.), p. 252.

ETHNOGRAPHIC REFERENCES

Andamanese: Coon, 1948, Chap. 6; Radcliffe-Brown, 1922.

Aztecs: Coon, 1948, Chap. 15; Murdock, 1935, Chap. XIII; Thompson, 1933; Vaillant, 1941.

Crows: Lowie, 1935; Murdock, 1935, Chap. X.

Eskimos: Birket-Smith, 1936; Coon, 1948, Chap. 4; Murdock, 1935, Chap. VIII; Rasmussen, 1908, 1931.

Incas: Means, 1931; Murdock, 1935, Chap. XIV.

Iroquois: Morgan, 1901; Murdock, 1935, Chap. XI.

Karieras: Radcliffe-Brown, 1931, Part I.

Samoans: Murdock, 1935, Chap. III; Turner, 1884.

Western Shoshoni: Steward, 1938.

Chapter 16

RELIGION

1. WHAT RELIGION IS

As we have noted in previous chapters, human cultures everywhere include patterns of social organization, designed to regulate the social interactions of individuals. Within a particular society, the members can understand the behavior of most people and they may even predict how an individual will react in given situations. Similarly, every culture includes a body of techniques—its technology—by means of which its participants produce their food, clothing, shelters, tools, and weapons. Within this area of knowledge, events are, in general, predictable: wood, properly treated, may be made into a bow or a shelter; clay, appropriately selected and manipulated, can be shaped into pottery vessels; stone, rightly chipped or ground, yields tools, weapons, and other artifacts.

But it is also true that human beings sometimes fail to behave predictably and that techniques prove undependable. An ordinarily even-tempered person falls into an inexplicable rage, a faithful wife or husband suddenly deserts his spouse, or an apparently healthy individual sickens and dies for no apparent cause. A favorite bow, hitherto sound, breaks; a piece of stone, despite careful handling, cannot be shaped into a tool or weapon; a mass of clay, though treated in the usual manner, fails to hold its shape or produce an adequate vessel. Careful hunting does not produce game, an unexpected rain or hail storm destroys a season's crop, or a herd, despite all precautions, is depleted by disease. Despite knowledge and time-tested techniques, many everyday activities are subject to failure—not the failure

469

that results from lack of skill or knowledge, but a failure that is inexplicable, unpredictable, and therefore mysterious.

As a result of events like these, disturbing to the even tenor of daily activity, every society that we know develops certain patterns of behaving, designed to guard, by one means or another, against the unexpected, and better to control man's relationships to the universe in which he lives. It is this area of culture that we shall call religion.

Because no people have achieved complete certainty either in interpersonal relations or in technology, religion is inevitably a part of every culture. To be sure, the forms of religious behavior vary enormously from one society to the next; there are almost countless differences in belief, ritual, and other aspects of religious practice. But we must not be deceived by these differences and dismiss all religions but our own as mere conglomerates of magical practices and superstitions. With our knowledge of medicine, it perhaps seems strange that the Navahos hope to cure tuberculosis by an elaborate nine-day ceremony, or that the treatment of disease among nonliterate peoples so frequently calls for praying, dancing, and singing rather than for careful treatment in a hospital or clinic. The fact is, of course, that few nonliterates share our considerable medical knowledge; to them, illness and disease, with few exceptions, can be treated only as unexpected events, not controllable by ordinary means. And it should not be forgotten that even in our own society there are many who quite sincerely believe that disease is best cured by prayer and faith rather than by medical knowledge.

Religious patterns of behaving center, then, about the uncertainties of living, and are particularly evident at times of crisis. Sometimes these are so-called life crises, such as birth, adolescence, marriage, illness, and death; some or all of these occasions are, in nearly all societies, the stimuli for ritual and ceremony. Other crises affect the society as a whole, like a food shortage, for example, in an Eskimo village. At such a time, the families in the village will come together, and, under the direction of a religious leader called a shaman, attempt to discover by magical means the cause of the shortage. Similar group ceremonies frequently mark a change of season, especially when, in an agricultural community, such a change results in a radical change of activity. Examples are found in harvest rituals, ceremonies to prepare fields for planting, and religious activities, like the Hopi Snake Dance, intended to bring rain to a growing crop.

It follows from what we have said that religion, like other patterns of culture, is not to be separated from the total cultural matrix. Religious patterns of behaving are in fact inextricably combined with both technology and social organization and find much of their meaning in this combination. To illustrate this point, let us turn for a moment to the gardening activities of the Trobriand Islanders, a Melanesian people who live north of the eastern tip of New Guinea.

The Trobrianders, according to Malinowski, are expert horticulturists, who work hard and systematically to raise their crops, principally yams, taros, and coconuts. Their land is fertile and well-watered, and their tools, though made of stone, shell, and wood, are sufficient to work the soil. Native techniques of horticulture are indeed more than adequate. Malinowski tells us that the Trobrianders "produce much more than they actually require, and in any average year they harvest perhaps twice as much as they can eat." [1]

Nevertheless, it would be a mistake to describe Trobriand gardening wholly in technological terms. To the native, gardening involves a veritable maze of technical and magico-religious procedures, neither of which may be separated from the other. The garden magician, as he is designated by Malinowski, is an important village official, preceded only by the village chief and sorcerer. Each year he performs

. . . a series of rites and spells over the garden, which run parallel with the labour, and which, in fact, initiate each stage of the work and each new development of the plant life. Even before any gardening is begun at all, the magician has to consecrate the site with a big ceremonial performance in which all the men of the village take part. This ceremony officially opens the season's gardening, and only after it is performed do the villagers begin to cut the scrub on their plots. Then, in a series of rites, the magician inaugurates successively all the various stages which follow one another—the burning of the scrub, the clearing, the planting, the weeding and the harvesting. Also, in another series of rites and spells, he magically assists the plant in sprouting, in budding, in bursting into leaf, in climbing, in forming the rich garland of foliage, and in producing the edible tubers. [2]

To sum up this section, it is now evident that religion includes all those patterns of behaving whereby men strive to reduce the uncertainties of daily living and to compensate the crises which result from the unexpected and unpredictable. Through religion men attempt to control, by magic, prayer, sacrifice, and numerous other ritual devices, the area of their universe which does not consistently yield to the secular technology. In so doing, men presuppose a world of supernatural beings, related to and in-

[1] Bronislaw Malinowski, *Argonauts of the Western Pacific* (New York and London: copyright 1932 by E. P. Dutton & Co., Inc., and Routledge and Kegan Paul Ltd.), p. 58.
[2] *Ibid.*, p. 300.

terested in man, who are variously called spirits, demons, deities, and gods. To communicate with these beings, and to secure their aid or assuage their anger, there are men with special powers and abilities, such as priests, shamans, magicians, or sorcerers, who serve as media between the human society and the supernatural world.

In the sections that follow we shall examine the major aspects of religion in some detail, to gain a greater understanding of both the nature and variety of religious beliefs and practices.

2. THE CONCEPT OF IMPERSONAL POWER

One of the most interesting and widespread of religious phenomena is the belief in a generalized and impersonal force, influence, or power that exists invisibly throughout the universe, and which may be possessed, to a greater or less degree, by gods, men, the forces of nature (such as the sun, moon, rain, or thunder), and natural objects such as pools, rivers, sticks, and stones. It should be emphasized that this force or power is wholly impersonal, that it is never embodied as such in a supreme god or deity. Gods may possess greater or less amounts of power but they are never the embodiments of power.

The notion of an impersonal power is, rather, a kind of explanatory principle, used to account for experiences out of the ordinary or events which cannot otherwise be explained. Thus, the Algonkin Indian term for impersonal power—*manitou*—is applied, not only to holy beings (gods or spirits) and to religious practitioners (priests and shamans), but as well to anything that is remarkable, wonderful, or inexplicably unusual. Similarly, Codrington says that *mana* (the Melanesian term for impersonal power) is that which "works to effect everything which is beyond the ordinary power of men, outside the common processes of nature." Codrington illustrates this point as follows:

If a man has been successful in fighting, it has not been his natural strength of arm, quickness of eye, or readiness of resource that has won success; he has certainly got the *mana* of a spirit or of some deceased warrior to empower him, conveyed in an amulet of a stone around his neck or a tuft of leaves in his belt, in a tooth hung upon a finger of his bow hand, or in the form of words with which he brings supernatural assistance to his side. If a man's pigs multiply, and his gardens are productive, it is not because he is industrious and looks after his property, but because of the stones full of *mana* for pigs and yams that he possesses. Of course a yam naturally grows when planted, that is well known, but it will not be very large unless *mana* comes into play; a canoe will not be swift unless *mana* can be brought to bear upon it, a net will not catch many fish, nor an arrow inflict a mortal wound.[3]

In Polynesia, the concept of *mana* works similarly to justify and rationalize a complex social system whereby individuals are ranked according to their birth and achievements. Polynesian communities are characteristically divided into social classes, which range from the chief and his family at the top of the social scale through many intermediate rankings to the war captives and slaves at the bottom. Rank, together with the ability to serve successfully in its functions, is direct evidence of the possession of *mana* and a measure of its quantity. Chiefs, as long as they are successful, have the greatest amount of *mana,* and may be superseded only by certain priests when these are actually possessed by their tutelary divinities. At other times, priests rank below the chiefs. Divinities, of course, by virtue of their divine nature, have more *mana* than humans, but they, too, are ranked among themselves and so do not all have the same degree of *mana.*

Mana thus accounts for social position and for successful achievement. But it also accounts for failure. Should a famous warrior be killed and eaten by the enemy, it is clear that he has somehow lost the *mana* which made him famous. The chief's *mana* is believed to protect him and his village from disaster, but should the village suffer defeat in war, many illnesses and deaths, or any other misfortune, it is proof that the chief has lost his *mana* and that he must, accordingly, be replaced by another.

The same is true of *mana* possessed by natural objects or artifacts. A stone of unusual shape may be buried in a garden; if exceptional crops result, the stone has *mana.* But should later crops fail to be exceptional, the stone has lost its *mana* and so become just an ordinary object of no value. A weapon with which a warrior is successful, or a canoe that is fast and handles well, are said to possess *mana* and are so enhanced in value. But should the weapon break for no apparent reason, or the canoe fail to perform, their *mana* has been dissipated.

Mana, in parts of Polynesia, is obtained by inheritance: the child takes *mana* from both his parents and so has more than either. In other regions of Polynesia, *mana* must be achieved by careful observation of the proprieties and by successful performance as a warrior, priest, chief, or craftsman. But even where none is inherited, achievement is also important, for the possession of *mana* can be evidenced only by successful performance, as we have already seen.

Similarly, artifacts—such as tools, weapons, canoes, and other manu-

[3] R. H. Codrington, *The Melanesians* (Oxford, 1891), pp. 118–120.

factured articles—are given *mana* by careful construction and a rigorous performance of all the ritual details pertinent to their building. Building a canoe, for example, requires both the craftsman's art and that of the religious practitioner (the craftsman usually is also a priest of his art), so that each step of the long and tedious process of building a canoe may be accompanied by the appropriate ceremony. Lacking such ritual observance, the canoe lacks *mana,* and is therefore no more than a miscellaneous assemblage of pieces of wood. Again, of course, even a properly constructed canoe may fail to exhibit the *mana* supposedly imparted to it in the building—should it, for example, turn out to be a slow and clumsy craft—for the test of *mana* lies ultimately in performance.

Another function of *mana,* and illustrative of its power, is that of taboo. One who possesses *mana* may lay a taboo, or prohibition, upon a bit of property and so forbid all others (of lesser *mana*) to touch or use it for fear of supernatural punishment. An especially interesting example of taboo is given by Linton, who witnessed the following incident in the Marquesas:

Very little authority was exercised over children, and practically none over the eldest who, as has been explained, outranked his parents. These infant family heads could do practically anything they pleased. In the valley of Puamau, I once visited the local chief, who had a boy of eight or nine. When I arrived, the chief and his family were camping in the front yard, and the boy was sitting in the house looking both glum and triumphant. He had had a quarrel with his father a day or two before, and had tabooed the house by naming it after his head. Until he lifted the taboo, no one in the family could enter the house.[4]

Taboo also resides in gods, men, and artifacts possessing great *mana.* A high chief, possessed of such *mana,* cannot be touched by one of lesser *mana,* for his person is itself taboo, and is believed to be physically dangerous to others. Among some Polynesian groups, the highest sacred chief virtually lives alone, for no one may approach him, use anything he uses, enter his house, or even allow the shadow of the chief to fall upon him. Similarly, the weapons of a famous warrior, possessed of much *mana* by virtue of successful performance in warfare, are taboo to warriors whose *mana* is less than that of the possessor of the weapons.

To sum up, it is now clear perhaps that the concept of impersonal power —whether it be the *mana* of Melanesians and Polynesians, the *manitou* of Algonkin Indians, or the many similar concepts of other peoples—is in essence an attempt to regularize and rationalize the uncertainties and ap-

---

[4] Ralph Linton, "Marquesan Culture," *The Individual and His Society* by Abram Kardiner (New York: copyright 1939 by Columbia University Press), pp. 158–159.

parent irregularities of human experience. As an explanatory principle, impersonal power is complete and self-sufficient. It accounts for all in the past and present and provides as well advance explanations for future events. Exceptional success, outstanding leadership, unusual performance, and all that is divine, supernatural, and wonderful is so because it possesses power. The power is amoral—neither good nor evil—and so it accounts equally for god and demon, priest and sorcerer, the outstandingly good man and the successful scoundrel. Though power may be either inherited or acquired through successful performance, it may always be lost. Accordingly, the concept of power rationalizes both success and failure, for while success indicates the possession of power, failure just as inevitably means its absence.

3. PERSONALIZED SUPERNATURALS

Though beliefs in an impersonal power are widespread, it must not be assumed that such beliefs preclude the conception of gods, spirits, and other similarly personalized supernaturals. In Melanesia and Polynesia, for example, where, as we have noted, *mana* is a dominant religious pattern, we also find a wide variety of personalized supernaturals. The same is true of other areas; indeed, it may be said that in no area that we know of is religion confined to the conception of impersonal power.

Animism, the most general of beliefs having reference to supernatural beings, is defined by Tylor, one of the first to use the term, as follows:

It is habitually found that the theory of Animism divides into two great dogmas, forming parts of one consistent doctrine; first, concerning souls of individual creatures, capable of continued existence after the death or destruction of the body; second, concerning other spirits, upward to the rank of powerful deities. Spiritual beings are held to affect or control the events of the material world, and man's life here and hereafter; and it being considered that they hold intercourse with men, and receive pleasure or displeasure from human actions, the belief in their existence leads naturally, and it might almost be said inevitably, sooner or later to active reverence and propitiation. Thus Animism, in its full development, includes the belief in souls and in a future state, in controlling deities and subordinate spirits, these doctrines practically resulting in some kind of active worship.[5]

It should be noted that animism, especially where it involves the belief in spirits who dwell in pools, trees, or other similar things, must carefully be distinguished from animatism, the doctrine that certain objects or nat-

[5] E. B. Tylor, *Primitive Culture* (Boston, 1874), Vol. I, pp. 426–427.

ural phenomena which we should consider inanimate are themselves capable of sentient action and movement. Animatism apparently never gives

rise to religious sentiments, nor does it inspire the worship of the object said to be animated. The California Indian who believes that a tree may kill him, if it so desires, by dropping one of its branches upon him does not therefore venerate the tree nor believe that the tree contains a spirit to be worshiped. He merely avoids trees or exercises great care when passing under them. On the other hand, the same Indian may avoid a certain pool because of the belief that it is inhabited by a malevolent spirit who will drag him under to be drowned, and he may further attempt to propitiate such a spirit by offerings. Animism, illustrated by the second example, is, then, a belief or set of beliefs in supernatural beings, whether they originate in the souls of once living creatures or have existed from the beginning of time as supernaturals, who may dwell in natural phenomena such as trees, pools, and mountains, in artifacts, such as weapons, houses, or boats, or who may simply exist invisibly in some portion or all of the universe.

Fig. 16:1. Zuñi supernatural being as impersonated in a ceremony (the Shalako).

The variety and types of supernatural beings in which men believe is so great as almost to defy either enumeration or classification. There are, first, the great and more remote gods or deities who commonly are believed to control the universe or some aspect of it and who are frequently held to be the creators of the present world. Next comes an enormous division of spirits, found in many varieties and with highly diverse characteristics. Spirits are usually closer to man and more concerned in his daily actions.

They may be beneficent, malevolent, or neutral toward men; they may dwell in certain localities (pools, mountains, towns, houses, and so on) or range the universe without limit; they may function as guardian spirits for temples, homes, or even individuals; they may be awesome, terrifying, lovable, or mischievous; or they may combine some or all of these functions and characteristics.

A final broad category of supernaturals includes the souls of the dead, the ghosts, who, freed by the death of the body, nonetheless retain an active interest and even a membership in the society of the living. These, too, may be beneficent or malevolent and possess many of the functions and characteristics of spirits. But they differ from spirits, not only in their origin, but as well in their greater affinity for man's society and in the fact that they more closely resemble man in appetites, feelings, emotions, and behavior.

Merely to illustrate the variety of supernatural beings in a single culture, and to apply our very rough classification, let us turn again to the Chiricahua Apaches. As we have noted before, the Chiricahuas are a nomadic, food-gathering folk, who live in small communities in the semiarid mountain country of New Mexico and Arizona. (See Chapter 13, § 3.)

Despite the fact that the Chiricahua pantheon is only loosely organized, it is possible roughly to distinguish our three classes of supernaturals—gods, spirits, and ghosts. In the first category, we find four major divinities: Life-Giver, White Painted Woman, Child of the Water, and Killer of Enemies. Life-Giver is the least defined of these, a "nebulous and remote Supreme Being," [6] according to Opler, who is credited with the creation of the universe but who is never described as a personality and is indeed only rarely referred to in both myth and ceremony. It is quite possible, as Opler says, that

Life-Giver is apparently a symbolization of supernatural power as such, the reservoir from which particular power grants and ceremonies flow. The European influence in this greater personalization of diffuse supernatural power can be inferred from the synonyms for Life-Giver, which are Yusn (from the Spanish *Dios*) and "He Sits in the Sky." [7]

Here, then, is a possible illustration of how a concept of supernatural and impersonal power (as described and illustrated in § 1) may be in a process of transformation, through culture contact, to that of a Supreme Being.

[6] Morris E. Opler, *An Apache Life-Way* (Chicago: copyright 1941 by University of Chicago Press), p. 280.
[7] *Ibid.*, ftn. 21, p. 281.

White Painted Woman, Child of the Water, and Killer of Enemies are far more concrete gods and figure prominently in both myth and ceremony. Child of the Water was most important at the beginning of time, when he, with the small aid of his older but far less effective brother, Killer of Enemies, made the earth habitable for man by ridding it of dangerous monsters. Now, as Opler says, "he is almost a sky-god, magnificent and rather remote" [8] and direct contact between him and the Chiricahuas occurs only rarely. "For ceremonial purposes, White Painted Woman is the feminine counterpart of Child of the Water, and the time of her direct impingement upon worldly affairs, too, is at an end." [9] Together with these deities, there are many others, mentioned frequently in the myths, but no longer actively concerned with the Chiricahuas. Among these are the malevolent monsters killed by Child of the Water—the Giant, the great Eagles, the Buffalo Bull, and the Antelope.

The Chiricahua Apache spirits are far more numerous and much more intimately concerned with present-day people. Among the more important of these supernaturals are the Mountain Spirits, the representatives of a "people" said to live in the holy mountains. The Mountain Spirits not infrequently visit the Apaches, particularly on the occasion of ceremonies, and they play a considerable role in the mythology and as a source of the so-called Masked Dancer rites. They are held in great "fear and reverence" by the Apaches, according to Opler, who goes on to say:

It is evident from some descriptions of the Mountain People that they are considered not only the denizens of a given mountain but also the custodians of the wild life ranging in the vicinity. Often . . . stories have the "holy homes" of the Mountain People richly populated with game animals. . . .

Anyone who is in the vicinity of a home of the Mountain People . . . sprinkles pollen toward the holy place and prays, "Protect us from enemies and do not let harm befall us while we are near you." Those who are in need are advised to appeal to the Mountain People: a man [i.e., a shaman] . . . said, "Any time you are in trouble or in danger from animals, pray to the Mountain People, and they will come from the mountains and protect you." [10]

There are also Water Beings (a beneficent spirit, called Controller of Water, and one who is malevolent, Water Monster), and a host of others, associated with natural phenomena or with animals that are particularly important as a source of power for curing. One of the animal spirits, Coyote, deserves special mention for his prominence in the myths. In these

[8] *Ibid.,* p. 281.
[9] *Ibid.*
[10] *Ibid.,* p. 280.

stories, Coyote plays many roles: he is the butt of tricksters, he ignores and flagrantly violates Chiricahua morals, and, on occasion, he functions as the innovator who brought to the Chiricahuas some of their most valued cultural possessions.

Finally, we find the ghosts of the dead as a third category of Chiricahua supernaturals. The dead are greatly feared by the Chiricahuas, and every effort is made to obliterate their memories as soon as possible. Occasionally, however, the ghosts of the dead do not remain in the underground afterworld to which they should retire, but return to visit, often in dreams, their living friends and relatives. Such visits are greatly dreaded, as indication that the one visited is soon to die himself. Innumerable precautions are therefore taken to avoid any reference to the dead, so as to stave off possible ghostly visitations.

To sum up, it is evident that the supernaturals we have called spirits play the largest role in Chiricahua Apache religion. The gods are few and remote from most daily activity; their role was played in the creation of the world and in making it fit for human habitation. Ghosts, though supernaturals, are feared but not worshiped; the Chiricahuas do not venerate the ghosts of the dead but seek rather to avoid them and to obliterate all memory of them.

Spirits, on the other hand, are prominent in everyday affairs, and especially so in rites and ceremonies, which are dedicated mainly to curing. Every adult Apache, man or woman, may have a familiar spirit, from whom he receives the access to supernatural power necessary to effect cures. Thus, some have power from owl, snake, and bear, three animal spirits feared and respected for their power, while others have power from spirits of game animals important in Apache economic life. Power from the Mountain Spirits enables a man to present the Masked-Dancer rite, an important ceremony for curing and community welfare. In brief, then, spirits among the Chiricahuas are the media through which the people obtain access to supernatural power and so the ability to cure illnesses, stave off death and misfortune, and otherwise ameliorate the troublesome problems of existence.

4. BAGANDA SUPERNATURALS: THE GHOSTS OF THE DEAD

Though a great many religions are like that of the Chiricahua Apaches in emphasizing the role of spirits, there are others in which the ghosts of the dead take on the more significant role. This is particularly true among the African peoples south of the Sahara, and a good example, to be described in the following, is found in the culture of the Baganda of East Africa.

The Baganda, we have noted before (Chapter 14, § 7), are horticulturists and cattle herders who live in the hilly and well-watered grass lands of Uganda. Their gods are far more numerous and better defined than those of the Apache. They fall into three major classes: clan gods, the deified ghosts of former kings, and tribal or "national" gods. Both clan gods (one for each of thirty-six clans) and those from former kings are, in essence, deified ancestors: they are ghosts of the dead who are not reincarnated, as ordinary ghosts, but raised to the status of deities. Clan gods represent the ancestor of the clan and are worshiped only by their descendants, the living members of the clan they represent. Kingly gods are honored by all—as they were indeed during their lives as kings—but are especially reverenced and used as consultants by the royal clan. Deified kings, then, probably represent an outgrowth from clan gods, the more numerous and important because of the position of authority which the royal clan occupies. Both clan gods and deified kings, it is evident, spring from a cult of the ghosts of the dead, to be described below.

Each of the so-called national or tribal gods has a temple and a cult of priests, supported by contributions from the royal treasury. These gods form the support of the kingdom and the country, and are honored and reverenced by all, royalty and subjects. The national gods are arranged, roughly, into a kind of hierarchy, each of them having a particular area of greatest influence and particular functions for which he is responsible.

Of greatest historical importance is the "father of the gods," Katonda, who is said to have created the universe and all that is in it. Katonda, however, once the creation was achieved, left the universe to his descendants, and he accordingly has but a small and relatively unimportant cult today. He is therefore remote from modern Baganda life, a rather abstract creator god who no longer functions significantly in everyday affairs.

Mukasa, the god of Lake Victoria, is truly the dominant Baganda deity today. He provides fish and controls storms. More important, he is the god of fertility: he sends twins, received with great rejoicing by the Baganda, and provides children to childless women. He is responsible for good crops and increases in the cattle herds, and he serves in general to stimulate and protect good living for all. Even the king frequently consults Mukasa, especially at times of crisis, gives generously to his temples, and provides him with many rich sacrifices.

The remaining gods have lesser functions: Walumbe, the god of death; Kaumpuli, the god of the plague, who is kept hidden in a hole in the earth by his priests; Kibuka and Nende, the gods of war, an important economic activity among the Baganda; Dungu, the god of hunters; Musuka, the rainbow god and special patron of fishermen; Gulu, the god of heaven, and Kitaka, the god of earth; Musisi, who lives in the earth's center and controls earthquakes; Nagawonyi, the goddess who sends rain, protects the growing crop, and receives the first fruits of the harvest; and Nabuzana, the goddess who has special charge of child-bearing women and whose priestesses function as midwives to the Baganda.

Spirits, too, are found among the Baganda, and are particularly associated with streams, lakes, wells, trees, hills, and all other such phenonema of nature. Shrines are often built for the spirits, to serve as their dwellings and the repository for offerings. When a Baganda crosses a stream, takes water or fish from a river or lake, chops down a tree, or otherwise alters the landscape, he is careful to propitiate the resident spirit by leaving an offering. The hills are especially sacred because of the many spirits who live there, even to the extent of providing sanctuary to those who have incurred the wrath of the king or his chiefs.

Most important of all to the Baganda are, however, the ghosts of their dead. When a person dies, his soul leaves his body and is immediately transformed into a ghost, invisible but nonetheless subject to much the same appetites, passions, and feelings as the living. The ghost feels cold, pain, and heat; he may be kindly and affectionate, or angry and vindictive; he may even suffer a second death by fire or by drowning. He is actually still a member of the society, the clan, and the family to which he belonged while alive, and though he exists, as it were, on a supernatural plane, this fact enhances rather than decreases his importance to his relatives and friends.

A newly made ghost goes first to Walumbe, the god of death, and there gives an account of his life. He then returns to the grave in which his former body is buried and takes up residence in a little shrine built for him at the head of the grave. The wives who have borne him children, and who survive him, live also at the grave, tending his gardens, his domestic animals, and his shrine. If these proprieties are well observed, and if suitable offerings are provided at the shrine, the ghost does not disturb his living relatives and friends, but functions, though invisibly, in much the same role as he played during his lifetime.

Should a ghost be annoyed, however, by the neglect of his shrine or grave, or by any improper action of his survivors, he may become malevolent and bring illness, misfortune, or even death to his relatives and friends. On such occasions, a shaman (religious practitioner) must be called upon for advice. The shaman may seek to propitiate the ghost by offerings and by repairing whatever omissions have occurred with respect to shrine and grave. If these fail, and a patient continues in his illness, the shaman may try to catch the ghost and kill him by fire or by drowning. The ghosts of one's father's sisters are said to be particularly and uniformly malevolent and must frequently be so disposed of. Malevolent ghosts sometimes take possession of the living, causing delirium and attacks of frenzy. In such cases, the shaman seeks to exorcise the ghost by making the patient inhale the smoke of burning herbs.

Two years after a person's death, his ghost is reincarnated by entering the body of a newly born child, a member of the same clan and family. The identity of each child is determined at the naming ceremony, when, with appropriate ritual, the child's father's father recites, in the presence of the baby, the names of his deceased clan relatives. The child, it is believed, will laugh when the proper name is spoken, as a sign that it recognizes the name it bore in a previous incarnation. When this has happened, that is, when the ghost of one deceased has been so reincarnated, his grave and shrine are abandoned, since the ghost, now again a soul in a human body, is no longer to be served and propitiated.

The Baganda, it is evident, achieve, through their beliefs in ghosts and reincarnation, a cyclic social continuity which links the society of the living with both the dead and those who are yet to be born. Most of the Baganda leave the society of the living only temporarily, providing of course their ghosts are properly treated and so encouraged to return. It is probable, though data are lacking, that malevolent ghosts, especially if they suffer a second death, are not reincarnated. It is by this avenue that illness and misfortune may be rationalized.

Note, too, that kings are not reincarnated but are made immediately into gods. It is not impossible, though historical verification is lacking, that we have in this deification of kings the sources of the national gods; they are perhaps deified ancestors of renown, whose remembrance has been lost to the Baganda of today.

5. THE GODS OF THE AZTECS

Among the Baganda we have noted the beginnings of a godly hierarchy, with a number of tribal or national divinities, each more or less specialized in function, and each honored by a temple and cult. Nonetheless, the Baganda gods are in general less important than the ghosts of the dead; the national gods represent, as it were, a form of religious specialization, the province of a limited number of priests or other religious practitioners.

This tendency toward specialization in religious belief is even farther advanced among the Aztecs of Mexico, whose supernatural beings are to be described in this section. The Aztecs, as we have said before, were a powerful and warlike people who, at the time of the Spanish Conquest in 1520, dominated most of present-day Mexico. While their basic economic dependence was on horticulture, we noted also the presence of extensive trade, external and internal, an almost continuous aggressive warfare for conquest, and the development of numerous specialized arts and crafts. (See Chapter 15, § 7.)

Like the other peoples whose supernaturals we have described, it is probable that the Aztecs also peopled their universe with gods, spirits, and ghosts. We know little of their concepts of ghosts; however, it is clear that the souls of most of the dead went to a place called Mictlan, an underworld home of the dead, and, though this was not a place of punishment, it was pictured nevertheless as a dreary and uninviting spot. Other ghosts were more fortunate. Those who died of drowning, lightning, or diseases like dropsy and leprosy, went to a paradise called Tlalocan, the residence of the rain gods or Tlalocs, where they enjoyed perpetual summer and all they wanted to eat and drink. Warriors killed in battle, women who died in childbirth, and victims sacrificed as offerings to the gods went to the home of the sun, an even more attractive place than the country of the Tlalocs. Warriors' souls were believed to appear during the day, after having accompanied the sun to the zenith, as humming birds, while the souls of women who died in childbirth escorted the descending sun to the horizon and then spent their nights on earth in the guise of moths. But, though offerings were made to the dead at ceremonies taking place at stated times after their demise, there is no evidence that the Aztecs had any such elaborate cult of the ghosts as we have described for the Baganda.

Spirits also played some role in Aztec religion, though our knowledge is again fragmentary. Hosts of spirits are reported for springs, fields, mountain-tops, households, and individuals (guardian spirits). There were also, apparently, many minor deities, similar to the clan gods of the Baganda, that served as tutelary divinities of families, clans, occupational and trade groups, and many similar social segments. It is notable that the latter appear to be closer to spirits than to ghosts, as among the Baganda.

But the Aztec gods far outshone these lesser supernaturals. There were literally hundreds of gods, specialized in a great variety of functions. They were apparently not too well organized into a hierarchy, or pantheon; single gods often appear with a variety of names and are even differently represented in paintings and carvings. The attributes of gods are also frequently confusing, with considerable overlapping as between one god and another. Part of this confusion undoubtedly springs from inadequate reporting; our only first-hand accounts of Aztec religion are from Spanish priests and soldiers. In part also, it is likely that the Aztecs, as a result of years of conquest and the gradual absorption of alien peoples, adopted many foreign gods to their own earlier, and probably much more limited, stock.

No one of the Aztec gods stood out as a supreme deity. Indeed, the idea of an organized assemblage of gods, with one as the supreme ruler, is relatively rare. It was apparently approached by the Inca of Peru, who regarded the sun as at least a dominant divinity, but is much more common in the older religions of the Near East, and in the offshoots of those found in ancient Greece and Rome. The concept of a single, all-powerful deity is even rarer, and is apparently lacking among all nonliterate peoples. As we know it in Old World history, it seems to have appeared first in Egypt, about 1400 B.C., and after many centuries diffused into Asia Minor. Here, about 800 B.C., the concept emerges in Judaism and Zoroastrianism, and later in Christianity and Mohammedanism. Even in these religions, however, we find constantly cropping up the concept of other, opposed divinities, such as the evil principle symbolized by Satan, and numerous lesser supernaturals, as represented by angels, cherubim, and saints. These are, to be sure, regarded more as derived divinities than divinities in their own right; they possess divine power solely by virtue of their attachment to the supreme being.

To return to the Aztecs, it seems clear that four of their deities stood out as more powerful and important than the rest. One of these was called Tezcatlipoca, who was said to be omniscient, all-seeing, and possessed of eternal youth. In one of his dual characters, he personified the breath of life and had the functions of judging and punishing sinners, humbling the haughty and overbearing, presiding over feasts and banquets, and serving as the patron of military schools. In his second character, symbolized by his representation with a black face, limbs, and body, Tezcatlipoca was the god of darkness, even the malevolent enemy of mankind, and served as the patron of those who practiced black magic, sorcery, and witchcraft. Here, then, is a god that combines into one character both a beneficent and an evil—or at least antisocial—principle.

Quetzalcoatl, the "plumed serpent," had a much wider range in Mexico and Central America, and was found, under various names, among many peoples. To the Aztecs, Quetzalcoatl was the divinity of wind and air, the special patron of the priesthood. According to myth and legend, he brought to the Aztecs the calendar and all their priestly arts and sciences. Once he headed a rich and peaceful empire in Mexico but, yielding to temptation under the machinations of enemies, he fell from his high position, traveled eastward, and disappeared into the ocean. The Aztecs, however, confidently expected Quetzalcoatl to return as a Messiah to restore the golden age, and, when Cortes, the Spanish conqueror, first appeared, the Aztecs thought for a while that he was Quetzalcoatl. This of course gave Cortes a great advantage, even though the Aztecs soon discovered their mistake.

The third of the four great Aztec divinities was Huitzilopochtli, the god of war and more remotely of the sun and of horticulture. He was especially important to the Aztecs, and perhaps original with them rather than borrowed from alien peoples. His great importance lay in his connection with war, which, as we have seen, was a major activity of the Aztecs, and in his patronage of agrarian arts, also basic to Aztec economy.

Finally we find the Tlalocs, apparently a group of divinities in control of rain, water, thunder, and the mountains. As we noted earlier, the land of the Tlalocs was one of the special "heavens" of the Aztec, reserved for people who died in certain specified ways. As gods of rain and water, the Tlalocs were of obvious importance to a nation of cultivators.

In addition to these, there were many separate gods: for each phase of growing maize plants and all other cultivated plants; for fire, lightning, the planets, the sun, and the moon; for the many regional divisions of the empire. There were the god of death and the underworld; the god of hunters and the morning star; the goddess who had charge of sexual sins, confession, and purification; and, finally, the many gods for warriors, weavers, traders, and other similar groups. All these, and more, had their special cults, priests, and ceremonies. The Aztec calendar of rites and ceremony was long and complicated, and, we may be sure, was in charge of a trained priesthood, men and women who devoted their lives to this calling.

It is perhaps worth noting here that as gods assume greater importance in a religion, there is apt to appear as well a greater organization of religious ceremonies and a specialized body of priests to conduct them. Usually, too, an elaboration of supernaturalism is apt to occur in societies which produce an economic surplus and are thereby enabled to support the priests, temples, and cults which are involved. We shall return to this point in later sections.

6. RELIGIOUS PRACTITIONERS: THE SHAMAN

In all systems of religion, individuals are required to perform, or at least assist at the performance of, certain activities by means of which supernatural beings (gods, spirits, or ghosts) are in some fashion propitiated or influenced. In many societies, the prayers of individuals and other similar activities form the bulk of religious acts, but there are few or no societies in which such behavior is not supplemented and guided by religious practitioners. There are nearly always some persons in the society who, by virtue of special training, personality characteristics, or both, are regarded as more skilled than others in influencing or making contact with supernatural beings. To these persons a social group or an individual in difficulties too great for his own personal powers will turn for assistance. Full-time, or in smaller societies with relatively simpler cultures, part-time, religious practitioners are apparently universal.

The term "shaman," in its widest sense, refers to a man or woman who serves a society as a part-time religious practitioner. Sometimes, as among the Eskimos, the shaman appears to be emotionally somewhat unstable, easily subject to epileptic-like fits or frenzies and to self-hypnosis. This is not universally the case, however, for in many societies the shaman is not required by his profession to do more than perform routine and somewhat monotonous rituals. We shall exemplify both varieties, using the Eskimos to illustrate the more emotional shamanistic procedure and the Chiricahua Apaches for the other.

Among the Polar Eskimos, we find that shamans are numerous: almost every family will have one, and there may be several in each winter village. Both men and women may become shamans but, though these practitioners are paid for their services, there are none who devote full time to shamanism. Shamans are always older and highly respected individuals, successful in other pursuits as well as in their religious activities.

To become a shaman, an individual must be visited by spirits while walking alone. When such a visitation occurs, the individual seeks advice from an older and well-established shaman and, under his guidance, has a number of religious experiences during which he talks to one of the outstanding divinities—the oldest and the most powerful of the spirits. This being gives the novice his personal guardian spirit or familiar and instructs him in shamanistic procedures.

Shamans are believed to possess unusual powers; among other things, they are said to call forth or suppress storms and banish or summon game animals. Their most important function is, however, to cure disease, which is thought to result from the loss of the soul. Soul loss is serious, for if the patient does not recover his soul, he will eventually die.

Curing rites take place only when requested of a shaman by a patient. The shaman then initiates the rite by speaking to his familiar spirit in a special tongue, reserved for these occasions and very different in vocabulary and style from the ordinary language. The shaman gradually works himself into a frenzy by singing spirit songs, beating on a drum, and dancing in a wild and uncontrolled manner. As he approaches the state of frenzy, he trembles and groans, and he may sometimes foam at the mouth or become rigid and apparently insensible to pain. He repeatedly calls upon his familiar spirit, and urges him to recover the soul of the patient.

Should the patient recover, the ceremony has been successful. Though no punishment is specifically meted out to shamans who fail in cures, a consistently unsuccessful shaman will, like a similarly unsuccessful physician in our society, fail to receive calls from patients, and so suffer both economic loss and a lowered prestige. Shamans, if they so desire, can turn their powers to evil purposes, by stealing and hiding the souls of their victims, and so causing them to sicken and die, unless the soul is restored by another shaman. Accordingly, especially powerful shamans are regarded with both respect and fear, and treated with great circumspection lest they retaliate by magical means.

Like the Eskimo, any adult Chiricahua Apache may become a shaman, and most adults have at one time or another undergone the vision experience necessary to become one. In the Apache vision experience, which may occur in dreams or when awake, a spirit, usually in the form of an animal or one of the Mountain People (see § 3), speaks to the visionary and offers him access to supernatural power. If the person so approached is responsive, he is transported, in his vision, to the home of the supernatural being, taught a ceremony or rite, and returned to the place from which he started. So instructed, the shaman is now usually prepared to administer the rite, once his familiar spirit (the supernatural who appeared in his vision) gives the signal. Contact with the spirit is maintained, however, and especially in the actual performance of the rite, or in the preparations that are made for it.

Ceremonies may also be learned from other shamans, without the vision experience. It is assumed, in these instances, unless indications to the contrary appear, that the spirit who first transmitted the ceremony approves the transfer and the recipient. Shamans, as they grow old, not infrequently so transmit their ceremonies to younger relatives and friends.

As among the Eskimos, the primary function of the Apache shaman is to cure disease. He may also use his power to search for lost objects, to discover the location of enemy warriors, to find and capture fugitives from justice, to bring success in warfare, love, games, and other enterprises, and to weaken the enemy and provide invulnerability from attack. But the ceremonies of the Apaches, and the performance of the shaman in them, afford a decided contrast to those of the Eskimos, as will be made evident in the following generalized description.

The Apache shaman goes into action only when called upon by a patient, who approaches him with certain specified ceremonial gifts. He need not accept every case that is offered, but chooses those he wants. The shaman, once he has accepted a patient, also controls the time and the place of the ceremony, and may even limit the number of participants and visitors he will permit to attend.

Once these preliminaries are determined, the shaman begins by rolling a cigarette and blowing smoke to the four directions, saying each time, "May it be well," and perhaps intoning a brief prayer for peace and security. He then addresses a prayer to his familiar spirit for aid in curing the patient, describes how he acquired the ceremony, and expands upon its virtues. At this point, the shaman may mark the patient—and others who are present—with pollen or some other similarly sacred substance.

Following this, the shaman begins to sing a series of songs (obtained from his familiar spirit) and to intersperse these with prayers. In this manner he seeks to call the spirit and to have him indicate, by some sign (apparent, usually, only to the shaman) the nature of the patient's disease and the techniques to be used in curing it. When this indication comes, the shaman performs any one of a number of acts, depending on the information received. He may administer medicinal herbs, suck foreign objects from the patient's body, or simply intensify the singing and praying to the accompaniment of various other ritual actions. At the end of the ceremony, the shaman not infrequently imposes certain food restrictions on the patient or gives him an amulet to be worn for further protection. In all this, we call especial attention to the deliberate nature of the shaman's actions, as compared to the frenzied behavior of those among the Eskimos. While Apache shamans may sometimes "struggle" with their familiar spirits, urging and pleading with them in repeated songs and prayers, they never put themselves into fits or trances.

Apache shamans, like those of the Eskimos, are paid for their services, though none make their living by this means alone. A failure to cure does not irreparably injure a shaman's prestige, unless of course it occurs too frequently. Apache shamans, too, may occasionally—or even consistently —use their powers for witchcraft and black magic, to injure and even kill people instead of curing them. Moreover, exceptionally successful curers must ultimately pay their familiar spirits for their success—such payment consisting either of the shaman's own life or that of one of his younger relatives. Accordingly, the successful shaman, especially if he is old and still apparently healthy, may be regarded by his relatives and associates with respect mixed with almost pathological fear—the fear that they may be called upon to recompense the source of his power.

To sum up, the shaman may be described, first, as a part-time specialist in religious functions, unlike the priest, who, as we shall see in § 7, devotes all his working time to these ends. The shaman, because he is found in societies which do not possess the economic facilities to support an organized religious institution, performs his religious duties in addition to others necessary to make a living.

Secondly, the shaman receives his powers either through direct experience with supernatural beings in dreams or visions, or, less often, from another shaman who has had such direct experience. He may not, like the priest, receive power simply by virtue of training and membership in a religious group, for the society to which he belongs does not possess such groups.

Third, because shamanism involves direct contact with supernatural beings, the shaman is usually a person who is emotionally less stable than his fellows, and so more than ordinarily susceptible to visions and dreams. In societies, like the Eskimo, where a shamanistic performance involves the shaman in fits, frenzies, trances, and the like, these psychological characteristics are of course emphasized.

Finally, it may be mentioned that the shaman usually functions in small, relatively private ceremonies, given at the instance of a single supplicant, in difficulties which he cannot control unaided. This is not always the case, however, as is seen when an Eskimo shaman holds a ceremony for a whole village to alleviate poor hunting conditions, or when an Apache shaman conducts a Girl's Puberty Rite (see § 9), a public ceremony attended by all in the local group and sometimes by members of other local groups as well. In these functions, the shaman is more like the priest, who ordinarily is in charge of group ceremonies.

7. RELIGIOUS PRACTITIONERS: THE PRIEST

The priest, in contrast to the shaman, is a full-time religious practitioner, who gains his powers very largely through his association with an organized religious group, and not alone through his ability to establish contact with supernatural beings. Priests are usually prepared for their profession by a more or less intensive training, and their performance, though on occasion not unlike that of the shaman, is ordinarily the result of such training rather than the result of inspiration or possession by a god or spirit. Though priests may of course conduct rites and ceremonies of a relatively private nature, they are most often in charge of an established calendar of rituals, laid down by the cult to which they belong, and performed at more or less regular intervals by all or some of the cult membership. The existence of priests in a society usually presupposes, then, a relatively high degree of religious organization.

We are of course familiar with religious practitioners of this sort in our own society, for the description given above applies in general to priests of the Roman Catholic and Eastern Orthodox churches, to ministers, pastors, and preachers in Protestant churches, and to rabbis in Jewish religious organizations. Among nonliterate peoples, full-fledged priesthoods occur in many societies, particularly in West and East Africa (for example, among the Dahomeans and Baganda, respectively) and among the Aztecs and Incas of the Americas. These societies, it should be noted, are technologically well advanced and practice economies which permit considerable specialization and a more or less intricate division of labor. In societies lacking such economic organization, priesthoods and organized religious groups tend also to be absent.

Fig. 16:2. Zuñi priest of one of the ceremonial societies.

There are, however, numerous societies whose religious practitioners share some of the characteristics of both priests and shamans. This is true, for example, among the Zuñi, a horticultural, pueblo-dwelling people of New Mexico, whose economic and social organization is not unlike that of the Hopi. (See Chapter 12, §§ 4, 6, and Chapter 13, § 8.)

All Zuñi adult males are members of a kiva society which performs sacred dances at appropriate intervals. A male may also become a member of a curing society, especially if he has been treated for an illness by the society, and so participate in its rituals. If he exhibits in high degree the personality characteristics valued by the Zuñi, such as sobriety of conduct, piety, and lack of social aggressiveness, he may be given a formal office in a kiva or curing society by its leaders—usually called priests. Subsequently, as vacancies occur, he may rise through a series of offices to become the head priest of a society, and if this be one of certain designated societies, he may become one of the small group of head priests who actually govern the Zuñi village.

The behavior of Zuñi priests, while in many ways not unlike that of shamans, is the result of long and careful apprenticeship in kiva and curing society rituals. In the main, this behavior is marked by sobriety, reverence, and respect, involves the careful and exact performance of long and complex rituals, and the recitation or singing of painstakingly memorized prayers and sacred songs. In brief, the Zuñi religious practitioner derives his special powers and influence from membership in an organized cult (the kiva or curing society), and not from a personal visitation from supernatural beings in dreams and visions. Among the Zuñi, a man who performed by personal revelations in the manner, let us say, of an Eskimo shaman, would probably be regarded as demented, and perhaps even killed or tortured for witchcraft. The one characteristic shared by the Zuñi religious practitioners with the shaman is that he is a part-time specialist who, like men who are not priests, must engage in farming, hunting, and gathering to make a living. Zuñi priests gain only respect and high position for their work; they are not supported as paid professionals.

Support for a priesthood comes only, as we have said, in societies in which the economic organization permits full-time specialization in religious activities. A good example is found among the Dahomeans, who live in West Africa in the French colony of Dahomey. Like the Baganda of East Africa, the Dahomeans are organized as a kingdom, once large and powerful but now reduced to a puppet state under French control. The Dahomeans are primarily agricultural and, though they lack the highly developed cattle complex of the East Africans, they do possess a number of domestic food animals, including sheep, goats, pigs, poultry, and a few cattle. In economic organization, the society is quite as advanced as the Baganda, with considerable trade and a complex specialization of labor.

Dahomean religion, while dominated by ancestor worship, is also marked by a large number of great or public gods, who are believed to support and protect the kingdom and the people. These are divided into three major hierarchies or pantheons: of the Sky, the Earth, and the Thunder. Most important, but in no sense a supreme deity, is Mawu, the moon goddess who rules the Sky pantheon with her husband Lisa, the sun god. These are the parents of most of the other gods, who have been assigned their domains by Mawu. Of the many lesser divinities in the Sky pantheon, Gu, the god of metals and of warfare and the giver of tools and weapons, is the most prominent. It need hardly be added that warfare is one of the principal economic supports of the kingdom.

The Earth pantheon is ruled by a twin pair called Sagbata, the first-born of Mawu, whose mating produced all the others, all of whom are males. Sagbata is extremely important to the Dahomeans since it is this divinity, or divine pair, who insures abundant crops. Sagbata also punishes evildoers by causing grainlike eruptions on their bodies, and so is also the god of small pox and other skin diseases. The Thunder pantheon, finally, is ruled by Xevioso, the second son of Mawu. He has general control over rain, thunder, fire, and the sea, but delegates some of this to Agbe, a particular god of the sea, and to numerous lesser deities in charge of various kinds of rain and thunder, of the waves and other aspects of the ocean, and of specific bodies of water.

Each pantheon has its own cult and sect of adherents. Not all Dahomeans belong to a cult, and many are only nominal members, as, in our own society, many people are only Christians or Jews in name. Members of the royal clan never join the cults—they worship only their clan gods and ancestors—and there is considerable opposition to the cults on the part of the government, which suspects them of subversive activities. Nevertheless, the cults do possess large numbers of adherents, divided into numerous temple groups. The cults appear to be equal in status, though the Sky cult, with the most elaborate ritual, has fewer members than either of the other two.

The establishment of a temple—and there are scores in Dahomey, each devoted to a particular god of one of the pantheons—requires a long and elaborate series of rites and sacrifices. In the course of these, an image of the god is installed on a platform inside a circular house of mud and thatch. Each temple has a full-time chief priest or priestess, a number of part-time assistant priests drawn from the older cult members who know the rituals, a group of lay initiates called "wives" of the god, and a body of novices who are undergoing initiation and who live in special dwellings on the temple grounds. The priests and the temples are supported by gifts from their adherents, whose families must give a large sum of money at their initiation, and may receive as well some support from the government. Ceremonies are usually of three kinds: secret rites performed within the temple by the chief priest alone, rituals performed in the temple for initiated members, and large public spectacles. Though in other portions of West Africa, cults similar to these—called secret societies—are often powerful agencies in government, the Dahomean kings have shorn their cults of any political power and keep them under strict surveillance.

It is clear, of course, that the Dahomean priesthood is little organized, as compared, let us say, with the many tight hierarchies of priests in our own western European civilizations. As cultures grow in importance and in the number of their participants, religious organizations, like political forms, tend to increase both in numbers of adherents and in the complexity of their organization. Dahomean religious organization stands, as it were, at the beginning of such development, while our own religious groups are the result of many centuries of growth and specialization.

8. MAGIC AND RELIGION

Magic, in the words of Frazer, involves two basic assumptions: first, "that like produces like, or that an effect resembles its cause; and, second, that things which have once been in contact with each other continue to act on each other at a distance, even after the physical contact has been severed." [11] The first assumption, according to Frazer, underlies what may be called homeopathic or imitative magic; the second, contagious magic.

A well-known and very widespread instance of imitative magic is found in the belief that an enemy may be injured or killed by injuring or destroy-

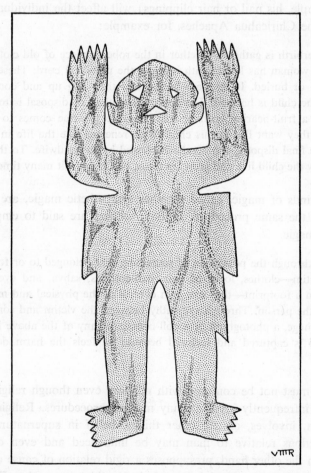

Fig. 16:3. Doll of handmade paper used by some Mexican Indians in witchcraft. After von Hagen.

[11] Sir James Frazer, *The Golden Bough*, Abridged Ed., one vol. (New York: The Macmillan Co., 1928), p. 11.

ing an image of him. The magician prepares the image very carefully, making it of mud, clay, wood, or some other like material. Various incantations or charms may be recited, to identify the image with the intended victim. Then the image is damaged or destroyed. It is believed, of course, that the victim will suffer just in those places on his body that the image is injured; thus, a knife or point inserted into the arms or legs of the image will cause wounds in the arms or legs of the victim. Similarly, if the image is destroyed, the victim will die.

Contagious magic finds illustration in another widespread belief: that harm, or good, done to something once closely associated with an individual (for example, his nail or hair clippings) will affect the individual as well. Among the Chiricahua Apaches, for example:

> The afterbirth is gathered together in the robe or piece of old clothing upon which the woman has knelt. With it is put the umbilical cord. These must not be burned or buried. If they are buried and then dug up and consumed by animals, the child is harmed. The approved method of disposal is to place the bundle in a fruit-bearing bush or tree "because the tree comes to life every year, and they want life in this child to be renewed like the life in the tree." Before the final disposal, the bundle is blessed by the midwife. To the tree she says, "May the child live and grow up to see you bear fruit many times." [12]

Both kinds of magic, called together sympathetic magic, are often involved in the same procedure. In Bali, witches are said to employ sympathetic magic,

> by which through the possession of something that belonged to or formed part of the victim—clothes, locks of hair, nail-cuttings, saliva, and even the soil taken from a footprint—they can gain control of the physical and mental condition of the person. Through sympathy between the victim and something of his—his image, a photograph or a doll containing any of the above ingredients —his soul is captured and tortured because he feels the harm done to his image.[13]

Magic must not be confused with religion, even though religious practices not infrequently involve many magical procedures. Religion, as we have seen, involves, among other things, belief in supernatural beings, whose actions relative to man may be influenced and even controlled. Magic, on the other hand, presupposes a rigid relation of cause and effect, unaffected by supernatural beings. It is for this reason that Frazer and

[12] Morris Edward Opler, *An Apache Life-Way* (Chicago: copyright 1941 by University of Chicago Press), p. 8.
[13] Miguel Covarrubias, *Island of Bali* (New York: Alfred A. Knopf, 1938), p. 351.

others have regarded magic as analogous to science, with its equal dependence on the assumption of a rigidly ordered universe. We must not, however, regard magic as the forerunner of science, as is sometimes done. The antecedents of science lie, not in magic, but rather in the practical knowledge of the outside world, in the homely techniques of trial and error, and in the testing of hypothesis by careful experiment.

To illustrate the role of magic in religion, let us present a highly abbreviated account of Navaho curing, there as among the Chiricahua Apaches the most important function of the religious practitioner. The Navaho believes that illness is the result of neglect of certain restrictions on his behavior, sorcery, contact with dead bodies or with ghosts, and a number of similar factors that impair his harmony with the universe. When he becomes ill, he resorts first to divination, a magical procedure whereby a shaman determines the nature of his disease. Divination, among the Navahos, commonly takes one of two forms: ritual trembling and gazing. In ritual trembling, the diviner's body begins to shake, first gently in the arms and legs but increasing in force until the whole body shakes violently. In the course of this seizure the diviner, guided by his power or familiar spirit, sees the symbol of some ceremony and so, because ceremonies are linked to particular diseases, is enabled to diagnose the illness of the patient. Gazing means looking with concentration at the sun, moon, or one of the stars. It is sometimes accompanied by trembling, but the diviner, in this practice, usually sees the symbol of the ceremony diagnostic of the disease as an after-image of the object on which he has fixed his gaze.

The next step is to be cured of the illness, first by reviewing one's past behavior with a shaman to discover and confess the specific acts responsible for the illness. After this, the ceremony appropriate to the illness must be performed, to expel the evil produced in the patient by his actions and to attract good in its place. Evil is expelled literally by taking emetics and cathartics, by sweating, fasting, bathing, and strict continence. In the course of the ceremony good is attracted to the patient by placing him on a sand painting and so allowing him to absorb the power of the deities depicted therein.

Here is an excellent example of sympathetic magic, for the sand paintings of the divinities possess the power to heal by virtue of the fact that they are precise representations of these deities. By placing the patient on the sand painting, rubbing his body with sand taken from the representations of the deities, and touching the patient with various articles contained in the shaman's ceremonial bundle, the powers of the supernatural beings so symbolized are conveyed into the patient's body, to fill him with good and restore him to health.

Magic, to sum up, is a body of techniques and methods for controlling the universe, on the assumption that if certain procedures are followed minutely, certain results are inevitable. It presupposes an orderly universe of cause and effect, not one in which events may occur unpredictably at the whims and fancies of supernatural beings. Nonetheless, magic is frequently associated with religion, as a technique with which to attain certain desired religious ends. It is, indeed, a method of compelling, by its own logic, the aid of the supernaturals: to the Navaho, the contact of the patient with the sand pictures of the supernaturals results inevitably in a flow of curative power from these gods and spirits to the patient.

It is easy, of course, to come to the belief that magic attains desired results. An enemy whose image is destroyed occasionally dies; the pouring of water from a pottery bowl is sometimes followed by rain; the Navaho patient not infrequently gets well. And if magic fails, there are many reasons: the complex procedure prescribed was incorrectly performed; other and more powerful magicians worked toward a contrary end; the universe is large and incompletely known and so certain inimical forces may have prevented success. Successes are remembered where failures are forgotten; in the absence of written records, successes are easily overestimated. Finally, to men who know and understand little of the universe, the belief in magic is comforting. Despite failures, magic affords the hope that, if the proper manipulations are made and the appropriate formulae recited, the universe may become more predictable and knowable, and eventually both understood and controlled. So magic, in many ways, fulfills both the psychological functions of religion and the practical functions of science.

9. RITUAL AND CEREMONY

Magic, insofar as it is connected with religious observances, is only one of the ways in which men seek to control the supernatural powers. Another, which is far more intimately linked to religion, is found in ritual and ceremony, both of which are directed toward the supplication and appeasement of supernatural beings. Where magic, as we have noted, compels supernatural aid in various ways, ritual and ceremony operate on the assumption that divine beings, like men, can be moved to pity, appealed to for justice, pleased by sacrifices and offerings, and, if they are malevolently disposed, propitiated and even bought off by gratifying their desires and appetites.

A ritual may best be defined, perhaps, as a prescribed way of performing religious acts, that is, of praying, singing sacred songs, dancing to the gods, making sacrifices, or preparing offerings. A ceremony, on the other hand, involves a number of interconnected and related rituals, performed at a given time. The Sunday morning service, at many of our Protestant churches, exemplifies a ceremony, which may include such rituals as reciting the Lord's prayer, singing prescribed hymns, and performing the sacrament of communion.

A more useful distinction may be drawn, however, in terms of the functions of rituals and ceremonies. At one extreme are those which center about individual life crises —rituals and ceremonies that mark such occasions as birth, naming, puberty, marriage, illness, and death. These are often called rites of passage. At the other extreme are so-called rites of intensification, that is, rituals and ceremonies that mark occasions or crises in the life of the community as a whole, such as the need for rain, defense against an epidemic or pestilence, preparations for planting, harvests, the initiation of communal hunting or fishing activities, and the return of a successful war party. Some rituals and ceremonies may serve both functions; an example is found in the Navaho ceremony called the Night Chant, given ostensibly to cure an individual of some illness, but actually serving

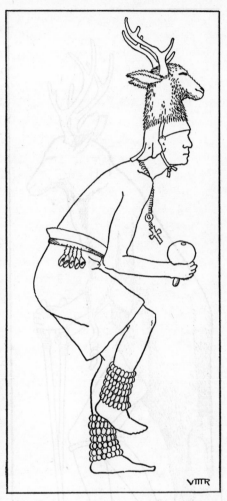

Fig. 16:4. Deer dancer, a performer in a Yaqui ceremony.

as well to enhance the well-being of the whole community. To illustrate these matters in more detail, let us describe some of the salient features of the Girl's Puberty Rite, an important Chiricahua Apache ceremony.

When an Apache girl experiences her first menstruation, this event, which marks her transition from girlhood to young womanhood, is celebrated by a rite of passage. This is called a "little ceremony," to distinguish it from the more elaborate Puberty Rite, of which it is a highly abbreviated form. It takes only a few hours and is attended only by the girl's family and some of their friends. An older woman serves as the girl's sponsor and attendant, and takes her through a brief ritual to insure good health and long life, while a shaman sings a number of sacred songs dedicated to the same end. At the end of these rituals, the family of the girl distributes gifts of food, tobacco, and other articles to the guests and onlookers.

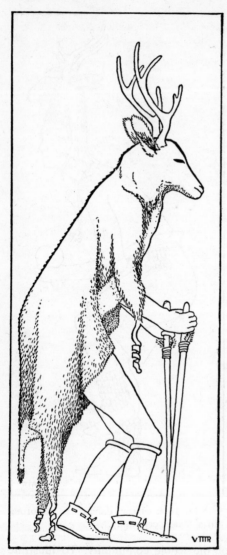

Fig. 16:5. Taos deer impersonator.

"Little ceremonies" necessarily occur at irregular intervals, since they are set by physiological changes taking place in particular individuals. Later, however, the girl goes through the longer and more elaborate Girl's Puberty Rite, often in company with other girls who have also passed their first menstruation and experienced the "little ceremony." This ceremony, though it does in fact celebrate the onset of puberty, is also a rite of intensification, designed to bring blessings, not only to the girls, but to the whole community, and to welcome these young women as prospective wives and mothers. Today, the Girl's Puberty Rite occurs but once a year as a regular annual event, and it is likely that a similar—but perhaps more frequent—regularity marked its performance in aboriginal times.

The Girl's Puberty Rite is made up of many rituals. On the morning of the first day, the shaman in charge directs the construction of the ceremonial structure, a large tipi, built especially for the occasion. Materials are brought together, holes are dug to receive the four main poles, and tall spruce trees selected to form this substructure. The shaman recites a prayer and, to the accompaniment of a rattle, sings the sacred songs which must accompany the building. It is a solemn ritual, to produce a ceremonial home, linked symbolically to White Painted Woman, an important Chiricahua divinity.

Many of the remaining rituals center of course about the adolescent girl. She must be dressed in a certain specified manner by her attendant, and taught to observe ritual restrictions on her eating, drinking, and other activities. Every morning of the four-day ceremony, the attendant leads the girl to a space before the entrance to the ceremonial tipi, "paints" her with sacred pollen, and gives her a ritual massage or "molding," praying the while that the girl may lead a good life and live long. Then the girl makes four ceremonial runs to the east, passing clockwise around a basket of ritual objects placed a few paces from the ceremonial structure. Many of the onlookers may run with her, to share her blessings and to pray, as they run, for good health and a long life. As the ritual comes to an end, the girl's family throw out presents of food to the crowd.

At night, the girl and her attendant are ritually conducted inside the ceremonial tipi by the shaman. There, while the girl alternately rests on an untanned hide and dances slowly back and forth, the shaman sings a long series of songs, interspersed with prayers, to conduct the girl "symbolically through a long and successful life." As one of Opler's informants puts it:

We think of a woman's life as blocked out in parts. One is girlhood, one is young womanhood, one is middle age, and one is old age. The songs are supposed to carry her through them. The first songs describe the holy home and the ceremony. Later come the songs about the flowers and the growing things. These stand for her youth, and as the songs go through the seasons the girl is growing up and reaching old age.[14]

In the meantime, another important series of rituals is going on in the cleared space before the ceremonial structure. Here appear a number of masked dancers, dressed to represent the Mountain Spirits, who perform about a big fire to the accompaniment of singing and drumming by a group of men seated near the tipi entrance. The masked dancers are in charge of a second shaman, who has spent many hours preparing them ritually for their dancing. In the course of the ceremony, the dancers may conduct cures if called upon to do so by patients in the audience; they bless the fire and the ceremonial structure; and they bring an aura of holiness and well-being to the entire enterprise.

It is clear, then, that the Girl's Puberty Rite is made up of many rituals, each with its specific function, combined into a loosely organized whole. The purpose of the ceremony is twofold: to insure long life, happiness, and

[14] Morris Edward Opler, *An Apache Life-Way* (Chicago: copyright 1941 by University of Chicago Press), p. 117.

good health to the girls on their entrance to young womanhood, and to bring similar blessings to the community as a whole. Finally, the ceremony provides the people who attend with an eagerly anticipated social occasion, where they may feast, sing, engage in social dancing and courtship, and renew old friendships.

10. THE ROLE OF RELIGION IN HUMAN SOCIETIES

The primary function of religion has already been mentioned in other connections: it provides an organized picture of the universe and establishes a more or less orderly relationship between man and his surroundings. Religion thus reduces fears and anxieties, and gives man, not only a greater feeling of security in the uncertain present, but as well the hope of a tolerable future. Frequently the organization of the universe established by religion reflects extraordinarily close and intimate relations, not only with the world of the supernatural, but also with animals, plants, and other aspects of nature.

We have already noted one such association, exemplified in the ancestral cult of the Baganda. Similar cults exist among many African and Melanesian peoples, and are perhaps most complexly developed among the Chinese. Simpler examples are legion. Among the Yaqui and Mayo Indians of northwestern Mexico, for example, the dead are regarded quite literally as continuing members of the family. There are special ceremonies when the dead are supposed to return and eat the essences of food prepared for them; prayers for the dead find an important place in every ceremony. Literate families keep books containing the names of their dead on the house altar, and these names are recited in prayers, with a special prayer for those whose names may have been forgotten. The dead do not have great powers, though they may retaliate against neglect, and they frequently mediate both with the saints (the Indians are nominally Catholic) and with the divinities of the forest. Finally, here as among the Baganda, most people believe that new-born children are reincarnated ancestors, so establishing a continuous cycle of birth, death, and rebirth.

Among the Zuñi of New Mexico we find a similar conception. Here the dead become members of a great company of rain spirits—the *kachinas*—whose good offices in bringing rain to the crops are essential to Zuñi survival. During the winter ceremonial season, the *kachinas* and other divinities come back to the village to mingle companionably with men, where they are impersonated and entertained in a long and spectacular cycle of ceremonies. Here again there is no sharp break between man and his dead, even though the latter are not reborn into the community of the living.

Australian totemism, which we discussed earlier in another connection

(Chapter 13, § 7), provides an excellent instance of relationship between man, the spirits of the dead, and nature. As we noted previously, there are numerous sacred places, called totem centers, in the country of an Australian band which are favorite spots for a certain animal species or areas of concentration for a species of plant, and in which the spirits of the dead reside. Conception is caused when one of these spirits enters the body of a woman; the child, then, is not only a reincarnated ancestor but also is related to the totem center from which his spirit came and to which it will return at death. Those whose spirits come from the same totem center form a cult, whose duty it is to observe, and see that others observe, certain restrictions on hunting and eating the animals or plants also associated with the totem center. The totem cult also performs ceremonies, at the totem center and elsewhere, to cause increase in the species associated with it. These relationships among man, the spirits of the dead, totem centers, and totem animals and plants link the band closely to its environment and to the animal and plant life which shares it with man and on which he depends for subsistence.

Largely on the basis of Australian data, Durkheim and later Radcliffe-Brown suggested that things of importance to a people, such as their sources of food, often find a place symbolically in their religious beliefs. This often appears to be true, as in Australia, where totems are nearly always the principal food plants and animals; among the Pueblo Indians, where cultivated plants play an enormous role in religious symbolism and belief; or among the Indians of the Plains, where the buffalo plays an equally large role in ritual and ceremony. There are other factors, however. Thus, the village-dwelling Yaquis of Mexico have no ceremonies related to crops or cultivation, their principal economic mainstay, but the animals and spirits of the forest play a large role in their belief and ceremonial. In part this may have a psychological explanation: farming is easy for the Yaquis and their crops seldom fail, and correspondingly, they fear the deserts and forests and dislike to spend even a single night in them. Accordingly, it may be that the practical security of farming activities requires no bolstering in religious activity, which reflects, instead, their apprehensions and fears of the deserts and forests that surround their villages.

As Durkheim also pointed out, religion often implies a distinction between sacred and profane (or better, secular) periods of living. Among the Australians, religion receives scant attention when the band during the secular seasons wanders about in search of food. Sacred seasons, correspondingly, are filled with religious activities, and are also periods when the easy availability of food permits large groups, made up of several bands, to gather.

Redfield has applied this concept to contrastive studies, pointing out that the sacred pervades much of life's activities in smaller nonliterate societies. In larger societies, with improved technologies and a larger body of exact knowledge, the area of activity regarded as sacred is smaller and that regarded as secular larger. With the large, urbanized social units of modern Europe and America, the sacred is still less important in daily life and is limited, where it exists at all, to formal occasions and special observances.

Religion functions importantly in reinforcing and maintaining cultural values. Though few religions apparently are as explicitly linked to ethics and morality as, for example, Christianity and Judaism, it is probably true that all or most religions tend, implicitly at least, to support and emphasize particular culturally defined standards of behavior. The concepts of *mana* and taboo (see § 2) exemplify this. As we have noted, the mere possession of *mana,* and its consequent power of taboo, is not enough in most Melanesian and Polynesian societies; the possessor of *mana* must also demonstrate in his behavior the virtues and capabilities required by his position. Similarly, as we noted among the Chiricahua Apaches, the shaman is expected to use his supernatural power for curing and for the good of the community; otherwise, he is regarded as a sorcerer, to be feared, avoided, and, in extreme cases, to be killed. Religion has other functions, and, in particular societies, may ostensibly be little concerned with moral values, but there are few if any instances, except perhaps in periods of rapid social change, where religious beliefs stand in opposition to socially approved values.

Another frequently occurring function of religion, which is served principally by ritual and ceremony, is the preservation of knowledge. Among many nonliterate people, ceremonies are dramas that symbolically re-enact culturally important procedures, particularly in the production of food. Among horticultural peoples, the ceremonial round may emphasize over and over again the steps necessary to make a successful crop. So, too, do hunting peoples frequently hold dances in which the movements of important food animals are imitated and the techniques of the hunter illustrated. Navaho ceremonies symbolically re-enact the myths of creation, the actions of the deities in creating the world and the things to be found in it. All such procedures, though they may place too great an emphasis on the traditional and so discourage innovation, nevertheless insure the retention of culturally valued techniques and procedures.

Finally, it is evident that rituals and ceremonies, together with uniformities of belief, contribute largely to social participation and social solidarity. We have seen, for example, that the Girl's Puberty Rite of the Apaches is not only a religious occasion but also a social event. The people of the local group, and often those of neighboring local groups, come together to participate in a common activity in an atmosphere heavily charged with emotion. In this fashion individuals renew and reinforce their identification with the social unit as a whole, and so gain, not only a heightened social cohesion, but also a greater individual security.

11. SUMMARY

Religion is, in the main, a response to the need for an organized conception of the universe and to have a mechanism for allaying anxieties created by man's inability to predict and understand events which do not apparently conform to natural laws. All peoples have devised some solution, however imperfect, to these problems, and though the solutions vary almost infinitely in detail, there are many broad concepts which occur again and again and are diffused over wide areas.

All peoples have some concept of supernatural power, related in some fashion to man, and more or less subject to his influence and control. The kinds of supernatural power vary from society to society. Widespread is the belief in impersonal supernatural power, as illustrated by the concept of *mana*. Also widespread are beliefs in personalized supernaturals, such as gods, spirits, and the ghosts of the dead. None of these concepts is of course mutually exclusive; we frequently find all of them in a given culture. There are, however, differences of emphasis: in some areas the concept of impersonal power is dominant, while in others gods, spirits, or ghosts may dominate a system of religious beliefs.

Methods of contacting, influencing, and controlling supernatural power are equally varied. Magic is often an important technique, both in religious activities and outside them. In contrast to magic, whereby supernaturals may be commanded if one is given the appropriate knowledge, we find ritual and ceremony, in terms of which the supernatural powers are appeased or cajoled into friendship with man. Among the mechanisms employed for these purposes are prayer, offerings, sacrifices, the singing of sacred songs, dances, and dramas re-enacting the doings of divinities and so bringing them close to man.

Universally, some individuals are believed to be more effective than others in establishing contact with supernatural powers. At one extreme is the shaman, who acquires this facility by divine inspiration in visions or dreams, and who may renew this contact in frenzies, trances, or simply by re-enacting in rituals the original experience. At the other extreme is the priest, who possesses power by virtue of training and membership in a cult, and who is generally a full-time practitioner in contrast to the shaman, who is only a part-time specialist in religious activities. Priests are usually found only in societies advanced enough in technology and economic organization to support full-fledged religious organizations, with temples, cults, and established ceremonial calendars. It should be noted, however, that, in societies like the Zuñi, the difference between shamans and priests is not as great as indicated above; the Zuñi religious practitioner, except that he serves only part time, has much the same functions and training as the priest.

It should be mentioned here—though we did not do so in the preceding —that religious beliefs, and often as well the details of ritual and ceremony, are usually preserved and recounted in myths. In some areas, such as Polynesia, the mythology is very elaborate and provides, as it were, a synopsis of the view of the universe more fully detailed in the totality of religious activities. The telling of myths is not seldom itself a religious activity, like a rite or ceremony, and is frequently an important part of more elaborate ceremonies. We shall have more to say of mythology in Chapter 18.

The function of religion and of its associated ritual and ceremony seems everywhere to include the psychological one of allaying anxieties and fears, and of providing for the interaction of man with the supernatural world. Usually, too, religion provides a more or less orderly account of man's place in the universe and his relations to the environment and to the animals, plants, and other phenomena of nature that make it up. Finally, religious occasions, particularly in the case of ceremonies, are also social functions, which help to develop social cohesion and group solidarity. The individual participant in such occasions experiences a variety of emotional satisfactions, not the least of which is in his more complete identification with the group and the consequent enhancement of his own security.

COLLATERAL READING

Boas, Franz. "The Origin of Totemism," *Race, Language and Culture*. New York: The Macmillan Co., 1940. Pp. 316–323.

Durkheim, Emile. *The Elementary Forms of the Religious Life*. (Trans. J. W. Swain.) New York: The Macmillan Co., 1915.

Frazer, Sir James G. *The Golden Bough*. One vol. Abridged Ed. New York: The Macmillan Co., 1928. Chapters III, IV.

Howells, W. W. *The Heathens, Primitive Man and His Religions*. New York: Doubleday and Co., 1948.

Malinowski, Bronislaw. "Magic, Science, and Religion," *Science, Religion, and Reality*, ed. J. Needham. New York: The Macmillan Co., 1925.

Radin, Paul. *Primitive Religion, Its Nature and Origin*. New York: The Viking Press, 1937.

Tylor, Edward B. *Primitive Culture*. First American Edition. Boston, 1874. Vol. I, Chapter XI; Vol. II, Chapters XII–XVIII.

ETHNOGRAPHIC REFERENCES

Aztecs: Coon, 1948, Chap. 15; Murdock, 1935, Chap. XIII; Thompson, 1933; Vaillant, 1941.

Baganda: Murdock, 1935, Chap. XVII; Roscoe, 1911.

Balinese: Covarrubias, 1937.

Chiricahua Apaches: Opler, 1941.

Dahomeans: Herskovits, 1933, 1938; Murdock, 1935, Chap. XVIII.

Eskimos: Birket-Smith, 1936; Murdock, 1935, Chap. VIII; Rasmussen, 1908, 1931.

Marquesans: Linton, 1939.

Navahos: Kluckhohn and Leighton, 1946.

Trobrianders: Coon, 1948, Chap. 10; Malinowski, 1932.

Zuñis: Cushing, 1920; Eggan, 1950, Chap. IV; Stevenson, 1904.

Chapter 17

LANGUAGE

1. LANGUAGE AND SPEECH

Earlier in this book (Chapter 8) we mentioned that men live in organized clusters called societies and that members of such clusters universally share a number of distinctive modes or ways of behaving which, taken as a whole, constitute their culture. Among these characteristic patterns of behavior, and an essential part of every culture, are certain ways of speaking known as language. Just as each human society has its own culture, distinct in its entirety from every other culture, so every human society has its own language.

Not all languages, however, are restricted in their scope to a single uniform speech community, all of whose members share the same modes of speaking. This is, indeed, only rarely the case, for it occurs mainly in very small nonliterate societies which are sharply distinctive in language from the peoples who surround them. In larger and more complexly segmented societies, like our own, the language may be divided into numerous types and dialects, which resemble each other only in certain general features, while at the same time they differ in many details. According to Bloomfield,

the main types of speech in a complex speech-community can be roughly classed as follows:

(1) *literary standard,* used in most formal discourse and in writing (example: *I have none*);

506

(2) *colloquial standard,* the speech of the privileged class (example: *I haven't any* or *I haven't got any*—in England only if spoken with the southern "public school" sounds and intonation);

(3) *provincial standard,* in the United States probably not to be differentiated from (2), spoken by the "middle class," very close to (2), but differing slightly from province to province (example: *I haven't any* or *I haven't got any,* spoken, in England, with sounds or intonations that deviate from the "public school" standard);

(4) *sub-standard,* clearly different from (1), (2), and (3), spoken in European countries by the "lower middle" class, in the United States by almost all but the speakers of type (2–3), and differing topographically, without intense local difference (example: *I ain't got none*);

(5) *local dialect,* spoken by the least privileged class; only slightly developed in the United States; in Switzerland used also, as a domestic language, by the other classes; differs almost from village to village; the varieties so great as often to be incomprehensible to each other and to speakers of (2–3–4) example: *a hae nane*).[1]

In studying a language, then, as in studying all of a culture, we must assume the existence of communities within which the ways of speaking and behaving are shared by all the members. In such communities, called speech communities, there occur, among others, certain events known as utterances, or single instances of speech produced at given times and places by individual speakers. The linguist collects and records utterances, and by comparing these one with another abstracts the ways or modes of speaking which, as we have said, constitute the language of the speech community. A language, like the culture of which it is a part, is then an abstraction from behavior (specifically, from speaking) and is not to be confused with a mass of specific utterances or, for that matter, with dictionaries or lists of phrases. No one can observe a language directly; he can only observe and record what people say and, from such utterances, abstract the patterns of language manifest therein.

To illustrate the difference between language and speech, we need only consider some of the ways in which we ourselves speak, and observe in particular the limits which our language, English, sets on our speech. Take, for example, the utterances *Sing!, March!, Go!,* and *Come!* Each of these is made up of a single word and each has the same intonation pattern or pitch. The same words, spoken with a slight rise in tone, yield quite different utterances: *Sing?, March?, Go?,* and *Come?* From this comparison (and many others like it) we may note two characteristic patterns of the

---

[1] Leonard Bloomfield, *Language* (New York and London: copyright 1933 by Henry Holt and Co. and George Allen & Unwin Ltd.), p. 52.

English language: (1) that commands (e.g., *Sing!*, *March!*, *Go!*, and *Come!*) have a high-level intonation which contrasts markedly with (2) the rising intonation of interrogatives like *Sing?*, *March?*, *Go?*, and *Come?* These patterns—the command (or imperative) and interrogative intonations—it should be emphasized, are not in themselves utterances, but are rather modes of speaking peculiar to certain classes of utterance.

If we now compare utterances like *Sing!* with others illustrated by *Bill!* or *John!*, we may note another pattern characteristic of commands in English. For *Bill!* and *John!*, though they are spoken with the same intonation as *Sing!*, are not commands but exclamations, utterances occurring under a strong stimulus, such as surprise at seeing the individuals so named. They differ from commands in that they include words which, like *Bill* and *John*, are nouns rather than verbs. Thus we derive another pattern of English: that commands have not only a characteristic high-level intonation but are made up of a verb, with or without modifiers. In contrast, nouns spoken with a high-level intonation are classed, not as commands, but as a kind of exclamation (there are also other varieties). A language is made up of statements like these, which describe as accurately as possible the particular ways of speaking which characterize the speech of a given community. Needless to say, the examples given are very simple ones; most of the patterns descriptive of a language are far more complicated.

2. *"PRIMITIVE" LANGUAGES*

In discussing the several aspects of culture in preceding chapters, we have had frequent occasion to contrast the cultures of nonliterate peoples with those of large urbanized communities, such as our own. We have noted, in such contrasts, that nonliterate peoples frequently possess cruder or less developed technologies, or that their systems of social organization or religious belief are relatively simple and uncomplicated. When we come to the study of language, however, this does not appear to be true, for the languages of nonliterate peoples, even those with the crudest technologies, are apparently not less well developed or more primitive than the languages of so-called civilized folk.

This statement may come as a surprise to most readers, for popular opinion tends toward a contrary view. We are often told that "primitive" peoples have "primitive" languages; that "primitive" languages have only a few hundred words as compared to the many thousands of, let us say, English; that "primitives" are not infrequently obliged, because of the poverty of their languages, to eke out their utterances with manual and facial gestures; or that "primitives" have neither the vocabulary nor the grammar to express the finer and subtler nuances of meaning.

All these statements—and many others like them—are pure mythology. For though languages of nonliterates certainly differ from our own and, indeed, from each other, these differences are essentially of the same order as those which distinguish unrelated languages of modern European, American, and Asiatic peoples. There are differences in pronunciation, in word structure and meanings, in the structure of phrases and sentences, and in grammar, but none of these indicates that some languages are, either in structure or in function, inferior to others. As Edward Sapir has said, all languages, of nonliterates or others, have the same "fundamental groundwork," to wit: "a clear-cut phonetic system," that is, a system of significant sounds, each of which is consistently differentiated from all the rest; a specific association of sound-groups (words and parts of words) with definable areas of meaning; and "provision for the formal expression of all manner of relations," that is, for a complete and systematic grammar. All this, Sapir continues, "meets us rigidly perfected and systematized in every language known to us." [2]

As illustration of these views, let us consider briefly some of the characteristics of the Navaho language, today spoken by some 60,000 Indians living in Arizona and New Mexico. The Navaho system of significant sounds includes thirty-four consonants and eight vowels. Some of these are wholly unknown in English—examples are found in the so-called glottalized consonants, pronounced with a simultaneous closure and release of the vocal cords in the larynx. Similarly, English has sounds lacking in Navaho: our *r* (in such words as *race* and *run*) or the initial *th* sounds of such words as *think* and *this*. But this does not mean that the Navaho sound system is incompletely formed or "primitive," for there are no criteria by which we can judge whether this sound or that is more or less necessary. All we can demonstrate in contrasting Navaho sounds with those of English is the wide difference between them; there is no evidence that one is better or more efficient than the other as, for example, a machine-age technology is more efficient than one based on stone tools.

It is probable that the Navaho vocabulary is somewhat smaller than that of English, if we take Webster's unabridged dictionary as a compendium of English words. But it must be remembered that Webster includes many words which are highly specialized and unknown to numerous speakers of English. Any dictionary of English must do this, for it is written, not for one uniform English-speaking community, but for many divergent ones.

[2] *Language* (New York: copyright 1921 by Harcourt, Brace and Co., Inc.), p. 22.

The term English, as we have noted, has reference to many language types and dialects, not to one alone, whereas Navaho, as a language designation, refers only to the speech ways of a single, small, and relatively undifferentiated society.

Furthermore, the Navaho vocabulary is not truly a small one. As best as we can count its words—and this is no easy task—they run to many thousands, and there is ample evidence that the language has potentialities for many thousands more. It turns out, in fact, with Navaho as with any other language, that the size of a vocabulary is not determined by strictly linguistic factors, but rather by the nonlinguistic culture. A language has as many words as may be needed by the speech community to express itself, and should its culture broaden to require the expression of new concepts, the language will immediately adapt to this need by the coinage or borrowing of new terms. Indeed, this has happened many times in Navaho where, by reason of contact with Spaniards and Americans, the culture and the vocabulary have considerably increased in volume.

Navaho grammar, like the sound system, is so different from that of English that it is difficult to express the difference in a brief space. We shall consider only a few points. Navaho nouns have no separate plural forms; whether one says *one horse* or *two horses,* the Navaho word for *horse* is spoken in precisely the same way. Certain English words—*sheep* is a good example—are similar in this respect, though this is exceptional where in Navaho it is the rule.

But this does not mean that Navaho has no means of indicating plurality in respect to nouns; it means only that such indication, where it is necessary, is made by other means. We may illustrate by English *sheep:* the expressions *two sheep* or *many sheep* indicate plural concepts quite as well as *two horses* and *many horses.* The only difference lies in the fact that in the first two phrases (*two sheep* and *many sheep*) plurality is expressed only in the adjectives *two* and *many,* whereas in *two horses* and *many horses,* it is expressed twice, once in the adjectives *two* and *many* and again in the ending -*s.* In Navaho, when it is necessary to indicate plurality, this is expressed by a separate word, not by an ending or (as in English *mice*) by a special form of the noun.

The grammar of the Navaho verb is exceedingly complex, far more so than that of the English verb. Our verbs are conjugated in relatively few forms; a regular verb, like *work* for example, has but four inflected forms: *work, works, worked,* and *working.* The greatest number of inflected forms is found in the verb *to be: am, are, is, was, were, be, been,* and *being,* a total of eight. No Navaho verb is so simply inflected, for even the regular verbs of Navaho have a minimum of sixty different inflected forms.

Where English verbs are conjugated mainly for tense—a distinction like that between *he works, he worked, he will work*—this feature is lacking in Navaho verbs. These are, instead, conjugated mainly for aspect, that is, in terms of whether the action denoted by the verb is incomplete, complete, in progress, or repeated. The Navaho equivalent of English *work*, in the third person of these four aspects, may roughly be translated: *he works* (in the sense of engaging in an action as yet incomplete), *he has (finished) working, he is working* (without regard for beginning or ending), and *he works repeatedly, over and over again.*

The fact that Navaho lacks regular tense indication in the verb is not, however, to be interpreted as a mark of primitivity; note that English verbs contain no regular marker for aspect, certainly no less important than tense. In brief, as we go from language to language, all we can find in their sound systems, vocabularies, and grammars are differences, sometimes greater, sometimes smaller. These differences cannot be evaluated as more or less primitive, or more or less advanced. As Sapir has said:

There is no more striking general fact about language than its universality. One may argue as to whether a particular tribe engages in activities that are worthy of the name of religion or of art, but we know of no people that is not possessed of a fully developed language. The lowliest South African Bushman speaks in the forms of a rich symbolic system that is in essence perfectly comparable to the speech of the cultivated Frenchman.[3]

3. THE DIVERSITY OF LANGUAGE

No less striking than the universality of language is its extraordinary diversity. There are probably thousands of distinct languages spoken in the world of today, not to mention numerous ancient idioms of which we have only scanty written records, and probably many others that have been lost without a trace. Linguists customarily divide the languages of the world into stocks or families (we shall later, § 7, see how this is done). In this section, our purpose is simply to provide a brief summary of the languages of the world and their classification, as far as it is now known.

Most important to us is the far-flung Indo-European family of languages which includes most of those best known to us. It is usually divided into nine subgroups: Germanic (including, among others, German, English, the Scandinavian languages, and Dutch), Keltic (mainly Gaelic and Welsh), Baltic (Lithuanian, Lettish, and others), Slavic (principally Rus-

---

[3] *Language* (New York: copyright 1921 by Harcourt, Brace and Co., Inc.), pp. 21–22.

sian, Polish, Czech, Bulgarian, and Serbo-Croatian), Romance (the languages derived from Latin, such as French, Spanish, Italian, Roumanian, and Portuguese), Greek, Indo-Iranian (including Persian, Kurdish, and many modern languages of India), Armenian, and Albanian. These languages, some of which, like English, have spread to many areas of the world, are now spoken by nearly 900 million people. Though many are obscure and little-known tongues, others (e.g., English, French, German, Spanish, and Russian) are exceedingly important for an understanding of the complex cultures of the western world.

Though most of the languages of Europe belong to the Indo-European family, there are a number of less important tongues that do not. Basque is one of these, spoken by some one million people in the Pyrenees and unrelated to any other known tongue. Traces, in scattered inscriptions, are also found of older non-Indo-European languages, once spoken in the European area but now extinct. Some of these, like Basque, may represent the remains of an earlier European population, wiped out or assimilated to the Indo-European-speaking invaders.

The other non-Indo-European languages of Europe (Finnish, Lappish, Hungarian, and Esthonian) belong to the large Finno-Ugric family. This family includes as well Carelian, Olonetsian, Ludian, Vespian, Livonian, and Ingrian (spoken in the portions of Russia adjacent to Finland) and four others (Cheremiss, Permian, Mordvinian, and Ob-Ugrian) which are scattered further east in northern Russia. Except for Finnish and Hungarian, few of these languages are important in the modern world. The total number of Finno-Ugrian speakers is about 16 or 17 million, with most of these speaking Hungarian (10 million), Finnish (3 million), Esthonian (one million), and Mordvine (one million). Samoyedic, a small group of languages spoken by about 18,000 people living along the Yenisei River in Siberia, is sometimes said to be related remotely to Finno-Ugric.

As we move eastward from Europe we encounter three more large families of languages: (1) the Turkic or Altaic (Turkish, Tartar, Kirghiz, and others) spoken by about 39 million people in southwestern Asia, plus a small, remote group, the Yakut, with about 200,000 speakers, in northeastern Siberia; (2) Mongolian, with about 3 million speakers who live for the most part in Mongolia; and (3) Tungus-Manchu, with fewer than a million speakers, located north of the Mongolians. Still farther north and east are found a cluster of languages, usually called the Hyperborean group, a geographical rather than a linguistic classification. These communities are mostly small and nonliterate (the Chukchi, Koryak, and Kamchadal, with a total of some 10,000 speakers), and we know too little of their languages to state their relationships with accuracy.

In eastern and southern Asia we find the great Sino-Tibetan family, of which Chinese, in its many different languages, is the most important subgroup. In addition to Chinese, the family includes Tibetan, Tai (or Siamese), Burmese, and a number of lesser known languages. The total number of speakers for Sino-Tibetan probably approaches 450 million, but nearly all of these (about 400 million) speak Chinese languages.

On the southern fringes of Asia we find, beginning in the west, the languages of the Caucasus mountains (a little-known group having considerable linguistic diversity and about 4 million speakers); the Dravidian family, in southern India, which includes such languages as Tamil (about 18 million speakers), Malayalam (6 million speakers), Canarese (10 million speakers), and Telugu (24 million speakers), plus numerous smaller groups; Munda, spoken by about 3 million people on the southern slopes of the Himalayas and in central India; and Mon-Khmer, made up of Annamite (some 14 million speakers) plus a number of idioms scattered over southeastern Asia, the Nicobar Islands, and some portions of the Malay Peninsula.

Japanese, with about 70 million speakers, is apparently unrelated to any other group, as is also Korean, with 23 million speakers. In northern Sakhalin and the adjacent coast around the mouth of the Amur River is Giliak, a far less important but also isolated tongue. Ainu is another such language, spoken by about 20,000 people of a very simple culture who today live in the northern portions of the Japanese archipelago.

Except for the languages of the Australian aborigines and a small cluster of Papuan languages spoken in New Guinea, all the languages of Oceania belong to a single stock, Malayo-Polynesian. This includes Malay (3 million speakers), Javanese (nearly 50 million speakers), Tagalog (in the Philippines with 1.5 million speakers), and numerous others in Melanesia, Micronesia, and Polynesia. Languages of the Malayo-Polynesian family are also spoken in Madagascar.

Africa is also complex linguistically. Most important, in terms of culturally advanced groups, are Semitic and Hamitic in northern and northeastern Africa. Semitic includes ancient Hebrew and its modern descendants, Arabic, Ethiopic, and numerous languages (e.g., Phoenician, Babylonian, Assyrian, and others) which are known only from written records. The Hamitic stock includes Egyptian, known only from records dating as early as 4000 B.C., and Berber, Tuareg, Kabyle, and other less significant modern tongues. Hamitic, together with Cushitic (a group of languages spoken south of Egypt) is sometimes said to be remotely related to Semitic.

South of the Sahara and extending in a broad belt across Africa are the so-called Sudanic languages. These are extremely numerous, and apparently very diverse, and no one is as yet certain as to their precise inter-relationships. There are some 50 million speakers estimated for the Sudanic group. Still farther south and extending to the tip of Africa is the great Bantu family of languages, also estimated to have some 50 million speakers. There is little doubt that the Bantu languages are related linguistically to each other, and some have said that Bantu may eventually be tied in with certain languages of the Sudanic group. The last two language families of Africa are very small and spoken by about 300,000 peoples of relatively simple cultures in southwestern Africa. These are the Bushmen, with about 50,000 speakers, and Hottentot, with about 250,000.

The most diverse linguistic area to be found anywhere in the world is North and South America. Where the Indo-European family of languages is spoken by about 900 million people, the population of the New World, less than one-twentieth of this number, speaks more than 1,000 different languages, divided into a minimum of 125 distinct families. Note, too, that the American aboriginal tongues are in no wise derived from those of the Old World, even remotely, but represent wholly unrelated forms.

Some American Indian language families are spread over considerable territories: Eskimo-Aleut, on the coasts of the Arctic from Alaska to Greenland; Athapaskan, in northwestern Canada, Alaska, and in smaller enclaves on the Pacific Coast and in New Mexico, Arizona, and Texas; Algonkin, over much of northeastern and midwestern United States, Canada south and east of the Athapaskans, and in two or three places in the northern plains; Siouan, the languages of many of the Plains Indian tribes; Uto-Aztekan, from Utah south through much of Mexico; Carib and Arawak, which extend from the West Indies through much of eastern South America; Tupi-Guarani, on the coast of Brazil; Araucanian in Chile; and the Kechuan family, spread by Inca conquests from Colombia to southern Peru.

Other language stocks are much smaller and we often find regions of incredible linguistic diversity, such as California, the North Pacific Coast, parts of Mexico and Central America, and many areas of South America. In California, according to Kroeber, we find 135 languages belonging to 21 families, though the aboriginal population was probably somewhat less than 150,000. In this region, it is not at all unusual to find three or more tribes, living in more or less constant contact within a restricted territory and each speaking a language of a totally different stock.

As our brief review of world languages demonstrates, there are few if any areas of culture which are so diverse as language. The range in modes of speaking is almost beyond description, and yields one of our most valuable storehouses of data for the comparative study of human behavior.

4. THE ANTIQUITY OF LANGUAGE

The enormous diversity of modern languages and the fact that every known speech community, of ancient or of modern times, has a fully developed language suggests that language is of great antiquity—as old as any other aspect of man's culture. It is wholly probable, and indeed quite likely, that man learned to speak at the same time, some million or more years ago, that he took his first few steps in accumulating a cultural tradition.

Evidence for this view must of course be indirect, for speaking, unlike the making of stone tools for example, leaves no traces behind. Our written records of speech are, in anthropological terms, extremely modern. Writing of any sort does not appear in human history before 4000 B.C. and even then is confined to very few societies. Many Indo-European languages (e.g., English) had no written records until the eighth or ninth centuries A.D., and our oldest record of an Indo-European tongue (the Indic Rig-Veda) is probably no earlier than 1200 B.C. In very many modern languages of nonliterate societies, there are of course no written records at all.

Justification for the view that language belongs, in age, with the crudest techniques of tool-making known to archeology, rests solely on the hypothesis, discussed elsewhere in this book, that culture came into being only when man learned to symbolize (see Chapter 8, § 11). Without this ability, the earliest hominids were no more advanced than the modern chimpanzee: they could and did learn but they did not accumulate learned patterns of behaving and transmit these as organized wholes to succeeding generations. Approximately one million years ago we find definite evidence, in archeological deposits, that hominids were not only capable of using tools but were also transmitting this knowledge to their descendants, who, very slowly, were improving and adding to these techniques. Some means of symbolizing is essential to this process.

The question may well be raised however: Need this early technique of symbolizing have been language? Is it not possible that early man symbolized by other means, that is, by gestures of one sort or another? Speaking, as many have suggested, may have been preceded by an earlier period of "gesture languages."

To answer this question, we need merely point out that we know only a few systems of communication based on gesture, and that these are extremely crude. (It goes without saying that we eliminate the gesture systems, like those taught to the deaf, which merely substitute manual symbols for oral or written ones.) One, perhaps the best known, exists among the

American Indians of the Plains. Like all gesture systems, it is limited in the number and definiteness of its symbols, and most important, is used only as a secondary means of communication between peoples who already possess spoken idioms. Wherever gesture systems occur, they appear to develop by reason of linguistic diversity, that is, to supply a rough means of communication between peoples who speak mutually unintelligible tongues. If this is true, then modern gesture systems are no relic of an early and primitive form of symbolizing; they are merely secondary systems to be used when, and only when, the infinitely superior means of communication by oral symbols fails. Incidentally, the oft-heard tale that American Indians used gestures to supplement the poverty of their spoken forms has, as modern studies of these languages amply demonstrate, no basis in fact whatever.

Another factor also suggests that oral language is man's earliest means of symbolizing. Speaking, unlike manual gestures, employs organs relatively free to take on this secondary function. A man using his arms and hands in work cannot gesture; he must stop what he is doing to communicate by manual gestures. Moreover, he must also get his audience to pay close visual attention to him, lest they lose a movement of significance. Speaking and hearing, on the other hand, can take place simultaneously with many other operations. The vocal organs are only seldom so occupied that speaking is impossible, and this is even more true of the hearing apparatus. In short, speaking and hearing employ precisely those organs which are most convenient for their purposes and which permit men to communicate and employ symbols along with their other work, and indeed to make symbolizing an important accompaniment of their work. We may say, then, with Sapir:

We are forced to believe that language is an immensely ancient heritage of the human race. . . . It is doubtful if any other cultural asset of man, be it the art of drilling for fire or of chipping stone, may lay claim to a greater age. I am inclined to believe that it antedated even the lowliest developments of material culture, that these developments, in fact, were not strictly possible until language, the tool of significant expression, had itself taken shape.[4]

5. THE STRUCTURE OF LANGUAGE

When we hear a language spoken for the first time, its utterances give the impression of a confused babbling, with no apparent order or meaning. But this confusion, once we become accustomed to the strange new sounds,

[4] Edward Sapir, *Language* (New York: copyright 1921 by Harcourt, Brace and Co., Inc.), p. 23.

is soon reduced to order. We begin to see that the sounds of the language are relatively few, and that these recur over and over again in the same and different combinations. Certain groups of sounds similarly recur with greater or less frequency and whole utterances occur in characteristic sets or patterns. After a time, it becomes apparent that the foreign speech, like our own or any other, is controlled and guided by a definable structure.

This structure, upon analysis, has two major aspects: phonological and grammatical. By phonological structure or phonology we mean (1) that the speakers of a language employ a finite number of distinctive sounds, called phonemes, and (2) that these phonemes are combined only in certain characteristic sequences. Grammatical structure or grammar refers to the fact that every utterance spoken in a given speech community follows one or other of a finite series of meaningful arrangements, peculiar to the language of that community.

To take midwestern American English as an example, we may note that it contains, according to Bloomfield, 41 phonemes—no more and no less. Most of these, like the consonants *p, t,* and *k* (often written *c* in English spelling), may begin an utterance, as illustrated by the words *pan, tan,* and *can.* Two consonants, however, never begin an utterance; these are the final consonant of *sing* (which is represented by the complex *-ng,* phonetically written *-η,* and not *-g*) and the medial consonant of *measure* (spelled *-s-* but written phonetically *-ž-*). Note, too, that while most consonants may end an utterance, *h* (as in *hand*) never does, and *w* (as in *was*) and *y* (as in *yes*) in the final position (as in *sow* or *they,* respectively) have a very different sound.

Similar rules govern combinations of consonants. Thus, while *l* may follow *p* (as in *play*), *k* (as in *clay*), and many other consonants, it never occurs (initially in an utterance) after *t, d,* the initial sounds of *thick* or *ship,* or after *h.*

The rigidity of phonological patterns like these is illustrated by our difficulty in learning foreign patterns different from our own, even where familiar sounds are involved. A native English speaker has no difficulty with the sound *-ž-* in such words as *measure, pleasure, rouge,* or *garage* (where it occurs medially or finally) but may find it hard to pronounce it at the beginning of words, as in French *Jean* or *gendarme.* Similarly, though all speakers of English are perfectly accustomed to the phoneme that begins words like *shave* and *ship* or that which begins *lash* or *laugh,* the combination of these, as in German *schlaf* ("*sleep*"), offers considerable difficulty. Our native patterns of pronunciation, as Whorf has pointed out, become fixed at six years of age or even earlier and from that time on (unless we learn another language) govern our speaking so firmly that "no sequence of sounds that deviates from it can even be articulated without the greatest of difficulty." [5]

Grammatical patterns are similarly rigid: they provide a set of molds into which we are obliged (if monolingual) to cast our speech and from which little deviation is tolerated. In English, for example, it is quite impossible to hear an utterance like *the run men* for *the men run;* in this type of sentence, the verb must come after the noun. Similarly, *a house white,* though understandable, is a rare substitue for *a white house* (compare French *une maison blanc*), for in English, in most instances, an adjective precedes the noun it modifies. Elements of compounds, like *railroad,* or of derived words, like *worker* (*work* plus the ending *-er, one who*) can only be spoken in this order, not in any other. A more subtle pattern distinguishes questions like *the man?* from statements like *the man;* the former is always spoken with a final high pitch and the latter with a final low pitch.

In these and numerous other instances, we quite unconsciously arrange our utterances in set, native patterns and rarely conceive of arranging them otherwise, even when we invent in fun a nonsense language. Lewis Carroll's phrase, *the mome raths outgrabe* (from "Jabberwocky" in *Through the Looking-Glass*), is English in grammar, despite the fact that the words are not. *The mome raths* quite clearly parallels structures like *the black dogs,* and functions as the subject of the sentence, which is completed by the verblike form *outgrabe.* Note, too, that *the mome raths,* a plural expression (as denoted by the suffix *-s* in *raths*), *takes* a plural verb, *outgrabe.* If we change *raths* to *rath,* the sentence must take a singular verb: *the mome rath outgrabes.*

Grammatical analysis makes use of two basic concepts: that of the morpheme and that of arrangement. A morpheme is a combination of one or more phonemes which has a unitary meaning, that is, which cannot be divided into separate elements each of which has meaning. English forms like *dog, cat,* and *horse* are morphemes, for they cannot be divided into smaller meaningful units. But a word like *worker* has two morphemes: *work* and the ending *-er.* This ending may also be found in the following words: *sing-er* ("one who sings"), *sail-or* ("one who sails," the spelling of the ending being irrelevant), and *runn-er* ("one who runs"). Morphemes which may make up the content of an utterance (as *go* or *come* in the utterances *Go!* or *Come!,* respectively) are called free morphemes. The rest are bound morphemes, like the *-er* of *work-er* or the *-s* of *book-s,* for these never occur in an utterance save as part of a larger derived form.

Arrangement has two aspects: morphological, which refers to arrange-

[5] B. L. Whorf, "Linguistics as an Exact Science." Reprinted from *The Technology Review,* Vol. 43 (1940), p. 62, edited at the Massachusetts Institute of Technology.

ments of morphemes and larger elements which result in words, and syntactic, which refers to arrangements which result in phrases and sentences. According to Bloomfield, there are at least four basic types of arrangement: order, phonetic modification, modulation, and selection. We shall illustrate these, for both morphological and syntactic constructions, in the following paragraphs.

Order has reference to the sequence in which the parts of words, phrases, and sentences are customarily spoken in a given language. In the English sentence, *The boys run,* we note, first, two major divisions: *The boys* (the subject or actor) which precedes *run* (the predicate or action). *The boys,* a phrase, has similarly two parts: *The* (a definite article) followed by *boys* (a plural noun). *Run,* of course, is but a single morpheme and needs no further analysis. But *boys* has again two elements: *boy* (a free morpheme) plus *-s,* a bound morpheme signifying the plural. In each division made in the analysis above, order is significant, whether it pertains to the sentence as a whole or to any of its constituent phrases and words.

Phonetic modification refers to the fact that morphemes may sometimes be spoken in two or more ways, depending on the other morphemes with which they may be combined. In English, morphemes are not infrequently so modified: examples are found in the suffix *-r* of *wait-r-ess* (which is the same as the *-er* of *waiter*) and the initial morphemes *dep-, wid-,* and *leng-* (from *deep, wide,* and *long,* respectively) of *dep-th, wid-th,* and *leng-th.* These are compulsory modifications (we do not say *wait-er-ess, deep-th, wide-th,* or *long-th*). Optional modifications occur in such English constructions as *can't* (from *can not*), *shouldn't* (from *should not*), and *haven't* (from *have not*), where the contracted forms may alternate more or less freely with those which exhibit no phonetic modification at all.

Modulation, the third basic type of arrangement, includes the patterns of stress and intonation which frequently accompany utterances or parts of utterances. In English, for example, the compound *blackbird* has but one major stress (on the element *black-*) as contrasted with two major stresses on the phrase *black bird.* Similarly, English sentences are marked by characteristic intonations which distinguish one type from another, even when they contain the same morphemes. Thus, *The book,* with final low pitch, is a statement, whereas *The book?,* with final high pitch is a question. In English, too, stress frequently differentiates nouns from verbs. As examples, compare *contrast* (stress on first syllable), a noun, with *contrast* (stress on second syllable), a verb; *contract* (initial stress, noun) and *contract* (final stress, verb).

Where pitch or intonation is used in English only to distinguish sentences, it is frequently used in other languages to differentiate words. In

Chinese, we are told, the syllable *man* many mean "deceive" or "slow," depending on the pitch with which it is spoken. So also in Navaho: the word *bìnìˀ* (with a high pitch on *bí-* and a low one on *-nìˀ; ˀ* is a glottal stop) means "his mind," while *bìnìˀ* (with a low pitch on both syllables) means "his land." Compare also Navaho *bìtàà* ("his father"), *bítáá* ("his forehead") and *bìzèè* ("his medicine"), *bízéé* ("his mouth").

In all languages that we know, morphemes, words, phrases, and other constituents of utterances are divided by various criteria into numerous classes and subclasses. Utterances may differ, then, in respect to the kinds of elements that make them up. It is this factor that we call selection— the classification of the constituents of which the utterance is constructed. We may illustrate by contrasting the English utterances *Go!* and *John!,* one of which is a command and the other a type of call. Both employ the same intonation pattern and there is no difference in order or phonetic modification, since both utterances have but one morpheme. The difference between them is solely a matter of selection: *go* is an infinitive verb and *John* a proper noun.

To summarize this section, it is now evident that every language includes:

(1) A set of distinctive sounds or phonemes, finite in number, and a definable pattern or phonology in terms of which these phonemes are combined;

(2) A large number of morphemes, free and bound, which in their totality make up its lexicon; and

(3) A set of arrangements (features of order, phonetic modification, modulation, and selection) whereby its morphemes are combined to make words, phrases, and sentences.

These three features, taken together, make up the structure of a language; the ways, manners, or modes which guide and control the speech behavior of the members of a speech community. Conversely, any utterance heard in a given speech community can be fully described in terms of the phonology and grammar of the language of that community.

6. LINGUISTIC CHANGE

Though linguistic structures, at any given point in their history, may appear to be rigid and unchanging, this appearance is illusory. In actual fact, all living languages (that is, all languages still being spoken) undergo continual change, manifest in both their phonological and their grammatical structures. Ordinarily this change is too minute to be observed in actual process; it becomes apparent only when we contrast languages at different points in their history or when we observe that two or more mutually unintelligible tongues are nevertheless derived from a common source, as the modern Romance languages are from Latin.

English affords us a good example of linguistic change. Its first written records appear about 900 A.D., and from that time on we have a more or less unbroken line of documents connecting the oldest recorded English with that of the present. Linguists customarily divide the history of the English language into three main periods: Old English (or Anglo-Saxon), from 900 A.D. to about 1100 A.D., Middle English, from 1100 to about 1550, and Modern English, from 1550 to the present. During this relatively brief span (little more than a thousand years), English has altered so radically in both phonology and grammar as to make it quite impossible for a native speaker of Modern English to read either Middle or Old English without a good deal of special study.

We can illustrate some of the changes in English phonology from 900 A.D. to the present by comparing the following words as they occur in Old English, Middle English, and Modern English.

Old English	Middle English	Modern English
mann	man	man
stān	stōn	stone
dǣel	dēl	deal
wīn	wīn	wine
drēam	drēm	dream
dēop	dēp	deep
sunu	sune	sun
hūs	hūs	house
mōd	mōd	mood
fȳr	fīr	fire

Note that the differences of sound are greater than is indicated by the orthography. Old English and Middle English *a* is pronounced roughly as in *pot* (the macron, e.g., *ā*, indicates length); Old English *ae* as in *man;* Old and Middle English *ī* as in *see;* Old English *ē* and the vowel of Middle English *dēp* roughly like the *é* of French *été* (but longer); Middle English *ē* in *dēl* and *drēm* as in *bed;* Old and Middle English *ū* as in *boot;* Old English *ō* and the vowel of Middle English *mōd* as in German *Sohn;* Middle English *ō* in *stōn* roughly like the British English *law;* Old English *ȳ* as the *u* of French *une*. In Old English vowel combinations, as in *drēam* and *dēop,* both vowels are pronounced.

We may note further that the differences in pronunciation between Modern English and its earlier forms are consistent and systematic, not random.

The vowels *ā, ū,* and *ȳ* of Old English, for example, nearly always become *o* (as in *stone*), *ou* (as in *house*), and *i* (as in *mice*) in Modern English, provided of course we compare these in words that have been retained in the language since Old English times. Examples of these regular phonetic correspondences are found in the following pairs: *stān, stone; hāl, whole; bāt, boat; gāt, goat; gān, go; hūs, house; mūs, mouse; cū, cow; lūs, louse; hū, how; fȳr, fire; mȳs, mice; lȳs, lice; brȳd, bride; hwȳ, why.* By means of similar phonetic correspondences we may eventually link up all the phonemes of Old, Middle, and Modern English, thus summarizing in systematic form all the changes in habits of pronunciation that have taken place in English-speaking communities during the past thousand years, insofar as these are reflected in written documents.

But differences in phonology are not the only ones which separate Old, Middle, and Modern English forms, for these may also differ in grammar. Old English *stān,* for example, had a total of six case forms: *stān,* nominative singular; *stāne,* dative singular; *stānes,* genitive singular; *stānas,* nominative plural; *stānum,* dative plural; and *stāna,* genitive plural. In the Middle English period, these reduced to four: *stōn,* nominative singular; *stōne,* dative singular; *stōnene,* genitive plural; and *stōnes* in the remaining three cases (genitive singular, nominative plural, and dative plural). Today English has but two forms: the general singular *stone* and the form *stones,* which functions indifferently as a genitive singular (written *stone's*), a genitive plural (written *stones'*), and a general plural.

Verbs, too, were conjugated differently in Old and Middle English as compared with the present. The Old English verb *bindan* "to bind," for example, had the following forms in the present indicative singular: first person *binde,* second person *bindest* or *bintst,* and third person *bindeth* or *bint.* These were retained essentially unchanged through most of the Middle English period, but today there remains only *bind* for the first and second persons *(I bind, you bind)* and *binds* for the third *(he binds).*

It is clear from these examples, few as they are, that Old, Middle, and Modern English, though obviously distinct languages (or better, sets of languages), are nevertheless linked in a continuous historical tradition. Old English is a set of languages spoken in England until 1100 A.D., when, by slow changes, it merged into a new set of languages which we have called, collectively, Middle English. In the same fashion, linguistic change being continuous, the Middle English languages gave way to the many modern forms of English now spoken, by reason of migration and colonization, both in England and in numerous other areas of the world. Both Old English and Middle English, once the languages of many thousands of people, no longer exist, save in the scanty recordings preserved in ancient documents.

7. THE COMPARATIVE METHOD

While written records afford us the best and most direct evidence of linguistic change, such records, for a great many languages, are unavailable. Writing, as we have noted before, is a relatively recent invention, no more than 6,000 years old, and even then is confined to only a few speech communities. Linguistic change, like language itself, is evidently much older. There is no reason to believe that unrecorded languages are less subject to change than those for which we have ancient documents.

The evidence that all languages change is found in the fact that groups of modern tongues reveal, on careful examination, the same sorts of resemblances in phonology and grammar that we have just noted between Old, Middle, and Modern English. Ways of speaking in modern English are similar to those of modern German, Dutch, Swedish, Norwegian, and Danish, even though these idioms, like the older forms of English, are languages very different from modern English. To illustrate this point, let us compare English, German, and Swedish in respect to the following words.

English	German	Swedish
brother	bruder	broder
daughter	tochter	dotter
door	tür	dörr
father	vater	fader
foot	fuss	fot
hair	haar	hår
heart	herz	hjärta
knee	knie	knä
man	mann	man
mother	mutter	moder
son	sohn	son

As a result of resemblances like these, which in the languages concerned are so numerous as to affect almost every aspect of the vocabulary, it is inferred that English, German, and Swedish are modern divergent varieties of an earlier protolanguage common to all three. English ways of speaking, in modern times, represent one set of divergences from those of the earlier speech community, whereas German and Swedish ways of speaking represent two other sets of divergences, different both from each other and from English. The resemblances between English, German, and Swedish, too many to result from coincidence, are evidence of their common origin in the remote past, and hence of the fact that all three languages have changed, though in different ways, from their common ancestor.

This means of describing linguistic change is called the comparative method. It involves, as our example above illustrates, a sorting of the vocabularies of the languages compared to ferret out the forms which are cognate to each other, that is, the forms which, in each of the languages compared, represent modern divergences from a single prototype form and hence are historically connected. Where investigation reveals many such cognates between two or more different tongues, these languages are presumed to be members of a single stock or family, or to be connected historically to a single protolanguage. If thorough comparison of two or more languages discloses no cognates, there can be no relationship between them.

Further examination of the cognate forms of related languages reveals, as in the case of Old, Middle, and Modern English, that their divergences in pronunciation may be reduced to orderly statements of phonetic correspondence. A sound correspondence evidenced in one set of cognates is ordinarily paralleled by scores of others containing the same sounds. Note, for example, that the correspondence of English and Swedish *d* (in *daughter–dotter* or *door–dörr*) to German *t* (in *tochter* and *tür*, respectively) is found also in the following sets: *dew, dagg, tau; death, död, tod; deep, djup, tief; day, dag, tag; deaf, döv, taub; dear* (expensive), *dyr, teuer; dance, dansa, tanzen; dive, dyka, tauchen;* and *dream, drömma, träumen.* Similar correspondences may be set up between nearly every English phoneme and its Swedish and German counterpart.

It is this systematic correspondence between the sounds of different contemporaneous languages that, like the same order of correspondence between different historical periods of the same language, truly evidences their common origin. Random similarities between languages, on the other hand, do not mean that they have a common antecedent, but only that such similarities are due to chance. Thus, it is mere coincidence that the English *ma* ("mother") resembles Navaho *-má* ("mother"). Borrowing may also account for some similarities, as in the case of Navaho *mósí* ("cat") from English *pussy.*

It is by the use of the comparative method that linguists divide the languages of the world into separate stocks or families. As we noted in § 3, there are many such families of languages—a reflection both of the diversity of modern tongues and the antiquity of language as a human faculty. As more and more languages are studied and compared intensively with each other, we may expect that the number of linguistic stocks will decrease. Families now apparently unrelated will eventually be shown to be related, though remotely. But it is not likely, by the comparative method alone, that we shall ever be able to demonstrate the common origin of all modern tongues. The rate of divergence of languages is too rapid, in relation to the great time span of human history, to make it probable that enough remains of a possible primeval uniformity of speech to link all present-day languages into a single great family.

8. MEANING AND SEMANTIC CHANGE

In studying the phonology and grammatical structure of languages we need not analyze the meanings of linguistic forms in any detail. We need only assume that each form (whether a morpheme, word, or phrase) has a meaning and that this meaning is wholly or in part different from that of other forms in the same category.

It is obvious, however, that languages exist in a social setting; people use them continually in all their activities, and very few human interactions are conducted without the use of language. It is by reason of this fact that linguistic forms are said (somewhat vaguely) to possess meanings, and that these meanings are supposedly determined by the ways in which the forms are used by human beings.

The meanings of linguistic forms are not easy to determine; they are by no means as fixed and definite as phonemes or structural features. Where the phonology of a given language may be so accurately described that we may predict, in that speech community, the precise phonological features of any possible word, phrase, or sentence, the same is not true of meanings. English *dog,* for example, has one sense in *Rover, the dog,* another in the expletive *Dog!,* and still a third in *He's a gay dog.* To say *Rover's in the dog-house* is definitely not the same as saying *John's in the dog-house* (that is, *John's in trouble*), a usage inexplicable in terms of the former sentence alone. Similarly *house* has three quite distinct meanings in the phrases *a good house, the fall of the house of Usher,* and *a White House spokesman.*

These difficulties in respect to meanings derive from the fact that linguistic forms are necessarily applied to a wide variety of different situations in everyday life. No language exists which provides specific forms for every single item in the flow of experience, nor is such a language conceivable, for it would soon acquire so large a stock of forms as to be unusable. In actual fact, linguistic forms apply, not to single experiences, but rather to larger or smaller categories of experience. These categories are not the same in every speech community but are unique to a given language, for they represent the cumulation of a long historical tradition. The system of meanings that prevails in a speech community, like the culture of which it is a part, is not one determined by science or logic but is an inventory developed quite unconsciously by generations of speakers and, like the structural features of language, subject to constant change.

Though little is as yet known of semantics (the study of meanings), certain facts are already clear. One is that most linguistic forms, regardless of the language, appear to have two sets of meanings: nuclear and marginal or metaphoric. This may be illustrated by our word *head* which, in its nuclear sense, refers to a part of the body. In its several marginal meanings, however, it is used in such phrases as *the head of the state, the head of a nail, the head of a street,* or *the head of a glass of beer.* Similarly, we note the word *mouth* in *the mouth of a cave, the mouth of a river,* and the colloquial compound *mouth-piece* for *lawyer.*

But this is not all. Linguistic forms frequently take on emotional associations or connotations in addition to their nuclear and marginal denotative meanings. These are of many different varieties. Some carry class connotations, that is, certain forms are conceived as more elegant or learned than others and mark the speakers as members of a social elite. *Lady* (even in such compounds as *wash-lady, cleaning-lady,* or *char-lady*) is considered more elegant than *woman; he isn't* and *he did it* more refined than *he ain't* or *he done it;* and *I saw nobody* more correct (socially) than *I didn't see nobody.*

Very often the connotations of a phrase or word will restrict its usage to particular situations. One who disregards such a restriction may be considered improper, irreligious, or even, in some societies, be subjected to severe punishment. In English, many of the words referring to excretory or reproductive functions are strictly tabooed as obscenities; learned Latin or Greek derivatives must be used instead. Less improper forms, at least among some speakers, are religious terms (like *God, Jesus, damnation,* or *Hell*) used as expletives. Many English speakers also avoid terms having ominous connotations, such as those referring to death and the names of certain diseases and natural phenomena.

Tabooed forms may be quite numerous in many societies, particularly among nonliterate peoples. Among the Navahos, for example, certain animals, like the snake, the bear, or the owl, may never be named in casual conversation; instead, various circumlocutions, like *the flat-footed one* for the bear, must be used. Similarly, a Navaho never gives his own name casually, nor does he permit anyone else to call him by name. Among these people, names are not used as means of identification as with ourselves, but are rather very special characteristics of the individual's personality. Especially tabooed among the Navahos are any words referring to death; and when a person dies, no one must refer to him again, even remotely, unless this is absolutely necessary.

Meanings, like other aspects of language, are in constant process of change. Some of the commoner types of semantic change may be tabulated as follows.

(1) Narrowing, where the meaning of a form becomes more restricted in scope. Examples: *meat* from Old English *mete* ("food"), *deer* from Old English *dēor* ("beast"), *garage* from a French word denoting any storage place.

(2) Widening, where the meaning of a form is enlarged. Examples: *barn* from Old English *bern* ("a storage place for barley"), *quisling* (roughly, "traitor") from the name of a Norwegian who accepted a post under the German occupation during World War II, *victrola* and *kodak,* originally trade names for the products of particular manufacturers.

(3) Degeneration, where a form takes on an unfavorable meaning, or one which is improper or obscene. Examples: *knave* from Old English *cnafa* ("boy, servant"; compare the German cognate *Knabe,* "boy"), *madam* (keeper of a brothel) from an earlier (and still used) honorific. Degeneration often results in the formation of euphemisms, words or phrases used as preferred substitutes for degenerated forms, tabooed in polite society. Thus, *to die* and *undertaker,* because of their ominous significance, are often replaced by *to pass away* and *funeral director* or *mortician,* respectively.

(4) Elevation, where the meaning of a form rises in the social scale, losing an earlier unfavorable significance. Examples: *knight* from Old English *cniht* ("servant, young disciple"), *marshal* from an older French word meaning "a caretaker of horses (mares)," *bishop* from an earlier Greek word meaning "overseer."

(5) Metaphor, where an earlier metaphorical or marginal meaning becomes nuclear. Examples: *pen* from the Latin *penna* ("feather") used especially of quills and secondarily of feathers employed as writing instruments; German *Kopf* ("head") from an earlier word meaning "cup, bowl, pot" secondarily applied to the head; *fare* (as payment for passage), a derivative of Old English *faran* which had the nuclear meaning "to go."

(6) Metonymy, where a meaning shifts to another close to it in space or time. Examples: *cheek* from Old English *cēace* ("jaw") and *jaw* from Old French *joue* ("cheek"). See also the word *stomach* which, as a euphemism, is often applied, not only to the organ it properly designates, but to all of the abdomen.

(7) Synecdoche, where a form referring to a whole narrows to a part of the whole, and vice versa. Examples: *stove* from an earlier word meaning "heated room," *town* from an earlier Germanic form meaning "fence," and *bureau,* earlier a writing desk but now customarily applied to a whole office or government department.

(8) Hyperbole, where a later meaning is weaker than an earlier. Examples are particularly frequent in colloquial speech and slang. The word *awfully* is today used in many trivial contexts where it formerly was limited

to far stronger expressions. The same is true of curses in English and other European languages and such expressions as *lousy, putrid,* or *stinking.*

(9) Litote, the opposite of hyperbole. Thus the phrase *protective custody,* in Nazi Germany, acquired a far grimmer meaning than it had had before. So also the verb *to strafe,* as used in modern warfare, derived from the German *strafen* ("to punish").

The factors making for semantic change are for the most part undetermined. In a few instances, however, it can be shown that cultural innovations of a nonlinguistic nature often result in changes of meaning. English *acre,* for example, derives from Middle English *acer,* "a field small enough to be plowed by a man and a yoke of oxen in one day" and this in turn from Old English *aecer,* "a cultivated field." These shifts are almost certainly linked with the increasing economic significance of land and the correlated need for measuring it accurately.

Similarly, in Navaho, we can show that the introduction of the horse changed the meaning of a word from *dog* to *horse.* Navaho *béeš* once meant "flint" or "knife," the instrument presumably named after the material of which it was made. When metal knives came into use, *béeš* took on its modern meaning, "metal" (retaining the older "knife" as well), and flint came to be designated by a new term.

But the problem of meaning cannot be resolved merely by analyzing particular items; we must instead examine the total systems of meaning that exist in human cultures. This aspect of semantics, the role of language in culture, will be treated in the section that follows.

9. THE ROLE OF LANGUAGE IN CULTURE

We customarily view linguistic forms as more or less neutral counters standing for items and categories of experience which, except for their differing names, are essentially alike to all speakers and observers. This view is encouraged by much of our language teaching, where the student frequently learns only to substitute the words and phrases of a foreign idiom for the supposedly equivalent ones of his native tongue. There is, we assume, a real class of animals known to speakers of English as *horses,* to the French as *chevaux,* to the Germans as *Pferde,* and so on through as many speech communities as we know. It is taken for granted that horses are alike to all observers, whatever their language, and that these observers differ only in the words they use to denote the class of experience subsumed under *horse* and its apparent equivalents.

But this view of language receives a rude jolt when we encounter the fact of connotation as described in § 8, or even when we discover that denotations may be both nuclear and marginal. The French word *chou,* for example, may be replaced in its nuclear sense by English *cabbage,* but this translation is obviously impossible in the French endearment *Mon chou* ("my darling") or in the idiom *faire chou blanc* ("miss one's aim, fail"). Similarly, of course, the *head* of *Put a head on* (a glass of beer) or the *dog* of *John's in the dog-house* cannot be translated by the French *tête* or *chien* or the German *Kopf* or *Hund.*

These difficulties, and many other similar ones, suggest that linguistic forms are not merely neutral counters, arbitrarily linked to areas of experience known to all men. It appears rather, as Whorf has said, that

. . . we dissect nature [the flow of experience] along lines laid down by our native languages. The categories and types that we isolate from the world of phenomena we do not find there because they stare every observer in the face; on the contrary, the world is presented in a kaleidoscopic flux of impressions which has to be organized by our minds—and this means largely by the linguistic systems in our minds. We cut nature up, organize it into concepts, and ascribe significances as we do, largely because we are parties to an agreement to organize it in this way—an agreement [implicit and unstated] that holds throughout our speech community and is codified in the patterns of our language.[6]

The problems of meaning and communication suggested by these views can best be brought to light by what Whorf has called "contrastive linguistics," the plotting of "the outstanding differences between tongues— in grammar, logic, and the general analysis of experience."[7] Contrastive studies are the more revealing when we choose languages remote from each other and spoken by peoples of widely divergent cultures. It is in such comparisons that we arrive at the principle of linguistic relativity,

which means, in informal terms, that users of markedly different grammars are pointed by their grammars toward different types of observations and different evaluations of externally similar acts of observation, and hence are not equivalent as observers but must arrive at somewhat different views of the world.[8]

Simple examples of such divergent views are not difficult to find. In English, the expression *that house,* by virtue of its place in the series *this*

[6] B. L. Whorf, "Science and Linguistics." Reprinted from *The Technology Review,* Vol. 42 (1940), p. 231, edited at the Massachusetts Institute of Technology.
[7] "Languages and Logic." Reprinted from *The Technology Review,* Vol. 43 (1941), p. 266, edited at the Massachusetts Institute of Technology.
[8] B. L. Whorf, "Linguistics as an Exact Science." Reprinted from *The Technology Review,* Vol. 43 (1940), p. 61, edited at the Massachusetts Institute of Technology.

house, that house, these houses, those houses, defines, roughly, a singular house at some distance from the speaker. But among the Kwakiutl Indians of British Columbia, according to Boas, a similar expression belongs to a more complex series, to wit:

1. the house (singular or plural) visible near me.
2. the house (singular or plural) invisible near me.
3. the house (singular or plural) visible near thee.
4. the house (singular or plural) invisible near thee.
5. the house (singular or plural) visible near him.
6. the house (singular or plural) invisible near him.[9]

Kwakiutl, it is evident, has six demonstratives where English has but four (that is, *this, that, these, those*). In Kwakiutl, one must specify visibility or invisibility as well as location in reference to the speaker, the person addressed, or some third person. Note, however, that the English distinction between singular and plural is not required in Kwakiutl, for all six of the Kwakiutl demonstratives refer indifferently to one or more than one.

In Eskimo, Boas continues, demonstratives are even more specific. An English expression like *that man* must appear in one of the following forms: *that man near me, that man near thee, that man near him; that man behind me, that man in front of me, that man to the right of me, that man to the left of me, that man above me, that man below me,* and so on for person addressed (thee) and the third person (him).

To take a more complex and revealing example, suppose we attempt to translate the English sentence *I give it to him* into Navaho, assuming just the literal sense of presenting another with a gift. At first, we can find no Navaho equivalent, for there is no Navaho verb that has the meaning *give.* But if we persist, we find not one but twelve Navaho forms which are at least the rough equivalents of our English sentence. All these are simple verb expressions, for in Navaho the verb is quite often as expressive as a whole phrase or sentence in English.

The first part of all twelve verbs (called the prefix complex) is the same. It may be written *bàaniš-,* where *b* and *n* are pronounced much as English *p* and *n,* respectively, *š* is like *sh* in *ship, a* is about the same as the vowel of *palm,* and *i* is like the vowel of *sit.* The vowel *a* is doubled to indicate that it is long; it has about twice the duration of *i. Bàaniš-* is made up of four morphemes: *b-,* from *bi-* ("him"), *àa-* ("to, toward"), *ni-* ("completively"), and *š-* ("I"). Arranged in this way, these morphemes together have the meaning "I cause it completively to him," obviously only a partial meaning as *bàaniš-* is only part of a larger form.

[9] Franz Boas, "Introduction," *Handbook of American Indian Languages, Part 1,* Bulletin 40, Bureau of American Ethnology (Washington, D. C., 1911), pp. 40–41.

To complete the Navaho form we must add one further morpheme, a verb stem. Twelve of these may be used, the choice depending on what sort of object is referred to by the "it" of the prefix complex. If this is a living object, the stem -*tèeh* ("a living object moves") is added to form *bàanìstèeh* ("I cause it [a living being] to move completively to him" or, roughly, "I give a living being to him"). Similarly, we can form *bàanìškàah* ("I cause a container with contents to move completively to him"), *bàanìsté* ("I cause a ropelike object to move completively to him"), and so on through a total of twelve categories of objects to be given. If the speaker is in doubt as to the nature of the object given, he uses *bàanìš²àah* ("I cause a round solid object to move completively to him" or "I cause it [unknown] to move completively to him").

It is clear, then, that the notion expressed by English *give,* as a separate category of action, does not exist in Navaho. Rather, the Navahos speak of giving as a special instance of "objects moving," where an agent causes an object of a particular type to move completively from himself to another. The act of giving, in other words, is differently conceived in the two speech communities, and this difference is codified in their styles of speech.

To conclude this section, it would appear that language functions far more importantly in a culture than simply as a neutral device to represent or symbolize the flow of experience. A language does more: it furnishes the categories and divisions of experience in terms of which its speakers cope with the universe about them. Sapir, in an article called "The Status of Linguistics as a Science," made this fact amply clear when he said:

Language is a guide to "social reality." Though language is not ordinarily thought of as of essential interest to the students of social science, it powerfully conditions all our thinking about social problems and processes. Human beings do not live in the objective world alone, nor alone in the world of social activity as ordinarily understood, but are very much at the mercy of the particular language which has become the medium of expression for their society. It is quite an illusion to imagine that one adjusts to reality essentially without the use of language and that language is merely an incidental means of solving specific problems of communication or reflection. The fact of the matter is that the "real world" is to a large extent unconsciously built up on the language habits of the group. No two languages are ever sufficiently similar to be considered as representing the same social reality. The worlds in which different societies live are distinct worlds, not merely the same world with different labels attached.[10]

[10] *Language* (Charlottesville, Va.: Linguistic Society of America), Vol. 5, pp. 207–214 (1929), p. 209.

10. WRITING

In our own society, where nearly everyone early learns to read and write, we often confuse language with writing and frequently speak of writing as though it were a special kind of language. The "written language" is contrasted to the "spoken language," with the former being regarded as somehow more accurate and precise than the latter. In some circumstances, indeed, we speak as though nonliterate peoples (that is, peoples who lack a writing) also lack a language and so can communicate with each other, if at all, only with the greatest difficulty.

The error implicit in these beliefs is obvious: language and writing, though clearly related, are not the same. They are, in fact, two very different aspects of culture. Writing, roughly defined, is a set of techniques for the graphic representation of speech, whereas language, as we have seen, is a complex of patterns which governs or controls speaking. All of us learn to speak early in life; with minor and unimportant exceptions, we have acquired all our habits of speaking before we are six years old. But we do not ordinarily learn to read and write until much later, if at all, and this learning has, on the whole, very little effect upon our speaking habits. Literate peoples, then, possess two cultural techniques related to language: the art of speaking, which they share with all humans, literate or not, and that of writing or representing their spoken forms graphically, a cultural possession which distinguishes them from nonliterate societies.

Writing probably originated from drawing, a technique as widespread among human beings as language itself. But we must emphasize that drawings, even in the form of conventionalized pictographs, are not the equivalents of writing. A drawing may well serve to recall an event, or even, as among the Plains Indians, to tell a story. Narrative drawings, however, often miscalled "picture-writing," differ from true writing in that the pictographs are not tied specifically to spoken words, syllables, or sounds, but may be interpreted by any of a number of equivalent utterances. The pictograph $\wedge$, as used by the Plains Indians, stands simply for a dwelling, whatever word might be used to name it, whereas our graphic symbol *house* is linked specifically to one spoken word and no other. The Plains Indian $\wedge$ can be read *house, dwelling, tipi, tent,* or any similar equivalent, but *house* can stand only for this word and no other.

True writing began, then, when conventionalized graphic symbols (derived, it would seem, from earlier pictographs) became associated with the sounds of a language. In all the earliest writings known, many or most of the symbols are logographic, that is, they stand for words, particular combinations of speech sounds. Some early systems are also syllabaries, in which the symbols stand for syllables rather than whole words. While logographic systems of writing still exist (as in Chinese) and many peoples (e.g., the Japanese and some of the peoples of India) still employ syllabaries, most modern systems are alphabetic, that is, the graphic symbols represent, more or less accurately, the distinctive sounds or phonemes of the languages written. The history of the development from the earliest known logograms to modern alphabetic writing is very complicated and still imperfectly known. We shall summarize only the major developments in the following paragraphs.

Writing was certainly invented twice in human history and possibly oftener. The earliest invention occurred in the Near East, probably among the Bronze Age Egyptians. It is possible that this invention spread, with many changes, throughout Europe and Asia, so giving rise to all modern systems of Old World origin, but many scholars believe that Chinese writing (and possibly other systems) were invented independently. Later, and quite independently of the Near East, writing was invented by the Mayas, an American Indian people of Guatemala and Yucatan. But Maya writing gave rise to no modern forms and today even the few surviving Maya records are undecipherable. The Aztecs of Mexico also possessed a writing, very like that of the Mayas, and probably derived from it.

The earliest Egyptian writing was a mixed system, combining logograms and even pictographs with symbols which stood for syllables. Later it became standardized to some twenty-four characters, each of which stood for a consonant plus a vowel. In this form the Egyptian writing was taken over by a neighboring people who spoke a Semitic language.

These people reworked the Egyptian system to suit the needs of their language. Each symbol came to represent a consonant alone; vowels were not represented at all. Semitic writing thus became alphabetic, in that each symbol stood for a single sound. It was, of course, incompletely alphabetic in that the vowels were not represented. This was no great handicap in a Semitic language where the vowels may easily be supplied from the arrangement of consonants in a word and the context in which the word appears.

The alphabet so formed spread quickly to all the Semitic-speaking peoples of the Near East, including the Phoenicians, traders living at the eastern end of the Mediterranean and the founders of the city of Carthage in North Africa. As a result of trading contacts with the Phoenicians, and probably under the stimulus of trade which requires written records, the Greeks soon took over the Phoenician alphabet, adapting it to their uses as the Semites had adapted the Egyptian syllabary.

The Greeks made many changes in the Phoenician alphabet, but the most important of these was the invention of vowel symbols. Greek, like

English, cannot be written intelligibly in consonants alone; vowels must also be represented. The Greeks, however, did not create many new symbols; rather they simply reinterpreted some of the Phoenician characters, especially those which were not necessary to the writing of Greek consonants. Thus the Phoenician aleph (a consonant pronounced deep in the throat) became the Greek vowel alpha, and two Phoenician symbols for *h*-like or breath sounds (absent in Greek) became Greek epsilon and eta, both vowels. Greek *o* was made from another Phoenician consonant, and *i* and *u* from two more.

From the Greeks, in a long series of borrowings extending over centuries, the alphabet spread to the Romans, the Germanic-speaking peoples, and so to all of Europe. At the same time, there was also a spread from the Near East eastward, for it is probable that the Indian systems of writing are from the same source as the Semitic and European. In all these borrowings, modifications were made: in the values of the signs used, in the form of the writing, and in numerous other details. Indeed, the history of writing is extraordinarily complex, and there still remain many problems yet unsolved. Whole systems of writing are still undecipherable in large part; an excellent example is found in the ancient inscriptions of Crete. And most of the later systems, though well known in general, still offer many problems of interpretation. Scholars are even today in doubt, for example, as to the proper reading of many Greek and Latin characters, or even of a number of particulars in the writing of Old English.

Nevertheless, it is clear that writing has a history definitely apart from that of language. Our central point, that language exists independently of a system of writing, should never be lost sight of. Writing adds a valuable set of techniques to a culture, but it adds nothing to the language.

Though writing marks an important step in the development of human cultures, it does not in itself provide all the features of long-distance communication, the keeping of accurate records, and the spread of learning so frequently attributed to it. In many societies writing remained a technique restricted to a small elite and even prohibited to the bulk of the population. Among the Mayas and early Egyptians, writing apparently functioned mainly as a magico-religious device; it was an art difficult to learn and laborious to perform. And even though the development of extensive trade in the Near East caused the spread of writing to secular uses, it still remained in the province of a few, highly skilled specialists.

True literacy and the spread of learning and education came only when writing was supplemented by means, like printing, for the rapid duplication of written records.

11. SUMMARY

Language, like the culture of which it is a part, is an abstraction, derived from observation and analysis of human behavior. The behavior studied is speaking, and a language may therefore be briefly defined as the ways of speaking prevailing in a given society.

We note further that languages, like cultures, are extremely divergent; no two societies possess precisely the same ways of speaking. Unlike certain aspects of culture, however, there are apparently no "primitive" languages, that is, there are no languages which, like certain crude stone-using technologies, are inferior or less well developed than others. It is this high development of languages everywhere, plus their diversity, that leads us to conclude that language is one of the oldest, if not the oldest, of human faculties.

We may go even further. Symbolizing, we have seen, is a prerequisite to culture, and language is one of man's most important means of symbolizing. It is therefore probable that no true culture was possible until language had itself come into being, or, at least, that language accompanied in development man's first steps in building a cultural tradition.

Contrastive and comparative studies of languages reveal that each has a distinctive structure (1) in respect to its significant sounds or phonemes and the ways in which these are combined in connected speech and (2) in respect to its grammar, or its ways of arranging morphemes into words, phrases, and sentences. Linguistic structures, though at any one time rigid and unyielding, are nonetheless subject to continual change. As a result of such change, and the spread of peoples over the areas in which they live, single languages frequently give way to clusters of many related idioms.

Comparative studies enable us to relate languages, one to another, and group them into stocks and families. Evidence of such relationship is best summarized in series of phonetic correspondences, whereby the phonemes of one language are seen to be regularly divergent from those of others in the same family. The languages belonging to a single stock are thus said to be derived, through a longer or shorter period of change, from a single original language. However, since this technique of classifying languages depends on the observation of similarities and regular divergences among modern tongues (or idioms known through documentary records), it does not carry us far into man's history. Languages are as old as culture and linguistic change has gone on as long. Consequently, though it is possible that all modern languages go back to a single source, their divergences today are so great as to provide no evidences of such a relationship.

Languages, by virtue of their functions in human societies, are linked to systems of meaning. The meanings of linguistic forms are, however, difficult to determine with precision; they are never so definite and systematized as phonological or grammatical features. Meanings also change through time, often quite independently of structural changes. Much semantic change can be related to changes in nonlinguistic culture, but there is also much that cannot be explained so simply.

The study of meanings also illuminates the role of language in human society, other than the self-evident one of providing a means of communication. It seems clear that linguistic symbols, and the ways of arranging and classifying them, profoundly influence our views of both the physical and social worlds, even to the extent that peoples with different languages may be said to live in different worlds of reality. Meanings, then, are not isolated bits of experience, arbitrarily associated, in different languages, with differing linguistic forms. There is rather a system of meanings for each language, organized according to certain basic premises or assumptions, much as culture taken as a whole is an organized interpretation of human experience, unique for each society.

Writing must be treated separately from language, for it reveals upon analysis a distinctive history and a distinctive function in human societies. Where a language may be described as a set of ways of speaking, so may writing be defined as a set of techniques for representing speech graphically. As compared with language, writing is a recent innovation, no more than a few thousand years old. All peoples speak, and all possess languages of essentially the same level of development. But writing is relatively rare, existing only among peoples more advanced in culture, and there are many societies in which it is lacking altogether. Writing is an extremely important basic invention, certainly necessary to the highly complex civilizations of the present day. Together with other inventions, such as printing, it makes possible long-distance communication, the keeping of accurate records, and the systems of education and research so vital to present world cultures.

COLLATERAL READING

Bloomfield, Leonard. *Language*. New York: Henry Holt and Co., 1933.

Hall, Robert A., Jr. *Leave Your Language Alone!* Ithaca, New York: Linguistica, 1950.

Karlgren, B. *Sound and Symbol in Chinese*. London: Oxford University Press, 1923.

Mallery, Garrick. *Picture Writing of the American Indians*. Tenth Annual Report, Bureau of American Ethnology, Washington, D. C., 1893.

Mandelbaum, David (ed.). *Selected Writings of Edward Sapir in Language, Culture, and Personality.* Berkeley: University of California Press, 1949. See especially: "Language" (pp. 7–32), "Dialect" (pp. 83–88), "Language and Environment" (pp. 89–103), "Communication" (pp. 104–109), "The Grammarian and His Language" (pp. 150–159), "The Status of Linguistics as a Science" (pp. 160–166), "Central and North American Languages" (pp. 169–178).

Sapir, Edward. *Language.* New York: Harcourt, Brace and Co., 1921.

Schlauch, Margaret. *The Gift of Tongues.* New York: Modern Age Books, 1942.

Sprengling, Martin. *The Alphabet.* Chicago: Oriental Institute Communications, 12, 1931.

Sturtevant, Edgar. *An Introduction to Linguistic Science.* New Haven: Yale University Press, 1947.

Chapter 18

THE ARTS

1. NATURE AND ORIGIN OF THE ARTS

Broadly defined, art must be considered as one of the universals of human culture. No culture is known in which some form of esthetic expression does not occur. This does not mean, of course, that all art forms are always represented or that the various types of esthetic expression are equally developed in every culture. Yet from its universality we may conclude that need for esthetic expression corresponds to some fundamental characteristic of human beings. On the other hand, the ways in which these needs are satisfied are culturally determined and, like other aspects of culture, have acquired a wide range of functions and become integrated with many other aspects of culture.

In our own culture we tend to think of the arts as a fairly well-defined group of activities, usually carried on by specialists. Painting, sculpture, music, professional dancing, the drama, the opera, the writing of fiction and poetry, are all generally recognized as "Art," at least if done under certain circumstances and with certain qualities. Less frequently we recognize other activities as being at least potentially "artistic." Fabric design, furniture design, ceramics, household decoration, and so on are sometimes recognized as having artistic elements, although they usually are considered as belonging to the practical or applied arts, rather than to the so-called fine arts. Nevertheless, all these and many other activities have one element in common; it is generally recognized that they may be carried on in ways which are more or less satisfying to the performer and the beholder. In other words, all have an "esthetic" component.

538

It is this esthetic component which we shall recognize as the basis for our broad definition of the arts. For purposes of our discussion, we shall consider any activity as related to the arts in which the resulting performance or the object made, over and above its possible efficiency or utility, affords a greater or less satisfaction to the one who produces it or to those who may view it.

This broad definition means that we may regard such things as dress and bodily ornamentation, for example, from the standpoint of art. Basketry decoration, the painting or modeling of pottery, the carving of a canoe prow or a house post, and all forms of dancing, music, and story-telling, then, are among the things which may be examined from the standpoint of their artistic component.

Although art in some form is universal among humans, there is no evidence that it goes back to the beginnings of the human species. Köhler's chimpanzees, it is true, hung strings and rags about themselves, smeared themselves with paint, and engaged in single-file circuits of a post in which they stamped one foot harder than the other, although not in unison. It may be that from such crude impulses in the basic primate stock arose the human needs for artistic expression, but we have no direct evidence that such is the case.

The earliest direct evidence of artistic activity occurs with Neanderthal man, who collected mineral pigments, such as ochre, and may well have used them for the decoration of the body. The beautiful stone-chipping of the Solutrean period likewise suggests derivation from esthetic impulses. There seems no practical purpose served by the beautifully regular retouching technique applied over the entire surface of such artifacts as knives and points. This conclusion is reinforced by the finding of caches of exceptionally fine examples of chipped implements which apparently had never been used. It seems likely in this case that once the perfect mastery of stone-chipping was acquired, esthetic satisfaction was derived from expressions of special virtuosity in the technique. Such satisfactions are widely known among modern human groups, where some people at least take pleasure in exceptionally well-made implements. Among ourselves, a well-made and designed machine or building gives satisfaction to most people quite apart from its purely utilitarian purposes.

Everyone in our culture, of course, recognizes the carving, modeling, and painting of the Aurignacian and Magdalenian as an artistic expression. Such realistic representation of nature is common among ourselves, although it is relatively rare among nonliterate groups. Among Paleolithic man, however, representational art probably was closely connected with religious or magical beliefs. In part our own representational art movement also was originally closely associated with religion, although today most of it is secular or nonreligious.

On the beginnings of such arts as the dance, music, and story-telling we have no information, for these leave no concrete evidences in archeological deposits. It might be noted, though, that one famous Magdalenian cave painting apparently shows a sorcerer (or perhaps a supernatural being?) engaged in some sort of dance. Further, since dancing, music, and story-telling or literature exist without exception in all contemporary societies, it is not improbable that these arts, like painting and modeling, go back at least to the Paleolithic and perhaps to the very beginnings of human culture.

A word may be added here on the subject of so-called primitive art, and the assumption so often implicit in this phrase, that the art forms (whether paintings, carvings, decorations, or narratives) of nonliterate peoples are universally crude in execution and childlike or immature in conception. This notion, like so many other popular ideas on primitive cultures, is far from accurate. To be sure, the art forms of some nonliterate peoples are less well executed than our own, particularly where the execution depends on crude tools and inferior techniques. But even this is not always true. Paleolithic paintings, for example, despite a crude technology, are often excellently done. The Pueblo Indians decorate their pottery with great skill and apparently have known this art for centuries. Art in wood, on the North Pacific coast of America, in Melanesia, Polynesia, and Africa, is extraordinarily well done, despite comparatively poor tools, and Eskimo carvings in bone and ivory have few equals anywhere. Finally, there is nowhere any weaving art superior to that of the ancient Peruvians, whose tapestries, in point of technique, have been favorably compared with the best that Europe has produced.

Maturity and sophistication in conception is, of course, another matter: it is no easy task to contrast widely divergent cultures on this point, and to grade them with respect to each other. Nevertheless, it is certain that no art, however simple the culture from which it springs, may be considered childlike or immature. There is sophistication and maturity in the art of all peoples, if only we know enough of the culture that produces it to be capable of understanding and appreciating it. Consider, for example, Navaho sand-paintings, designs made of colored vegetable and mineral materials against a background of buckskin or sand. There are hundreds of these, depicting the holy people and abstractions of sacred powers. "These highly stylized paintings," according to Kluckhohn,[1] "serve, in somewhat the fashion of medieval glass painting, to make visible and concrete the holy

---

[1] Kluckhohn and Leighton, *The Navaho,* p. 132.

figures and religious concepts of The People." Taken together, the Navaho sand-paintings are symbolic of an enormously complex myth cycle, recounting the creation of the universe, the preparation of the world for habitation by man, and the origins of most rituals and ceremonies. There is nothing immature or childlike in these conceptions, however strange and unusual they may appear to persons of a foreign culture.

In summary, then, we may consider the arts as including any activity with an esthetic component. Activities with such components are universal among contemporary peoples, although we cannot effectively trace the history and origin of the arts. The arts probably arise out of psychological needs of man, although there is much to be learned in this regard, but like other such activities, they are culturally conditioned and controlled and are related to other aspects of culture. In subsequent sections we will consider some of the functions and cultural interrelations of the arts, the relation of the arts to the individual, art as a form of communication, and art as cultural tradition. As we shall see, these necessarily overlap to some degree.

2. ART AND THE INDIVIDUAL

The totality of the processes involved in the production of a work of art have probably never been studied with anything like scientific accuracy and detail. Yet it is clear that many factors operate in artistic production, each of which is necessary to the completed procedure. Among these factors, two certainly stand out as paramount: the culture and period in its history in which the artist participates, and the people with whom he lives and works, whether these be critics, collaborators, or simply his friends and relatives. While in this section we shall concentrate on the individual and his relationship to art, we cannot neglect either the social or the cultural setting in which the artist does his work.

In one sense, all of art is produced by individuals. Even when many people collaborate, as in a dramatic production, a ballet, a symphonic concert, or the writing and production of a motion picture, the many forms, actions, and patterns that make up the completed production do not arise spontaneously. All may be traced ultimately to the contributions of this individual or that. Groups as such create nothing; the act of creating is always an individual's action.

Nevertheless, it is a mistake to conclude that a work of art, even a painting or a novel, is exclusively the production of one person, or that a group product, such as a motion picture, can be reduced to a mere sum of individual contributions. Actually, the processes of artistic production are far more complicated; the artist, in effect, gives expression in his productions

to sentiments, emotions, and ideas that arise through and by his interactions with others. It is in this sense that all art owes its inception to its
social and cultural setting rather than to the artist alone. The unique genius
of the artist lies in his sensitivity to the social and cultural milieu, and in his
ability to respond in an esthetically satisfying medium.

To exemplify this point is difficult, for, as we have said, no one has
really studied the artist at work. But we can sometimes infer something of
the process of artistic creation from an analysis of the work produced. Numerous studies of literature illustrate such analysis, and demonstrate that
no artist truly works in isolation but is continually subject, in one way or
another, to many influences originating in his culture, his historical period,
and in the people with whom he lives. Similar illustration may be found in
nonliterate societies, particularly in the telling of myths and legends. The
story-teller truly interacts with his audience and may frequently add to the
tale and embellish it in response to their reactions to his performance. He
will also adapt his tale to particular cultural circumstances by illustrating
and developing the plot in terms of current events and happenings known
to the audience and himself. In this way, the tale gradually changes in both
form and content, as it is told over and over again by different narrators,
to different audiences, and at different times in the history of a people.

In our society, the individual artist—that is, the painter who paints a
picture or the novelist who writes a book—is customarily given great prominence; his dependence on other people and on his culture is frequently
overlooked. In other societies, and particularly among nonliterate peoples,
works of art—such as the stories told, the songs sung, and decorations on
pottery, basketry, and other media—are often anonymous, or at least the
individual artist is given only a subordinate role in their production. It is
this difference that we recognize when we speak of folk art, in which, as
in the art of nonliterates, the role of the individual as creator is much reduced, if not lost altogether.

The anonymous nature of folk art and the art of nonliterate peoples has
frequently led to the observation that everyone in a folk or nonliterate society is an artist, whereas in our society the artist is usually a professional.
In one sense this is true, for folk arts and those of nonliterates are often
practiced, to some degree, by nearly everyone. Most Navaho adults are at
one time or another story-tellers; many Navaho men sing at ceremonies
or social dances; and nearly all Navaho women weave decorated blankets.
But it may be worth while to examine this observation in more detail, and
so learn more of the role of the individual in the arts. Are all members of
a nonliterate society artists? Are they all equally able? Are no differences
recognized between artists?

Unfortunately there are few concrete studies which enable us to answer these questions directly. One of the best researches in this field is a study by the late Lila O'Neale of the basket-weavers of the Karok and Yurok Indians of Northwest California.[2] These two groups, almost identical in culture, are widely known as technically skillful basket-makers. The baskets are in a variety of shapes and have a geometric ornamentation which is generally admired in our culture. In her investigation of these people, Miss O'Neale found that many women make baskets; in aboriginal times, probably every woman did so, for baskets are an important part of the household equipment. Yet considerable differences in skill, both in weaving and in the use of design, are evident. These differences are clearly apparent to the Indians themselves; they recognize that one woman is a better artist than another. The superior weaver appears to get some satisfaction from this recognition, but also to get satisfaction from her own feeling of ability and skill.

The designs placed on baskets today vary considerably, but there is clear distinction between old design elements and new. There are also traditional ways of placing designs on baskets of different shapes. Approved originality in design consists of making slight variations in the traditional design elements or motifs, and in their placing on the basket. Variations or completely original innovations are more apt to be accepted and perhaps copied, however, if the weaver is a recognized leader in the field. Innovations by a poor weaver are certain to be criticized and are not copied. According to Miss O'Neale, "Far from being deadened by a craft in which so much is reduced to conformity, the women of the two tribes have developed an appreciation of quality, design-to-space relationships, and effective color dispositions which are discriminating and genuine." [3]

In the preceding case, we are dealing with a craft which imposes technical limitations on the artist to begin with, and which takes years of instruction and practice before great skill can be developed. In addition there are conventions as to what is acceptable and what is not. Yet within this framework there are recognized differences of ability. There is also limited but real originality. Artists appear to have developed conscious esthetic standards and apparently derive satisfaction both from achieving these standards and from the recognition accorded them by others.

Such evidence as we have indicates that other arts among nonliterates are similarly regarded, at least to some degree. There are recognized standards in all artistic activities, whether it be painting designs on pottery,

[2] "Yurok-Karok Basket Weavers," *University of California Publications in American Archaeology and Ethnology,* XXXII, 1–182, 1932.
[3] *Ibid.,* p. 165.

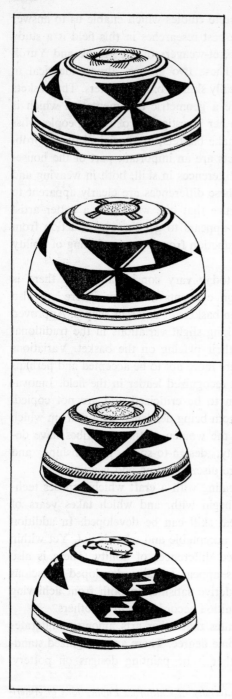

Fig. 18:1. Variations in design elements and their placing in California Indian baskets. After O'Neale.

weaving cloth, carving wood, dancing, or telling stories, and there are as well recognized differences in ability. The maker or performer gets satisfaction from his skill or virtuosity, in his creativeness within the limits imposed by the culture, and from the recognition of his fellows.

In our own society, there is considerable evidence that the same factors operate, although with varying force among different individuals. Some artists, writers, and others have seemed indifferent to the recognition of their fellows, while some have derived their principal satisfaction from such recognition. In a society which supplements recognition with monetary rewards, the latter have usually fared better economically.

It is not assumed, of course, that an artist works only to gain personal gratification, whether by his own creativeness or by recognition from others. Artists frequently have something to say, some emotion or idea that they hope to communicate to others who may view their productions. This is particularly true in our own society, and probably occurs as well in others. Indeed, there are some who believe that all of art everywhere communicates, whether or not the artist is conscious of such communication, and whether or not a society recognizes the art medium as a means of communication. However this question may be answered, it appears that emotions and ideas are more explicitly expressed in such fields as painting, literature, and the dramatic arts than in others. We shall discuss the communication function of the arts further in the section that follows.

3. ART AS COMMUNICATION: CONVENTIONS AND FORMAL SYMBOLS

In the preceding paragraph, it was suggested that the artist often seeks to convey ideas and emotions. In so far as he succeeds, he is communicating to his fellows. In the discussion of the Yurok and Karok basketry, it was pointed out that the artist operated within a closely limited set of conventions. Such conventions are always present where communication is achieved.

This statement may be challenged by many artists in our society. In part, this is because the conventions within which the artist operates, whether in our own society or a nonliterate society, are very largely unconscious, just as is most of cultural behavior. The literary artist, for example, operates within the framework of a system of symbols known as language, and language is taken for granted by most artists. Linguistic conventions, though in many ways rigid and unyielding, do of course allow for a certain degree of individuality and originality in the arrangement and handling of their elements. But these variations are severely limited; even an e. e. cummings, whose innovations are after all mainly in writing rather in language, will not write in nonsense syllables. A Joyce or a Stein achieves certain effects by violating some writing and linguistic conventions, but, in so doing, limits his audience, at least until these innovations come more widely to be understood and appreciated. And it should not be forgotten that an unknown artist, or one of lesser stature, cannot so easily persuade his readers to tolerate radical innovations of writing and linguistic expression; his variations on the commonly accepted conventions may cause him to lose touch with his readers altogether. In short, the literary artist is bound rather closely by both a system of language and a system of writing that language; a bondage he cannot escape if he seeks to communicate to any but a chosen few.

Similarly, in the field of painting, we accept in the first place the convention of two-dimensional representation of three-dimensional space. That this is a convention, and that the interpretation is learned, is indicated by reports that some peoples in Oceania, who have no two-dimensional art, are at first incapable of recognizing and interpreting photographs. In our own culture, of course, everyone is familiar with two-dimensional representation from a very early age. With a few exceptions, most modern painters still operate within the convention of two-dimensional representation, however much they may ignore other conventions.

In the theater, likewise, a room is commonly represented with only three sides; the fourth is, of course, removed that the audience may view the action. Audiences accept this convention without question, despite its arbitrary and artificial character. Indeed, in recent years, audiences have even become accustomed to central staging, where all of the walls are dispensed with, and the actors are surrounded by an audience on all four sides.

More elaborate and rigid conventions may depend upon formal symbols, which differ very little from the symbols used in language. In our own religious art, for example, a golden ring or halo above the head of a figure is used to denote a divine being and is so understood by most people in our society. It would have no such meaning to an ancient Mayan who, on the other hand, would find no incongruity in a human figure with one arm ending in a serpent symbol to identify him as a particular deity. Symbolism, then, can be of two kinds, the acceptance of certain basic conventions upon which a whole art form is based, such as representing three-dimensional space on a two-dimensional canvas, and the use of particular symbolic items, such as a halo. In our own culture the use of specific symbols in art is relatively rare and mainly associated with religious art. In other cultures, such as that of the ancient Mayas, the number of specific symbols is very great.

One of the truly great art expressions of the world is that of the Maya Indians of Central America, an art which maintained itself with varying but high quality over nearly two thousand years. The Mayas were extremely skillful painters and sculptors, and were able accurately to represent the human body in its most difficult positions, that is, as reclining, full face, three-quarter face, and so on. Their artists had also made a rather able development of perspective a number of centuries before it began to develop in European painting. Despite its technical excellence, however, much of Maya art is incomprehensible at first sight to people of our culture. Two major reasons exist for this. One was the Maya convention which deemed large vacant spaces in a composition to be undesirable. Accordingly, they filled these spaces with elaborate and ornate designs, and even used wholly meaningless elements merely to fill space. The second, and in some ways more important reason, was the high degree of religious symbolism involved. Maya art was primarily a religious art and incorporated a large number of formal symbols. These all conveyed significant meaning to a Maya; to the modern observer unversed in Maya art, they are apparently meaningless insertions and even distortions of the main figures.

Not all art traditions utilizing formal symbolism are related directly to religion. The Indians of the North Pacific coast developed a great art tradition which is even harder for a person of our culture to understand than is that of the Maya. Again the element of formal symbolism is large. The North Pacific coast Indians represent a great many animal forms as well as mythical beings. The latter, of course, would not be understandable without knowing the religious beliefs, but even representations of animals often may not be recognized by the untrained observer.

Fig. 18:2. Haida carved plate, illustrating the shark design adapted to a round, flat surface.

The North Pacific coast Indians seek, first, to adapt the form of the animal represented to the object to be decorated, and second, to represent, as far as possible, the whole animal. They do not, however, attempt a realistic view; as Boas has said, "with the exception of a few profiles, we do not find a single instance which can be interpreted as an endeavor to give a perspective and therefore realistic view of an animal." [4] Animal representations are, then, "combinations of symbols of the various parts of the body of the animal," so arranged "that the natural relation of the parts is preserved, being changed only by means of sections and distortions, but so that the natural contiguity of the parts is observed." [5]

[4] Franz Boas, "The Decorative Art of the Indians of the North Pacific Coast," *Bulletin of the American Museum of Natural History*, 9, 123–176 (1897), p. 176.
[5] *Ibid.*

As an example, let us describe briefly a wooden box, decorated with a carving or painting of the beaver. The front of the beaver is represented on the front of the box, the sides of its body on each side of the box, and the tail on the back of the box. On the bottom of the box is a view of the beaver's underside, and on the top, a similarly disconnected view of the beaver's back. In brief, the animal is, as it were, sectioned by the artist, and each section represented separately, but in its proper relation to other sections, on the object to be decorated.

Excellent designs are thus achieved, but of course the animal represented is completely unrecognizable to anyone ignorant of North Pacific coast culture. To the native, however, the representation is clear and unmistakable, for included in every design are formal symbols identifying the animal. Thus, the beaver representation in the example given above will show two large incisor teeth, a scaly tail indicated by an ovaloid area hatched in a particular way, and a stick held between the forepaws. However differently a beaver may be pictured on objects of differing size and shape, these symbols will always be included, and so identify the picture to the initiated viewer.

It is obvious, from the above examples, that visual art operates through symbolism to some degree and that it will convey certain meanings to persons familiar with the symbols. Similar circumstances could be demonstrated for the other arts also. As a vehicle for communication, however, the arts operate on a much broader and more subtle scale than through symbolism. Their effectiveness seems to stem from the fact that in general the arts entertain, they produce a certain "suspension of disbelief," and generally have some emotional quality to them. These other aspects of communication should be examined briefly.

4. ART AS COMMUNICATION: FUNCTIONS

One of the main functions of the arts as communication is to reinforce belief, custom, and values. In some art traditions this function may be extended to instruction or propaganda. Thus religious art, whether expressed in the architecture of churches, in the presentation of religious scenes, or in the images of saints, serves first of all to create the emotional and intellectual atmosphere considered proper for religious exercises. It also serves as a constant reminder of aspects of belief, and, in the form of drama, it may take on a direct instructional purpose.

For example, throughout the Middle Ages, the church, confronted with the problem of a large illiterate population in Europe, developed dramatic representations of important religious events or dogmas (the so-called mystery plays), both to educate and to reinforce knowledge of fundamental Christian doctrine. This device was transferred to Latin America for use in educating the Indian, where it met with considerable success, and still persists in many places. Often such religious dramas are coupled with the dance, as in the Mexican "Pastores," one of the better known, but far from the only survival, of the mystery plays in Latin America. Plays and pageants for children are common in many of the churches in the United States as well, particularly around Christmas, and are commonly used, in many primary schools, to teach young children. Adult schools for illiterates also use dramatic performances as teaching devices, especially in modern China.

Fig. 18:3. Pueblo dance mask used in religious ceremonies.

Such use of the arts is common among many nonliterate peoples as well. The Pawnees, for example, have a ceremony before planting time in which the whole routine of the proper planting and care of corn is reviewed. Similar ceremonies occur among a number of northwest Amazon tribes, where many religious ceremonials and dances occur before planting time, interspersed with long recitatives regarding the proper planting and care of the plants appropriate to the season. In this way conservation of knowledge on a practical level is interwoven with religious belief, artistic performance involving drama, music, dance, and poetry, and a social occasion of considerable importance.

The study of nonliterate myth and folk tale again provides many similar examples, in which beliefs and value systems are reinforced and transmitted to the young. Such functions are not always obvious from the mere reading of tales, but often become clear when the setting of the story-telling is examined. Many Indians of western North America, for example, tell elaborate tales centering around the mythical figure of Coyote. Coyote is usually represented as a trickster who indulges in more or less malicious pranks as well as activities of the grossest and most immoral character, judged by both native standards as well as our own. Such tales are frequently told in the presence of the young. Almost invariably, however, Coyote meets with misfortune as a result of his behavior. The adults treat the stories as extremely funny, making clear that their laughter is at the improper behavior of Coyote and pointing the moral at the end that no good can come of such behavior. The parallel between the inevitable triumph of virtue and the discomfiture of vice in our own popular literature, from the so-called comic strip to many motion pictures, seems obvious.

The function of the arts in reinforcing knowledge, beliefs, attitudes, and values is fairly easily recognized in a simple homogeneous society. In a complex and heterogeneous society such as ours, the problem becomes more difficult, for not all groups within our society have the same beliefs, attitudes, and values. We may agree that virtue should always triumph, but definitions of virtue differ from group to group. The successful labor leader who wins better wages, hours, and working conditions may be a proper hero to members of his union, but he must be portrayed as a villain to satisfy most members of the employing group in our society. Making a motion picture about a real labor problem—certainly a significant aspect of our culture—is fraught with great difficulties, for a motion picture is very costly to make and hence must draw sizable audiences. The common assertion that commercialization of the arts is at the root of this problem seems an inadequate explanation. A ceremonial among nonliterates, which may give rise to expressions of design, dance, music, drama, and poetry, may involve many weeks of labor by virtually the entire group—the weaving of special baskets, the making of ceremonial regalia, the extensive rehearsals, the accumulation of large quantities of food—and hence economically requires much greater outlay proportionately than the making of a motion picture. The real point may be that in the homogeneous society everyone is agreed as to the nature and purposes of the performance. The motion picture, on the other hand, can at best satisfy only a portion of the members of a society and the temptation is strong to make it appeal to the widest possible audience. In the attempt to offend the fewest people, the motion picture product, then, is often trivial and inane.

On the other hand, the motion picture offers many possibilities for presenting, under the guise of entertainment, the viewpoints of special groups. Controlled primarily as they are by large financial interests, motion pictures are criticized by some as presenting a view of American life and aspirations conforming to that of bankers and employers. On the other hand, as motion pictures are made by individuals who are essentially employees, some people suspect the movies of being colored by contrary views. Pictures dealing with religion, race relations, labor relations, politics, and other similarly controversial topics almost always draw strong criticism from one group or another, to say nothing of Congressional investigations.

Although the element of communication is most obvious in such things as motion pictures and the radio, it is present frequently in most forms of art. Moods and emotions may be communicated rather than ideas, especially in music, the dance, poetry, and many forms of painting. And it must not be forgotten that an important function of the arts is the evoking of pleasure. The dance, for example, in our own society is very largely devoted to the pleasure of the participants, if we except the relatively small amount of professional dancing. Most young people in our society participate in dancing, and it has come to be closely associated with many other aspects of our culture, such as those which govern social occasions, courting procedures, and mate selection. It remains one of the few arts in our culture in which great numbers participate rather than being the observers of professional activities.

The whole problem of the arts as a means of communication is a very large one and, despite the very considerable literature, much research remains to be done. In the last two sections we have tried merely to indicate a few of the problems and to discuss some of the very general conclusions that seem obvious. It is clear, however, that the problem is not confined to our own culture, where most of the research has been done by psychologists and sociologists, but that it presents universal aspects common to all cultures.

5. ART AS CULTURAL TRADITION

In the preceding sections, we have noted that art invariably involves the use of conventions and symbols. The use of symbols, in art as in language, implies a body of common understandings among the members of a society, and carries as well the implication that these understandings are transmitted from generation to generation. While the conventions and symbols of art are, at any particular time, more or less rigid and conservative, they do undergo change through time, just as any other aspect of culture.

Symbols and conventions afford perhaps the best indication that the arts belong to culture and partake in cultural processes and change. It is obvious, however, that all other aspects of art are likewise culturally determined. Techniques, the choice of subject matter, the preference or emphasis on this or that art, the functions of the arts, attitudes toward art and the artist—all these are cultural in character. To illustrate these points, we shall present a concrete example, drawn from a study of the potter's art among the Pueblo Indians.

The region around Kayenta in northeastern Arizona was occupied by a Pueblo people with a special local pottery-making tradition which lasted from about 700 A.D. to about 1300 A.D. In the course of this 600-year-long pottery tradition, it underwent numerous changes in techniques, forms, and most particularly, in the character of the painted designs utilized. It is the painted designs, which we shall discuss in subsequent paragraphs.[6]

During a period known as Pueblo I ($\pm$750–900 A.D.), the dominant pottery was decorated with poorly painted black designs on a white background. These were built upon a foundation of horizontal lines encircling the vessel. From these lines depended enrichments, such as ticks, dots, hooked triangles, and other geometric forms, and, in other cases, the spaces between lines were filled by various elements set in panels. (See Figure 18:4a.)

The second period, Pueblo II (900–1100), had two phases. The earlier was marked by a development of Pueblo I design but with thicker lines (Figure 18:4b). Some new fillers appeared but the fussier decorations of Pueblo I disappeared. On the inside of bowls, the layout became radial (Figure 18:4c) in appearance, although this was accomplished, actually, by widening the band with filled panels until it nearly covered the interior of the bowl. The changes were gradual and represent the development of a unified tradition.

In the later phase of Pueblo II, two new styles appear. One shows many characters of the earlier style but with much more careful painting and design layout. Treatment of design elements changed, and many new elements, such as interlocking scrolls and frets, appeared. (See Figure 18:4d.) Bowl interiors were treated quite differently: they were usually divided into three sections, the two outside being occupied by characteristic fillers modified to fit the shape (Figure 18:4e). The second late Pueblo II design was simpler, with banding lines from which depended outlined figures, or with outlined fillers between lines, the figures then being filled with hatching (Figure 18:4f and g).

Although these three Pueblo II designs can be clearly distinguished from one another, there are many individual pieces of pottery which show elements from two or more. Or perhaps this can be better put by saying that

[6] Ralph Beals, George Brainerd and Watson Smith, "Archaeological Studies in Northeastern Arizona," *University of California Publications in American Archaeology and Ethnology*, 44, 1–236, 1945.

Fig. 18:4. Kayenta pottery designs: (*a*) Pueblo I designs, (*b, c*) early Pueblo II designs, (*d, e, f*) late Pueblo II designs, (*g, h*) designs on Pueblo II orange ware, (*i*) a Pueblo III design, (*j*) a late Pueblo II design, (*k*) a Pueblo III, orange ware design. After Beals, Brainerd, and Smith. See text for discussion.

many elements were common to the three traditions. The two late Pueblo II traditions, while using decorative elements in common with the earlier, seem to represent the effects of influences from outside the area under study. We also find in Pueblo II an orange pottery, usually covered with a red slip or coating on which were sometimes painted black designs, similar, on the whole, to those on the black-on-white pottery of the same period (Figure 18:4g and h).

Pueblo III (1100–1300) saw a tremendous variety of black-on-white pottery decoration. On certain large jars the layout of the design involved an elaboration of the hooked triangle which we saw as a type of enrichment in Pueblo I, which shows, on the one hand, the continuity of some elements of the tradition, and on the other, the degree to which modification can occur. Great elaboration of design occurred on this basis, together with much development of scrolls or interlocking S designs (Figure 18:4i). Yet despite the apparent great richness of design in this period, close analysis reveals a quite rigid group of conventions within which the elaboration occurred. Moreover, the major part of the stock of designs and types of layout can be shown to be derived from a slightly earlier black-on-white pottery development which occurred in the Flagstaff area to the southwest. In other words, there is actually a fairly sharp break between the black-on-white pottery designs of Pueblo II and those of Pueblo III in the Kayenta area.

The case is quite different when we turn to the orange ware pottery of Pueblo III. Shortly before the beginning of Pueblo III black-on-white types, there appeared a great flowering of the orange ware types with polychrome decoration of red, black, and white paints in various combinations. To a very considerable degree, the design layouts and the motives used are those from the late Pueblo II black-on-white pottery (cf. Figure 18:4j and k). For perhaps a hundred years, both black-on-white and orange ware polychrome were at their climax in richness of design and abundance. In some instances they were certainly made by the same potters (evidenced by complete outfits for both types together with partially completed vessels found in the same graves), yet almost at no point are they identical in either design layout or design elements. In the case of polychrome pottery, we have a continuous tradition going back to the Pueblo I black-on-white, modified and elaborated, it is true, and enriched by some infiltration of outside influences. In the case of the black-on-whites, we have a discontinuity, with the Pueblo III black-on-whites derived mainly from outside, although utilizing a modification of the old spurred triangle in layouts of design, and developing quickly a great local richness and variation. Indeed, in the latter part of Pueblo III, the period of great cliff dwellings and open, large, multiple houses, there seems even marked differentiation in pottery decoration from town to town.

The great pottery tradition of the Kayenta area came to an end with the abandonment of the area about 1300. We could trace its influences among the ancestors of the modern Hopis, and perhaps even into modern Hopi pottery, but this seems unnecessary for our point.

The function of the decorated pottery of the Kayenta area is not certain. Cooking vessels were made in a different unpainted ware not described in this section. It is possible that the painted pottery was used for storage and perhaps for water-carrying. It also seems likely that some, at least, of the pottery was used for ceremonial purposes. The decoration can only have been made for esthetic purposes. The variety and character of the decoration preclude the possibility that it had symbolic values to any extent. It seems reasonably certain that the decoration represented an esthetic design tradition which gave satisfaction to the maker through exercise of skill and taste, within the limits of the conventions of the group, and gave pleasure to the observer or user.

To recapitulate, then, Kayenta pottery design developed in black-on-white designs in Pueblo I, either through a wholly local development, or more probably, through the local adaptation of a design tradition borrowed from elsewhere. Through a long period of time it flourished through gradual enrichment and growth of skill, influenced from time to time by stimuli from other regions, but always keeping its distinctive local character.

At the beginning of Pueblo III times, attention focused on the previously little decorated orange ware, and there was a great efflorescence of design and the addition of new colors, still basically in the same design tradition. Because of the general appearance of polychrome pottery in the Southwest about this time, we can guess that the stimulus for the new development came from outside, but again it was, in detail, primarily a local development. Shortly after the beginning of this efflorescence in orange ware, strong outside influences resulted in a considerable modification of black-on-white design. Although some influence in layouts of design persisted, in the main the elaborate Pueblo III decorative development in black-on-white came from borrowed designs and motives. Yet this borrowed design tradition had come from a related tradition so that there is no absolute break.

As an art movement, then, we have a tradition continuing over some six hundred years with fairly narrow limits to the conventions employed. Within the limits of this tradition, however, there were opportunities for originality and change which took place through both internal developments and external influences. At no time was there a complete break with the past, nor, if one viewed the whole area of painted pottery-making in the Southwest, would there be any doubt of the distinctiveness and continuity of the tradition. In the detailed study of this art form, we can see illustrated the general principles of cultural continuity and culture change.

With such a relatively limited area and concrete geometric designs it is possible to follow the movement as a cultural tradition fairly easily. But wherever we have a long documented tradition, we may see similar processes at work in other cultures. Painting in our own culture, in a general way, seems to indicate the same sort of history, although it is harder to document exactly. We shall summarize this history briefly in the section that follows.

6. ART AS CULTURAL TRADITION: EUROPEAN ART

The great tradition of painting in Euro-American culture began with the Renaissance. The development of perspective, perhaps the influence of the rediscovery of Greek civilization, the patronage of the church, the great intellectual ferments associated with the beginnings of the age of exploration all apparently contributed to a great efflorescence of an art which had been relatively dormant although not absent in earlier periods.

A major characteristic of painting in the Renaissance was its realistic character. Great attention was paid to painting human and animal figures with correct anatomy. Landscapes show plausible if not exact trees, streams, hills, or buildings. Exact conformance to the conventions of perspective was required. Certain general, although not usually expressed, rules of composition were developed. Symbolism was present but confined mainly to religious art. However, since much of early Renaissance art was religious, the amount of symbolism was considerable. Individual variation was in technical skill and virtuosity and in the individualization of landscapes and figures, particularly the human figure.

This tradition flourished through succeeding centuries, and seems not to have been seriously challenged until virtually the early part of the present century and the development of abstract schools of painting. (This term as used here covers a variety of developments, but space does not permit additional elaboration.) Abstract artists in part turned inward, devoting themselves primarily to the expression of inner and personalized emotions and observations. Public reaction, on the whole, was adverse, because the new type of interest, for its failure to conform to the older conventions, did not communicate. Artists condemned the public for its inability to appreciate the new art, yet this lack of appreciation was the inevitable result of abandoning one set of conventions for another. The small but appreciative audience for modern art forms must be viewed as a group who have begun to understand the new conventions. It is difficult to see how any artist who wishes to paint for anyone but himself can avoid either conforming to existing conventions or the establishment of new conventions which are understood by his audience. Virtually all modern artists, indeed, continue to conform to the convention of two-dimensional representation of three-dimensional objects. Others have entered upon a high degree of symbolism as well, employing, however, the less well-established symbols of psychoanalysis.

On the whole, the public has so far failed to absorb or understand the new conventions. On the other hand, the tradition of Renaissance art has continued to flourish among popular and commercial artists. Advertising art, particularly that of our "slick paper" magazines, must be regarded as a direct continuation of the art tradition of the Renaissance.[7] It is true that there has been change of detail and, to some extent, a change of function. It perhaps is not irreverent, however, to suggest that the religious painting of the Renaissance was in effect a form of advertising.

The present period, then, is one in which most of the public and some of the artists are continuing in a long-established art tradition, in a fashion not dissimilar to the development of the pottery-painting tradition of the Kayenta region. For some decades, however, we have had a group of artists interested in a different type of art and endeavoring, unconsciously at least, to establish a new set of conventions. It would, in this connection, be interesting to know how the artists were regarded who first introduced the new Pueblo black-on-white tradition into the Kayenta region. Very likely they evoked the kind of responses so common in our society when new, radical, or modern art forms, whether in painting, sculpture, or music, are first presented to the public. Modern art is frequently condemned (both by critics and the layman) as meaningless, crude, and fuzzy in conception and execution, childlike, or even disgusting or obscene. These critics, like most Americans, are steeped in Renaissance art conventions, and deeply resent efforts to alter this tradition or to establish a different set of conventions. It is indeed entirely impossible to say at this time whether the innovations of modern art will succeed or not, but we may expect, at the least, that the Renaissance tradition will undergo slow but continuous change, and that there will be further changes of function, similar to that which has occurred with the movement of the tradition into the field of commercial and popular art.

[7] We are indebted for this idea to a suggestion by S. MacDonald Wright, although he is not responsible in any sense for the interpretation and development we have given here.

7. MUSIC

Our discussion has so far been couched in very general terms, with illustrations drawn mainly from various kinds of pictorial and decorative art. In this and the following section we shall offer a brief discussion of other art forms: music, poetry, and prose narratives.

Of all the arts, music perhaps best illustrates the effect of cultural tradition in determining both social and individual standards of what is desirable and approved. The influence of the cultural tradition on standards of musical appreciation results often in a kind of physiological conditioning, to the extent that music which is pleasing and satisfying to members of one society may be no more than a physically painful cacophony to those of another. An excellent example is found in our own reaction to Chinese music.

As is the case with most music outside the western European musical tradition, Chinese music uses a different scale from our own. In both scales each note represents a physically determinable sound wave. This, reaching the human ear, causes vibrations which the nervous system transmits to the brain of the listener. Any musical scale can thus be described, in physical terms, as a set of wave lengths of varying size with fixed intervals between them. The major difference between the Chinese scale and our own rests in the use of a different system of intervals between the fixed points of the scale. It is these intervals rather than the absolute pitch of each note which the ear "perceives," and which cause acceptance or rejection of a particular type of music.

To the Western ear, Chinese music seems meaningless, inharmonious, and often downright unpleasant. To the Chinese, our music sounds much the same. Inasmuch as the physiological apparatus for the perception of sound is identical among the two peoples, we must conclude that the difference in appreciation is due to cultural conditioning.

This fact becomes clearer if we examine the history of Western music itself. Over a period of several centuries we find that various kinds of intervals within our own scale have varied in popularity. Sound combinations which one century considered dissonances have become commonplaces in another. Thus, little more than half a century ago, Debussy was considered a radical in music. Most people considered his work ugly and full of dissonance. Today his works are generally regarded rather highly, for people have, through repetition, become accustomed to the intervals he employs. The history of the development of jazz likewise shows the influence of conditioning. Intervals once condemned as "barbaric" in early jazz music have in many cases crept into so-called "classical" music and are accepted today.

Such innovations are continuing. The late Arnold Schoenberg, for example, experimented with an entirely new arrangement of intervals, creating in effect a new twelve-note musical scale. For years his work was condemned by many, and public performances of his music were almost unknown. Only a small group of people gave them any appreciation. It is too early to say whether the work of Schoenberg will have a lasting influence on contemporary music, but it is interesting to observe that in recent years some of his works have been performed by major symphony orchestras in concerts for the general public. Perhaps most people are still puzzled, or even repelled, by Schoenberg's music, but many people who formerly would have rejected it entirely now find it at least interesting for an occasional performance. In the light of the past history of musical changes, it is entirely possible that in another half century Schoenberg's music will be entirely accepted and that the work of earlier composers will be considered insipid, meaningless, or even ugly.

In a somewhat similar fashion, the music of nonliterate peoples seems to most of those reared in European traditions to be a formless and meaningless jumble of sounds. On analysis, this proves not to be the case. It is true that the music of many nonliterate peoples emphasizes rhythm rather than melody, and that it is performed mainly by singing and simple percussion instruments rather than by a number of instruments producing different tones. Similarly, the melodic intervals usually differ from our own, and harmony or tonal accompaniments to the melody are rare. Nevertheless, the studies of musicologists have clearly shown that the music of all nonliterate peoples shows very definite patterns, and is not in the least random or chaotic. Usually, in any particular nonliterate society, there exist only a few acceptable patterns for the opening and closing phrases of songs, while the series of melodic phrases making up the song are of standard length, and utilize a limited number of combinations of intervals, with other possible combinations rarely if ever appearing. Moreover, certain patterns can be shown to extend beyond a single tribe, and it is often possible to map out areas of common or similar musical tradition just as it is possible often to establish culture areas for other phases of culture. The implication is that the formation and spread of a particular musical style follow the same general processes as may be found in the origin and spread of a particular type of harpoon or other similarly tangible artifact class.

The occasions for music, among many nonliterate peoples, are extraordinarily varied and numerous. In Robert Lowie's account of the Crow Indians, to which we have frequently referred, songs are mentioned in connection with almost every activity. Mothers sing, and even compose, lullabies to their children. In many cases the children learn these as they grow older, sing them while playing, and sometimes all the children in the camp will learn a particular song. Young men wander through the camp at night, playing flutes to amuse and entertain their sweethearts, and not infrequently a young man may compose a love song to be sung outside the tipi of the girl he loves. Many men have their own sacred songs, which are learned in the course of their contact with supernatural powers in vision experiences, and which are sung at times of grave personal crisis or in ceremonies and rituals. Ceremonial occasions are replete with singing, a principal technique of appealing to the supernatural powers.

Songs are also used to build up a martial and aggressive spirit for war parties. When a war party returns successfully, and its members distribute their booty, the recipients of gifts will compose and sing songs of praise, recounting the brave deeds and extolling the generosity of the warriors. There are also mourning songs to honor the dead. But perhaps most frequent are songs of mockery, sung to ridicule a member of the society who has in some fashion failed to conform to accepted standards of Crow behavior. Clearly, music plays a most important role in Crow life, and the same appears to be true of many, if not all, nonliterate societies.

An interesting musical event, reminiscent of our own musical competitions, occurs among the Eskimos. During the spring, when many Eskimo families come together for feasts and ceremonies, there are frequent song contests. A man who has been injured by another, whether by theft, the destruction or misuse of his property, or by another means, will compose a song ridiculing his opponent and challenge him to a contest. If the challenge is accepted, the injured man, to the accompaniment of furious drumming, will mock his opponent in song, accuse him of a long series of misdeeds, refer disrespectfully to his relatives, and otherwise expose him to ridicule. The opponent appears not to listen but in his turn sings a similar song, returning the charges in kind. No other hostilities take place; there is simply a long exchange of satirical and derogatory songs, which may go on for many evenings, and may even continue, at intervals, over several years. The spectators attend these contests with great interest, urging the contestants to their best efforts, and judging the skill with which each contestant composes and sings his songs.

To the Eskimo songs and singing play a large role in all activities. Rasmussen quotes the following "views on how a song is born in the human mind," given to him by a Netsilik Eskimo of Boothia Peninsula:

Songs are thoughts, sung out with the breath when people are moved by great forces and ordinary speech no longer suffices.

Man is moved just like the ice floe sailing here and there out in the current. His thoughts are driven by a flowing force when he feels joy, when he feels fear, when he feels sorrow. Thoughts can wash over him like a flood, making his breath come in gasps and his heart throb. Something, like an abatement in the weather, will keep him thawed up. And then it will happen that we, who always think we are small, will feel still smaller. And we will fear to use words. But it will happen that the words we need will come of themselves. When the words we want to use shoot up of themselves—we get a new song.[8]

8. POETRY AND PROSE

In many cases it is difficult to separate poetry from song. As among the Crows, most poetry is sung. Discussion of poetry likewise is hampered by its figurative and allusive language, often coupled with elaborate symbolism, qualities difficult to render in translation. Nevertheless the poetry of nonliterates clearly follows culturally determined traditions and often is of considerable charm even in translation.

Frequently poetic expressions are very brief, emphasizing in vivid form some cultural ideal. Lowie gives the following two songs or chants, revealed in visions to Crow warriors:

Whenever there is any trouble, I shall come through it. Though arrows be many, I shall arrive. My heart is manly.

Eternal are the heavens and earth; old people are poorly off; do not be afraid [that is, do not be afraid of dying on the war-path].[9]

Densmore quotes one of a Papago woman's curing songs as follows:

> Brown owls come here in the blue evening,
> They are hooting about,
> They are shaking their wings and hooting.[10]

Similarly, a Chippewa song is translated by Densmore:

> I hear the birds before the day,
> I see the flowers beside the way.
> How can you sing, happy and free,
> How can you sing so close to me
> When I have lost my sweetheart? [11]

[8] Knud Rasmussen, *The Netsilik Eskimo*. Report of the Fifth Thule Expedition 1921–24, Vol. VIII, No. 1–2 (Copenhagen: copyright 1931 and used by permission of Gyldendalske Boghandel, Nordisk Forlag, and Rudolf Sand & Rudolf Sand, Jr.), p. 321.

[9] Robert H. Lowie, *The Crow Indians* (New York: copyright 1935 by Rinehart & Co., Inc.), p. 104.

[10] Frances Densmore, "American Indian Poetry," *American Anthropologist,* 28, 448–449 (1926), p. 448.

[11] *Ibid.,* p. 449.

The Polynesians are especially noted for their chants, which are applicable to many occasions, and often include long historical genealogies. The following example, without a genealogy, is given by Peter Buck; it is sung on the death of a chief.

Alas, the bitter pain that gnaws within
For the wrecked canoe, for a friend who is lost.
My precious heron plume is cast on Ocean's strand,
And the lightning, flashing in the heavens,
Salutes the dead.

Where is authority in this world, since thou hast passed
By the slippery path, the sliding path to death?
Lone stands Whakaahu mountain in the distance,
For thou art gone, the shelter of thy people.
Flown has my singing bird that sang of ancient learning,
The keel of Tainui, the plug of Aotea,
Now bewailed by women's flowing tears.
Beautiful lies thy body in thy dogskin tasseled cloak,
But thy spirit has passed like a drifting cloud in the heavens.
All is well with thee who liest in state on chieftain's bier.
Ah, my precious green jade jewel, emblem of departed warriors!
The dragon emerged from his rocky fastness
And sleeps in the house of death.[12]

Famous for their long sea voyages, the following chant expresses a major Polynesian preoccupation:

The handle of my steering paddle thrills to action,
My paddle named Kautu-ki-te-rangi.
It guides to the horizon but dimly discerned.
To the horizon that lifts before us,
To the horizon that ever recedes,
To the horizon that ever draws near,
To the horizon that causes doubt,
To the horizon that instills dread,
The horizon with unknown power,
The horizon not hitherto pierced.
The lowering skies above,
The raging seas below,
Oppose the untraced path
Our ship must go.[13]

[12] Peter H. Buck, *Vikings of the Sunrise* (New York and Philadelphia: copyright 1938 by Frederick A. Stokes Co. and J. B. Lippincott Company), pp. 282–283.
[13] *Ibid.*, p. 40.

The poems given above illustrate a preoccupation with cultural ideals, with nature and supernatural forces, and the sheer expression of emotion so common in the poetry of all peoples. Similar examples are legion in non-literate societies; the items quoted are by no means unusual. The following poem (or song) was composed by Orpingalik, the Netsilik Eskimo, who gave the definition of song we quoted in § 7. Orpingalik calls his song "My Breath," and explains: "This is what I call this song, for it is just as necessary to me to sing it as it is to breathe." [14] The translation, made as close as possible to the Eskimo original, is by Rasmussen in collaboration with Orpingalik.

> I will sing a song,
> A song that is strong.
>   Unaya—unaya.
> Sick I have lain since autumn,
> Helpless I lay, as were I
> My own child.
>
> Sad, I would that my woman
> Were away to another house
> To a husband
> Who can be her refuge,
> Safe and secure as winter ice.
>   Unaya—unaya.
>
> Sad, I would that my woman
> Were gone to a better protector
> Now that I lack strength
> To rise from my couch.
>   Unaya—unaya.
>
> Dost thou know thyself?
> So little thou knowest of thyself.
> Feeble I lie here on my bench
> And only my memories are strong!
>   Unaya—unaya.
>
> Beasts of the hunt! Big game!
> Oft the fleeing quarry I chased!
> Let me live it again and remember,
> Forgetting my weakness.
>   Unaya—unaya.

[14] Knud Rasmussen, *The Netsilik Eskimo* (Copenhagen: copyright 1931 and used by permission of Gyldendalske Boghandel, Nordisk Forlag, and Rudolf Sand & Rudolf Sand, Jr.), p. 321.

Let me recall the great white
Polar bear,
High up its back-body,
Snout in the snow, it came!
He really believed
He alone was a male
And ran towards me.
    Unaya—unaya.

It threw me down
Again and again,
Then breathless departed
And lay down to rest,
Hid by a mound on a floe.
Heedless it was, and unknowing
That I was to be its fate.
Deluding itself
That he alone was a male,
And unthinking
That I too was a man!
    Unaya—unaya.

I shall ne'er forget that great blubber-beast,
A fjord seal,
I killed from the sea ice
Early, long before dawn,
While my companions at home
Still lay like the dead,
Faint from failure and hunger,
Sleeping.
With meat and with swelling blubber
I returned so quickly
As if merely running over ice
To view a breathing hole there.
And yet it was
An old and cunning male seal.
But before he had even breathed
My harpoon head was fast
Mortally deep in his neck.

That was the manner of me then.
Now I lie feeble on my bench
Unable even a little blubber to get
For my wife's stone lamp.

The time, the time will not pass.
While dawn gives place to dawn
And spring is upon the village.
    Unaya—unaya.

But how long shall I lie here?
How long?
And how long must she go a-begging
For fat for her lamp,
For skin for her clothing
And meat for a meal?
A helpless thing—a defenceless woman.
    Unaya—unaya.

Knowest thou thyself?
So little thou knowest of thyself
While dawn gives place to dawn,
And spring is upon the village.
    Unaya—unaya.[15]

Little has been done so far in the purely literary analysis of the poetry of nonliterate peoples. Although extensive collections exist for some groups, most of these have been translated, more or less adequately, into English or some other European tongue, and precise analysis can only be made by studying poetry in the original language. Such features as prosody, rhyme, alliteration, and other similar poetic devices are necessarily lost in translation. Yet even in translation, certain literary characteristics may be seen, such as the parallel structure evidenced in the Polynesian sea chant given above. The few comparative studies so far made emphasize the fact that the poetry of all societies, like their music, adheres to well-defined standards of form, and employs a common stock of poetic images and other literary devices, which is often as standardized and as complex as our own.

Literary forms in prose, written or merely told, are found among all peoples. Major types include narratives (such as myths, legends, and other tales), proverbs, riddles, and puns. While prose narratives, like songs, appear to be universal, proverbs and riddles appear to be most frequent in the Old World, and are relatively very rare among the aboriginal peoples of the Americas. Puns are probably universal, but are so dependent upon an intimate knowledge of the languages in which they occur as to be extremely difficult to collect.

Among most nonliterate peoples, prose narratives are almost endless

[15] *Ibid.,* pp. 321–323.

and often of great functional importance. In many instances, two major types may be discerned: myths and legends. Myths are usually stories laid in another world, quite different from that of the present, and stories in which the principal actors are gods, spirits, and other supernaturals. Legends, on the other hand, recount events which took place in the world as it is today, though often at some earlier time. Men are actors in legends, though supernaturals, too, not infrequently play important roles. The distinction between myths and legends, though a convenient one, is none too sharp; there are many tales which cannot easily be ascribed to one or the other category.

Myths frequently are concerned with origins—the creation of the universe and its various aspects, the origin of important cultural aids such as fire, the origins of significant food animals and plants, the beginnings of death or illness, the origins of the society itself and of its clans or other social segments, and the origins of ceremonies and rituals. We find many such tales among the Navahos; for example, a recent collection lists such titles as the origin of the Night Chant (an important curing ceremony), the people of the lower world (an episode in the creation story), the origin of the Salt Clan, the origin of horses, the building of the first hogan (or Navaho house), and the first louse.

Other myths center about the actions of a culture hero or spirit, often individualized under the name of some animal. These tales are not infrequently arranged in a cycle or connected series of episodes. An example is found among the Mescalero Apaches, who tell a long cycle of stories dealing with Coyote, a trickster who is pictured sometimes as a human, sometimes as an animal. Coyote undergoes a host of experiences, now with this animal, now with that, which illustrate almost infinitely his dominant characteristics of greed, cupidity, cunning, and gluttony. Coyote is also impious and often stupid, and the stories of his adventures frequently evoke roars of laughter from the audience. But, at the end of this long cycle of tales, and after Coyote has run the gamut of his adventures, he is possessed by the culture hero, a divinity, and made the instrument of creation. Through him, the present universe and all living things of the earth, excepting only man, are brought into being. Once this has been accomplished, Coyote is himself reduced to the status of an animal, and the culture hero, together with other divinities, completes the creation and makes the world habitable for man.

Legends are more mundane in content, though these tales, too, include their share of the wonderful, the awesome, and the supernatural. Among the Mescaleros, there are numerous tales related of the Mountain Spirits and of man's contacts with them. These are, in a sense, vision experiences, which tell how a person, often caught up by some crisis or dangerous situation, is assisted by the Mountain Spirits, taken to their holy home, instructed in a ceremony, and returned to his people.

Proverbs and riddles are exceedingly common in Africa, where they function as a kind of repository for the wisdom of the group. In some parts of Africa, indeed, proverbs are used much as legal precedents are used in our courts; both the complainant and the defendant, in West African court procedure, quote proverb after proverb to support their claims.

As with the other forms of art, the prose literature of a group shows a definite style and reflects aspects of the culture. In a recent study of Hawaiian literary style, it is pointed out that the choice of subject and the treatment of character reflect the aristocratic society of aboriginal Hawaii. The tales characteristically use hyperbole or exaggeration, especially with respect to the hero of a tale, colorful metaphors and similes, symbolism, great emphasis on details such as long name lists, antithesis and repetition. Humor is abundant but is mainly based either on punning or on scatological reference; sarcasm is rare. Certain Polynesian linguistic features, which make alliteration and repetition or parallel structure easy, are extensively developed.

In general, tales show their derivation from the cultural and social setting in which they occur more clearly than other art forms. The function of tales is likewise more obvious usually than with other arts; in most cases they clearly either afford explanatory statements about the universe and its origins or emphasize group values and ideals, often with a definitely didactic purpose. Very often a single tale will combine several such functions. With all the reasonably obvious functional significance of the tale, however, it should not be overlooked that the tale also entertains. Tales are not told simply to impress the young or one's fellows with proper and improper ways of behavior, or to explain the gods; they are also told because teller and his hearers enjoy the process.

9. SUMMARY

Though not all of the arts are equally developed, nor even represented, in every culture, there are no societies which lack artistic activities altogether. Moreover, it seems clear that art was a part of culture from its earliest beginnings, though its traces are few even in Paleolithic cultures and restricted to art forms like painting and sculpture. It is the universality of art and its probably great antiquity that suggests that artistic activities apparently satisfy some deeply rooted psychological need, common to all mankind.

Art forms are numerous and include such major activities as pictorial or representational arts (for example, painting and sculpture), literary arts (including the songs and stories of nonliterate peoples), the dramatic arts, and decorative arts. Art is defined as an activity which, over and above its practical or utilitarian values, also brings satisfaction both to the artist and to those who participate in his work as beholders, audience, or collaborators. It is this esthetic component that distinguishes art from other aspects of culture.

Works of art, like tools, weapons, and other artifacts, are of course made by individuals, working alone or in collaboration with others. Groups or societies, as such, produce nothing. Yet it should also be understood that no artist lives in isolation; he is always a member of a particular society and he always participates in a particular culture. As such, his work is profoundly influenced by the cultural patterns of his times, and becomes, not an entirely individual product, but a product of the culture as well.

In addition to the fact that artistic activities result in esthetic satisfactions to artists, performers, audiences, or participants, they also have other functions. One such function is communication; to a greater or less degree, all arts serve as media for the communication of emotions, ideas, attitudes, and values. The efficiency with which the artist communicates depends on the degree to which the conventions and symbols he uses are understood and appreciated by his fellows. In small and homogeneous societies, there is often only a single system of conventions and symbols, common to all members of the society. In large heterogeneous societies, on the other hand, conventions and symbols may differ from one group to another within the society, and so often restrict the artist's audience. Systems of conventions and symbols, though they vary in their rigidity from one society to another, always allow for some degree of individuality and innovation, even in nonliterate societies. Changes in systems of conventions and symbols are slow, and come about through innovations by individual artists or by the adoption of new ideas from other cultures.

Because art serves often as a medium of communication, it functions also to conserve and reinforce beliefs, customs, attitudes, and values. Nearly all arts have this function, though it is perhaps most evident in the literary and pictorial arts. In some instances, the arts may be used for instructional purposes or to propagandize; an instance is found in the so-called mystery plays of the medieval European church.

COLLATERAL READING

Beals, Ralph L.; Brainerd, George W.; and Smith, Watson. "Archaeological Studies in Northeast Arizona," *University of California Publications in American Archaeology and Ethnology*, 44, 1–236, 1945.

Boas, Franz. *Primitive Art*. Oslo: Institut f. Sammenlig. Kultur, VIII, 1927.

————. *Race, Language and Culture*. New York: The Macmillan Co., 1940. See "The Development of Folk-tales and Myths," pp. 397–406; "The Growth of Indian Mythologies," pp. 425–436; "Mythology and Folk-Tales of North American Indians," pp. 451–490; "Stylistic Aspects of Primitive Literature," pp. 491–502; "Representative Art of Primitive People," pp. 535–540; "The Decorative Art of the North American Indians," pp. 546–563.

Day, A. Grove. *The Sky Clears, Poetry of the American Indians*. New York: The Macmillan Co., 1951.

Luomala, Katherine. "Polynesian Literature," *Encyclopedia of Literature*, ed. J. T. Shipley (New York, 1946), pp. 772–789.

McCurdy, George G. *Human Origins*. New York: D. Appleton and Co., 1924. Vol. I, Chapter VII.

Malinowski, Bronislaw. *Myth in Primitive Psychology*. New York: W. W. Norton and Co., 1926.

Métraux, A. "South American Indian Literature," *Encyclopedia of Literature*, ed. J. T. Shipley (New York, 1946), pp. 857–863.

O'Neale, Lila M. "Karok-Yurok Basket Weavers," *University of California Publications in American Archaeology and Ethnology*, XXXII, 1–182, 1932.

Radin, Paul. *Primitive Man as Philosopher*. New York: D. Appleton-Century and Co., 1927.

Roberts, H. H. "Primitive Music," *Encyclopedia of the Social Sciences*. New York: The Macmillan Co., 1933. XI, 150–152.

————. "Musical Areas in Aboriginal North America," *Yale University Publications in Anthropology*, No. 12, 1936.

Thompson, Stith. *The Folktale*. New York: Dryden Press, 1947.

Voegelin, Erminie. "North American Native Literature," *Encyclopedia of Literature*, ed. J. T. Shipley (New York, 1946), pp. 706–721.

ETHNOGRAPHIC REFERENCES

Crows: Lowie, 1935.
Netsilik Eskimos: Rasmussen, 1931.
Polynesians: Buck, 1938.

Chapter 19

EDUCATION AND THE
FORMATION OF PERSONALITY

1. THE SCOPE AND NATURE OF EDUCATION

Education to most people has come to mean the activities that go on in the formal institutions of our society known as schools, supplemented perhaps by readings and lectures that are less formally organized. When we discuss the problems of education, we are usually talking about the problems of schools, colleges, and universities, or of such related questions as adult education, the training of teachers and other professionals, and vocational education. To the social scientist, and especially to the anthropologist, education is a much wider process, and includes all of learning, formalized and unformalized, that results in the acquisition of culture by the individual, the formation of his personality, and his socialization, that is, his learning to accommodate himself to living as a member of a society.

Many educators similarly realize that education in our society includes much more than schooling alone. Individuals acquire their patterns of behavior, their techniques, their attitudes and opinions, and their value systems from many sources, among which the school, college, or university often plays but a minor role. These sources include, among others: the family, which exercises almost exclusive control over the infant and child during his earliest, and perhaps most important, formative years; friends, associates, and age mates, whose influence on the individual is important throughout most of his life; and the mass media of communication, that

570

is, newspapers, magazines, books, radio, television, and motion pictures, influences that play an especially large role in the forming and confirming of attitudes, opinions, and value systems.

Among nonliterate peoples, where formal systems of schooling are little developed or lacking entirely, education is even more obviously a function of individuals and groups who are not professional teachers. In these societies, all or most of an individual's education comes from his family, friends, associates, and age mates, for the mass media of communication are of course lacking in nonliterate societies. Moreover, education in these societies is largely an unconscious and unplanned process; the infant, child, youth, and adult learns more from participation than from precept, in the system of mutual obligations that exist between kin, in the processes of economic organization, in ritual and ceremony, and in the telling of myths and legends. We shall illustrate these techniques in the sections that follow.

Education, then, is in all societies a continuous process, which begins with the birth of the child and carries on, with greater or less intensity, throughout the entire life of the individual. By virtue of this process, the individual learns the ways of his culture and comes to participate more or less fully in it. He also acquires a personality—a complex pattern of "rational faculties, perceptions, ideas, habits, and conditioned emotional responses" [1]—which is derived in part, perhaps, from certain genetically controlled capacities or predispositions, in part from the many statuses and roles the individual assumes during a lifetime, and in part from the training given to him in a particular culture. And if the educational process is successful, as it usually is, the individual also becomes socialized to a greater or less degree, that is, he learns to accommodate himself to living with others in his society and to integrate his own desires and ideals with the systems of values common to the group.

We do not mean to imply in the foregoing that either the culture as a whole or the educational process specifically reduces all individuals in a given society to one or other of a prescribed series of personality types, each characteristic of the age-group, status, or role to which the individual belongs. Individuals differ as such in all societies, and, as far as we now know, the range of variation is essentially the same for all societies. As Linton puts it:

Due to the superficial adjustments which individuals make to status personalities and to the great extent to which the content of personality is controlled

---

[1] Ralph Linton, *The Study of Man* (New York: copyright 1936 by Appleton-Century-Crofts, Inc.), p. 464.

by culture, an investigator's initial impression of the members of an alien society is that all those in any particular status are much alike in personality. This is quite on a par with his other initial impression that they all look very much alike. As soon as he comes to know Indians or Polynesians or Malagasy as individuals, he becomes conscious not only of marked differences in the basic organization of their personalities but also of striking similarities between those personalities and those of individuals with whom he is familiar in his own society . . . At the same time, different societies seem to show differences in the relative frequency of occurrence of the various psychological types. There can be little doubt that some of them show a higher proportion of introverts or megalomaniacs or paranoids than others.[2]

In the sections that follow, we shall discuss the process of education, as herein defined, in more detail, and illustrate it in widely divergent cultures.

2. THE INFANT

At birth the infant has a minimum of personality and a complete absence of knowledge. He does make certain responses to his environment, as when frightened by a loud noise or a sensation of falling. He responds to lights, sucks under certain circumstances, and reacts to comfort and discomfort, both internal and external. According to some psychologists, he has already experienced frustrations through the constrictions put upon movement in the womb, and presumably at birth has begun to seek relief from frustration by aggressive actions against his environment. In other words, to some extent his personality has begun to form. According to the same school of psychologists, birth itself is a major traumatic experience which leaves irremediable effects upon the personality. For a time after birth, according to this group, tensions are built up in the infant through hunger and other bodily functions, and these tensions are relieved by feeding and evacuation. Feeding and evacuation form, for a time, the major preoccupations of the infant, and its early associations with its environment, and more especially with the other humans in its environment, are hence conditioned by these factors. The mother particularly is associated with warmth, comfort, and with release of the tensions associated with hunger.

The point of major interest here is the possible effect of these experiences and conditions upon the formation of personality. Most psychologists today are inclined to attribute the formation of personality entirely to the operation of the cultural and physical environment. Anthropologists, on the whole, are not disposed to go that far, but to believe that there is also an inherited biological component in personality formation. They are led

[2] *Ibid.,* p. 484.

to this conclusion because of their experience in finding individuals, in quite different societies, who have very similar personalities; indeed, many feel that much the same range of personality types is present in any culture. Linton, for example, suggests that personality is the result of three factors: the inherited biological element, the operation of culture and environment upon the individual, and the effect of unique or idiosyncratic experiences of the individual.

Just what the biological determinants of personality may be is still obscure. They may be associated with constitutional types, endocrine balances, or any one of a number of other physiological factors. While some of these factors probably have genetic determinants, it seems unlikely that there are specific genetic determinants operating directly on personality. Instead, such biological factors as exist relate to capacities or potentialities for personality development rather than to personality as such. Essentially the infant has no personality at birth, but develops one gradually through the interaction of the organism with its physical, social, and cultural environment.

Each culture prescribes certain conventional ways of rearing an infant. Thus, in some cultures, the infant is nursed whenever it cries, allowed to take as much time as it wishes, is played with by various members of the family, and is permitted much freedom of movement. In other cultures, the infant may be nursed only at specified hours, is hurried in its nursing, and not only may be neglected between feedings, but may be tightly bound in a cradle, thus restricting even its arm movements, and removed only twice a day for cleaning. As the child grows older, there are similar variations in prescribed treatment. All these differences are believed to make for profoundly different effects on the infant's development of personality, as we go from one culture to another.

On the other hand, it is unlikely that any two infants, even in the same society, have precisely the same experiences. Parents vary somewhat in the closeness with which they adhere to culturally prescribed routines. Moreover, especially as the infant develops into the child, each individual will have unique experiences. One child may be stung by a bee at an early age, wander into the woods and become lost, be knocked over by a running adult, and so on, while another child may have none of these experiences or have them at a much later age. These variations in idiosyncratic experience, like cultural differences in child-training routines, almost certainly modify the formation of the personality.

In addition to personality development, we may note as well the beginnings of socialization in the infant. He starts gradually to identify certain aspects of his environment. If he is not restrained, he early begins exploration of his own body and its potentialities, as well as that part of the environment he can see and touch. He identifies certain individuals and, we may surmise, becomes conscious of differences in their relationships to himself. The father may be identified, for example, as one who may play with but not feed the infant. The infant also experiments with his vocal apparatus in making a variety of sounds. As he approaches the transition toward childhood, he begins the process of identifying certain sound sequences with meanings, and begins to manipulate such objects as he can reach and handle or that may be given to him by others.

A rather detailed account of the period of infancy is given by Du Bois in her study of the people of Atimelang on the island of Alor in the Dutch East Indies. Among these people the mother stays in the house four to six days after birth, and devotes herself exclusively to feeding and fondling the infant. Warm baths are given the infant every two or three days, continuing until the child can walk, after which cold baths are given. The mother's brother, and secondarily her sisters and mother, have primary responsibility for the physical needs of the mother and child during the four- to six-day period after birth; the father is excluded during this period. The exclusion of the father in part reflects the claims of the mother's kinsfolk on the child.

The father of the child, although excluded, is under many obligations. If he works too vigorously, the child's soul may stray and the child die unless the father can remember the transgression, locate the place where it was committed, and by a ritual return the child's soul. Similarly, the child may become sickly through the anger of spirits, and the father must then pay for a diviner to determine the trouble and provide the subsequent sacrifices.

The descent of the mother from the house is marked by a simple ceremony. Premasticated bananas and vegetable gruels are added to the infant's diet, although for some time the child apparently may often reject the food. The infant is the center of attention, being passed from hand to hand and fondled by people of both sexes and all ages. Fondling consists of rocking and joggling the child, and caressing him on limbs and trunk with mock bites.

Ten days to two weeks after birth, if it is the busy season, the mother begins to work in the fields. The child is left with some older sibling, a grandparent, or the father. Consequently it is often deprived of food, although premasticated bananas or gruel may be offered or some other nursing mother may occasionally suckle the child. Indeed, few children are not at one time or another suckled by another woman.

The child is never left alone, nor is it laid down, except in the house or on the veranda. It spends most of its time in a carrying shawl, slung over one shoulder with the infant under the opposite arm in a half-lying, half-sitting position. When the mother returns from the fields she nurses and fondles the child, giving it the breast whenever it is restless. At other times the child may be quieted by stroking the genitals. At night the child sleeps with the mother alone until, when the child is able to sit up or crawl, the mother resumes intercourse with the father. After this, the child may still sleep on the same mat with his parents, or he may be placed with another adult or older sibling.

No efforts are made at verbal training in infancy beyond repetitions of the infant's name, although songs may be sung to pacify it. Neither is there any effort to urge the child to walk until it has itself learned to pull itself up on its feet. No attempt at toilet-training is made in the prewalking period, and there are no expressions of disapproval or dislike if the child soils itself. The child has increasing opportunities for movement and crawling as it grows. Between the twelfth and eighteenth month the child begins to walk. Weaning does not take place until after the child walks.

This picture of infancy affords some unusual features. The most marked of these perhaps is the fact that the infant is not always nursed when hungry or restless, owing to the absence of the mother in the fields. In other cultures, a child would be taken to the fields by the mother and nursed when necessary. Another unusual feature is the very early feeding of gruels and premasticated foods, although many nonliterate peoples begin such feeding earlier than is usually the case among ourselves. A third important point is the relative freedom of movement of the young child, for the carrying shawl does not unduly restrict his activities.

With respect to the latter point, many American Indians show a marked contrast. The child is fastened to a rigid cradle board which confines all body movements. In some cases also both arm and head movements are restricted. Although the child may be nursed more frequently, it is often removed from the cradle board only once or twice a day for cleaning. At this time it may be fondled and at other times it may be rocked and lullabies sung to it. If it cries excessively, though, it may be set to one side or even hung in its board to a tree outside camp until it has exhausted its rage and quieted down. Although the child may get a little opportunity to crawl as it grows older, substantially it spends its life in the rigid confines of the cradle board until it is of an age to walk. As a result, it has been noted that infants' muscular coordinations and spacial perceptions are very retarded, although these develop rapidly once the infants are out of the cradle board.

The psychological implications of these differences in treatment are not

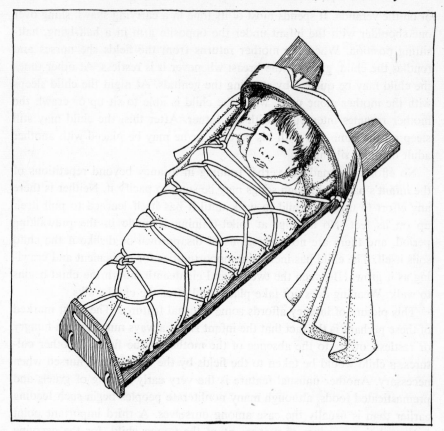

Fig. 19:1. Child fastened to a cradle board.

yet entirely clear. It has been suggested, however, that the stoicism and patience ascribed to many American Indians may arise from their infant confinement. Others ascribe quietness, docility, and lack of interest in spontaneous play to the same cause. Whatever the validity of such specific ascriptions may be, all our present knowledge of psychology strongly suggests that the various infant experiences will have both immediate and latent effects upon the behavior of the individual.

An important point about this period of infancy is that the educational process, whether concerned with personality formation, learning a language, or establishing rudimentary social relationships and discriminations, is often unconscious, both with the child and with the adults in the environment. Moreover, this is largely true of the entire educational process in nonliterate societies. Only rarely are the procedures and objectives of education made entirely explicit. In our own society this is of course mainly true of those parts of education which lie outside the formal educational process, and it is only in recent years and only among a relatively sophisticated stratum of population that we find conscious attempts to form the child's personality, usually by sets of rules and attitudes which change radically each decade.

3. CHILD-TRAINING AMONG THE ALORESE AND THE CROWS

The transition line between infancy and childhood is an arbitrary one, which we have set, for convenience and strictly in cultural terms, at about the time when the child begins to walk and talk. At this time, the child is not only learning to get about more efficiently by himself, but he is also entering, through speech, into a vast new world of experience and training. Both these faculties clearly assist in broadening the child's personality and in hastening the process of socialization.

As the infant grows into the child, his increasing interest in and exploration of the environment may be encouraged, hampered, or very largely ignored, depending on the culture into which he is born. Some restraints, however, will always be placed on his activities. The child will be kept from walking into the fire, seizing harmful objects, eating injurious substances, or violating religiously sanctioned rules. And perhaps more important, the child will be subjected to a more or less rigorous training in the control of his bodily functions, and to a more or less abrupt change in feeding habits.

Du Bois' account of the Alorese child again gives a more concrete picture. For a time after a child begins to toddle, he is still placed in the carrying shawl for nursing or for moving any considerable distance. For a time he will be placed in the shawl whenever he insists. But by the time a child is two and a half or more, he rarely is placed in the shawl. This is a period of diminishing bodily contacts with others and lessening physical support.

When the child can walk it is turned out to play during the day under the casual supervision of an older child or aged adult. Feeding is much less satisfactory from the child's point of view; while his mother is in the fields, he receives only such food as the older children will give him, usually in response to begging or screaming for food. Weaning begins about this time also, though if another child is expected, the process may be accelerated. It is rare in any case for a child to nurse longer than three or four years, and almost never is a child suckled after another child is born. Weaning is begun by pushing the child away gently, but if he is persistent he may be slapped, or, if this is not adequate, be sent to the house of a relative for a few days.

It is likely that this picture, as in the case with most anthropological accounts, overestimates the importance of nursing as giving food satisfactions. Normally the flow of milk is interrupted with the resumption of the normal menstrual cycle in women, and in any case it usually ceases at about fourteen months. In cases of prolonged nursing, then, the breast is given primarily as a pacifier and not a source of food. Important psychological correlations with the length of the nursing period undoubtedly exist, but interpretations in terms of food satisfactions are equally certainly erroneous.

Toilet-training is not initiated in Alor until the child can walk and is old enough to understand explanations. The child accompanies the mother to a privy or outside the village. Generally within a few months the child has learned sphincter control and to clean himself. Bladder control seems to come a little later, and to have even less emphasis placed upon it. More drastic than toilet-training seems to be the shift to the cold bath every two or three days. As most children either have lesions of yaws or cuts and abrasions which are painful on contact with water, and the mothers are rather rough in their scrubbing of children, tantrums and rages during baths are common, often lasting half an hour after the end of the bath.

Regular sleeping habits are not enforced. Both in the village and within the household there may be a good deal of movement at night. There may be a dance outside, a youth may return from courting, a member of the family may wish to recount a dream, or someone may get hungry and put on the pot for a midnight snack. Children consequently often take naps at odd times during the day.

Talking is picked up without conscious training on the whole, although adults tease and ridicule children for errors in speech. Five-year-olds may show a fluency in cursing when thwarted. This may be related to the fact that as soon as a child can walk he will be ordered about by any adult, at first to fetch and carry and go on errands, but later for more demanding tasks. Rebellion develops early and modes of escape from onerous duties are found somewhat later. Most striking in the Alorese picture of childhood is the lack of consistency in the behavior of adults toward children. The children are teased, ridiculed, neglected, praised, and rewarded in completely unpredictable fashions; in other words, discipline is entirely inconsistent. Temper tantrums in children are numerous and appear to be the outcome of this erratic and inconsistent treatment.

In later childhood, temper tantrums tend to disappear as the child acquires some devices for dealing with its environment, even though discipline becomes harsher, and adds physical violence or threats thereof to teasing and ridicule. Boys receive very direct training for their adult roles. However, they must forage now for their own food much of the time; they form gangs, steal, or become "fags" for young men. Although boys receive less direct teaching than girls, they have many more opportunities to be present at events which give them indirect instruction about the adult society in which they must live. Girls, while less privileged in some ways, receive consistent training in women's activities and are allowed to participate in them. Lack of training and praise, together with harsh discipline, create uncertainty and self-distrust in the child. Children have few defenses against adults, although they can and frequently do run away, and may be sheltered by an adult relative if their treatment has been too harsh.

This picture may seem to belie the general statements about education made earlier. Nevertheless, the treatment of children is not unrelated to the requirements of the adult culture. Much of the valued activity of the adult culture centers about financial transactions in which bargaining, chicanery, deceit, and mistrust are common. Given the values of Alorese culture, a training which leaves children distrustful of their environment and their fellows seems functional.

Quite otherwise is the case in different cultures. Although Plains Indian treatment of infants is restrictive and the discipline accorded small children often harsh, much of childhood is rather carefree and protected. Among the Crows, for example, while small children who cry or have tantrums may have water poured down their noses, older children associate freely with their age mates in games which often are play reproductions of adult activities. Boys hunt rabbits and birds, shoot at marks, play with captured buffalo calves, or kill them in simulated hunts. Girls often build miniature tipis, and boys and girls join together in playing house. The boys hunt or steal food, and though they may be beaten if caught, such minor thefts are usually treated by adults with good-natured toleration; the girls prepare the food. Groups of children will sometimes set up their own mock caravans when a band is on the march, pitching their own miniature tipis at a little distance when camp is made. Boys form societies aping adult societies and even steal one another's "wives" as the adult Foxes and Lumpwoods (men's societies among the Crows) steal each others' unfaithful wives. Girls visit the tipis of boys as if coming to marry them and are given food by indulgent parents. Groups of boys play at taking scalps (of coyotes, wolves, or rabbits) and visit the tipis of their parents singing victory songs and receiving gifts of food.

Crow children grow up to respect the aged, to be stoical, brave, generous, and on the whole well adjusted to the demands of adult life. The transition to full participation in adult activities is an eagerly awaited privilege undertaken under the friendly guidance of elders. When young people, especially males, are forced to undergo hardship in vision quests or on the warpath, this is to test their worthiness as adults or to aid them to acquire prestige and supernatural power. Only those who fail to conform to behavioral standards, weaklings, cowards, or orphans, are apt to receive mistreatment. Beatings are rare, and if public ridicule is sharp and frequent, public praise for good behavior is freely given.

Despite the necessary omission of many details, the examples given suggest clearly that there is some educational preparation for adult life in each case, although that of the Alorese seems less adequate than among many other groups. Likewise it seems clear that differences in treatment and education must produce differences in personality or at least in the frequency of certain personality types, which in part are related to the different demands placed on the adult individual in various cultures.

4. CHILD-TRAINING: THEORETICAL ASPECTS

In recent years many anthropologists and psychologists have laid great emphasis on toilet-training and feeding as primary determinants of the child's developing personality. It has been noted, for example, that toilet-training begins very early in some societies and is quite severe. The child may be forced to the proper behavior and punished in various ways for minor lapses. In other societies, the matter may be handled very laxly, as we have already noted for the Alorese. Most societies, probably, fall between these two extremes, as is the case among the Tarascan Indians of Mexico.

The Tarascans do not attempt early toilet-training of the child. After the child can walk easily, however, he is urged to care for himself properly or to make his needs known. Children who soil themselves or wet their garments often are not changed for some time. The mother either ignores the child or explains what has happened; the child must follow the mother about, whimpering and uncomfortable, until she chooses to change him. If learning proves unusually slow, the child may be deprived of water or his food intake regulated, particularly at night. Physical punishment is usually lacking, however. Most families treat their children affectionately; they are carried about and cared for, not only by their mothers but also by their fathers and older siblings. They show little or no fear of strangers, particularly if a parent is talking to the stranger in a friendly fashion. Frequently, at the slightest encouragement, they are even friendly or affectionate to strangers. Shyness and awkwardness with others does not begin until shortly before adolescence, a change in behavior that can hardly be attributed to toilet-training.

While there seems to be little doubt that toilet-training and feeding play perhaps a significant role in personality formation, our knowledge seems not yet adequate to speak of them as major factors. Training children to avoid ceremonial objects may be quite as rigorous as toilet-training; thwarting the child's actions or desires to handle objects would seem quite likely to have as much effect on his personality as food deprivations, provided of course the child's needs at the time are satisfied.

Moreover, most psychological interpretations, even though they do not emphasize unduly toilet-training and feeding processes, assume that the adult generally occupies a role of either frustrating the child in his activities or compelling the child to do things he does not wish to do. As a result the child is said to experience frustrations and tensions which result in aggressive behavior, tantrums, or internalized or hidden anger and aggression. The parent most active in training and discipline is apt to be hated and feared, although this may necessarily again be hidden. Mitigation of the effects of the frustrations and compulsions may occur if there is a warm and affectionate treatment.

This explanation seems one sided. It assumes that the child has "natural" responses to all situations. Such obviously is the case with such a thing as hunger, but most of the situations encountered by the child are culturally created. To these the child can have no "natural" response but must learn a response. Even though there may be a number of alternative responses, the child is normally unaware of the alternatives and is not frustrated by being "forced" to accept that considered proper by the adults. Moreover, at a relatively early age children become eager to ape adult activities. In our own culture children of less than one year often are anxious to eat with a spoon and drink from a cup. Unless there is punishment for failure to perform according to adult standards, the adult who facilitates use of spoon or cup appears, not as forcing the child and frustrating his "natural" desire, but as a beneficent being who aids the child to accomplish his wishes. In more purely social situations, when the child encounters a stranger, the parent often puts the child at ease by showing him the proper behavior. Similarly, the adult frequently is in a position of helping the child to improve his manipulation of the physical environment, whether it be throwing a ball, wielding a hammer, or shooting a bow and arrow. The more extreme emphasis on the role of the parent in creating frustrations and hence becoming the object of concealed aggression seems a very simplistic and inadequate hypothesis. The development of personality is continuous, at least well into adult life, and often adults fail to show the personality which, according to more extreme current theory, should be produced by their childhood training. Additional study of later influences on personality formation is needed before we will have a coherent and adequate theory. This fact has been recognized by Ralph Linton, who has contributed much to current theory, but who is now concentrating his attention on the post-childhood phases of personality formation.

One reason we believe that current theory regarding culture and personality must be regarded with reserve is that it is largely based upon psychoanalytic concepts. Generally speaking, the great advances in learning theory made by psychologists in recent years and the important contributions of social psychologists such as the late Kurt Lewin and his followers have been little employed by anthropologists. Psychoanalytic concepts are still in the clinical stage where they have produced striking results in the treatment of patients in our culture. But the concepts are still empirical and lack scientific verification in very large part. In one sense psychoanalysis is in the state of medicine a hundred years ago, before the development of scientific medicine.

This criticism should not be understood as condemning the entire culture-personality approach. In our opinion some of the most fruitful and exciting work in anthropology at the present time is being done in this field. It is a frontier field, however, and as such most of the work must be regarded as exploratory and provisional. It cannot command too much space in an introductory text. We have given this much space to it because newcomers to anthropology are most apt to encounter the work of such brilliant pioneers as Margaret Mead, Ruth Benedict, Cora Du Bois, and Abram Kardiner (the latter a psychoanalyst). Students should be able to place this work in perspective with relation to the totality of anthropology.

Education during childhood results not only in personality formation but also in the child's socialization. It is, indeed, in this period that socialization begins in earnest, that the child begins, in other words, to learn his culture and especially those cultural patterns that govern his relations to others, both children and adults.

The earliest learning of this sort is with relation to the kinship group. The child is in constant contact with his parents, siblings, and a varying number of other relatives. If the family is an extended one, the contacts with other relatives may be close. By precept and example the child learns the names or terms by which he should address each person in his environment, and more importantly, he gradually learns the behaviors expected of him and which he may expect from others.

Sometimes the inculcation of behaviors is deliberate. Not only is the child told repeatedly, but little examples may be given. The western Apache, for example, may send a child to ask a favor of a particular relative, a favor which would not be granted by any one except such a relative.

By practical example, then, the child discovers that a relative whom he calls by a certain term may be counted upon to act in a given way.

If antagonisms exist, these also are inculcated in the child. The Nisenan Indians of California may indicate a given individual to the child many times, with comment: "That man killed your uncle; be careful of him; sometime he must be killed in revenge." People who are otherwise untrustworthy, lazy, inveterate borrowers, and so on, may similarly be pointed out. Conversely, persons worthy of emulation, who are industrious, brave, or possess other qualities admired by the society are held up to the child as models.

In most cultures the child begins at an early age to emulate his parents. By five or six, a Tarascan boy accompanies his father to the fields or woods. At first he may merely watch his father's blanket while his father plows; or, if the expedition is for firewood, he may carry a single stick home in his own special tumpline, a small replica of his father's. Before adolescence he may be going alone with a burro to get firewood. By fourteen he is capable of a day's work with ox team and plow. Similarly, the Tarascan girl at three or four accompanies her mother to the fountain for water, carrying her own miniature jar, a replica of her mother's. By seven or eight she is doing her stint at the grinding stone, making tortillas, sweeping the house and yard, and perhaps washing clothes. By nine or ten she may be going alone to the mill with corn to be ground. Both boys and girls not infrequently care for their younger siblings, carrying them on their backs while they play games. By early adolescence, both sexes have acquired a reasonable facility in the basic techniques of making a living and running a house.

The Tarascan Indian is perhaps unusually early in learning the basic techniques. In many groups, full competence comes later; this seems especially true in hunting groups such as the Crows, where the dangers and physical exertions are too great for the boys to take full part. Yet at an early age, Crow boys are taught to play with and later to make weapons, and as early as seven or eight may be engaged in hunting birds or other small game close to the camp or home. Even a Tarascan boy, although he knows the techniques of farming, will not have acquired all the knowledge necessary to be a successful farmer. Normally, for some time his father directs his activities and advises him. This may continue long after marriage, although in part the advice may be given by surrogates or substitutes for the parents, such as the boy's uncles or godparents of his marriage.

During childhood, the individual usually receives a considerable amount of instruction in basic attitudes, standards, and values. We have already mentioned the use of the folk tale among the Indians of western North

America. In his study of primitive education, George Pettitt points out many other examples of the use of stories to inculcate attitudes and ideals. Plains Indian stories, for example, glorify the successful warrior and prepare the child to seek achievement in war, one of the dominant social and economic activities of these groups. In Chapter 16 we pointed out the educational function, as well, of rituals and ceremonials. Pettitt further elaborates this point also.

Pettitt deals with a number of other mechanisms for education. In the matter of discipline, for example, resort may be had to supernatural powers. The child may be told of one or more supernatural beings who are able to see all transgressions and will punish them. Sometimes these supernatural beings are impersonated by masked men as, for example, the Zuñi A'doshlĕ. According to Pettitt,

The A'doshlĕ have bulging eyes, protruding teeth, and a mat of tangled hair. The husband of each pair carries a huge knife with which to cut off heads, and the wife bears a huge basket in which to carry off children and a large crooked stick with which to catch them. At the time of the annual ceremony they make a perfunctory dance and then begin to search for bad children, of whom they have, presumably, been notified in advance. The parents of the bad children make apparently herculean efforts to repel the terrible A'doshlĕ. They barricade the door of the house, and beat drums and pans. In recent years they have carried the mummery to the point of firing guns over the heads of the A'doshlĕ. But all of this is of no avail. The A'doshlĕ are supernaturals. They break through the barricade—thereby demonstrating to the children that punishment for misbehavior is as inevitable as the rising of the sun. The old woman with the crooked stick puts it around bad girls and drags them over to a metate to grind them up. The old man whirls his knife in the face of bad boys. There is a threat in reserve that they will eat up bad children. They go so far as to bite the child in the neck. The elders of the family add to the dramatic effect by evincing great fear themselves. To demonstrate further that this discipline comes from the outside, the A'doshlĕ frequently lecture the parents, sometimes seriously if one happens to be lazy or otherwise remiss. Only when the visiting disciplinarians have been bought off with presents of meat and meal will they consent to forego more drastic punishment. Meanwhile the shouting has been listened to by neighboring children from the darkest corners of their respective homes.[3]

That this type of discipline is highly effective cannot be doubted, however much it might be criticized by a modern child psychologist. Moreover, it may be effective at a very early age. At Cochiti, an Indian pueblo (and

[3] George A. Pettitt, "Primitive Education in North America" (Berkeley, Calif.: courtesy of *University of California Publications in American Archeology and Ethnology*), XLIII, 1–182, p. 34.

many other places), the owl is said to be a supernatural who punishes bad children. Parsons reports that when a Cochiti woman imitated the hooting of an owl in answer to a question about what she would do to frighten a child into being good, a three-year-old was panic-stricken and buried his face in his mother's lap.

Other coercive means are used to inculcate proper behavior in children. Praise and ridicule are widespread among nonliterate peoples as a potent means of encouraging both young and adult to behave properly. Praise seems usually to be universal—any adult will praise a child for doing something meritorious—but it is especially used within the family. Thus a Crow Indian father, for example, gives feasts for his son, especially when the latter has done something meritorious, at which the father, other relatives, and guests make speeches extolling the youth.

Just as common is ridicule for the child who fails to conform. Sometimes ridicule is anonymous where, at night, a whole camp may start shouting out the ridiculous actions of some individual. More commonly, it is the individual's fellows and more particularly certain relatives who may be the source of the ridicule. The function of joking relatives in this connection has already been described in Chapter 13. Because of the extensive use of praise and ridicule from early childhood on, many nonliterates are highly sensitive to both, abnormally so from our point of view.

Another system of rewards often used to encourage learning is the granting or withholding of the privileges of maturity. This will be further elaborated in the discussion of adolescence.

One aspect of education among both nonliterates and ourselves which has been little explored is the function of the age group itself. In most societies, children and adolescents spend a good portion of their time with their approximate age mates; examples are found in the play groups and "gangs" so common among ourselves. In every such age group, there are obvious differences in the knowledge and sophistication of its members. Some of the children are older than the rest and frequently teach the younger ones, both by precept and example. Evidence of such teaching is found in the fact that many children's games, songs, rhymes, techniques of making and handling toys, and the like, are passed from one generation of children to the next without the intervention of adults. Other cultural items are similarly transmitted. In our society, for example, where there is often great reticence between parents and children concerning sexual matters, the child not infrequently obtains much of his first, and often inaccurate, sexual knowledge from his older age mates. The same is probably true in other societies as well, and of other cultural patterns, but we have as yet no really dependable studies of this important area of education.

5. PUBERTY AND ADOLESCENCE

The beginning of adolescence is usually associated with puberty, that is, with the beginnings of physiological maturity and the first functioning of the sexual organs. In girls, puberty is definitely marked by the onset of menstruation, enlargement of the breasts, and other indications of maturity. Among boys, the period is not so clearly marked; there is only a gradual change which is indicated by an increased growth of body and face hair, the alteration of the voice, and changes in bodily weight and proportions. In both sexes, however, the onset of puberty and adolescence is accompanied by numerous changes in both personality and behavior.

Among many nonliterate peoples, the youth, at puberty or very shortly thereafter, is ready to assume the cultural status of an adult. The boy has learned the techniques necessary for economic self-sufficiency, and though he may still be regarded as a very young man, he is nevertheless classed as an adult and not as a child. Girls similarly have been taught in the techniques appropriate to their sex, and not infrequently marry very soon after their first menstruation.

In our society, of course, the case is quite different. The adolescent, male or female, has not yet completed his preparatory schooling at puberty, and if he hopes to learn a profession, such as medicine, he must spend many years at school before he attains his goal. Marriage, for both boys and girls, usually is deferred long beyond puberty; the adolescent is discouraged from marriage until he attains a greater or less economic self-sufficiency and he is also forbidden extramarital sexual experiences. In most cases, indeed, adolescents are regarded as children rather than as young adults: parental authority is not relaxed and the adolescent is given little or no increase in responsibilities.

It is this treatment of the adolescent, made necessary perhaps by the elaboration of our culture and the long time needed for a child to attain adult status, that accounts in large part for the considerable emotional conflicts that mark the period in our society. Margaret Mead has shown, for example, in her studies of Samoa that emotional crises in adolescence are apparently culturally produced, and not an inevitable concomitant of physiological maturity. Samoan children, at an early age, are completely educated about sex and related matters. At puberty, both sexes enter almost immediately into adult forms of behavior, sexually as well as in other ways. In short, the period of adolescence in Samoa is transitional between childhood and adulthood, culturally as well as physiologically; the adolescent is given greater freedom and more responsibility than the child even though he has not yet achieved adult status. As a result, adolescence in Samoa is apparently relatively free of emotional difficulties.

Our society takes little or no cognizance of puberty in any ritual or ceremonial sense. To be sure, an adolescent boy may be twitted about his changing voice, his immature beard, or his changing attitudes toward girls, but there is no ritual activity that marks a change in his social status. Similarly, our society does not emphasize a girl's first menstruation but regards this event, rather, as a highly personal affair, and even as something to be hidden or to be ashamed of. The closest thing to a puberty ritual in our culture is the coming-out or debutante party, more a social than a ceremonial affair, and even then restricted to a relatively small segment of the population.

If we make little of the onset of adolescence, other societies formally recognize the period and often make it the key point for intensive educational practices, usually connected with ritual observances. These are apparently more frequent for boys, though girls' adolescence rites are also very common.

Girls' puberty rites very frequently take place at the first menstruation. In many cases, the ritual is only a family affair—a rite of passage—like the "little ceremony" mentioned in Chapter 16, § 9, for the Chiricahua Apaches. Commonly, at this time, the menstruant is segregated, for she is believed to possess magical or supernatural influences of possible danger to others, and subjected to numerous restrictions on her behavior. Among some California Indians, for example, the girl is secluded in a special hut built for that purpose, forbidden certain foods, required to use a tube for drinking and a specially made stick to scratch herself, and required to bathe and exercise in a prescribed way. Among the Chiricahua Apaches, as we have seen, the "little ceremony" is followed by an elaborate Girl's Puberty Rite in which one or more pubescent girls are the center of attention. During this time, the girls are said to be imbued with supernatural power and even to have the power of healing others and of bringing them blessings. The primary function of the rite is to safeguard the girl at a crucial point in her life, and to focus all supernatural power on the task of insuring her a long, fruitful, and happy life. Secondarily, the rite functions much as a debutante party, for the girl is now a woman ready for marriage and is so introduced, as it were, to the members of the local group and band.

Boys also go through special rituals which formally admit them to adult status or to its initial stages. Such ceremonies are extremely widespread, and some elements of them seem to have a world-wide distribution, which suggests either that these elements are very old, or that they are simple enough to have developed independently in many diverse societies. Most frequent and striking of these elements is the idea that the boy dies and is resurrected as a man. In some cases women and young children are simply told that the boy, who has disappeared for the time of the ceremony, has died and later comes back to life; in others, an actual simulation of death is observed. The boy is rendered unconscious and later revived. Among some African tribes, boys may be secluded for as much as a year; on their return home they must pretend not to know their own village, their friends, or their families, and go through a period of supposed education about them.

The symbolism of this action is evident. The child has now become an adult. As an adult he is required to exhibit an adult personality and to take on adult behavior and responsibilities. In effect, one personality has died, a new one has come into existence. The dramatization of death and resurrection in ceremonies such as these effectively symbolizes the change in the boy's personality and impresses him with the importance of his new role.

Other widespread observances at this time include the infliction of a "tribal mark." Actually, these marks are apparently symbols of adult or quasi-adult status. These include circumcision in many parts of Australia, Africa, and Asia, tattooing and scarification throughout much of the Old World and in parts of the New, changes in styles of cutting the hair, perforation of the ears, nasal septum, or the lips to receive ornaments (although this is sometimes done in infancy), permission to wear adult clothing and ornamentation, and other like procedures.

A feature of most of the formal initiations into adult status is a period of training and education. Among the Hopis, the boy is initiated into a *kiva* in a ceremony which includes whipping and other ordeals. The boy learns for the first time, at least in theory and apparently in actuality in most cases, that the masked impersonators of the supernatural *kachina* are really his relatives and fellow townsfolk. He is given an initial period of education in the religion and mythology of the group, an educational process which may last for many years as he strives to rise in the religious hierarchy which he now discovers is the real social force in the community.

The Onas of Tierra del Fuego induct all boys into adult status through a group initiation ceremony held in a special conical hut. The initiation lasts two or more months; the boys are given special instruction and are told the origin myth. Masked impersonators of supernaturals are revealed to be human at the close of the initiation. Girls' puberty ceremonies among the Onas are individual, but special instruction is also given.

In addition a special school is held for boys who wish to become shamans or doctors. The candidates sing and fast in hopes of gaining a guardian spirit. Once the spirit is acquired, the neophyte receives instruction from an older shaman. Similar schools or individual training for specialized callings are recorded for many nonliterate peoples. It is clear that formal instruction, at least in some matters, is a widespread practice.

Initiatory rites and induction to adult status may sometimes be employed as means of discipline and social control. Boys may not be permitted to go through the initiation until they have shown physical fortitude or the ability to carry on adult activities. In Australia, where the society is frequently controlled by the aged, initiations are actually a series of rituals covering many years. At each step, the individual gains more freedom of action in the society, but not until he is a mature man does he conclude all the initiatory rites. As these rituals are religious in nature and involve the progressive imparting of secret information, the elders are able to hold a monopoly of power.

The length of the peroid of adolescence varies greatly in different cultures. Among the Tarascan Indians, marriage follows very shortly after puberty. Girls may be married by fourteen or even earlier, and it is not uncommon for a girl of fifteen or sixteen to have two children. Boys are one or two years older than girls at marriage. This does not mean, however, that either girls or boys are considered fully educated at marriage. The first year after marriage is usually spent in the household of the groom's parents. The girl works at household tasks under the supervision of her mother-in-law, the boy works in the fields or at some other occupation under the direction of his father. Only after the first child is born do the couple set up their own establishment. In addition the godparents of the marriage, an older couple, selected by the bride and groom to be ceremonial sponsors at the wedding, retain a continuing responsibility for the young couple, visit them frequently, and give advice concerning personal relations as well as other behavior.

In some nonliterate societies marriage occurs much later. Among the Masai of East Africa, as we noted in Chapter 14, § 1, the young man must spend from ten to fifteen years as a warrior before he can marry. During this period he accumulates the property necessary to set up a household and to assume the position of an "elder" in his native village. Among the Plains Indians, similarly, a young man often may not marry until he has gained some war honors, or otherwise proved himself able in adult activities. In most nonliterate societies, however, marriage follows soon after the physiological maturation, as symbolized by initiation or puberty ceremonies. At this time, both boys and girls are considered able to undertake most of their responsibilities as spouses and parents, even though, as among the Tarascans, they may still be required to work under the supervision of parents or parents-in-law for a time. It should be noted, too, that the extended family, so common among nonliterates, and the equally common pattern whereby the newly married live in close association with either the wife's or the husband's relatives, enormously simplify the economic burden of the newly married.

In complex societies, however, and more particularly in our own, the elaboration of techniques, understandings, and interrelationships has become so great that education is still incomplete with puberty. For a substantial portion of our population it continues for a considerable number of years. Achievement of economic self-sufficiency, regarded by most people in our society as a necessary prelude to marriage, usually takes several years more. As a result, the age of marriage has become progressively higher, and many professional people, whose education takes many years of advanced study, do not marry until they are in their thirties. Distortion of the personality and neurotic difficulties of many sorts are often traced to this deferment of marriage.

6. LEARNING A WAY OF LIFE: APACHE INFANCY

In the preceding sections, we have described educational processes in a piecemeal fashion in respect to differing periods in the individual's life cycle. We shall now give a unified picture of education in a single society —that of the Chiricahua Apache Indians—and so illustrate the learning of a way of life very different from our own. Much of Chiricahua Apache culture has been described elsewhere in this book: we already know the Chiricahuas therefore as a seminomadic food-gathering peoples who lived formerly in southeastern Arizona and southwestern New Mexico. Today they live on a reservation in eastern New Mexico.

The Chiricahuas conceive life as a path along which the individual travels, moving slowly from birth through infancy, childhood, adolescence, and adulthood to death. Much of this path, in Chiricahua belief, is beset with dangers, such as illness and misfortune, brought about in part by the individual's own carelessness or ignorance, and in part by the machinations of sorcerers. To guard against these dangers, the individual must be protected by ritual and ceremony, that he may travel the path of life precisely as it was traveled by the supernatural culture heroes of the mythical period, and so gain both long life and happiness. Much of a Chiricahua's education, accordingly, is bound up with ceremony, itself a teaching device of considerable importance, though the Chiricahuas by no means neglect training in techniques, skills, and patterns of social behavior.

The child receives his first contact with ritual soon after birth. The midwife washes the new-born baby in tepid water, lays it on a soft robe, and then performs a simple rite—strewing pollen and ashes to the four directions, presenting the baby similarly to each direction, and accompanying this procedure with prayers and other acts characteristic of her particular ritual. Later, usually the fourth day after birth, a shaman who knows the proper rituals makes a cradle for the child, and attaches to this cradle a number of amulets to guard the baby from harm. The child spends most of his time laced tightly into the cradle but with his head and arms free for some movement. He is nursed whenever he cries, and he is taken periodically from the cradle to be bathed and dusted with a powder made from willow bark. As the baby grows more active, beads and jingles are hung from the canopy of the cradle to amuse him.

When the child is old enough to crawl, he is allowed increasing amounts of time outside the cradle. He is carefully watched, however, to prevent his coming into contact with things that may injure him. Dogs are kept away from the encampment, for they may bark or otherwise frighten the child. Fretful children may be rocked in their cradles, with one of the parents or some other adult singing lullabies to them.

Some time between the ages of seven months and two years, a shaman is hired to perform the ceremony known as "Putting on the Moccasins." This is to celebrate the first attempts of the child to walk, and, in the course of the ceremony, the child receives his first moccasins and often a new outfit of buckskin clothing as well. Numerous rituals are performed to bless the child and to insure for him good health and a long life. The ceremony is also a social occasion, attended by the family and their friends, and, after the ceremony is finished, there is much feasting and giving of gifts.

The following spring—the season when everything begins to grow—a shaman is selected for the first hair-cutting rite. With considerable ritual and the usual prayers for good health and long life, the shaman crops the child's hair closely, leaving only one or two locks. Ideally, this ceremony should be performed four times in successive springs. After this the hair is allowed to grow long for both male and female children. About the time of the first hair-cutting rite, weaning begins. The child is provided with light foods, so that he will not demand the breast so much, but if this is not effective, he may simply be deprived of breast feeding or discouraged from it by smearing the nipples with sour or peppery substances.

During the period just described, the child's world is pretty much limited to the encampment of the extended family, and even to the wickiup of his own primary family. In an earlier chapter (Chapter 13, § 3), we described this environment and the complex social relations, based on kinship, that unite the members of the encampment. Even as an infant, it may be noted, the child is early brought into contact with a variety of relatives—his parents and older siblings, his mother's sisters and their families, and his maternal grandparents. He may also be taken to visit his paternal relatives at the encampment from which his father came.

7. LEARNING A WAY OF LIFE: APACHE CHILDHOOD

As the infant grows into childhood, he increases his knowledge of this social environment and of the many techniques practiced and artifacts used. In particular, he learns how to behave toward his kinsfolk: he establishes close and intimate relations with his siblings and cousins of the same sex, he learns of "avoidance" and "respect" relatives (see Chapter 13, § 3), he learns that maternal uncles and grandparents are especially friendly adults, very much interested in teaching and aiding him.

Moreover, as he grows older and understands more, he is constantly told, both by his parents and other relatives, how to act. Chiricahua adults take the problem of rearing and training children very seriously, for the behavior of children reflects on the extended family, and those whose children misbehave may be severely criticized. One of Opler's informants summarized the admonitions he received during childhood in the following words:

As far back as I can remember my father and mother directed me how to act. They used to tell me, "Do not use a bad word which you wouldn't like to be used to you. Do not feel that you are anyone's enemy. In playing with children remember this: do not take anything from another child. Don't take arrows away from another boy just because you are bigger than he is. Don't take his marbles away. Don't steal from your friends. Don't be unkind to your playmates. If you are kind now, when you become a man you will love your fellowmen.

"When you go to the creek and swim, don't duck anyone's children. Don't ever fight a girl when you're playing with other children. Girls are weaker than boys. If you fight with them, that will cause us trouble with our neighbors.

"Don't laugh at feeble old men and women. That's the worst thing you can do. Don't criticize them and make fun of them. Don't laugh at anybody or make fun of anybody.

"This is your camp. What little we have here is for you to eat. Don't go to another camp with other children for a meal. Come back to your own camp when you are hungry and then go out and play again.

"When you start to eat, act like a grown person. Just wait until things are served to you. Do not take bread or a drink or a piece of meat before the rest start to eat. Don't ask before the meal for things that are still cooking, as many children do. Don't try to eat more than you want. Try to be just as polite as you can; sit still while you eat. Do not step over another person, going around and reaching for something.

"Don't run into another person's camp as though it was your own. Don't run around anyone's camp. When you go to another camp, don't stand at the door. Go right in and sit down like a grown person. Don't get into their drinking water. Don't go out and catch or hobble horses and ride them as if they belonged to you the way some boys do. Do not throw stones at anybody's animals.

"When a visitor comes, do not go in front of him or step over him. Do not cut up while the visitor is here. If you want to play, get up quietly, go behind the visitor, and out the door." [4]

The children are early made aware of sex differences; boys are encouraged to play together and at games in which they imitate activities pertinent to their sex. Girls, too, form into groups, and often join with the women in their daily activities, performing tasks suitable to their age and strength. At the earliest possible age, both boys and girls are made aware of the dangers that threaten the local encampment from hostile aliens, and are taught to remain quiet when enemies may be near.

Discipline, though at times firm and decisive, is not severe; Chiricahua adults are on the whole gentle and indulgent toward their children. The child may, however, be frightened into good behavior by adults' invoking of a dreadful and shadowy being who, the young are told, captures and eats noisy or disobedient children. Other supernaturals are similarly used, in particular one of the Mountain Spirits called the Gray One, whom the children see impersonated in ceremonies. Finally, the children soon acquire the adults' dread of owls, bears, snakes, and ghosts, all of which symbolize the power of evil.

Young children are given corporal punishment only as a last resort. If, however, a child is unusually obnoxious, he may be sent off on a wild goose chase in search of some nonexistent object. As boys and girls grow older, however, serious breaches of etiquette, manners, or morals may bring physical punishment, together with loud scoldings. Boys who are disobedient or who fight a good deal may be obliged to fight publicly with various individuals until they have received a thorough beating.

More often, however, the child is guided in his behavior by telling him

[4] Morris Edward Opler, *An Apache Life-Way* (Chicago: copyright 1941 by University of Chicago Press), p. 27.

myths, legends, and personal narratives. Story-telling sessions occur frequently during the winter evenings, and children are often required not only to attend but also to stay awake and listen. The story-teller, when children are present, is always careful to point the moral of his tales. Older men will also emphasize the need for training in this or that technique by relating personal experiences in which their skills saved them from various dangers.

In these story-telling sessions the child gets the ideological background necessary to an understanding of his culture, and especially to an understanding of the supernatural world and the rites and ceremonies which are used to deal with it. Gradually he absorbs the Apache view that much of success in life depends on the favors of the supernatural powers. This is reinforced by rituals which center about the child and also by his witnessing the important community ceremonies that go on about him. The child also learns, of course, the fears which are manifested in his community—of ghosts, of witchcraft, and of other forces that may be malevolently inclined.

But children are not continually preached at nor harassed by fears; actually they spend much of their time in games. Both sexes make and play with dolls and miniature household equipment. Boys play at hunting and war, and may even imitate in play the dancers and singers they see and hear in ceremonies. So they learn these sacred rites, at the same time discovering that sacred songs, rituals, and ceremonies are the personal property of shamans, not to be performed without supernatural inspiration or the guidance and permission of those who own them.

As they approach puberty, training in adult techniques and activities becomes more intensive for both sexes. Boys are taught to make and handle weapons, to hunt, to care for themselves in camping expeditions, and to engage in other activities, such as the semisacred hoop and pole game, appropriate to males. Girls are kept busy preparing for marriage and the duties of caring for a household. The girl early learns to care for younger children, to find and prepare vegetable foods, to make and use household equipment, to make clothing, and to cook. It should be noted that much of this training, for both boys and girls, comes easily, for the children are eager to imitate their elders so that they may be included in adult activities and gain the good will and approval of their kin.

8. LEARNING A WAY OF LIFE: APACHE PUBERTY AND ADOLESCENCE

As we have noted earlier (see § 5), the Apache girl at puberty goes through two ceremonies, the "little ceremony" at her first menstruation, and the more elaborate puberty rite shortly thereafter. The latter ceremony, among other things, is an announcement of the girl's readiness for marriage. After the ceremony, she is carefully guarded until her marriage takes place. She may elude her guardians and elope, or she may even succeed in having a clandestine affair (for which she will be severely punished if it is discovered), but ideally her marriage is arranged by her parents, who go to considerable lengths to secure a husband suitable in character, status, and family connections. The girl usually enters marriage well equipped to carry on the obligations of adult life, made easier by the fact that she continues to live, with her husband, in the extended family of her rearing. Marriage marks the end of a girl's preparatory education, though she continues of course to learn more through practical experience as a wife and mother.

The boy's training at puberty is both harsher and more carefully directed than that of a girl. Great emphasis is laid on physical fitness for the adult male. He must often depend on his strength, skill, and fleetness of foot to save him from death or injury in hunting and warfare. Accordingly, boys are made to rise before daylight and run long distances, often while carrying a heavy pack. They must also bathe in icy water during the winter and dry off away from the fire. Boys have many duties which have value in their training, such as caring for horses and acting as scouts and camp guards, when they must slip noiselessly through the brush looking for the tracks of hostile aliens. Especially are they trained to care for themselves when alone in the wilderness: how to find food or go without when necessary, how to find water, where to sleep safely, and the proper techniques of camping in bad weather and finding their way in rough or difficult country.

When a boy reaches puberty his training becomes more formal and passes partly out of the hands of the family. While emphasis on physical fitness and ability to handle weapons continues, the boy has to demonstrate his ability to a wider circle of people, and more emphasis is placed on group training. Boys run in groups, and engage in contests of various sorts, both of skill and physical prowess. Boys are matched for individual fights, and there are also mock group fights with slings or with small bows and arrows. In foot races, sometimes an adult on horseback follows and whips those who lag. Boys also get practice in handling and riding horses and are taken on hunts. Sometimes as early as fourteen a boy is a skillful hunter and dangerous warrior. Those who are outstanding in the training period early achieve recognition and so lay a sound basis for their adult status.

During this period the attitudes of parents change toward the boys. While in childhood indulgence marked the relations of father and son, the father now insists on strict compliance with the tasks laid on the boy. No conscious cruelty is practiced; rather the attitude is that a good father owes it to his children to make them ready to cope with any emergency in their adult lives.

At about sixteen the boy volunteers to go on raiding parties as a novice. Although protected from danger, he must meet the same exacting physical standards as the adults. Usually four expeditions as a novice are required before a boy is considered a full-fledged adult. He receives definite instruction before his first party so that he knows both what to expect and how to conduct himself in any contingency (such as being separated from his party and having to make his own way home). Often shamans take part in the preparation, and the novice is identified with the supernatural. Older men treat novices with some reverence, and at the same time the novice is under food and behavior restrictions and is the object of ritual behavior. He is also required to act as servant to the older warriors and to do many of the menial tasks necessary to a war party.

If a boy comports himself properly, after his fourth trip as a novice he is regarded as an adult. He is now a warrior on an equal status with others of a raiding party. He may participate in the war dance and is expected to be in the front rank when there is fighting. He likewise shares in the gains of a war party, for much of Apache raiding is to steal horses and to secure other economic benefits. Marriage may follow soon after the boy has completed his training as a warrior and has gained sufficient status as a hunter to be welcomed by the family of his sweetheart.

Like the girl, the boy who has passed his novitiate has many things to learn from practical experience as a husband and father. Most important, perhaps, is the gaining of supernatural power, for most Apache men hope, sooner or later, to have a vision experience or dream which will bring them into direct contact with a supernatural being. This experience, the Chiricahuas believe, not only enhances an individual's status in the community, but insures as well that he will live long and enjoy both health and well-being. An adult with access to supernatural power has his own protection against the inimical forces of the universe. Throughout his life, therefore, he continues to seek more power and so gain increased knowledge and potential control over supernatural forces. Women, too, may seek power, particularly after the age of child-bearing, but in the main, these activities seem predominantly masculine.

In summary, then, the Chiricahua Apaches, a small society that has but a precarious existence in a none-too-rich environment, seek first to protect their children against harm and to give them the affection and support necessary to their growth and development. The child learns much through more or less unconscious observation and participation, but there is as well a good deal of purposeful direction, on the part of adults, in teaching the child techniques, social relationships, and the values and ideals of Chiricahua culture. As the child grows to maturity and adulthood, he is prepared to assume his place in the society and in his turn pass on to his children the skills, knowledge, and wisdom he himself has acquired.

9. SUMMARY

All cultures include educational mechanisms, which are both unconsciously applied and purposively directed. The function of these mechanisms is to train the young in the common behavior patterns and understandings that make up much of the culture. Not only must the child be taught the necessary skills and associated knowledge by which he must make a living, he must also be socialized by learning the accepted ways of dealing with his fellows, and he must acquire a working relationship with the universe through understanding the supernatural forces about him. In addition the society, through its culture, seeks to mold individual personalities to acceptable types. Among Plains Indians, for example, a high premium is placed on individual military exploits and consequently on aggressive and individualistic personalities. While this type apparently predominates, there are of course individuals who fail, for whatever reason, to conform. If these are males, they may find avenues of recognition through extraordinary supernatural powers, by becoming transvestites and adopting women's dress and ways, or they may simply muddle along as more or less unhappy and despised misfits. It is probable that all societies include such maladjusted individuals, for though culture is a major force in molding the personality, no society succeeds in reducing all its members to a single personality type.

A point of great significance here, which we have not previously mentioned, is that once a society has established a range of personality types compatible with its culture, there is a strong tendency, on the part of individuals who fit these types, to perpetuate and conserve the cultural tradition. This point has great importance to problems of social and cultural change, and especially so to colonial administrators and others who seek to change native cultures. Even when such efforts are directed at raising living standards or protecting natives against exploitation by others, they may fail completely because the changes in culture required demand personalities the society cannot produce. It may well be, as many anthropologists have pointed out, that successful modifications in a culture must begin with modifications in the area of education and child-training.

Throughout early life, and often continuing until advanced adulthood, individuals are instructed, directly and indirectly, in the ways of their culture. In nonliterate societies we only very rarely find formal agencies, such as schools, directed toward this purpose. Instead, the educational process is primarily in the hands of the family, and to a lesser extent in the charge of other social units, such as the warrior units of the Masai. Ceremonies, particularly those given at puberty, story-telling, and games frequently serve secondarily as educational mechanisms.

In larger and more complex nonliterate societies, we not infrequently find the beginnings of schools or training centers, usually in preparation for puberty ceremonies. Thus, many West African peoples require their boys to serve a novitiate in a secret society or cult, during which they gain a more or less formalized education in ritual and ceremonial matters. Similarly, among the Indians of ancient Peru, the sons of the Inca nobility attended a "university" at Cuzco, the capital, where they were instructed in the history of the royal lineage, the technique of making and reading a recording device called the *quipu,* and the arts of war and government.

While much learning in nonliterate societies is from willing imitation of adult activities and play, compulsion, with attendant rewards and punishments, is not infrequently resorted to. Sometimes particular relatives exercise discipline, either directly by means of corporal punishment and other devices, or indirectly through praising the successful and subjecting the deviant to ridicule. Supernatural beings are often invoked to frighten children into proper behavior, and sometimes these supernaturals are impersonated by disciplinarians who whip or otherwise administer both physical and psychological punishments.

Among most nonliterates the major preparatory education is complete at puberty and the children, after only a brief adolescence, pass on to marriage and adult status. This is of course in marked contrast to our own culture, where formal schooling normally continues throughout adolescence and not infrequently extends far into the adult years as well.

It may be noted also that, where nonliterate societies are small and the culture homogeneous, the education is essentially the same for all children, excepting only differentiation by sex. Adults, though they may have varying roles in the educational process, nevertheless share the same body of understandings and goals. Education in these societies is geared, therefore, to more or less well-defined aims, the same for all members of the society, and reiterated over and over again in ritual, story-telling, and in numerous other ways.

In our own society, and even in some of the larger and more complex nonliterate societies, the situation is quite different. Class-oriented education appeared, for example, in Peru, where the children of the nobility received training in history, religion, warfare, and government denied to the children of the *purics* or householders. For the latter, there was training only in specifically designated techniques, and in blind allegiance and explicit obedience to the Inca rulers. In our own society, education is carried on by many agencies—the family, the age group, the school, and the mass media of communication—and these efforts are not infrequently unintegrated, confusing, and downright contradictory. The child is therefore often confronted with wide divergences between ideals and behavior, as when the ideals of cooperation and public service he is taught in school are found to conflict with competitive and individualistic ways of making a living. As Ruth Benedict has pointed out, we teach our children one set of values and then expect them to live by another. It is not surprising, therefore, that education in our society frequently fails to accomplish its ends, or that children emerge into adult life often unequipped either technically or emotionally to carry on successfully their adult roles.

COLLATERAL READING

Dennis, Wayne. *The Hopi Child.* New York: D. Appleton-Century Co., 1940.

Kardiner, Abram. *The Individual and His Society.* New York: Columbia University Press, 1939. Parts I, III.

Leighton, Dorothea, and Kluckhohn, Clyde. *Children of the People.* Cambridge: Harvard University Press, 1947. Part I.

Linton, Ralph. *The Cultural Background of Personality.* New York: D. Appleton-Century Co., 1945.

Mead, Margaret. *Coming of Age in Samoa.* New York: W. Morrow and Co., 1928.

————. *Growing Up in New Guinea.* New York: W. Morrow and Co., 1930.

Pettitt, George A. "Primitive Education in North America," *University of California Publications in America Archaeology and Ethnology,* XLIII, 1–182, 1936.

ETHNOGRAPHIC REFERENCES

Alorese: Du Bois, 1944.

Australians (Aruntas): Coon, 1948, Chap. 7; Murdock, 1935, Chap. II; Spencer and Gillen, 1927.

Chiricahua Apaches: Opler, 1941.

Crows: Lowie, 1935.

Masai: Forde, 1950, Chap. XIV; Hollis, 1905.

Nisenans: Beals, 1933.

Onas: Steward, 1946, Vol. I, pp. 107–125.

Tarascans: Beals, 1946.

Zuñis: Cushing, 1920; Eggan, 1950, Chap. IV; Stevenson, 1904.

Chapter 20

PROBLEMS OF CULTURE CHANGE

1. INVENTION AND DIFFUSION

We have now completed the definition and description of culture that we began in Chapter 8. Our description of culture in its many aspects is of course not exhaustive; we have dealt only with the major categories, illustrating these sufficiently to give some idea of man's almost infinitely varied behavior. And we have noted that every human society, literate or non-literate, has a distinctive culture, which governs the behavior of its members relative to their environment, their social interactions, and the world of the supernatural.

But we have also noted, incidentally, throughout the preceding pages, that cultures are never static and unchanging. This fact indeed is obvious even to the most inexperienced observer. Our grandparents, for example, follow somewhat different ("old-fashioned") modes of behavior, evident in their dress, their speech, and their manners. Old books, newspapers, and photographs yield similar evidence; it is an interesting example of cultural change just to read over the advertisements in older newspapers and magazines. In short, just as contemporaneous cultures may differ more or less in rough proportion to their separation in space, so do single cultures differ slightly as between adjacent generations, more widely from one century to the next, and so on increasingly as the time periods compared are more and more distant from each other. Cultures do not of course change at the same rate—a given time span may witness great changes in one culture and very little in another. One of the most important problems that confronts the anthropologist—and indeed the social scientist generally—

is to analyze and classify the data of culture toward the end of better understanding the phenomena of cultural change and cultural stability.

As noted in Chapter 8, we may distinguish between the term "culture" and the phrase "a culture" in part as follows: "culture" refers to the totality of the designs for living practiced by man at all places and times, whereas a culture has reference to a single set of designs for living found in a particular society at some point in its history. This distinction is important in the study of cultural change, for it is evident that a change in culture can come about only by invention, as when some innovation in technology, social organization, religion, or language is made a part of man's cultural apparatus taken as a whole. A change in a culture, on the other hand, may arise either from an invention made within a particular society, or by virtue of intersocietal contact and the consequent borrowing or diffusion of a cultural item from one society to another.

It is evident, then, that every cultural pattern, whether it involves a technique, a mode of behavior toward relatives, a manner of speaking, or a form of religious worship—and every product of these patterns—has its origin in an act of invention, performed by someone somewhere. While some cultural patterns and products undoubtedly remain within the culture of their origin, subject only to slow modification through time, others just as certainly diffuse to neighboring cultures and hence are subject, not only to the modifications imposed by time, but also to diverse modifications put on them by the various cultures into which they are accepted. Both invention and diffusion, then, are fundamental to the study of cultural change.

Inventions are of two major types: primary or basic inventions, which involve the discovery of a new principle, and secondary or improving inventions, which involve only the application of a principle already known. The bow exemplifies a basic invention: someone had to discover, probably by accident, that a slender piece of wood bent by stretching a cord between its ends furnished a source of power hitherto unknown. We do not know when or where the first bow was made (it probably occurred near the end of the Paleolithic in some portion of the Old World), or how the original inventors used the new implement. But it is clear, from subsequent history, that the principle of the bow has been applied to a host of secondary inventions, including the bow used to propel arrows, the bow drill used to bore holes or to make fire by friction, and the musical bow and all other instruments (such as the harp, piano, violin, and banjo) that employ a taut string to produce a musical note. In a similar fashion, the discovery that steam, exploding gasoline vapors, and electricity furnish new sources of power has made possible the bulk of modern machines and vehicles, driven by one or other of these means.

The old adage—that necessity is the mother of invention—is, like so many others, less true than false. It is true of course, especially in our own society, that many secondary inventions and even some basic inventions are the result of consciously directed research and experimentation. But this is rare in other societies and only recent in our own; it is probable that most of the inventions man has made came about quite accidentally, as unforeseen results of handling and perhaps playing with materials and techniques. Skilled craftsmen, it has been observed in all societies, frequently enjoy exploring the potentialities of techniques they are using by trying different combinations of devices and attempting to expedite and improve their results. It is this kind of curiosity, coupled with experience and skill in craftsmanship, rather than necessity, that brings about basic inventions and that probably also results in new applications of known principles.

Except for the numerous inventions well documented in the recent history of our own culture, we know very little of the origins of the major inventions in human history. The control and use of fire, the bow in its many applications, the techniques that make up agriculture and animal husbandry, and many other important inventions—the history of all these is known only in very general terms. Indeed, all we know of most of the fundamental inventions on which the present European, Asiatic, and American cultures rest—including the wheel, the arch, the calendar, writing, the techniques of domesticating plants and animals, and the techniques of working metals—is that these occurred somewhere in the Near East and its environs at various periods between 10,000 B.C. and the beginning of the Christian era. From their place of origin, these inventions spread by diffusion until they reached their present distribution, undergoing numerous modifications and elaborations on the way by means of secondary inventions.

We must not assume, however, that all invention took place in the Old World. The American Indians, notably those of Mexico, Central America, and Peru, probably developed plant domestication, metallurgical techniques, writing, and the calendar (among other inventions) quite independently. After 1492, many of the products of New World inventions were incorporated into Old World cultures; for example, corn, beans, squash, and many other New World domesticated plants found their way into the agricultural complexes of Europe, Asia, and Africa, and the working of platinum into the Old World metallurgical technology. Present-day technologies, as represented in modern European and American cultures, have therefore a complex history, for the elements go back to widely diverse sources, scattered over the whole world.

Anthropologists not only cannot establish in detail the time and place of many inventions but they still have much to learn both of the processes of invention and diffusion and how these processes relate to cultural change. The Near East, as we have noted, witnessed for a time a large number of basic inventions in technology which were accompanied by major innovations in social and political organization, religion, and a host of other features of the nontechnological culture. A similar phenomenon may be noted for China, where, at one period, there appeared such important inventions as silk-weaving, paper-making, printing by movable type, gun powder, and the mariner's compass. In Central America, too, the Maya Indians produced, apparently over a brief period of time, such significant innovations as a calendar, writing, a system of mathematics and astronomy, and a distinctive architecture, together with large cities and a complex form of political organization. Finally, some historians have asserted that four important innovations set off, in the European Renaissance, a great cycle of cultural change which has persisted in Europe and America to the present day. These innovations (and it is notable that all but printing, which may have been reinvented in Europe, came to Europe by diffusion) are paper and printing, which accelerated the spread of knowledge, gun powder, which aided in the building of great conquest states, and the compass, which made possible the development of navigation and the subsequent period of exploration, overseas commerce, and colonization.

These examples suggest that basic innovations, whether due to invention or diffusion, do not occur singly but in clusters, and that there is probably some functional relationship between them. Some anthropologists maintain, in fact, that basic technological inventions, particularly those having to do with the food quest, invariably set off cycles of rapid social and cultural change and so stimulate innovations in all other departments of culture. The evidence for this view is still scanty, however, for there are some areas of culture, such as language, the arts, and systems of religious belief, where innovations are apparently independent of technology, or at least where innovations are not easily related to technological change.

Our emphasis in the discussion of cultural change thus far has been primarily on technology, for the material evidence provided by archeology provides a far richer historical perspective for this aspect of culture than it does for nonmaterial aspects. The less abundant evidence for the nonmaterial aspects of culture nevertheless suggests that the same processes operate. Some individuals speculate about the universe, organize new systems of thought, or modify old ones. Others enjoy playing with such things as kinship systems, as Elkin has shown for northwest Australia.[1] In this

[1] A. P. Elkin, "The Complexity of Social Organization in Arnhemland," *Southwestern Journal of Anthropology*, 6, 1–20, 1950.

region in recent years there has been a penetration of the complex eight-class system. Elkin's evidence suggests that the change is not because of felt inadequacies in the earlier system but because of greater prestige for the eight-class system and the fact that some individuals enjoy showing their proficiency in understanding and operating the more complex form. Changes likewise develop slowly through the fact that each individual and generation cannot perfectly reproduce the behaviors of their parents, hence modifications and secondary developments constantly arise, although these may be within certain limits imposed by the environment and the technology. Societies likewise borrow kinship usages, new words, new habits or fashions, or new religious beliefs, altering them subtly or obviously to fit their own cultural patterns and attitude systems.

Even if we accept the view that cultures change as total configurations rather than simply by the adding of discrete innovations, many basic problems still remain. We do not know, for example, why periods of cultural innovation, such as those mentioned above for the Near East, China, Central America, and Europe, occur when they do, nor do we know why some cultures change more rapidly than others. And though some innovations in culture may be viewed as the result of technological change, we must still determine the factors which effect changes in technology, and the precise manner in which technological innovations bring about others. These problems, and some of the solutions that have been proposed, will form the subject matter of the sections that follow.

2. CULTURAL EVOLUTION

Anthropology as a scientific discipline began about the middle of the nineteenth century. At that time scholars were turning increasingly to the study of culture—not only the advanced cultures of Europe, America, and Asia, but also the cultures of what we have called nonliterate peoples. The stimuli to these studies came in the main from two sources: an increasing knowledge of the prehistory of Europe as recovered by archeological research, and an increasing knowledge, from travelers, missionaries, and soldiers, of the artifacts, techniques, customs, and beliefs of nonliterate peoples.

These data posed a challenging problem—the relation of nonliterate cultures to the great civilizations of Europe and America. Previously this question had been answered by the so-called degradation theory, based on the assumption, largely from theology, that man had been created a civilized or semicivilized being. Nonliterates, then, were those who had fallen from this high original status of civilization, whose cultures had been degraded, for whatever reasons, to a status only a little above that of the animals.

But this hypothesis obviously offered many difficulties. Increased knowledge of nonliterate peoples made it plain that there is no simple division between civilized and degraded—the nonliterates themselves revealed many differences in cultural achievement. More serious was the fact that archeology revealed, for Europe itself, not the original status of civilization, but rather that European civilization had its sources in cultures not unlike those of contemporary nonliterates.

As a result of these discoveries, and in an attempt to synthesize and organize the growing body of data on nonliterate peoples, we find the beginnings of the first truly scientific thinking on anthropological problems —a body of doctrines called cultural evolutionism. These doctrines, theories, and hypotheses are best presented in Edwin B. Tylor's *Primitive Culture,* first published in 1865, and Lewis H. Morgan's *Ancient Society,* 1877.

Though the concept of evolution had already been developed in the biological sciences (Charles Darwin's *The Origin of Species* was published in 1859), there is little evidence that this work had much influence on cultural evolution. Cultural evolution is no mere extension of Darwinism to cultural data—though it obviously belongs, as it were, to the same intellectual climate. It is rather an independent development. Cultures were not conceived as differentiating in time, like genera and species, from a single ancestral form. Instead, cultural evolutionism conceived culture, wherever and whenever it was found, as developing progressively through time and as following essentially the same sequence of development among all the peoples of the earth.

The emphasis of the cultural evolutionist on progress, or progressive evolution, arose, in part at least, as an answer to the theory of cultural degradation. To Tylor and Morgan it was axiomatic that all tribes and nations had in general progressed in culture, though with occasional relapses and of course in differing degrees. "The history of the human race," said Morgan, "is one in source, one in experience, and one in progress." [2]

From the undeniable fact that living and historic peoples exist and have existed in differing states of culture, the evolutionist proceeded to construct a sequence of cultural stages, or as Morgan calls them, statuses. The most elaborate sequence is outlined by Morgan, who sees culture beginning in (1) a lower status of savagery—wherein man was but little advanced over the animals—and progressing therefrom to (2) a middle and (3) an upper status of savagery, along with certain advances in techniques, social organization, and religion. From here culture moves into (4) a lower, (5) a middle, and (6) an upper status of barbarism, these advances again being

[2] *Ancient Society* (Chicago, 1907), p. vi.

marked by the slow acquisition of techniques and the development of more advanced social institutions. Finally, culture achieves the seventh status, that of civilization, marked by the invention of phonetic writing and the beginnings of European culture as it is known today. This sequence, the evolutionist maintained, is a necessary and predetermined one, made so, according to Morgan, by the "natural logic of the human mind and the necessary limitations of its powers." [3]

Evidence of the culture of each of these stages is to be found among modern and historic peoples, according to the evolutionists. Thus, the cultures of the Australians and Polynesians bear witness to the type of culture in the middle and upper statuses of savagery, respectively, the culture of the Iroquois to that of the lower status of barbarism, the culture of the Zuñis to that of middle barbarism, the culture of the Homeric Greeks to that of upper barbarism, and our own modern cultures, in all their historical development, to that of civilization. The lower status of savagery, it will be noted, has no analogs in modern or historic societies; it is, rather, a projected period, necessary to bridge the gap between the earliest status finding an analog in known societies and the cultureless status of man's prehominid ancestors.

It should be emphasized that this scheme purports, not to unravel the history of given cultures or peoples, but only to sum up the evolution of culture as such. It is the evolution of *culture* that is being summed, not the history of *a* culture or of *a* people. A given society might well move, by virtue of contacts with other more advanced folk, from a culture representative of savagery directly to one representative of civilization, and so omit the status of barbarism entirely. It is only culture, in all of its aspects, that is said to evolve progressively from the earliest status of savagery, through all the intermediate statuses, until it finally flowers in civilization.

None of the evolutionists attempted to apply this hypothesis to the whole of culture—it was applied rather to selected aspects, such as art, religious belief, the family, or marriage, and not infrequently these were considered wholly without regard for the total cultural contexts from which they came. Accordingly, the results are often wholly untenable, as, for example, with Morgan's attempt to describe the evolution of familial systems. Here he maintains, first, that the monogamous primary family of our society is necessarily preceded by patrilineal clans, matrilineal clans, a "consanguine" family based on group marriage, and a period of promiscuous intercourse, in that order. There is, of course, no proof of this sequence. Indeed, as we have noted earlier, the monogamous primary family appears to be all but universal in human societies, and is found, not

[3] *Ibid.,* p. 18.

only among civilized peoples, but as well in numerous nonliterate cultures. (See Chapter 13.)

Despite these strictures, it should not be assumed either that cultural evolutionism is dead or, even more mistakenly, that the evolutionists contributed little or nothing to anthropology. Even Robert H. Lowie, one of the severest critics of evolution in culture, believes that stages of cultural development may well be established and writes: "[Evolution] is very far from dead, and our duty is merely to define it with greater precision." [4] Some attempt has been made, mainly by Leslie White, to achieve this greater precision, and we shall return to this topic in a later section (see § 7).

As to the positive contributions of the evolutionists, these are considerable. Among others we may list the following:

(1) The evolutionists were the first to recognize and employ the concept of culture, and to free this concept from its earlier entanglement with the concept of race. Tylor's definition of culture, which is significantly still widely quoted, emphasizes this point. "Culture or Civilization," he said ". . . is that complex whole which includes knowledge, belief, art, morals, law, custom, and any other capabilities and habits acquired by man as a member of society." [5]

(2) The evolutionists were among the first to recognize the possibilities of a science of culture, that is, to see that cultural phenomena are not random or haphazard but subject, like the phenomena of physics and biology, to scientific law and generalization. While many of their own attempts to systematize cultural data are subject to serious criticism, the evolutionists did bring order to the study of culture, a first prerequisite to successful research. In this sense, then, it may well be said that the evolutionists provided an initial base for a science of cultural anthropology, not explicitly recognized by those who preceded them.

(3) By their own attempts to systematize cultural data, and the criticisms these received, the evolutionists stimulated an enormous amount of consciously directed field research, almost unknown before their day, when scholars had, for the most part, to depend for data on the writings and reports of untrained observers.

3. BOAS AND THE AMERICAN SCHOOL

The methods and researches of Franz Boas and his students in the United States, which centered primarily on aboriginal America, stand in

[4] *The History of Ethnological Theory* (New York: Farrar and Rinehart, 1937), p. 27.
[5] *Primitive Culture* (Boston, 1874), Vol. I, p. 1.

sharp contrast to those of the evolutionists. In art, indeed, Boas' methodology developed as a critical response to evolutionism, a theory of culture he strongly opposed as a premature philosophical or logical synthesis based more on speculation than on careful scientific research. Boas turned instead to field research on narrowly restricted problems, so delimited that the researcher could maintain a strict control over the many variables inherent in cultural data. It was Boas' belief that the study of many such problems might eventually produce a self-consistent and scientifically sound body of theory.

There is little evidence, however, that Boas ever achieved any such theory; at least he never wrote anything like a systematic statement of his theories and method. He did achieve, rather, together with many of his associates and students, a method of research into cultural problems which is strictly empirical in its approach. To illustrate this method, we shall review briefly a part of his study of the mythology of the Tsimshians, an Indian tribe on the coast of British Columbia. This study, according to Leslie Spier, is "a characteristic example of the empirical methods of the school of anthropology founded by Boas," and "expresses some of the fundamental postulates of this school." [6]

Boas' study is in part an attempt to work out the distribution of folk tales within the area (the Northwest coast) in which the Tsimshians live, and by this means to account for the origins and history of Tsimshian myths. He compares, therefore, Tsimshian tales with those of their neighbors and discovers that, though no two peoples in the area tell a given tale in precisely the same way, the versions found in the several tribes are more or less similar to each other. Thus one tale, "The Prince Who Was Deserted," occurs in twenty versions. Comparing these, Boas finds that the tale may be broken down into five incidents or motifs, each of which has from one to nine variants. Incident I is told in nine variants (numbered 1–9), II in eight variants (1–8), III in only one, IV in two variants (1, 2), and V in six variants (1–6). Among the Tsimshians, the tale includes all five incidents, each of which, however, is told in a particular variant as follows: I.1, II.1, III, IV.1, and V.1. The Masset have a simpler version, with only three incidents: I.9, II.3, and V.2; incidents III and IV are omitted entirely. The Tlingit version omits only incident III, and the remaining four are told in the following variants: I.3, II.1, IV.1, and V.4. Similar variations are noted in the remaining versions of the tale, no two of which are identical.

---

[6] "Historical Interrelation of Culture Traits: Franz Boas' Study of Tsimshian Mythology." Analysis 31 in S. A. Rice (ed.), *Methods in Social Science* (Chicago: copyright 1931 by University of Chicago Press, pp. 449–457), p. 457. Boas' study may be found in the *31st Annual Report, Bureau of American Ethnology* (Washington, D. C., 1916), pp. 20–1037. Our summary is drawn mainly from Spier's analysis.

As a result of this analysis, which is applied to seventy-five separate Tsimshian tales, many of which are far more complex than the one used for illustration, Boas comes to the following conclusions.

(1) The similarities between the tales told by the Tsimshians and their neighbors result on the whole, not from independent and parallel inventions, but rather from borrowing or diffusion.

(2) The tales, however, do not diffuse as single items or traits of culture—as is shown by ways in which the versions differ from tribe to tribe —but rather each incident diffuses quite independently of the rest and has therefore its own unique history of diffusion.

(3) Each tribe tells its version of a tale as a unified whole, so demonstrating that the diffused incidents which make it up, despite their disparate origins, are secondarily reinterpreted by the receiving culture, presumably to fit a prevailing literary tradition. This also fits in with the fact that the incidents vary in the telling from one tribe to the next, as a result, presumably, of this secondary reinterpretation.

Spier, in his analysis of Boas' Tsimshian study, finds in it an illustration of a view of culture common to the American school. In this view, cultures are conceived as made up of discrete traits, that is, isolable items, like the incidents of Tsimshian tales, which may be particular patterns of behaving or the results in artifacts of such patterns of behaving. These culture traits are fashioned primarily as the result of historic factors, in which diffusion plays a dominant role. A particular culture, then, while it may include a few traits independently invented or conceived, is made up for the most part of traits which have come to the culture from widely divergent sources. The majority of American anthropologists, according to Spier,

have come to view every culture as a congery of disconnected traits, associated only by reason of a series of historic accidents, the elements being functionally unrelated, but believed to be related by the bearers of that culture because of the interpretation the traits have undergone.

This view . . . strikes boldly at the proposition that there is any inherent sequence of cultural forms. The presence of the traits, the relations in which they stand, and the modifications they undergo are due to specific historical determinism.[7]

It is evident that this concept of culture, presented here in a somewhat more extreme view than is held by many of the American school, specifically rejects any notion of generalizing on cultural change. If both the presence of a culture in a given society and the modifications it may un-

7 *Ibid.,* p. 455.

dergo are the result of "specific historical determinism," there is little hope that these determinants may be subject to law or generalization. But this does not mean of course that cultural evolution does not take place; Boas and his school do not so much refute evolution as avoid it in favor of particularistic historical researches. This concentration on historical problems and on the phenomenon of diffusion has been characteristic of the American school, and has given rise to two further methodological tools—the culture area and the age area—to which we shall now turn.

4. THE CULTURE AREA AND THE AGE AREA

The culture area and the age area were first explicitly formulated by Clark Wissler, a contemporary of Boas, in three books: *The American Indian* (1917), *Man and Culture* (1923), and *The Relation of Nature to Man in Aboriginal America* (1926). As two of these titles suggest, both the culture area and the age area were developed first in relation to American Indian studies, though both concepts have since been applied to other ethnographic regions. Concepts similar to the culture and the age area, according to Kroeber, "have long been in use in the biological sciences," and were indeed used in anthropology before Wissler but only "implicitly, or without methodological formulation." [8]

Taken by itself, the culture area is simply a device for classifying cultures—or, more aptly, clusters of culture traits—in respect to geographic regions. It arose actually as a way of arranging cultural data in museums (Wissler was for years a curator at the American Museum of Natural History); it was only later that Wissler and others made use of it as a tool in historical studies.

In attempting to classify the enormous amount of data available on American Indian cultures, Wissler noted:

(1) That particular culture traits (whether these consist of artifacts like tools, containers, or shelters, or of specific modes of social organization or religious belief) tend to cluster in given regions—therefore called culture areas—and to be confined to such regions. In aboriginal America, according to Wissler, there are fifteen such culture areas, notably in the Great Plains of North America (the Plains area), the Pacific coast south from Alaska to Oregon (the Northwest coast area), southwestern United States extending into northern Mexico and Lower California (the Southwest area), eastern South America from the Guianas to Argentina (the

---

[8] A. L. Kroeber, "The Culture-Area and Age-Area Concepts of Clark Wissler." Analysis 17 in S. A. Rice (ed.), *Methods in Social Science* (Chicago: copyright 1931 by University of Chicago Press, pp. 248–265), p. 248.

Tropical Forest area), Argentina south to the southern tip of South America (the Patagonian area), and the west coast of South America from Ecuador to about the middle of Chile (the Andean area).

(2) That the peoples or "tribes" of a given culture area, though by no means identical in culture, each possesses, to a greater or less degree, the traits characteristic of the area.

(3) That some of the peoples of a given culture area—ideally those who live in or near its geographic center—have all or nearly all of its characteristic traits. The cultures of these peoples are said to be typical of the area and to constitute its culture center.

(4) That the remaining peoples of a given culture area—ideally those who live concentrically about its geographic center—have fewer of its characteristic traits, the number decreasing in rough proportion to their distance from the culture center.

(5) That the peoples who live at the borders of the area have mixed or marginal cultures, in that the traits of their cultures are derived from more than one culture center.

To illustrate, let us describe briefly the Plains area of North America. Here is found a cluster of twenty characteristic traits, including among others: the hunting of bison for food (and a characteristic lack of horticulture or fishing); the use of the skin tipi as a dwelling; the dog-travois (a pair of poles hitched to the dog with the free ends dragging, used to transport burdens); round shields; skin containers (and a lack of pottery or basketry); a circular arrangement of tipis in camp (the camp circle); an emphasis on warfare with war honors and male military societies; the vision experience as a primary means of seeking supernatural guidance; and the sun dance, an elaborate religious ritual. Eleven tribes, more or less centrally located, have all or most of these traits. Tribes at a greater distance from this culture center have fewer of its characteristic traits, but substitute others, for example: pottery for skin containers, horticulture rather than exclusive reliance on hunting, earth-covered houses instead of tipis, and so on. Marginal tribes, living at the borders of the area, have the fewest Plains traits, combining these with an equal number of traits from adjacent areas. Culture centers, Wissler points out, are relatively easy to determine; the borders of culture areas tend to be indeterminable. Only rarely, if at all, can sharp lines be drawn between adjacent culture areas.

Used simply as a classificatory device, the culture area is convenient and widely employed. Herskovits and others have set up culture areas for Africa, mainly south of the Sahara; Linton worked out culture areas for Madagascar; and several attempts—Bacon's is the most recent—have been made to divide Asia into culture areas. Even such large and rather poorly defined regions as Indonesia, Melanesia, Micronesia, and Polynesia in the South Pacific may be said to comprise culture areas.

Wissler, however, attempted to give the culture area a greater historical significance by combining it with the age area. The age area rests on two assumptions: (1) that culture traits tend to diffuse equally in all directions from their point of origin, and (2) that the area over which a trait has diffused gives some indication of its age relative to other traits diffused within the same region. Thus, if two traits, A and B, diffuse outward from the same source, but A has diffused over a wider area than B, then A is older than B.

Returning now to the culture area, we may view its culture center as the point of origin (at least within the area) of its characteristic traits, or, as Kroeber has said, the center is "a locus of superior productivity."

This center, normally maintaining itself for some time, tends inevitably to radiate culture content or forms to a surrounding zone, which in turn imparts the contribution of a more peripheral belt, while the center, in the interim, is likely to have advanced to subsequent phases of development which normally obliterate more or less the earlier ones.[9]

It follows, then, that the traits at the margins of a culture area (where these belong to the area) represent its earliest stratum of culture (since they have diffused most widely) while, as we move closer to the center, the age of the culture traits found there lessens. The center of a culture area thus becomes, not only the region in which its typical culture is found, but also the region in which this culture has existed for the longest time. Correspondingly, the cultures of the margins and the zones intermediate to the margins and the center, provide the means whereby the history of the culture at the center may be reconstructed.

Much criticism has been leveled at this means of reconstructing culture history by use of the culture and the age area. It has been pointed out that age-area determinations are of dubious validity: culture traits only rarely, if at all, diffuse equally in all directions from their center of origin and hence many qualifications must be placed on the notion that traits with differing areas of diffusion differ also in age. Geographic and social factors may impede the spread of a trait in one direction and accelerate it in another. Thus traits may diffuse more rapidly along trade routes than in other directions; a trait complex, like horticulture without irrigation, may fail to diffuse to an unsuitable region, for example, a semiarid desert; and

[9] A. L. Kroeber, "The Culture-Area and Age-Area Concepts of Clark Wissler." Analysis 17 in S. A. Rice (ed.), *Methods in Social Science* (Chicago: copyright 1931 by University of Chicago Press, pp. 248–265), p. 254.

certain culture traits, like ceremonial elements, features of language, or the characteristics of a clan system, may diffuse less readily than culture traits like tools, shelters, containers, or items of clothing.

Even more important is the fact that diffusion appears always to be a selective process: a people apparently never accept all the traits that come to them and new elements that might be acceptable at one point in their history may equally be rejected at another. To exemplify this point, it will be helpful to review briefly the known history of the Ghost Dance, a modern American Indian ritual which, during two periods in recent history, spread far and wide among some American Indian tribes. The Ghost Dance was designed to restore the dead by ceremonial means and so to cause a return to the glories and freedom of the older aboriginal life, away from domination by the whites. It appealed particularly to those Indian tribes who suffered heavily under white control and who were too weak to resist the whites by military means.

The Ghost Dance appeared first in 1870 among the Paiutes of Nevada, at a time when the Paiutes were undergoing considerable economic difficulties and decimation by disease. From the Paiutes, the Ghost Dance spread rapidly to other Indians in Nevada and much of California, all of whom lived under essentially the same difficulties as the Paiutes. Certain Indians of northern California, however, though subject to similar economic stringencies and ill health, failed to take over the Ghost Dance, even though it was made known to them. The reason lay in their active fear of the dead, a fear which was strong enough to inhibit any participation in a ceremony designed to restore the dead to life. The ceremony was also rejected by the Plains Indians but for a different reason. At this time, 1870, the Plains Indians were still strong enough to resist the whites through warfare; they needed no ceremonial palliative for their ills.

The 1870 Ghost Dance soon died out, to be revived in 1890 by a descendant of the originator. This time the California Indians, disintegrated and disillusioned, had nothing to do with the new movement. But the Plains Indians, who had arrived at a critical condition similar to that of the Paiutes in 1870, eagerly took over the new Ghost Dance, reinterpreting its promise to mean the return of the bison and the old hunting and war-making existence and the destruction of the whites by the ancestral ghosts. The Navahos, however, though also in a critical condition, still rejected the Ghost Dance—and for the same reason, an active and dominant fear of the dead, that had led the Indians of northern California to reject the 1870 ceremony.

It is clear from this example—and many similar ones may be cited—that diffusion is no mechanical process, the same for all aspects of culture at all times. It is rather an exceedingly complex process, subject to many conditions, cultural, sociological and geographical.

5. THE EXTREME DIFFUSIONISTS AND THE CULTURE HISTORICAL SCHOOL

The nineteenth-century evolutionists, as we have noted, tended to underestimate diffusion as a factor in the building of cultures—it was their view that cultures changed more or less independently and mainly through inventions and innovation. Similarities between cultures were explained for the most part as the result of the like operation of the human mind under like circumstances. American anthropologists, on the other hand, emphasize diffusion as a process, though they are careful to limit its effects and are cautious in ascribing cultural similarities, especially where these occur between widely separated regions, to diffusion. Nevertheless, they have made the point, axiomatic today, that by far the bulk of any culture comes by borrowing; invention is a rare process in the history of most cultures, and nearly all basic inventions seem to have been made only once or twice in all of cultural history.

It is because of this rarity of invention that some anthropologists fall into the error of placing too great an emphasis on diffusion. Instead of allowing each case to be judged on its merits, these scholars ascribe the same universality to diffusion that the early evolutionists ascribed to invention. They tend, therefore, to connect historically even widely dispersed traits, provided these show any similarity of form whatever. Two schools of anthropology rest on this basis: the extreme diffusionists, a small and ephemeral group headed by the Englishmen Sir Grafton Elliott Smith and W. J. Perry, and the culture historical *(Kulturkreis)* school, founded by the Germans Fritz Graebner and E. Foy and carried on today by the so-called Vienna group led by Fathers Wilhelm Schmidt, Wilhelm Koppers, and Martin Gusinde.

The first of these theories of culture is presented in Elliott Smith's three works, *The Migration of Culture* (1917), *Elephants and Ethnologists* (1924), and *Human History* (1929), and most elaborately in Perry's *The Children of the Sun* (1923). In these books, Smith and Perry hold that true civilization occurred but once in human history, in Egypt, and spread from this center throughout the world, even to such remote areas as Mexico and Central America. The complex of traits which emerged in Egypt included a number that were especially important in tracing its spread: sun worship, great monolithic monuments, the building of pyramids, mummification of the dead, the dual organization of society, and a high regard for gold and pearls. Before the origin and spread of this complex of traits, the peoples of the world had only the bare essentials of culture, similar perhaps to what is possessed by the Australian aborigines. The Egyptians, once they had risen above this state, pushed outward in all directions in a vast colonizing effort, bringing their civilization, in more or less complete form, to all of the areas now marked by complex cultures. To some peoples of course this civilization never came, or having come, became degraded in various ways.

In this conception of the growth of culture, the whole world is regarded as a single culture area, with Egypt as the principal culture center. Wherever similarities between different cultural regions are found—as, for example, between Egypt and the Mayas and Aztecs—these are assumed to be the result of migration and diffusion, however remote from each other the peoples concerned may be. Essential to the method is Smith's and Perry's easy interpretation of cultural similarities: thus, for example, they assume without question that the pyramidal structures of the Mayas and Aztecs are sufficiently like those of the Egyptians to be derived from that source. But the likeness between Egyptian and Mexican pyramids is really only superficial; all we can say is that these structures in the two regions are more or less of the same shape. The Egyptian pyramids are, however, pointed structures with inside chambers, and they served as enormous tombs in which the kings were buried. Mexican (both Maya and Aztec) pyramids, on the other hand, are truncated substructures on which small temples or altars are placed, with elaborate staircases leading to the top. They rarely have inside chambers but are solid and were, in fact, often made simply by shaping a natural hill and facing it with stone. These differences, both in form and function, far outweigh the similarities, and suggest that the Mexican pyramidal monuments were invented quite independently of the Egyptian.

While few scholars today take the work of Smith and Perry seriously, the latter did perform an important service in focusing attention on the spread of culture in the Old World. An outstanding contribution of this sort is their relating of megalithic monuments and tombs of Mediterranean and Atlantic Europe, crude as these are, to the far more complex pyramidal tombs of Egypt. Much of the interrelationship through migration and diffusion of Europe with the Near East has been clarified under the stimulus of studies like these.

The *Kulturkreis,* or culture historical school, though also diffusionist, is more moderate than the extreme diffusionists, and has shown a good deal more vitality and persistence. The method—best treated in Wilhelm Schmidt's *The Culture Historical Method of Ethnology* (translated by

S. A. Sieber, 1939)—is still followed by many European scholars and is strong as well in many countries of South America. Like the extreme diffusionists, the culture historical school regards diffusion as a more or less mechanical process, and tends to ignore the cultural and sociological factors that, as we have seen, so strongly condition the acceptance or rejection of diffused traits. Schmidt and his co-workers, however, do set up rigorous standards whereby to evaluate similarities between widely dispersed traits; they do not, like the extreme diffusionists, take any similarity, however slight, as evidence of connection by diffusion.

The culture historical school derives most, if not all, of modern culture from a limited number of trait complexes or *Kulturkreise*. These, it is assumed, are a set of more or less "pure" or unmixed cultures, which originated in various places in the Old World at different periods in antiquity. From these centers of origin they diffused widely, eventually to give rise, in one fashion or another, to all subsequent cultures.

There is of course no direct evidence of these *Kulturkreise*—their existence in antiquity must be inferred from an intensive comparative study of known modern and historic cultures. Where, then, two areas in the modern world—even though these be remote from each other—illustrate the same complex of traits, the cultures of these areas are said to result from the same stream of diffusion and hence be historically connected. In some instances the cultures of a given region may be the resultant of several streams of diffusion, so stratified as to be easily distinguishable. In other cases, however, the several streams of diffusion may have mixed with each other to bring about modifications and even innovations in the original trait complexes.

It is easy to see that this hypothesis, like that of the extreme diffusionists, rests too heavily on diffusion conceived as a mechanical process; no allowance is made for the functional adaptations and reinterpretations that diffused traits must certainly undergo. Moreover, the culture historical method assumes as well a considerable cultural stability; that the *Kulturkreise* may today be recognized implies that cultures have changed only very slowly and in relatively unimportant details. To be sure, there are cultural complexes of high stability and perhaps of great antiquity—one such appears to be the association of puberty initiation rites with the infliction of tribal markings, the use of masks and bullroarers, and the exclusion of women, which is found in areas as widely separated as Australia and Tierra del Fuego. It is doubtful, however, whether these are common; certainly there are as many, if not more, examples of highly unstable trait complexes. Finally, it should be noted that at the Wenner-Gren Foundation Symposium held in New York in 1952, Wilhelm Koppers stated that he and his associates now reject the earlier *Kulturkreise* as being inadequate and unnecessary for the use of their historical method.

All three of the diffusionist schools we have examined—the American, the Smith-Perry, and the culture historical—though differing greatly in their conception of diffusion and its importance to the building of culture, have in common an antievolutionist bias and a resulting determination to interpret cultural phenomena almost wholly in historical terms. Their thesis appears to be that a culture may only be understood if its history is known or at least can be reconstructed. Against this it may be urged that historical data, where available, only increase our knowledge of a culture; they neither account for its presence nor help to define the conditions under which cultures change. The kind of history known for nonliterate cultures is even less helpful, for it is itself only barely reconstructed from studies of the spatial distribution of culture traits, and is usually too sketchy even to provide adequate descriptions of the process of change. If cultural anthropology is to be more than a purely descriptive discipline, its phenomena must be studied also with a view to generalization; and historical researches, however precisely and carefully conducted, do not of themselves lead to such generalization.

6. FUNCTIONALISM AND RELATED CONCEPTS

As we have noted, the several historical schools of anthropology—and notably the American school—tend to view single cultures as congeries of disconnected traits, disparate in origin and history, and "associated only by reason of a series of historic accidents." [10] They deny, moreover, that any "functionally primary relationship can be posited between a congeries of genetically unrelated traits," and insist that "only from the point of view of the bearer of the culture have they any necessary relation, since he views them through the spectacles of rationalization." [11]

This conception of culture was soon challenged, especially by the functionalists led by Bronislaw Malinowski. Functionalist theory is developed in some detail in Malinowski's many writings (which begin about 1920), but the most complete treatment may be found in his *A Scientific Theory of Culture and Other Essays* (1944) and *The Dynamics of Culture Change* (1945). Malinowski maintains, first, that every living culture is a func-

[10] Spier, "Historical Interrelation of Culture Traits: Franz Boas' Study of Tsimshian Mythology." Analysis 31 in S. A. Rice (ed.), *Methods in Social Science* (Chicago: copyright 1931 by University of Chicago Press, pp. 449–457), p. 455.

[11] *Ibid.*

tioning and integrated whole, analogous to an organism, and that no part of a culture may be understood except in relation to the whole. It is the functioning of a culture trait in the total system of a culture that explains it and reveals its true identity; a trait is to be understood, not by reconstructing the history of its origin and diffusion, but rather by the ways in which it influences and is influenced by the other elements within the system. In this view, it is evident, history plays no role; a culture is studied simply as its exists on a single time plane, and not in terms of its historical or evolutionary development.

The second aspect of Malinowski's theory is an attempt to account for culture itself, to determine the ultimate function of human cultures and so account for their presence among men. Again he does not see this as a historical problem, and still less as an evolutionary problem. Instead, Malinowski tries to relate culture, in all its principal aspects, to human needs, that is, to set up a correlation between man's requirements as a biological organism and his ways of meeting these requirements that will hold generally for all of mankind.

As Malinowski sees it, men everywhere must satisfy seven basic biological needs if they are to survive: metabolic, reproductive, and the needs for bodily comfort, safety, movement, growth, and health. To each of these, in every society in the world, we find some kind of cultural response, listed respectively as a commissariat, a system of kinship, shelter, means of protection, activities, training, and hygiene. Malinowski cautions, however, against the view that biological needs are forces that send men off in a blind search for satisfactions. Each pair of needs and responses (for example, metabolic needs and the commissariat) are rather to be viewed as inseparable, or as the biological and cultural aspects, respectively, of the same phenomenon. The routine needs of living are everywhere indissolubly bound to organized and ever-present routines of satisfaction, otherwise human societies could not exist.

The cultural responses to basic biological needs set up in turn certain derived needs, cultural rather than biological in nature, that are also common to all mankind. To illustrate, we may contrast the metabolic need for nutrition, which is met by certain techniques for obtaining food, with the derived need for training the participants in a culture in the proper use and application of these techniques. Such training is obviously no less necessary to human survival than the acquisition of food itself, but it is less directly related to the biological need that underlies both. Derived needs, taken together, divide into four principal cultural imperatives, each of which finds a response in a broad division or aspect of culture. Thus, economic systems are a response to the imperative that tools, implements, and other material necessities be made, used, maintained, and replaced. Institutions of social control are a response to the imperative that prescriptions and codes be established to regulate human behavior in all of its aspects. Education is the third category—a response to the imperative that the participants in a culture and its institutions must be recruited, trained, and provided with the knowledge necessary to the performance of their roles. Fourth and last is political organization, the response to the imperative that authority within each society must be defined, equipped with powers, and provided with the means of enforcing them.

Malinowski's view of culture is distinctive, among other things, for his use of the concept of function and his emphasis on a nonhistorical approach to the understanding of cultural phenomena. It is perhaps this latter feature that links Malinowski to A. R. Radcliffe-Brown, who is frequently but mistakenly classed with Malinowski as a functionalist. Radcliffe-Brown's views on culture have not been summarized in any systematic theoretical work; they are perhaps best given in his "Methods of Ethnology and Social Anthropology" (*South African Journal of Science,* Vol. 20, 1923), "The Present Position of Anthropological Studies" (*Report of the Centenary Meeting, British Association for the Advancement of Science,* 1932), and his articles on "Primitive Law" and "Social Sanction" in the *Encyclopedia of the Social Sciences* (1935).

Unlike Malinowski, Radcliffe-Brown directs his attention to the study of society rather than to culture, and regards himself more as a sociologist or social anthropologist than a student of culture. A society, he maintains, is, like an organism, made up of interfunctioning and interdependent parts. Just as the parts of an organism function together to maintain the whole, so do the usages and institutions found in a society contribute to the maintenance and persistence of the social organism. This is indeed the principal, if not the only, function these usages and institutions have, taken as a whole, that is, to insure the persistence of the society itself. Radcliffe-Brown does not, like Malinowski, attempt to explain society or culture by reference to biological considerations; he devotes himself instead to a comparative study of societies themselves, taken as the given data of the science of social anthropology.

His objective in such studies is neither historical nor evolutionary; he quite firmly rejects both these approaches in favor of nonhistorical researches. Radcliffe-Brown seeks rather to achieve the following ends:

(1) Precise descriptions of functioning social structures as these exist in various parts of the world. The usages and institutions found in human societies are to be described with especial reference to their role in maintaining the social structure.

(2) A systematic classification of social phenomena together with a suitably exact terminology.

(3) Formulation of the general laws that underlie social phenomena, by scientific methods paralleling those of the natural sciences.

While it cannot be reported that Radcliffe-Brown or his followers have produced much, as yet, in the way of social laws or generalization, it is true that he has at least cleared the way for a generalizing science of social anthropology. His work, according to Redfield, "clarifies sharply the distinction between the historical and the scientific approaches to anthropology, and . . . affords one procedure and one set of concepts for pursuing the scientific approach." [12]

The work of Malinowski and Radcliffe-Brown has turned many American anthropologists from their earlier concentration on historical studies to a new interest in examining and redefining their methods and approach. This is reflected, for example, in Linton's analysis of the culture trait, which, he finds, has at least four aspects or characteristics: form, use, function, and meaning. These are defined as follows:

(1) The form of a trait includes such features as shape, dimensions, methods of manufacture, and all else that contributes to its visible or observable substance. Forms, whether of material or nonmaterial traits, are readily observable and easily transmitted from one culture to another.

(2) Use, also easily observed and transmitted, includes the ways in which a people employ the trait. An ax, for example, may be used to chop down trees, or it may be specialized to some use in warfare (the cutting off of enemy heads) or to a particular ritual purpose. Use is not necessarily bound to form, for traits of similar or identical forms may have quite different uses in diverse cultures.

(3) The function of a trait is wider than its use—it consists of the place of the trait in the total culture. To a forest people, for example, the ax may function in a larger complex of traits bound to horticulture and the clearing of land for the production of crops. In another society, however, lacking horticultural techniques, the ax may function in a wholly different context, say that of building shelters, canoes, and other similar constructions. Again we find no necessary relation of function to either use or form; the three are quite independent of each other.

(4) Meaning, finally, refers to the totality of associations that the people in a society attach to a given trait. Thus, in the Amazon forest where stone is unknown except in objects obtained in trade, the stone ax is a treasured

---

[12] Robert Redfield, "Introduction." In Fred Eggan (ed.), *Social Anthropology of North American Tribes* (Chicago: copyright 1937 by University of Chicago Press, pp. vii–xii), p. xi.

implement, to be carefully guarded, used, and cared for. This meaning would obviously be lacking among peoples who live where stone is abundant and where axes, lost or dulled with use, may be replaced without too much difficulty. Meaning is again an independent feature and one which, like function, is not easily, if at all, transmitted from one culture to another.[13]

This more complex definition of a trait, it is evident, throws a new light on trait distribution studies, the concepts of the culture and age area, and the historical inferences that may be drawn by these means. It emphasizes, too, the interconnectedness of cultural elements and the extreme difficulty of determining the criteria of similarity among the traits of diverse cultures.

Another and more important effect of functionalist theory is the emergence of the concept of integration in culture, the interconnectedness of traits in their webs of function and meaning. Modern anthropologists, for the most part, now reject the concept that cultures are only random assemblages of traits. Cultures are viewed rather as integrated wholes, with their constituent traits firmly knit together. We have, however, already discussed this view of culture (the guiding one of this book) in another place; see Chapter 8, especially §§ 7, 8.

7. RECENT STUDIES RELATED TO CULTURAL EVOLUTION

Though the problems raised by the early evolutionists have been largely neglected since Morgan's time, there are many modern anthropologists who believe with Lowie that these problems require more precise formulation. In a few instances such formulation has been attempted, in greater or less detail. We shall review briefly three of these: the work of Julian Steward (particularly, his "Cultural Causality and Law: A Trial Formulation of the Development of Early Civilizations," *American Anthropologist*, 51, 1–27, 1949), V. Gordon Childe's *Man Makes Himself* (New York: Oxford University Press, 1939), and Leslie White, particularly his "Energy and the Evolution of Culture," *American Anthropologist*, 45, 335–356, 1943.

Steward has made a number of studies relating technology and environment to the development of social and political groups; we reviewed one of these, in part, in an earlier chapter (see Chapter 15, § 2). In the paper cited above, he points out that, with few exceptions, modern anthropologists have not attempted "to formulate cultural regularities in generalized

[13] Ralph Linton, *The Study of Man*, pp. 402–404.

or scientific terms." While not denying that "cause and effect operate in cultural phenomena," their studies have centered more on "cultural differences, particulars, and peculiarities" than on the "perfectly legitimate purpose of making scientific generalizations from . . . the recurrent cultural patterns, sequences, and processes in different cultures." [14]

Steward proposes therefore to attempt such a formulation, not "to achieve a world scheme of culture development . . . but to establish a genuine interest in the scientific objective and a clear conceptualization of what is meant by regularities." [15] This formulation is in no sense final: "Any formulations of cultural data are valid provided the procedure is empirical, hypotheses arising from interpretations of fact and being revised as new facts become available." [16]

To achieve his formulation, Steward compares the sequence of cultural development in the arid and semiarid regions of Mesopotamia, Egypt, India, China, the north Andean area of South America, and Meso-America. He concludes that the several archeological periods of each center, despite many differences in detail, may be grouped into five eras: preagricultural, an era of incipient agriculture, a formative era of basic technologies and folk culture, an era of regional development and florescence, and an era of cyclical conquests. The cultures of each era, whatever the area in which they are found, display certain regularities or recurrent features, sufficiently distinctive to be subject to a "rough, cursory, and tentative" formulation. The formulation

applies only to the early centers of world civilization. The eras are not "stages," which in a world evolutionary scheme would equally apply to desert, arctic, grassland, and woodland areas. In these other kinds of areas, the functional interrelationship of subsistence patterns, population, settlements, social structure, co-operative work, warfare, and religion had distinctive forms and require special formulations.[17]

Childe's work covers the field of Old World prehistory, a subject in which he is an acknowledged expert. The archeologist, he points out, customarily divides Old World prehistory into four major periods: the Paleolithic, Neolithic, Bronze Age, and Iron Age. The cultural data that define these periods, Childe maintains,

. . . disclose not only the level of technical skill and science attained, but also the manner in which their makers get their livelihood, their economy. And it is

[14] *Op. cit.,* p. 1.
[15] *Op. cit.,* p. 2.
[16] *Op. cit.,* p. 3.
[17] *Op. cit.,* p. 23.

this economy which determines the multiplication of our species, and so its biological success. Studied from this angle, the old archaeological divisions assume a new significance. The archaeologist's ages correspond roughly to economic stages. Each new "age" is ushered in by an economic revolution of the same kind and having the same effect as the "Industrial Revolution" of the eighteenth century.[18]

In Childe's view, then, culture in the Old World, and by implication elsewhere, developed successively through four stages, each marked by a revolution of the economy, which revolutions "reacted upon man's attitude to Nature and promoted the growth of institutions, science, and literature— in a word, of civilization as currently understood." [19]

This formulation rests, obviously, on a kind of economic determinism, the notion that economic changes, resulting from technological improvement, are primary factors in culture change. It is perhaps pertinent to ask how technological and economic changes, aspects of culture change itself, come to be regarded as independent variables, producing dependent changes in the rest of the culture. Further, it may be noted that Childe's stages are scarcely of the same order of significance. Surely there is far greater significance in the Neolithic revolution, which added food production to man's cultural equipment, or to the Industrial Revolution, which gave him power-driven machines, than to the relatively minor changes in tool-making materials that distinguish the Bronze and Iron Ages from each other and the Neolithic.

White is the most explicitly evolutionary of the three anthropologists here discussed; indeed, he is almost the only modern anthropologist who has devoted himself seriously to the problem of cultural evolution. In general, he follows Morgan rather closely; his work may almost be regarded as a modern restatement of Morgan's thesis, though White has added a good deal in the way of clarification and precision to Morgan's work.

According to White, man, like all other animals, exploits his environment or habitat to obtain from it the means of sustaining life and perpetuating his kind. Unlike other animals, however, man has developed culture to aid him in this process, and this culture, through the many millennia of man's existence on earth, has gradually become a more effective instrument in man's struggles to maintain himself. One important problem of anthropology, as White sees it, is to study this evolution of culture and to determine, not only the sequences of cultural development, but also the

[18] V. Gordon Childe, *Man Makes Himself* (New York: copyright 1939 by Oxford University Press), p. 39.
[19] *Ibid.*, p. 41.

factor or factors which are responsible for them. He finds this factor in the concept of energy, and formulates the following law of cultural evolution:

. . . culture develops when the amount of energy harnessed by man per capita per year is increased; or as the efficiency of the technological means of putting this energy to work is increased; or as both factors are simultaneously increased.[20]

To illustrate the working of this law, White applies it to Morgan's notion that culture evolved in three major stages, from savagery through barbarism to civilization. In the stage of savagery, White points out, man has access only to the energy of his own body, except perhaps for the rare and casual employment of fire, wind, and water. His culture in consequence is limited, both in technology and social organization, as is illustrated by such nonliterate peoples as the Australian aborigines.

Archeological evidence makes it clear that at one time all men were in this stage of cultural development, that is, during the Paleolithic, a period variously estimated at from 500,000 to 1,000,000 years in duration. During this time, culture evolved only as technology (the means whereby energy is expended) increased in efficiency, that is, as new tools and devices were invented. Today, though culture per se has evolved far beyond savagery, there remain some peoples whose cultures, still dependent on human energy alone, are even now in the stage of savagery. The point of importance here is that savagery denotes, not a time period in the history of culture, but a stage of cultural evolution, which may be illustrated from any period in world history.

The second stage of cultural evolution, barbarism, began with the domestication of plants and animals. Here, according to White, is a new source of energy, not merely a technological advance. As he puts it:

. . . when man domesticated animals and brought plants under cultivation, he harnessed powerful forces of nature, brought them under his control, and made them work for him. . . . Thus the difference between a wild plant and animal economy and a domestic economy is that in the former the return for an expenditure of human energy, no matter how large, is fixed, limited, whereas in agriculture and animal husbandry, the initial return for the expenditure of human energy augments itself indefinitely.[21]

Agriculture, which White considers more important to the evolution of culture than animal domestication,

[20] White, "Energy and the Evolution of Culture," *American Anthropologist*, 45, 335–356 (1943), p. 338.

[21] *Ibid.*, pp. 341–342.

. . . increased tremendously the amount of energy per capita available for culture-building, and, as a consequence of the maturation of the agricultural arts, a tremendous growth of culture was experienced . . . and the great cultures of China, India, Mesopotamia, Egypt, Mexico, and Peru came rapidly into being.[22]

We may cite archeological evidence to the effect that barbarism, as a stage of cultural development, first appeared some eight to ten thousand years ago in the Old World, later in the New. Not all peoples shared the new energy source; some, as we have noted, remain in the stage of savagery even today. Within barbarism, culture continued to evolve but only through technological gains—the addition of metals to stone for tool-making, the invention of the plow, the arch, the calendar, writing, and numerous other devices. But no new energy source appeared until the beginning of the nineteenth century and the Industrial Revolution, when man first discovered how to apply the energy from the burning of coal and other fuels to the driving of his machines. It is this discovery—not, as Morgan and Tylor thought, the invention of writing—that marks, according to White, the third stage of cultural evolution, or civilization.

Turning now to social organization, White finds that this aspect of culture *"is dependent upon and determined by the mechanical means with which food is secured, shelter provided, and defense maintained."* In short, *"social evolution is a consequence of technological evolution."* [23] But this is not all:

While it is true that social systems are engendered by, and dependent upon, their respective underlying technologies, it is also true that social systems condition the operation of the technological systems upon which they rest; the relationship is one of mutual, though not necessarily equal, interaction and influence. A social system may foster the effective operation of its underlying technology or it may tend to restrain or thwart it.[24]

White comes, then, to the following conclusion:

A social system may so condition the operation of a technological system as to impose a limit upon the extent to which it can expand and develop. When this occurs, cultural evolution ceases. . . . it can be renewed only by tapping some new source of energy and by harnessing it in sufficient magnitude to burst asunder the social system which binds it. Thus freed, the new technology will

---

[22] *Ibid.*, p. 343.
[23] *Ibid.*, p. 347.
[24] *Ibid.*, p. 347.

form a new system, one congenial to its growth, and culture will advance again until, perhaps, the social system once more checks it.[25]

It should be noted that White claims no originality for the thesis discussed; it is, he states: ". . . substantially the same as that advanced by Lewis H. Morgan and E. B. Tylor many decades ago." [26] White has, however, performed a useful service in clarifying the ideas of the early evolutionists and in bringing these ideas, long neglected, again to modern students. He has also answered many of Morgan's critics and in numerous instances shown that these criticisms were based on misconceptions rather than facts. It is plain, however, that cultural evolution no longer holds the dominant position it once held in cultural anthropology; today it is but one approach among many, and it serves only one line of anthropological interest. There are many problems of modern anthropology, historical and functional, which must be approached quite differently. We shall review some of these in the chapter that follows.

COLLATERAL READING

Boas, Franz. *The Mind of Primitive Man.* Rev. Ed. New York: The Macmillan Co., 1938.

———. *Race, Language and Culture.* New York: The Macmillan Co., 1940. See "The Methods of Ethnology," pp. 281–289; "Evolution or Diffusion," pp. 290–294; "History and Science in Anthropology: A Reply," pp. 305–311.

Dixon, R. B. *The Building of Cultures.* New York: C. Scribner's Sons, 1928.

Herskovits, Melville J. "The Processes of Cultural Change," *The Science of Man in the World Crisis,* ed. Ralph Linton. New York: Columbia University Press, 1945. Pp. 143–170.

Linton, Ralph. *The Study of Man.* New York: D. Appleton-Century Co., 1936. Chapters XVIII–XXVI.

Lowie, Robert H. *The History of Ethnological Theory.* New York: Farrar and Rinehart, 1937.

Malinowski, Bronislaw. *A Scientific Theory of Culture and Other Essays.* Chapel Hill: University of North Carolina Press, 1944.

———. *The Dynamics of Culture Change.* New Haven: Yale University Press, 1945.

Morgan, Lewis H. *Ancient Society.* Chicago, 1907.

Perry, W. J. *The Children of the Sun.* London: Methuen and Co., 1923.

Radcliffe-Brown, A. R. "Methods of Ethnology and Social Anthropology," *South African Journal of Science,* XX, 1923.

———. "The Present Position of Anthropological Studies," *Presidential Address, British Association for the Advancement of Science,* 1930.

[25] *Ibid.,* p. 348.
[26] *Ibid.,* p. 351.

Rice, Stuart A. (ed.) *Methods in Social Science*. Chicago: University of Chicago Press, 1931. Analyses 17–19, 31.

Schmidt, Wilhelm. *The Culture Historical Method of Anthropology*. (Trans. by S. A. Sieber.) New York: Fortuny's, 1939.

Smith, Sir Grafton Elliot. *Human History*. New York: W. W. Norton and Co., 1929.

Tylor, Edward B. *Primitive Culture*. First American Ed., Boston, 1874. Vol. I, Chapters I–IV.

White, Leslie. *The Science of Culture*. New York: Farrar, Straus, and Young, 1949.

Wissler, Clark. *Man and Culture*. New York: Thos. Y. Crowell Co., 1923.

———. *The Relation of Nature to Man in Aboriginal America*. London: Oxford University Press, 1926.

Chapter 21

ACCULTURATION AND APPLIED ANTHROPOLOGY

1. THE PROBLEM OF ACCULTURATION

As we have noted, much of cultural change takes place by way of diffusion, the spreading of culture elements and complexes from one society to another. Diffusion occurs inevitably when peoples of diverse cultures are in contact, whether that contact be hostile or friendly, direct or through the medium of intervening peoples. But we have also noted that diffusion is no mechanical process, that, as in the case of the Ghost Dance (see Chapter 20, § 4), societies may accept or reject new culture elements, depending on whether or not the new elements fit into the total patterning of the receiving culture. Cultures, because they are integrated wholes, do not merely add or subtract traits in the process of change; each new element accepted is, rather, fitted into a functioning whole, often undergoing considerable modification in the process, and, if it cannot be so fitted, it may not be accepted. The Ghost Dance, it will be remembered, was wholly unacceptable to tribes like the Navaho, in whose culture ghosts were regarded with extreme fear and dread.

During the past twenty-five years many anthropologists have become interested in a particular kind of cultural change—called acculturation—the study of which has contributed much both to the concept of culture itself and to our understanding of cultural change as a whole. Acculturation refers broadly to cultural changes which take place when two peoples, sig-

628

nificantly diverse in culture, live in long and intimate contact with each other. Most acculturation studies, however, have been concerned with the contact of Euro-American and nonliterate peoples in such regions as Negro Africa, Oceania, and aboriginal America. In these instances—and perhaps this is true of all cases of acculturation—one of the peoples concerned (the Europeans or Americans) inevitably assume a dominant position in respect to the other, and hence frequently impose certain changes on the cultures of the subordinate nonliterate groups. The nonliterates, therefore, lose full freedom of choice in acceptance or rejection of particular culture elements, a factor which clearly distinguishes changes taking place through acculturation from changes which occur through the more general process of diffusion.

It should not be assumed, however, that dominant peoples necessarily employ force in imposing cultural changes on the subordinate group. Force is sometimes used, of course; we know, for example, that both Europeans and Americans have required nonliterates to attend schools and churches, to wear clothing, to work on plantations or in industrial establishments, and to give up such practices as cannibalism, head-hunting, intertribal warfare, and polygyny. More often the dominant group brings about cultural changes indirectly, frequently through the introduction of money or trade goods. The Hudson Bay Company, early fur-traders in northern Canada, completely revolutionized the aboriginal food-gathering economies in this region of offering trade goods for furs and so encouraging trapping as a specialized craft. The dominant group, by reason of the status, prestige, and riches it may confer, often creates internal pressures among the subordinate peoples to acquire the ways of life of their superiors and so improve their lot.

To illustrate these points, let us turn now to one of the great laboratories for the study of acculturation—Mexico. Here European and Indian cultures have been face to face for more than four hundred years, and the history of acculturation, which process still goes on today, is well known—better known, indeed—than for any other part of the world.

2. ACCULTURATION IN MEXICO

As we have previously noted, the first Spanish expedition under Cortes reached Mexico when it was dominated by the Aztecs of Tenochtitlan, a capital built on the present site of Mexico City. The Aztecs and their neighbors throughout central and southern Mexico lived in an urban society, that is, one characterized by relatively large cities supported by a highly developed system of garden cultivation, and having as well a high degree of occupational specialization, extensive commerce, and well developed socioeconomic classes. The government at Tenochtitlan had, in the two centuries preceding the coming of Cortes, expanded its control over many other peoples through a systematic and ruthless program of military conquests. Conquered peoples were not, however, drawn into a closely knit political system, but retained considerable freedom and local autonomy as long as they remained at peace with Tenochtitlan and continued to pay that city a fixed annual tribute.

When the Spanish arrived, they found many groups very restive under Aztec domination, and some of these gave them a friendly reception. By organizing native disaffection, the small unit of Spaniards, who were never more than 2,500 in number, raised a large native army and destroyed Tenochtitlan. After the fall of Tenochtitlan, many of the peoples formerly dominated by the Aztecs, and who had taken no part in the revolt, peaceably accepted the Spaniards as the successors to the Aztecs and continued paying tribute.

Even more remarkable than the conquest of a region of some five to ten million people by 2,500 Spaniards is the fact that the Spaniards were able to keep control, although after eighty years (at the end of the sixteenth century) there still were only about 20,000 Spaniards in the country. An examination of the record shows that this was the result of several processes. In the first place, the Spaniards simply moved into the position in the existing social structure which had previously been occupied by the Aztec upper class. Native rulers friendly to the new regime were allowed to keep their position, in some cases for nearly a century after the conquest. The native religion had been closely bound up with the power of the dominant Aztec group, and when it was defeated, lost much prestige. Christianity thus found easy acceptance among peoples who were already hospitable toward new religious ideas. For large segments of the population the Spanish Conquest made little change in political participation or economic life; they continued to cultivate their ancestral lands in much the same fashion as before and paid the same tribute to the government, now Spanish rather than Indian. While public religious performances changed radically, in many regions the "common man" continued to perform his household and agricultural rituals in the old traditional form.

All evidence points to a period after the Conquest in which the Indians tended to accept European culture with considerable eagerness and rapidity. In some areas, where the Spanish had been established as large landholders, the Indian was gradually brought under greater exploitation and control. His work habits were modified, the non-Christian elements of his religion eliminated, his dress changed, and often his language lost. While many food habits and techniques remained, in considerable part these were adopted also by the Spanish conqueror. In short, except for the Spaniards of the cities, who were in constant contact with the Old World, the distinction in culture between Indians and Spaniards tended to disappear except as the latter maintained their distinctiveness as members of the upper class.

In other regions Indians were put under the administration of missionary orders which attempted to prevent Indians from learning Spanish in order to protect them from the bad example of the Spanish layman. Self-governing Indian communities were formed and Indian titles to land maintained. The missionaries introduced many elements of European culture, carefully selected, which were accepted by the Indians either through force, persuasion, or interest, without at the same time losing all their Indian ways. When the missionaries were removed in the eighteenth century, the Indian societies still retained some cohesiveness, although they were not the same as in aboriginal times. The Indians could not speak Spanish and the secular priests who succeeded the missionaries did not learn Indian languages. The Indians were heavily exploited and disillusioned by their inferior role in the new Spanish-American society. Consequently they withdrew when they could to avoid all possible contact with the Spaniards. Definite movements to revive old ways developed in many areas, and new European elements were frequently rejected. But as many of the old ways had been forgotten, attempts at revival were often unsuccessful, and the new stable culture that emerged was an amalgam of Indian and European elements.

Today, then, Mexico is a region of many distinctive cultures, roughly to be divided, perhaps, into two main groups. The first of these includes the so-called Mestizo cultures, in many regional variants. The bearers of these cultures are Spanish-speaking and the descendants of those who, under the direct control of the conquerors, took over new ways of living, retaining only a very few elements of their aboriginal and pre-Conquest cultures. The second are the Indian cultures, which differ markedly, not only from the cultures of the Mestizos, but also from each other. Bearers of these cultures speak Indian languages in the main and know little Spanish. Except in respect to language, the Indian cultures, especially in their distinctive features, are mainly the result, not of the retention and development of pre-Conquest elements, but rather of the retention and readaptation of sixteenth- and seventeenth-century Spanish cultural traits, which have long disappeared from the non-Indian cultures of Mexico. In the Indian cultures, these elements, modified and reworked, have been so integrated with aboriginal cultural patterns as to result in wholly new cultural wholes, which are amalgams, not simple mixtures, of Spanish and Indian traits. The modern "Indian" cultures of Mexico are, then, certainly not Indian in the pre-Conquest sense, nor are they Spanish—they are rather new creations which have emerged from a fusion of both the Spanish and the Indian traditions. More recently, following the 1910 revolution in Mexico, Indians have been drawn into increasing contact with the rapidly industrializing national culture of Mexico and a new cycle of acculturation is under way.

This survey of a very complex history, brief as it is, shows the operation of such processes of acculturation as the use of force, directly and indirectly, the acceptance and rejection of new cultural elements, the modification of culture traits taken from one culture to another, and, most important, the revamping of whole cultures through the stimulus of day-to-day contact with a foreign cultural tradition. As acculturation studies progress, they reveal with increasing clarity the extreme complexity of cultural change. Even relatively small modifications, particularly when introduced under pressure, may have far-reaching effects on a society and its culture, and may often give rise to profound psychological conflicts or enforce major reorientations of ideas and values. Not infrequently acculturative processes result in considerable social disturbances and individual psychological maladjustments, which may be reflected in large-scale messianic religious movements, increases in antisocial behavior, and in much individual neurotic behavior. In extreme cases, whole societies may withdraw entirely, rejecting all innovation as necessarily evil. The significance of these findings becomes clearer in the sections that follow.

3. APPLIED ANTHROPOLOGY

While some anthropologists look with disfavor upon attempts to discover practical uses for their knowledge, few scientists, however devoted to "pure" and apparently impractical research, do not at bottom hope that at some time their findings may contribute to a better life for their fellow men.

The earliest important applications of anthropology were primarily in the sphere of colonial administration, a fact which has contributed to the disrepute in which application is held by many anthropologists. The Dutch, British, and somewhat later the French have long considered anthropology and the anthropological training of colonial administrators to be of great importance.

An important early use of anthropology was the development of so-called indirect rule. Studies of native law, social structure, and the identification of native leadership were utilized to establish types of administration which would cause the least disturbance of native life. In Indonesia, for example, tribal law was codified, the codes often varying from village to village depending on local conditions. Some modifications were often made (for example, head-hunting, where it existed, would be prohibited in the final codification), but the bulk of the existing customary law was given support and became binding upon the group.

Superficially desirable as this approach might be, it nevertheless became an obstacle to social change within the native group. Inequitable land tenure practices or autocratic local government, acceptable when the group was isolated from the rest of the world, became extremely difficult to change with the inevitable infiltration of new ideas and knowledge of conditions in other parts of the world. Inevitably also, the European administrators remained primarily interested in developing markets for European industrial goods and enlarging the production of raw materials. Finally, such policies often made it difficult for peoples to learn to manage their own affairs in relation to their widening contacts with the outside world.

Basically the problem involved is whether the administration is oriented toward maintaining a dominant-subordinate relationship or is directed toward aiding the people to develop an independent and equal status within a modern, unified, and industrializing world. In the first case, applied anthropology tends to become a process of finding out how best to persuade people to conform to the goals of the dominant culture, often with a minimum of cultural change. Even in the second case, where self-government and self-determination are the goals, administrators frequently think they know what is best, and the anthropologist again is primarily confined to the task of persuading people to accept administrative decisions "for their own good."

Most anthropologists in the United States tend to reject either of these functions as an unethical use of their knowledge. Nevertheless, there are times when such actions seem necessary and desirable. An extreme example is afforded by the inhabitants of Bikini atoll in the Pacific who were moved to another location when Bikini was selected as the site for testing atomic bombs. At first they found great difficulty in adjusting to this move, but with the help of an anthropologist were finally (at least at this writing) apparently reconciled to their new home and making a successful adjustment. This case history may be worth a brief treatment.

4. THE PROBLEM AT BIKINI

The inhabitants of Bikini were originally a conquering group who had expelled the original inhabitants and settled down under a relatively autocratic hereditary chieftain. About a hundred years later they were persuaded to accept the sovereignty of the powerful chieftain, Kabua, controlling a group of neighboring islands, to whom they paid a traditional tribute in return for reciprocal services. This paramount chief handled relations with Europeans, and when German, and later Japanese, control was established, the paramount chief paid all the taxes out of the tribute he received, paid for medical care, and took general responsibility for the welfare of all the islanders of the group.

With the selection of Bikini for the atomic test, the military governor of the Marshall Islands went to Bikini, explained the situation, and asked cooperation of the residents through consenting to removal. Unable to consult with their paramount chief and unused to having their opinion asked, the Bikinians acquiesced, and the problem of seeking a new home was faced. However, the decision, apparently freely made, actually was not understood; it was primarily a response of people used to accepting the decisions of someone in authority.

Land in this region is extremely scarce and usually densely populated; Bikini itself had a population of 167 on a total land area of 2.32 square miles, some of it unfit for cultivation. An invitation was extended from the paramount chief and the councils of the islands of Ujae and Lae to settle on one or the other. However, both these islands are much smaller and more densely settled than Bikini, and navigation for the evacuation ship would be difficult. Consequently an uninhabited island, Rongerik, belonging to a different paramount chief, was selected. Rongerik had many fewer resources than Bikini and produced poor coconuts, but it was thought this difficulty could be overcome. The fact that Rongerik was generally regarded as the former home of a dangerous female spirit whose malign influence still lingered on the island was not mentioned by anyone, partly because the Bikinians thought their stay would be only temporary. Nor was the fact that the use of this island involved transfer of allegiance to another paramount chief thought to be of importance.

It is impossible to detail here the complex social arrangements which were upset by the removal, the readjustments which it was necessary to make in Rongerik, or the reasons why the group came to the verge of starvation, partly through the meager resources available and partly through lack of will to struggle against what appeared to be a hopeless situation.

It was at this point that an anthropologist (Leonard Mason of the University of Hawaii) arrived on the scene to investigate the situation. In a short time he had discovered the underlying cause of the difficulties and the unanimous wish of the Bikinians to move from Rongerik—by this time to almost anywhere else.

Military government in this case acted quickly. Emergency food rations were flown in. The population was moved to Kwajalein temporarily where all were fed, housed, and clothed, and those who were willing secured well-paid employment in military construction operations. After several months, during which all available sites were investigated and shown to the leaders, the Bikinians voted to move to Kili, a small but rich southern island, where there is little doubt they can support themselves in a fashion equal to the best Marshall Island way.

Not all problems were solved at the time of the last report upon the group. Because of differences in the shore-line, the Bikinians need help in learning to manage small boats in heavy surf. They have not yet decided on how they will allocate their lands, a decision depending partly on their relationship with the paramount chief. Kili was an uninhabited island not under the jurisdiction of any chief. The islanders feel that their new land came from the United States government, and not from the chief. Moreover, the military government (superseded now by a civilian government) now takes responsibility for their health and welfare, functions that were formerly the responsibility of the paramount chief. Hence many Bikinians wish to deal directly with, and if necessary apparently pay tribute (taxes) directly to, the agency which is looking after their welfare. Some of the basic problems are alluded to by Mason who writes:

The speed and effectiveness of the Bikini resettlement during any particular phase was closely correlated with the type of individual in charge and with the amount of pressure applied from higher levels or by criticism from outside the government. . . . It has been observed on a number of occasions that administrative personnel in general tend to regard the Marshallese as children who can be easily satisfied with promises and to bring charges of laziness and inefficiency when Marshallese do not respond as expected. This is related to another common tendency of Americans in their relations with peoples of another culture, and that is to interpret what they see and hear in terms of American culture and its values, with a corresponding failure to comprehend what is really taking place.

. . . There appears to be an ambivalence in our whole approach to the problems of administering dependent peoples. On the one hand, we profess to respect and to preserve tradition and custom, while on the other, we attempt with a kind of missionary zeal to bring to the Marshallese that which we judge to be the best in our own culture and therefore the best for the Marshallese. This frequently leads us into embarrassing situations . . .[1]

The case of the Bikinians illustrates some of the difficulties in a dogmatic view of the proper function of applied anthropology. In this and similar situations, overwhelming forces and decisions made far from the area and incomprehensible to the people concerned, vitally affect their future. Problems are raised concerning which the people themselves can make no intelligent decision. (For instance, Bikinians were flown back to see the atoll after the atomic blast; the physical damage visible is small and it is impossible to explain the dangers of radiation to them; consequently they still do not understand why their return is impossible although they have finally accepted the fact.) Administrators are forced inevitably to make decisions for them; an anthropologist can frequently assist in forming the decisions that will be most satisfactory to the people involved. The more extreme view among some anthropologists is that we have no right to make such decisions nor to induce culture change in other peoples. The majority, however, would probably agree that at least in this case it was a responsibility of anthropologists to assist in developing the most satisfactory solution of an unavoidable problem.

5. OTHER APPLICATIONS OF ANTHROPOLOGY

In the United States, the more conscious efforts to develop applied anthropology came to a focus with the formation of the Society for Applied Anthropology in 1941. Within this society a considerable group, in collaboration with specialists in other social sciences, have devoted themselves in part to industrial problems. A somewhat specialized point of view has therefore developed among them, which is primarily applicable to industrial situations, although it has some utility elsewhere.

In brief, this group sees a properly functioning society as composed of individuals or groups who have worked out an adjustment to each other so that their relationships may be considered to be in a state of equilibrium. This state of equilibrium may not be static, but so long as the various parts change harmoniously, the state of equilibrium continues. From time to time, either through internal developments or outside influences, this state of equilibrium is disturbed. In industrial situations this may take the form

---

[1] Leonard Mason, "The Bikinians: A Transplanted Population," *Human Organization* (New York: copyright Spring, 1950, by Society for Applied Anthropology), Vol. 9, No. 1, pp. 5–15, p. 15.

of strikes, lockouts, growing grievances, slowdowns, and various other evidences of conflict including growth of individual tensions and insecurities.

Within such a situation, the role of the applied anthropologist is seen as restoring a state of equilibrium satisfactory to those involved. The last phrase is regarded as important, for it is insisted that the applied anthropologist occupy a neutral and impartial role. He must find the causes of grievances, tensions, and strained interpersonal relationships, and seek to re-establish equilibrium through education, mutual concessions, and the reorganization of institutional and interpersonal relationships.

Many people, including some anthropologists, look with disfavor on these attempts to control our culture. Some anthropologists feel that such work impairs the scientific viewpoints of the anthropologists and that they become mere agents of expediency in carrying out the administrative policies. Others feel that our knowledge of culture is still not sufficient, and that we are apt to forget that we do not have all the answers and hence to cease to do the fundamental research that is still necessary.

Attempts to control culture of course involve the lives and futures of many human beings. Serious responsibilities are assumed by those who would undertake such a task. Anthropologists and administrators must decide on objectives and determine values in many cases, although in a democratic society machinery exists for the determination of goals by the members of the group. Such techniques should be improved. Our knowledge is still so limited that mistakes are certain to be made. Control techniques may be used for nefarious purposes as in Nazi Germany. As a result, many people, both anthropologists and others, feel that no attempts at control should be used.

Perhaps it should be pointed out that much the same arguments were used when science began to show us how to control nature. Many people felt that interference with nature was sacrilegious, overlooking the fact that by his mere possession of culture man constantly interfered with and controlled nature. Science still has not found ways to control more than a limited part of nature. Moreover, applied science has made many mistakes. For example, during World War I, applied science made possible a great extension of farming in the drier regions of our own Middle West. The unforeseen results were serious erosion, more severe and devastating floods, and the so-called "dustbowl" conditions of the early thirties. Nevertheless, few people today would have us give up our scientific control of nature. The answer is not abandonment of science but the development of more and better science.

Applied anthropology is today very much in its infancy and will undoubtedly make many mistakes. The problems of culture, involving, as they do, millions of individual human beings, are among the most complex problems we face. Vastly more research is needed before we can achieve relatively good controls over culture. Unless we wish to continue to be the unwitting pawns of cultural forces rather than to control those forces, we must have vastly more science rather than less. University budgets for research into society and culture, that is, for the social sciences as a whole, must be greatly increased. Great research centers must be developed, similar to those existing for research in the physical sciences. Freedom of inquiry and discussion must be maintained. As Linton has said, the Greek scholars forged a key to the door to the natural sciences but were prevented from opening the door by the rise of dogmatism and intolerance. Not until modern times did conditions come about which permitted the use of the Greek key to open the door to the control of nature. The social sciences, Linton believes, are today in the position of the Greek natural sciences. The social sciences have forged a key to open the door to the understanding of society and culture. The threatening rise of dogmatism and intolerance would end, perhaps for centuries, any possibility of using the key that has been created.

6. ANTHROPOLOGY AND THE MODERN WORLD

Attempts to apply scientific method to social phenomena are relatively recent. In many parts of the world this possibility is still not recognized at all, and even in our own society many people either are not aware of the possibility or disbelieve in it. In part the scepticism with which social science is viewed by some natural scientists stems from the great complexity of social data and the impossibility in most cases of establishing experimental situations. Natural scientists, accustomed to the use of laboratory techniques and experimental method, are often dubious of social science results, pointing to the frequent lack of agreement among social scientists themselves. As a result, basic decisions about human affairs tend to be settled by polling the opinions of community leaders, whether or not they have the competence to render a decision.

This technique, called a kind of magic by Kluckhohn, is illustrated in the following incident. Several years ago, a scientist asked a considerable group of people in a university town how they would go about solving a problem confronting the public schools of the town. The group were presented with ten ways of making a decision, of which the first was substantially, "Find out what the leading business men, educators, ministers, and other community leaders think, and follow their opinion," to the last, which was in effect, "Hire an experienced investigator to ascertain all the facts and then form an opinion." The majority of the people questioned chose the first method; no one chose the last. In other words, even the most elementary steps of scientific method were rejected in favor of relying upon "leaders," who are supposed by some occult means to discover an answer.

A growing understanding of cultural forces and the gradual realization that the complex variety of human behavior is subject to orderly and discernible processes, is today rapidly dispelling these older views. When it is recognized that laboratory experiment is only one highly specialized technique of observation and not the sole method of science, the possibilities of a science of human affairs and behavior begin rapidly to develop, as in the past few years. More and more we realize that scientific method is by no means limited to laboratory techniques nor to any other single means of observation. It is instead a process of formulating hypotheses to explain known facts and of continuously subjecting these hypotheses to verification and reformulation by further and extended observations.

If we turn now to what anthropology has to offer the modern world, we may note that it contributes significantly to two major understandings. First, anthropology, especially by reason of the concept of culture, helps us understand and deal with those whose cultures are diverse from our own. Second, and equally important, anthropology gives us a better understanding of our own behaviors, institutions, and beliefs. Note here that anthropology only contributes to these understandings; it is neither the only contributor nor does it pretend to supply all the answers. A few concrete instances will clarify these points.

In the field of international relations, knowledge of the processes of culture often permits us both to understand the behavior of others better and so to conduct ourselves that we have better relations with others. Particularly important is the concept of cultural relativity, namely, the recognition that when other peoples react differently they do not do so from stupidity or maliciousness. Basically, as we have seen, human beings everywhere confront similar kinds of problems for which they have, through many thousands of years, developed solutions different from our own. These historically determined patterns of behavior are closely integrated to form a cultural whole which to its bearers justifies and makes reasonable their actions, ideas, and beliefs. What seems immoral to us may seem right and proper to them; conversely, much that we consider right and proper may appear positively immoral to others. Thus, for example, a woman delegate from Pakistan eloquently and successfully opposed a proposal in the United Nations to condemn polygyny. Millions who live in India believe that the killing of animals of any sort, let alone the eating of their flesh, is extremely wicked. The chief of an African tribe once said that

Europeans must be the wickedest people alive to kill millions of men in warfare without even the intention of using their flesh for food. To many other nonliterate peoples it is incredible that people in our society may starve while others still have food. No amount of justification on our part will convince these people that they are wrong, and conversely, many of us probably find it difficult, if not impossible, to justify cannibalism, or even polygyny.

Failure to understand these deeply rooted behavior patterns and the premises about the world that underlie them often results in our behavior becoming arrogant and ethnocentric, and in our failing to win people to points of view that are to our own best interests. An example of such ethnocentrism is given in the following report, written by an anthropologist, on a meeting of the American Council on Education (1950) devoted to problems of education in occupied countries. The report says, in part:

The report of Colonel .... on Japan was very discouraging because of the attitude and point of view. He painted a glowing picture in which everything is going beautifully in Japan and there are no problems. As a result of the United States program, Japanese character, personality, and culture have been entirely changed during the past five years and they are well on the road to American democracy. The ethnocentric approach on the part of most delegates and officials toward all of the occupied countries was almost unbelievable. Nearly every discussion and comment was predicated on the assumption that American institutions are perfect and that success in the occupied countries consists only in recasting them more nearly in our own image. It was implied that what is wrong with Japanese culture is that it is so unlike American culture . . . Japanese universities were thoroughly excoriated because they were copied after the European pattern and not the American pattern. Unquestionably, foreign nationals representing the occupied areas must have felt that most of the discussion was an unvarnished insult to their national cultures.[2]

Anthropological viewpoints become even more important in the various programs to raise the living standards of countries outside our general cultural heritage. These technical assistance programs, such as our own government's Point IV program or the technical aid program of UNESCO, are too often predicated on the view that if people only can be brought to live exactly like ourselves, their problems will be solved. Citizens of the United States particularly tend to have a missionary zeal to make the world over in our own image. Such an assumption of the "rightness" of our own way of behaving often is highly offensive to others and may seriously interfere with the success of technical aid missions.

[2] George Foster, "Reports of Committees and Representatives" (*American Anthropologist*, 53, 447–460, 1951), pp. 456–457.

On one very simple level, knowledge of the total cultural situation is basic to success. Often our technical methods are dependent upon very complexly interrelated factors, such as widespread literacy and mechanical knowledge, specialized production facilities, laboratories, land systems, and economic conditions. These are rarely duplicated in other countries. It should be obvious that teaching people to farm with tractors will not be successful if their economy will not support the purchase or maintenance of machines, if their land-holding system is based on small plots farmed by gardening techniques, and if their social system in part revolves about the mutual exchange of labor. In such cases, improvement of agricultural techniques must begin on a nonmechanized basis. The introduction of new plants or of new techniques of tillage, fitted into what the people already know and so presented as not to dislocate existing patterns of interpersonal relations, may be entirely feasible, and may produce far more useful results than premature attempts at mechanization.

Frequently technical aid programs also bypass recognized local leaders and social groupings, or ignore economic and ideological differences. Efforts to improve the care of children may founder upon economic considerations: people often do not have the money to buy the things the medical men think desirable. A number of years ago the Mexican government attempted to suppress the use by the Otomi Indians of *pulque,* a mildly alcoholic drink fermented from the juice of the agave or century plant. It was soon discovered that many of these Indians were totally lacking in any water supply and hence had no other source of liquid, but that even when water was available *pulque* was almost the only source of certain vitamins and minerals especially essential to the growing child. Efforts to introduce modern medicine often fail when, as among the Navaho Indians, there is a belief that disease is caused by supernatural forces, or, as in much of Latin America, there is no conception of micro-organisms as a cause of disease. Efforts to introduce a model public health program in a Latin American country failed because the directors from the United States were totally unaware of the existing class structure and ignored the only group of people who could have led the community to acceptance of the new ideas. In other cases, where a people were ridiculed for their folk concepts of disease, there was again failure to introduce and properly integrate into the culture badly needed medical practices. Examples like these may be multiplied endlessly.

Not all anthropologists agree, however, that it is ever justified deliberately to introduce changes in the cultures of others. They maintain, rather, that there is no such right, that all peoples should have the privilege to hold to their own cultures, unmolested by outsiders.

The difficulty here lies in the fact that world culture today is undergoing a major technical revolution through the expansion of industrialism. There is no reason to believe that this cultural revolution is less radical than, say, the Neolithic revolution which introduced the cultivation of food plants. Control of the industrial revolution, moreover, in the light of our present knowledge, at least, seems impossible. No culture today can remain in isolation, and cultures in contact, as we have seen, undergo changes. It is doubtful if all peoples who came in contact with the Neolithic revolution were entirely happy about it, but in large areas of the world they either had to accept it or be displaced by others. It is doubtful in the present situation, given the demands of technology and the present world order with its power structure, that many peoples can maintain even relative isolation or that peoples controlling needed natural resources or forming a power vacuum will have any opportunity of rejecting participation in the modern world.

The role of the anthropologist would seem to be to develop as much respect as possible for the cultural values of others and to aid them in making an adjustment to the modern industrial world which will be on their own terms rather than upon ours. Cultural relativity suggests that many customs we may reject represent values in another culture which must be respected. Just as we have accepted, internationally and nationally, the right of a man to his own religious beliefs, we must be prepared in large part to accept the right of a man to his own culture.

Such a viewpoint is sometimes misunderstood. An anthropologist, who should have known better, once reacted violently to this proposition, asserting that it means that we must not interfere with the right of the Eskimos to kill their grandparents. In a certain sense this is quite correct. Although probably the majority of the peoples of the world, including quite likely many thoughtful Eskimos, regard the killing of grandparents as undesirable, the practice, given the native conditions of Eskimo life, is all but inescapable.

The reasons for this must be fairly clear to those who have assimilated the many references to the Eskimos in this book. Under aboriginal conditions, the Eskimos have a very limited food supply which cannot be enlarged under their native technology. The supply is ordinarily sufficient to maintain children and working adults, but it is only rarely, if ever, enough to support any considerable number of the aged or sick, unable to work. To prohibit the killing of grandparents (too old or ill to work) is, therefore, to endanger all and even, quite literally, to condemn the group as a whole to slow starvation and death.

Under such conditions it would seem that we have no right to interfere with the Eskimo customs with respect to grandparents unless we are willing to aid them to reach a condition of economic security which will enable the group to survive and still feed the grandparents. Such a course, naturally, means embarking upon programs designed to help people to help themselves. In some cases it means, temporarily at least, undertaking programs which opponents have characterized as "giving a quart of milk to every Hottentot." If we are not willing to undertake such programs, then we should not criticize other peoples for following customs necessary to their survival.

When we turn to the role of anthropology in helping us understand ourselves, cultural relativity again may be badly misunderstood. The shock of discovering that behavior we consider bad may be condoned or even approved in other cultures, sometimes leads uncritical students to believe they can abandon all behavior rules. Such a viewpoint is quite unjustified, for all cultures have moral rules with deep historical roots and functional reasons for their existence within the given culture. What is bad in one culture may be good in another, and vice versa, for precisely the same reasons—the rules are necessary to the proper functioning of the culture and to the adequate adjustment of the individual to his own environment. To respect the customs of others does not mean that these customs are equally to be practiced in our culture.

The culture of the Euro-American peoples is deeply imbedded in Judeo-Greco-Christian backgrounds. While the values of this background have undergone slow change through the centuries, they cannot be ignored by a member of our culture. It may be that not all our values are of universal validity for other cultures, or that the values of other cultures may in some degree be better than our own, but until some scientific method of studying values can be developed, we must for the most part insist merely upon their validity within a given culture. To respect the validity of another culture is not to deny the validity of our own; when we recognize that a Moslem is bound to his culture, we should likewise recognize that we are bound to ours. At the same time, we must not fail to recognize that values, like all the rest of culture, are subject to change, and that the values of an earlier period in our history need not necessarily be of equal importance today.

Anthropology in the modern world, then, has the important function of helping us to understand ourselves and our culture. Through intensive studies of many cultures, we learn that, while all peoples have broadly similar capacities and face the same problems of living, they are subject in each society to differing natural conditions and have hence developed diverse ways of meeting their problems. These ways of living are complexly integrated into a cultural totality—a set of techniques, habits, customs, beliefs, and institutions, each set characteristic of a given people. Through this understanding, we learn as well that our own behavior is similarly conditioned by a culture, one among many others. As we learn more about culture—how it is integrated, its historical and evolutionary development, the processes of cultural change, and the complex relation between culture and individual behavior—anthropology becomes increasingly useful in the understanding and direction of human affairs.

Anthropology is of course not the only social science that deals with human behavior, nor does it supply answers to all social problems. Rather it offers, through its central concept of culture and its intensive comparisons of many diverse cultures, an integrative framework which aids all of social science in the analysis and understanding of our own very complex civilization. As such it may contribute heavily to the ultimate goal of gaining the same scientific controls over social and cultural phenomena that we now possess in the field of the natural sciences, and, even more important, to the solution of the problem of using such controls for the benefit of all mankind.

COLLATERAL READING

Hallowell, A. Irving. "Sociopsychological Aspects of Acculturation," *The Science of Man in the World Crisis,* ed. Ralph Linton. New York: Columbia University Press, 1945. Pp. 171–200.

Herskovits, Melville J. *Acculturation, the Study of Culture Contact.* New York: J. J. Augustin, 1938.

Hunter, Monica. *Reaction to Conquest.* Oxford: Oxford University Press, 1936.

Keesing, Felix M. "Anthropology in Colonial Administration," *The Science of Man in the World Crisis,* ed. Ralph Linton. New York: Columbia University Press, 1945. Pp. 373–398.

Linton, Ralph (ed.). *Acculturation in Seven American Indian Tribes.* New York: D. Appleton-Century Co., 1940.

Linton, Ralph. "Present World Conditions in Cultural Perspective," *The Science of Man in the World Crisis,* ed. Ralph Linton. New York: Columbia University Press, 1945. Pp. 201–221.

Redfield, Robert. *The Folk Culture of Yucatan.* Chicago: University of Chicago Press, 1941.

———. *The Village that Chose Progress.* Chicago: University of Chicago Press, 1950.

Tax, Sol (ed.). *Acculturation in the Americas.* Chicago: University of Chicago Press, 1952.

Tax, Sol, and Others. *Heritage of Conquest: the Ethnology of Middle America.* Glencoe, Illinois: Glencoe Free Press, 1952.

(Note: Many additional articles on applied anthropology may be found in the journal, *Human Organization,* published in New York by the Society for Applied Anthropology.)

APPENDIX

Ethnographic Bibliography

Beals, Ralph L. *Cherán: A Sierra Tarascan Village*. Smithsonian Institution, Institute of Social Anthropology, Washington, D. C., 1946.

———. "Ethnology of the Nisenan," *University of California Publications in American Archaeology and Ethnology,* XXXI, 335–414, 1933.

Birket-Smith, K. *The Eskimos*. New York: E. P. Dutton and Co., 1936.

Bogoras, V. G. *The Chukchee*. American Museum of Natural History, Memoirs, 11, 1904–09.

Buck, Peter H. *Vikings of the Sunrise*. New York: Frederick A. Stokes Co., 1938.

Childe, V. Gordon. *Man Makes Himself*. New York: Oxford University Press, 1939.

Cole, Fay-Cooper. *The Peoples of Malaysia*. New York: D. van Nostrand Co., 1945.

Coon, Carleton S. *A Reader in General Anthropology*. New York: Henry Holt and Co., 1948.

Covarrubias, Miguel. *Island of Bali*. New York: Alfred A. Knopf, 1938.

Cushing, F. H. *Zuñi Breadstuff*. New York: Museum of the American Indian, Heye Foundation, 1920.

Du Bois, Cora. *The People of Alor*. Minneapolis: University of Minnesota Press, 1944.

Eggan, Fred. *Social Organization of the Western Pueblos*. Chicago: University of Chicago Press, 1950.

Forde, C. Daryll. *Habitat, Society and Economy*. New York: E. P. Dutton, 1950.

646

Herskovits, Melville J. *Dahomey: An Ancient West African Kingdom.* New York: J. J. Augustin, 1938.

———. *An Outline of Dahomean Religious Belief.* American Anthropological Association, Memoir 41, 1933.

Hollis, A. C. *The Masai.* Oxford: the Clarendon Press, 1905.

Kluckhohn, Clyde, and Leighton, Dorothea. *The Navaho.* Cambridge: Harvard University Press, 1946.

Linton, Ralph. "Marquesan Culture" and "The Tanala of Madagascar," *The Individual and His Culture,* by Abram Kardiner. New York: Columbia University Press, 1939. Pp. 137–196, 251–290.

———. "The Tanala, A Hill Tribe of Madagascar," *Field Museum of Natural History, Anthropological Series,* 22, Chicago, 1933.

Lowie, Robert H. *The Crow Indians.* New York: Farrar and Rinehart, 1935.

Malinowski, Bronislaw. *Argonauts of the Western Pacific.* New York: E. P. Dutton, 1932.

Means, Philip A. *Ancient Civilizations of the Andes.* New York: Charles Scribner's Sons, 1931.

Morgan, Lewis H. *League of the Ho-Dé-No-Sau-Nee or Iroquois.* (Ed. H. M. Lloyd.) New York, 1901.

Murdock, George P. *Our Primitive Contemporaries.* New York: The Macmillan Co., 1935.

Opler, Morris E. *An Apache Life-Way.* Chicago: University of Chicago Press, 1941.

———. "An Outline of Chiricahua Apache Social Organization," *Social Anthropology of North American Tribes,* ed. Fred Eggan. Chicago: University of Chicago Press, 1937. Pp. 173–242.

Radcliffe-Brown, A. R. *The Andaman Islanders.* Cambridge: the University Press, 1933.

———. *Social Organization of Australian Tribes.* Melbourne: Macmillan and Co., 1931.

Rasmussen, Knud. "The Netsilik Eskimo," *Report of the Fifth Thule Expedition 1921–24,* VIII, No. 1–2, Copenhagen, 1931.

———. *The People of the Polar North.* London: K. Paul, Trench, Trubner and Co., 1908.

Rivers, W. H. R. *The Todas.* London: Macmillan and Co., 1906.

Roscoe, John. *The Baganda.* London: Macmillan and Co., 1911.

Schebesta, P. *Among Congo Pygmies.* London: Hutchinson, 1933.

Seligmann, C. G. and B. Z. *The Veddas.* Cambridge: the University Press, 1911.

Spencer, B., and Gillen, F. S. *The Arunta.* London: Macmillan and Co., 1927.

Stevenson, M. C. *The Zuñi Indians.* 23rd Annual Report, Bureau of American Ethnology, Washington, D. C., 1904.

Steward, Julian H. *Basin-Plateau Aboriginal Socio-Political Groups.* Bulletin 120, Bureau of American Ethnology, Washington, D. C., 1938.

————. (ed.) *Handbook of South American Indians.* Bulletin 143, Bureau of American Ethnology, Washington, D. C., 1946. (6 volumes.)

Swanton, John R. *Contributions to the Ethnology of the Haida.* American Museum of Natural History, Memoirs, VIII, Leiden, 1909.

Thompson, J. Eric. *Mexico before Cortez.* New York: Charles Scribner's Sons, 1933.

Titiev, Mischa. *Old Oraibi, A Study of the Hopi Indians of Third Mesa.* Peabody Museum of American Archaeology and Ethnology, Harvard University, Papers, 22, 16–301, 1944.

Turner, G. *Samoa.* London: Macmillan and Co., 1884.

Vaillant, George C. *Aztecs of Mexico.* New York: Doubleday, Doran and Co., 1941.

INDEX